REVELATION

FOUR VIEWS, REVISED & UPDATED

A PARALLEL COMMENTARY

STEVE GREGG

FOREWORD BY DR. ROBERT G. CLOUSE

THOMAS NELSON
Since 1798

NASHVILLE DALLAS MEXICO CITY RIO DE JANEIRO

WWW.THOMASNELSON.COM

Unless otherwise noted, Scripture taken from THE NEW KING JAMES VERSION. © 1982 by Thomas Nelson, Inc. Used by permission. All rights reserved.

The following publishers and authors have generously given permission to use extended quotations from copyrighted works:

A Commentary on the Revelation of John, by George Eldon Ladd, © 1972. Used by permission of Wm. B. Eerdmans Publishing Co., Grand Rapids, MI. All rights reserved.

The Book of Revelation (The New International Commentary on the New Testament), by Robert H. Mounce, © 1977. Used by permission of Wm. B. Eerdmans Publishing Co., Grand Rapids, MI. All rights reserved.

Interpreting Revelation, by Merrill C. Tenney, © 1957. Used by permission of Wm. B. Eerdmans Publishing Co., Grand Rapids, MI. All rights reserved.

The Revelation Record, by Henry M. Morris, © 1983. Used by permission of Tyndale House Publishers, Inc., Wheaton, IL. All rights reserved.

Lectures on the Revelation, by H. A. Ironside, © 1920. Used by permission of Loizeaux Brothers, Neptune, New Jersey. All rights reserved.

The Revelation: An Analysis and Exposition of the Last Book of the Bible, by Arno C. Gaebelein, ©1915. Used by permission of Loizeaux Brothers, Neptune, New Jersey. All rights reserved.

Revelation, by Charles Caldwell Ryrie, © 1968. Used by permission of Moody Bible Institute of Chicago, Moody Press, IL. All rights reserved.

The Revelation of Jesus Christ, by John Walvoord, © 1966. Used by permission of Moody Bible Institute of Chicago, Moody Press, Chicago, IL. All rights reserved.

More Than Conquerors: An Interpretation of the Book of Revelation, by William Hendriksen, ©1939. Used by permission of Baker Book House, Grand Rapids, MI. All rights reserved.

Revelation, by Geoffrey B. Wilson, © 1985. Used by permission of Evangelical Press, England. All rights reserved.

The Days of Vengeance: An Exposition of the Book of Revelation, by David Chilton, © 1987. Used by permission of Dominion Press, Ft. Worth, Texas. All rights reserved.

The Time is at Hand, by Jay E. Adams, © 1966. Permission granted by author.

Revelation: An Introduction and Commentary, by Homer Hailey, © 1979. Baker Book House, Grand Rapids, MI. Permission granted by author.

The Cosmic Drama, by Herschel H. Hobbs, © 1971. Word Books, Waco, Texas. Permission granted by author.

Page layout: Crosslin Creative

ISBN: 9781401676216

Printed in United States

19 20 LSCC 10 9 8 7 6

This book is dedicated with affectionate
gratitude to Chuck Smith, pastor of Calvary
Chapel in Costa Mesa, California, a lover of Bible
prophecy, and my first mentor in ministry.

Contents

Preface to the Revised & Updated Edition

For the fifteen years since the first edition of this book was published, I have hosted a daily Christian talk show on AM radio, discussing (and sometimes answering) callers' questions about the Bible. At the time of publication, I had spent the previous fourteen years as a lecturer at a small Bible institute in Oregon. For the twelve years prior to that, I had been a freelance, international Bible teacher. Despite the wearing of multiple hats, during almost forty-three years of ministry, I have not been a prolific book writer. In fact, I have not produced a book for publication since the appearance of this one in 1997.

When one writes so few books, he wants the few that he writes to be as good as they can be. Therefore, immediately after the publication of the first edition of *Revelation: Four Views* I began to see imperfections that I wished I could have avoided. It was on the occasion of the publisher's request to publish an *updated* and *expanded* version that I was invited to make alterations to the original. The primary changes in this edition are as follows:

1. The viewpoint that appears in the fourth column of the main body of the work is rightly called the *idealist*. I was aware of this, when writing in 1997, but I did not find many authors referring to their view by this name, even when it was their view. I assumed that they may not have preferred this label for their position, and I sought for an alternative name from their writings. Though authors taking this position floated a variety of possible labels (e.g., the *philosophy of history* view), there was none among them of which all seemed to approve. At that time, I decided to create a generic name for the viewpoint, and I settled upon the label *spiritual*. The ink was no sooner dry on the first copies of the book than I regretted this decision. *Idealist* is clearly the most widely recognized name for this view, and it is so named in this edition.

2. The first edition sported unused white space on many of its pages, owing to the fact that I could not find an equal amount of material for all four views in many cases, and the four-column format meant that when the treatment of one or two views extended considerably beyond that for the others, there often would be white space in the columns to which the commentary on the other approaches did not extend. In preparing this second edition, I have found more authorities than were available to me in 1997 from which to quote.

3. When I wrote *Revelation: Four Views*, I was not aware of Richard Bauckham's book, *The Theology of the Book of Revelation*, which had been published four years earlier. Also, in the years since 1997, a major commentary on Revelation by G. K. Beale has appeared. The importance of these two scholars in the modern evangelical world renders it essential that their work be included in a study such as this.

Apart from these few things, the second edition is very much like the first. I have been very encouraged by the many positive reviews the first edition received and am grateful to Thomas Nelson that a second edition in paperback was deemed a worthwhile project. It gave me another opportunity to delve into the fascinating exploration in which I continue to revel. I wish you equal revelry in your own exploration.

Steve Gregg, December 2012

FOREWORD

BY DR. ROBERT G. CLOUSE

Steve Gregg has given Christian scholarship an excellent book combining the four major ways to interpret the book of Revelation. By approaching the Apocalypse with a verse-by-verse parallel commentary, his work will lead the reader to reopen the discussion of this section of Scripture and expose many people for the first time to outlooks other than their own.

Revelation is a unique book, in that a person seems either to make everything of it or else to make nothing of it. In many churches sermons on the Revelation are so numerous that they become a hermeneutical method of interpreting the whole Bible, while among other groups the book is seldom mentioned. In two areas, specifically, one's understanding of the Revelation is both revealed and shaped, and in both of these Steve Gregg's work is helpful to all students of the Revelation. The first area concerns how the Millennium of chapter 20 is understood, and the second concerns the basic way interpreters approach the Revelation.

Those who make the most use of the book of Revelation generally use it to present a premillennial view of the earthly reign of Christ. Interpretations of this coming age have been labeled postmillennial, amillennial, and premillennial. The postmillenarian believes that the kingdom of God is extended through Christian preaching and teaching as a result of which the world will be Christianized and will enjoy a long period of peace and righteousness. The new age will not be essentially different from the present, and it emerges gradually as an ever larger share of the world's population is converted to Christianity. During this age the church assumes a greater importance, and many social, economic, and educational problems are solved. The period closes with the second coming of Christ, the resurrection of the dead, and the final judgment.

In contrast to the above view, the amillennialist believes that the Bible does not predict a period of universal peace and righteousness before the end of the world. Instead, good and evil will coexist until the second coming of Christ when the dead will be raised and the last judgment held. The so-called Millennium is seen as a symbol of the present age of the church.

The third major interpretation, premillennialism, affirms that the Lord's return will be followed by a period of peace and righteousness before the end of the world, during which Christ will reign as king in person. Usually, premillenarians have taught that the return of Christ will be preceded by certain signs such as the regathering of Israel to their ancient homeland, the preaching of the gospel to all nations, a great apostasy, wars, famine, earthquakes, the appearance of the Antichrist, and a great tribulation. Detail concerning this tribulation are sought in the middle chapters of Revelation.

In addition to presenting the three main views on the Millennium, the author devotes the majority of the commentary to presenting the four ways in which interpreters have approached the main sections of Revelation: the *preterist, historicist, futurist,* and *idealist* approaches. A *preterist* is one who believes that most of the prophecies of the Apocalypse have been fulfilled in the past. The *historicist* (or *presentist*) considers the events of Revelation now in the process of fulfillment, while the *futurist* believes that the bulk of the book refers to the events to come. The *idealist* views the Revelation as a great drama involving transcendent truths such as the conflict between righteousness and unrighteousness or the victory over Satan.

Regardless of the perspective on Revelation each may hold, many students of prophecy are intolerant of those who cannot in good conscience agree with them. I hope that such individuals will read this unique and helpful contribution. Steve Gregg approaches all the views of the Revelation in a judicious, kindly, and evenhanded manner. I trust this book will reach a wide audience of those who wait patiently and prayerfully for the coming of the kingdom of our Lord Jesus.

Robert G. Clouse
Editor of *The Meaning of the Millennium: Four Views*
Professor Emeritus
Indiana State University

INTRODUCTION TO THIS COMMENTARY

The researches of many learned commentators
have thrown much darkness upon this subject,
and if they continue, we may be certain that
we will soon know nothing about it at all.

—attributed to Mark Twain

WHY THIS COMMENTARY?

I looked for the book that you are holding for many years. Since I found that it did not exist, I wrote it.

For years, one of my responsibilities as a lecturer in an obscure Bible institute was to teach verse-by-verse through the book of Revelation. Though this was by no means the only book of the Bible that I was assigned to teach, I found none so difficult as the book of Revelation.

Strangely, I did not always regard Revelation to be so difficult to understand. In the beginning of my career, I knew of only one reasonable viewpoint to consider. I believed that there were two types of prophecy students—those who shared my views on Revelation and those who had not yet heard them convincingly presented. I was able to teach with confidence, since I was not aware of any responsible alternatives to my own view—with the exception that I knew some Christians were so unfortunate as to set the Rapture of the church at a time different from that in my system.

As I studied the subject over the years, however, I began to be unsettled by the discovery of details in the book that didn't seem to fit my paradigm. At one point, I actually came to the conclusion that I did not, and never would, understand the book of Revelation at all and would have to confine my teaching exclusively to the other books of Scripture.

As I talked with Christian friends and ministers from denominations other than my own and read the commentaries they recommended, I gradually became aware of several alternative approaches to Revelation that made at least as much sense as did mine. Some of these views had been around much longer than mine had been, and had been dominant Christian viewpoints earlier in history. In the course of the following decade, I found myself favoring first one view and then another as I became aware of the merits of each of the alternative approaches. Eventually, I came to appreciate the strengths of more than one position sufficiently to allow me to hold my own opinions lightly and to view those who espoused alternative views with respect.

By the time I began teaching in the Bible school in 1983, the only honest way I knew to teach the book of Revelation was to apprise my students of the best arguments for each significant approach. Since I was not bound to any denominational or theological position on this matter, I had nothing to lose if the students reached conclusions different from my own and nothing to gain by winning them over to "my side." Laboring under the conviction that those who teach can expect "a stricter judgment" (James 3:1), I felt that I should not conceal or pass over significant data that might help my students make better-informed decisions in their understanding of Scripture.

I found that the commentators fell into one of four basic camps, though there were variations upon particulars within each camp. It occurred to me that someone—somewhere—must have published a book that compared these four views side-by-side and passage-by-passage, which would save me much time and expense in my study and preparation.

After a decade of searching, I discovered that, although hundreds of commentaries had been published on Revelation, none had ever compared the four major approaches point-by-point in parallel columns. Most of the commentators acknowledged, in their introductions, the existence of four approaches, but they generally would give views other than their own short shrift and then seldom mention them again in the body of their works. Even though highly respected evangelical scholars have advocated each of the four views (suggesting that each is at least *plausible*), no book had previously presented readers with the best arguments for each view on a passage-by-passage basis.

That is why I wrote this book.

WHAT ARE THE FOUR VIEWS?
Approaches Included—and Excluded

I have limited my task in this volume to comparing four views consistent with the evangelical commitment to the inspiration of Scripture—that is, those regarding the book of Revelation as a genuine revelation from God to the author.

The commentaries that fit this description align themselves under four basic approaches. At this point, a brief description of these four approaches will lay the foundation for later elaboration.

The *historicist* approach, which is the classical Protestant interpretation of the book, sees the book of Revelation as a prewritten record of the course of history from the time of John to the end of the world. Fulfillment is thus considered to be in progress at present and has been unfolding for nearly two thousand years.

The *preterist* approach views the fulfillment of Revelation's prophecies as having occurred already, in what is now the ancient past, not long after the author's own time. Thus the fulfillment was *future* from the point of view of the inspired author, but it is *past* from our vantage point in history. Some *preterists* believe that the final chapters of Revelation look forward to the second coming of Christ. Others think that everything in the book reached its culmination in the past.

The *futurist* approach asserts that the majority of the prophecies of Revelation have never yet been fulfilled and await future fulfillment. *Futurist* interpreters usually apply everything after chapter 4 to a relatively brief period before the return of Christ.

What is generally called the *idealist* approach to Revelation does not attempt to find individual fulfillments of the visions but takes Revelation to be a great drama depicting transcendent spiritual realities, such as the perennial conflict between Christ and Satan, between the saints and the antichristian world powers, the heavenly vindication of the martyrs and the final victory of Christ and his saints. Fulfillment is seen either as entirely spiritual or as recurrent, finding representative expression in various historical events throughout the age, rather than in one-time, specific fulfillments. The prophecy is thus rendered applicable to Christians in any age.

Occasionally, writers will refer to what sounds like yet another interpretive approach to Revelation, which they call the *dramatic* approach. It views the book of Revelation as being composed like a Greek drama, divisible into seven acts, with each of these divided into seven scenes. This view of Revelation has received greatest attention among those embracing the *idealist* approach to Revelation and is not actually a fifth approach. Because it is a view only of the structural composition of the book, and not of the meaning of its prophecies, the *dramatic* approach to understanding Revelation would, theoretically, be compatible with any of the four major approaches.

This focus on the book as a genuine message from God likewise excludes from separate treatment a great number of modern commentaries taking a *literary-ana-*

lytical approach. These treatments are often more "concerned with sources from alleged periods and backgrounds (e.g., Egyptian, Zoroastrian, Babylonian, Jewish) and its final redactions"[1] than with the message of the book itself.

As Morris Ashcraft has put it:

> The literary-analytical approach begins with the assumption that Revelation was composed from different sources, which must be identified and dealt with accordingly. This approach is concerned with the interpolations, dislocations, sources and their evaluation. A common fault in this method is that the interpreter often stops short of the major question, What meaning did John intend to convey?[2]

More to the point, this approach raises questions as to whether the book is really the record of prophetic visions given to the seer, as it represents itself to be, or merely the literary production of a skilled editor, who disingenuously claimed inspiration for his work in order to bolster its credibility.

AIMS, SCOPE, AND PERSPECTIVE OF THIS COMMENTARY

Some students of the Bible may be looking for a commentary that will quickly resolve difficult passages in the book of Revelation by giving a definitive and incontestable meaning to its perplexing visions. They will not find this commentary answering to this purpose. Those who will most appreciate this volume will be those who want to do some thinking of their own, to reach conclusions that they can own with confidence (not just views they can borrow from one expositor or another), and who desire to have all the options laid out clearly before them, in order to assist them in this goal. Such readers will find in this work a unique help, unlike any other presently in print.

There is the distinct possibility that the initial result of perusing these pages will be a diminished sense of certainty as to which view is correct. However, patient study can result in a rewarding outcome. One of the chief aims I have had in writing has been to deflate, in some degree, the unjustified dogmatism and theological provincialism that has often been the result of exposure to teachers who provide no options from which to choose but their own.

Solomon warns us that "The first one to plead his cause seems right, until his neighbor comes and examines him" (Prov. 18:17), and "He who answers a matter before he hears it, it is folly and shame to him" (18:13). Many of us have been put in a position to answer matters of great controversy without really having heard any of the alternatives presented fairly for our consideration—and this deficiency is not only found among the taught, but also among those who teach. *It is probable that merely by reading the introduction of this book, the student will become more familiar with the principal interpretive options than are many pastors who regularly teach from the Revelation.*

The book's very name in the Greek New Testament is *The Apocalypse,* which means the "unveiling" or "uncovering"—though many seem to have found it to be more of an "obscuring." Was it *this difficult* to the original readers? We may never know, but it is likely that they understood it better and with less difficulty than we do. They shared the Revelation author's knowledge of the culture and of the kind of literature that Revelation is. This knowledge, like that of the original languages, is something that we, who are two thousand years removed from the original audience, must learn through specialized study. It is my hope that this commentary will be an effective tool in helping readers gain some of this knowledge—after, perhaps, shaking up much of what they think they already know.

I have presented in parallel columns the four leading views advocated by Christian scholars and teachers throughout church history. This presentation encourages readers to understand the views by a comparison of the strengths and weaknesses of each. My object has not been to advocate any position above another—and I have intended that my own opinion should not be evident. My purpose is not to advance a particular view that I, personally, find most credible, but to provide the best possible presentation of each view on every passage in Revelation—allowing respected authorities from each viewpoint to speak for themselves.

In my research for this project, roughly a dozen commentaries for each view (nearly fifty commentaries in all) were consulted, in order to draw from them the clearest explanations and the most cogent arguments for each approach. My goal was to give approximately equal treatment for each approach. At any given passage, if one view actually receives more consideration than others, this does not reflect conscious favoritism toward that approach on my part. A larger treatment of one approach may simply reflect the greater number of opinions within that view to be surveyed.

Readers may be curious to know which approach to the book of Revelation this author personally favors. It has not been my desire to showcase my own opinions (which have changed a number of times, and may yet change in the future). I have not regarded my own view of Revelation to be definitive, immutable, or supremely important. In the course of my research for this book, I have become increasingly convinced that as Albertus Pieters wrote:

None of these schools of interpretation can claim any monopoly on scholarship or faith. Each group numbers many fine scholars and devout Christian believers. Therefore complete certainty in regard to the interpretation of the Apocalypse is not to be had. It is our duty to do the best we can, to study the various systems and accept the view that seems to us right, but always with a certain amount of reservation and of respect for the opinions of others.[3]

THE FORMAT OF THE COMMENTARY

The format adopted for parts 2 through 6 of the commentary (Revelation 4–19) is that of a four-column parallel commentary that runs across two facing pages. In these portions of the commentary, a section opens with a title, a reference to the Scriptures commented on, and the text of the Scripture itself from the New King James Bible. This material is then followed by the presentation of the four major approaches, following this order, left to right across a two-page spread: the *historicist,* the *preterist,* the *futurist,* and the *idealist.*

The four-column format cannot be employed for every portion of the book. It is not until the beginning of chapter 4 that the four views really part company (and the radical differences apply only to chaps. 6–19). Thus the first three and the last three chapters of Revelation are not debated on the same basis as are the chapters in the middle of the book. There is by no means unanimity as to the meaning of these opening and closing sections, however.

Concerning the seven letters to the seven churches (chaps. 1–3), there are not four distinct opinions among commentators, though there are portions of those chapters that lend themselves more to one than to another of the four approaches. The commentary for this section is, therefore, not set in parallel columns. However, in these chapters, the reader will find special comparative notes highlighting features thought to favor one approach over another or those that are explained differently from different viewpoints.

Likewise, the debate over chapters 20 through 22 historically has not turned so much on whether one is *a futurist,* a *preterist, and so forth,* as on whether one is or is not a *millennialist*—and if so, of what variety. When we reach chapter 20, we will be obliged to exchange the four-view format for one comparing the *three* millennial viewpoints.

For the sake of following a complete train of thought, some readers may find it helpful to study one particular approach all the way through the book—or at least through a major section—before examining another of the views on the same material. This may allow the flow of an argument to be grasped with greater ease and the strength of each position to be individually assessed. However, the commentary is laid out in a manner that allows access at a glance to all four interpretations of any given verse on the same page.

NOTES

1. J. W. Bowman, "Revelation" in IDB, vol. 4. (Nashville: Abingdon, 1962), 61.
2. Morris Ashcraft, Hebrews: "Revelation" in BBC, vol. 12 (Nashville: Broadman, 1972).
3. Albertus Pieters, *The Lamb, the Woman and the Dragon* (Grand Rapids: Zondervan, 1937), 42.

INTRODUCTION TO THE BOOK OF REVELATION

Attempting to understand the book of Revelation is no small undertaking, and presents special challenges unique to its case. This is because among the New Testament writings, Revelation is unique in its *genre*, its *purpose*, and its *method* of communicating its message. It would be naive to assume that one can do justice to the interpretation of this book without responsibly dealing with some of the special interpretive considerations that apply uniquely to it. The original readers probably instinctively took these factors into consideration, but our cultural distance from them renders it necessary to face the difficulties deliberately and to consider them as introductory considerations.

WHAT MANNER OF BOOK IS THIS?

Many have never recognized that Revelation, like most of the books of the New Testament, was written in the form of an epistle. It has the traditional opening and close, common to nearly all of the biblical epistles. After a brief introduction, apparently written by another hand, which speaks of John in the third person (1:1–3), we find the true beginning of the epistle, in verse 4: *"John, to the seven churches which are in Asia."* This resembles, in form, the opening of every one of the Pauline epistles, as well as those of James, Peter, and Jude.

That the book was a letter intended for a specific contemporary audience is seen, for example, in verse 11: "What you see, write in a book and send it to the seven churches which are in Asia: to Ephesus, to Smyrna, to Pergamos, to Thyatira, to Sardis, to Philadelphia, and to Laodicea."

The close of the book, too, is typical of a biblical epistle: *"The grace of our Lord Jesus Christ be with you all. Amen"* (22:21). Every epistle of Paul's, as well as Hebrews, closes with a similar benediction.

Thus the first step toward gaining a correct understanding of Revelation is to recognize that it is an epistle to a particular group of Christians, bearing a message intelligible and relevant to them at the time it was written. This means that we must seek first to discover how it applied to, and would have been understood by, its original readership, just as we would do in studying any other epistle in the New Testament. Only secondarily do we transfer truths to our own modern circumstances. This is how responsible readers approach 1 and 2 Corinthians, Galatians, James, or any other New Testament book, and it is also the most responsible way to approach this epistle of John known as *The Apocalypse of Jesus Christ.*

In two important respects, though, Revelation differs from all other New Testament epistles. These differences present unusual challenges with reference to the interpretation of Revelation:

1. *Unlike other biblical epistles, Revelation is a prophecy,* as it repeatedly affirms itself to be (1:3; 22:7, 10, 18, 19). It came to John as a series of visions, not unlike the prophecies of Daniel or Zechariah. It is the only book of prophecy in the New Testament.

Other epistles *contain* prophecies, but only this book *identifies itself as* a prophecy. The function of prophecy, according to Paul, is to speak "edification, encouragement, and comfort to men" (1 Cor. 14:3). These aims are accomplished through a combination of preaching and prediction—or as some put it, through *forthtelling* the word of the Lord for the present, as well as *foretelling* future events.

Chapters 2 and 3 of Revelation contain oracles of the Lord concerning the contemporary situations of the seven churches of Asia Minor. These chapters contain the only letters in the Bible dictated directly by Jesus. As in most prophetic preaching in the Old Testament, their message is one of comfort to the afflicted saints, coupled with a call for the disobedient to repent.

The predictive element is prominent in chapters 4 through 22, which are concerned with events to occur "after these things."

2. *Revelation's message is written in the style of apocalyptic literature,* a distinct literary genre, popular in John's time, but obscure to modern readers. Between 200 BC and AD 100, Jewish and Christian writers produced a large number of noncanonical literary works that, because of their similarities to Revelation (*The Apocalypse*), are now referred to as *apocalyptic.* Some examples known to us would include the books of *I Enoch, 4 Ezra, The Apocalypse of Baruch, The Book of Jubilees, The Assumption of Moses, The Psalms of Solomon, Testaments of the Twelve Patriarchs, The Sibylline Oracles,* and so forth. While first-century Jews and Christians were fond of reading this kind literature, no other book of the New Testament was written in this style.

Ways in Which Revelation Is Similar to Other Apocalyptic Writings

While exhibiting feature unique to its case, in several important respects Revelation resembles other apocalyptic works of its time. For example:

1. In both Revelation and other apocalyptic writings, *angels appear commonly as tour guides and interpreters.*

2. Like the other books of its genre, Revelation was *written during, or in anticipation of, a time of intense persecution of believers.* Suffering at the hands of enemies has been a recurrent feature of the history of the people of God. Seasons of persecution of Jews or Christians are the setting in which most apocalyptic books appeared. Some scholars have referred to these works, in general, as "tracts for hard times." Revelation was clearly written at just such a time of difficulty for some of the readers. The author describes himself as a "companion in the tribulation" with his readers (1:9). One of the recipient churches had lost a member through martyrdom (2:13), and others were warned of impending tribulation, imprisonment, and testing (2:10; 3:10). One of the main themes of the predictive portion of the book is that great suffering lies ahead, and martyrdom is a recurring motif.

3. Another obvious similarity between the canonical Apocalypse and its noncanonical counterparts is the *use of vivid images and symbols* (monsters and dragons, symbolic numbers and names, etc.) *in the portrayal of conflict between good and evil.* A failure to take full account of this feature has led to some rather outlandish teachings on this book by some whose rule of interpretation is "always literal, unless totally absurd" (unfortunately, not everyone's sensor is equally calibrated for measuring the *absurdity quotient* of a given theory). Though this rule may be a good one when dealing with literature written in a strictly technical genre, the case is exactly opposite when studying apocalyptic literature, where symbolism is the rule, and literalism the exception.

A very good illustration of such symbolism can be seen in the prelude and postscript added to the biblical book of Esther by an anonymous hand, centuries after its composition. These additions can be found in any Bible containing the *Apocrypha,* and are typical of the apocalyptic style of the period that produced them. At the beginning of the book, someone writing in the guise of Mordecai, reports an alleged dream, described as follows:

> Behold, noise and confusion, thunders and earthquake, tumult upon the earth! And behold, two great dragons came forward, both ready to fight, and they roared terribly. And at their roaring every nation prepared for war, to fight against the nation of the righteous. And behold, a day of darkness and gloom, tribulation and distress, affliction and great tumult upon the earth! And the whole righteous nation was troubled, they feared the evils that threatened them, and were ready to perish. Then they cried to God and from their cry, as though from a tiny spring, there came a great river, with abundant water, light came, and the sun rose, and the lowly were exalted and consumed those held in honor. (chap. A 4–10)

Then follows the book of Esther, after which the same pseudo-Mordecai sums up as follows:

> I remember the dream that I had concerning these matters, and none of them has failed to be fulfilled. The tiny stream which became a river, and there was light and the sun and abundant water—the river is Esther, whom the king married and made queen. The two dragons are Haman and myself. The nations are those gathered to destroy the name of the Jews. And my nation, this is Israel, who cried out to God and were saved. (chap. F 2–6)

These samples are particularly instructive to us since we know the story of Esther from the prose section of the book and can see how the symbols are being used by an apocalyptic writer to correspond to actual events. We can also easily recognize certain similarities here to the book of Revelation, written in the same genre—dragons, angels, earthquakes, rivers, light, tribulation, and so forth, which symbolically represent ordinary characters and events in the story.

Such apocalyptic imagery is also found in some canonical books of the Old Testament (e.g., Isaiah 24, Daniel, Ezekiel, Zechariah) and in Jesus' Olivet Discourse (Matthew 24; Mark 13; Luke 21).

In Revelation, impersonal phenomena are personified. For example, Death and Hades are represented in chapter 6 as a horseman and his footman, respectively. Like actual characters, they are later cast into the lake of fire (chap. 20). Various entities are symbolically portrayed as animals (e.g., a Lamb, a serpent, monstrous beasts, mutant locusts, etc.). Two spiritual communities, depicted as a harlot and a bride, are given symbolic names, like Babylon, Sodom, Egypt, and Jerusalem. A real woman is symbolically called "Jezebel." Political upheavals are described in terms of cosmic disruptions: the sun and moon darkened, stars falling, every island and mountain disappearing, and so on. This imagery is typical of apocalyptic literature and would have been recognized as such by readers in the first-century church.

4. As in other apocalypses, *numbers in Revelation generally convey larger concepts, rather than functioning as mere statistical data.* The most evident of these is "seven"— the number of completeness or perfection (compare Deut. 28:7, 25; Ps. 12:6; 119:164; Prov. 9:1; 24:16). In Revelation, there are seven churches, seven seals, seven trumpets, seven bowls, seven thunders, seven beatitudes, and so on. Fractions such as one-third and multiples of twelve (e.g., 24 and 144,000) also seem to be used in nonliteral ways that transcend their value as mathematical figures. The number ten and multiples thereof seem to function similarly. For this reason, it may be unwise to press for literal interpretations of certain time periods mentioned in Revelation. Very arguably, "a thousand years" means "a very long time" (as in

Ps. 90:4 and 2 Pet. 3:8), contrasted with passages where "ten days" (2:10), "one hour" (17:12), and the indefinite "a little while" (20:3) would seem to convey briefer periods in equally nonspecific terms.

Ways in Which Revelation Differs from Other Apocalyptic Writings

While the similarities between Revelation and other writings of it genre are striking, scholars are quick to point out features not found in those other works and unique to the biblical apocalyse. For example:

1. Unlike other Jewish apocalyptic books, *Revelation claims to be a prophecy inspired by God.* Though Revelation's universal acceptance had to wait until the fourth century, the church came to recognize the divine inspiration of this book and has, for that reason, recognized it as part of the legitimate canon of Scripture. Other apocalyptic writings of the same period do not make explicit claims of being inspired by God and were not recognized as Scripture by the historic Christian church.

2. *Revelation identifies its true author by name.* While other apocalyptic writers preferred to adopt pseudonyms, identifying themselves as famous persons of much earlier times, such as Enoch, Abraham, Ezra, Solomon or (as seen above) Mordecai, John was a known contemporary with his readers and identifies himself by name repeatedly in the book.

3. *Revelation actually predicts the future.* The noncanonical apocalyptic writings merely appear to do so. When, for example, they use as a pseudonym a famous figure, like Solomon, they write about their own times from the perspective of that figure's time. The apocalyptic author thus *appears* to write about the future, though the "predictions" are, in fact, a retelling of the author's own recent history. By contrast, Christians have become convinced that the book of Revelation actually is what it claims to be: a prophetic epistle, written in the apocalyptic mode, predicting future events under the inspiration of the Holy Spirit.

WHO WROTE IT?

Earliest Viewpoint

The authorship of a book often determines the authority it carries, and especially in the case of a book being considered for inclusion in the Bible. New Testament books are thought to carry apostolic authority. Since the apostles were specifically appointed by Christ to speak on His behalf to the church, their writings and those of their close companions, who wrote under their supervision, are regarded as Scripture.

The authorship of Revelation is disputed—and important. If the book was written by one of the apostles, its inclusion to the canon should be universally recognized. However, if the author was not an apostle, but some otherwise unknown Christian writer, his book would belong, along with the *Didache*, the *Shepherd of Hermas*, and the *Epistle of Barnabas*, in the collection of writings that the early church found edifying, but not finally authoritative.

There was no dispute among the apostolic fathers (that is, those living a generation or two after the apostles themselves) as to the authorship of the Revelation. The author identifies himself four times simply as "John" (1:1, 4; 21:2; 22:8), expecting that, without further self-description, he would be known to his audience. The earliest fathers—e.g., Justin Martyr (d. 165), Irenaeus (c. 180), Clement of Alexandria (d. 215), Tertullian (d. 220)—unanimously identified this author with John, the son of Zebedee, one of the twelve apostles, and the "beloved disciple" of Christ, to whom the writing of the fourth Gospel and three epistles is also attributed. If this is so, then the book of Revelation certainly belongs in our New Testament.

Later Proposals

While accepting its place in the canon, Dionysius of Alexandria (mid-third century) did not believe Revelation to have been the work of the apostle. Eusebius (c. 325), followed by a number of modern commentators, attributed the book to another John, a presbyter thought to have been mentioned in an ambiguous statement of Papias. This Papias was a second-century writer from whom we derive much of our understanding of the origins of New Testament books. His works have not survived, except in the form of quotations found in Eusebius' *Ecclesiastical History.* In one passage, Papias described his methods of gathering information about the apostles (whom he refers to as "the elders"). The ambiguity of his statement has given rise to the theory of "the Presbyter John" as an alternate to the apostle for the authorship of the Apocalypse. Papias wrote:

> For I have never, like many, delighted to hear those that tell many things, but those that teach the truth. . . . But if I met with anyone who had been a follower of the elders anywhere, I made it a point to inquire what were the declarations of the elders. What was said by Andrew, Peter or Philip. What by Thomas, James, John, Matthew or any other of the disciples of our Lord. What was said by Aristion, and *the presbyter John*, disciples of the Lord.[1]

Scholars differ as to whether "the presbyter John" is a reference to the apostle or to another John, otherwise unknown to us. The main argument for the latter thesis is that Papias mentions the apostle John separately, before mentioning the presbyter John, suggesting the existence of two notable men named John. If this is the case, it may have been this presbyter who wrote Revelation. However, simply making this suggestion does not make it true. There may have been dozens of Johns in the early church. This would not help us in determining which of them was our author of interest. The overturning of the strong, early tradition of apostolic authorship should require convincing evidences.

Revelation and John's Other Writings

A principal reason given for doubting the apostolic authorship is that the Greek style and grammar of Revelation are greatly inferior to that of the fourth Gospel and three epistles, which are also traditionally attributed to the apostle John. On this basis, some have asserted dogmatically that the same author certainly could not have written Revelation and the other books attributed to John. The gospel and epistles of John are written in a good literary Greek style, whereas Revelation's "grammar is perpetually stumbling, its idiom is that of a foreign language, its whole style that of a writer who neither knows nor cares for literary form."[2]

A. T. Robertson puts it more delicately, writing that "there are numerous grammatical laxities in the Apocalypse, termed by Charles a veritable grammar of its own."[3] But Radermacher described the book as "the most uncultured literary production that has come down to us from antiquity."[4]

In Defense of the Apostolic Authorship

1. In answer to these things, defenders of the apostolic authorship point out that John is described, in Acts 4:13, as "unschooled" and may have been incapable of writing cultured Greek. His other writings, having been written from Ephesus, may owe their polished style to the use of an amanuensis (a kind of secretary) not available on Patmos, where Revelation was written. Alternatively, Revelation may not reflect John's characteristic style, and its sloppiness may be accounted for by the haste with which he sought to write down visions as they occurred or by his excited mental state.

2. The fact that the author provides no information clarifying his identity, beyond his given name, also supports the traditional theory of authorship. It seems unlikely that any person in the early church, other than the apostle, would have been so well known as to be able to identify himself simply as "John" and expect to be recognized by all the churches.

3. Many special concepts and expressions are unique to Revelation and John's other writings. Assuming that the apostle wrote the latter (a point not universally

agreed upon), these similarities would seemingly argue for the apostolic author-ship of Revelation as well.[5]

For example, the Greek term "Logos" ("Word") as a referent to Christ, is found only in John's Gospel, John's first epistle, and in Revelation (John 1:1; 1 John 1:1; Rev. 19:13). Similarly, "the Lamb" is found, as a messianic title, only in the fourth Gospel and in Revelation (John 1:29, 36; Rev. 5:6, etc.). Both books also contain the promise, found nowhere else, that the "water of life" will be given to "him that thirsts" (John 7:37f.; Rev. 22:17).

Other typically Johannine expressions in Revelation include the unique "keep . . . from" (Gr. *tēreo ek;* John 17:15; Rev. 3:10), and a particular form of the Greek word for "true" (*alethinos*), which appears nine times in John, four times in 1 John, and ten times in Revelation, but only five times elsewhere in the New Tes-tament. Similarly, the concepts of the "first resurrection" (John 5:24–29; Rev. 20:5), Satan's being "cast out" (John 12:31; Rev. 12:9, 13), and the idea of "over-coming" the world (or Satan) are found exclusively in John's writings (e.g., John 16:33; 1 John 2:13, 14; 5:4, 5; Rev. 12:11; 21:7, etc.). Strangely, John and Revela-tion both make paraphrastic use of Zechariah 12:10, though neither properly quote it (John 19:37; Rev. 1:7). As F. F. Bruce observed:

> Revelation certainly comes from the same environment as the other Johannine
> writings. Whatever differences there are between this book and the Fourth Gos-
> pel, both present one who is called 'the Word of God' and 'the Lamb of God' saying
> to His followers, 'In this world you have trouble. But take heart! I have overcome
> the world' (John 16:33); whatever differences there are between it and the First
> Letter of John, both encourage the people of Christ with the assurance: 'This is the
> victory that has overcome the world, even our faith' (1 John 5:4).[6]

In the early church, the apostolic authorship of the book of Revelation faced all of the same challenges to its acceptance as it faces today, yet those living closest to its source found the theory plausible nonetheless. Perhaps we cannot know for cer-tain that the author was not another John, but there probably is not sufficient evi-dence to overturn the consensus of the early church: namely, that of the candidates for author of the Apocalypse, the apostle John seems the most likely.

DATE AND HISTORICAL SETTING

To understand any New Testament book, it is valuable to establish the time it was written and to sketch pertinent features of its historical and cultural context. In deciding among the various possible approaches to Revelation in particular, such considerations can be altogether determinative. As mentioned above, the book of Revelation was written during a time of persecution and trial for some of the recipient churches. It seems to have been written with a mind to encourage the believers that, even if they should be called upon to suffer, or even to die, for their faith, yet their vindication (and the doom of those who persecute them) is sure and not far off. Such a message would be a useful encouragement regardless when it was written, since the church has often been called upon to suffer, and the vision of the reigning Lamb and the vindicated martyrs transcends local, contemporary situations. However, commentators often suggest that the magnitude of the crisis described in Revelation requires that we identify it with one of the imperial persecutions of the Roman emperors.

Altogether, there were ten emperors who are believed to have persecuted Christians. Only two of them, however, did so within the lifetime of John—namely Nero, who reigned from AD 54 to 68, and Domitian, who reigned from 81 to 96.

Most modern scholars appear to favor the later date, in the time of Domitian, for the writing of Revelation, placing it at about AD 96. There have been many advocates of note, though, who have defended an earlier date, in the reign of Nero—perhaps 67 or 68. Many modern evangelicals, especially those taking the *preterist* approach, favor the earlier date, since that would make the book predate the fall of Jerusalem in 70, allowing for the possibility that the book may be predicting that event. Not all who have defended the early date have been *preterists, but, for the other three approaches, the date of writing is not nearly so crucial. For the other viewpoints, as G. K. Beale observes:*

> One can in fact affirm the early date or the late date without the main interpretative approach being affected. Under either dating position the book could be understood as a polemic against Rome and especially against compromise with ungodly Roman culture. The early date allows for an anti-Jerusalem focus but does not demand it. [7]

There are respectable arguments, and impressive advocates, favoring both dates. We will consider, individually, the primary evidences adduced in support of each view.

Written During Nero's Persecution

In favor of the earlier date of writing (during Nero's persecution), several internal evidences are presented.

1. *The temple still standing.* Among the most important arguments for a Neroean date of writing is the apparent existence of the temple in Jerusalem at the time of

writing (11:1–2), and the tension between the church and its Jewish detractors (e.g., 2:9; 3:9), both of which, it is argued, changed when Jerusalem was destroyed by the Romans in AD 70. The active persecution of the churches by the Jews would seem less likely to be a feature of a post-70 date, since (one would think) the Jews of the diaspora would feel demoralized and disempowered than before the destruction of their nation.

These evidences are inconclusive, however. First, because the temple described in Revelation 11 is part of a symbolic vision and need not have been seen while its earthly counterpart was standing. It could even be a *future* temple that is depicted, even as Ezekiel saw a temple in his vision at a time when no temple stood in Jerusalem (Ezek. 40–48). Second, it is not evident that Jewish persecution of Christians came to a grinding halt with the overthrow of the Jewish State. In fact, the Jews in Smyrna took an active role in the martyrdom of that town's Christian leader Polycarp in the second century.

2. *The sixth king.* Another important argument for a Neronean date is based upon the cryptic passage in Revelation 17:10, which speaks of the king currently reigning at the time of writing: "There are also seven kings. Five have fallen, one is, and the other has not yet come. And when he comes, he must continue a short time." Unless the term "kings" here is taken as "kingdoms" (i.e., Egypt, Assyria, Babylon, Media-Persia, Greece, Rome), a natural understanding of this statement would be that five Roman emperors had fallen, and the sixth was reigning at the time of writing. Since Nero was the sixth man to be recognized as emperor of the Roman Empire, this would seemingly place the date of writing sometime within his reign.

3. *The number of the beast.* A further confirmation of the earlier date is often found in the identification of Nero with the number "666," which can, with some ingenuity, be demonstrated to fit his name (see *preterist* comments at 13:18). John's assumption that the wise among his first-century readers would be able to identify the name of the beast from the gematria[8] suggests that the one represented as "the beast" was a known entity at the time of writing. No other prominent man living in John's lifetime can easily be identified by this number.

4. *The Muratorian Canon.* In addition to these internal considerations, there are also a number of external evidences for the earlier date of composition. One of the most ancient surviving documents of the ancient Latin church is called the *Muratorian Fragment,* which provides a list of the New Testament books accepted as canonical by the church around the year 170. In this fragment, we read: "Apostle Paul himself, following the example of his predecessor John, writes by name to only seven churches." The assertion that Paul, who probably died around AD 67, in

writing to seven named churches, was following the lead of *his predecessor* John, who had also (earlier) written to seven churches, can only be understood to mean that Revelation was written before Paul's death—that is, in the sixties. This testimony is as early as that of Irenaeus, upon whose statements the case for the later date largely rests. The contrasting testimony of Irenaeus is usually preferred over that of the Muratorian Canon, however, due to Irenaeus' connections to persons closely associated with John.

5. *Clement of Alexandria* (AD 150–215) relates an anecdote about the later years of John's life, beginning with the words, "Hear a story that is no mere story, but a true account of John the apostle that has been handed down and preserved in memory. When after the death of the tyrant he removed from the island of Patmos to Ephesus . . ."[9] Since the story goes on to relate a very active (almost athletic!) physical life of the Apostle, many scholars believe that "the tyrant" alluded to must have been Nero, not Domitian. At the time of Domitian's death, John would have been nearly one hundred years old, yet Clement's story describes him as riding on horseback in hot pursuit of a young bandit who was a lapsed Christian. If Nero was Clement's "tyrant," then Clement is saying it was under Nero's rule that John was banished to Patmos and wrote the Revelation.

6. *Other New Testament books.* Interestingly, there are possible cases of the citation of passages from Revelation by other New Testament writers, who are known to have died before AD 70. James, in his epistle, refers to "the crown of life which the Lord has promised" to give to those who endure testing (James 1:12). There is no such statement of the Lord on record, other than that found in Revelation 2:10, which promised "a crown of life" to those who endure trial. Was James familiar with the book of Revelation?

Similarly, the apostle Peter may be referring to Revelation 21 (if not Isaiah 65) when he mentions God's "promise" of "new heavens and a new earth in which righteousness dwells" (2 Peter 3:13). While Peter might have promises either in Isaiah or in Revelation in mind, his reference to the new heavens and new earth as being the dwelling place of "righteousness" might favor the latter, since righteousness is not a prominent part of the description given in Isaiah.

Since James and Peter both died prior to AD 70, and could not be quoting from the book of Revelation unless it had been written prior to their deaths, these examples can be included among the external evidences for an early date of Revelation.

Among the well-known scholars who have held to the early date of Revelation have been Jay Adams, Adam Clarke, Alfred Edersheim, J. B. Lightfoot, John A. T. Robinson, Philip Schaff, and many others. The early date was the prevalent theory among Bible scholars of the nineteenth century. In 1893, William Milligan, who favored the late date, admitted that "recent scholarship has, with little exception, decided in favour of the earlier and not the later date."[10] Likewise, church historian, Philip Schaff, writing in 1910, asserted, "The early date is now accepted by perhaps the majority of scholars."[11] Dr. Kenneth Gentry lists over 130 notable scholars and commentators who favored the early dating of Revelation.[12]

Written During Domitian's Reign?

On the other hand, numerous evidences are also presented for a later date, during the reign of Domitian. Well-known advocates of this date include: Robert Mounce, Albert Barnes, B. B. Warfield, Donald Guthrie, John Walvoord, Merrill Tenney, and perhaps most other commentators of the twentieth century. There are a number of internal evidences that have commended themselves to scholars as favoring this date.

1. *Return of Nero?* Many believe that emperor worship is alluded to in Revelation 13 and that the references to a "mortal head wound that healed" allude to a well-known superstition that arose after Nero's death, claiming that he would, in fact, return at the head of the Parthian armies to again conquer Rome. It is claimed that emperor worship was not enforced until the time of Domitian and that he was widely regarded as a "second Nero," making him the best candidate for the current persecutor of John and his companions.

In response to this, it may be argued that, since John wrote prophetically, references to the reign of Domitian (if they are found in Revelation) need not have been written contemporaneously with that reign. John may well have written decades (or centuries!) earlier than the events that he predicted. It is logically possible that a true prophet, writing in the time of Nero, could write predictions that would be fulfilled in the time of Domitian. Therefore, we may be looking in the wrong place for clues concerning the time of writing when we try to fit the events described in the prophetic portions of the book into the time of writing.

This particular argument also raises questions as to whether John actually belied this so-called *Nero Redivivus* myth, and if so, whether such an adherence to the superstition would adversely impact his claim to inspiration.

2. *The extent of the persecution.* Another argument for the later date is that Nero's persecution never extended far beyond the city of Rome itself, whereas Domitian's persecution of Christians (it is claimed) spanned the whole empire. Since the churches addressed in Revelation were in what is now Turkey, they would be

sufficiently distant from Rome to be immune to Nero's persecution, though they would have suffered under Domitian's rule.

It is not necessary to believe that the seven churches in Asia were suffering as the result of any emperor's decree, whether Nero's or Domitian's. The letters make no mention of imperial persecutions, and give no indication that the churches were currently experiencing trouble from any but local antagonists. In fact, there is no evidence that all seven of the churches were experiencing any persecution in their vicinities at the time of writing (some were complacent, self-confident, and lukewarm).

If Nero, or any emperor, persecuted Christians in Rome, Christians in other parts of the empire might well have faced local persecution incidentally at the same time, as their local enemies may have taken advantage of the general antichristian attitude of the emperor to justify harassing the churches in their localities. Besides this, many scholars, including those supportive of a late date, have said that there is no historical proof that there was an empire-wide persecution of Christians even in Domitian's reign. This undermines the very premise upon which this argument rests.

3. *Conditions in the churches.* Support for the later date of Revelation is also sought by appeal to the conditions prevailing in the seven churches *at the time of writing.* Some believe that the degree of spiritual decline found in the churches at Ephesus (which had left its first love), Sardis (which was dead, having only a reputation for being alive), and Laodicea (which was lukewarm) would suggest the passage of considerable time since their founding. Since the persecution of Nero's time happened less than a decade after these churches were founded, it is thought that there would not be sufficient time for the necessary degree of spiritual decline to have occurred, prior to Nero's death in 68.

Yet the loss of first love in Ephesus is a condition that can happen to a church in a very short time, as the experience of many modern congregations can demonstrate. Paul marveled that the Galatian churches had so severely regressed almost immediately after he had left them as infant congregations (Gal. 1:6). The founding of the churches in Sardis and Laodicea is not recorded in Scripture, and we know nothing of the original state of these congregations. For all we know, their poor state might not represent any significant decline, as they may never have risen much above the condition in which Revelation describes them. Paul's Corinthian correspondence demonstrates the alarming degree of carnality to which a church can degenerate in as little as two years after its founding. There is nothing incredible about the suggestion that similar scenarios may have applied to Ephesus, Sardis, and Laodicea as well.

4. *The existence of the church in Smyrna.* Some believe that the church of Smyrna (addressed in Rev. 2:8–11) did not exist in the lifetime of Paul, who may have lived up until about AD 67. This would make it unlikely that there would be a church there to address within the time of Nero's reign. Since there was a church in Smyrna when Revelation was written, this has been used as an evidence for the later date of writing.

The belief that there was no church in Smyrna in Paul's lifetime is based upon a statement from Polycarp, who was the bishop of that very church in the second century. Polycarp wrote in a letter to the church at Philippi:

Among [you at Philippi] the blessed Paul labored, who are praised in the beginning of his epistle. For concerning you he boasts in all the churches who then alone had known the Lord, for we had not yet known him *(Letter the Philippians,* 11:3).

Notably, Polycarp does not actually state that the church in Smyrna did not exist in Paul's lifetime, but that the Smyrnans "had not yet known" the Lord at the time when Paul wrote his epistle to the Philippians, which was probably no later than AD 63.[13] This would allow sufficient time for the church to come into existence in Smyrna before AD 68.

5. *The prosperity of Laodicea.* The city of Laodicea was destroyed in an earthquake in AD 60 or 61 and required many years to rebuild. Yet, when Revelation was written, the church in that city claimed to be "wealthy, and have need of nothing" (3:17). Many commentators feel that the city could not have recovered sufficiently during the decade of the 60s to have allowed such a self-confident attitude to prevail in the Christian congregation there.

Of course, this is a rather subjective suggestion. A city, though still under reconstruction, might well be feeling proud of the rapidness of its recovery within a few years after surviving a great earthquake. Furthermore, the church's self-confidence might have had nothing to do with the city's physical circumstances. The boasts may have been an expression of pride from a sense of spiritual self-sufficiency. This arrogance could exist regardless of the state of the city's physical recovery.

External Evidences for the Later Date

The foregoing internal evidence we have considered for the late date of Revelation has been ambiguous at best. The strongest argument for the later date is based on the testimony of extrabiblical sources. Several church fathers indicate that Domitian was emperor when John wrote Revelation. All of them, however, seem to base their information on the important testimony of Irenaeus, found in a passage wherein he wrote:[14]

> Now since this is so, and since this number [666] is found in all the good and ancient copies, and since *those who have seen John face to face testify*, and reason teaches us that the number of the name of the beast appears according to the numeration of the Greeks by the letters in it . . . We will not, however, incur the risk of pronouncing positively as to the name of Antichrist; for if it were necessary that his name should be distinctly revealed in this present time, it would have been announced by him who beheld the apocalyptic vision. *For that was seen no very long time since, but almost in our day, towards the end of Domitian's reign* (emphasis mine).

If Irenaeus is saying that the vision was seen at this late date, then his witness carries considerable weight. In view of the unchallenged claim that Irenaeus knew Polycarp, who in turn knew the apostle John, he might well be expected to have accurate information regarding the time of John's imprisonment on Patmos.[15] Several other church fathers, possibly following the lead of Irenaeus, indicated the same time frame for the date of the writing of Revelation. But is this the correct understanding of Irenaeus' words?

While the *importance* of Irenaeus' testimony may be undisputed, the same cannot be said about his *meaning.* The main ambiguity debated by scholars concerns *what* or *who* it was that was *seen* toward the end of Domitian's reign? Was it *the vision* which John "beheld"? or was it *the Apostle himself,* who was "seen . . . face to face" by those who testify?

The phrase "That was seen . . ." may be a corruption of an original that read, "He was seen . . ." If this is true, then it only proves that John lived into the reign of Domitian, though he may have written the Apocalypse much earlier. Irenaeus, then, would not be commenting on the time of the writing of the Apocalypse.

Those who originally translated Irenaeus' work into English complained of the poor condition of the manuscript evidence for his work. They wrote:

> The great work of Irenaeus, now for the first time translated into English, is unfortunately no longer extant in the original. It has come down to us only in an ancient Latin version, with the exception of the greater part of the first book, which has been preserved in the original Greek, through means of copious quotations made by Hippolytus and Epiphanius. The text, both in Latin and Greek, is often most uncertain.[16]

Since the text is admittedly "uncertain" in many places, there is room for uncertainty concerning any preferred reading of the statement of Irenaeus. Early-date scholars have put forward plausible arguments concerning this passage.

Early-Date Responses to Irenaeus

In *The Beast of Revelation*, Dr. Kenneth Gentry marshals seven strong reasons, some linguistic, some contextual, and some logical, for interpreting Irenaeus' statement as meaning that it was John—not John's vision—that was seen during the principate of Domitian.[17]

For example, early in the passage, Irenaeus refers to the number 666 as appearing in "all the . . . ancient copies" of the book of Revelation. This presupposes that the book had been around a good long while before this statement was written. If there were copies of the book that were ancient, was not the original more ancient still? Yet, in Irenaeus' estimation, the time of Domitian's reign was not considered to have been very ancient history, for he speaks of that reign as occurring "almost in our day." How could Irenaeus speak of "ancient copies" of a work whose original had been written "almost" in his own time?

With reference to his mention of Domitian's reign, there are grounds for believing that Irenaeus was speaking of the time of *John's last being seen* by the brethren, rather than the time of John's having seen the apocalyptic vision. Kenneth Gentry paraphrases what he believes to have been Irenaeus' thought as follows: "It is not important for us to know the name of the beast (or Antichrist), which was hidden in the number 666. Were it important, why did John not tell us? After all, he lived almost to our own era, and spoke with some men I have known."[18]

If this is indeed Irenaeus' main point, then how would it serve his purpose to speak of the time when Revelation was written? His intention would be to emphasize the accessibility of John to explain the number of the beast, had he wished to do so.

Gentry's arguments, modern sentiments notwithstanding, undermine the case for the Domitianic date of writing of the Apocalypse, insofar as they depend on one's interpretation of Irenaeus. Further, any independent arguments advanced in favor of the *preterist* approach, which plausibly apply the prophecies of Revelation to the fall of Jerusalem in AD 70, would also argue for a date of writing prior to that date. At the very least, the *possibility* of the early date keeps the *preterist* approach legitimately in the debate.

STRUCTURAL PARALLELISM IN REVELATION

What are we to make of the sequence of visions in Revelation? How are they organized? There is no reason to insist on a strictly chronological sequence to the unfolding of events predicted in Revelation, though some approaches have a tendency to assume such a sequence. It should be remembered that when John says, "After these things I saw . . ." (as he frequently does), he is referring to the sequence in which he saw the visions—not necessarily implying anything about the chronological order in which the visions would find fulfillment in events.

A certain amount of parallelism is to be observed in Revelation, regardless of which of the four approaches one takes. That is, some portions double back to cover the same ground as was covered in previous sections. Scholars do not agree as to how many parallel sections are present. *Some futurists* identify two parallel sections, seeing chapters 4 through 11 as a complete description of the Tribulation, and chapters 12 through 19 as another description of the same period.

Those who take the *idealist* approach usually identify as many as seven parallel segments in the book. The first segment (chaps. 1–3) is concerned with the seven letters to the seven churches, and has application to the entire church age. The second segment (chaps. 4–7) deals with the same period under the figure of the breaking of seven seals. The third section (chaps.8–11) covers the same period by employing the symbols of seven trumpet judgments. Chapters 12 through 14, chapters 15 and 16, chapters 17 through 19, and chapters 20 through 22 present four additional views of the church age (with the exception of the last, which extends beyond the present age), making seven altogether. Some authorities point out that each segment contains a reference to the Second Coming of Christ as its culmination (e.g., 1:7; 6:14–17; 11:18; 14:14–20; 16:20–21; 19:11; 20:9).

Daniel, it has been observed, contains parallel sections. This is especially apparent in Daniel's chapters 2 and 7, both of which cover the reigns of the same four successive kingdoms, symbolically depicting them as four metals and four beasts, respectively, and chapter 8 revisits two of the four. Similarities between Daniel and Revelation are universally acknowledged, and some feel that one of those similarities is the retelling of the same story repeatedly using different symbols.

Many passages demonstrate the presence of some parallelism in Revelation: The "beast" is seen at war with the saints in the midst of chapter 11, but emerges initially in chapter 13. "Babylon" is described in her glory, in chapter 17, but is twice, earlier, been declared to have already "fallen" (14:8; 16:19). Every mountain and island are removed in 6:14, but flee away again in 16:20. Three different places describe a great "battle" (16:14; 19:19; 20:8)—possibly the same battle in each case. The mention of three-and-a-half years occurs five times and may refer, in each case, to the same period emphasizing its different features (11:2, 3; 12:6, 14; 13:5). There is no question that chapter 12 has at least two parallel segments (12:6

and 12:13–17). These data seem to be equally problematic for any interpretation that looks for chronologically sequential fulfillments.

The implications of these parallels affect one's chronological placement, for example, of the "thousand years," or the Millennium. If the events of Revelation 20 *must* follow the events described in chapter 19, where many interpreters find the Second Coming of Christ, then the Millennium in chapter 20 should be anticipated as coming after the Second Coming of Christ. This is no doubt one of *premillennialism's* significant assumptions. But if the Second Coming is seen in chapter 19, and chapter 20 doubles back to start a new parallel section, then one might see in the binding of Satan (20:1–3) the beginning of the Gospel Age, as does the *amillennialist.*[19]

A correlation between the seven *trumpet* judgments and the seven *bowl* judgments has often been observed, suggesting the possibility of parallelism between the sections:

A. The first of each affects the earth (8:7; 16:2).

B. The second of each affects the sea (8:8; 16:3).

C. The third of each affects the rivers (8:10; 16:4).

D. The fourth of each affects heavenly bodies (8:12; 16:8).

E. The fifth of each affects men (9:1; 16:10).

F. The sixth of each affects the Euphrates (9:13; 16:12).

G. The seventh of each is the end (11:15; 16:17).

Notwithstanding these observations, however, it is difficult to sustain the contention that all seven sections are truly parallel to each other. The seven alleged references to the Second Coming may not all describe that event (see commentary following). The battles mentioned might not all be the same battle. The parallels noted between the *trumpets* and the *bowls* may be merely stylistic, since very different events are described in the two sequences. Also, since the seven *bowl* judgments are called "the seven last plagues" (15:1), it sounds as if they bear a chronological, not synchronous, relationship to the previously mentioned plagues (e.g., the *trumpets*).

Parallelism in Revelation does not, in itself, undercut any of the major approaches. It does, however, militate against making firm chronological predictions based on a passage's position in the book.

REVELATION'S USE OF THE REST OF SCRIPTURE

Though scholars debate the degree to which Revelation may have been influenced by noncanonical writings, there is little question that the Apocalypse contains recycled materials previously employed in other canonical books. The symbols of the book of Revelation are not generally novel or new, most of them having previously been introduced in other portions of Scripture and are deliberately echoed in John's prophecy. The book has been called "a rebirth of images," since it takes imagery familiar from hundreds of Old Testament passages and reworks them into new applications. For example, the symbol of "the two olive trees" as a designation for the two witnesses in chapter 11 is an echo of Zechariah 4:3, 11–14, where the two olive trees are evidently Zerubbabel and Joshua, the high priest. Yet Revelation, while taking the identical phrase, applies it to different characters.

Unlike most other books of the New Testament, Revelation does not contain even one direct quotation from the Old Testament. However, there are hundreds of allusions to images and expressions from the Old Testament, and from the New Testament as well (especially the other writings of John).

It has been calculated that Revelation draws upon concepts and imagery from Isaiah (79 times), Daniel (53 times), Ezekiel (48 times), Psalms (43 times), Exodus (27 times), Jeremiah (22 times), Zechariah (15 times), Amos (9 times), and Joel (8 times).

The principal historical matrices from which the images frequently are taken are: a) the Exodus, b) the end of the Babylonian exile, and c) the life of Jesus. We will examine these individually.

Images Drawn from the Exodus

The book of Revelation is replete with echoes of the Jewish exodus from Egypt:

- The evil power that persecutes God's people is spiritually called Egypt (11:8);

- The plagues of darkness, hail, locusts, boils, frogs, water turning to blood, etc., all recall similar plagues sent against Egypt prior to the Exodus;

- Christians are said to be "freed" by the blood of Christ (1:5 marg.), just as the Jews experienced freedom from Egypt only after shedding the blood of the Passover lamb;

- The dragon that persecutes the woman (12:3ff.) recalls Egypt, which is called a dragon in Ezekiel 29:3 and Psalm 74:13;

37

- Like Israel of old, the woman, having escaped the dragon, is nourished in the wilderness (12:6, 14);

- As Israel, having safely crossed the sea, sang the "song of Moses," so also the redeemed sing "the song of Moses and the Lamb" (15:3).

A further connecting link between the thought of Exodus and that of Revelation is the reference in the latter to the tabernacle and its furnishings. In Exodus, Moses was told to build the tabernacle after a pattern revealed to him on Mount Sinai (e.g., Exod. 25:40). The book of Hebrews tells us that this earthly tabernacle was a model of a heavenly counterpart (Heb. 8:1–5; 9:1–9). John apparently saw that heavenly tabernacle, for he describes golden lampstands (1:12), hidden manna, associated with the ark of the covenant (2:17), the ark itself (11:19), the altar of sacrifice (6:9), the altar of incense (8:3–5), and the holy of holies (11:1; 15:8). There are other possible references to the tabernacle, as, for instance, the marked likeness of the New Jerusalem to the holy of holies (see comments on chap. 21).

From these data, we may rightly conclude that the message of Revelation somehow is connected, in principle, with the significance of the original exodus of Israel. Exactly what that connection is, will be a matter to be debated among the various approaches.

Images Drawn from the End of the Exile

As Israel had spent centuries in bondage in Egypt, so did Judah later spend seventy years in exile in Babylon. And just as God delivered Israel from Egypt, and allowed them to resettle the land promised to their fathers, so also He delivered the remnant from Babylon, bringing them back to their ancestral land. The return of the Jewish captives from the exile in Babylon was like another exodus, and is sometimes compared, in the Old Testament, with the original exodus.[20] Both "exoduses" thus provide imagery for the message of the Apocalypse. Insofar as the historical exodus from Egypt somehow informs the message of Revelation, so far also does the historical "exodus" from Babylon. In Revelation, the siege of the beloved city (20:9) and the repeated declarations of the fall of Babylon (14:8, ch.18) call to mind the historical period of this latter deliverance. In Revelation, the fall of Babylon is seen as being effected, in part, by the drying up of the river Euphrates and invading kings of the East (16:12), as was the case when ancient Babylon fell to the Medes and the Persians in 539 BC.

Images Drawn from the Life of Christ

The historical life of Jesus also provides imagery for some of the visions in Revelation. Christ's death, resurrection, and victory over Satan are matters of frequent reference (e.g., 1:18; 2:8; 5:6, 9; 12:10, etc.). His birth and ascension are probably depicted in Revelation 12:5.

The ministry of "two witnesses," in chapter 11, mirrors the earthly career of Christ. Their ministry is described as lasting three-and-a-half years (v. 3), as did His. They are slain in the same city "where our Lord was crucified" (v. 8). After three days, they rise from the dead and ascend into heaven (vv. 11–12), and the persecuting city is consequently smitten (v. 13), as Jerusalem was in AD 70.

Obviously, the book of Revelation is not predicting the historical exodus, the return of the exiles from Babylon, or the earthly ministry of Jesus, since those things occurred prior to its writing. Nor are we to anticipate a literal replay of these unique historical occurrences. However, Christ, through John, is presenting his message in language reminiscent of these events, no doubt in order to highlight the similarity *in principle* of the events he is predicting to those of the past.

ADDITIONAL INTERPRETIVE CONSIDERATIONS

Certain issues bear upon the interpretation of Revelation that do not enter into the consideration of how most other books are interpreted. Some pivotal issues include these:

- the geographical scope of the visions;
- the meaning of the "coming" of Christ in Revelation; and
- the meaning of the "thousand years" (the Millennium) in Revelation.

Adherents to the various major approaches will understand these issues differently. It is important, in assessing the four approaches, to understand the alternative ways in which these issues are viewed by each.

The Geographical Scope of Revelation

In Revelation we read frequently of "all those who dwell on the earth" and of events affecting the "whole world." Because of these and similar expressions, our first impression is likely to be that the judgments described in the book are global in extent. Whether this initial impression is to be trusted or not depends, to a large extent, upon the context and the meaning of the Greek word usually translated as "earth" and the usage of the word "world."

The word used in the Greek text for "earth" is *ge,* which can be translated as "earth" or as "land" with equal legitimacy, depending on context.[21] In any place where the intended meaning is "land," it opens the possibility that reference is being made to the land of Israel, which is often denoted in Scripture by no more elaborate a designation than the expression "the land."

In the Old Testament (and, arguably, in the New as well) the Gentile nations are symbolically called "the sea" in contrast to "the land" (i.e., Israel).[22] Thus, phrases like "those who inhabit the earth (or land)"[23] and "kings of the earth (or land),"[24] if not understood globally, could be references to the people of Israel and their rulers, respectively.

In Revelation, as elsewhere in Scripture, the decision whether to translate *ge* as *land* or *earth* is largely determined by context. There may be some help in observing that sometimes the word is in contrast to "the sea,"[25] suggesting that "land" may be the intended meaning, as when John sees an angel with one foot on the "land" (*ge,*) and one foot on the sea (10:1). At other times, the word is contrasted with "heaven,"[26] which would favor, in such contexts, the translation as "earth," as when John sees a new heaven and a new "earth" (*ge;* 21:1). Unfortunately for this method of determining the meaning, the word is sometimes contrasted with heaven and with the sea in the same passages![27]

Likewise "the world" normally speaks to us of the planet earth. But to biblical writers it often was limited in scope to the Mediterranean "world" or the Roman Empire (see Luke 2:1; Col. 1:6). Similar passages that employ language that sounds universal but where the scope is actually limited to the Roman Empire would include Daniel 7:23, Acts 2:5, and Colossians 1:6, 23. Thus in Revelation, a statement about "the time of trial which shall come upon the whole world to test those who dwell on the earth" (Rev. 3:10) could refer to an empire-wide crisis, which would especially place stress upon those who dwell in Israel.

Such a meaning could not be proved from linguistic considerations alone, and would have to be determined contextually as part of the flow of the thought of the passage. Different approaches would incline differently in these determinations. *Futurist* and *idealist* interpreters would usually incline toward seeing these expressions in the universal and global sense. *Preterists* and *historicists* usually understand them in terms of a narrower scope, as limited to Israel or to the Roman

Empire. Final decisions about this kind of language will ultimately hang on the larger considerations, depending on which of the four approaches carries greatest weight in the judgment of the interpreter.

The "Coming" of the Lord In Revelation

At least twelve times (possibly more) the book of Revelation promises or warns that Christ is going to "come." In most cases, the impression is given that his coming will not be very far distant. Evangelicals today commonly apply such references to what we usually call the *Second Coming* of Christ—meaning his final appearance in glory to judge the world at the end of history.

Adherents to each of the four approaches surveyed in this book anticipate the literal return of Christ at the end of the age, and (with few exceptions) all find reference to this eschatological coming in the book of Revelation.[28] Such a finding might seem abundantly obvious to those familiar with only one approach to Revelation. However, when we carefully assess the way this terminology is used, we find that other interpretations are also plausible. It is instructive to consider at least three factors relevant to Revelation's references to Christ's "coming":

1. Christ is occasionally said to "come" in a spiritual sense.

> Behold, I stand at the door and knock. If anyone hears My voice and opens the door, **I will come in to him** and dine with him, and he with Me. (Rev. 3:20)

> And I will pray the Father, and **He will give you another Helper** . . . the Spirit of Truth . . . I will not leave you orphans; **I will come to you**. (John 14:16–18)

> Jesus answered and said to him, "If anyone loves Me, he will keep My word; and My Father will love him, and **We will come to him and make Our home with him**. (John 14:23)

Each of these passages includes a promise to Christ's disciples that he will "come" to them, though his Second Coming is not intended in any of them. It seems clear in the two passages in John (and probable, in the Revelation passage) that what is being promised is Christ's coming in the person of his Spirit to dwell within the believer. Thus the coming of the "Spirit of Truth" is spoken of as synonymous with the coming of Christ himself to his disciples (John 14:16–18), and Paul can speak of the "Spirit of God" or the "Spirit of Christ" dwelling in us (Rom. 8:9) as synonymous with "Christ" dwelling in us (Rom. 8:10).

2. Temporal judgments upon nations are "visitations" from God.

The language of prophecy often expresses a perspective different from that of ordinary historical narrative or prosaic literature. The prophets recognized in the great political upheavals of history the acts of the sovereign God (Amos 3:6) exercising his prerogative of "removing" and "raising up" rulers and empires (Dan. 2:21). The conquest of one nation by another through invasion and war were little more than God's means of judging the former—a nation that had been "weighed in the balances and found wanting" (Dan. 5:27). The use of one nation's military machine for the punishment of another sinful nation did not require that the nation so used be aware of its being an instrument in the hands of God (Isa. 10:5–15). God is working invisibly behind the affairs of men, unperceived except by the prophetic vision. A consequence of this prophetic perspective is the frequent occurrence in Scripture of the language of God's "coming" to a nation to judge it, even though what is envisaged is not a visible appearance of God, but a military conquest. Thus Isaiah, predicting the invasion of Egypt by the forces of Assyria, can write, "Behold, the Lord rides on a swift cloud, and will **come** into Egypt" (19:1). Similar language, when applied to Christ (Matt. 24:30), is apt to be applied by the average western reader to his Second Coming, though the language, when used in Isaiah, clearly does not allow this identification.

Similarly, other prophetic oracles, when describing national judgments, which are political and military in nature, express these phenomena in terms of God's "coming" against the land of his enemies:[29]

For [the LORD] **is coming** to judge the earth [or land], (Ps. 96:13; 98:9)

For behold, **the** Lord **comes out of His place** to punish the inhabitants of the earth [or land] for their iniquity. (Isa. 26:21)

For behold, **the** Lord **is coming out of his place**; He will **come down** and tread on the high places of the earth [or land]. (Mic. 1:3)

Even so, in Revelation Christ threatens at times to "come" to various churches in order to redress the wrongs being perpetrated by them.

He warns the church at Ephesus: "Repent and do the first works, **or else I will come to you quickly** and remove your lampstand from its place—unless you repent." (Rev. 2:5)

This threat probably had nothing to do with the Second Coming, since the effects of Christ's "coming" to Ephesus would not be the end of the age, but merely the removing of that church's lampstand from its place—a likely symbol for the extinction of that congregation (which now has been fulfilled).

Christ threatened to "come" to at least two other churches as well:

To Pergamos:

"Repent, **or else I will come to you quickly** and will fight against them with the sword of My mouth." (Rev. 2:16)

To Sardis:

"Remember therefore how you have received and heard; hold fast and repent. Therefore if you will not watch, **I will come upon you as a thief**, and you will not know what hour I will come upon you." (Rev. 3:3)

Since these churches no longer exist, and will thus not be affected at the future Second Coming, it is probably best to apply the language to a temporal judgment upon those churches and not His eschatological coming. It is necessary, in studying Revelation, to take this use of language into consideration.

3. He is coming quickly.

One other important observation we must make concerning this aspect of the message of Revelation is that Christ's "coming" is repeatedly said to be near at hand.

For example, *the church in Philadelphia* was promised: "Behold, **I am coming quickly**! Hold fast what you have, that no one may take your crown" (Rev. 3:11). On two other occasions he makes the identical promise: "Behold, **I am coming quickly**!" (Rev. 22:7, 12). In light of these statements, we may draw three possible conclusions:

1. They refer to the Second Coming, and were untrue, since that event did not occur shortly after the words were written;

2. They refer to the Second Coming, but we must not take the expression "quickly" to mean "very soon"; or

3. They do not refer to the Second Coming, but to some event that actually occurred shortly after the time of writing.

The first option does not sit well with evangelicals (like myself) who accept the inspiration of Scripture and the canonicity of the Apocalypse, since the inclusion of failed prophecies would seemingly render the author a false prophet and his book a deception.

The second option is taken by many evangelicals, who explain "quickly" in a variety of ways. Some take it to mean "suddenly when the time comes, but not necessarily soon." Others suggest that it means "certainly," without implying anything about timing.

Commonly, interpreters suggest that the Lord's coming really was "near" at the time of writing, but not as men count "nearness." Since "a day to the Lord is as a thousand years," the Second Coming has not really been long delayed—only two days, so far!

To this last suggestion, it has been replied that, while two thousand years may be a short time in God's way of thinking about time, it is nonetheless a very long time to those of us whose entire lifetimes generally fall short of one hundred years. Had the book of Revelation been written *to God,* rather than to humans, it might be of some comfort to him to know that the consummation was not very far distant—only two thousand years. But this would give little comfort and communicate no information of value to readers for whom two thousand years is not in any sense a short while.

When Paul told Timothy that he intended to come to him shortly (1 Tim. 3:14; 2 Tim. 4:9), it is unlikely that Timothy was expected to take into consideration that Paul, an inspired writer, was reckoning in divine terms and that, if Paul were not to come until a thousand years later, he should not be thought to have defaulted on his promise. It is hard to believe that the repeated words of comfort to the suffering churches that Jesus would come quickly (Gr. "without delay") were intended to convey anything other than their natural meaning to the human recipients. If this was reckoned on God's timetable, and not on man's, then these frequent time notices actually communicate no information, and would seemingly only serve to raise false hopes in the readers.

The third option, that the promises of his soon coming refer to some event that actually occurred shortly after the time of writing, is credible if we take into consideration the fact that the "coming" of Christ can refer to historical judgments, as discussed above. Jesus, when on earth, spoke of some event, to which he referred as his "coming," as scheduled to occur within the lifetime of his own contemporaries:

Assuredly, I say to you, **there are some standing here** who shall not taste death **till they see the Son of Man coming** in His kingdom. (Matt. 16:28)

And **they will see the Son of Man coming** on the clouds of heaven with power and great glory. . . . So you also, when you see all these things, know that it is near—at the very doors. Assuredly, I say to you, **this generation will by no means pass away** till all these things take place. (Matt. 24:30, 33–34)

Some evangelicals—being made unnecessarily uncomfortable by these statements and wishing to salvage their status as true predictions of the Second Coming—have interpreted the expression "this generation" in various ways. The phrase has been made out to mean "this race," or "the generation that sees the signs of the Second Coming," etc.—despite the fact that Jesus spoke of "this generation" in at least four other verses in Matthew, from which no plausible meaning can be taken but "those living at this time."[30] In any case, the similar phrase, "there are some standing here who shall not taste death till . . ." is not so easy to reinterpret. Both passages seem to tell us that something He called "the coming of the Son of Man" was to occur within the generation of Jesus' first followers.

Rather than being embarrassed by these inspired predictions or reinterpreting them beyond recognition, some interpreters find it more honoring to Christ simply to acknowledge that he told the truth in rather natural language. This approach indeed challenges our natural tendency to read every reference to the "coming" of the Son of Man as a reference to his eschatological appearing, but if such a challenge is necessary in order to make biblical and historical sense of the statement, this may not be too great a concession to make.

To acknowledge that some significant event that occurred shortly after it was predicted is in some passages referred to as a "coming" of the Lord renders intelligible some of these troublesome verses. It allows for a more natural understanding of another prediction made by Jesus: "For assuredly, I say to you, you will not have gone through the cities of Israel before **the Son of Man comes**" (Matthew 10:23). It also vindicates James from the charge of making a gross miscalculation when he wrote (with an unmistakable allusion to Matthew 24:33):

> The coming of the Lord is at hand. . . . Behold, the Judge is standing at the door! (James 5:8–9)

Some of the above statements have been applied by interpreters to the transfiguration or to Pentecost, though chronological considerations rule out the possibility that Matthew 24 or James predicts either of those events. *Many preterists* point out that Christ's "coming" in judgment upon the rebel city of Jerusalem occurred within the generation of those to whom Jesus spoke (Matt. 24:34), before all of them had died (Matt. 16:28), and brought an end to their opportunities to evangelize the cities of Israel further (Matt. 10:23). *Preterists* and some *historicists* believe that this judgment is depicted in some portions of the book of Revelation. Most other approaches find ways of applying all such references to the future Second Coming.

None of these considerations challenge the validity of the doctrine of the Second Coming, but they demonstrate that there is more than one event or phenomenon that can be spoken of as a "coming" of Christ. This fact should caution interpreters against jumping to immediate conclusions when they encounter such expressions in Revelation, and requires that we carefully consider the overall context of each statement through the eyes of the differing approaches.

The Millennium in Revelation

It may surprise many to learn that the greatest issue of controversy related to the book of Revelation, from earliest times to the present, has not been over the identity of the two witnesses, or the meaning of the number "666," or the timing of the Rapture in relation to the Tribulation. Already, in the third century, the watershed issue in the interpretation of the Apocalypse was defined in terms of one's understanding of the meaning of the "thousand years" in Revelation 20. The term "Millennium" (from the Latin: *mille* = thousand, and *annus* = years) has generally been adopted to refer to this period. In all the Bible, only this one chapter, occurring near the end of Revelation, mentions the thousand-year reign of the saints with Christ. Those acquainted with the history of interpretation (see discussion below) will realize that it is no exaggeration to call this the most controversial chapter in the Bible. The likelihood that this chapter refers to the same period as that depicted in the many Old Testament passages describing the golden age of the Messiah's reign (e.g., Ps. 72; 110; Isa. 2:1–4; 11:1–11; Ezekiel 34; Daniel 2; etc.) means that one's understanding of the Millennium determines much of what one thinks about the fulfillment of scores of Old Testament prophecies as well.

Despite the importance of the subject, the question of the chronological relation of this period to Christ's Second Coming, and that of whether these passages are to be understood literally or in a spiritual sense, have never been answered with unanimity by the church. Three Christian views on the Millennium may be distinguished from one another: 1. *premillennialism*, 2. *postmillennialism*, and 3. *amillennialism*.

1. Premillennialism (once known as *chiliasm)* is the belief that the second coming of Christ will precede the millennial kingdom. Taking a mostly literal approach, premillenarians expect a period of one thousand years' duration, during which Christ will reign with his saints here on earth prior to the establishment of the eternal new heavens and new earth. The millennial reign will be characterized by international peace and justice resulting from the universal enforced rule of Christ over saved and unsaved alike. At the end of this time, Satan's brief period of freedom will put humanity to one final test just before the final judgment.

There are two principal varieties of premillennialism: 1) *historic premillennialism* and 2) *dispensational premillennialism* or, simply, *dispensationalism.* The latter differs from the former in its emphasis on the continuing centrality of national Israel in God's eschatological program and in anticipating a Rapture[31] of Christians to heaven before the beginning of the Tribulation.[32]

Premillennialism has been accused by its critics of promoting a pessimistic outlook for the temporal future—though, if this is what Scripture teaches, premillennialists can hardly be faulted for such pessimism. This view is most likely to be held by those adopting a *futurist* approach to Revelation (e.g., Walvoord, Ryrie, Gaebelein, Ironside, etc.).

2. *Postmillennialism* teaches that Christ will return at the end of the millennial period. According to this camp, the millennial kingdom will be established through the evangelistic mission of the church. This enterprise will be so successful that all, or most, people will become Christians, resulting in a lengthy period of peace on earth before Christ's second coming. Many great evangelical leaders, including Benjamin B. Warfield and Jonathan Edwards, were postmillennialists, as are a growing number of modern evangelicals, known as *Christian Reconstructionists.* The latter group place emphasis on the need to reform, through law and the Gospel, the political and cultural spheres, as a part of bringing the world systems into greater conformity to the demands of Christ, the King. Postmillennialists are often (though not always) inclined toward the *preterist* approach to Revelation (e.g., Chilton, Gentry, DeMar—though not Rushdoony, who is an *idealist* postmillennialist), since their optimistic view of the future works better if the disasters described in Revelation are seen as belonging to a time now past, rather than to the end of history.

3. *Amillennialism* understands the thousand years of Revelation 20 as a symbolic number representing an indefinitely long period of time, which happens to correspond to the entire span of time from the first coming of Christ until his second coming. In other words, the Millennium is the same as one might call the "Church Age." Most aspects of chapter 20 (like most aspects of the rest of Revelation) are taken as symbolic. The binding of Satan happened spiritually at the cross; the reign of the saints is the present age; the loosing of Satan is a final period of deception coming on the world in the end of the age; the fire from heaven that devours the wicked is the second coming of Christ. Those embracing this understand-

47

ing have included virtually every theologian from Augustine through the Reformation, and there are many adherents today. Amillennialists are found in the ranks of several of the various approaches to Revelation, including *historicists* (e.g., Martin Luther), *preterists* (Jay Adams), and *idealists* (William Hendriksen), but only rarely among *futurists* (Abraham Kuyper).

It should be remembered that the various approaches to Revelation are not linked inseparably to any particular millennial position, so that one's eschatology does not necessarily dictate which general approach to Revelation is to be preferred.

HISTORY OF INTERPRETATION
The Early Church

Full-length commentaries on Revelation[33] from the first three centuries of the church have not survived for us to examine, with the exception of that of Victorinus of Pettau (d. 303), which seems to have come down to us in a form altered from its original state. Of this, Swete writes:

> Of the commentary of Victorinus in general it is impossible to speak with confidence until it is before us in a form nearer to that in which it came from his pen. But the extract published by Haussleiter from what appears to be the original work confirms the statement that Victorinus held firmly by the chiliastic *[premillennial]* *interpretation* of Apoc. xx.[34]

We know that Melito of Sardis (170), Irenaeus (180), and Hippolytus of Rome (220) all wrote complete commentaries on Revelation, but none of these have survived to the present. There are fragments of exposition on Revelation to be found in Justin Martyr (d.165), Melito, Irenaeus, and other early fathers. In his writings, Tertullian (d. 220) quoted from eighteen of the twenty-two chapters.[35] From these, we can know what these men believed about a number of the subjects in Revelation, and can extrapolate from them what their general view of the book must have been.

Views of Ante-Nicene Western Fathers

Papias (c.130), bishop of Phrygian Hierapolis, interpreted the Millennium as a future golden age on earth, and "embellished his description of it with features drawn from Jewish sources."[36] His millennial (in those days, called *chiliastic*) ideas were followed, in the main, by Justin, Irenaeus and Tertullian, and Lactantius

(d. 320). It is on this basis that premillennialists today often claim that the early church was uniformly premillennial. This conclusion, however, is not wholly trustworthy in light of the evidence.

We do not have access to very much that was written in the first four centuries of the church, and a large variety of interpretations may have been held for which no documentation has survived. Justin Martyr (a premillennialist), writing on this very subject, left clear testimony to the presence in his day of alternative viewpoints in the church. In his *Dialogue With Trypho*, Justin wrote:

> I and many others are of this opinion [premillennialism], and [believe] that such will take place, as you assuredly are aware; but on the other hand, I signified to you that many who belong to the pure and pious faith, and are true Christians, think otherwise.[37]

It seems clear that there were "many" whom Justin regarded as "true Christians" and "who belong to the pure and pious faith" who did not hold to his brand of premillennialism—or possibly not to premillennialism at all. That he did not regard them as heretics serves to illustrate that the early church would not have agreed with dispensationalist John F. Walvoord's assessment that premillennialism is of comparable importance to the doctrines of verbal inspiration, the deity of Christ, substitutionary atonement, and bodily resurrection.[38] The evidence suggests that the development of eschatological systems was not a chief priority among the earliest Christians. Thus, many of the principal fathers neglected to say enough about their views on this subject to enable us to determine their exact sentiments. We are certainly at liberty to question the validity of sweeping statements of dispensationalists like Charles C. Ryrie, when he asserts that "Premillennialism is the historic faith of the Church."[39] A more accurate statement of the case would be that the eschatological fragments of the relatively few writers whose works we can examine bear witness to the premillennial convictions of those particular writers.

In addition to his expectation of a thousand-year terrestrial kingdom and a restored Jerusalem (based on Revelation 21), Irenaeus identified the first beast of Revelation with Paul's man of sin and considered a possible identification of 666 with the word *Lateinos* (meaning, "Roman"), suggesting Rome. Based upon 17:12, he believed that the empire would be divided into ten kingdoms and Rome reduced to ashes.[40]

In his tract, *On Christ and Antichrist*, Hippolytus identified the two witnesses of chapter 11 as Enoch and Elijah. The pregnant woman of chapter 12 was seen as the church, and the whore Babylon as Rome. He saw the first beast as the Roman Empire, to be wounded to death but restored under Antichrist. The second beast was seen as ten kingdoms that will replace the empire.[41]

In Rome, Tertullian understood the book similarly. To him, Babylon is Rome; the two beasts are the Antichrist and the false prophet who wage war with the church. There will be a bodily resurrection, followed by a kingdom of a heavenly order but having its seat on earth.[42]

Thus the western fathers of the Ante-Nicene church whose works have survived took a quasi-literal and *eschatological* approach to the Book of Revelation. They lived, of course, too early in history for them to take a *historicist* approach, such as that which later arose and which spread the fulfillments of the prophecies over the space of over 1,800 years. Events, which later *historicists* would view as ancient history, were, in those days, present and future realities. This means that the fathers would have spoken *futuristically*, even if they were identifying the prophetic events with the same phenomena that *historicists*, and some *preterists*, now associate with past fulfillments.

The Alexandrian Fathers

The Alexandrian fathers rejected chiliastic views (Millennialism). These fathers introduced an allegorical approach to Revelation. Origen (c. 185–254) repudiated the literal interpretation of the chiliasts as "Jewish."

Prior to Origen, Clement of Alexandria (c. 150–215) interpreted the twenty-four elders as a symbol of the equality of Jew and Gentile in the church; locusts' tails as the mischievous influence of immoral teachers; and the many-colored foundation stones of the New Jerusalem as the manifold grace of apostolic teaching.[43]

Origen interpreted the seven-sealed roll as Scripture, to which Christ alone has the key; the white horse rider, he believed, represents the opening of heaven by the Divine Word through the white light of knowledge which he imparts to believers.[44]

Methodius followed the Alexandrian approach as well. In his exposition, the male-child of 12:5 represents the baptized soul in which Christ is born; the dragon's seven heads are the seven greater sins; his ten horns are intended to contrast with the ten commandments; the beast is a symbol of fleshly lust.[45]

This allegorizing method of interpretation, which did away with the expectation of specific historical fulfillments, eventually displaced the eschatological approach, though both are found together in the commentary of Victorinus in 303. Victorinus' commentary followed the allegorizing approach. It appears that Augustinian editors may have altered it, however, because in its present form it champions *amillennialism,* whereas Jerome (c. 345–420) listed Victorinus. along with Tertullian and Lactantius, as a *chiliast* (that is, a premillennialist).

Tyconius (c. 390), a Donatist, also followed the allegorizing method, though he did not rule out altogether the possibility of historical fulfillments. He applied the Millennium to the interval between the first and second advents of Christ. "His interpretation was taken over by Jerome and Augustine and became normative in the church for the next eight centuries."[46]

Augustine (c. 354–430), in *The City of God,* interpreted Revelation 20 in the same manner as did Tyconius. The same general allegorizing method was followed in the commentaries of Primasius (c. 550), Alcuin (c. 735–c. 800), Rabanus Maurus (c. 775–c. 836) and Walafrid Strabo (c. 807–c. 849). Swete summarizes:

> Primasius, Cassiodorius, Apringius, Bede, Beatus, and most of the writers on the Apocalypse who followed them in the earlier centuries of the Middle Ages, were content with a mystical exegesis which varied in its details according to the fancy of the individual expositor or the needs or ideas of his time.[47]

During this general period, two commentators stand out as exceptions to the trend of Tyconius:

Andreas of Cappadocia (early sixth century) produced the greatest of the Greek commentaries. Swete regards him as "perhaps the best known of ancient expositors of the Apocalypse, and certainly none of them is more edifying or, in his own way, more attractive."[48] This work blends the methods of Irenaeus, Origin, and Tyconius and makes its own contribution in suggesting some historical fulfillments alongside mystical interpretations. Andreas saw Babylon as the world opposing the church in general, but more specifically identifies the seven kings (17:10) as seven embodiments of the world power, the sixth being Rome and the seventh Constantinople. He remains, with Tyconius and Augustine, amillennial.

The Development of Historicism

In the West, Berengaud (ninth century) also combined the mystical with the historical interpretation. As with later *historicists,* Revelation is seen as covering the whole course of human history, but with a broader range of history in view. The first six seals are applied to the period from Adam to the fall of Jerusalem; the first six trumpets represent the preaching of the word from times of patriarchs to the age of Christian martyrs; the two witnesses are Enoch and Elijah prior to the second coming of the Lord; the first beast is Antichrist with seven deadly sins as heads;

51

the second beast is seen either as a follower of Antichrist or of all followers of Antichrist taken collectively; Babylon is pagan Rome, but as representing more generally the devil's city; the ten horns are interpreted as the successive incursions of barbarians which broke up the Roman Empire. As with modern *amillennialists*, the 1,000 years extend from the ascension of Christ to the end of the world; and the first resurrection is seen as the present condition of saints.[49]

The development of a "more concrete *historicism*"[50] can be seen in the works of Anselm of Havelberg (1129–1155) and Rupert of Deutz (1111–1129), though the later *historicism* emphasizing a chronological division of the book came from Joachim of Floris (1130–1201), who also originated the earliest forms of postmillennialism.[51]

Joachim's *historicism* was taken over by most of the Franciscans, especially in Paris, and influenced many in Europe during the thirteenth and fourteenth centuries. Though Joachim was loyal to the Church of Rome, many during this period who followed his system began to find in Revelation's first beast a symbol of the Roman papacy. It was this element in *historicism* that later galvanized the Reformers in their resistance to Rome.

Martin Luther (c. 1500) was one of the first commentators to see Revelation from chapter 4 onwards as a prophetic survey of church history. The particulars of John Calvin's interpretation are not known, since Revelation is the only New Testament book upon which he did not produce a commentary. However, Luther's general approach to Revelation was followed by virtually all the Reformers and by Protestants well into the nineteenth century. The papacy was consistently identified with Revelation's beast and with Babylon.

Coming to the defense of the papacy, Spanish Jesuits presented two alternative approaches to the *historicism* of the Reformers. One response was that of Francisco Ribera (1537–1591), a professor at Salmanca, who taught that John, in Revelation, only foresaw events of the near future and of the final things at the end of the world, but had none of the intervening history in view. The Antichrist was defined as a future individual who would arise in the end times. Babylon was seen as Rome—not under the popes—but in a future corrupted state. This was the beginning of many of the ideas that later developed into features of the modern *futurist* approach to Revelation.

Another Jesuit scholar, Luiz de Alcazar (1554–1613), introduced a *preterist* approach to Revelation, in which chapters 4 through 11 were interpreted as depicting the church's struggle against Judaism, culminating in the fall of Jerusalem in AD 70; while chapters 12 through 19 reflect the church's struggle with paganism, ending in the fall of Rome in 476; and chapters 20 through 22 as the triumph of the church in papal Rome.

In the seventeenth and eighteenth centuries, Protestant scholars further developed the details of Luther's *historicism*. "In England Joseph Mede and two eminent Cambridge mathematicians, Sir Isaac Newton and William Whiston, found minute fulfillments of St. John's prophecy from the days of Domitian to their own."[52] A similar system was followed on the Continent by Vitringa and Bengel.

The Rise of Literary-Critical and Dramatic Approaches

In this same general period, the great Dutch Protestant theologian, Hugo Grotius (1583–1645), introduced two departures from the general Reformed approach to Revelation: (1) He was the first Reformed exegete to give up the identification of the papacy with the Antichrist; and (2) He understood some of the visions to reflect the period before and some the period after the fall of Jerusalem. Grotius, according to Bruce, "may . . . be regarded as the pioneer of the literary-critical approach to the book."[53] He is widely regarded as a *preterist*,[54] and Swete says that he "trod generally in the steps of Alcasar."[55]

At the end of the eighteenth century, a view was proposed by Eichhorn, which would today be called the *dramatic* approach, and it is fundamental to the approach of many modern interpreters of Revelation from the *idealist* camp. On this view, Revelation is a great poem, or drama, divisible into acts and scenes, having as its theme the progress and victory of the Christian faith.

The nineteenth century presented new challenges to those of the continuous-historical persuasion. *Historicists* had not expected history to continue quite so long, and now interpreters had to find room for the new historical data, like the French Revolution and its results.

The Rise of the Futurist Approach

For approximately two centuries, Protestants had regarded *futurism* as a product of the papacy's self-defense against the claims of the Reformers. Non-Catholics had generally shunned it, though a form *of futurism* was adopted by the Fifth Monarchy Men in the seventeenth century. "Their excesses brought it into disrepute, but it was renewed in the 19th century by the early teachings of the Plymouth Brethren and by the Bible Conference movement in the 19th and 20th centuries."[56] The official entrance of the *futurist* approach to Revelation into Protestant circles came through Samuel R. Maitland, librarian to the archbishop of Canterbury, around 1827. The Plymouth Brethren leader, John Nelson Darby, then incorporated it into his dispensational theology, for which he is most remembered. Other Protestant scholars who began to embrace *futurism* included Isaac Williams in England, and Stern, Bisping, and others on the continent.[57]

The Development of the Idealist Approach

Meanwhile, others like Auberlen were developing the modern *idealist* interpretation that holds that the point of Revelation is to reveal a *philosophy of history*. Specific persons or events are referred to only when they were outstanding examples of a principle.

By the end of the nineteenth century a new attitude toward Revelation was developing amid the liberal scholarship in Germany, which soon spread to England and America. This was the *literary-critical* approach, mentioned earlier. This system of research concerns itself primarily (exclusively?) with the literary source materials used by the apocalyptic author and his method of utilizing them for his purpose. Historical or eschatological fulfillments of the visions are not looked for in actual time and space.

The Contemporary Conservative Protestant Scene

Conservative Protestant commentaries (those that do not follow the literary-critical approach) in the nineteenth and twentieth centuries have been divided:

The *historicist* approach continued into the nineteenth century in the writings of E. B. Elliott *(Horae Apocalypticae,* 1847), A. J. Gordon, Albert Barnes, and others. To my knowledge, the only modern commentaries that still espouse this view today have not come from recognized scholars (not that this fact should condemn them), but from Seventh-Day Adventists and essentially self-published authors who are desirous to reintroduce this viewpoint to a modern readership.[58] Eugene Boring would seem to be correct when he writes, "Although widely held by Protestant interpreters after the Reformation and into the twentieth century, no critical New Testament scholar today advocates this view."[59]

The *preterist* approach was defended in the nineteenth century by Moses Stuart (1845) and in the early twentieth century by James Snowden (1919). Preterism has had a recent resurgence in the writings of *Christian Reconstructionists* like Gary DeMar, David Chilton and Kenneth Gentry.

One of the first popular presentations of the *futurist* approach, and the most influential, was that of J. A. Seiss *(Lectures on the Apocalypse,* 1909). During the twentieth century, the *futurist* approach to Revelation (mostly in its dispensational form) became the most familiar view among Christian laypeople and in the secular culture as well! This popularity was facilitated by various factors. The publication of the *Scofield Reference Bible* in 1909, as well as the Bible Conference Movement in America and Britain, propelled dispensational *futurism* to a place of prominent visibility among Protestant laypeople. In the early to middle decades of the twentieth century, many Bible institutes sprang up, especially in America (the most important being Dallas Theological Seminary) to promote the same viewpoint. Graduates from these schools have produced a never-ending stream of books and publications advocating various opinions within this same approach to Revelation. Christian television, radio, movies, novels, and electronic media, were utilized to very great advantage by dispensational advocates of *futurism*, with the result that many Christians and non-Christians alike believe that the book of Revelation is, and always was, universally understood to be a foreglimpse of the end of the world. The publication of the phenomenally successful *The Late Great Planet Earth* by Hal Lindsey in 1970 and the best-selling Left Behind *novel* series published from 1995 to 2007 wove dispensational *futurism* into the very fabric of American pop culture.

Apocalyptic Futurism has been advocated by sound scholars, such as Walvoord, Mounce, and Ladd, to be sure, as well as by innumerable cranks and eschatological faddists, who have often given Bible prophecy a bad name by their repeated speculations concerning the date of the Second Coming, and by their assigning of tenuous correspondences between Revelation's visions and the specific developments in an ever-changing modern political milieu.

However, *futurism* has not grown-up without rivals. Beginning in the twentieth century, the *idealist* approach also received wide acceptance in modern evangelical commentaries, though various labels have been attached to it. Since Eichhorn, in the eighteenth century, the dramatic nature of the book has intrigued many students of its students. In 1939, William Hendriksen popularized this view in his book *More Than Conquerors*, though the view was found in a number of works earlier in the twentieth century as well. At the time of this writing, the most respected commentaries in the evangelical academy seem to be those espousing such an approach.

The *preterist, futurist,* and *idealist* approaches will all be with us for some time to come, and the *historicist* approach has an abiding voice in the classic commentaries of Matthew Henry, John Wesley, Adam Clarke, Albert Barnes, and others, which show no signs of vanishing from evangelical libraries (and may, for all anyone may predict, experience a resurgence). This fact gives all four evangelical viewpoints a right to be heard by a contemporary audience, and that is why they are afforded a comparison in this volume.

ANALYSIS OF THE FOUR APPROACHES

1. The Historicist Approach: Revelation Surveys the Whole of Church History.

Modern commentaries presenting this approach are rare to nonexistent, though an abbreviated list of the luminaries of the past who took this view would have to include Huss, Wycliffe, Tyndale, Luther, Calvin, Zwingli, Melanchthon, John Knox, Sir Isaac Newton, John Foxe, John Wesley, Jonathan Edwards, George Whitefield, Charles Finney, C. H. Spurgeon, Matthew Henry, Adam Clarke, Albert Barnes, E. B. Elliott, H. Grattan Guinness, and Bishop Thomas Newton.

In our time, *historicism* is clearly not in vogue. My reason for including it in this volume alongside the other approaches is that it survives in most of the classic commentaries of the past few centuries, which are still published and used today. It is too early to pronounce as finally deceased a view whose advocates continue to speak in print to modern readers of their works. Modern Seventh-Day Adventists also, with their widely promoted "Revelation Seminars," present their own version of this approach, connecting at many points with the views of the historic Protestant commentators. In addition, I have heard of a small movement of evangelicals who are trying to revive respect for this view as the true understanding of the book of Revelation. Who can say whether they might succeed?

Those who teach this view believe that God revealed, in advance, events spanning the entire church age, through the symbolic visions of the Apocalypse. For example, the breaking of the seven *seals* (chaps. 6–7) is usually identified with the barbarian invasions that brought down the Western Roman Empire. The trumpet judgments then turn to the fall of the Eastern Roman Empire. The scorpion-tailed locusts that come out of the bottomless pit and the serpent-tailed horses, of the fifth and sixth *trumpets*, respectively, (chap. 9) unanimously recognized as Mohammed's Arabs, followed by the Turks, attacking Constantinople. The two "beasts" (chap. 13) represent different aspects (political and priestly) the corrupt Roman Church.

A unique characteristic of this line of interpretation is its advocacy of what is called the "year-for-a-day principle" when dealing with designations of time in Revelation. It is believed that the time periods are literal and exact, but are cast in a symbolism that represents a year as a day. On this principle, five months (150 days) is taken to designate 150 years. The significant period of 1,260 days is interpreted as the same number of years. "An hour, and a day, and a month, and a year" becomes (depending whether a year is 360 days or 365 days) 391 years and 15 days, or 396 years and 106 days.

In support of this procedure, appeal is made to Ezekiel 4:4–6, in which the prophet was required to lie on his left side for 390 days, and upon his right side for 40 days, representing the same number of years of judgment decreed upon Israel and Judah respectively. This principle is then extrapolated to apply to "prophetic time" in all plausible cases in Daniel and Revelation.

Though this principle is said to apply universally to prophetic time periods (at least in Daniel and Revelation), yet it is not applied with total consistency. The "thousand years" of Revelation 20 presents a notable exception. If the day-for-a-year principle were to be applied consistently here, the so-called Millennium would be 360,000 years long. *Historicists,* generally, do not apply the principle to this period. Other examples in which "prophetic time" is *not* calculated on the day-for-a-year principle include Isaiah 7:8 (65 years), Isaiah 16:14 (3 years), Isaiah 23:15 (70 years), Jeremiah 29:10 (70 years), Matthew 20:19 (3 days). The existence of such a large number of inexplicable "exceptions" raises legitimate questions about this principle's general applicability.

Like *preterism and futurism,* the *historicist* approach is able to align specific historic events with certain details in Revelation, though this process often involves a fair degree of conjecture. By way of criticism of this view, *preterist* Professor Moses Stuart accused *historicists* of setting the reader of Revelation "afloat upon a boundless ocean of conjecture and fancy, without rudder or compass."[60] Yet *historicism* claims for itself some interesting success stories.

Sometime around 1690, it is reported, *historicist* interpreter Robert Fleming was invited before the English court of William of Orange, King William III, to lecture on Bible prophecy. The king asked the man of God when the temporal power of the papacy in Europe would fall. Fleming's reply was published in his 1701 book entitled *Apocalyptic Key.* Concerning the fall of the papacy as the ruling power in Europe, the prophecy scholar wrote: "I say this judgment will begin about AD 1794 and expire about 1848." This prediction was made approximately one hundred years prior to the projected dates. *Historicist* apologists point out that in 1794 the French Revolution's "Reign of Terror" occurred, which, they say, marked the beginning of the end of the pope's temporal power in Europe. In the year 1848, the pope was temporarily driven from Rome.[61]

One nonnegotiable feature of classical Protestant *(historicist)* exposition is the assertion that the papacy is the Antichrist. Since the principal advocates of this view were the Reformers, this identification leaves the interpreters open to the charge of forcing their exegesis into an ideological straightjacket for partisan reasons, for the sake of maintaining the diabolical nature of their opponents.

57

Interestingly, though, this view of the papacy was held prior to the Reformation by the Franciscans, and by precursors to the Reformation, like Huss and Wycliff.

On the other hand, assuming this identification to be correct, the *historicists* see in all other approaches to Revelation Satanically-inspired smokescreens to obscure the true identity of Antichrist. They assert, specifically, that *preterism and futurism* are both inventions of the Jesuits, designed to neutralize the bad publicity given to the pope by the Reformers.[62]

Though few today seem to credit this approach, the preface to Albert Barnes' *Notes on Revelation* (1884–85 edition) demonstrates that it is not without impressive historical confirmations:

> Up to the time of commencing the exposition of this book, I had no theory in my own mind as to its meaning. I may add, that I had a prevailing belief that it could *not* be explained, and that all attempts to explain it must be visionary and futile . . . In this state of things, the utmost that I contemplated, when I began to write on it, was to explain, as well as I could, the meaning of the language and the symbols, without attempting to apply the explanation to the events of past history, or to inquire what is to occur hereafter. . . . Beginning with this aim, I found myself soon insensibly inquiring whether, in the events which succeeded the time when the book was written, there were not historical facts of which the emblems employed would be natural and proper symbols, on the supposition that it was the divine intention, in disclosing these visions, to refer to them. . . . To my own surprise I found, chiefly in Gibbon's *Decline and Fall of the Roman Empire*, a series of events recorded, such as seemed to me to correspond, to a great extent, with the series of symbols found in the Apocalypse. . . . It was such, in fact, that if it had been found in a Christian writer, professedly writing a commentary on the book of Revelation, it would have been regarded by infidels as a designed attempt to force history to utter a language that should conform to a predetermined theory in expounding a book full of symbols. So remarkable have these coincidences appeared to me in the course of this exposition, that it has almost seemed as if he had designed to write a commentary on some portions of this book.(vi–viii).

Though he rejects this approach, Albertus Pieters grants that *historicism* has some impressive aspects:

> That some points in the interpretation, as developed by these expositors, seem excellently to fit the history, must be frankly conceded. One of the best, in my judgment, is the identification of the fifth trumpet with the rise of Mohammedanism and of the sixth trumpet with the coming of the Turks. The things there seen in the vision would surely be appropriate symbolical descriptions of those great calamities. Yet an occasional hit of this kind does not prove anything with regard to the system as a whole.[63]

When one examines the verse-by-verse expositions of the *historicists*, I think one will have to say that the scheme makes more than a few "occasional hits." In fact, the development of history has been shown to fit the outline of the book of Revelation so nearly that in the days when this view predominated, it was said that a missionary might go to heathen lands armed only with a copy of Gibbon's *Decline and Fall of the Roman Empire* in one hand and Barnes' "Revelation" in *Notes on Revelation* in the other, and prove beyond question the inspiration of Bible![64]

Most modern scholars, however, find little good to say about this approach. F. F. Bruce, for instance, wrote:

> No important contribution to the exegesis of Revelation was made by [*historicists*], whether J. A. Bengel in Germany or Joseph Mede, Sir Isaac Newton and William Whiston in England—eminent as these exegetes were in other fields of study. The book itself has suffered in its reputation from the extravagances of some of its interpreters, who have treated it as if it were a table of mathematical conundrums or a divinely inspired *Old Moore's Almanack*.[65]

One of the weaknesses of the *historicist* approach is seen in the inability of its advocates to agree upon the specific fulfillments of the prophecies. Moses Stuart (*preterist*) charged that "Hitherto, scarcely any two original and independent [*historicist*] expositors have been agreed, in respect to some points very important to their bearing upon the interpretation of the book."[66]

For example, while most *historicists* see the seven *trumpets* as pertaining to the Islamic forces attacking the eastern Roman Empire, they disagree among themselves about the preceding section (the seven *seals*) as to whether they refer to the defeat of the Western Roman Empire by Huns and Vandals, or to the destruction of Jerusalem by the Romans. Walvoord (*futurist*) asserts, "At least fifty different systems of interpretation have arisen from the historical view alone."[67] If the prophecies' meanings cannot be identified with certainty, even after their fulfillments, the value of the prophecies to the readers of any period, whether before or following the fulfillments, is called into serious question.

Another criticism of *historicism* has been that it is too flexible in the service of its advocates, allowing most of them to identify their own times as the culmination of history. Walvoord (*futurist*) criticizes *historicism* on these very grounds, saying "its adherents have succumbed to the tendency to interpret the book in some sense climaxing in their generation."[68]

Historicism is criticized as being too parochial, failing to take the development of the church throughout the world into consideration. Tenney (*futurist*) has made this observation:

The Historicist view which attempts to interpret the Apocalypse by the development of the church in the last nineteen centuries, seldom if ever takes cognizance of the church outside Europe. It is concerned mainly with the period of the Middle Ages and the Reformation and has relatively little to say of developments after AD 1500.[69]

George Eldon Ladd (*futurist*) also finds fault with the *historicist* position. "The view has little to commend it," he writes, "for the Revelation would in that case have little to say to the churches of Asia to which it was addressed." The *historicist* might counter that the only approach more vulnerable to this particular criticism than *historicism* would have to be *futurism!*

2. The Preterist Approach: Fulfillment Is in the Past, Shortly after the Time of Writing.

Among those identifying themselves as *preterists*, there are two very different types:

1. Many exegetes whose method is actually *literary-critical* have chosen to label their approach as *preterist* or, alternately, as *contemporary-historical.* The writers to whom I refer are not *preterist*, in the evangelical sense. They are referred to by Pieters as "Left Wing" of *preterism.*[70] They apply the term to themselves because they believe that contemporary elements of John's own day can be identified in the symbolic language he uses. But they do not generally insist upon any actual fulfillment in ensuing events of the things prophesied in the Apocalypse. They almost all believe in a date of writing in Domitian's reign (i.e., AD 95–96) and believe that John's desire for a soon vindication in the coming of the kingdom was expressed in his prophecy, but failed to be fulfilled. Of such scholars, Albertus Pieters wrote:

> Some of these writers have no respect whatever for the Apocalypse as an inspired writing . . . This seriously affects their exegesis. In their opinion, the writer knew nothing of the future by inspiration, and hence an interpretation that has been falsified by history does not on that account seem to them inadmissible.[71]

2. In contrast, those who hold to the classical *preterism* of centuries past take a high view of the inspiration of Scripture and they date the book of Revelation prior to AD 70. They are capable of pointing out many details in Revelation that they believe were fulfilled in the fall of Jerusalem, and some see in the later chapters the prediction of the fall of Rome and beyond to the second coming of Christ. Some of these (the *full-preterists*, as they are usually called) hold that none of the prophecies in Revelation look beyond the judgment of Jerusalem, but this is presently a

minority position among *preterists*. What I am representing as *preterism* in this volume is this inerrantist, early-date *preterism*, which has had worthy, conservative advocates for several centuries.

On this view, the book has only such value to modern readers as does any fulfilled prophecy in the Bible (e.g., most prophecies of the Old Testament), but to the early readers, who were enduring persecution from the Jews and the Romans at the time, it served as a promise of soon deliverance and of the vindication of those who died as martyrs.

This view has the advantage of immediate relevance to the original readers, a feature we would strongly expect to find in any epistle.

Preterism also is the only view that does not have to seek an alternative to the literal sense of passages like Revelation 1:1 and 19, which affirm that the events predicted "must shortly come to pass" and "are about to take place;" and like Revelation 22:10, where John is told *not* to seal up the book, because "the time is at hand." The deliberate contrast between these instructions and those given to Daniel is striking. Daniel was commanded to seal up his book because it would not be immediately fulfilled (Dan. 12:9). If sealing a prophecy is appropriate because there is to be a significant delay in its fulfillment, then John's being told not to seal his prophecy suggests that the fulfillment would be immediate. In fact, the words of the angel affirm this very meaning. A degree of stretching, even of desperation, is sometimes discernible in the comments of non-*preterists* on such passages.

Another point favorable to the early-date *preterist* approach is that the prophecies of Revelation exhibit many points of correspondence with the fall of Jerusalem as recorded in horrendous detail by the historian and eyewitness, Flavius Josephus. Since Josephus was not a Christian and probably never had opportunity to read Revelation, these correspondences seem to bolster the credibility of this interpretation, just as appeal to Gibbon's history of Rome enhances the plausibility of the *historicist* approach.

The Olivet Discourse in Mark 13 (and parallels) is often called the "little apocalypse," because many believe that the discourse covers, more succinctly, the same information as does Revelation. In fact, since the discourse is included in Matthew (chap. 24), Mark (chap. 13) and Luke (chap. 21), but not in John, some have suggested that Revelation might be regarded as John's expanded version of the Olivet Discourse. J. Stuart Russell points out the significant amount of subject matter common to the discourse and the Apocalypse:

> What do we find in our Lord's prophecy? First and chiefly the *Parousia* [the principal Greek word for the "coming" of Christ]; then wars, famines, pestilence,

earthquakes; false prophets and deceivers; signs and wonders; the darkening of the sun and moon; the stars falling from heaven; angels and trumpets, eagles and carcasses, great tribulation and woe; convulsions of nature; the treading down of Jerusalem; the Son of man coming in the clouds of heaven; the gathering of the elect; the reward of the faithful; the judgment of the wicked. And are not these precisely the elements which compose the Apocalypse.[72]

The Olivet Discourse was given as a response to the disciples' question concerning the timing of the destruction of the temple in Jerusalem (see Mark 13:1–4 and parallels), and can arguably be viewed as answering their inquiry. Since Revelation appears to share the same subject matter as does the discourse, *preterists* think it fair to assume that Jerusalem's destruction in AD 70 is the concern of both prophecies. Some *preterists* believe that the book of Revelation looks no further into the future than the Jewish holocaust in AD 70.[73] Others,[74] however, believe that the first half of Revelation describes the fall of Jerusalem, the second half predicts the fall of the Roman Empire, and the final chapters describe the second coming of Christ.

The principal criticism of the *preterist* approach is its heavy dependence on the pre-AD 70 date of writing, which is defensible but not undisputed (see earlier discussion under *Date and Historical Setting*). If the book was written after that date, it obviously cannot be predicting events that occurred in that year.

Another problem associated with the *preterist* approach is related to its alleged roots. Critics have traced the origins of *preterism* to the Jesuit Luis de Alcazar (1554–1613), who formulated it to refute the Reformers' *historicist* view and their identification of the pope as the Antichrist. Thus *preterism* is said to share similar disreputable origins *with futurism* (see below), with both of them being Roman Catholic responses to Protestantism.[75]

However, elements of the *preterist* approach to both Revelation and the Olivet Discourse were held by some much earlier than Alcazar's time. In the early fourth century, the church historian Eusebius, after reviewing Josephus' description of the destruction of Jerusalem in AD 70, wrote:

> It is fitting to add to these accounts the true prediction of our Saviour in which he foretold these very events. His words are as follows: 'Woe unto them that are with child, and to them that give suck in those days! But pray ye that your flight be not in the winter, neither on the Sabbath day. For there shall be great tribulation, such was not since the beginning of the world to this time, no, nor ever shall be' [Matt. 24:19–21].[76]

This quote indicates that Eusebius recognized in the Olivet Discourse (and the great tribulation) a description of Jerusalem's destruction by the Romans. It is the same belief that *preterists* hold concerning that discourse, though Eusebius did not extend the application to Revelation, since he held to the later date of writing, and did not accept its canonicity (which had not yet been universally established).

Early in the sixth century Andreas of Cappadocia wrote a commentary on Revelation that is still in existence. Though he did not take the *preterist* approach, he knew of some who did. Commenting on Revelation 6:12, he wrote: "There are not wanting those who apply this passage to the siege and destruction of Jerusalem by Titus." Also at Revelation 7:1, he wrote: "These things are referred by some to those sufferings which were inflicted by the Romans upon the Jews."[77]

Another commentary on Revelation written (probably) in the sixth century by Arethas[78] says of Revelation 6:12: "Some refer this to the siege of Jerusalem by Vespasian." On Revelation 7:1, Arethas writes: "Here then, were manifestly shown to the Evangelist what things were to befall the Jews in their war against the Romans, in the way of avenging the sufferings inflicted upon Christ." At 7:4: "When the Evangelist received these oracles, the destruction in which the Jews were involved was not yet inflicted by the Romans."

These data prove that something like the modern *preterist* understanding at least of the early part of Revelation existed in the church as much as a thousand years before the time of Alcasar, and cannot, therefore, be traced ultimately to him.

One additional objection to this view is that, if Revelation was written concerning Jerusalem's destruction, it would seem more appropriate that the message be sent to the Jews in Palestine, rather than to churches in Asia, eight hundred miles away. The fact that John wrote to the Asian churches, rather than the Jerusalem church, weighs against the likelihood that his message focused upon the fall of Jerusalem.

A response to this criticism may involve several considerations:

a) The Jerusalem church had already received a very similar warning from Christ Himself, when He was among them (Matt.24; Mark 13; Luke 21). Additionally, Eusebius reports that the church there did receive a special revelation, given to "approved men," prior to the Roman siege of the city, warning them to flee the city. Thus, they would not additionally require the Apocalypse to further warn them;

b) The churches of Asia would find as much value in prophecy and its fulfillment as would Christians in any place or time, including ourselves. This would especially be true of those churches (like Smyrna and Philadelphia) which were experiencing persecution from the Jews in their cities. The fall of Jerusalem was not some ordinary disaster of little concern to people at some distance away. It represented a *sea change* in the manner by which people, the world over, would view God, the Christian movement, and the sacrificial system. It signaled the passing of one divinely established order in favor of an entirely new divinely established order. It was so important an event (for all Christians) that Jesus saw in it the fulfillment of "all that was written" (Luke 21:20–22)

c) John was intimately involved in the lives of the Asian churches at this point in history, counting Ephesus—not Jerusalem—as his home congregation. That he would be commissioned to write to those under his oversight seems natural enough, regardless of the contents of his message.

3. The Futurist Approach: Everything after Chapter 3 Awaits Fulfillment in the Future.

The *futurist* approach is held by the majority of the most-popular, contemporary evangelical writers and Bible teachers. It has so dominated the Christian media, in fact, that many Christians (and virtually all non-Christians) are unaware even of the existence of other approaches.

The best-known variety of *futurism* today is that taught by dispensational teachers. This is the camp of J. N. Darby, C. I. Scofield, Clarence Larkin, Charles Ryrie, John Walvoord, Hal Lindsey, Jack Van Impe, J. Vernon McGee, Chuck Swindoll, David Jeremiah, most Baptists, most Pentecostals, the Calvary Chapel Movement, the Plymouth Brethren, Evangelical Free Churches, and most nondenominational, evangelical churches.

The principal difference between the dispensationalist view and *other futurist* views of Revelation would probably be the fact that the former places the Rapture of the church at Revelation 4:1, while most *others* would place it later (e.g., in chap. 19).

According to this view, Revelation divides into three sections, defined in 1:19, where John is told to write "the things which you have seen, and the things which are, and the things which shall be after these things." Following this outline, chapter 1 describes the first division, or the things John had *seen,* which means the vision of the glorified Christ on Patmos. Chapters 2 and 3 describe the things "which are," that is, the present realities of the churches (or the Church Age),[79] and everything after chapter 3 describes events, which were not only future at the time of writing, but are still future from our own standpoint.

The majority of the material (chaps. 6–19) is thought to describe a seven-year (or, sometimes, a three-and-a-half-year) tribulation period, followed by the return of Christ (chap. 19), a thousand-year reign of Christ on earth (chapt. 20), and the renewal of creation (chaps. 21–22).

Like *historicists,* many *futurists* understand Revelation to be chronologically continuous, though some see two parallel sections of Revelation (chaps. 4–11 and chaps. 12–19), both of which describe a future time of tribulation.

Belief in *the futurist* approach frees the reader to take a more literal view of the visions, reducing the difficulties of interpreting what other views see as symbols. Of the various approaches to Revelation, the *futurist* is most likely to take a literal interpretation,[80] since it alone has the luxury of doing so. For example, there has never been a time in the past when a third of the sea turned to blood, killing a third of the fish and sinking a third of the ships (Rev. 8:8–9). If this is to have a literal fulfillment, it must still be in the future. Other approaches, which apply it to past events, must take the passage nonliterally.

The same is true of other events anticipated in Revelation, such as hailstones of a hundred pounds weight, locusts that sting like scorpions, two prophets who die in Jerusalem and rise again in three-and-a half-days only to be publicly translated into the heavens for all to see, a mandatory mark applied to the forehead or right hand of every noncompliant citizen, and so on. Henry Morris makes this point:

> It is inevitable that literalistic expositors of Revelation will be primarily futurists since practically none of the events of Revelation 4–22 have yet taken place in any literal sense. Many futurists do accept a cyclical development, but probably most (including myself) follow a strictly chronological approach.[81]

The desire to understand Revelation literally may be the leading factor favoring the adoption of a *futurist* approach, although most of the elements of the tribulation that they believe to be revealed in the book do not arise from the *literal application* of any particular passage.

For example, a major feature of the tribulation expected by *futurists* is its seven-year duration, divided in the middle by the Antichrist's violating a treaty he had made with Israel and setting up an image of himself in the rebuilt Jewish temple in Jerusalem. Yet none of these elements can be said to arise from the literal interpretation of *any* passage in Revelation.

Similarly, there is no passage in Revelation, which when literally applied, will yield a prediction of an anti-Semitic Antichrist figure, cobra helicopters, a global cashless economic system, or nuclear war—all of which are features common to many dispensationalists' view of the tribulation.

The *futurist* believes that Revelation 20 describes a period of world peace and justice, with Christ reigning on earth from Jerusalem—though no part of this description can be found in the chapter itself if taken literally.

These observations do not mean that the *futurist* scenario cannot be true. However, such a tribulation as is popularly taught must be derived by reading into the passages in Revelation features that are not plainly stated there.

Dispensationalists themselves often must grudgingly admit to the necessity of recognizing some symbolism in Revelation, all the while clinging, as much as possible, to the literal hermeneutic that is their boast in contrast to most other theological systems. An example is Walvoord's treatment of symbolic numbers. After giving a list of the most prominent numbers found in Revelation, he writes:

> These numbers may be understood literally, but even when understood this way, they often carry with them also a symbolic meaning. . . . Though the symbolism is not always obvious, the general rule should be followed to interpret the numbers literally unless there is clear evidence to the contrary. The numbers nevertheless convey more than their bare numerical significance.[82]

In the pages immediately following, Walvoord lists twenty-six images in Revelation that he believes must be understood symbolically (that is, *nonliterally*). Charles Ryrie, another prominent dispensational *futurist* writes:

> The concept of literal interpretation always raises questions since it seems to preclude anything symbolic, and the book obviously contains symbols. . . . Futurists do recognize the presence of symbols in the book. The difference between the literalist and the spiritualizer is simply that the former sees the symbols as conveying a plain meaning.[83]

Henry Morris, who believes he has written probably the "most literal" commentary on Revelation, acknowledges, "Many futurists still employ much symbolism, while others take most of these future events in a very literal sense."[84]

In one sense, there is a strong psychological appeal to the *futurist* approach. Many of us would like to have a divinely inspired channel of insight into the future. *Futurists* believe that to reveal the future in advance is in keeping with God's character and methods throughout Scripture, and sometimes see in this book just such a tool of prediction.

Confidence in this approach is enhanced whenever a commentator is able to match current geopolitical events with his interpretation of Revelation, as when Hal Lindsey reported that the Red Chinese claimed they could field an army of an estimated "200 million armed and organized militiamen"—the very number of the invaders mentioned in Revelation 9:16.[85]

That the Euphrates is to be dried up to allow passage for the "kings of the East" (Rev. 16:12) finds its alleged confirmation in the fact that "this kind of thing has been made technically possible by the Russians' recent construction of a dam near the headwaters of the Euphrates."[86]

Some *futurists*, most commonly those of the dispensational camp, are very fond of finding this kind of evidence in support of their view of Revelation. In fact, every generation of futuristic interpreters for the last 150 years or longer has been able to gain confidence, by comparing their own times with the prophecies of Revelation, that they themselves were living in the time of fulfillment.[87]

Not all *futurists* are dispensationalists and not all approve of engaging in what some refer to as "newspaper exegesis." There are notable *futurist* scholars who reject the dispensational distinctives. An example would be Dr. Theodor Zahn, who in 1929 was the foremost conservative scholar in Germany in the field of New Testament literature and exegesis. Some more recent *futurists* have, like Mounce and Ladd, temper their *futurism* with a touch of *preterism* and/or *idealism*. They take Revelation less literally, and refer to dispensationalism as "extreme." They remain *futurists*, however, in that they anticipate a future Antichrist arising to persecute the saints in a future tribulation period, and they do anticipate a literal thousand-year reign of Christ on earth.

It is not surprising that the *futurist* approach, more than any of the others, has appealed to popular sentiments. However, some biblical scholars have complained that *futurism*, like *historicism*, renders the book of Revelation about 90 percent irrelevant to the original readers, since, on this view, they lived nearly two thousand years prior to its fulfillment (despite the book's repeated affirmations of the near fulfillment of the prophecies[88]). If we go along with dispensational interpreters in finding the Rapture of the church at Revelation 4:1, then the book becomes largely irrelevant, not only to the original readers, but also to all Christians of any age. This is because the church will be in heaven before the majority of the prophecies begin to unfold, neither experiencing nor witnessing their fulfillment. This leaves it far from obvious why Christians should take an interest in such events—or why God should wish to reveal them to us.

Some critics object to *futurism* on the basis of its origins. Francisco Ribeira, a Spanish Jesuit, is said to have originated this approach to Revelation in 1585 for the purpose of refuting the *historicist* view, and the Reformers' insistence that the "beast" was the papacy. Ribeira taught that the "Antichrist" had not yet come and would be an individual arising "in the last days." Protestants rejected this view for over two hundred years, but it was finally introduced in Protestant circles by

Samuel Maitland in 1827 and popularized in the works of J. N. Darby, the founder of dispensationalism, beginning in 1830. Protestant interpreters sometimes still look upon this approach with suspicion because of these roots.

It may be noted that, unlike the *historicist* and *preterist* approaches, the *futurist* approach cannot be tested from history. One may evaluate the *historicist* and the *preterist* approaches partially on the basis of their claims that actual and documentable events have occurred in history, which correspond with their interpretation of Revelation's predictions. The *futurist* view, however, cannot be verified or falsified in this manner, since the things predicted have not yet occurred. In the absence of certain knowledge of the future, it can be argued that anything *might* yet happen to fulfill the *futurist's* expectations. The dispensationalists, in particular, do not stand ever to be embarrassed by future developments, since they believe that they will be raptured before any of the predicted events occur. Whether this invulnerability to falsification is an asset or a liability to *futurism* is not a matter of universal agreement.

4. The Idealist Approach: No Single Fulfillment; Only Transcendent Principles and Recurrent Themes.

I am using the label *idealist* to include all approaches that do not look for individual or specific fulfillments of the prophecies of Revelation in the historical or futuristic sense, but affirm only that spiritual lessons and principles (which may find recurrent expression throughout history) are symbolically depicted in the visions. Though this kind of approach is sometimes unfairly associated with theological liberalism, it is entirely consistent with a high view of inspiration of Scripture, and there are many commentaries by theological conservatives who believe that John had the visions revealed to him exactly as he claims, but who believe that their meaning is to be spiritually understood in a sense that would be edifying to believers of any age.

D. T. Crafer traces the modern emergence of this view to William Milligan:

There is one other method of interpretation worthy of mention; it is that associated with Milligan himself. He divorces the book almost completely from history, and finds in it little more than a noble expression of those great principles of the divine government whose operation we can trace in every age of the world.[89]

It was not easy to choose a label for this approach. Many writers refer to it, but they prefer differing ways of designating it. The most common name for the view is the *idealist*. Some commentators call this view the *nonliteral, allegorical*[90] or the *symbolic, poetic*[91] interpretation; others call it the *philosophy of history school.*[92] In the first edition of this book, I labeled it the *spiritual* approach, but I have revised it to reflect the more commonly known label: *idealist.*

According to this view, the great themes of the triumph of good over evil, of Christ over Satan, of the vindication of the martyrs and the sovereignty of God are played out repeatedly throughout visions of Revelation, without reference to single historical events. The battles in Revelation may be seen as referring to spiritual warfare, to the persecution of Christians, or to international conflict in general throughout history. The beast from the sea may be identified as the satanically in-spired political opposition to the church in any age, and the beast from the land as the opposition of pagan or corrupt religion to Christianity. The Harlot represents either the compromised church or the seduction of the world in general. Each bro-ken *seal* or sounded *trumpet* depicts some reality (e.g., famine, war, natural disas-ter) that may be observed in history, on a recurring basis, as part of the sovereign outworking of God's purpose in history.

Milligan puts it this way: "While the Apocalypse thus embraces the whole pe-riod of the Christian dispensation, it sets before us within this period the action of great principles and not special incidents."[93]

One advantage of this view is that it avoids the problem of harmonizing specific passages with specific fulfillments—a difficulty which has plagued the *historicist, futurist,* and *preterist* views—and makes every passage relevant and edifying to any generation of Christians.

The significant disadvantage of the *idealist* position is that the book of Revela-tion itself claims to be predicting events "that must shortly come to pass" (1:1), giv-ing the impression that some fulfillment, in some particular historical setting, is intended.

For this reason, most modern commentators, both of the evangelical wing and of the *literary-critical* type, have intermixed some of the commitments of the *idealist* approach with one of the other historically based approaches. This is not a difficult merger to effect, as Pieters rightly observes:

> [*Idealist*] interpretations combine readily with those of the Preterists or of the His-toricists, because any symbol, understood by them to refer to a certain force or tendency may be considered fulfilled in any event in which such a force or ten-dency is dominant.[94]

Most commonly, the combination is with late-date *preterism,* as Walvoord points out when discussing the trend of liberal scholarship: "Contemporary liberal works usually follow a combination of the preterist and the symbolical methods of interpretation, disregarding the strictly historical interpretation as well as the futurist."[95]

This is observable, not only among liberals, but also in many modern evangelical writings on Revelation. Though evangelical commentators commonly list the *idealist* (or some equivalent designation) as one of the approaches alternate to their own, they employ its methods in their actual comments. The most common tendency is to mix the *idealist* approach with the *preterist* and then either call their view *preterism*, leave their view unlabeled or give it an original name.

Typical of this blending of approaches is that of Harvey J. S. Blaney expressed in *The Wesleyan Bible Commentary:*

> John anticipated a great persecution, of which he had tasted a sample, which would be followed by the destruction of the evil forces of the world and the establishment of a rule of righteousness and peace of permanent duration. But the delay of that Kingdom has made the truths contained in this book applicable to all ages in the struggle of right against evil while the church continues to wait and expect the return of its Lord and Savior.[96]

Blaney describes himself as a *preterist*, but ends up without any actual historical fulfillment and is left making the same application as does anyone who takes the *idealist* approach. This is extremely common with modern neo-evangelical commentators on Revelation. In fact, Pieters asserts: "Today, scholars are prevailingly in favor of this system [*preterism,*] either unchanged, or combined with the ideas of the Philosophy of History [*idealist*] School."[97]

Leon Morris and Michael Wilcock are among those who follow such a procedure without hazarding a name for their mixture. Earl Morey also attempts the same, but refers to the result as "the *classical* approach." Herschel H. Hobbs and Homer Hailey (alliteration unintentional) take the same approach, but call it the *historical background* view.

William Hendriksen and his 1939 book, *More Than Conquerors,* fall into this same general category, though he calls his view *progressive parallelism.* He has given it this name because he sees Revelation as a series of seven segments parallel to each other, each concerned with the entire Church Age, but depicting the age with different symbols in each segment. His is thus similar with what has been called the *dramatic* approach. This understanding of the structure of Revelation was championed prior to the appearance of Hendriksen's book (e.g., Erdman's *The Revelation of John* in 1936)[98] and is followed to a greater or lesser extent by several modern treatments (e.g., Wilcock and Wilson).

Hendriksen's interpretation is essentially *idealist* in character, with some *preterist* or *historicist* elements. A. T. Robertson categorizes this view as another kind of *historicism*, and calls it *synchronous historicism*, but since no specific historic fulfillments are identified, it seems more appropriate to include it under the rubric of the *idealist* approach. Indeed, Hendriksen's sixth and seventh propositions about the Book of Revelation identify his approach as a combination of *idealism* and *preterism*, respectively:

> PROPOSITION VI. *The seals, trumpets, bowls of wrath, and similar symbols refer not to specific events, particular happenings, or details of history, but to principles—of human conduct and of divine moral government—that are operating throughout the history of the world, especially throughout the new dispensation. [idealism]*[99]

> PROPOSITION VII. *The Apocalypse is rooted in contemporaneous events and circumstances. Its symbols should be interpreted in the light of conditions which prevailed when the book was written. [preterism]*[100]

Occasionally, *futurism* is even thrown into the *idealist/preterist* mix. After surveying the four principal approaches, for instance, George Eldon Ladd—who is largely a *futurist*—concludes that "the correct method of interpreting the Revelation is the blending of the preterist and the futurist methods." However, he also says "The beast is both Rome and the eschatological antichrist—*and, we might add, any demonic power which the church must face in her entire history*"[101] (emphasis mine). Thus he combines not only the *preterist and futurist* approaches, but the *idealist* as well.

This is also Mounce's approach. Like Ladd, he is largely a *futurist* in his treatment of the major prophecies of Revelation, but we find *idealism* combined with *preterism* and *futurism* in his view of the beast:

> In John's vision the beast is the Roman Empire [*preterism*] . . . Yet the Beast is more than the Roman Empire. In a larger sense, it is the spirit of godless totalitarianism that has energized every authoritarian system devised by man throughout history [*idealism*]. At the end of time, the Beast will appear in its most malicious form. It will be the ultimate expression of deified secular authority [*futurism*].[102]

Although many of these scholars combine the *idealist* approach with others, and use innovative labels, or none at all, to describe their preferred amalgam, the *idealist* interpretation has a character entirely of its own and sees Revelation from an entirely different perspective than do the more strictly historico-eschatological approaches. As J. Barton Payne has observed:

Allegorizing commentators may treat the Apocalypse according to principles of mystical interpretation . . . or according to theories of liturgical, poetic, or dramatic literary forms such as have been proposed by modern critics; but all writers of this type unite upon reducing the book's 'real' teaching to certain matters of timeless truth, or at least to interpretations that are devoid of concrete, historical specification.[103]

That is the distinctive feature that makes an interpretation fall into the *idealist* category in this volume. The authors that I cite for this view include some from among the ranks of those who identify themselves by some other label or even with one of the other viewpoints. It is because of the spiritualizing element in their interpretations that I have placed in the *idealist* column when quoting them there.

NOTE

This commentary covers all of the book of Revelation. The commentary on chapters 4–19 is arranged in four parallel columns that run across two facing pages. These provide the reader with the four main approaches to these chapters in side-by-side columns. On several occasions this arrangement results in a blank page or column because there is no further commentary for the views on that page. This isn't an error. These pages appear as they do in order to keep the parallel-column layout consistent and easy to use. For your convenience, these pages refer to the page number where those views continue.

Notes

1. Eusebius, *Ecclesiastical History*, 3:39:4.
2. J. H. Moulton, W. F. Howard, and N. Turner, *Grammar of New Testament Greek*, vol. 2, part 1, 3.
3. A. T. Robertson, *Word Pictures in the New Testament*, vol. 6. (Nashville: Broadman, n.d.), 273.
4. *Neutestamentliche Grammatik*, 3.
5. Although some will argue that the whole Johannine corpus, rather than coming from one writer, emerged from a "Johannine community."
6. F. F. Bruce, ed., *Revelation, in the New International Bible Commentary* (Grand Rapids: Zondervan, 1979), 1594.
7. G. K. Beale, *The Book of Revelation* (Grand Rapids: Eerdmans, 1999), 4.
8. Languages like Hebrew, Greek and Latin use letters of the alphabet for numbers. *Gematria* or *gimatria* is the practice of assigning a numerical value to a word or phrase, based upon the sum of the values of the individual letters. The number 666 is an example, in Rev. 13:18.
9. Clement, *Miscellanies* 7:17

10. William Milligan, *Discussions on the Apocalypse* (London: Macmillan, 1893), 75.

11. Philip Schaff, *History of the Christian Church* 3rd ed.(Grand Rapids: Eerdmans, 1950 [1910]) 1:834.

12. Kenneth Gentry, *Before Jerusalem Fell: The Dating of the Book of Revelation* (Tyler, TX: Institute for Christian Economics, 1989), 30–38.

13. Some advance a theory of an Ephesian origin of Philippians, placing the date of writing as early as AD 57.

14. Iraneus, *Against Heresies* 5:30:1, 3.

15. Though Irenaeus, of course, was not infallible. His historical accuracy has sometimes been questioned in view of his assertion that Jesus lived to be over fifty years of age *(Against Heresies,* 2:22:5).

16. Alexander Roberts and W. H. Rambaut in *The Writings of Irenaeus,* vol. 1, trans. 1880. Cited by Gentry, *Before Jerusalem Fell (Tyler, TX: Institute for Christian Economics),* 49.

17. Gentry, *Before Jerusalem Fell,* 152–56.

18. Ibid., 153.

19. Some *postmillennialists* view this situation about the same as do the *amillennialists.* Alternatively, most *postmillennialists* do not see the Second Coming in chap. 19, but rather interpret the vision as the spread of the gospel in the present age.

20. E.g., Isa. 11:15–16; 43:1–6; 51:9–11; Jer.16:14–15; 23:7–8

21. This is also true of the Old Testament equivalent Hebrew word *erets.*

22. See, e.g., Isa. 60:3–5; Dan. 7:2ff. Compare Rev. 10:2; 12:12 with notes there.

23. Rev. 3:10; 6:10; 11:10; 13:8, 12, 14; 14:6; 17:8.

24. Rev. 6:15; 16:14; 17:2, 18; 18:3, 9; 19:19; 21:24

25. Rev. 7:1–3; 10:2, 8; 13:11.

26. Rev. 12:4, 9; 13:13; 20:9, 11.

27. Rev. 10:5–6; 12:12; 14:7; 21:1.

28. With the exception of the "fully-realized *preterists*" who believe that since AD 70 there remains nothing further of prophecy to be fulfilled, e.g., J. Stuart Russell in *The Parousia.*

29. In the Old Testament examples, the word "earth" is the Hebrew *erets* and could be translated "land."

30. Matt. 11:16; 12:41, 42; 23:36.

31. A term derived from the Latin *raptus,* referring to the "catching up" into the air of believers who are alive at the time of the Second Coming, cf. 1 Thess. 4:16.

32. In dispensational parlance, this term refers to a period of seven years at the end of the present age, identified with the time of judgments and calamities described in Revelation 4–19. The name "Tribulation" is taken from Matt. 24:21 and Rev. 7:14.

33. Nearly all commentators who endeavor to survey the history of interpretation of Revelation express indebtedness to H. B. Swete's excellent work. I must also register my indebtedness to Swete, but also to Tenney, Bruce, Walvoord, and, especially, Wainwright, for their helpful summaries.

34. H. B. Swete, *The Apocalypse of St. John* (New York: Macmillan, 1906), ccix.

35. Ibid., cx.

36. Bruce, "Revelation" in the IBC, 1,594.

37. Chap. 1, xxx.

38. John Walvoord, *The Millennial Kingdom* (Findlay, OH: Dunham, 1959), 16.

39. Charles Ryrie, *The Basis of the Premillennial Faith* (Neptune, NJ: Loizeaux Brothers, 1953), 17.

40. See Swete, ccvii f.

41. *Ibid.*, ccviii.

42. *Ibid.*, ccix.

43. *Ibid.*, ccviii.

44. *Ibid.*

45. *Ibid.*, ccix.

46. Bruce, "Revelation" in IBC, 1594.

47. Swete, *The Apocalypse of St. John*, ccx.

48. *Ibid.*, ccxi.

49. *Ibid.*, ccxif.

50. Merrill C. Tenney, "Revelation" in *Zondervan Pictoral Encyclopedia of the Bible*, vol. 5 (Grand Rapids: Zondervan, 1975), 97.

51. Walvoord, *The Millenial Kingdom*, 18.

52. Swete, *The Apocalypse of St. John*, ccxiv.

53. Bruce, "Revelation" in IBC, 1595.

54. e.g., Walvoord, *The Millenial Kingdom*,17.

55. Swete, *The Apocalypse of St. John*, ccxiv.

56. Tenney, "Revelation" in *Zondervan Pictoral Encyclopedia of the Bible*, 97.

57. Swete, *The Apocalypse of St. John*, ccxv.

58. e.g., Miller *[Revelation: A Panorama of the Gospel Age*, 1991) and Robert Caringola *[The Present Reign of Jesus Christ*, 1995). Caringola told me in a telephone conversation that no American scholar had published a commentary from the historicist viewpoint in the past fifty years.

59. M. Eugene Boring, "Revelation" in *Interpretation: A Bible Commentary For Preaching and Teaching,* James Luther Mays, ed. (Louisville: John Knox, 1989), 49.

60. Quoted in editor's preface to Barnes' "Revelation" in Notes (Grand Rapids: Baker, 1884–85), xii. Essentially the same accusation has been made by Stuart's opponents about his own *preterism*. Professor Bush critiqued Stuart's *preterism* as leaving the church "cut loose from every chronological mooring, and set adrift in the open sea, without the vestige of a beacon, lighthouse, or star . . ." (Ibid., xiii). I have *found futurist* writers to quote Stuart verbatim in their criticizing *every* view that rivals their own. It seems that each view seems hopelessly subjective to critics who champion alternative positions.

61. This example cited by Barnes, in Notes, 370, and Caringola, *The Present Reign of Jesus Christ*, 3.

62. See above heading, History of Interpretation.

63. Albertus Pieters, *The Lamb, the Woman, and the Dragon* (Grand Rapids: Zondervan, 1937), 48.

64. Ibid..

65. Bruce, "Revelation" in IBC., 1595.

66. Moses Stuart, *A Commentary on the Apocalypse, 2* vols. (Andover, MA: Alien, 1845), v.

67. John Walvoord, *The Revelation of Jesus Christ* (Chicago: Moody, 1966), 125. Sensing the vulnerability of *futurism* to the same criticism, Walvoord adds: "While even in *the futurist* school minor variations will be found in various expositors, the general conclusion that these chapters picture future definite events is the important coherent factor." *Historicists* may respond that their view also pictures definite events, albeit events generally past, and that this definiteness provides the same "important coherent factor."

68. Ibid., 19. The comment seems oblivious to the vulnerability of his own dispensational *futurism* to precisely the same charge. The same criticism of *historicism* is made by J. Barton Payne, who regards it as "a sure proof of the illegitimacy of this approach." *Encyclopedia of Biblical Prophecy* (Grand Rapids: Baker, 1973), 593.

69. Tenney, "Revelation" in *Zondervan Pictoral Encyclopedia of the Bible*, 96.

70. Pieters, *The Lamb, the Woman, and the Dragon*, 42.

71. Ibid.

72. J. Stewart Russell, J. Stewart, *The Parousia: A Critical Inquiry into the New Testament Doctrine of our Lord's Second Coming* (Grand Rapids: Baker,, 1887, rpr. 1983), 375f.

73. E.g., Russell.

74. E.g., Jay Adams and David S. Clark.

75. For this criticism, see, for example, the footnote to p. xiii of the editor's preface to Barnes' "Revelation" in *Notes*.

76. Eusiebus, *Ecclesiastical History*, Book III, chap. 7.

77. Both citations from Andreas taken from Kenneth Gentry, *The Beast of the Revelation* (Tyler, TX: Institute for Christian Economics, 1989), 107.

78. Cited by Gentry, *The Beast of the Revelation*, 107. Gentry mentions that this dating for Arethas is asserted by Stuart and Fausset, but that Swete and Aland place the date of Arethas later, c. AD 914.

79. Frequently identifying the seven church epistles with successive divisions of church history from the beginning to the present.

80. This is most likely to be the case when the commentator is a dispensationalist. Non-dispensational futurists, like Robert Mounce, do not encourage a literalistic approach and advocate a full appreciation for the symbolic character of apocalyptic literature.

81. Henry M. Morris, *The Revelation Record: A Scientific and Devotional Commentary on the Book of Revelation* (Wheaton, IL: Tyndale House, 1983), 26.

82. Walvoord, *The Revelation of Jesus Christ*, 28.

83. Ryrie, *Revelation*, 9. It is not explained how the *futurist*, more than the *spiritualizer*, sees in the symbols a plain meaning. It will become clear that all of the approaches believe that they assign plain meanings to the symbols in the book.

84. *Morris, The Revelation Record*, 26

85. Hal Lindsey, *There's a New World Corning* (Eugene, OR: Harvest House, 1973), 140.

86. Ibid., 221

87. In 1973, dispensationalist Hal Lindsey wrote: "For those of us who know what the prophets have taught, picking up our morning newspaper is practically a traumatic experience. Headline after headline screams out a confirmation of these remarkable predictions." [Ibid., 99–100). Forty years later, some dispensationalists still make the same kind of claims, though the current headlines *scream out* a very different geopolitical landscape from that of the 1970s.

88. E.g., Rev. 1:1, 3; 22:10.

89. In *Gore's New Commentary*, 680.

90. E.g., Walvoord; Payne calls it *allegorized*.

91. E.g., G. R. Beasley-Murray.

92. E.g., Pieters, Hobbs, and Hailey.

93. William Milligan, *The Book of Revelation* (London: Hodder & Stoughton, 1889), 153.

94. Pieters, *The Lamb, the Woman, and the Dragon*, 41.

95. Walvoord, *The Revelation of Jesus Christ*, 18.

96. J. S. Blaney, "Revelation," in *The Wesleyan Bible Commentary*, ed. Charles Carter (Grand Rapids: Eerdmans, 1969), 419.

97. Pieters, *The Lamb, the Woman, and the Dragon*, 44.

98. Though Hendriksen's book is often cited as the definitive work on this position, he himself acknowledged that "This view, in one form or another, is adopted by R. C. H. Lenski [*Interpretation of St. John's Revelation*, 1935], S. L. Morris, *The Drama of Christianity* [1928], M. F. Sadler, *The Revelation of St. John the Divine* [1894], B. B. Warfield, *Biblical Doctrines* [1929]" (Hendriksen, *More Than Conquerors: An Interpretation of the Book of Revelation* [Grand Rapids: Baker, 1939], 19). In fact, Albert Barnes, writing in 1851, evidenced an awareness of this position, though he disregarded it in *Notes*, 189).

99. Hendriksen, *More Than Conquerors*, 43.

100. Ibid., 45.

101. George Eldon Ladd, *A Commentary on the Revelation of John* (Grand Rapids: Eerdmans, 1972), 14.

102. Mounce, *What Are We Waiting For? A Commentary on Revelation*, 65.

103. Payne, *Encyclopedia of Biblical Prophecy*, 593.

PART I

THE SEVEN LETTERS

REVELATION 1—3

WHAT IS THE SIGNIFICANCE OF CHRIST'S COMMISSION TO JOHN?
WHAT DO THE SEVEN CHURCHES SIGNIFY?

⧖ HISTORICIST APPROACH:

- John is given a vision of Christ, who announces that he is to write of things that would soon begin to take place, and which would extend through the entire age of the church.
- Seven churches in Asia received these letters, but they represent seven periods of church history, each exhibiting the special features of the respective original church.

⧖ PRETERIST APPROACH:

- Christ appears to John on Patmos, commissioning him to write things that would soon afterward find fulfillment in the fall of Jerusalem.
- The letters reflect the conditions prevailing in seven churches in the Roman province of Asia prior to the Jewish war of AD 66–70.

⧖ FUTURIST APPROACH:

- While a prisoner on the isle of Patmos, John sees a vision of Christ, commanding him to write of events that would be fulfilled at the end of the present age, just prior to the Second Coming.
- Some *futurists* take the letters in the same manner as do the *historicists*, while others take them more as do the *preterists* or those taking the *idealist* approach.

⧖ IDEALIST APPROACH:

- The symbolic vision of Christ depicts His glorious character and sovereignty, conveying Christ's sovereign involvement in the affairs of the world and of the church, including his intimate concern for His suffering servants.
- The churches resemble churches that might exist at any time throughout the church age, and the letters are applicable to any churches that may share their conditions. The number seven is symbolic, suggesting application to the whole Christian church of all ages.

INTRODUCTION

REVELATION 1:1—3

¹The Revelation of Jesus Christ, which God gave Him to show His servants—things which must shortly take place. And He sent and signified it by His angel to His servant John, ²who bore witness to the word of God, and to the testimony of Jesus Christ, to all things that he saw. ³Blessed is he who reads and those who hear the words of this prophecy, and keep those things which are written in it; for the time is near.

These first three verses speak of John in the third person, suggesting that they were written by the custodians of the epistle, who may have added them at the time of publication as a brief prologue and endorsement of the work. Similar editorial endorsement appears at the end of John's Gospel, where some anonymous hand penned the closing words: "This is the disciple who testifies of these things, and wrote these things; and we know that his testimony is true" (John 21:24). We are left to guess the identities of those to whom "we" refers. "We" may have been members of a "Johannine community" (a group of John's disciples) or simply the church leaders (probably in Ephesus) who preserved and probably published John's work posthumously. Not all commentators agree with such an assessment, though. Mounce, for instance, thinks this opening section "appears to have been added by the author himself after completing the book."[1]

The expression, **Revelation of Jesus Christ** (v. 1), presents a certain ambiguity. The Greek allows that Jesus Christ could be either the subject being revealed or the one doing the revealing. The former idea—that it is Christ himself who is being revealed, or *unveiled*—would agree well with the general contents of the book, especially of the present chapter, and of chapters 5, 14, and 19, in which John sees pictorial representations of Christ.

The latter alternative—that the book contains information revealed through Christ—seems to agree with the rest of the verse, which suggests that the material of the visions was revealed first to Christ by God (the Father), then by Christ to an angel, who passed it along to John. John then bore witness (beginning at verse 4) to the visions, putting them into this written form.

The phrase, **the testimony of Jesus Christ** (v. 2), possesses the same ambiguity as does **the revelation of Je-**

sus Christ in verse 1. It could refer to John's testimony *concerning* Christ (i.e., the gospel), or else to the message which Christ himself testified to John. The first option seems to work best here and in verse 9, since, in both places, "the testimony of Jesus" is coupled with the word of God. While one could argue that, since "the word of God" is a word *from* God, "the testimony of Jesus" must therefore be a testimony *from* Jesus, yet both can be ways of describing the gospel message. Since John is the one bearing witness in verse 2, "the testimony of Jesus Christ" more likely refers to the testimony about Christ as borne by John.[2]

Blessed is he who reads (v. 3). This beatitude is the first of seven in the book.[3] Initially, the blessing is pronounced upon the reader—probably the person who would read the book publicly in the assembly. Beyond that, the blessing is for those of the congrega-tion who hear and obey. That this blessing extends also to those who hear and obey in later generations is no doubt intended as well.

In this beatitude the book is first identified as a prophecy (v. 3). The prophetic character of this revelation is reaffirmed in 22:7, 10, 18, and 19. In one place we are informed that the testimony of Jesus (discussed above) is "the spirit of prophecy" (19:10).

The prophecy here is said to pertain to events whose time is near (v. 3). This is affirmed repeatedly. The things revealed, according to verse 1, must shortly take place, and a few verses later, we are told that John wrote of "things which are about to take place" (so reads the Greek of verse 19).[4] On the surface, this gives us the impression that John expected the fulfillment of the prophecies to occur very shortly after he wrote them. However, see comparative note box below.

SPECIAL COMPARATIVE NOTE ON 1:1–3:

"must shortly take place . . . the time is near"

Of the four approaches we are considering in this commentary, the early-date *preterist* is the most comfortable with such statements about near fulfillment, taken at their face value. This approach views the book as written shortly before AD 70 and predicting the fall of Jerusalem, which occurred in that year. Later-date *preterists* would apply the fulfillment to the fall of Rome centuries after John's time or, possibly, to the downfall of Domitian.

Historicists would see the fulfillment as *beginning* shortly after John's time, but extending long beyond, through the entire age of the church.

To the *idealist* interpreters, the time is always near, since the visions transcend any particular time period and may, in principle, recur or continue unceasingly throughout all times.

Futurists suggest that the terms "shortly" or "near" have some meaning other than that which first comes to mind. There are essentially two alternatives:

(1) The word "shortly" means "quickly" or "suddenly"—thus meaning that there will be a rapidity of fulfillment whenever the proper time may come, but that may be thousands of years later than John's time. This view is taken by Walvoord, Ryrie, and Lange, among others. Though this may deal adequately with the word "shortly," it does not dispense with the problem of "the time is near."

(2) The second alternative is to suggest that "shortly" means "soon" and that "the time is near" may be taken literally, but that John is speaking according to God's way of reckoning time and nearness. Since a day to the Lord is as a thousand years and a thousand years is as a day (2 Pet. 3:8), even an event two thousand years removed might be regarded as "near" from God's perspective. This is the view of Alford, Fausset, Vitringa, Henry Morris, and others. Perhaps the greatest question suggested by this proposal is whether the original human readers of Revelation would share God's perspective and would view such distant events as being "near."

GRACE AND PEACE FROM THE TRIUNE GOD

REVELATION 1:4–6

[4]John to the seven churches which are in Asia: Grace to you and peace from Him who is and who was and who is to come, and from the seven Spirits who are before His throne, [5]and from Jesus Christ, the faithful witness, the firstborn from the dead, and the ruler over the kings of the earth. To Him who loved us and washed us from our sins in His own blood, [6]and has made us kings and priests to His God and Father, to Him be glory and dominion forever and ever. Amen.

These verses read like the opening of most of the biblical epistles. The author first identifies himself and his readers (v. 4), who belong to **the seven churches** (named in v. 11). The letter most likely was a circulating epistle, to be read (and perhaps copied) by one church and then passed along to the next. The epistle of Paul to the Galatian churches and the epistles of James and Peter were handled similarly, since each addresses several churches. Many scholars believe that Paul's epistle to the Ephesians was such a circular epistle, probably sent to many of the same churches addressed in Revelation.[5] These churches were in Asia, which was not, referring to the continent, but to a Roman province, identified with modern Turkey.

Like most New Testament letters, this epistle begins with a benediction of grace and peace upon the readers. In other letters, this **grace and peace** generally are spoken of as coming from God the Father and from Jesus. In Revelation, the source of the grace and peace is described in more elaborate terms, which most commentators decode as references to the Father, the Son, and the Holy Spirit.

It is the Father **who is and who was and who is to come** (v. 4). Though it is possible to apply this language to Christ, He is mentioned separately in the following verse. **He who is** seems to echo the words to Moses at the burning bush: "I am who I am" (Exod. 3:14). The expression **who is to come** can simply mean "who shall be."

The seven Spirits who are before His throne (v. 4) is one of the more perplexing expressions in the book of Revelation. Commentators usually take it to mean "the sevenfold Spirit of God"—a reference to the Holy Spirit as described in Isaiah 11:2. He is there called the Spirit of the Lord, of wisdom, of understanding, of counsel, of might,

of knowledge, and of the fear of the Lord. This explanation probably has more in its favor than most alternatives. If this is the correct identification, then the greeting has moved from a focus upon the Father to a focus upon the Holy Spirit, to be followed in the next verses by a focus upon the Son. While most epistles wish the readers grace and peace from the Father and from the Son,[6] this is the only one to include the Spirit as well.

The description of Jesus (v. 5) gives Him three titles, all of which carry comforting implications for Christian readers facing persecution.

As **the faithful witness**, Jesus has set the example for those called to bear witness in a hostile world. Paul reminded Timothy that, when on trial for His life before Pilate, Jesus "witnessed the good confession" (1 Tim. 6:13). Thus the church of Smyrna is urged by Jesus to "be faithful until death" (Rev. 2:10), and Antipas, who was killed in Pergamos, is crowned with the epithet "My faithful martyr" (Rev. 2:13)—which is the same expression as is here given to Christ.[7]

The second title for Christ is **the firstborn from the dead**, a term first found in Paul's writings (Col. 1:18), arising from his understanding of Psalm 2:7: "You are My Son, Today I have begotten You." Paul understood this "begetting" to be a reference to the resurrection of Christ (Acts 13:33).

Thereafter, the title "firstborn from the dead" as well as the similar expression, "the first fruits of those who have fallen asleep" (1 Cor. 15:20), came to suggest the resurrection of Christ, seen as the guarantee of a later resurrection of believers (1 Cor. 15:23). Mentioned here, it reminds those who are called upon to be faithful until death that Jesus' faithfulness was vindicated by resurrection from the dead. His vindication came first; theirs will follow.

In calling Jesus **the ruler over the kings of the earth**,[8] John is lifting the horizon of his readers' perspective above the earthly rulers, some of whom may have been the visible source of their sufferings, to Him who sits enthroned above the kings of the earth, exercising absolute sovereignty over them (Prov. 21:1; Dan. 2:21; 4:17). In times of persecution, the kings of the earth who "set themselves . . . against the LORD and against His Anointed" (Ps. 2:2) loom large in the view of the afflicted church. But when the veil is pulled aside, as it is here, to reveal the One who "sits in the heavens and laughs" (Ps. 2:4), who has not relinquished any part of His sovereignty to tinhorn tyrants, the church takes courage and comfort—and such encouragement may be the principal reason God sent these visions to the exile on Patmos.

No doubt to encourage faith for the present, John mentions the love of Jesus toward the churches, illustrated in what He already has done in sacrificing himself (v. 5). This affirmation reads differently in different Greek texts. That which is followed in the KJV and the NKJV reads as above: **Who loved us and washed us from our sins in His own blood**, whereas the text followed by the bulk of modern translations has it: "Who loves us and *freed* us from our sins by his own blood." The difference between the past tense in one case and the present tense in the other does not alter significantly the meaning of Christ's love for the churches. The present tense may indicate that the love of Christ for His people is not a thing of the past, appearances to the contrary. Being "washed" by the blood of Jesus is a scriptural concept,[9] though the idea of being "freed" by the blood of Jesus— seen as a parallel to Israel's having been freed from Egypt by the blood of the Passover lamb—may be preferred, in view of the frequent use in Revelation of the Exodus motif (see introduction). Jesus' death is thus seen as accomplishing a second exodus: as Israel was delivered from the bondage of Egypt, Christians are delivered from the bondage of sin. This theme of a second exodus is found repeatedly in the prophets of the Old Testament,[10] and also appears in other New Testament passages.[11]

The expression **kings and priests** (v. 6) also is found in 5:10. In both passages, the redeemed of humanity—the church—is so described. An alternate textual reading gives the phrase as "a kingdom of priests," which changes the sense considerably.[12] The newer translations usually favor the latter reading, based on its similarity with Exodus 20:6, from which it apparently is taken. This is one of the many New Testament verses that give to the church titles originally applied to Israel (cf. 1 Pet. 2:9–10), suggesting that God's kingdom is now to be associated with the church rather than Israel. Most ancient kingdoms had official religious systems, with an elite priesthood. The kingdom of God does not *possess* a priesthood, but is itself God's priesthood on the earth. The church is "a holy priesthood" and a "royal priesthood" (1 Pet. 2:5, 9). Protestants have based their doctrine of the priesthood of believers on passages like this, focusing primarily on the priestly privilege of access to God. The principal function of priests, however, was to mediate between God and men. As God's priesthood in the world, the church mediates to bring men to God, both by the priestly function of teaching the nations the ways of God (Lev 10:10–11; Matt. 28:19–20), and by the offering of spiritual sacrifices (Isa. 66:20; Rom. 15:16).

The reference to Christ's God and Father (v. 6) calls to mind the words of Christ recorded elsewhere by the same apostle: "I am ascending to My Father and your Father, and to My God and your God" (John 20:17).

The greeting closes with the shortest of the seven doxologies, or ascriptions of glory to God, of the book—speaking only of **glory and dominion** (v. 6). The subsequent doxologies speak of "glory and honor and thanks" (4:9); "glory and honor and power" (4:11); "power and riches and wisdom, and strength and honor and glory and blessing" [a sevenfold ascription] (5:12); "blessing and honor and glory and power" (5:13); "blessing and glory and wisdom, thanksgiving and honor and power and might" [another sevenfold ascription] (7:12); "salvation and glory and honor and power" (19:1).

THE LORD WHO IS COMING

REVELATION 1:7—8

[7]Behold, He is coming with clouds, and every eye will see Him, even they who pierced Him. And all the tribes of the earth will mourn because of Him. Even so, Amen. [8]I am the Alpha and the Omega, the Beginning and the End," says the Lord, "who is and who was and who is to come, the Almighty."

With the words, **Behold, He is coming**, we are introduced to the great theme of the book. The comfort that this promise contains for the suffering believers, and the warning for the obstinate, will be elaborated upon throughout the remainder of the book. There is not total agreement among interpreters, however, as to the precise import of the announcement. Is this referring to the ultimate appearing of Christ at the end of history as we know it, or to something else? Various options are considered in the special comparative note on verse 7.

SPECIAL COMPARATIVE NOTE ON 1:7

Behold, He is coming (v. 7). But precisely what event is being announced? The *futurist* approach takes this statement somewhat literally, seeing in it a prediction of the Second Coming of Christ in the clouds at the end of the present age. This seems to many to be the most natural way to understand the expression and is apt to be followed by most who favor the *historicist* and the *idealist* approaches as well.

The *idealist* approach may see this as one of several references to the Second Coming, though this approach is also at liberty to spiritualize the coming as does Rushdoony: "This Christ comes continually in the clouds of judgment over history."[13]

The most elaborate arguments for an alternative meaning of this verse are presented by some *preterist* commentators, who suggest that the passage does not predict the literal Second Coming, but is a figurative description of Christ's coming in vengeance to destroy Jerusalem, not in person, but using the Roman armies in AD 70. This understands Christ's "coming" in the same way as does Rushdoony (see above), though limiting the reference to a single event. Such interpreters note the following considerations:

The principal features of the prediction are: (a) Christ **coming**, (b) His coming **with clouds;** (c) **every eye will see Him, even they who pierced Him; and (d) all the tribes of the earth** [or land] mourning at His coming.

(a) The expression ***coming*** the Lord is used in many contexts that do not appear to be referring to the Second Coming (e.g., Rev. 2:5; 3:20; cf. Deut. 33:2; Isa. 19:1; Zech. 1:16; Mal. 3:1–2; Matt. 10:23), thus leaving open the possibility of another meaning here;

(b) The specific language of the Lord coming ***with clouds*** is used in the Old Testament with reference to historic judgments not associated with the end of the world (Isa. 19:1; Ps. 104:3) and may be so understood here as well;

(c) Jesus placed the time of His "coming with the clouds" within the lifetime of some of His contemporaries (Matt. 16:28; 24:30, 34; 26:64). This would allow one to understand ***they who pierced Him*** as the actual generation that crucified Christ, which would be the natural understanding to the literalist. In agreement with this suggestion, we find that the "coming of the Lord" is announced, elsewhere in Revelation, to be impending at the time of writing (3:11; 22:20);

(d) The judgment of Jerusalem is implied by the expression ***all the tribes of the earth*** (which can be translated, "all the tribes of the land [Israel]") ***will mourn.*** The Old Testament passage which is alluded to is a prophecy concerning "the inhabitants of Jerusalem" (Zech. 12:10). This view finds further support in the fact that Israel is divisible into tribes, whereas the earth is generally divided into nations.

Many will not find these arguments sufficient to overthrow the more dominant opinion, and the ultimate decision on the meaning of this passage will, in the final analysis, depend upon the reader's view of Revelation as a whole.

Who is the speaker in v. 8? The expression **who is and who was and who is to come** has previously been used of God the Father (comments, v. 4). However, the expression fits equally well when applied to Christ (cf. Heb. 13:8: "Jesus Christ is the same yesterday, today, and forever"). The Speaker here is able to take upon himself the Old Testament title *El Shaddai* (the Almighty), a name used interchangeably with Yahweh[14] (Gen. 17:1, etc.). The expressions, **Alpha and the Omega, and the Beginning and the End** are here used for the first time in Scripture, but are later (v. 17) amplified by the addition of "the First

85

and the Last," a title for Jehovah in Isaiah 44:6. All these titles (which are essentially synonymous in meaning) are combined in Revelation 22:13, where they seem to be applied to Jesus (see 22:12, 16). Even in 1:17–18, the speaker identifies himself as the one "who lives, and was dead, and behold, I am alive forevermore," a reference that points unmistakably to Christ. Revelation, then, attributes to Jesus Christ titles uniquely attributed to Yahweh in the Old Testament. This data is death to any theology that withholds full deity from Jesus Christ; it illustrates why Revelation is said to present a "high Christology."

THE SETTING OF THE REVELATION

REVELATION 1:9—11

⁹I, John, both your brother and companion in the tribulation and kingdom and patience of Jesus Christ, was on the island that is called Patmos for the word of God and for the testimony of Jesus Christ. ¹⁰I was in the Spirit on the Lord's Day, and I heard behind me a loud voice, as of a trumpet, ¹¹saying, "I am the Alpha and the Omega, the First and the Last," and, "What you see, write in a book and send it to the seven churches which are in Asia: to Ephesus, to Smyrna, to Pergamos, to Thyatira, to Sardis, to Philadelphia, and to Laodicea."

Again the author identifies himself by name. He does not call himself "the Apostle," but by the more humble term, **your brother** (v. 9). Although John was **on . . . Patmos** (v. 9) when he saw the visions, he may not have written the book in its present form until some time after his return to his home in Ephesus.

That John was on the island **for the word of God and for the testimony of Jesus** (v. 9) has been taken by some to mean that he went there as a missionary of his own accord, though church traditions indicate that John was banished to this island by the emperor. Rulers used banishment to an island as a means to rid themselves of influential troublemakers, without having to kill them. An early tradition holds that John previously had been sentenced to be dipped in boiling oil. Whether he was miraculously preserved through this ordeal or banished to an island instead of carrying out of the original sentence, nobody knows. Since John suggests that he was his readers' **companion in the tribulation**, the suggestion that he was experiencing persecution is preferred. **Patmos** is a rocky, crescent-shaped island about thirty-seven miles southwest of the mainland of Asia Minor (modern Turkey), where the seven recipient churches were located.

Some *futurist* commentators feel that the sentence, **I was in the Spirit on the Lord's Day** (v. 10), would be better translated, "I was [carried] in the Spirit unto the day of the Lord." This would be a way of saying that the Spirit carried John into the future so he could observe the actual "day of the Lord," i.e., the Second Coming and its precipitating events at the end of the age.

The majority of expositors, including most *futurists*, however, take **in the Spirit on the Lord's Day** to be a reference to John's state of mind on the first day of the week—our Sunday. This day has been known as "the Lord's Day" in Christian tradition since at least as early as the *Didache* (late first or early second century), since it was the day of Christ's resurrection. On this view, John was far from his home on this regular day of worship, possibly with his home church on his mind, when his reverie was interrupted by the announcement that he was to transcribe a letter to send to that very church, among others.

The seven churches were mentioned in verse 4, but they are now named in verse 11. There were at least three other churches known to have been in Asia at this time,[15] but the number may here have been limited to seven because of the symbolic value of that number. Seven, being the number of completeness, could suggest that the message to the seven churches is applicable to the total church throughout the world. The cities are listed in the logical order in which they would likely receive the letter. Assuming Ephesus would receive the letter first, the letter would travel northward then east and southward again in a horseshoe-shaped route.

THE APPEARANCE OF CHRIST

REVELATION 1:12—16

¹²Then I turned to see the voice that spoke with me. And having turned, I saw seven golden lampstands, ¹³and in the midst of the seven lampstands One like the Son of man, clothed with a garment down to the feet and girded about the chest with a golden band. ¹⁴His head and hair were white like wool, as white as snow, and His eyes like a flame of fire; ¹⁵His feet were like fine brass, as if refined in a furnace, and His voice as the sound of many waters; ¹⁶He had in His right hand seven stars, out of His mouth went a sharp two-edged sword, and His countenance was like the sun shining in its strength.

Those who describe Revelation as a drama divisible into seven "acts" of seven scenes each, usually see this portion as a sort of "opening vision," introductory to the seven "scenes" in chapters 2 and 3, that is, the seven letters. Each successive "act" is said to be similarly introduced by an opening vision.

Having heard the **voice** of Jesus, John **turned to see** (v. 12) Him who had spoken. The first thing that caught his attention was the **seven lampstands** of gold, recalling the seven-branched lamp, by whose light the priests offered their incense in the tabernacle. As verse 20 informs us, these lampstands represent the seven churches addressed in the letter. The church is the light of the world (Matt. 5:14; Phil. 2:15; Eph. 5:8–13). It may be signifi-

cant that John's vision of Christ was set in the midst of the churches (v. 13), suggesting that it is in the gathered assemblies of Christians that the presence of Christ resides on earth today (Matt. 18:20).

The description of Christ in verses 13–16 is the only description the Bible gives of His features, though this (like the descriptions in 5:6; 14:14; 19:11–13) is, without doubt, a symbolic rather than a literal description. Students of Daniel will note that the description agrees, to a great extent, with that of the messenger who brought the information to Daniel in his final vision (cf. Dan. 10:5–6), with the following exceptions:

(1) Daniel's messenger had His **golden band** around His waist, where-

as Jesus here has His **about the chest** (v. 13);

(2) His voice in Daniel was like that of a multitude. Here it is compared with **the sound of many waters** (v. 15);

(3) the countenance in Daniel had the appearance of lightning, but in Revelation it is **as the sun shining full strength** (v. 16);

(4) the following particulars in John's vision are not found in Daniel: white **head and hair** (v. 14), a **sword** coming from the mouth (v. 16), and the **seven stars** in **His right hand** (v. 16).

The general character of the vision is one of the glory of Christ, the shining face being reminiscent of that which John had seen on the Mount of Trans-figuration decades earlier (Matt. 17:2). According to the various expositors, the **golden band** worn across the chest is an emblem of high rank in the ancient world, and the long, linen garment is probably priestly. White **hair** is the emblem of age and honor—and possibly wisdom. The flaming **eyes** convey the idea of piercing vision, and the **feet like fine brass** suggest the irresistibility of His judgment as He will later tread the "great winepress of the wrath of God" (Rev. 14:19). The **two-edged sword** from His mouth can hardly refer to anything other than His word (Heb. 4:12; Eph. 6:17), and the meaning of the **seven stars** is given in verse 20.

THE COMMISSIONING OF JOHN

REVELATION 1:17–19

[17]And when I saw Him, I fell at His feet as dead. But He laid His right hand on me, saying to me, "Do not be afraid; I am the First and the Last. [18]I am He who lives, and was dead, and behold, I am alive forevermore. Amen. And I have the keys of Hades and of Death. [19]"Write the things which you have seen, and the things which are, and the things which will take place after this."

John's reaction resembles Daniel's. Both fell prostrate at Christ's feet; John was as dead (v. 17), while Daniel "retained no strength" and "was in a deep sleep" on his face (Dan. 10:8–9). Both were restored to their normal posture by the imposition of a hand on their heads and words of assurance. Here Jesus iden-

89

tifies himself in terms discussed earlier (see comments on v. 8).

Christ possesses **the keys of Hades and of Death** (v. 18), because His own resurrection from the dead has also secured the resurrection of His followers who are faithful unto death (2:8, 10). This may also have been the meaning of Jesus' statement at Caesarea Philippi that "the gates of Hades will not prevail" against the church (Matt. 16:18). Since Jesus holds the keys to the gates of Hades and Death, He can unlock and open those gates to resurrect the saints in the last day.

John is told to **write** three things (v. 19). The **things** which he has seen would most naturally refer to the vision just described, although it might refer to things John had seen much earlier. The Gospel of John contains information that the author had personally "seen" (John 19:35), but no commentator, to my knowledge, has suggested that Jesus was here commissioning John to write both the Gospel and the Apocalypse. It is not known whether John had already written the fourth Gospel at the time of this vision.

SPECIAL COMPARATIVE NOTE ON 1:19

"The things which are, and the things which will take place after this."

Dispensational *futurist* interpreters believe that **the things which** are the developments pertinent to the church age, and John's record of these things is found in chapters 2 and 3 of this book, in the form of the seven letters to the churches. Some dispensationalists think that the seven letters foresee the entire church age from John's day until the Rapture (see note: The Interpretation of the Letters, page 91).

The dispensationalists also believe that "these things" (Gr. *meta tauta*) in the phrase "after these things" (more literal than **after this**) is a reference to the church age. On this view, the recurrence of the phrase in Revelation 4:1 (see *futurist* note there) signals the Rapture of the church and the end of the church age.

The things which will take place after this could be more literally translated "the things which *are about to* take place after these things," a fact that is seized upon by *preterists as* another evidence for their belief that the fulfillment of the book would be quick in coming. If the book was written prior to AD 70, it would thus refer to the fall of Jerusalem.

A MYSTERY EXPLAINED

REVELATION 1:20

[20]"The mystery of the seven stars which you saw in My right hand, and the seven golden lampstands: The seven stars are the angels of the seven churches, and the seven lampstands which you saw are the seven churches."

Jesus now explains one of the mysteries of the book: the meaning of the stars and the lampstands. The latter is intelligible enough. The **lampstands** represent **the seven churches** named above (see note on v. 12). The explanation of the seven stars, however, raises more questions still. These are **the angels of the seven churches**. But how are we to understand these "angels" of the seven churches? They are as mysterious as the "seven spirits of God" (v. 4), with whom they are somehow associated in 3:1. Whether the "angel" of each church refers to a heavenly being, like a guardian angel, or to an earthly messenger (Gr. *angelos* simply means *messenger*), like a pastor or bishop, has been disputed. In each of the letters that follow, the angel of each church is addressed as the recipient. Since these angels no doubt are expected to pass along to the churches the information communicated to them by Christ, many commentators feel they must be visible, human messengers in contact with the congregations. We may justly conceive of the communication between God and His heavenly angels as being somewhat more direct than to require letters posted to them by apostles.

SPECIAL COMPARATIVE NOTE ON CHAPTERS 2 AND 3: THE INTERPRETATION OF THE LETTERS

Since they are not primarily predictive in character, the interpretation of the seven letters is not a matter of great controversy among the four approaches surveyed in this commentary–with one exception:

Interpreters of the *preterist*, and the *idealist* schools, and many *futurists* as well, understand the letters to be addressed to the actual, historic churches named in them, and by extension to any churches that may find themselves in similar circumstances to theirs. Beyond this, they seek no additional, hidden meaning behind them.

However, those of the *historicist* school, and some of the *futurist* school, have called attention to certain parallels between the individual letters and successive periods of church history, from John's day until the end. They conclude that the seven letters present a panorama of the age of the church.

On this view, the letter to *Ephesus* is said to describe the church during the apostolic age until about AD 100. *Smyrna*, the church enduring persecution, is likened to the church from about 100 till 313, which suffered under a series of Roman emperors. *Pergamos* is a church compromised with carnality and false doctrine, much as the church became from Constantine's Edict of Toleration (313) until the rise of the papacy (about 600). *Thyatira* is seen as the papal church until the Reformation (from 600 to 1500) and *Sardis* as the church during the Reformation itself (from 1500 to 1700). *Philadelphia* is regarded as corresponding to the church that experienced a resurgence of missionary activity (1700 to present), followed by the *Laodicean* church, which was lukewarm, and is likened to the liberal churches of modern times. More specific comments to this effect will be found in the comments on each of the letters.

Though this concept arose originally within the *historicist* camp of interpreters, it is today found chiefly among *futurist* commentators—particularly among many (but not all) dispensationalists.

Many *futurist* commentators today, along with all *preterist* and *idealist* interpreters, generally ignore this application altogether, or critique it on the grounds that nothing in the text of Revelation would in any sense suggest that the letters to contemporary Christian congregations should be given this secondary meaning, and that it violates the commitment to literal interpretation espoused by many.

Exponents of the view in question are able to find interesting parallels in history that convince them that such an approach is intended in Revelation (see comments at relevant passages). Those who criticize the position say that the whole church of any particular period can hardly be regarded as one homogenous entity that fits the description found in a given letter. For example, unless we are to reject the most natural understanding of these chapters, we must assume that the first-century church contained all seven types of churches represented in the letters, since the letters are ostensibly applicable to seven churches existing side by side in the first century.

Also, ever since the Reformation, whenever a new "period" has been introduced, there has not been a passing of the previous type of church, but simply the addition of another kind existing alongside. Today there continue to be churches of the pre-Reformation type, the Reformation type, the "missionary" type, and the liberal type (said to be represented by Thyatira, Sardis, Philadelphia, and Laodicea).

Those of the Reformed traditions also object to the identification of Sardis with the Reformation church, since that church is described as having only a reputation for being alive, while it is in fact dead.

THE STRUCTURE OF THE LETTERS

The structure of the seven letters exhibits a high degree of symmetry. They follow a consistent pattern, beginning with the address, which is always **"To the angel of the church of** [the city] . . ." This is invariably followed by the identification of Christ as the sender of the letter, usually (though not in every case) describing him in terms drawn from the vision of chapter 1.

Jesus' first message to each church is: "**I know your works**." The churches' works are sometimes commendable and sometimes requiring censure.

In three of the seven (Ephesus, Pergamos, and Thyatira), the churches' *good* works are initially acknowledged, though there is the disclaimer: "Never-theless **I have a few things against you** . . ."

Two churches (Smyrna and Philadelphia) are commended without any such complaint, while two other churches (Sardis and Laodicea) receive only the complaint without any commendation. The five churches receiving rebuke (all except Smyrna and Philadelphia) are summarily commanded to **repent**, with some stated threat attached if they fail to do so.

Each letter ends with a command to **hear what the Spirit says to the churches** and an encouraging promise **to him who overcomes.** The order of these two elements is inexplicably reversed in the last four letters.

LETTER TO EPHESUS

REVELATION 2:1—7

[1]"To the angel of the church of Ephesus write, 'These things says He who holds the seven stars in His right hand, who walks in the midst of the seven golden lamp-stands: [2]"I know your works, your labor, your patience, and that you cannot bear those who are evil. And you have tested those who say they are apostles and are

not, and have found them liars; ³and you have persevered and have patience, and have labored for My name's sake and have not become weary. ⁴Nevertheless I have this against you, that you have left your first love. ⁵Remember therefore from where you have fallen; repent and do the first works, or else I will come to you quickly and remove your lampstand from its place—unless you repent, ⁶But this you have, that you hate the deeds of the Nicolaitans, which I also hate. ⁷"He who has an ear, let him hear what the Spirit says to the churches. To him who overcomes I will give to eat from the tree of life, which is in the midst of the Paradise of God."'

With a population of approximately 250,000, **Ephesus** was the largest and most important city in the Roman province of Asia. The city was devoted to the cult of Artemis (Latin: Diana) and had a temple to the goddess that was regarded as one of the seven wonders of the world. The **church of Ephesus** had been established by Paul, who continued to minister there three years after its founding (Acts 20:31). In addition to Paul, Ephesus had benefited from the personal ministries of Apollos, Priscilla and Aquila, and Timothy, who was residing there when Paul sent him the two letters found in our New Testament. John probably had lived there before being banished to Patmos. No doubt he was eager to hear what Jesus would have to say to those at his home church while he was in exile.

The reference to Christ as the one **who holds the seven stars in His right hand and who walks in the midst of the seven golden lampstands** (v. 1) may call attention to the fact that, while the church's heavenly existence is secure in the sovereign care of Christ, he must visit the earthly counterparts to inspect and correct their conduct and attitudes. As a priest in the temple tends the lamps to keep them from growing dim or going out, Christ moves among the churches to attend to the purity and brightness of the light they give to the world.

Christ affirms His knowledge of the church's positive traits. There was no defect in their **labor, patience,** or intolerance of **those who are evil** (v. 2). They were exercising discernment toward **those who say they are apostles and are not**, and had uncovered some frauds. Paul, in his final visit with this church's elders, had forewarned them of wolves that would arise to harm the church (Acts 20:28ff). In the second century, Ignatius, bishop of Antioch, commended this church for its loyalty to the truth that had effectively prevented any false sect from gaining a hearing among its members.[16]

In particular, a group of false teachers called **Nicolaitans** (v. 6) had attempted to insinuate themselves into the church fellowship, but had found the shepherds alert and had been exposed. A tradition having the support of some of the early church fathers identifies the Nicolaitans with the followers of Nicolas, who was one of the seven men selected to serve the church in Acts 6:5, but later became a heretical teacher. Some modern commentators (e.g., F. F. Bruce) suggest that Nicolas was a disciple of the Gnostic heretic Cerinthus. Whoever the Nicolaitans may have been, their teaching is compared, in verse 15, with that of **Balaam**, who advocated sinful license in idolatrous practices and sexual immorality. Jesus shared the Ephesian church's hatred for this movement, which also had some advocates in the church of Pergamos (v. 15).

Though the Christians had **not become weary** (v. 3) in well doing, they had become negligent in the most important area: **you have left your first love** (v. 4). Whether love of God or of one another is intended is not specified, though the two likely are not to be sharply differentiated (John 13:34f; 1 John 4:20f). The loss of love is no minor defect, but constitutes a **fallen** state of the church, requiring that they **repent and do the first works** (v. 5) if they are to avoid the threatened judgment. Their present **labor** (v. 2), which was not lacking in quantity, differed from **the first works** (v. 5) by the absence of the **first love,** which had driven the earlier works. Like Martha, a church may become so engrossed in religious work that it neglects the "one thing needed" (Luke 10:42). No amount of religious orthodoxy, labor, or loyalty can make up for a deficit in Christian love (1 Cor. 13:2–3).

The warning that Christ **will come to you quickly and remove your lampstand from its place** (v. 5) can hardly refer to His Second Coming and almost certainly speaks of the total extinction of the church in that location.[17] Indeed, today there is no city or church in the Turkish location that was once Ephesus.[18] Islam has been established in this region that Paul had once thoroughly evangelized (Acts 19:10). How different might the history of that region have been had the church continued to practice its first love (Eph. 1:15)?

As Jesus frequently had said to His disciples while on earth, He now says to the churches, **He who has an ear, let him hear** (v. 7).[19] But since the voice of Christ is now communicated through His abiding Spirit, the statement is modified slightly: **let him hear what the Spirit says**. Though each church received its own personalized letter from the Lord, the message of the Spirit is directed **to the churches** collectively. The Spirit of God still has relevant warnings in these letters to churches in every place and time.

Each letter contains a promise to the believer **who overcomes**. Though it is not specified precisely what is to be overcome, John's other writings speak of both Jesus and the believer overcoming "the world" (John 16:33; 1 John 5:4–5). This implies the continued successful resistance of the world's corrupt moral and spiritual influence. Five of the seven churches were beginning to exhibit a worldly spirit in one respect or another, but all seven had some within them who were at least capable of resisting the corrupting influence in order to gain the prize. In this case, the prize will be **to eat from the tree of life, which is in the midst of the Paradise of God** (v. 7). The name Paradise—from a Persian word meaning "pleasure park"— had originally been applied to the garden of Eden in the Septuagint, the Greek Old Testament (Gen. 2:8; Ezek. 28:13). It was the location of the original **tree of life**. After Adam and Eve fell, God barred sinful man from access to the fruit of this tree, the eating of which would have conferred eternal life (Gen. 3:22). In the New Testament, Jesus and Paul apply the term spiritually to the place of the departed spirits of the faithful (Luke 23:43; 2 Cor. 12:4), and in Revelation 22:2, the tree of life is seen growing in the New Jerusalem. Thus the promise to the overcomer translates into a guarantee of life in the eternal state, following the resurrection.

Among *historicists* and some *futurists*, Ephesus is said to represent the condition of the church of the apostolic age, until the end of the first century.

LETTER TO SMYRNA

REVELATION 2:8–11

[8]"And to the angel of the church in Smyrna write, 'These things says the First and the Last, who was dead, and came to life: [9]"I know your works, tribulation, and poverty (but you are rich); and I know the blasphemy of those who say they are Jews and are not, but are a synagogue of Satan. [10]Do not fear any of those things which you are about to suffer. Indeed, the devil is about to throw some of you into prison, that you may be tested, and you will have tribulation ten days. Be faithful until death, and I will give you the crown of life. [11]"He who has an ear, let him hear what the Spirit says to the churches. He who overcomes shall not be hurt by the second death."'

Smyrna (modern Izmir) was the second largest and reputedly the most beautiful city in Provincial Asia and is the only city of the seven that is still in existence today. Smyrna was the first city of Asia to build a temple to *Roma*,

96

the spirit of Rome, in 195 BC. In John's day it was a city that had been "resurrected from the dead," in that it had been destroyed seven hundred years earlier and had lain in ruins for three hundred years. This fact may be alluded to in Christ's reference to His own resurrection in the greeting: **who was dead, and came to life** (v. 8). Of all the letters, that to Smyrna is the most brief and is one of only two that receives no rebuke, nor any call to repentance from Christ. In John's time, the Christians in Smyrna, like John himself (1:9), were experiencing **tribulation** (v. 9), which was going to continue and, possibly, intensify. In a later generation, the famous church father Polycarp would be the bishop of this church and would suffer a notable martyrdom. Though the thought that Polycarp may have **been the angel of the church in Smyrna** (v. 8) has some appeal, it cannot be seriously entertained, since this would place the date of the book of Revelation unreasonably late.

To the suffering church, Jesus identifies himself as **the First and the Last**, reminding them that he **was dead, and came to life** (v. 8). The recollection of His suffering and vindication prepares the way for His exhortation that they, too, should **be faithful until death** (v. 10) in order that they might also be crowned with eternal life.

As usual, Christ affirms His awareness of their circumstances: **I know your works, tribulation, and poverty** (v. 9). It is sometimes necessary to be reminded of this in times of suffering, since God may seem distant at such times. Though they are poor in material things, He testifies on their behalf, **but you are rich.** James, in his epistle states that God has "chosen the poor of this world to be rich in faith and heirs of the kingdom" (James 2:5)—a probable allusion to Luke 6:20, but also fitting well with this evaluation of the Smyrnian Christians. This contrasts sharply with Jesus' assessment of the Laodicean believers, who think themselves rich, but are poor by His reckoning (3:17).

As in the case of the Philadelphian church (3:9), the troublers of the church in Smyrna were **those who say they are Jews and are not** (v. 9)—in other words, unbelieving Jews, whom Jesus here considers to be **a synagogue of Satan** (cf. John 8:44). Smyrna had the largest Jewish population of any Asian city. If this was written prior to AD 70, then it was a period in which the main adversaries of Christianity were the Jews. The church there was understandably harassed more than most.

The Christians should not **fear any of those things which [they] are about to suffer** (v. 10), even as Jesus had previously taught His disciples not to fear those who can "kill the body, and after that have no more that they can do" (Luke 12:4). Peter likewise instructed the churches of this region, "even if you should suffer for righteousness' sake . . . do not be afraid of their threats, nor be troubled" (1 Pet. 3:14). Fearlessness, however, may not necessarily mean the total absence of dread, but rather the refusal to succumb to intimidation, so that threats of harm do not turn them back from their duty to Christ.

The church in Smyrna was soon to become a special object of diabolical malice, as the **devil is about to throw some of you into prison . . . you will have tribulation** (v. 10). God has a purpose for this, however, namely, **that you may be tested**. Such testings are not to be feared, but should be cause for rejoicing (Matt. 5:11–12; James 1:2), since they are intended to produce endurance and result in the glory of God (Rom. 5:3f.; James 1:3f.; Pet. 1:7). Since the persecution is said to be instigated by **the devil,** and since the Jews of Smyrna were **a synagogue of Satan** (v. 9), it is probable that the persecution here, as elsewhere, was brought about by the local Jewish community (cf. Matt. 23:34; Acts 13:45; 14:19; 17:5, 13; 1 Thess. 2:14–16).

In the case of the Smyrnians, the duration of testing is limited to **ten days** (v. 10). History has not recorded any period of ten days that was endured by these Christians, though surviving records are very limited. Some commentators consider the ten days to refer to ten actual waves of persecution, or to the ten emperors who allegedly persecuted the churches throughout the first three centuries.[20] Other interpreters think that the "ten days" is in contrast to the much longer time designations in the book, and simply suggest that the tribulation for this church will be of relatively short duration.

Jesus does not promise that He will protect His people from martyrdom, but that, if they remain **faithful until death**, they shall receive **the crown of life** (v. 10). Though this may refer to an actual crown to be worn upon the head, it may simply be a symbol of eternal life itself. The possession of eternal life is a crowning glory, even as is the present experience of "lovingkindness and tender mercies" with which the Lord has already crowned us (Ps. 103:4). James almost sounds as if he is referring to this promise to the Smyrnian church when he writes, "Blessed is the man who endures temptation; for when he has been approved, he will receive the crown of life which the Lord has promised to those who love Him" (James 1:12), though the suggestion of a later date for James than for Revelation would be very unconventional. To be crowned with eternal life is to be exempted from **the second death** (v. 11), which is later equated with the lake of fire (20:14).

In comparison with all of the other letters, except Philadelphia, the call for this church to "repent" is conspicuous by its absence.

Among *historicists* and some *futurists*, Smyrna is believed to represent the church during the period of persecution under the Roman emperors. This began with the brief but severe persecution under Nero in AD 64, but became more focused and deliberate under Domitian and many of his successors, from about 95 till 313. The tenth of these, it is said, began under Diocletian and lasted ten years (303–313). The year-for-a-day interpreters *(historicists)* believe that the **ten days** (v. 10) of tribulation promised to the Smyrnian Christians correspond to the ten years of this final persecution. "The ten days of Smyrna is one of the greatest arguments for the messages of the seven churches being applied to successive ages. This divine time measure forces the issue."[21]

LETTER TO PERGAMOS

REVELATION 2:12–17

[12]"And to the angel of the church in Pergamos write, 'These things says He who has the sharp two-edged sword: [13]"I know your works, and where you dwell, where Satan's throne is. And you hold fast to My name, and did not deny My faith even in the days in which Antipas was My faithful martyr, who was killed among you, where Satan dwells. [14]But I have a few things against you, because you have there those who hold the doctrine of Balaam, who taught Balak to put a stumbling block before the children of Israel, to eat things sacrificed to idols, and to commit sexual immorality. [15]Thus you also have those who hold the doctrine of the Nicolaitans, which thing I hate. [16]Repent, or else I will come to you quickly and will fight against them with the sword of My mouth. [17]"He who has an ear, let him hear what the Spirit says to the churches. To him who overcomes I will give some of the hidden manna to eat. And I will give him a white stone, and on the stone a new name written which no one knows except him who receives it."'

Pergamos, or Pergamum, was the provincial capital of Asia. If Ephesus was the "New York City" of Asia, Pergamos was its "Washington, DC." The city was noted for many things. It had the second largest library in the world—containing 200,000 volumes—exceeded only by the library at Alexandria, Egypt. Besides being the oldest city of Asia, Pergamos was the first to erect temples to Caesar Augustus, to Zeus, and to the serpent-god Asclepius. The latter was considered the god of healing, and people would journey to Pergamos seeking cures for their ailments. In this sense, it was a sort of "Lourdes" of the ancient world. The reference to **Satan's throne** (v. 13) may allude either to the Roman authority seated in Pergamos or to the other demonic, idolatrous practices occurring there. Beale writes:

> The reference to "Satan's throne" may also have been brought to mind because of the conical hill behind Pergamum which was the site of many temples, prominent among which was the throne-like altar of Zeus, which itself would have been sufficient to arouse the thought of the devil's throne.[22]

The **church of Pergamos** is the only one of the seven known to have had a martyr—**Antipas . . . who was killed among you** (v. 13), about whom nothing more is known. His death did not deter the faithful of the church from their loyalty to Christ. In referring to Antipas as **My faithful martyr**, Jesus dignifies him with the same eulogy as is used of Jesus himself in Revelation 1:5 (where the word "martyr" is translated "witness" in most versions).

Since this church was in the Roman capital, the persecution that claimed the life of Antipas likely was carried out by Roman authority. This may account for Christ's identifying himself as **he who has the sharp two-edged sword** (v. 12), a reminder that the sword of Christ (v. 16) was more to be feared than that of Rome.

While the church had managed to **hold fast to [Christ's] name and did not deny [His] faith** (v. 13), not all of its members had remained entirely faithful to the Lord. The church is charged with losing some ground to the world, for there were some among them who held **the doctrine of Balaam** (v. 14), and some who held **the doctrine of the Nicolaitans** (v. 15), detested by Christ himself. Of the doctrine of Balaam, we are told that he **taught Balak to put a stumbling block before the children of Israel, to eat things sacrificed to idols, and to commit sexual immorality** (v. 14) a fact mentioned in the Old Testament narrative only on the occasion of Balaam's death (Num. 31:16). Peter anticipated the coming of teachers who would follow "the way of Balaam . . . who loved the wages of unrighteousness" (2 Pet. 2:15). What Balaam did, he did for money. Whether those in Pergamos were teaching false doctrine for pay, or simply teaching false doctrine, we do not know. What is evident is that sexual immorality and compromise with idolatry were being tolerated and even advocated by some in the church. In the second century, these same issues would be principal features of the gnostic heretics. Whereas the Ephesian church had no tolerance for the "deeds of the Nicolaitans" (2:6), this church was seeing the encroachment of an actual "doctrine" of the same group (see comments at 2:6).

Though the whole church is called upon to **repent,** it is only the offenders against whom Jesus threatens to **fight . . . with the sword of My mouth** (v. 16.). What form this judgment will take is not specified, though it probably does not refer to the Second Coming, since this church no longer exists.

Those who overcome, abstaining from the allure of fornication and the idolatrous feasts, will participate in a feast of their own. Jesus will give them **some of the hidden manna** (v. 17). There was a tradition among the Jews that Jeremiah had taken the ark of the covenant, containing a golden pot of manna, with him when he fled to Egypt before the Babylonians destroyed Jerusalem. Some taught that, at the initiation of the kingdom age, Jeremiah would return, bringing the ark with him, and would serve a feast of the manna that had been hidden for centuries in the ark. Some Jews of Jesus' day thought He might be Jeremiah (Matt. 16:14). When He fed the multitudes with a few loaves, the people began to say, "This is truly the Prophet who is to come into the world" (John 6:14). Jesus responded that He was the true manna that came down to give life to the world (John 6:32–33). The Pergamos overcomers are promised that they will commune with Him at His feast in the kingdom, since they refuse to commune with demons at the idolatrous meals (see 1 Cor. 10:14–22).

Much speculation has attended the interpretation of a **white stone** (v. 17). In one view, it is a token of vindication or acquittal, referring to the practice of a judge handing an accused criminal either a black stone signifying condemnation or a white stone indicating acquittal. The message then would be that, though the Christians may stand condemned in the Roman courts, they will be justified at the bar of eternal justice.

Another view is that the white stone was a token given to contestants in the Greek games as they completed their race, to be traded in later for their actual awards.

Perhaps the prevailing view among commentators holds that a white stone with a person's name written upon it served as a sort of pass for admission to certain functions, like the feasts in the idol temples. If this view is correct, the meaning here would be that those who do not compromise themselves with idols will receive "a pass" admitting them into the messianic feast of the kingdom.

Among the *historicists* and some *futurists*, Pergamos is seen as representing the imperial church after Constantine (313–606), wherein the church ceased to be officially persecuted and obtained access to the portals of political power. Pergamos, it is alleged,[23] means "married to power." It was during this time that the institution of the papacy had its inception. In 313, the Decree of Coronation made Rome ("where Satan's throne is") the center of Christendom.[24] Like Israel in the days of Balaam, the church of this period was being seduced into immorality and the worship of idols through the rise of the papal system. Some[25] who take this approach have suggested that Antipas does not refer to an individual, but to a class of men opposed ("anti-") to the popes ("papas"), which men were martyred in great numbers in Rome and Constantinople. Christ threatens to fight this institution with the sword out of His mouth—e.g., His Word.

LETTER TO THYATIRA

REVELATION 2:18—29

[18]"And to the angel of the church in Thyatira write, 'These things says the Son of God, who has eyes like a flame of fire, and His feet like fine brass: [19]"I know your works, love, service, faith, and your patience; and as for your works, the last are more than the first. [20]Nevertheless I have a few things against you, because you allow that woman Jezebel, who calls herself a prophetess, to teach and seduce My servants to commit sexual immorality and eat things sacrificed to idols. [21]And I gave her time to repent of her sexual immorality, and she did not repent. [22]Indeed I will cast her into a sickbed, and those who commit adultery with her into great tribulation, unless they repent of their deeds. [23]I will kill her children with death, and all the churches shall know that I am He who searches the minds and hearts. And I will give to each one of you according to your works. [24]"Now to you I say, and to the rest in Thyatira, as many as do not have this doctrine, who have not known the depths of Satan, as they say, I will put on you no other burden. [25]But hold fast what you have till I come. [26]And he who overcomes, and keeps My works until the end, to him I will give power over the nations. [27]'He shall rule them with a rod of iron; they shall be dashed to pieces like the potter's vessels'—as I also have received from my Father; [28]and I will give him the morning star. [29]"He who has an ear, let him hear what the Spirit says to the churches."'

Lydia, Paul's first convert in Philippi, was from the city of **Thyatira** (Acts 16:14). The purple cloth she sold was a major product of that city. However, Thyatira was known for little else of importance. Of the seven cities of Asia mentioned in Revelation, Thyatira was the least significant, though the church there received the longest letter. It is known that the city had many trade guilds, and it would have been difficult to make a living without participating in one of them. Yet the guilds practiced idolatrous rites at their gatherings, which Christians could not countenance. Therefore, the Christians in Thyatira may have been hard pressed to support themselves and their families without resorting to some measure of compromise with idolatry.

There arose in the church a self-professed prophetess, symbolically called **Jezebel** (v. 20) due to the similarity of her influence upon the church to that of the original Jezebel upon Israel. This woman apparently taught that idolatrous practices were permissible, encouraged fornication, and indulged in the same herself with members of the church. This error in the church was similar to the "doctrine of Balaam" in the church at Pergamos, the difference being that, in Thyatira, the doctrine was promoted by a woman and there were men committing fornication with her (v. 22). It is possible that the prophetess was representing her insights as

"the deep things of God" (comp. 1 Cor. 2:10), that is, as reflecting a superior enlightenment concerning the exercise of grace—as was the case (and still is) with many antinomians[26] (cf. Rom. 6:15; Jude 4). If this is so, there is a deliberate irony in Christ's categorizing these teachings as **the depths** (or the "deep things") **of Satan** (v. 24).

Christ reveals himself to this church as **the Son of God** and informs them that His **eyes** are **like a flame of fire**, and His **feet like fine brass** (v. 18). Both of these characteristics suggest impending judgment. His piercing vision sees all and can therefore not fail to judge rightly, whereas His feet, with which He will tread upon the wicked in the winepress of God's wrath (14:19f.; Isa. 63:1–4), are of irresistible strength, like brass. Jesus will judge the wicked in the church (vv. 22f.) with a judgment none can thwart or resist.

In many respects, **the church of Thyatira** was a good church. The Christians apparently had no shortage of **works, love, service, faith, and . . . patience**, and their works were increasing: **the last are more than the first** (v. 19). There is a striking contrast between this church and that in Ephesus, for the church in Thyatira was not defective in love, whereas Ephesus had abandoned its first love. But, while Ephesus had no tolerance for error and false messengers, Thyatira's fault was a willingness to **allow that**

103

woman Jezebel, who calls herself a prophetess, to teach and seduce My servants to commit sexual immorality and eat things sacrificed to idols (v. 20). This contrast points up the difficulty of striking a balance between a generous and forgiving love and a proper intolerance for heresy and sin in the church.

Jezebel was not a problem of recent origin. The church had tolerated this woman's influence for some time. All the while, Jesus had not yet brought judgment because He wished to give Jezebel **time to repent** (v. 21). However, the patience of Christ was in this case unrewarded, for **she did not repent**. Now there was nothing left for Jesus to do but to intervene for the protection of the purity of His church: **I will cast her into a sickbed** (v. 22), whether literally or figuratively (i.e., a sickbed as opposed to her preferred bed of fornication) is not certain. This "sickbed" may not be a literal illness, but rather a reference to the **great tribulation** that will befall her and **those who commit adultery with her**. This tribulation may be a direct judgment from God or some disaster resulting from political, social, or economic upheaval. A perplexing aspect of the judgment is the threat to **kill her children with death** (v. 23). Her "children" may be her followers or her natural offspring. In any case, even at this late date the consequences can yet be averted if **they repent of their deeds** (v. 22).

Even as God's destruction of Egypt became an occasion of fear to the surrounding nations in Moses' day, the downfall of this corrupt movement in the church will be a wake-up call for the morally lax in all the churches who hear about it, because **all the churches shall know that I am He who searches the minds and hearts** (v. 23).

There are those in Thyatira who **do not have this doctrine** (v. 24). When God judges, the righteous have nothing to fear, since God's wrath is not indiscriminate. Each man will receive what his deeds warrant: **I will give to each one of you according to your works** (v. 23).

Christ has **no other burden** (v. 24) to place upon those who have remained undefiled by the errors of Jezebel, other than that which lies upon Christians generally—namely to not lose their grip on their convictions: **hold fast what you have till I come** (v. 25). Whether the Second Coming is in view here, or the arrival of the Judgment threatened to Jezebel and her followers, is not stated clearly, though the latter may better fit the context.

Here the overcomer is described as the one who **keeps My works until the end**, with whom Christ will share His own **power over the nations** (v. 26). The fulfillment of this promise has been variously applied: (a) to reigning with Christ over the unsaved nations during a future Millennium (20:4), (b) to participating in the reign of the saints with Christ after death in heaven (another way of understanding 20:4), or (c) to reigning over Christians of lower rank in the new earth, assuming there will be varying degrees of authority awarded to various saints (see Matt. 25:21, 23; Luke 19:17, 19; 1 Cor. 15:41f.).

The paraphrase of Psalm 2:9 **'He shall rule them with a rod of iron; they shall be dashed to pieces like the potter's vessels'** (v. 27), appears, in context and without punctuation, to apply to the overcoming believer. In the psalm itself, it is clearly Christ who wields the rod of iron (as also in Rev. 19:15), which no doubt accounts for the translators in this case using quotation marks. Citation of the psalm points out that the authority of the exalted believer is not his own, but derived from the authority of Christ.

I will give him the morning star (v. 28). In a later chapter, Jesus identifies himself as the Bright and Morning Star (22:16). Thus as He is the "hidden manna" promised to the overcomers of Pergamos (v. 17), so is He the "morning star" that will be given to the overcom-

ers of Thyatira. The promise may convey the idea that those who continue to hold forth their lamp in the present night, they will live to see the dawning of a new day.

In the view of *historicists* and some *futurists,* Thyatira represents the church of the period of papal triumph and persecution (606–1517). "It is the middle church of the seven, and likewise covers the Middle Ages."[27] Thyatira (says Caringola) means "to be ruled by a woman." In this case, the woman is likened to Jezebel in the days of Ahab and Elijah. This woman made immorality and idolatry official policy for the society. Uriah Smith wrote: "A more striking figure could not have been used to denote the papal abominations."[28] As Jezebel caused Israel to worship the mother goddess Ashtaroth (called the "Queen of Heaven" in Jer. 44:17, 18, 25), so the church in the Middle Ages introduced the worship of Mary, "the Queen of Heaven." Jesus threatens to "kill her children with death." Some say that refers to the terrible plagues, including the Black Death (beginning 1347), that decimated the European population in the Middle Ages.

LETTER TO SARDIS

REVELATION 3:1—6

¹"And to the angel of the church in Sardls write, 'These things says He who has the seven Spirits of God and the seven stars: "I know your works, that you have a name that you are alive, but you are dead. ²Be watchful, and strengthen the things which remain, that are ready to die, for I have not found your works perfect before God. ³Remember therefore how you have received and heard; hold fast and repent. Therefore if you will not watch, I will come upon you as a thief, and you will not know what hour I will come upon you. ⁴You have a few names even in Sardis who have not denied their garments; and they shall walk with Me in white, for they are worthy. ⁵He who overcomes shall be clothed in white garments, and I will not blot out his name from the Book of Life; but I will confess his name before My Father and before His angels. ⁶"He who has an ear, let him hear what the Spirit says to the churches."'

The city of **Sardis**, the old capital of Lydia, had become famous for its red dye and woolen goods. Twice in its history it had been conquered—by Cyrus, in 549 BC, and by Antiochus the Great, in 218 BC—because of failing to keep adequate watch. It may be with allusion to this historical fact that Jesus exhorted the church to **be watchful** (v. 2) against the encroachment of sin, which might conquer the church. The city was known for its immorality, and this may have made it more challenging for the Christians of the city to remain pure, since there were only **a few names even in Sardis who have not defiled their garments** (v. 4). Tragically, this is one of the two churches (Laodicea be-

ing the other) that receive no commendation from the Lord. The only thing good about the church as a whole (not considering the remnant of overcomers, vv. 4–5) was its reputation. The church had a **name** that it was alive, but in this respect, it was greatly overrated: but **you are dead** (v. 1). There were indeed **works** in the church, but Christ complains that he did not find them **perfect before God** (v. 2). What it is that renders these works imperfect is not specified. Perhaps their motivation lacked love (1 Cor. 13:1–3) or they were not works springing from faith (Gal. 5:6). Once a church has a good reputation in the public eye, it is possible to mechanically continue in the

106

same activities but lose the original motivation that made it great. The incentive to good works can shift from a desire to serve and please God to simply a desire to maintain the good public face that the church has come to enjoy.

What little life actually remains (v. 2) in Sardis is, unfortunately, **ready to die**, and the church is commanded to **strengthen** whatever is left of that original spark of life that had nearly gone out. There was some backtracking to be done. The Christians needed to **remember** and **hold fast** to the manner in which they had formerly **received and heard** (v. 3). Such could not happen unless the church would **repent** of its present state of mind.

Having previously been warned of the need to **be watchful** (v. 2), the church is now apprised of another consequence they can expect to befall them if they fail in this: **if you will not watch, I will come upon you as a thief** (v. 3). The language employs imagery elsewhere associated with the Second Coming of Christ (for the thief motif, see Matt. 24:43; 1 Thess. 5:2; 2 Pet. 3:10). Yet there is the possibility that some more immediate visitation of judgment is described here by the same imagery. In this case, the failure to watch seems to be the reason that they **will not know what hour I will come** (v. 3) upon them, whereas, in the case of the Second Coming of Christ, even for those who are watching, He will come "at an hour you do not expect" (Matt. 24:42, 44).

Turning to the remnant of overcomers in Sardis (vv. 4–5), Jesus' words emphasize that He knows His own "by name" (John 10:3). There are a **few names** (v. 4), in Sardis who are overcomers, to whom Christ gives a two-pronged promise in v. 5:

(a) **I will not blot out his name from the Book of Life**. This is a difficult statement to harmonize with the concept of the believer's inevitable perseverance. There are two classic ways to remove the impression that this passage denies the doctrine of perseverance of the saints. One is to suggest that the Book of Life is not the list of the redeemed, but rather contains the names of all people living at a given time. Removal of one's name from the book would thus signify physical death but not damnation (but cf. 20:15). A second suggestion is that the warning is merely hypothetical—meaning that no one will ever have their name removed in actuality, since it is not said that some *will* have their names removed, only that some *will not* (but cf. 22:19);

(b) **I will confess his name before My Father and before His angels**—an allusion to the promise Jesus made to those who would faithfully confess him before men (Matt. 10:32).

Jesus mentions twice that these few in Sardis will wear **white garments** (vv. 4, 5), perhaps in contrast with the red woolen goods for which the city was renowned. The supreme compliment is paid by the Lord to these nonconformists in the church: **for they are worthy** (v. 4)—not unlike the eulogy pronounced over the rare men of faith in Old Testament times, "of whom the world was not worthy" (Heb. 11:38). The expression "they are worthy" is used later in Revelation with an entirely opposite meaning (Rev. 16:6, translated in the NKJV "it is their just due"). Since they do not "run with the pack," Jesus guarantees, **they shall walk with me** (v. 4).

The *historicists* and *some futurists* see Sardis as representing the church at the time of the Reformation (1517–1793). This extends from the time of Luther to that of Wesley. This movement ended the Dark Ages and brought refreshing signs of life to the church, though, it is said, Jesus did not find its works perfect before God. The Reformation went a certain distance in discarding unscriptural traditions and in restoring biblical authority in the church, but, in the opinion of some (e.g., the Anabaptists), it did not go far enough.

LETTER TO PHILADELPHIA

REVELATION 3:7—13

[7]"And to the angel of the church in Philadelphia write, 'These things says He who is holy, He who is true, He who has the key of David, He who opens and no one shuts, and shuts and no one opens: [8]"I know your works. See, I have set before you an open door, and no one can shut it; for you have a little strength, have kept My word, and have not denied My name. [9]Indeed I will make those of the synagogue of Satan, who say they are Jews and are not, but lie—indeed I will make them come and worship before your feet, and to know that I have loved you. [10]Because you have kept My command to persevere, I also will keep you from the hour of trial which shall come upon the whole world, to test those who dwell on the earth. [11]Behold, I am coming quickly! Hold fast what you have, that no one may take your crown. [12]He who overcomes, I will make him a pillar in the temple of My God, and he shall go out no more. I will write on him the name of My God and the name of the city of My God, the New Jerusalem, which comes down out of heaven from My

God. And I will write on him My new name, ¹³"He who has an ear, let him hear what the Spirit says to the churches."'

The city of **Philadelphia** had a relatively small population in John's day, due to the fear of earthquakes, with which the city was plagued. Historically, the inhabitants had frequently been forced to move out of the city due to its instability. Philadelphia had been destroyed by earthquake in AD 17, and even though it had been rebuilt, many people still were fearful about living in town and remained instead in the surrounding countryside. For this reason, the church there may have been small, though it remained a significant church in the region at least until the twelfth century, and a small congregation has been in the location even in modern times.

This letter was sent to encourage the church concerning a time of tribulation. As was the case in Smyrna (2:9), the present troublers of the church in Philadelphia appear to have been the local **Jews** (3:9). A worse calamity, of broader proportions, however, was coming, and Jesus promises to preserve the church through it. As in the letter to the church in Smyrna, this church receives no rebuke nor call to repentance.

Jesus identifies himself as the One who is **holy** and **true** (v. 7). This is the first of the letters not to take its introductory description from features found in chapter 1.o Nonetheless, else- where in Revelation Jesus is declared to be both holy (15:4) and true (19:11)— and is also said to be "holy and true" (6:10). The reference to Jesus having the **key of David** (v. 7), so that he **opens and no one shuts, and shuts and no one opens** is an allusion to Isaiah 22:22, in which the same privilege and prerogative is assigned to a man named Eliakim, who was steward over the house of King Hezekiah. This man had the power either to admit persons or to deny entry into the king's house. Jesus is claiming to have a corresponding right with reference to admitting people into God's presence. As a matter of fact, He tells the church that He has chosen to admit them: **I have set before you an open door** (v. 8). The mention that no **one can shut** it may imply that the Jews in Philadelphia (mentioned in v. 9) sought to exclude the Gentiles from God (cf. Matt. 23:13; 1 Thess. 2:15f.), but Jesus had made access available to them through himself. Though persecuted and having only **a little strength**, the congregation had managed to remain faithful. He commends them that they **have kept my word, and have not denied My name** (v. 8).

As in 2:9, Jesus again refers to the persecuting Jews as the **synagogue of Satan**. They **say they are Jews and**

are not, but lie (v. 9)—they are not real Jews in Christ's sight because "If you were Abraham's children, you would do the works of Abraham" (John 8:39), and "He is not a Jew who is one outwardly . . . but he is a Jew who is one inwardly" (Rom. 2:28f.). Although, prior to AD 70, the principal systematic persecution of Christians came from the Sanhedrin and synagogues of the Jews, both Christians and Jews later became the targets of Roman persecution—a development that would bring an end to biblical Judaism, but which would not be able to extinguish Christianity.

That the persecuting Jews would one day be forced to **come and worship before your feet** (v. 9) does not mean that the believers will be worshiped as deities, but they will be sitting enthroned with Christ (3:21), before whom, someday, every knee shall bow (Phil. 2:10). Though they are presently seeking to exclude the Gentiles from the love and favor of God, the day will come when these Jews will be forced to acknowledge **that I have loved you** (v. 9). Jesus had previously expressed a concern that "the world might know" that God loves His disciples (John 17:23). The day will come in which His desire will be fulfilled.

What is meant by the promise, **I also will keep you from the hour of trial which shall come upon the whole world, to test those who dwell on the earth** (v. 10)?

Dispensational *futurists* find in this statement a promise of the pre-tribulation Rapture. **Taking the hour of trial which shall come upon the whole world** to be suggestive of a global crisis, it is thought that this refers to a future tribulation period. Since Jesus promises to *keep* [the church] *from* this terrible time, it is argued that the church must be removed from the earth prior to the tribulation of the last days. However, this passage is capable of alternative interpretations.

Those of other approaches would not agree that the "hour of trial" is to be identified with a period of a few years at the close of history. Even if this identification is allowed, however, it is far from clear that the removal of Christians from the earth would be the only possible way in which Jesus could *keep* His people *from* the wars and plagues anticipated to occur at that time. For example, Jesus prayed thus for His disciples: "I do not pray that You should take them out of the world, but that You should keep them from the evil one" (John 17:15). The words "keep . . . from" in the latter verse are the same Greek words (*ek tēreō*) that are found here in Revelation. Non-dispensationalists argue that "keeping from" does not require removal from the planet, since Jesus specified that His prayer was not that the disciples be taken out of the world.

To the *idealist*, the time of trial is generic. All people the world over experience times of trial. From time to time in history there are international conflicts and crises that threaten the peace and safety of believers as well as unbelievers. Through all such trials, the believer, who has kept faith with the Lord, is secure in God's care.

Preterists argue that an empire-wide crisis would satisfy the normal use of the terminology in Revelation 3:10. **The whole world** is a term used to designate the Roman Empire in Luke 2:1 and elsewhere. That it is to **test those who dwell on the earth** (or "land," i.e., Israel) may suggest that there is a crisis that will shake the whole empire and put the Jews, in particular, into special peril. In AD 68, the death of Nero, and the civil wars that followed, greatly threatened the stability of the Roman Empire, until Vespasian was made emperor in AD 70. During this same period (66–70), the Jews were embroiled in a fight for the survival of their nation against the Romans . . . a fight which they lost. *Preterism* suggests that this judgment on Jerusalem is what is implied in the promise, **I am coming quickly!** (v. 11).

The church will weather the storm, but the Christians will have to **hold fast what you have, that no one may take your crown** (v. 11). The overcomer will be made **a pillar in the temple of My God** (v. 12). Assuming a familiarity with the concept of the church being the temple of God (1 Cor.

3:16; Eph. 2:20–22; 1 Tim. 3:15; Heb. 3:6; 1 Pet. 2:5), faithful confessors will possess positions of stability and support. Such pillars are earthquake-proof, so that, unlike the citizens of Philadelphia, who had frequently been driven out of their city by quakes, the overcomer **shall go out no more**. Three inscriptions will be written upon the believer who endures: (1) **the name of My God**, and (2) **the name of the city of My God, the New Jerusalem**, and (3) **My new name** (v. 12). Having the name of God and of Christ written upon oneself is probably like a slave bearing the brand of his master. Further along, we will hear an angel expressing concern that the judgments not begin until "we have sealed the servants of our God on their foreheads" (7:3). Those thus sealed are later seen to have the "Father's name written on their foreheads" (14:1)—a contrast to those who have the name/mark of the beast upon their foreheads (13:16ff.). Such a mark on the believer is not a visible tattoo, but the seal of God's ownership, a concept Paul equates with the believer's possession of the Holy Spirit (Eph. 1:13; 4:30). The writing of the **New Jerusalem** upon the believer suggests citizenship there (cf. Ps. 87:5–6). This Jerusalem is described in symbolic detail in chapter 21.

In the systems of the *historicists* and *some futurists*, Philadelphia is taken to represent the church at the time of the

111

Great Awakening (from 1793) and beyond. This began with the era of Wesley, Whitefield, Edwards, Finney, and Moody, whose activities ranged from the early eighteenth to the late nineteenth centuries. The "open door" that Christ had placed before this church refers to the great opportunity for evangelistic harvesting. This period will continue until the return of Christ, overlapped in the latter days by the Laodicean period.

LETTER TO LAODICEA

REVELATION 3:14–22

[14]"And to the angel of the church of the Laodiceans write, 'These things says the Amen, the Faithful and True Witness, the Beginning of the creation of God: [15]"I know your works, that you are neither cold nor hot. I could wish you were cold or hot. [16]So then, because you are lukewarm, and neither cold nor hot, I will vomit you out of My mouth, [17]Because you say, 'I am rich, have become wealthy, and have need of nothing'—and do not know that you are wretched, miserable, poor, blind, and naked—[18]I counsel you to buy from Me gold refined in the fire, that you may be rich; and white garments, that you may be clothed, that the shame of your nakedness may not be revealed; and anoint your eyes with eye salve, that you may see. [19]As many as I love, I rebuke and chasten. Therefore be zealous and repent. [20]Behold, I stand at the door and knock. If anyone hears My voice and opens the door, I will come in to him and dine with him, and he with Me. [21]To him who overcomes I will grant to sit with Me on My throne, as I also overcame and sat down with My Father on His throne. [22]"He who has an ear, let him hear what the Spirit says to the churches."'"

Laodicea, by all accounts a very prosperous city in John's day, was noteworthy on a number of counts. It was a banking center, which is obviously related to its general wealth. Laodicea also was a producer of black wool clothing and carpets. The city was the location of a famous medical school and the producer of a powder substance used to treat ailments of the eye.

The city's water supply originated from hot springs six miles away at Denizli. In the process of traveling through the aqueduct to Laodicea, the water became tepid—neither hot nor cold. Allusions to these local distinctives may be detected in Christ's choice of words used to address **the church of the Laodiceans** (v. 14).

The state of the church in Laodicea was one of self-satisfaction and complacency. Apparently the Christians, like the city itself, enjoyed a high degree of comfort and prosperity—a factor that led to a diminished zeal for the things of God. The letter to the Laodiceans shares with Sardis the unhappy distinction of lacking any commendation from the Lord.

Jesus calls himself the **Amen** (v. 14). Though this word appears nine times in Revelation, and numerous times throughout the rest of Scripture, this is the only time it is used as a title or name. It is a Hebrew expression of strong affirmation, meaning "so be it." In John's Gospel accounts, on no less than twenty-five occasions, Jesus prefaced His remarks with the rabbinical "Amen, amen"—translated "most assuredly" in the NKJV (the familiar "Verily, verily" of the KJV). Paul wrote of Christ: "For all the promises of God in Him are Yes, and in Him Amen, to the glory of God through us" (2 Cor. 1:20). Christ affirmed the truth of the promises by fulfilling them (cf. Rom. 15:8). Coupled, as it is here, with the phrase the **Faithful and True Witness** (cf. 1:5), the emphasis is clearly upon the truthfulness of the testimony that Jesus brings, either in general or in His specific, present warning to this church.

Seemingly unrelated to the above self-designations, Jesus next identifies himself **as the Beginning of the creation of God** (v. 14). It should not be assumed that this makes Christ out to be a created thing. The Greek word translated **Beginning** is *arch*, which carries the concept of the "beginning, origin, active cause." Rather than the "first thing created," the expression could be understood to mean "he who is the Origin (Source, Creator) of the creation of God."

Paul instructed the Colossian church to pass along his letter to the church of Laodicea (Col. 4:16). If these instructions were followed, then this church would have been familiar with the Colossian epistle, where the role of Christ as Creator is strongly affirmed: "He is the image of the invisible God, the firstborn over all creation. For by Him all things were created . . . All things were created through Him and for Him" (Col. 1:15, 16). Thus there is little likelihood that the Laodiceans would interpret Jesus' words here to mean that He was a created being.

In comparing the spiritual state of the church to the nauseating tepid waters of the city, Jesus describes the community of believers negatively as **neither cold nor hot** (v. 15), and, positively, as **lukewarm** (v. 16). No direct explanation tells how this metaphor corresponds to a spiritual state, but the command to **be zealous and repent**

113

(v. 19) suggests that the lukewarmness represents a deficiency in zeal for Christ.

The statement, **I could wish you were cold or hot** (v. 15), raises the startling prospect that Jesus, though wishing for all believers to be hot, would actually find coldness less offensive than lukewarmness. Perhaps we should not find this too surprising. Those who zealously oppose Christ (cold), and those who zealously serve Him (hot), have one thing in common: *they both take Him seriously.* The one who neither opposes nor serves offers Christ the ultimate insult—affirming His existence, but not taking Him seriously.

Such a condition places a church in jeopardy of being ejected from the very body of Christ: **I will vomit you out of My mouth** (v. 16). The image of Jesus vomiting is an undignified and shocking one, and its use here warns us that He is not to be taken lightly.

The general attitude of the church is represented in the quote: **'I am rich . . . and have need of nothing'** (v. 17). Wealth has a way of imparting a false sense of self-sufficiency—the very antithesis of the beggarliness of spirit commended in the Sermon on the Mount (Matt. 5:3). The church had not always been in this state, but had become wealthy, and now the insidious, corrupting influence of mammon[29] had caused a loss of zeal for the things of God. In striking contrast to the church at Smyrna, which Jesus called "rich,"

though in a state of poverty (2:9), the Laodicean church, though materially affluent, was in God's sight **wretched, miserable, poor, blind, and naked** (v. 17). Each descriptive word was ironic, in view of the local medical school, the banks, the eye salve, and textile industry for which the city was famed.

I counsel you—though He might boldly command, Jesus takes instead the role of Counselor (cf. Isa. 9:6), conveying more of a sense of advising one in His best interests. His counsel (v. 18) is this:

(1) **to buy from Me gold refined in the fire, that you may be rich**, because they are **poor** (v. 17). The refined gold implies character that has been refined through affliction (cf. Job 23:10; 1 Pet. 1:6–7). Luxury is not known for its character-building qualities;

(2) **to buy . . . white garments, that you may be clothed, that the shame of your nakedness may not be revealed**. In all likelihood, the Laodicean Christians were well-dressed. The suggestion of their shameful nakedness before Christ must have stunned them. Later in Revelation, we read of a bride dressed in "fine linen, clean and bright," which is said to represent "the righteous acts of the saints" (19:8). Righteous acts apparently are the garments required, and lacking from this church;

(3) **to . . . anoint your eyes with eye salve, that you may see**. The

church had a vision problem. Despite the fact that a world-renowned eye salve was produced in that very city, the church had lost its spiritual perception. Peter indicates that people who have failed to persevere in Christian growth are "shortsighted, even to blindness" (2 Pet. 1:9).

Jesus' approach in this letter is bluntly confrontational (to the point even of neglecting the traditional opening commendation), but the harshness of His tone is a manifestation of His love for His servants: **As many as I love, I rebuke and chasten** (v. 19). It is the Father who is said to chasten His children in Proverbs 3:12. Here it is Jesus taking this responsibility—perhaps another instance of the Revelation identifying Christ with God.

The command, be zealous and repent (v. 19), may either suggest that they are to repent of the sin of lacking zeal, or else that Jesus wants them to repent zealously.

Behold, I stand at the door and knock (v. 20). Familiar as an evangelistic text for sinners, this verse, in context, actually expresses Christ's feeling of being an outsider from His own church, desiring to be invited back in. If the church will not dine with Christ, then, **if anyone hears My voice and opens the door, I will come in to him and dine with him, and he with Me**. Dining with Christ may have eucharistic connotations: although Jesus may not be attending the church's love feasts, He will commune privately with any individual who welcomes Him. To such overcomers as respond to this offer, Christ will not only commune but also allow them **to sit with Me on My throne** (v. 21). Reigning with Christ also is promised to the overcomers in Thyatira (2:26f.), and additional references to the co-regency of the saints are found in 5:10 and 20:4. Opinions concerning the exact time of this fulfillment depend upon one's eschatological system—it could be in the Millennium; or after death, reigning in heaven prior to the Second Advent. It could be a spiritual reign of saints in this life or a literal reign over the new earth. Theories abound.

The present and accomplished enthronement of Christ is stated clearly enough: **as I also overcame and sat down with My Father on His throne** (v. 21). The Christians had already deduced this from Psalm 110:1—"The LORD said to my Lord, 'Sit at My right hand, till I make Your enemies Your footstool'" (Mark 16:19; Acts 2:33–35; 1 Pet. 3:22; 1 Cor. 15:25).

Among *historicists* and some *futurists*, it is generally argued that Laodicea represents the lukewarm sector of the church in the end-times (possibly beginning near the end of the nineteenth century). The scholarly assault on the Bible, epitomized and exacerbated by the publication of Darwin's *Origin of*

Species (1859), put tremendous pressure upon the church to conform to modern thought or lose academic respectability. Many theologians succumbed to this pressure and began subjecting the Bible to "scientific methods" of analysis. Such analysis, though far from objective or conclusive, became fashionable in many seminaries and denominations, resulting in a loss of respect for the Bible as a genuine revelation from God. In many cases, secular psychology, sociology, anthropology, philosophy, and whatever social trend became popular in secular thinking (e.g., the breakdown of biblical models of marriage and sexuality), have displaced the Bible in its authority to dictate norms for the church. Modern churches that have gone this route are said to be represented by this Laodicean church. They are lukewarm, and Christ says that they nauseate him. Those applying the seven church letters to eras of church history believe that both the Philadelphian and the Laodicean types of church will exist together until the coming of Christ.

Having considered what the Spirit had to say to each of the seven churches individually, we are prepared to proceed to the main theater, where the pageant of heavenly scenes of later developments is presented for the edification of all seven of the churches—and, as we think, of the entire church of all times, as their symbolic number doubtless suggests.

SUMMARY OF CHAPTERS 1–3

Having considered Christ's assessment of the current state of the seven churches, we are prepared to go on to the prophetic events about which He wished for them to be informed.

In the view of the *historicists*, the letters contain a cryptic reference to the conditions in which the whole church would be found at varying times in her history. The church of Ephesus represents the church in John's own day, while the church in Laodicea stands for the church in the end-times.

The *preterists* consider the letters to apply to little else than the contemporary situation of the seven churches as they existed in John's time. As with all biblical epistles, however, application to similar churches of any time is acknowledged.

Futurists may side with the *historicists* or, alternatively, with the *preterists* and the *idealist* interpreters with reference to the application of the letters, though they see the reference to the "things which shall take place after this" (1:19) as referring to the end of the present age.

 Idealist interpreters see the purpose of the book as communicating to the whole church the facts of God's sovereignty in history and His vindication of the righteous. The seven churches symbolize the church of all times, and the letters apply to any churches in which the relevant circumstances prevail.

NOTES

1. Robert H. Mounce, "The Revelation Record: A Scientific and Devotional Commentary on the Book of Revelation" in the NICNT, 63.
2. The matter is more complex than may immediately appear. The words "witness" and "testimony" are important words in Revelation. Whereas the emphasis is most often upon the Christian as the witness to Christ and having the testimony of Christ (6:9; 1:7; 2:11, 17; 19:10; 20:4), yet Christ is also called the faithful witness (1:5; 3:14) and is found testifying (22:18, 20).
3. The others are found at 14:13; 16:15; 19:9; 20:6; 22:7, 14.
4. The same point is emphasized at the close of the book (22:6, 10).
5. Based on the textual variant of Eph. 1:1, which lacks the phrase "who are in Ephesus"— thus leaving the recipients unspecified.
6. E.g., Rom. 1:7; 1 Cor. 1:3; 2 Cor. 1:2; Gal. 1:3; Eph. 1:2, etc.
7. The words "martyr" and "witness" are both *martus* in Greek.
8. Recalling another Pauline expression, echoed elsewhere in Revelation: "King of kings and Lord of Lords" (1 Tim. 6:15; Rev. 19:16).
9. Heb. 9:14; John 1:7.
10. E.g., Isa. 11:16; Mic. 7:15, 18–19.
11. E.g., Luke 9:31(Gr.); 1 Cor. 5:7.
12. Both readings affirm the priesthood of believers. The difference is between "kings" and "a kingdom" (i.e., the subjects of a king).
13. Rousas John Rushdoony, *Thy Kingdom Come: Studies in Daniel and Revelation* (Fairfax, VA: Thoburn, 1978), 87.
14. When written in all capital and small capital letters, LORD translates the Hebrew word *YHWH*, which has traditionally been rendered "Jehovah" or "*Yahweh*."
15. In Colosse, Hierapolis, and Troas.
16. Ignatius, *To the Ephesians*, 6:9.
17. This is noted by Walvoord (*The Revelation of Jesus Christ*, 57), who quotes Alford for confirmation.
18. Known today as Ayasaluk.
19. Cf., Matt. 11:15; 13:9, 43; Mark 4:9, 23; 7:16; Luke 8:8; 14:35.

20. "In popular Christian thought the idea has prevailed that there were ten great persecutions of the church that were practically universal in scope, by Nero (AD 64), Domitian (AD 95), Trajan (AD 112), Marcus Aurelius (AD 177), Septimus Severus (late second century), Maximinus (AD 235), Decius (AD 250), Valerian (AD 257), Aurelian and Diocletian (AD 303). It is true that widespread persecution was promoted by Decius, Valerian, and Diocletian, but earlier persecutions were local in character or relatively mild in execution." Ladd, *A Commentary on the Revelation of John.*

21. Caringola, *The Present Reign of Jesus Christ,* 50.

22. G. K. Beale, *The New International Greek Testament Commentary: The Book of Revelation* (Grand Rapids: Eerdmans, 1999), 246

23. Caringola, *The Present Reign of Jesus Christ,* 50

24. Ibid.

25. William Miller, *Miller's Lectures,* cited in Caringola, *The Present Reign of Jesus Christ,* 55.

26. *Antinomianism:* from the Gr. *anti* (against) and *nomos* (law). This view, found among the Gnostics, held that believers who had saving "knowledge" were under the restraint of no law—and might even show superior insight by casting off moral restraint.

27. Caringola, *The Present Reign of Jesus Christ,* 58.

28. Uriah Smith, quoted in Caringola.

29. Cf. Mark 4:19; 10:23; 1 Tim. 6:9f.

PART II

THE SEVEN-SEALED SCROLL

REVELATION 4–7

WHAT EVENTS DO THE MYSTERIOUS SCROLL AND ITS UNSEALING REPRESENT? WHEN DO THESE EVENTS OCCUR?

⏳ HISTORICIST APPROACH:

- The unsealing of the scroll represents the beginning of the fall of the Roman Empire.
- The seal-sequence begins with the reign of Domitian (who died AD 96) and follows the decline of the empire through the invasions of the Goths and Vandals in the fourth and fifth centuries.
- Alternative historicist opinions are surveyed in commentary.

⏳ PRETERIST APPROACH:

- The unsealing of the scroll represents the judgment of God upon Jerusalem (AD 66–70); 144,000 Judean Christians escape to Pella.
- The four horsemen represent the Roman invasion of Israel to quell the Jewish rebellion (AD 66), bringing bloodshed, civil war, famine, death, and ultimately the fall of Jerusalem in AD 70.

⏳ FUTURIST APPROACH:

- The scroll and its unsealing represent the Rapture of the church and the beginning of the Great Tribulation (4:1, according to dispensational view); 144,000 Jews of the end-times are sealed (saved).
- In the end times, the Antichrist rides forth conquering on the white horse; war, famine, and cosmic disturbances (possibly nuclear war) follow.

⏳ IDEALIST APPROACH:

- The scroll and its unsealing represent God's dealings with mankind, seen in cycles of war, martyrdom, and judgment recurring repeatedly throughout history.
- The visions underscore God's sovereignty in the rise and fall of earthly kingdoms and His protection of the saints in the midst of political upheavals, without tying these experiences to specific Historicist events.

THE THRONE-ROOM VISION

REVELATION 4:1–3

[1]After these things I looked, and behold, a door standing open in heaven. And the first voice which I heard was like a trumpet speaking with me, saying, "Come up here, and I will show you things which must take place after this."[2] Immediately I was in the Spirit; and behold, a throne set in heaven, and One sat on the throne. [3]And He who sat there was like a jasper and a sardius stone in appearance; and there was a rainbow around the throne, in appearance like an emerald.

⏳ HISTORICIST

On this passage, E. B. Elliott in *Horae Apocalyptica* explains:

In the two preceding chapters of the Apocalypse, "the things that were,"—the state of the church then existing—had been described to the Evangelist. Then . . . the scene passed from his view of the seven lamps and the heavenly High Priest that walked amog them. It remained that the promised revelation should be made of things future—the things that were to follow on the state then present of the church and of the world.

Matthew Henry writes:

[After these things], that is, not only "after I had seen the vision of Christ walking in the midst of the golden candlesticks," but "after I had taken his messages from his mouth, and written and sent them

⏳ PRETERIST

By being caught up to heaven, and seeing the throne of God, John is treated to a vision comparable to that theophany in the first chapter of Ezekiel. Thus the throne of God, and God upon it, are depicted in both places. There is a similarity, also, in the import of Ezekiel's and John's prophecies, in that the former devotes the first half of his book to prophecies related to the judgment of Jerusalem, which is also the subject of John's Apocalypse. The only difference being that Ezekiel's visions concerned the first destruction of Jerusalem, in 586 BC, by the Babylonians, whereas John foresees the second destruction, in AD 70, administered by the Romans. Both prophets see these disasters as having God as their Author, who sits enthroned on a throne of sovereignty and of judgment.

⌛ FUTURIST

This passage marks one of the major turning points in the book of Revelation. Everything in the previous chapters concerns "things which you have seen" and "the things which are" (1:19). We now come to **things which must take place after this** (v. 1). To the dispensational view, **after this,** or, more literally, "after these things" [*meta tauta*] means after "the things of the church," or "after the church age." Thus the material in Revelation after this point will be fulfilled after the church is gone.

Some believe that John's transportation to heaven may be viewed as a type of the Rapture of the church, and the mention of **a voice . . . like a trumpet** (v. 1) here may recall the language of the Rapture passages in 1 Corinthians 15:51–54 (which refers to "the last trumpet") and 1 Thessalonians 4:16–18 (which refers to the "voice of the archangel and the trumpet of God"). Dispensational *futurists* note that the church is not seen hereafter on the earth—only in heaven (7:9–17). As Walvoord puts it,

> The word *church,* so prominent in chapters 2 and 3, does not occur again until 22:16, though the church is undoubtedly in view as the wife of the Lamb in Revelation 19:7. . . . Saints who come to know the Lord in this period are described as saved Israelites or saved

⌛ IDEALIST

To those who divide the book into seven segments, this verse is the beginning of section 2 or Act2. The opening words, **After these things** (v. 1), do not mean "This is what will happen next," but rather, "This is the vision I saw next." The entire church age, depicted from an earthly standpoint in chapters 1 through 3, will now be viewed again—this time from a heavenly viewpoint. As Beale writes:

> Being ushered into the spiritual, timeless dimension of God's heavenly council means that the time of the events that John sees in vision may be difficult to determine precisely. Some of the symbols may be descriptive symbolism in that they portray what has taken place up to the present. Or they may contain determinative symbolism predicting what will come to pass . . . they all probably have a mixture of past, present, and future elements.[2]

John is again said to be **in the Spirit** (v. 2). This probably means that he was not bodily removed from Patmos, but that he was given spiritual vision inTto the heavenly courts. His view of God's **throne** (v. 2) reassured the persecuted churches that, despite their difficulties, God was still (and always is) in ultimate control of the situation. The emphasis on God's sovereignty in Revelation is seen in the repeated mention of "throne" or "thrones" (forty times in

121

⧗ HISTORICIST *(continued)*

to the several churches, according to his command, after this I had another vision." John is given a vision intended to call attention to the sovereignty of God over history and the unique privilege of Christ to unfold the future.

Matthew Henry, again, observes:

He saw a glorious one upon the throne. This throne was not empty; there was one in it who filled it, and that was God, who is here described by those things that are most pleasant and precious in our world: *His countenance was like a jasper and a sardine-stone;* he is not described by any human features, so as to be represented by an image, but only by his transcendent brightness.

In the subsequent breaking of the seven seals (chaps. 6–8), and the events that this action calls forth, the vision gives a glimpse of the conquests of Imperial Rome for three hundred years, culminating in Constantine's establishment of Christianity as the religion of the empire. The seven trumpets that follow (chaps. 8–11) foretell the fall of the Western, and then the Eastern Roman Empires, to the end of the world. Thus the seals and trumpets give the secular, political history from John's time forward. At 11:19, however, a new view commences, referring to the internal affairs of the church. ⧗

⧗ PRETERIST *(continued)*

In this chapter, we are introduced, most probably, to a heavenly courtroom scene. The Judge sits **on the throne** (v. 2) where, as we shall see in chapter 5, He is about to hand down sentence upon the accused. The plaintiffs are the martyrs of Christ, whose complaint against their persecutors is recorded later in the vision (6:9). The accused (Jerusalem) is about to be condemned. The repetition of the expression **after this** [Gr. *meta tauta*—literally, *after these things*] at the end of verse 1 identifies the present material as the previously announced "things that are about to happen after these things [again, *meta tauta*]" (1:19, literally rendered). Since John was told (in the first century) that these things were "about to take place," a first-century fulfillment is to be looked for. The seven-sealed book (5:1) is God's sentence against Jerusalem, and the subsequent breaking of the first six seals depicts the Jewish crisis of AD 66–70: the war between the Jews and Rome, issuing in the utter destruction of the Jewish capital, state, and religious system. ⧗

⌛ FUTURIST *(continued)*

Gentiles, never by terms which are characteristic of the church, the Body of Christ.[1]

Those futurists who reject the dispensational view do not place the Rapture of the church here, but they agree with the dispensationalists that the future Tribulation is the subject matter of the following chapters (4–19). In response to Walvoord's points stated above, they would say that the word "church" is used in the Apocalypse only with reference to individual congregations, thus leaving unaddressed the question of the universal church and its whereabouts. "The church," conceived as a global entity, is mentioned nowhere in Revelation—either before or after chapter 4. They further note that the terms "saints" (5:8; 8:3–4; 11:18; 13:7–10; 14:12; 15:3; 16:6; 17:6) and "redeemed" (5:9; 14:3–4) are indeed (contr. Walvoord) "terms which are characteristic of the church, the Body of Christ," when found elsewhere throughout the New Testament. ⌨

⌛ IDEALIST *(continued)*

this book; only fifteen times in the rest of the New Testament).

The Inhabitant of the throne is likened to **jasper** (v. 3), which is elsewhere said to be clear as crystal (21:11), and is otherwise unknown. Probably a diamond is intended, representing the purity of God on His throne. The **sardius** (or carnelian) stone is red, calling to mind God's avenging wrath. The green of an **emerald** is here the principal color of the **rainbow,** a symbol of God's mercy or grace (Gen. 9:12–15) [Morey]. ⌨

THE TWENTY-FOUR ELDERS

REVELATION 4:4—5

[4]Around the throne were twenty-four thrones, and on the thrones I saw twenty-four elders sitting, clothed in white robes; and they had crowns of gold on their heads. [5]And from the throne proceeded lightnings, thunderings, and voices. Seven lamps of fire were burning before the throne, which are the seven Spirits of God.

⌛ HISTORICIST

Without attempting to identify the **twenty-four elders** (v. 4), Adam Clarke suggests that the image may be taken from the smaller Sanhedrin at Jerusalem, which was composed of twenty-three elders. Barnes speaks for many other expositors of this school when he recognizes in the twenty-four elders "the church triumphant—redeemed—saved—as rendering praise and honour to God; as uniting with the hosts of heaven in adoring him for his perfections and for the wonders of his grace."

Ezekiel saw twenty-five men in a vision (Ezek. 8:16; 11:1), representing the high priest and the heads of the twenty-four orders of priests. Here, the Lamb replaces the high priest of that vision, and the church replaces the corrupt priesthood of Ezekiel's day.

Clarke believes (see note at 1:4) that the seven spirits are angels, thinking it

⌛ PRETERIST

Jay Adams does not follow the apparent majority in seeing the **twenty-four elders** (v. 4) as representing the church (e.g., David Clark), or "the representative assembly of the Royal Priesthood, the Church" (e.g., Chilton). He understands them to be distinguished from the church in 5:9f., where some manuscripts read "men," "them," and "they" in place of "us" and "we." Nor does he follow others in seeing them as angels, since they are distinguished from angels throughout chapters 5 and 7. Instead, he follows Pieters in suggesting:

> The twenty-four elders probably do not represent any particular group. . . . They are included to complete the picture of the heavenly court. . . . They are here to create the proper effect. Later in the book, they help carry the story forward, much as the chorus in a Greek tragedy. . . . Beyond this,

⏳ FUTURIST

Henry Morris appears alone in suggesting that the **twenty-four elders** (v. 4) are the first twenty-four ancestors of Christ (Adam through Pharez) listed in Genesis 5 and 11.

Ladd and Mounce both understand the elders to be angels, not human. Mounce describes them as "an exalted angelic order who serve and adore God as the heavenly counterpart to the twenty-four priestly and twenty-four Levitical orders (1 Chron. 24:4; 25:9–13) functioning both in the royal and the priestly."

The majority opinion among dispensationalists (e.g., Gaebelein, Ryrie, Walvoord, Lindsey, and others) identifies the twenty-four elders as the New Testament saints, who were raptured into heaven (in v. 1). Gaebelein writes: "There is only one possible meaning. They represent the redeemed, the Saints in glory. They are Priests (clothed in white) and they are Kings (crowned); they are the royal priesthood before the throne."

Their presence before the throne of God, prior to the unleashing of the various tribulation judgments, is seen as proof of a pretribulational Rapture. Hal Lindsey sees a further indicator that the church has been raptured at this point in the fact that the **seven lamps of fire** (v. 5), which were the seven churches on earth in chapter 1 (v. 20), are now **before the throne** in heaven. Ryrie

⏳ IDEALIST

The **twenty-four elders** (v. 4) are the "celestial representatives" of all the redeemed, glorified and enthroned, who worship continuously. Their **white robes** symbolize their purity. Their **crowns** [Gr. *stephanos*] suggest "victory and joy, not political authority" (Morey). Leon Morris agrees, but specifies that they are *angelic* representatives of the whole body of the faithful. The number twenty-four recalls the twelve patriarchs and the twelve apostles (brought together in Rev. 21:12–14), and therefore suggest the redeemed of both the Old and the New Testament times. This view has the support of Hendriksen, Hailey, Hobbs, and Wilcock. The number twenty-four also recalls the priesthood, which was divided in David's time into twenty-four courses for logistic reasons (1 Chronicles 24). Since these elders do priestly functions—like burning incense (5:8)—they depict the church in its character as a "royal priesthood" (1 Pet. 2:9). Wilson thinks they are angelic princes of the highest rank who perform priestly functions before the throne (compare 5:8 with 8:3–4).

Lightnings, thunders, and voices (v. 5) describe the fearsome power of God, and possibly His sovereignty over the forces of nature. The seven lamps, identified with the seven Spirits of God, represent the Holy Spirit. ⏳

HISTORICIST *(continued)*

inappropriate that the Holy Spirit be designated as seven in number.

Matthew Henry, however, agrees with the majority in identifying the seven spirits with the Holy Spirit, but he explains the numerical problem by appealing to the "various gifts, graces and operations of the Spirit of God in the [seven] churches of Christ." Elliott, also accepting this identification, sees it as a "necessary inference from the association of these seven Spirits with the Father and the Son in chap.1:4."

PRETERIST *(continued)*

they seem to do nothing, and represent nothing.[3]

The **lightnings, thunderings and voices** (v. 5) recall Mount Sinai, where God first established His covenant with Israel. Similar phenomena are mentioned here to suggest the end of that covenant and its replacement with another. The writer of Hebrews (citing Hag. 2) likened the overthrow of the first covenant (publicly demonstrated by the destruction of Jerusalem and the temple in AD 70) to the time of its establishment at Sinai, but the latter would be accompanied by even more fearful phenomena (Heb. 12:18–29).

⌛ FUTURIST *(continued)*

and Walvoord do not follow Lindsey in this, rather tending to see the seven lamps and seven spirits as representing the Holy Spirit. ✦

THE FOUR LIVING CREATURES

REVELATION 4:6—11

[6]Before the throne there was a sea of glass, like crystal. And in the midst of the throne, and around the throne, were four living creatures full of eyes in front and in back. [7]The first living creature was like a lion, the second living creature like a calf, the third living creature had a face like a man, and the fourth living creature was like a flying eagle. [8]The four living creatures, each having six wings, were full of eyes around and within. And they do not rest day or night, saying: "Holy, holy, holy, Lord God Almighty, Who was and is and is to come!" [9] Whenever the living creatures give glory and honor and thanks to Him who sits on the throne, who lives forever and ever, [10] the twenty-four elders fall down before Him who sits on the throne and worship Him who lives forever and ever, and cast their crowns before the throne, saying: [11] "You are worthy, O Lord, to receive glory and honor and power; for You created all things, and by Your will they exist and were created."

HISTORICIST

In Ezekiel's vision of the throne of God (Ezekiel 1), creatures similar to these were seen under the throne, as if bearing it up. Albert Barnes points out that "it was not unusual for the thrones of monarchs to be supported by carved animals of various forms, which were designed undoubtedly to be somehow emblematic of government—either its stability, vigilance, boldness or firmness. Thus Solomon had twelve lions carved on each side of his throne."

In the case of God's throne, the creatures are not carved, but **living creatures** (v. 6). The rabbis said that

PRETERIST

David S. Clark sees the **four living creatures** (v. 6) as "angels, or archangels around the throne." Chilton identifies them with Ezekiel's cherubim (Ezekiel 1 and 10). Adams, in apparent agreement, says the creatures, like the twenty-four elders, are neither angels nor men,

> since they . . . are distinguished from both in chapters 5 and 7. They are rather to be identified with the Cherubim of Ezekiel, to which they most closely conform. Their function is to guard and bear the throne of God. In this

FUTURIST

The **sea of glass** (v. 6) is the heavenly model for the "molten sea" (laver) in Solomon's temple (2 Chron. 4:2–6). According to Gaebelein, "Now it is solidified because no more water is needed for the cleansing of the Saints."

Of the many interpretations of the **four living creatures** (v. 6), Walvoord prefers the idea that they represent "the attributes or qualities of God presented to John here as living entities." This is also the opinion of Ironside. Ryrie gives this as one possible option also, since "they are said to be 'in the midst of' the throne."

Ladd follows the rabbinic interpretation of the four faces on Ezekiel's cherubim, seeing the four creatures as four aspects of nature: wild beasts, domesticated animals, human beings, and flying creatures. He suggests two possible interpretations that he says may both be correct: (1) They represent the praise and adoration extended to the Creator by the totality of His creation; (2) they are angelic beings used by the Creator in executing His rule and divine will.

Henry Morris believes them to be angelic beings, an alternative Walvoord also admits as possible. Lindsey thinks they are angels "who represent the four portraits of Christ that we find in the four Gospels." The idea that the lion, ox, man, and eagle portray, respectively, Christ as King (as in Matthew), Servant (as in Mark), Son of Man (as in Luke),

IDEALIST

The **four living creatures** (v. 6) recall the description of the cherubim (Ezekiel 1) and seraphim (Isaiah 6) combined into one image. Bauckham writes:

> They are heavenly beings whose existence is entirely fulfilled in the worship of God. Their ceaseless worship at the heart of all reality, around the divine throne, represents the theocentric nature of all reality, which exists ultimately to glorify God. They are therefore the central worshippers whose worship is taken up by wider circles.[4]

They may simply be unusual celestial beings who belong to neither class but bear similarities to both. Or they may be a symbolic picture of the creation, which praises God, as do the redeemed (v. 4).

Beale remarks:

> The four living beings represent the whole of animate life. They are performing the function that all creation is meant to fulfill. That is, all things were created to praise God for his holiness and glorify him for his work of creation. 5:13 bears out that this is not only the ideal purpose for all creatures but also that some day this purpose will actually be fulfilled, not only in heaven but also on earth, since it is an anticipation of the consummation.[5]

⧗ HISTORICIST *(continued)*

the **lion** (v. 7) was chief of wild beasts, the ox (**calf**) the chief of domestic beasts, the **eagle** the chief of birds, and **man** the chief of all "intellectual creatures." Elliott reminds us of the appearance of similar creatures in Ezekiel 1 and 10, and thus identifies them with an order of angels, even identifying them with the seraphim of Isaiah 6, "for they are symbolized as *burning lamps of fire . . .* to identify them with the *Seraphim,* or *burning ones,* seen beside the throne by Isaiah."

Barnes thinks "they are symbolical beings designed to furnish some representation of the government of God—to illustrate, as it were, that on which the divine government rests, or which constitutes its support—to wit, power, intelligence, vigilance, energy." By contrast, Adam Clarke thinks the four creatures may represent the whole of creation. Matthew Henry thinks they signify the ministers of the gospel as the twenty-four elders signify the whole church.

In that they **cast their crowns before the throne** (v. 10), they acknowledge His authority as the source of their own. ⓠ

⧗ PRETERIST *(continued)*

passage, they serve the purpose of emphasizing the majesty of the vision. Like the elders, they are to help the revelation unfold.

In this respect, the passage continues to resemble features of Ezekiel's throne (or throne-chariot) vision at the beginning of that book, and thus continues to call to our minds the principal subject matter of Ezekiel's prophecy as well, namely God's imminent judgment on the apostate city of Jerusalem.

Though the imagery clearly is taken from Ezekiel's cherubim, there is the one marked difference, of course, in that the cherubim of Ezekiel, though of the same number, had sixteen faces among them, since each of the four cherubim had four faces, whereas these living creatures appear to have only one face each.

Chilton compares the four faces of the living creatures with "the middle signs in the four quarters of the Zodiac," namely, Leo (the **lion**), Taurus (the bull, or **calf**), Aquarius (the **man**), and Scorpio. He explains that a figure of an **eagle** was used for Scorpio in ancient times. As the heavens declare God's glory, he says, so do these continually. ⓠ

FUTURIST *(continued)*

and Son of God (as in John) goes back at least as far as Victorinus. Ryrie approves this view, although Walvoord seems to join Alford in condemning this notion as excessively speculative.

IDEALIST *(continued)*

The redeemed (the twenty-four elders) follow the lead of the creation (the living creatures) in glorifying God. Here God's worthiness to be worshiped is connected to His having **created all things** (v. 11). Though cherub-like in appearance, the creatures' song (v. 8) resembles that of the seraphim (Isaiah. 6).

THE SEALED SCROLL

REVELATION 5:1–4

[1]And I saw in the right hand of Him who sat on the throne a scroll written inside and on the back, sealed with seven seals. [2] Then I saw a strong angel proclaiming with a loud voice, "Who is worthy to open the scroll and to loose its seals?" [3] And no one in heaven or on the earth or under the earth was able to open the scroll, or to look at it. [4] So I wept much, because no one was found worthy to open and read the scroll, or to look at it.

⌛ HISTORICIST

This **scroll** in the hand of God contained information of great importance, as is seen by the pains taken to find a person qualified to open it and disclose its contents. The opening of the scroll would require the breaking of seven wax seals. Documents were often sealed by persons in authority, and while breaking a seal was no great difficulty, it could not be done by anyone other than one having proper authorization.

The scroll itself may represent "the purposes and designs of God relative to His government of the world and of the Church" (Clarke). Matthew Henry thinks so, describing the contents of the book as "the designs and methods of divine Providence towards the church and the world." Barnes identifies the contents of the book simply as "future events." All three of these expositors see the vision as intended to show that no one other than Jesus can disclose the

⌛ PRETERIST

In Jay Adams' view, the **scroll** with the **seven seals** is the sentence handed down by the judge against Jerusalem for its part in shedding "all the righteous blood" of the martyrs (Matt. 23:35). John has entered the courtroom at the end of the trial, just in time to hear the sentence delivered—if only one can be found worthy to execute it! Judgment is due, but only He who is without sin may "first cast a stone at her." Initially, no one is found to qualify, resulting in great grief for John, since this would mean that the martyrs' blood must go unavenged.

Adams and Pieters suggest that the seven seals are positioned in a row along the overlapping edge of the rolled-up scroll, requiring that all seven be broken before the scroll begins to be opened. On this view, the breaking of each seal does not produce action, but only gives occasion to introduce the leading characters

132

⏳ FUTURIST

Henry Morris, in agreement with many dispensational interpreters (e.g., Ironside, Criswell, Lindsey), wrote, "But what is this remarkable scroll? It is nothing less than the title deed to the earth itself." Walvoord notes, "Roman law required a will to be sealed seven times as illustrated in the wills left by Augustus and Vespasian for their successors." The mighty judgments of the Tribulation period that are unleashed by the opening of the document all are part of God's reclaiming for Himself the control of the earth, which was forfeited to Satan by the fall of Adam and Eve long ago. The "redemption of the purchased possession" (Eph. 1:14) is accompanied by long-overdue punishments upon the usurpers who have "destroyed the earth" (Rev. 11:18) and defied their Creator. Ryrie writes:

> Actually, we are not told in this chapter what the book contained, but when the seals are broken in chapter 6 the judgments of God are poured out on the earth. When the seventh seal is opened, the trumpets sound (8:1) and when the seventh trumpet blows, Christ is said to receive the kingdoms of this world (11:15).

Under Jewish law, real estate that had been forfeited by a man could be redeemed (bought back) by any near kinsman (Lev. 25:25). To redeem the earth, forfeited by man, the redeemer

⏳ IDEALIST

Bauckham writes:

> After the revelation of God's sovereignty in heaven . . . the question of how his sovereignty is to become effective on earth is raised. John sees in the right hand of the One seated on the throne a sealed scroll (5:1). This contains the secret purpose of God for establishing his kingdom. Its contents are, in fact, what is to be revealed to John as the content of his prophecy for the churches."[7]

According to Morey, the **scroll** is the "redemptive plan of God" seen as "God's Last Will and Testament." Some think it is the Lamb's book of life (cf. 3:5; 13:8; 20:12, 15; 21:27), containing the names of all who are saved. The reason that it is written inside and on the back is that there are too many names to be contained on the inside alone.[8]

It is in the right hand, a symbol of God's power and authority. Since it is written inside and out, all available space has been filled, so nothing can be added to God's plan. It must be a ***strong angel*** with a **loud voice** who issues the summons, so that every person **in heaven and on the earth, and under the earth** may hear of the challenge. The question is not whether anyone *strong enough* to break the seals can be found, but whether any will be ***worthy*** to do so. John weeps because there seems to be none worthy to step forward, and God's

REVELATION 5:1—4

HISTORICIST *(continued)*

future dealings of God in history. John's tears are an expression of disappointment. He had gotten his hopes high that he would see a disclosure of the future; with the failure to find any **worthy** parties **in heaven or on earth or under the earth**, it appeared those hopes were to be left unsatisfied.

PRETERIST *(continued)*

in the ensuing drama. The actual judgments only begin with the sounding of the seven trumpets in chapter 8.

Alternatively, David S. Clark simply sees the scroll as containing "the future," while David Chilton understands it to be a testament document representing the New Covenant. The big question, then, becomes: "Who is worthy to be the Mediator of this New Covenant?" Chilton writes: "But the coming of the New Covenant implies the passing away of the Old Covenant [Hebrews 8:13], and the judgment of apostate Israel."[6]

FUTURIST *(continued)*

must be a kinsman (hence a man, not an angel) and must come forward with the purchase price in hand—something that no one in the universe could do except Jesus (see 1 Pet. 1:18–19).

IDEALIST *(continued)*

purposes must therefore be delayed or hindered. No man but Christ is worthy to execute the plan of God, symbolized by breaking the seals and opening the scroll.

THE APPEARANCE OF THE LAMB

REVELATION 5:5—6

⁵But one of the elders said to me, "Do not weep. Behold, the Lion of the tribe of Judah, the Root of David, has prevailed to open the scroll and to loose its seven seals." ⁶ And I looked, and behold, in the midst of the throne and of the four living creatures, and in the midst of the elders, stood a Lamb as though it had been slain, having seven horns and seven eyes, which are the seven Spirits of God sent out into all the earth.

⌛ HISTORICIST

Matthew Henry and Adam Clarke both see in the double designation of Christ a reference to His dual nature. According to the flesh, He is **of the tribe of Judah** (v. 5), but as touching His divine nature, He is **the Root of David.** Some (e.g., Barnes) interpret the latter expression as essentially synonymous with the Old Testament phrase, "a Rod from the stem of Jesse, and a Branch . . . out of his roots" (Isa. 11:1), later referred to as "a Root of Jesse" (Isa. 11:10).

Henry and Clarke, however, with many others, see the title **Root of David** as describing, not Christ's ancestry, but David's. That is, Christ is not only David's "Son," but also David's "source" or "Root" (cf. Christ's enigmatic question in Matt. 22:45).

Expositors agree in seeing the **seven horns** (v. 6) and the **seven eyes**

⌛ PRETERIST

The absence of a qualified person to loose the seals and open the scroll has provided the dramatic setting for the introduction of the Hero of Revelation, usually depicted in this book as the **Lamb** (v. 6). Comparing Christ with a lamb is not a reference to His gentleness, since He is portrayed in the following chapters as anything but gentle (cf. 6:16)! His role as the Sacrificed One explains His being likened to a lamb (cf. John 1:29). The fact of His having been slain is emphasized (v. 6) because Christ, having sacrificed Himself, **prevailed** (v. 5) over the forces of evil (Col. 2:15; Heb. 2:14). As the One slain by the leaders in Jerusalem, He shares the same grievance against her as do the other plaintiffs (e.g., 6f.), namely that, as a victim of her injustice, He has the right to be vindicated against Jerusalem (Luke

⧖ FUTURIST

Judah is called a lion in Genesis 49:9. The oft-repeated expression, **Behold!** (v. 5), is similar in meaning to our exclamation, "Surprise!" John had wept at the prospect of no one qualifying to open the scroll. The unexpected news that a lion-like Judean had qualified for the task changed his chagrin into hope. But this announcement was not the end of the surprises. John writes, "I looked— and surprise!" It was no lion at all, but **a Lamb** (v. 6) that had stepped forward. From the viewpoint of those in heaven, He is recognized as a conquering Lion, though to human eyes, Jesus seemed a mere lamb.

Ryrie thinks that the **seven eyes** (v. 6) "represent the fullness of the Spirit of God." Of the same, Walvoord writes, "This may be a reference to seven angels." Morris sees in the **seven horns** (v. 6) a reminder of the invasion of Jericho, when seven "trumpets of ram's horns" were sounded. These ideas are intriguing when one considers that seven angels with seven trumpets become a focal point of the action after the seventh seal is broken in chapter 8. ⧖

⧖ IDEALIST

That Jesus is here connected to Judah's tribe, and particularly David's line, is a way of underscoring His messianic qualifications, since the prophets foretold that the messiah would come through that pedigree. The designation **Lamb** (v. 6) for Christ is found twenty-eight times in Revelation. John the Baptist declared that Christ was like a sacrificial lamb (John 1:29). In this portrayal, the image of a lamb is not strictly adhered to, since the figure has **seven eyes,** an emblem of omniscience, and **seven horns,** suggesting omnipotence. These two traits qualify Christ to be the ideal judge, prosecutor, and executioner, even as His having **been slain** and His lamb-like innocence qualify Him to be the ideal Savior. Remember that this is a symbolical drama, so we should not expect Him to have this peculiar appearance in reality, nor is it uniformly used as a way of describing of Him throughout the remainder of the book (e.g., 6:2; 14:14; 19:11ff.). ⧖

⌛ HISTORICIST *(continued)*

as representing "all power" and "all knowledge and wisdom," respectively. They do not agree on the identification of the "seven spirits of God." Henry, and most others, seeing them as the Holy Spirit, and Clarke as angels of providence. ⬙

⌛ PRETERIST *(continued)*

11:50f.). He who was like a lamb in His sacrifice has become like a **Lion** (v. 5) in avenging the righteous blood that was shed. ⬙

THE WORSHIP OF THE LAMB

REVELATION 5:7—10

[7]Then He came and took the scroll out of the right hand of Him who sat on the throne. [8]Now when He had taken the scroll, the four living creatures and the twenty-four elders fell down before the Lamb, each having a harp, and golden bowls full of incense, which are the prayers of the saints. [9]And they sang a new song, saying, "You are worthy to take the scroll, and to open its seals; for You were slain, and have redeemed us to God by Your blood out of every tribe and tongue and people and nation, [10] and have made us kings and priests to our God; and we shall reign on the earth."

⌛ HISTORICIST

Adam Clarke writes that "the whole Church of God . . . acknowledge[s] that Jesus Christ is alone worthy and able to unfold and execute all the mysteries and counsels of God." The celebration of redemption is linked with the celebration of exaltation of those redeemed: "We shall reign on the earth." Of this, Matthew Henry points out:

⌛ PRETERIST

The taking of the scroll by the Lamb provokes an outburst of worship and praise in heaven, and a **new song** (v. 9) is introduced. In Revelation 4:11, they had sung an "old song" of praise to God for His older work of creating all things. The new song praises Him for His new work of redemption in Christ. This worship is accompanied by the priestly

138

FUTURIST

The appearance of the Lamb to open the scroll marks the beginning of the end of the present age. With the breaking of each seal, His Second Coming is brought another step nearer. The mention of **the prayers of the saints** (v. 8) reminds us that for almost two thousand years the church has been praying, in accordance with Christ's instructions, "Thy kingdom come; Thy will be done on earth as it is in heaven." The breaking of the seals paves the way for the fulfillment of this age-long desire of the saints to see the kingdom of God established.

The reign of the saints **on the earth** (v. 10)—as opposed to "in heaven"—is a reference to the millennial reign of the saints with Christ after He has returned to earth to establish His kingdom. Henry Morris writes: "Three times in the book of Revelation it is said that believers are to be made kings and priests (Rev. 1:6; 5:10; 20:6). These functions apply particularly in the millennial kingdom, when there is still need for them."

IDEALIST

This is the fulfillment of Daniel 7:9–14, where the One like the Son of Man approaches the Ancient of Days to receive dominion and a kingdom. Incense represents **the prayers of the saints** (v. 8; cf. Ps. 141:2), which saints are represented by the twenty-four elders offering them in this vision. The **new song** (v. 9) is the response of the redeemed to God's new redemptive acts in Christ in establishing the New Covenant, even as the older song of Moses (Exodus 15) was the response of the redeemed to God's older acts of redemption, associated with the Exodus and the establishment of the Old Covenant. This new song is the song of the church throughout the present age. In contrast to the song sung in 4:11, which praised God's work in creation, this song focuses on God's work of redeeming men from every nation through Christ. The royal priesthood of saints now spiritually **reign on the earth** (v. 10) through "their worship, their prayers and their witness in word and deed" (Morey).

REVELATION 5:7–10

HISTORICIST *(continued)*

Every ransomed slave is not immediately preferred to honour; he thinks it is a great favor to be restored to liberty. But when the elect of God were made slaves by sin and Satan, in every nation of the world, Christ not only purchased their liberty for them, but the highest honour and preferment, *made them kings and priests . . . and they shall reign on the earth.*

This **reign on earth** (v. 10) is taken either in the postmillennial sense to mean an ascendancy of Christianity in this world—the kings and governors being all Christians—prior to the Second Coming (Adam Clarke, Albert Barnes), or in the amillennial sense of a spiritual reign of the saints over their own spirits (no longer as slaves of sin) in the spiritual kingdom at the present time—the apparent view of Matthew Henry, along with many others.

PRETERIST *(continued)*

worship form of the offering up of **incense** (v. 8), which here represents **the prayers of the saints**—most likely the Christians who are being persecuted and are pleading for deliverance (cf. 6:10). This deliverance comes when their persecutors in Jerusalem are judged, after the seven seals of the scroll are broken. Making the redeemed **kings and priests** (v. 10), or as the more ancient manuscripts have it, "a kingdom and priests," implies that the original kingdom of priests, Israel (Exod. 19:5–6), has been done away with and replaced by the Church (cf. Heb. 7:12; 8:13).

⏳ FUTURIST *(continued)*

According to dispensational expectations, many unsaved people will live on
earth during the Millennium, and the
saints will reign over these people from
their headquarters in Jerusalem (cf.
Luke 19:17).

ANGELS AND CREATION JOIN THE SONG

REVELATION 5:11–14

[11]Then I looked, and I heard the voice of many angels around the throne, the living creatures, and the elders; and the number of them was ten thousand times ten thousand, and thousands of thousands, [12]saying with a loud voice: "Worthy is the Lamb who was slain to receive power and riches and wisdom, and strength and honor and glory and blessing!" [13]And every creature which is in heaven and on the earth and under the earth and such as are in the sea, and all that are in them, I heard saying: "Blessing and honor and glory and power be to Him who sits on the throne, and to the Lamb, forever and ever!" [14]Then the four living creatures said, "Amen!" And the twenty-four elders fell down and worshiped Him who lives forever and ever.

HISTORICIST

Clarke rightly observes that Christ receives the same praise as does God, which would be idolatry if He were not God Himself. On these verses, Henry writes:

> Indeed, it is just matter of joy to all the world to see that God does not deal with men in a way of absolute power and strict justice, but in a way of grace and mercy through the Redeemer. . . . All the world has reason to rejoice in this. The song of praise . . . consists of three parts, one part sung by the church, another by the church and the angels, the third by every creature.

Barnes notes:

PRETERIST

The song of 4:11 was sung by the twenty-four elders alone. In the song of 5:9–10, they were joined by the four living creatures. Now **many angels** (v. 11), numbering into millions, add their voices in attributing glory to the Lamb. This is the second song sung to the Lamb in this chapter. In the first (v. 9), He was declared to be "worthy to take the scroll and to open its seals." In the second (v. 12), He is proclaimed worthy to receive His due, described in the form of a sevenfold doxology. He is thus "doubly worthy"—first, to unleash judgments on His persecutors (i.e., by breaking the seals), and second, to get for Himself His rightful glory. Finally,

⧖ FUTURIST

The "myriads of myriads and chiliads of chiliads" of **angels** (v. 11, literally), who now join the song are not a literal number, but a way of saying "innumerable" angels. God's faithful angels (in contrast to those that fell) are countless. This language recalls that of Daniel 7:10—"A thousand thousands ministered to Him; ten thousand times ten thousand stood before Him." Compare also Psalm 68:17—"The chariots of God are twenty thousand, even thousands of thousands."

Those things attributed to Christ by the singing multitude speak not of His First Coming, which was in weakness and humiliation, but of His Second Coming, which is in **power . . . and strength and honor and glory** (v. 12).

When we are told that **every creature** (v. 13) in heaven, earth, and the sea now sing of the glory of God, this "must refer," writes Morris, "either to holy angels appointed to serve in these regions, or else to the animal creation—more likely the latter." That the creation glorifies God is declared in Psalm 19 and again in Psalm 148:7–10: "Praise the Lord from the earth, You great sea creatures, . . . beasts and all cattle; creeping things and flying fowl." Morris qualifies this statement, as seems necessary, "with the implied exception, no doubt, of those evil ones from whom the world is to be redeemed." ⧖

⧖ IDEALIST

The worship offered by the entire cosmos is equally **to Him who sits on the throne, and to the Lamb** (v.13). The frequent association of Christ with God, in this manner, in Revelation is a basis for the doctrine of Christ's deity. The Lamb is closely associated with the One on the throne repeatedly, in a manner that can only suggest comparable dignity—something that could never be afforded to any finite and created entity.

One example of why taking a literal approach to Revelation is problematic can be seen here, where every created thing in the universe is said to be singing God's praises. **Every creature** (v. 13) would have to include humans, yet many of them are still cursing and blaspheming throughout the judgments that follow. The vision succeeds in obtaining its desired effect, however, for one can hardly help but be thrilled when reading this description and picturing the scene as John experienced it. What a contrast to his circumstances on Patmos, to which he must have become oblivious by this time! ⧖

HISTORICIST *(CONTINUED)*

The whole universe, therefore, is sublimely represented as in a state of profound adoration, waiting for the developments to follow on the opening of the mysterious volume. All feel an interest in it; all feel that the secret is with God; all feel that there is but One who can open this volume; and all gather around, in the most reverential posture, awaiting the disclosure of the great mystery. 🕰

PRETERIST *(CONTINUED)*

every created being in the universe joins in this rising crescendo of praise and worship to both **Him who sits on the throne** and **the Lamb** (v. 13). When the praises have reached their highest point, **the four living creatures** add their **Amen!** (v. 14), and the **elders** fall on their faces. After all of this dramatic praise, it would seem difficult for the following chapters to avoid being anticlimactic—but they somehow manage to overcome this difficulty! 🕰

THE FIRST SEAL: THE FIRST HORSEMAN

REVELATION 6:1–2

[1]Now I saw when the Lamb opened one of the seals; and I heard one of the four living creatures saying with a voice like thunder, "Come and see." [2] And I looked, and behold, a white horse. He who sat on it had a bow; and a crown was given to him, and he went out conquering and to conquer.

HISTORICIST

The **white horse** (v. 2) and rider of the first seal refer to the period of Roman imperialism from the death of Domitian (AD 96) to the peace made by Commodus with the Germans in AD 180. This was the period of the five good emperors: Nerva (96–98); Trajan (98–117); Hadrian (117–138); and the two Anto-

PRETERIST

Jay Adams, following Pieters, suggests that the seven seals are in a row on the overlapping lip of the document, thus rendering it impossible even to begin opening the scroll until all seven seals are removed. In this view, nothing happens Historicistly until the seventh seal is broken in 8:1:

FUTURIST

With the breaking of the first **seal** (v. 1), the Tribulation begins. There are some *futurists* (e.g., Kuyper, Ladd, Morris), who see this rider on the **white horse** (v. 2) as Christ. Similarly, Ladd interprets this rider as the proclamation of the gospel in all the world. White, he argues, is always a symbol of Christ, something associated with Christ, or of spiritual victory. F. A. Jennings rejects this adamantly:

> The whole context and character of these seals absolutely forbid our thinking of this rider being the Lord Jesus, as so many affirm. His reign shall not bring war, famine, and strife in its train.[9]

He suggests that the rider "may be a personification of government or rule in the last days in the hands of Gentiles."

IDEALIST

As each of the first four seals is broken, **one of the four living creatures** (v. 1) says "Come" (preferred textually by most rather than **Come and see**— (v. 1). The call is not for John to come and see, since he need not go anywhere in order to see the visions, but the call is to the respective horsemen, emphasizing the divine origin of the events they represent.

According to Biederwolf, "Almost all scholars down to AD 150 took the image as a symbol of the preached gospel and its success." This is still the view of many modern commentators, including Alford, Hendriksen, and Hailey. Hendriksen writes: "Our Lord is riding forth victoriously, conquering and to conquer. That, in all probability, is the meaning of the rider on the white horse."

⧗ HISTORICIST *(continued)*

nines, Antoninus Pius (138–161) and Marcus Antoninus Aurelius (161–180). These five expanded Rome by military conquest until occupying most of the territories formerly ruled by the three preceding empires, Babylon, Medo-Persia, and Greece.

After noting that the Christians of John's day would probably have expected an immediate judgment from God upon Rome, Elliott writes:

> The first symbol under which the Roman people was represented . . . represented it somewhat strangely under the colour of triumph, prosperity, and health in the body politic . . . advancing the limits and the greatness of the empire.

The **bow** (v. 2) in hand may refer to the fact that Nerva (and the dynasty he established) was not of Roman but of Cretan descent. The Cretans were known as a race of bowmen, a fact commemorated on their coins by a figure of a Cretan with a bow in his hand.

Historian Gibbon refers to this period as the "Golden Age" of the Roman Empire. Toynbee has called it the "Indian Summer" of Rome's greatness. Barnes writes, "It was in general a period of prosperity, of triumph, of conquest— well represented by the horseman on the white horse going forth to conquest." In support of this he cites from Gibbon's *The Decline and Fall of the Roman Empire:* "If a

⧗ PRETERIST *(continued)*

A careful study of the passage shows that during the seal-breaking, no action takes place. The most that chapters 6 and 7 do is introduce the reader to the main characters, forces, and circumstances with which the rest of the section is concerned. They are preparatory to the action which will take place once the book is opened.

Others believe that, with the breaking of the first seal, the progression of events leading to the destruction of Jerusalem (in AD 70) begins. Horses represent war. The first four seals, when broken, release horses with their riders, hence, warfare and its accompaniments. David S. Clark writes:

> There is no reason for assuming that these four seals or four horses are successive events to the extent of representing successive ages. It is not true to fact that conquest comes in one age, war in another, famine in another, and death in another. They all belong to the same age; they are parts of the same affair; they all go together, conquest, war, famine, death. And if these symbols point to any specific time there is every reason to believe that they point to the very period in which John was writing and in which his churches were living; and that they had specific reference to the last days of the Jewish state, at the destruction of Jerusalem.

FUTURIST *(continued)*

Similarly, Mounce sees this seal as a symbol of conquest and militarism and invasion from without.

Most *futurists* (e.g., Walvoord, Ryrie, Lindsey, and others) believe that the **white horse** (v. 2) and its rider represent the Antichrist riding forth to conquer the world. The **crown given to him** (v. 2) is not a symbol of legitimate sovereignty (for then the word for crown would be *diadēma*), but a crown acquired by conquest (*stephanos*). Who "gives" the Antichrist these victories and this power? It is the dragon Satan (cf. Rev. 13:2 and 2 Thess. 2:8–10). Satan once told Christ that all the kingdoms of the world were his to give to whomever he wished (Luke 4:6). Here we see the one to whom Satan finally gives these kingdoms.

Gaebelein distinguishes between this rider and the Antichrist, though the things he says about this rider are the things most *futurists* would apply to the Antichrist:

> The rider here is a great counterfeit leader, not the personal Antichrist, but the little horn which Daniel saw coming out of the ten-horned beast (Daniel vii). We are now in the most solemn and ominous times the world has ever known. Many are the voices calling for a European confederacy and for some great leader, another Napoleon. . . . And the Lord will permit such a one to come, deceiving the

IDEALIST *(continued)*

However, Wilson expresses doubt about this identification:

> The rider on the white horse is often identified with Christ or the progress of the gospel in the world, but the Lamb who opens the seal cannot be expected to reappear as the rider thus sent forth.

Hendriksen answers this objection:

> An objection often advanced is that Christ cannot at the same time be the One who opens the seals and the contents of the first seal. But why should this be considered impossible? By the same process of reasoning should we not reach the conclusion that Christ cannot lay His right hand on John (1:17), for in that right hand He is holding seven stars (1:16)?

To many *idealists*, the four horsemen represent the universal sequence of conquest, war, famine and death, oft repeated in history, but here revealed as proceeding from God's sovereign purpose in judging a corrupt humanity. On this view, the **white horse** (v. 2) and rider represent the generic concept of military conquest, at whatever time or place in history it may occur, and is seen as God's way of raising up and removing kings (Dan. 2:21). The ebb and flow of political empires are in the hand of God. He does not always give such government as a people would prefer,

⌛ HISTORICIST *(continued)*

man were called to fix the period in the history of the world during which the condition of the human race was most happy and prosperous, he would, without hesitation, name that which elapsed from the death of Domitian to the accession of Commodus."

Alternatively, a few *historicists* (e.g., Matthew Henry and Adam Clarke) interpret the breaking of the seven seals essentially as do the *preterists.* That is, the whole vision applies to the fall of Jerusalem in AD 70. In the breaking of the first seal, they are inclined to see the progress of the gospel. Thus, Matthew Henry writes, "The convictions impressed by the word of God are sharp arrows."

The Treasury of Scripture Knowledge has comments that "this seems to be the representation of the person and dignity of Christ, and the mild and beneficent triumphs of his Gospel over all the powers of paganism."

Seventh-Day Adventist Pinkoski writes:

> Now because the first horseman with the crown carried a bow, that does not necessarily mean he is a bloodthirsty warrior—arrows can easily carry messages, and the message of Christianity spread fast in the first century. ⌂

⌛ PRETERIST *(continued)*

Since the holocaust of AD 70 was preceded by more than three years of war between the Jews and the Romans, some take this rider on the white horse to be Vespasian or Titus at the head of the Roman armies. Russell writes: "In this first scene we see the Roman invader advancing to the combat. Yet the war has not actually begun." He is **given** (v. 2) his crown (i.e., victories) by God Himself, who is sending these calamities upon the apostate city that killed the prophets and crucified Christ. "These are the days of [God's] vengeance" (Luke 21:22).

Alternatively, the rider could be Christ, seen as going forth to war against His murderers through the calamities about to be revealed. Each horseman is summoned by the heavenly authority, saying, "Come!"—a textual reading that many prefer to **Come and see** (vv. 1, 3, 5, 7). ⌂

⧗ FUTURIST *(continued)*

world so that they will say "peace and safety" (1 Thessalonians v:1–3). This coming leader of the revived Roman empire will go forth to conquer and become its political head.

Walvoord clearly has the same cross-references in mind, though he equates them all with the Antichrist himself:

> The rider on the white horse is none other than the "prince that shall come" of Daniel 9:26, who is to head up the revived Roman Empire and ultimately become the world ruler. . . . He is Satan's masterpiece and the counterfeit of all that Christ is or claims to be . . . the world ruler of the tribulation, the same individual described as the beast out of the sea in Revelation 13. 🕮

⧗ IDEALIST *(continued)*

but may give them oppressors that will serve His ends of judging a wicked society (Prov. 17:11).

Herschel Hobbs' *historicist background* approach sees the horsemen in the manner just described except that, in addition to the general meaning, they include the historical manifestation of these principles in John's own day (which he takes to be the time of Domitian). That is, the horsemen, in addition to representing conquest, war, famine, and death *in general,* also focus on these forces as agents of the coming downfall of the Roman persecuting power, thus encouraging the persecuted readers of John's day. 🕮

THE SECOND SEAL; THE SECOND HORSEMAN

REVELATION 6:3—4

³When He opened the second seal, I heard the second living creature saying, "Come and see." ⁴Another horse, fiery red, went out. And it was granted to the one who sat on it to take peace from the earth [or land], and that people should kill one another; and there was given to him a great sword.

⌛ HISTORICIST

This rider bears **a great sword**, and like the previous rider, is associated with the Roman Empire. It may be mere coincidence that Paul, writing of the Roman power said, "he does not bear the sword in vain" (Rom.13:4).

Most historicists relate **the second seal** (v. 3) to the period from the accession of Commodus (AD 180) to the accession of Diocletian (AD 284). As Elliott says, "It was the period of civil wars and bloodshed in the Roman Empire." This summary comment is expanded in Sismondi's *Fall of the Roman Empire:*

> With Commodus commenced the third and most calamitous period. It lasted ninety-two years, from 192 to 284. During that period, thirty-two emperors, and twenty-seven pretenders alternately hurled each other from the throne by incessant civil warfare [which]

⌛ PRETERIST

The second horseman represents the loss of peace from the "land" (a preferred translation to **earth**—v. 4) of Israel. Besides the war that the Jews were fighting against the Romans (suggested by the first seal), there were civil wars among the Jews themselves. J. Stuart Russell explains:

> The Jewish war, under Vespasian, commenced at the furthest distance from Jerusalem in Galilee, and gradually drew nearer and nearer to the doomed city. The Romans were not the only agents in the work of slaughter that depopulated the land; hostile factions among the Jews themselves turned their arms against one another, so that it might be said that "every man's hand was against his brother."

Josephus describes the situation in these terms:

⌛ FUTURIST

The **fiery red** (v. 4) color of this horse suggests bloodshed, and speaks of a time of war that comes upon the earth as the Tribulation progresses. Walvoord writes:

> The constant tension among nations and the ambitions of men have their climax in this period before Christ comes. Though 'wars and rumors of wars' (Matt. 24:6) are characteristic of the age, it is evident that warfare occupies a large place in the consummation of the age with a resultant great loss of life. There apparently is a series of wars, the greatest of which is under way at the time of the second coming.

Hal Lindsey identifies the rider on the red horse with Russia, with her Arab allies in the Middle East, attacking Israel (Ezekiel 38; Daniel 11), and places this at the midpoint of the Tribulation. Lindsey writes: "The war escalates until it involves all the major powers on the earth and becomes the greatest battle in the history of mankind—the Battle of Armageddon." Ray Stedman writes: "Understandably, many Bible scholars today view this 'large sword' as a symbol of the awesome power of the nuclear bomb." After raising the question of whether Revelation really does describe modern-day warfare, he concludes:

> We have to admit that it is only in our century, with its efficient,

⌛ IDEALIST

If the white horse represented conquest in general, then the **fiery red** (v. 4) horse represents war in general, or civil war in particular.

Empires established by conquest often dissolve as the result of the lack of internal solidarity, leading to revolution and revolt. The horrors and carnage of war are another means by which God judges sinful societies. "If a trumpet is blown in a city, will not the people be afraid? If there is calamity in a city, will not the LORD have done it?" (Amos 3:6). As the story of civilization is the story of war and conflict, the judgment of God can be seen everywhere throughout man's career. Friedrich von Schiller wrote: 'The history of the world is the judgment of the world.'[10]

Applying the principle to the concerns of the original readers, Hobbs points out that the Roman Empire, built through warfare, "would ultimately perish by it," thus fulfilling Jesus' axiom that "all who take the sword will perish by the sword" (Matt. 26:52).

On the other hand, Hendriksen and Hailey, who saw the white horse as Christ riding forth in the perpetration of the gospel, now understand the red horse to represent the persecution of the church that inevitably follows the spread of Christianity into heathen lands. Their argument rests partly on the parallel they see between this vision and the statement of Jesus in Matthew

⧗ HISTORICIST *(continued)*

taught the world on what a frail foundation the virtue of the Antonines had placed the felicity of the empire(vol. 1:36).

The **fiery red** (v. 4) horse rider thus depicts these civil conflicts that spelled the beginning of the end of the Roman Empire.

Alternatively, *historicist* Adam Clarke, agrees with *preterists* at this point, understanding the phrase **to take peace from the earth** (v. 4) as meaning "to deprive Judea of all tranquillity.[*sic*] . . . This was literally the case with the Jews, while besieged by the Romans." Also in possible agreement is Matthew Henry:

> The next three seals give us a sad prospect of great and desolating judgments with which God punishes those who either refuse or abuse the everlasting gospel. . . . Some understand them of the persecutions that befell the church of Christ, and others of the destruction of the Jews.

⧗ PRETERIST *(continued)*

Every city was divided into two armies encamped one against another . . . so the daytime was spent in shedding of blood, and the night in fear." (*Wars* 2: 18:2)

In the end, during the siege of Jerusalem, there was deadly fighting among three or four antagonistic Jewish camps within the besieged city. The Jews had rejected the Prince of Peace, who had said, while weeping over Jerusalem, "If you had known . . . the things that make for your peace! But now they are hidden from your eyes" (Luke 19:42). The next words Jesus spoke predicted the Roman armies invading the land and leveling the city of Jerusalem (Luke 19:43–44). What could speak more directly to the fulfillment of this threat than for Revelation to speak, as here, of one sent **to take peace** (v. 4) from the land? Zechariah also had predicted this as a consequence of the Jews' rejection of Christ (Zech. 11:10–14).

⌛ FUTURIST *(continued)*

high-tech approach to killing, that the fulfillment of these terrible predictions could even come about.

Henry Morris believes that this vision also speaks of a time of civil wars erupting within nations, organized crime running rampant, and individual feuds generating waves of murders. 🔷

⌛ IDEALIST *(continued)*

10:34: "I did not come to bring peace but a sword." In that passage, Jesus was warning the disciples about opposition they would receive for their loyalty to Him.

The word **kill** (v. 2) is *sphatto*, a word used elsewhere of the killing of Christ the Lamb (cf. 5:6) and of those whose souls were seen "under the altar" (6:9). It properly means "slaughter" and thus could point to the sacrificial character of the faithful martyrs' deaths. 🔷

THE THIRD SEAL; THE THIRD HORSEMAN

REVELATION 6:5—6

[5]When He opened the third seal, I heard the third living creature say, "Come and see." So I looked, and behold, a black horse, and he who sat on it had a pair of scales in his hand. [6]And I heard a voice in the midst of the four living creatures saying, "A quart of wheat for a denarius, and three quarts of barley for a denarius; and do not harm the oil and the wine."

⌛ HISTORICIST

Many see **the black horse** (v. 5) as the fiscal oppression imposed by some of the emperors of the third century. Taxes could be paid either in money or in produce—particularly in grain, oil, and wine. For the purpose of paying these taxes, produce was given a value of monetary equivalence. This is possibly the meaning of the statement, **A quart of wheat for a denarius, and three quarts of barley for a denarius** (v. 6). Elliott believes that the phrase **do not harm the oil and the wine** (v. 6) would be better translated "be not unjust in the oil and the wine."

Caracalla (218–222) granted citizenship to all free men in the empire, but only so he could tax them more. Gibbon refers to "the land tax, the capitation, and the heavy contributions of corn, wine, oil, and wheat, exacted from the provinces for the use of the

⌛ PRETERIST

The **scales** in the hand of the rider of the **black horse** (v. 5) seem to indicate that men must eat their bread by measure, as God warned the Jews that they would have to do if they rebelled against Him (Leviticus 26:26). This horse represents famine or shortage of food. The color black also is reminiscent of famine: "Our skin was black like an oven, because of the terrible famine" (Lam. 5:10). The **denarius** (v. 6) was a day's wage for the average laborer. In return for his work he is to get a mere **quart of wheat,** or about one person's daily ration. Thus a man would have to work a full day just to earn enough to fill his own belly. To feed a family, he must turn to cheaper grain, which costs only one-third as much.

The Jews in Jerusalem suffered terrible food shortages during the Roman siege. Though initially there was enough food stored up to last a long

⧗ FUTURIST

Most *futurists* understand this horseman to represent famine conditions brought on by the warfare in the previous seal during the future Tribulation. Few fail to point out that the **quart of wheat** (v. 6) mentioned was a man's approximate daily need for sustenance, while the amount of money (**a denarius**) was what a common laborer would earn in a day. Thus the expression meant that it would consume a day's wages to buy a day's supply of wheat, or the same price could buy enough cheaper grain to feed a few more mouths.

Henry Morris, taking a different course, sees in this seal a reference to the power of commerce to generate prosperity or calamity, inflation or depression, opulence or starvation. International capitalists will take advantage of the period of peace to gain full control of the oil, food, and money resources of the world.

This is similar to the view of Ray Stedman:

> Another possible explanation of the third seal is economic upheaval—inflation, recession, panic. . . . Inflation may well be the justification the Antichrist will use to impose rigid controls over buying and selling, as we shall see in Revelation 13.

On the enigmatic **do not harm the oil and the wine** (v. 6), Ryrie writes:

⧗ IDEALIST

Possibly as a consequence of war (the red horse), or simply as the result of God-ordained drought (Deut. 28:23–24), famine comes as a judgment upon sinners. It is one of the "four severe judgments" (Ezek. 14:21) by which God takes vengeance on corrupt societies. "When I send against them the terrible arrows of famine which shall be for destruction, which I will send to destroy you, I will increase the famine upon you and cut off your supply of bread" (Ezek. 5:16). In modern societies, this may simply refer to economic disruption and inflation.

A **denarius** (v. 6) was the average laborer's daily wage. Wilson explains:

> At these 'famine' prices, which were twelve times the ordinary rate, a man's daily wage would only buy enough wheat to support himself, and if he wished to provide something for his family he would have to buy barley instead. The command not to hurt the oil and the wine limits the extent of the famine. The drought is severe enough to destroy most of the cereal crops, but the deep-rooted olive and the vine are not seriously affected.

A common explanation of the reference to **the oil and the wine** (v. 6) is that these constitute luxuries, whereas grain is a staple of survival. Even in famine times, the rich somehow man-

⧗ HISTORICIST *(continued)*

court, the army and the capital" of this period. He also says, "The great body of Caracalla's subjects were oppressed by the aggravated taxes, and every part of the Empire crushed under the weight of his iron scepter."

Barnes also sees this seal as representing general economic deprivation caused by heavy taxation, but of a later period. Upon the abdication of Diocletian, Galerius assumed the title of Augustus and greedily raised real estate taxes to an unprecedented level. Oppressive laws demanded that land be heavily taxed based on its productivity. This led landowners to deliberately reduce grain production to avoid the high taxation. The practice of destroying crops to avoid taxes became so widespread that the government issued an edict forbidding the destruction of olive trees and grapevines (**do not harm the oil and the wine**—v. 6). These details are recorded by Gibbon and Lactantius (cited by Barnes).

Some *historicists* (e.g., Clarke and Henry) go along with the *preterists* in identifying this seal with the food shortages in besieged Jerusalem in AD 70. Adam Clarke mentions some commentators, known to him, who placed this dearth earlier still, identifying it with the famines predicted by the prophet Agabus (Acts 11:28), which, we are told, came upon the Jews in the time of Emperor Claudius. ⧗

⧗ PRETERIST *(continued)*

time, the warring factions in the city, out of sheer spite, regularly destroyed the grain stores of the opposing factions! Thus food became so scarce that Josephus records at least one case of a mother eating her infant (compare Deut. 28:53 and 2 Kings 6:28f.). It was with reference to this time that Jesus had said, "But woe to those who are . . . nursing babies in those days!" (see Luke 21:20–23; 23:28–29). Consider the verbal parallels between this horseman's decree and this description in Josephus:

> Many there were indeed who sold what they had for one quart; it was of wheat, if they were of the richer sort, but of barley, if they were poorer. (*Wars* 5: 10:2)

The statement, **do not harm the oil and the wine** (v. 6) could allude to the fact that some sacrilegious Jews pillaged the oil and wine from the temple. Josephus writes that John Gischala, the leader of one of the factions, confiscated the sacred vessels of the temple:

> Accordingly, drawing the sacred wine and oil, which the priests kept for pouring on the burnt offerings, and which was deposited in the inner temple, [John] distributed them among his adherents, who consumed without horror more than a hin in anointing themselves and drinking. (*Wars* 5: 13:6) ⧗

⌛ FUTURIST *(continued)*

Apparently luxury items will not be in short supply, but of course most people will not be able to afford them. This situation will only serve to taunt the populace in their impoverished state."

Ironside also believes the oil and wine represent luxuries. He writes: "The rich seem to escape a part of this judgment for the oil and the wine, the luxuries of the well to do, are not to be hurt." He adds: "They will receive their share of judgment later."

Walvoord does not see the oil and the wine as luxuries, pointing out that these were considered staples in the ordinary household in biblical times:

> There would be no money left to buy other things, such as oil or wine, which were considered essential in biblical times. To put it in ordinary language, the situation would be such that one would have to spend a day's wages for a loaf of bread with no money left to buy anything else. The symbolism therefore indicates a time of famine when life will be reduced to its barest necessities. ⌛

⌛ IDEALIST *(continued)*

age to maintain their luxurious lifestyles. Wilcock points out that this is one indicator that the third seal "stands for partial hardship rather than total famine."

Hobbs gives another angle on the expression **do not harm the oil and the wine** (v. 6), pointing out that, in AD 92, Domitian had endeavored to interfere with the cultivation of grapes in the provinces. The angry reactions of the people around Smyrna influenced the emperor to abandon the policy and not interfere with wine production. Thus, "do not harm . . . the wine" would convey to the Asian Christians that they need not fear for their vines, for Domitian would not hurt them. Moffatt considers this detail to be a "watermark of the Domitianic date" of the writing of Revelation.

An entirely different approach to the seals is that of Hendriksen and Hailey, who understand the second and third seals to be consequences that follow upon the first seal, which they took to be the advance of the gospel in the earth. The second seal represented bloody persecutions of the believers, whereas this third seal speaks of economic persecutions of the same. ⌛

THE FOURTH SEAL; THE FOURTH HORSEMAN

REVELATION 6:7–8

[7]When He opened the fourth seal, I heard the voice of the fourth living creature saying, "Come and see."[8]So I looked, and behold, a pale horse. And the name of him who sat on it was Death, and Hades followed with him. And power was given to them over a fourth of the earth, to kill with sword, with hunger, with death, and by the beasts of the earth.

⌛ HISTORICIST

The time of fulfillment, according to Barnes, is the twenty years from AD 248 to 268, encompassing the reigns of Decius, Gallus, Aemilianus, Valerian, and Gallienus. Barnes quotes Gibbon:

> From the great secular games celebrated by Philip to the death of the emperor Gallienus, there elapsed twenty years of shame and misfortune. During this calamitous period of time . . . every province of the Roman world was afflicted by barbarous invaders and military tyrants, and the ruined empire seemed to approach the last and fatal moment of its dissolution.

Gibbon also writes that, from the years 248 to 296, "five thousand persons died daily in Rome; and many towns that escaped the hands of the barbarians were entirely depopulated."

⌛ PRETERIST

The Greek word translated **pale** (v. 8) actually denotes a pallid yellowish-green. **To kill . . . with death** means "with pestilence," as the Hebrew word for pestilence, used about fifty times in the Old Testament, is translated in the Septuagint more than thirty times by the Greek word *thanatos* ("death").

Because of the internal fighting and starvation of the Jews, conditions in besieged Jerusalem in AD 70 could readily be described in the terms found here. The reference to the means of death, **sword, hunger, death** [i.e., *pestilence*], and **beasts of the earth** (v. 8), are a deliberate echo of Ezekiel 14:21, where "sword and famine and wild beasts and pestilence" are called God's "four severe judgments on Jerusalem." In Ezekiel, God used these means to inflict judgment at the time of the destruction of Jerusalem by the Babylonians in 586 BC,

FUTURIST

Applying these seals to the end times Tribulation, Kuyper writes:

> Death and Hell now attack human society, and the great destruction sets in, the first effect of which is bewilderment and general havoc, as a fourth part of the inhabitants of the earth is destroyed by the sword or by starvation or by deadly disease or by wild beasts.

Walvoord adds:

> The area covered by this judgment, described as the earth (Gr. gē), though sometimes only of the promised land given to Israel, is a general word referring to the inhabited world and in this context apparently extends to the entire earth. . . . Treated geographically it would be equivalent to the destruction of more than the entire population of Europe and South America.

Because of the current world population being so great, one fourth of the inhabitants would represent a number larger than those destroyed in Noah's day. Therefore, this would be the "Great Tribulation" of unprecedented magnitude spoken of by Jesus in Matthew 24:21. Since "Great Tribulation" is the term that technically refers to only the final three and a half years of the seven-year Tribulation, some (e.g., Walvoord) believe that these seals apply strictly to that end period. Others place

IDEALIST

The **pale horse** and its rider represent **Death** (v. 8) by various causes: sword, famine, death, and beasts of the earth. In a sense, this summarizes all four horsemen. **Hades** (v. 8), the place of the dead, follows close behind to receive the dead.

The first four seals are thus summarized by Swete: "This series of pictures repeats itself in history, and the militarism and lust of conquest . . . are among the forces set loose by the hand of Christ to prepare the way for His coming and the final publication of the secrets of the Sealed Book." The reference to the death of **a fourth of the earth** (v. 8) emphasizes the fact that we are not at this point seeing a global catastrophe, but only recurring instances of geographically limited judgments. Wilcock writes:

> The wiping out of a quarter of the human race sounds like a disaster of the first magnitude, until one realizes that nothing has been said to indicate that this is a single catastrophic event. After all, every man dies sooner or later, and what is probably meant here is that a sizable proportion of those deaths are the unnecessary ones caused by war and famine and kindred evils.

The recurring patterns suggested by these seals had a contemporary relevance to the original readers in that

⧖ HISTORICIST *(continued)*

Does this not correspond well with the figure of Death and Hades riding rampant in the earth?

Of the four judgments listed in verse 8, **sword, with hunger, with death** (pestilence), **and by the beasts of the earth,** Gibbon documents that three—sword, famine, and pestilence—did indeed wreak havoc in the empire and estimates that half (not the conservative *fourth* of Scripture) the human population of earth was killed in this period. Eusebius adds information about the **beasts of the earth** [dogs]:

> Death waged a desolating war with . . . famine and pestilence . . . Men wasted away to mere skeletons, stumbled hither and thither like mere shadows, trembling and tottering. They fell down in the midst of the streets. . . . Some indeed were already the food for dogs. (*Ecclesiastical History*, Book III, chap. 6.)

Elliott prefers to translate **a fourth of the earth** (v. 8) as does the Latin Vulgate, "over the four parts of the earth," referring to the four sections into which the Roman Empire was divided at that time. ⧖

⧖ PRETERIST *(continued)*

which was a precursor of this event, similar in detail and in significance, in AD 70.

Josephus describes the carnage and death in Jerusalem during the siege in the following terms:

> So all hope of escaping was now cut off from the Jews, together with their liberty of going out of the city. Then did the famine widen its progress, and devoured the people by whole houses and families; the upper rooms were full of women and children that were dying by famine; and the lanes of the city were full of the dead bodies of the aged. The seditious . . . as not enduring the stench of the dead bodies . . . had them cast down from the walls into the valleys beneath. However, when Titus, in going his rounds along those valleys, saw them full of dead bodies, and the thick putrefaction running about them, he gave a groan . . . and such was the sad case of the city itself (*Wars* 5: 12:3–4). ⧖

FUTURIST *(continued)*

the beginning of the "Great Tribula-tion" at chapter 11.

IDEALIST *(continued)*

they predicted the means by which the Roman persecutors would meet their end.

Hailey and Hendriksen interpret the seals in connection with their ef-fects upon the church, in contrast to the later trumpet judgments of God upon the unbelieving world. Of the fourth seal with its four severe judgments, the sword, famine, pestilence, and wild beasts, Hendriksen writes: "These four, moreover, are symbolical of *all* univer-sal woes which believers suffer along with the rest of humanity throughout the entire dispensation."

THE FIFTH SEAL

REVELATION 6:9—11

[9] When He opened the fifth seal, I saw under the altar the souls of those who had been slain for the word of God and for the testimony which they held. [10]And they cried with a loud voice, saying, "How long, O Lord, holy and true, until You judge and avenge our blood on those who dwell on the earth?" [11]Then a white robe was given to each of them; and it was said to them that they should rest a little while longer, until both the number of their fellow servants and their brethren, who would be killed as they were, was completed.

⌛ HISTORICIST

Most *historicist* interpreters take this to be the ordeal of the church under Diocletian, whose reign began in 284 but who did not begin to persecute Christians until 303. Gibbon writes: "Perhaps it was represented to Diocletian, that the glorious work of the deliverance of the empire was left imperfect so long as an independent people [the Christians] were permitted to subsist and multiply in it."

Others give slightly different dates for the age of martyrs: "This seal seems a prediction of the terrible persecution of the church under Dioclesian (*sic*) and Maximian, from AD 270 to 304, which lasted longer, and was far more bloody, than any or all by which it was preceded, whence it was called 'the era of the martyrs'" (*Treasury of Scripture Knowledge*).

⌛ PRETERIST

As the blood of sacrificial animals was poured out at the foot of the altar (Lev. 4:7), so the **souls** of the martyrs (slain like animals by the Jewish priests) are seen **under the altar** (v.9). "The soul [Heb. *nephesh*] of the flesh is in the blood" (Lev. 17:11). Their blood cries out for vindication, as did the blood of Abel (Gen. 4:10). The fact that the martyrs are asking for the avenging of their blood upon **those who dwell on the earth** [or land] (v. 10) suggests that their persecutors were still alive on earth at the time John saw the vision. Prior to AD 70, the main persecutors of the righteous Jews and Christians were the leaders of the Jewish nation, headquartered in Jerusalem (Luke 13:33). These thoughts are brought together by Jesus when He predicted:

FUTURIST

During the Tribulation, many believers will experience martyrdom at the hands of multiple antagonists, including the beast (11:7; 13:7, 15), the great harlot (17:6; 18:24), and the general populus (16:6).

These souls **under the altar** (v. 9) are persons martyred during that period. "The introduction of these martyred dead in heaven at this point immediately after the fourth seal seems to imply that these martyrs have come from the tribulation scene on earth" (Walvoord). Gaebelein, despite the mention of "souls," contends that "They are risen from the dead and are in glory with redeemed bodies."

To the dispensationalist, this scene applies to a time after the Rapture of the church, and the martyrs cannot, therefore, be identified with Christians of the church era. Their cry for vengeance indicates that they stand on other than Christian ground. "Christians are not supplicating for vengeance on their foes. The prayer for vengeance refers us to the imprecatory Psalms prewritten by the Holy Spirit in anticipation of the final persecution of Jewish believers" (Gaebelein). It seems that anyone converted after the Rapture must be martyred, "except the remnant of Israel, who are sealed for protection" (Phillips).

IDEALIST

This vision reveals the present state of those who have already died for their faith. They were "judged according to men in the flesh, but live according to God in the spirit" (1 Pet. 4:6). The picture of the martyrs presented here emphasizes the sacrificial character of their deaths. Thus, their souls are **under the altar** (v. 9), where the blood of sacrificial victims was poured in the temple (Lev. 4:7). Hobbs writes:

> Like the Lamb they had had their throats cut—this is the meaning of "slain" here and in 5:6. But it is a symbolic word. We are not to understand that these peoples' throats were cut any more than was that of Jesus . . . These martyrs had been sacrificed because of their faithfulness.

Whether these martyrs "represent all who suffer in any way for Christ's sake" (Wilcock), or stand particularly for those slain by Domitian (as Hobbs thinks), the vision reminds us that the martyrs of Christ from every age live on before God. They anticipate eventual vindication, which is not complete until their murderers have been brought to justice. They are, however, consoled by the giving of white robes, meaning they are pure and incapable of defilement. They are at rest: "Blessed are the dead who die in the Lord from now on. 'Yes,' says the Spirit, 'that they may rest from

⧗ HISTORICIST *(continued)*

Many details of this persecution are recorded by Gibbon and Neander, cited by Barnes. Constantine's conversion occurred during the battle of Milvain Bridge, in 312, which made him the sole ruler of the Western Empire. The following year, he issued the Edict of Toleration, granting to "Christians and to all others full liberty of following that religion which each may choose." This was the official end of the era of martyrs in the Roman Empire.

Adam Clarke, still agreeing with the *preterists* at this point, holds this seal to apply to Christians who died under Jewish persecutions in the early years of the church. He writes concerning the expression, **those who dwell on the earth** (v. 10): "Probably meaning the persecuting Jews; they dwelt 'upon the land,' a form of speech by which Judea is often signified in the New Testament." ⧖

⧗ PRETERIST *(continued)*

That on you [Jerusalem] may come all the righteous blood shed on the earth, from the blood of righteous Abel to the blood of Zechariah . . . whom you murdered between the temple and the altar. . . . All these things will come upon this generation (Matt. 23:35f.).

The destruction of Jerusalem in that generation was the sentence of the divine Judge in response to the cries of the blood (souls) of the righteous ones slain by her leaders. Russell writes:

It is impossible not to be struck with the marked resemblance between the vision of the fifth seal and our Lord's parable of the unjust judge (Luke xviii. 1–8): 'And shall not God avenge his own elect, which cry day and night unto him, though he bear long with them? I tell you that he will avenge them speedily' . . . This is more than resemblance: it is identity. ⧖

⧗ FUTURIST *(continued)*

Whether the vision pertains to those slain only in the first half (Gaebelein, Ryrie) or the second half (Walvoord), or throughout the entire Tribulation period is a debated point.

Moorehead believes that the martyrs in this vision are indeed church Christians killed during the Tribulation, and Mounce sees the vision as an interpretation of Christian martyrdom.

⧗ IDEALIST *(continued)*

their labors, and their works follow them'" (Rev. 14:13).

If praying for vengeance, such as we find here, seems a sub-Christian sentiment, Beale points out that theirs is a "prayer that the reputation of God and his people be vindicated," and that "he will be considered unjust if he does not punish sin."[11]

THE SIXTH SEAL

REVELATION 6:12—17

¹²I looked when He opened the sixth seal, and behold, there was a great earth-quake; and the sun became black as sackcloth of hair, and the moon became like blood. ¹³And the stars of heaven fell to the earth, as a fig tree drops its late figs when it is shaken by a mighty wind. ¹⁴Then the sky receded as a scroll when it is rolled up, and every mountain and island was moved out of its place. ¹⁵And the kings of the earth, the great men, the rich men, the commanders, the mighty men, every slave and every free man, hid themselves in the caves and in the rocks of the mountains, ¹⁶ and said to the mountains and rocks, "Fall on us and hide us from the face of Him who sits on the throne and from the wrath of the Lamb! ¹⁷ For the great day of His wrath has come, and who is able to stand?"

⌛ HISTORICIST

These great apocalyptic signs may symbolize the fall of paganism to Christianity in the Roman Empire, associated with Constantine's accession and conversion. The earthquake (v. 12) is a prophetic metaphor for political or spiritual revolutions. **Sun** (v. 12), **moon** (v. 12), and **stars** (v. 13) represent earthly dignitaries, political authorities, and great "lights" in the political or religious "heavens." Elliott calls this the dissolution of the "Pagan firmament." He writes: "According to the usual scripture use of such terms, it was to be considered as representing the ruling department in the polity; and its luminaries as the actual rulers and governing powers therein." He continues:

⌛ PRETERIST

Russell writes:

> "This is . . . 'the great and terrible day of the Lord' predicted by Malachi, by John the Baptist, by St. Paul, by St. Peter, and, above all, by our Lord in His apocalyptic discourse on the Mount of Olives. . . . It is impossible to overlook the connection between the seventeenth verse and the language of Malachi iii. 2, 'But who may abide the day of his coming?'"

The vision depicts the end of the Jewish state and the fall of its leaders. David Clark writes:

> It may doubtless be taken for granted that these convulsions of nature were seen in vision and are not to be looked upon as actual

166

⏳ FUTURIST

Mounce sees this seal, and the catastrophes that go with it, to be heralding the beginning of the last days through great cosmic disturbances. For example, the **earthquake** (v. 12) was a regular feature of divine visitation (cf. Exod. 19:18; Isa. 2:19; Hag. 2:6). He does not commit himself to a strictly literal interpretation of the phenomena mentioned, but sees them as "signs in the heavens" that are both symbolic and literal. The reader is thus left wondering whether some of the phenomena are literal and some symbolic, or if they are literal, but with symbolic significance. The former of these possibilities is favored by Gaebelein:

> Most of it is symbolical, yet at the same time great physical phenomena are also involved. The earthquake possibly means a literal earthquake. . . . Everything is being shaken in this poor world. The civil and governmental powers on earth all go to pieces; every class from kings to slaves is affected by it and terrorized. The political and ecclesiastical world is going to pieces.

Ironside takes the vision symbolically. He writes:

> It is therefore not a worldwide earthquake . . . but rather the destruction of the present order— political, social, and ecclesiastical—reduced to chaos; the

⏳ IDEALIST

Almost all *idealist* interpreters recognize, in this seal, the end of the world at the second coming of Christ. Beale writes: "The judgment of the world is depicted with stock-in-trade OT imagery for the dissolution of the cosmos. This portrayal is based on a mosaic of OT passages that are brought together because of the cosmic metaphors of judgment that they have in common."[15]

He refers to "the quarry of texts from which the description has been drawn," listing as examples the following Old Testament texts: Psalm 68:7–8; Isaiah 13:10–13; 24:1–6, 19–23; 34:4; Jeremiah 4:23–28; Ezekiel 32:6–8; Joel 2:10,30–31; 3:15–16; Amos 8:8–9; and Habakkuk 3:6–11.

Some[16] consider this too early in the book to portray the final judgment of the world at the Second Coming of Christ, since, in their view, John's vision does not deal with this until Revelation 20:11–15.

These interpreters would see these calamities as representing the judgment of God upon those who were oppressing the Christians in John's day, i.e., the Roman Empire.

The more common view[17] however, is that we do have the Second Coming of Christ presented here. The events of the first five seals are social and political upheavals that recur often in history, but this "great day of His wrath" represents a climax of all the cycles of

⧗ HISTORICIST *(continued)*

The general intent of this vision does not seem to me to have been difficult to understand. It surely betokened some sudden and extraordinary *revolution in the Roman empire*, which would follow chronologically after the aera [*sic*] of martyrdoms depicted under the Seal preceding, a revolution arising from the triumph of the *christian* [*sic*] *cause* over its enemies, and in degree complete and universal. No *partial* change would answer to the strength of the symbolic phraseology.

Some relate this vision to the division of the empire in 395 between the East, under Honorious, and the West, under Arcadius. This is taken as a portent of the eventual fall of the empire, which did not occur until 476.

Barnes applies this seal differently, seeing in it the invasions of the Roman Empire by the northern hordes of Goths and Vandals, between 376 and 418. Thus he sees the sixth seal as fulfilled by the same events depicted in the early trumpet judgments that follow.

Adam Clarke waffles at this point between the view of the *preterists*, that this is AD 70, and that of other *historicists*. He writes: "All these things may literally apply to the final destruction of Jerusalem, and to the revolution which took place in the Roman Empire under Constantine the Great. Some apply them to the 'day of judgment'; but they

⧗ PRETERIST *(continued)*

occurrences. As no one would assume that the four horses actually rode over the earth, but were symbolical representations of things that were to happen, so these convulsions of nature were probably to be understood in the same way.

The symbols of cosmic collapse do seem strange to modern ears, but the same are commonly used in the Old Testament, as denoting the end of temporal empires in prophecy—e.g., of Babylon (Isa. 13:10), of Edom (Isa. 34:4). and of Egypt (Ezek. 32:7–8). The same terms are used by Jesus in predicting the disaster that would befall the Jewish nation in that generation (Matt. 24:29, 34). David Clark writes:

> I am not sure but that it is a feature of biblical symbolism to make sun, moon, and stars, and such phenomena to represent the strong social and political powers, or men in high places like kings, princes, or priests, or high officials of church and state. And in confirmation you will notice that the following verses refer to just such men, as if to be a sort of commentary on these symbols.

J. Stuart Russell, anticipating the objection that the fall of Jerusalem was not as catastrophic as the language of this seal would suggest, writes:

> Prophecy is poetry, and Oriental poetry also, in which gorgeous

FUTURIST *(continued)*

breaking down of all authority, and the breaking up of all established and apparently permanent institutions.[12]

In contrast, ultradispensationalist,[13] E. W. Bullinger writes: "It is impossible for us to take this as symbolical . . . The difficulties of the symbolical interpretation are insuperable, while no difficulties whatever attend the literal interpretation."[14]

Ryrie (in company with Walvoord, Morris, and others) takes this passage quite literally (except in the case of stars falling, which he thinks refer to a meteor shower). He identifies six catastrophic events calculated "to strike terror into the hearts of men living on the earth . . . At this point men will know assuredly that the tribulation has begun, for they recognize it as 'the great day of his wrath.'" Henry Morris explains:

> The vast worldwide network of unstable earthquake belts around the world will suddenly begin to slip and fracture on a global basis and a gigantic earthquake will ensue. This is evidently, and naturally, accompanied by tremendous volcanic eruptions, spewing vast quantities of dust and steam and gases into the upper atmosphere. It is probably these that will cause the sun to be darkened and the moon to appear blood-red.

IDEALIST *(continued)*

judgment. The seals are a self-contained series, culminating in this ultimate judgment at Christ's eschatological coming in glory. There are additional cycles to come in the book (e.g., the seven trumpets and the seven bowls), which will bring us to the same climax in their respective turns.

Alford writes: "We may unhesitatingly set down as wrong all interpretations which view as the fulfillment of this passage any period except that of the coming of the Lord." Mention is made of seven structures of creation: earth, **sun,** and **moon** (v. 12), **stars** (v. 13), **sky, mountains,** and **islands** (v. 14) and seven classes of men: **kings, great men, rich men, commanders, mighty men, slaves,** and **free** men (v. 15), in order to symbolize the universality of the disasters.

Wilcock writes:

> The question of whether the earthquake, the darkened sun, and so on, are to be taken literally or metaphorically, misses the point. That day will spell the end of the entire universe as we know it (Heb. 12:26), and the end of the planets and galaxies as well as the end of the human institutions they may symbolize.

Wilson writes:

> With the opening of the sixth seal John is given his first vision of the end . . . The final shaking of the

⧗ HISTORICIST *(continued)*

do not seem to have that awful event in view."

Matthew Henry, in most respects a *historicist*, applies this seal in a *preterist* manner. He considers the **earthquake** (v. 12) to represent the shaking of the foundations of the Jewish religion and nation, the darkening of the heavenly lights to represent the fall of the chief governors and rulers of the land, the heavens being rolled back like a scroll to "signify that their ecclesiastical state should perish and be laid aside forever," and the moving of **every mountain and island** (v. 14) to be the general terror that should affect all men of perception. ⧗

⧗ PRETERIST *(continued)*

symbolical imagery is the vesture of thought. Besides, the objection is based upon an inadequate estimate of the real significance and importance of the destruction of Jerusalem. . . . It was a grand providential epoch; the close of an aeon; the winding up of a great period in the divine government of the world.

Not all the language is strictly symbolic. That the people of Jerusalem would seek refuge in **caves** (v. 15) and under the **rocks** (v. 16) at this time, for example, was predicted by Christ (Luke 23:28–31) and verified as historical by Josephus, who wrote:

> So now the last hope which supported the tyrants and that crew of robbers who were with them, was in the caves and caverns underground, [hoping] that after the whole city should be destroyed, and the Romans gone away, they might come out again, and escape from them. This was no better than a dream of theirs; for they were not able to lie hid either from God or from the Romans. (*Wars* 6: 7:3). ⧗

⧖ FUTURIST *(continued)*

Hal Lindsey contends that this seal describes the first nuclear exchange. A nuclear explosion will trigger the worst **earthquake** (v. 12) ever. The smoke will darken **the sun** and make **the moon** appear red. The falling **stars** (v. 13) are Russian bombs. This is similar to the view of Ray Stedman:

> The sun and the moon will appear darkened, probably as a result of dust and ash. This may well be the effect astronomer Carl Sagan has dubbed "nuclear winter," the darkening of the sun by clouds of dust and ash thrown up by the mass detonation of nuclear weapons.

⧖ IDEALIST *(continued)*

universe will convince the proudest rebels of their arrogant folly (v. 15) . . . John shows how the unleashing of God's judgment completely shatters what the ancients regarded as the fixed points of an ordered world. . . . This terrifying judgment reduces men of every class to the same condition of abject fear, as they vainly seek refuge in the caves and rocks of the mountains (Isa. 2:19).

THE SEALING OF GOD'S SERVANTS

REVELATION 7:1—3

[1]After these things I saw four angels standing at the four corners of the earth, holding the four winds of the earth, that the wind should not blow on the earth, on the sea, or on any tree. [2]Then I saw another angel ascending from the east, having the seal of the living God. And he cried with a loud voice to the four angels to whom it was granted to harm the earth and the sea, [3]saying, "Do not harm the earth, the sea, or the trees till we have sealed the servants of our God on their foreheads."

⌛ HISTORICIST

To Elliott, this chapter comprises the second half of the sixth seal. The four destructive angels, withheld until the sealing of God's servants is completed, are said to be the "threatening tempest of barbarians who would be unleashed against the Roman Empire through the sounding of the first four trumpets."

Similarly, Barnes, having earlier described the gathering of barbarians against Rome under the figure of the sixth seal, suggests that **the four winds** (v. 1), here seen as being withheld, have a double reference: (1) the impending wars that led to Rome's demise (agreeing with Elliott) and (2) to the moral laxitude in the days of Constantine and to later heretics like Arius and Pelagius. As the church was about to face its darkest period, it was necessary for God to identify His genuine

⌛ PRETERIST

The reason for inserting a vision of this sort here, prior to the breaking of the seventh seal, is that the first six seals have been described with a focus on their effect upon the apostate nation of Israel. The question naturally arises—and indeed is asked in the closing verse of chapter 6—whether anyone will be spared the effects of these judgments when they fall. Thus *before* any wind of disaster can blow across the land, we see that God has identified his faithful ones and set them apart for a separate fate.

Jerusalem twice fell to invaders because of God's judgment upon them: first, in 586 BC to the Babylonians; and second, in AD 70, to the Romans. Prior to the conquest in 586 BC, God took care to identify His own and to separate them for safety during the holocaust.

172

FUTURIST

One distinctive of many dispensational-ists is their unashamedly literal inter-pretation of **the four winds,** the **four angels,** and the **four corners of the earth** (v. 1), though Henry Morris points out that the latter expression is better translated "four quarters of the earth" (cf. 20:8). To those who take this literal approach, this passage offers evi-dence of the angels being in control of the natural elements (e.g., the winds). The mission of these four angels is "to prevent an outbreak of the fury of the elements. Very soon such an outbreak will occur . . . The purpose of the sus-pension is that a certain group may be sealed" (Ryrie). Walvoord writes:

> In contrast to chapter 6 which seems to give the chronological events of the great tribulation, chapter 7 does not advance the narrative but directs attention to two major groups of saints in the tribulation . . . A description of this is given . . . which is so plain that no one should question whether people will be saved after the rapture.

Isaiah 26:20–21 speaks of a time when the Lord will go forth to punish the inhabitants of the earth. It may well be that those sealed in this chapter are the ones of whom Isaiah writes, when he, in verse 20, exhorts:

Come, my people,

Enter your chambers,

IDEALIST

After these things I saw (v. 1) does not indicate a sequence of events, but only the order in which the visions were presented to John.

Beale points out that the signifi-cance of a "seal" was to authenticate or designate ownership. He says that the fact that the sealed are called "slaves" or "servants" of God underscores the idea of ownership, "since it was a common practice in the ancient world to mark slaves on the forehead to indicate who owned them and to whom they owed service."[18]

The **four winds** (v. 1) held in abey-ance are probably to be identified with the four horsemen who appeared earli-er. This suggestion is supported by Zechariah 6:5, where, concerning the four horses that appeared in his vision, the prophet is told "these are four spirits [or *winds*] of heaven." Thus, the sealing of God's people, as described in this vi-sion, has taken place prior to the break-ing of the first four seals.

The terrifying judgments described in the first six seals invite the natural inquiry, "What is to become of the faith-ful people of God in the midst of such mayhem and devastation?" What John saw here gave the answer to the ques-tion with which the previous chapter closes: "Who is able to stand?" The an-swer, of course, is those who have the seal of God **on their foreheads** (v. 3). It is clear from later developments in the

⌛ HISTORICIST *(continued)*

servants for spiritual preservation. Barnes sees a probable fulfillment of this prophecy of preservation in the beneficent attitude toward Christians shown by Alaric, the king of the Goths, when he was sacking Rome. Gibbon notes: "Alaric himself was heard to say that he waged war with the Romans, and not with the apostles."

Various alternative views see the sealing as referring either to a) the Albigenses and the Waldensians, b) to the time of the Reformation, or c) to the period after the fall of Napoleon Bonaparte.

Henry and Adam Clarke, largely *historicists*, agree with the *preterists* in seeing chapters 6 and 7 as pertaining mostly to the fall of Jerusalem in the first century.

Of the sealing **on their foreheads** (v. 3), Matthew Henry writes:

> God has a particular care and concern for his own servants in times of temptation and corruption. . . . The seal of God was set upon their foreheads, a seal known to him, and as plain as if it appeared on their foreheads.

Clarke writes, "It is worthy of remark that not one Christian perished in the siege of Jerusalem; all had left the city and escaped to Pella." ⌛

⌛ PRETERIST *(continued)*

This fact was symbolically portrayed to Ezekiel in a vision of an angel marking God's faithful with an ink mark on their foreheads. Following this marking, six angels with deadly weapons were dispatched against Jerusalem to slaughter its inhabitants (Ezekiel 9).

Here a similar vision is given to John prior to the second destruction of Jerusalem in his own day. This time, before **the four winds** (v. 1) are unleashed upon Israel, God's servants are sealed on their foreheads for their preservation. The last words in chapter 6 were: "The great day of His wrath has come, and who is able to stand?" (Compare the similar question and context of Mal. 3:2). The present vision answers this question. Those who survived the holocaust of AD 70 were those who possessed the seal of God (Eph. 1:13), that is, the Jewish believers in Christ. That the Jewish Christians in Jerusalem actually escaped to safety prior to the siege is a matter of history (see note at next section). ⌛

FUTURIST *(continued)*

And shut the doors behind you;
Hide yourself, as it were,
for a little moment,
Until the indignation is past.

Mounce understands the interlude of chapter 7 as "a stylistic feature repeated in the trumpet sequence (10:1–11:13) contrasting the security and blessedness which awaits the faithful and the panic of a pagan world fleeing judgment."

IDEALIST *(continued)*

book that this seal upon the forehead functions as an identification of who shall be exempted from later judgments. For example, the locusts of the fifth trumpet judgment are told that they are not permitted to hurt any person who bears this seal (9:4). Whenever God sends judgment on societies or civilizations, He is mindful of those who are His own and who bear His seal. The four horse judgments are *never* released upon the earth until God's redeemed are identified and sealed for special protection.

THE ONE HUNDRED AND FORTY-FOUR THOUSAND

REVELATION 7:4—8

[4]And I heard the number of those who were sealed. One hundred and forty-four thousand of all the tribes of the children of Israel were sealed: [5]of the tribe of Judah twelve thousand were sealed; of the tribe of Reuben twelve thousand were sealed; of the tribe of Gad twelve thousand were sealed; [6]of the tribe of Asher twelve thousand were sealed; of the tribe of Naphtali twelve thousand were sealed; of the tribe of Manasseh twelve thousand were sealed; [7]of the tribe of Simeon twelve thousand were sealed; of the tribe of Levi twelve thousand were sealed; of the tribe of Issachar twelve thousandwere sealed; [8]of the tribe of Zebulun twelve thousand were sealed; of the tribe of Joseph twelve thousand were sealed; of the tribe of Benjamin twelve thousand were sealed.

⌛ HISTORICIST

Elliott and Barnes see the 144,000 as symbolic of the entire church, "the Israel of God." According to Elliott, "the twelve tribes of Israel, and the 144,000 mentioned in them, designate respectively the visible professing Church in the Roman empire, and Christ's true Church, the election of grace, gathered out of it." These, as noted in the previous segment, arose after Constantine's conversion and were sealed to be preserved against the barbarian invasions about to be unleashed upon the empire in the first four trumpet judgments (ch. 8).

Elliott lays heavy emphasis on the distinction between the "confessing" church and the true church, because, as

⌛ PRETERIST

God always has had a remnant in Israel who are faithful despite widespread apostasy. God knows their number. He told Elijah of seven thousand who had not bowed the knee to Baal. When Jesus came, that remnant of the Jews who remained faithful to the God of Israel were those who recognized Jesus as the Messiah and followed Him. When Paul was discussing the calamity of widespread Jewish unbelief, in his generation, he qualified that general condition with the observation, "at this present time, there is a remnant according to the election of grace" (Rom.11:5).

This faithful remnant in the first century was the original core of what

FUTURIST

During the Great Tribulation, a godly remnant of 144,000 Jewish people will be **sealed** (v. 4) for protection from the later plagues (cf. 9:4). Gaebelein explains:

> The vision states clearly that the sealed company is "of all the tribes of the children of Israel." There are today perhaps a score or more of little sects who all claim to be the 144,000 . . . If the true interpretation of Revelation is seen, that this company is called after the rapture of the Church, these confusing theories will at once be rejected.

That these are *physical* Israelites (not to be confused with the church, as in the *historicist* and *idealist* approaches) is underscored by the division of the group into twelve tribes. The church is not divided into tribal divisions. Walvoord writes:

> It would be rather ridiculous to carry the typology of Israel representing the church to the extent of dividing them up into twelve tribes as was done here, if it was the intent of the writer to describe the church.

The sealing and preservation of these Jews will fulfill those passages that speak of God bringing Israel to repentance in the last days (Zech. 12:10–13; Rom. 11:26–32). The omission of the tribe of Dan from the list is consid-

IDEALIST

This company represents the church as the true and spiritual Israel. Hobbs gives three reasons for not understanding this vision to apply to ethnic Israelites: (1) such a view imposes a canon of literalism upon a passage belonging to a very symbolic book, (2) the book of Revelation does not elsewhere draw distinctions between the Jewish Christians and their Gentile counterparts, and (3) the sealing of this group, contrasted with the multiracial multitude in verses 9 through 17 (who are not sealed), would suggest that only Jewish believers, and not other Christians, are sealed by God for protection.

Beale points out that Israel lost track of their tribal identities in the long diaspora since 722 BC and AD 70. He anticipates the response that "though the Jews may not know their tribal identities, God does," to which he counters that the many centuries of intermarriage between Jews of various tribes (and with Gentiles) has done much to erode any legitimate confidence that distinct tribes even exist for God to identify.[21]

Wilson expresses a further reason for not taking this as ethnic Israel and speaks for many expositors:

> That ethnic Israel is not in view is confirmed by the irregular listing of the tribes. Judah is placed first as the Messiah's own tribe, Dan is omitted, Levi is included as an

⧗ HISTORICIST (continued)

he points out, after the christianization of the empire after Constantine's conversion, the visible church came to be infiltrated by many who had no true conversion—a process that eventually led to the corruptions he will associate with the papacy, later in the book. He derives evidence for this mixture of the true with the impostor from peculiarities in the listing of the tribes, wherein "there is an intermingling of the tribes sprung from the *bond-woman* with those sprung from the *free-woman*." This rather esoteric argument would not appeal to all.

Of course, since the sealing is seen as protection against the barbarian hordes, who would not know the difference between a professing Christian and a genuine believer, Elliott believes that the larger group would be spared along with the smaller.

Matthew Henry is a *historicist* who tends to follow the *preterists* in his general approach to the breaking of the seven seals:

> In this list the tribe of Dan is omitted, perhaps because they were greatly addicted to idolatry; and the order of tribes is altered, perhaps as they had been more or less faithful to God. Some take these to be a select number of Jews who were reserved for mercy at the destruction of Jerusalem; others think that time was past, and therefore it is to be more generally applied to God's chosen remnant in the world.

⧗ PRETERIST (continued)

we now call the church; many Gentile converts having been added to their company since that time. Just prior to the siege of Jerusalem in AD 70, the Jewish Christians in that city were warned by a prophetic oracle to flee from the city (echoing Jesus' own warning in Luke 21:20ff.). Historian Eusebius (c. 325) wrote:

> The whole body, however, of the church at Jerusalem, having been commanded by a divine revelation, given to men of approved piety there before the war, removed from the city, and dwelt at a certain town beyond the Jordan, called Pella.[19]

The normative view among evangelical *preterists* is that this 144,000 is a symbolic number representing the full number of Jewish Christians who escaped the doomed city before its destruction. There is no way of knowing the actual number of Judean Christians who escaped (it could have been this actual number), it is not necessary to speculate, since the number given is too perfectly rounded to be considered literal.

That this group lived in the first century is confirmed in another passage, which calls them the "firstfruits to God" (Rev. 14:4). Compare James 1:1, 18, which speaks of the Jewish believers as "firstfruits"). If this 144,000 referred to some future group living in the end-times (as the *futurists* believe), one

⏳ FUTURIST *(continued)*

ered by some an indicator that the Anti-christ will be of that tribe (cf. Gen. 49:17; Jer. 8:16). Alternatively, it may be that both Dan and Ephraim are omitted because of their involvement in idolatry.

Despite the silence of the text on the nature of their activities, Gaebelein asserts, "This sealed company also bears a great testimony. They are the preachers of the Gospel of the Kingdom."[20] Hal Lindsey has referred to the company as "144,000 Jewish Billy Grahams." Ray Stedman speaks of them as "Christ's Commandos."

Mounce and Ladd dissent from the above opinion. Not holding to the pre-tribulation Rapture thesis, they both believe the 144,000 to be symbolic of the church in the Tribulation. They are thus "the last generation church, not a select group, but the full number of faithful believers alive when that event takes place" (Mounce). ⏳

⏳ IDEALIST *(continued)*

ordinary tribe and Joseph replaces Ephraim.

Bauckham finds another significance in the numbering:

> The 144,000 are an army. This is implicit in the fact that 7:4–8 is a census of the tribes of Israel. In the Old Testament a census was always a reckoning of the military strength of the nation.[22]

The number 144,000 is symbolic, derived by multiplying 1,000, the basic military division in the camp of Israel (Num. 31:4–5), by 144 (twelve squared), symbolizing the faithful remnant of the Old Israel and of the New Israel—thus forming the true spiritual Israel, the church. In any age, it is the church that is preserved from God's judgments upon nations, though this does not mean the church does not suffer at the hands of sinners (6:9). ⏳

HISTORICIST *(continued)*

He thinks the former view is more probable.

⧗ **PRETERIST** *(continued)*

would expect them to be called the "last fruits."

AN INNUMERABLE MULTITUDE

REVELATION 7:9—17

⁹After these things I looked, and behold, a great multitude which no one could number, of all nations, tribes, peoples, and tongues, standing before the throne and before the Lamb, clothed with white robes, with palm branches in their hands, ¹⁰and crying out with a loud voice, saying, "Salvation belongs to our God who sits on the throne, and to the Lamb!" ¹¹And all the angels stood around the throne and the elders and the four living creatures, and fell on their faces before the throne and worshiped God, ¹²saying: "Amen! Blessing and glory and wisdom, thanksgiving and honor and power and might, be to our God forever and ever. Amen." ¹³Then one of the elders answered, saying to me, "Who are these arrayed in white robes, and where did they come from?" ¹⁴And I said to him, "Sir, you know." So he said to me, "These are the ones who come out of the great tribulation, and washed their robes and made them white in the blood of the Lamb. ¹⁵Therefore they are before the throne of God, and serve Him day and night in His temple. And He who sits on the throne will dwell among them. ¹⁶They shall neither hunger anymore nor thirst anymore; the sun shall not strike them, nor any heat; ¹⁷for the Lamb who is in the midst of the throne will shepherd them and lead them to living fountains of waters. And God will wipe away every tear from their eyes."

⧗ HISTORICIST

Elliott identifies this innumerable throng with the group sealed early in the chapter. In the former vision, they were sealed for preservation; here they are seen in their eternal blessedness. According to

⧗ PRETERIST

Having shown John the Jewish saints who would escape the Tribulation of AD 70, the Lord now shows him the great throng of Gentiles who will be saved as a result of God's disowning His

⧗ FUTURIST

According to the dispensational view, in addition to the salvation of the Jewish remnant (the 144,000), an even greater number of Gentiles will be brought to Christ by their testimony during the Tribulation. The palm-bearing company is identified with that multitude of Gentiles who come to faith in Christ and often must endure martyrdom for the stand they take.

The mention of **the great tribulation** (v. 14), when compared to Matthew 24:21, helps to identify the historical period to which this company belongs. Some writers (e.g., Walvoord) point out that this group is distinct from the twenty-four elders (who represent the church, already raptured in 4:1) in that **one of the elders** (v. 13) speaks here with John about the group in question, but is himself not one of them. The distinction between the church (raptured at Rev. 4:1) and all other saved people in Revelation is an important one to the dispensationalist. Both the 144,000 Jews and this great company of Gentiles are distinct from the church and did not respond to the Gospel of Grace, which was preached until the Rapture. Having missed the Rapture,

⧗ IDEALIST

The scene now shifts from earth to heaven. As the 144,000 represent the church as sealed by God on earth, the innumerable host is the church finally glorified in heaven. The church is here revealed to be made up of many nations, whereas the vision of the 144,000 used imagery that identified the church as the spiritual *Israel*. It is sometimes said that the 144,000 symbolize the "church militant" while on earth, whereas the innumerable multitude represent the "church triumphant" in heaven. Lenski writes of the two parts of this chapter that they provide *"the revelation of the church. Sealed—Glorified!"*

This great multitude appears with **white robes** (v. 9) and **palm branches** (v. 9), symbolic of purity and victory, respectively. Their earthly trials are over. Their robes are **washed** (v. 14) white (like those of the martyrs in 6:11), referring, in this case, to the imputed righteousness of God, through faith in the blood of Christ.

The symbolism of the passage is underscored by the mention of washing the robes and making them **white in the blood** (v. 14), since blood is not usually thought of as a whitening

⌛ HISTORICIST *(continued)*

Elliott and Barnes, showing these in heaven is intended to encourage the church of its heavenly triumph—a needed message at a time when the church was facing rapid spiritual decline after Constantine.

Barnes distinguishes those in this vision from those in the first part of the chapter:

> The design seems to be to carry the mind forward quite beyond the storms and tempests of earth—the scenes of woe and sorrow—the days of error, darkness, declension, and persecution into that period when the church should be triumphant in heaven . . . The multitude that John thus saw was not, therefore, I apprehend, the same as the hundred and forty-four thousand, but a far greater number—the whole assembled host of the redeemed in heaven, gathered there as *victors*, with palm-branches, the symbols of triumph, in their hands. The *object* of the vision is to cheer those who are desponding in times of religious declension and in seasons of persecution, and when the number of true Christians seems to be small, with the assurance that an immense host shall be redeemed from our world, and be gathered triumphant before the throne.

Matthew Henry and Adam Clarke, still viewing this section in the same manner as do the *preterists*, see the two

⌛ PRETERIST *(continued)*

unfaithful wife and seeking a new family (cf. Hos. 1:10; 2:23, and their applications in Rom. 9:24ff. and 1 Pet. 2:9f.). This is also spoken of in Isaiah 49:20–22. These ones **come out** (literally, "are coming out") **of the great tribulation** (v. 14) in the sense that their inclusion in God's kingdom resulted from that event, at which time Judaism came to a formal end and the universal gospel was proclaimed to all nations.

It is very common for the New Testament to view the mission to the Gentiles as a consequence of the judgment on Israel, even though Paul's ministry among the Gentiles (as well as other missionaries' work outside of Israel) occurred prior to the destruction of Jerusalem. This fact did not prevent Jesus from identifying the time when the kingdom would be taken from Israel and given to the Church as the time of the judgment of AD 70 (see Matthew 21:40–41, 43). Similarly, in the parable of the wedding feast, Jesus described the commissioning of the king's servants to go abroad with their invitation (to the Gentiles), only after the king had burned up the city of those first invited (Matthew 22:2–10). The inclusion of Gentiles was well underway before Jerusalem fell, but that aspect of the kingdom's propagation totally defined the movement after AD 70. Therefore, it is not strange to represent this multitude of Gentile believers as the up-shot of the

⏳ FUTURIST *(continued)*

they have responded to the Gospel of the Kingdom. They will enter the Millennium, but will forever have an inferior status to that of the church. Seiss refers to them as being "not first class saints." Here they are seen, as most understand it, in heaven, having come out of the Great Tribulation. Some, including Jennings[23] and Gaebelein, do not believe this scene is in heaven. This vision, according to Gaebelein, applies:

> to saved Gentiles on earth. . . . This great company therefore does not stand before a heavenly throne, but before the millennial throne on earth . . . The temple mentioned is the millennial temple (Ezek. xl–xliv). And then there is a description of the millennial blessings for these redeemed nations.

Not all *futurists* are dispensationalists, however, and some understand this palm-bearing company to be "the church after the tribulation is over, saved in the Kingdom of God, presumed martyred" (Ladd), and representing the "eternal blessedness of all believers when in the presence of God they realize the rewards of faithful endurance" (Mounce).

Seiss refers to "an otherwise creditable writer" known to him, who argued "upon the authority of the vision now before us, that there is no such thing as a rapture of the Church before the great

⏳ IDEALIST *(continued)*

agent. Lenski writes: "This blood and nothing else in the universe whitens us so that we may stand before God."

Through death, these believers "are coming" (as it reads literally) **out of the great tribulation** (v. 14). The mention of **great tribulation** may refer to the "intensification of troublesome times as the Age comes to an end" (Morey). Wilson argues that, since this picture is of Christians at any time in history, the Tribulation must be taking place throughout the church age:

> Here "the great tribulation" does not refer to any particular time of suffering, but includes all the afflictions through which the saints have passed on their way to glory.

A medley of images from Isaiah are employed to convey the blessed state attained by the glorified saints. The expression that God **will dwell among them** (v. 15) is more literally "will spread his tabernacle over them." This tabernacle protects the people of God from **hunger, thirst, sun,** and **heat** (v. 16). This alludes to Isaiah 4:6—"And there will be a tabernacle for shade in the daytime from the heat, for a place of refuge, and for a shelter from storm and rain," and Isaiah 49:10—"They shall neither hunger nor thirst, neither heat nor sun shall strike them."

The redeemed are forever in the care of the Lamb, who, like a shepherd,

⌛ HISTORICIST *(continued)*

groups as distinct, with the main differences between them being their respective sizes and their different ethnicities. Besides the significant remnant of Israel who are delivered from destruction, at the fall of Jerusalem, there is an even larger number to be saved out of every ethnicity.

Clarke writes: "This appears to mean the Church of Christ among the Gentiles, for it was different from that collected from the twelve tribes [described in verses 4–8]." Distinct from the large but measurable number (144,000) of *Jews* saved in the church, the number of Gentiles will be innumerable and of every ethnic category. "God will have a greater harvest of souls among the Gentiles than he had among the Jews. *More are the children of the desolate than of the married woman.* [Isa. 54:1]" (Matthew Henry). Of this company, Henry continues:

> They were invested with the robes of justification, holiness and victory, and had palms in their hands, as conquerors used to appear in their triumphs: such a glorious appearance will the faithful servants of God make at last, when they have *fought the good fight of faith and finished their course.* ⌨

⌛ PRETERIST *(continued)*

tribulation that befell the Jews in that year.

Alternatively, these are Christian *martyrs*, slain by certain Roman emperors after the fall of Jerusalem (the view of Adams, David S. Clark, and others). Adams writes:

> The vast Gentile multitude, coming out of the portending Roman persecution, is also introduced at this point . . . Note the heavy emphasis upon the glorious gains and blessings of faithful martyrdom in verses 9, 15, 16, and 17.

Clark writes:

> It has been thought by some that the terms used to describe this multitude are too inclusive or universal to fit the historical view of these chapters. In answer it may be said that the terms used to describe the multitudes that were in Jerusalem at Pentecost were almost as universal; for it is said that there were Jews from every nation under heaven. ⌨

FUTURIST *(continued)*

tribulation." This writer, says Seiss, "is sadly mistaken." 🔄

IDEALIST *(continued)*

will **lead them to living fountains of waters. And God will wipe away every tear from their eyes** (v. 17). This takes up the imagery from Isaiah 49:10—"for He who has mercy on them will lead them, even by the springs of water He will guide them," and Isaiah 25:8—"the Lord God will wipe away tears from all faces." 🔄

A BRIEF SILENCE IN HEAVEN

REVELATION 8:1

[1]When He opened the seventh seal, there was silence in heaven for about half an hour.

⧗ HISTORICIST

Elliott identifies this **silence** with the short period during which the 144,000 were sealed in the previous chapter. It represents the brief interval between the opening of the seventh seal and the first barbarian invasion to be seen in verse 7. This interval is thought to be "the seventy years that intervened between Constantine's victory over Licinius, followed by the dissolution of the pagan heavens, AD 324, and Alaric's revolt and the invasion of the empire, consequent on the death of Theodosius, AD 395." Elliott calculates that **half an hour** in heaven is precisely equivalent to seventy years of Roman history.

Albert Barnes writes that the half-hour silence was for effect to mark the solemnity of the events about to be reported. "Of course, this is a symbolical representation, and is designed not to represent a pause in the events themselves, but only the impressive and fearful nature of the events which are now to be disclosed." Matthew Henry suggests

⧗ PRETERIST

The brief **silence** in heaven contrasts sharply with the noise of praise and song that characterized the heavenly scene in chapters 4 and 5. Conspicuously missing are the "loud voices" of the martyrs inquiring how long it would be before they were avenged (6:10). Perhaps their cries have ceased because the requested vengeance upon their persecutors, the leaders of the Jews, had now commenced. For a short time, symbolically represented as **half an hour,** there would be no more such complaints heard in heaven. Soon, however, new persecutions of Christians by Rome would cause the righteous blood to again cry for vindication. This may be what is portrayed symbolically in the following verses, where prayers of the saints again are offered as incense to God. The "half hour" may be the period of time normally required by the priest in the temple to offer the daily incense. This "time of incense" was a time of silent prayer for the

⧗ FUTURIST

Concerning this interval of **silence,** Walvoord writes:

> Contained in the seventh seal are all the subsequent developments leading to the second coming of Christ, including the seven trumpets and the seven bowls of the wrath of God . . . [This silence] may be compared with the silence before the foreman of a jury reports a verdict; for a moment there is perfect silence and everyone awaits that which will follow.

Ryrie observes:

> With the opening of this last seal the book is now fully opened, and one would expect a holocaust to let loose. Instead there is silence . . . This is a silence of expectancy, for this is the last seal. It is also a silence of foreboding that precedes the onslaught of judgments. It lasts for half an hour (which may be understood just as literally as the other time designations in the book). 📷

⧗ IDEALIST

For a short time (symbolized by **half an hour),** heaven is in awestruck silence, anticipating the completion of God's purposes. It is the lull before the storm. Hailey points out that "[a] half hour is ordinarily a short period of time, but it seems long when one is waiting." What follows this silence is the blowing of seven trumpets, recalling the fall of Jericho at the blast of seven trumpets. It should be remembered that Jericho's fall also was preceded by a period of silence, as the Israelites circled the city seven days without a sound.

There is no unanimity on the question whether the seven trumpets, which follow, are the contents of the seventh seal, or whether one series (the seals) comes to an end and is punctuated with a brief silence, which anticipates another discreet series (the trumpets). The question, then, is, Do the seven trumpets *belong to* the seventh seal, occurring chronologically after the first six seals, or do they begin a fresh, new view of the same period from the beginning? 📷

⧗ HISTORICIST *(continued)*

two possible meanings of the silence in heaven: (1) that there was a brief period following the destruction of Jerusalem during which no complaints from the saints (as found in 6:9–10) were presented in heaven because all was temporarily peaceful for the church on earth. This silence was soon broken by the renewed prayers of the saints (8:3–5); or (2) that this is "a silence of expectation . . . The church of God, both in heaven and earth, stood silent to see what God was doing. ⧗

⧗ PRETERIST *(continued)*

attendant worshipers (Luke 1:10, 21). This would accord with the description of the ceremony by Alfred Edersheim.[24] In this case it will be an angel in heaven, not a priest in the temple, who is offering the incense (v. 5).

REVELATION 4–7 SUMMARY: THE SEVEN-SEALED SCROLL

The Lamb and the scroll are introduced to the reader in the vision of chapters 4 and 5. In some respects, this opening vision is more attention-getting than the events that follow, revealing, as it does, the throne of God in heaven and His unusual attendants enthusiastically worshiping Him for His holiness and His creative and redemptive acts. Not until the fifth chapter is John's attention drawn to the scroll in the hand of God, the contents of which are concealed by seven seals. A call goes forth throughout the universe for a champion to come and break the seals and open the scroll. Initially, none is found qualified to open the scroll, causing John great dejection. At the crucial moment, Christ appears, depicted as a slain Lamb, and takes the scroll from the hand of God on the throne. All the inhabitants of heaven rejoice because one has finally come who is worthy to break the seven seals and open the scroll. They burst into praise and adoration as the Lamb prepares to break the seals. Chapter 6 marks a major change in the action, as the Lamb successively breaks the seven seals that had formerly prevented the opening of the cryptic scroll. Wild and terrifying things then begin to transpire, beginning with four ominous horsemen, and do not let up until nearly the end of the book.

The adherents to the four approaches do not agree about the time frame or import of this dramatic vision. Even those within each individual camp often disagree with reference to the details of interpretation. Those of every persuasion are inclined to see the principal significance of this throne-room vision as an affirmation that God is sovereign over all, and the events that follow are the direct results of His righteous decrees. Most also agree that this vision underscores the unique qualifications of Christ to judge the wicked, based upon His sacrificial death. There is a wide range of opinions—not necessarily divided along the lines of the four approaches—about the exact identity of the scroll. Leading *historicists* take it to represent "the purposes and designs of God" or simply, "future events." To some *preterists* it is the sentence of the judge being handed down for execution, and to others it is the document representing the New Covenant. *Futurists* typically see the sealed scroll as the title deed to the earth, to be reclaimed by Christ in the final seven years of history. *Idealist* interpreters have alternately identified it as "the redemptive plan of God" or "God's last will and testament."

Where the four approaches divide most sharply, of course, is in the timing of the earthly events that result from the breaking of the seven seals.

Historicists spread the fulfillment of the prophecies of the whole book over the entire age of the church and connect this breaking of the seals with events occurring early in the history of the church. Some[25] take the breaking of the seals back as far as the fall of Jerusalem in AD 70 (in this instance agreeing with the early-date *preterists).* On this view, the breaking of the seven seals concerns the judgment of the Jewish commonwealth in the late sixties AD, culminating in the doom of Jerusalem in AD 70. The more characteristic view among the *historicists*[26] associates the breaking of the first seal with the death of Domitian (AD 96) and identifies the breaking of the other seals with events marking the prosperity of the Western Roman Empire and its degeneration, extending to the invasions of Goths and Vandals in the fourth and fifth centuries. The 144,000 sealed saints are the spiritual Israel (the church), preserved by God through these political upheavals.

Early-date *preterists* agree with those *historicists* who see the seal-breaking as fulfilled in the fall of Jerusalem. They point out the unmistakable similarities between the images used here and those of the Olivet Discourse (Mark 13, and Matthew 24; Luke 21:5–36), in which Jesus predicted the destruction of Jerusalem and the temple. The 144,000 represent the Judean Christians, who fled from Jerusalem prior to the siege and thus escaped the holocaust.

Futurists see in these chapters the beginning of the end-time Tribulation. The four horsemen represent the rise of the Antichrist, followed by global calamities in the form of war, famine, and death. The 144,000 are Jews converted during the Tribulation. Dispensationalists believe that the church will already have been raptured, so these Jewish believers are a part of Israel, not the church.

Idealist interpreters do not look for specific single fulfillments of the visions in Revelation. The four horsemen depict the recurring historic phenomena of conquest, war, famine, and death, without reference to any particular cases. Alternatively, the first horseman might depict Christ's gospel riding triumphantly through the earth. The point is that such events are sent into the world at the command of God and function as a part of His redemptive and retributive plan. The martyrs seen in heaven remind us that those in every age who have suffered for Christ will be vindicated, and the 144,000 represent the church throughout history.

Though the four approaches do not fully agree upon every detail of interpretation, there is not radical disagreement about the issues depicted in the opening throne room vision of chapter 4. Differences of general approach, however, begin to emerge in chapter 5 and become more conspicuous in chapter 6.

NOTES

1. Walvoord, *The Revelation of Jesus Christ*, in situ.

2. Beale, *The New International Greek Testament Commentary*, 319.

3. Jay Adams, *The Time is at Hand* (Phillipsburg, NJ: Presbyterian and Reformed Publishing, 1966), 61.

4. Bauckham, *The Theology of the Book of Revelation*, 33.

5. Beale, *The Book of Revelation*, 332

6. David Chilton, *The Great Tribulation*, (Tyler, TX: Institute for Christian Economics, 1997), 56.

7. Richard Bauckham, *The Theology of the Book of Revelation (Cambridge: Cambridge University Press, 1993)*, 73f.

8. Daniel Thambyrajah Niles, *As Seeing the Invisible: A Study of the Book of Revelation* (Whitefish, MT: Literary Licensing, 2012), 55.

9. F. A. Jennings, *Studies in Revelation* (n.p., 1937), 56.

10. Quoted in Geoffrey Wilson, *Revelation* (Durham, England: Evangelical Press, 1984), n.p.

11. Beale, *The New International Greek Testament Commentary*, 392.

12. H. A. Ironside, *Lectures on the Revelation*, (Neptune, NJ: Loizeaux Brothers, 1920), 114.

13. Ultradispensationalism is a subgroup within the dispensational camp, also known as *Bullingerism*.

14. E. W. Bullinger, *The Apocalypse*, 274. cited by Walvoord.

15. Beale, *The New International Greek Testament Commentary*, 396.

16. E.g. Hailey, Pieters, Dana, Summers.

17. E.g., Hendriksen, Hobbs, Moffatt, Wilcock, Wilson.

18. Beale, *The New International Greek Testament Commentary*, 410f.

19. *Ecclesiastical History*, Book III; chap. 5. See preterist note at 7:1–3.

20. "The Gospel of the Kingdom" is, to many dispensationalists different from the "Gospel of Grace," the latter being the gospel preached by the church in the present age, and the former being applicable only after the Rapture of the church.

21. Beale, *The New International Greek Testament Commentary*, 419.

22. Bauckham, *The Theology of the Book of Revelation*, 77.

23. Jennings, *Studies in Revelation*, 218ff.

24. Edersheim, *The Temple*, 167.

25. E.g., Clarke, Henry, and others.

26. E.g., Barnes, Elliott, and others.

PART III

THE SEVEN TRUMPETS
REVELATION 8–10

WHAT EVENTS DO THE SEVEN TRUMPET JUDGMENTS REPRESENT? WHEN DO THESE EVENTS OCCUR?

⧗ HISTORICIST APPROACH:

- The trumpets speak of a series of invasions against the Roman Empire (Vandals, Huns, Saracens, and Turks).
- The sixth trumpet brings the fall of Constantinople to the Turks (1453).
- The little book represents the Bible being made available to the masses of Europe after the invention of the printing press.

⧗ PRETERIST APPROACH:

- The first four trumpets correspond to disasters inflicted by the Romans on the Jews in the Jewish War (AD 66–70).
- The fifth trumpet probably depicts the demonic spirits rendering the besieged Jews irrational and self-destructive. The sixth trumpet refers to the Roman armies, who destroyed Jerusalem and slaughtered or deported all the Jews.

⧗ FUTURIST APPROACH:

- Either literally or symbolically, the trumpets represent calamities that will be endured by the unrepentant inhabitants of earth during the coming seven-year Tribulation.
- These may be supernatural judgments direct from the hand of God or merely the disastrous effects of man's improper stewardship of the earth and his abuse of technology (e.g., nuclear weapons).

⧗ IDEALIST APPROACH:

- Catastrophes reminiscent of the plagues of Egypt befall sinful humanity many times in history, demonstrating God's displeasure and, like trumpet blasts, warning of worse things to come upon the unrepentant.
- Sinful humanity typically absorbs these injuries with defiance, refusing to repent.

COALS OF FIRE CAST TO EARTH

REVELATION 8:2–6

²And I saw the seven angels who stand before God, and to them were given seven trumpets. ³Then another angel, having a golden censer, came and stood at the altar. He was given much incense, that he should offer it with the prayers of all the saints upon the golden altar which was before the throne. ⁴And the smoke of the incense, with the prayers of the saints, ascended before God from the angel's hand. ⁵Then the angel took the censer, filled it with fire from the altar, and threw it to the earth. And there were noises, thunderings, lightnings, and an earthquake. ⁶So the seven angels who had the seven trumpets prepared themselves to sound.

⌛ HISTORICIST

The **angel** (v. 3) who offers the **incense** is none other than Christ, acting in his priestly role in the heavenly sanctuary. The incense that He adds to **the prayers of the saints** (v. 3) makes them pleasant to God. **The saints** here, as in the fifth seal vision, are those slain by Rome during the era of the martyrs. Their prayer (Rev. 6:10) called for the vindication of their blood by the judgment of their murderers. At that time they were told to wait a little while longer—possibly the "half hour" of verse 1. In the present vision, their prayers have **ascended before God** (v. 4), signifying that they are about to be answered, as will be seen in the seven trumpet judgments which follow.

Alternatively, Barnes thinks these prayers are the church's unavailing

⌛ PRETERIST

The **censer** (v. 3) that was used in offering the saints' prayers for justice and vindication is now filled with coals of **fire from the altar** (v. 5), and the angel hurls it in judgment upon the land of Israel ("land" being the preferred translation to **earth** in verse 5). Chilton observes:

> The irony of this passage becomes obvious when we keep in mind that it is a prophecy against apostate Israel. . . . Now, when God's people were commanded to destroy an apostate city, Moses . . . ordered: "You shall gather all its booty into the middle of its open square and burn all its booty with fire *as a whole burnt offering* to the Lord your God" (Deut. 13:16; Judg. 20:40; cf. Gen. 19:28). The only

⧖ FUTURIST

The incense is associated **with the prayers of all the saints** (v. 4). "Who are the saints whose prayers are being heard here? At the very least they are the saints of the tribulation days who are living on the earth and who pray to God for an outpouring of His wrath on the godless of the earth" (Ryrie).

As Ironside puts it, "Here is the answer to the cry of His afflicted ones down in that scene of tribulation. The prayers went up to the Father, and judgment came down."

The incense is offered by one described as an **angel** (v. 3), whom many identify with Christ Himself, since He is acting in the role of priest. Henry Morris speaks in accordance with many others (e.g., Gaebelein, Ironside, Walter Scott), in saying:

> We are justified seeing in this angel none other than the Lord Jesus Christ appearing here in yet another of His many offices, this time in His gracious ministry of intercession, of conveying our own prayers to His Father, "now to appear in the presence of God for us" (Heb. 9:24).

Fausset does not think it necessary to identify this angel with Christ:

> The angel does not provide the incense; it is given to him by Christ, whose meritorious obedience and death are the incense, rendering

⧖ IDEALIST

As chapter 1, which introduced the seven churches, served as a prelude to Act 1 of the drama, and as chapters 4–5, which introduced the seven seals, served as a prelude to Act 2, so do these opening verses, which introduce the **seven angels** (v. 2), serve as a prelude to Act 3. Because the sixth seal in chapter 6 portrayed the end of the world and the day of wrath, the **seven trumpets** introduced here cannot follow the seals chronologically. The series of judgments represented by the seals synchronizes with those of the seals. Wilson, with many others, believes that "the vision covers the same ground again, but from a different point of view. The calamities described are typical judgments which recur throughout this dispensation, and should not be regarded as symbolizing particular events."

In this opening vision, **the prayers of all the saints** (v. 3) are seen to be ascending before God in heaven. They are offered up with **much incense,** to make them pleasant and acceptable to God. Lenski suggests that this incense "represents the intercession of Christ for his church, which adds power and efficacy to the prayers of the church." Hendriksen suggests a similar thesis. A seemingly less likely interpretation is put forth by Summers, who, remembering that incense was burned as part of the Roman celebrations of triumph, writes: "The incense of victory was thus

195

⧗ HISTORICIST *(continued)*

intercession that God would have mercy on the sinners—the imagery suggesting that Rome is beyond reclamation. He writes:

> The incense-offering; the prayers; the fearful agitations produced by the casting of the censer upon the earth, *as if the prayer was not heard, and as if the offering of the incense did not avail to turn away the impending wrath,* all are appropriate symbols to introduce the series of fearful calamities which were coming upon the world on the sounding of the trumpets.

By these judgments, the Roman Empire will be brought to desolation. The first four trumpets are four waves of barbarian hordes, which bring down the western part of the empire. The fifth trumpet brings the Saracens (Muslim Arabs), who attack the southern and eastern parts of the empire. The sixth trumpet invites the Turks, who conquer the eastern division of the empire. ⧉

⧗ PRETERIST *(continued)*

acceptable way to burn a city as a whole burnt sacrifice was with God's fire—*fire from the altar.* Thus, when a city was to be destroyed, the priest would take fire from God's altar and use it to ignite the heap of booty which served as kindling, so offering up the entire city as a sacrifice. It is this practice of putting a city "under the ban," so that nothing survives the conflagration (Deut. 13:12–18), that the book of Revelation uses to describe God's judgment against *Jerusalem.*

For Israel, the trumpet was an instrument used to rally the troops for war or to warn of an enemy invasion. Likening the upcoming judgments to the sounding of trumpets suggests that God Himself is making war against His enemies in apostate Israel.

Just as the downfall of Jerusalem, in this book, is likened to that of Sodom and Egypt (11:8), and to the fall of Babylon (14:18; 16:19), so is it, by the figure of these seven trumpets, likened to the fall of Jericho, which also involved the sounding of seven trumpets by seven priests (Josh.6:4, 20). ⧉

⌛ FUTURIST *(continued)*

the prayers of the saints well-pleasing to God.

On the question of the identity of this angel, Ryrie writes:

Some understand this to be Christ, our High Priest. Others regard him as an angel, and there seems to be no reason why an angel could not perform the functions described here.

Walvoord concurs:

There is no way to determine with finality which of these two views is correct, though the preponderance of opinion seems to favor regarding the angel as Christ in His work as High Priest.

⌛ IDEALIST *(continued)*

scattered upon the living coals of Christian intercession."

Since the **fire from the altar** (v. 5) is cast upon the earth from the same censer that had offered up the prayers of the saints, we are to understand that the retributive judgments of God come upon the earth in response to the prayers of the church. Such prayers, it would appear from the result, are prayers for vindication, but they are not offensive in the sight of God, due to the incense joined to them.

THE FIRST TRUMPET

REVELATION 8:7

⁷The first angel sounded: And hail and fire followed, mingled with blood, and they were thrown to the earth. And a third of the trees were burned up, and all green grass was burned up.

⌛ HISTORICIST

The first four trumpets represent the four great blows that fell upon the Western Empire from the beginning of the fifth century to its fall in 476. **Hail** is a symbol of God's judgment (Job 38:22–23), and the combination of **hail and fire** (or thunderbolts) recalls the plagues of Egypt in particular (Exod. 9:23; Ps. 18:13; 78:48; 105:32). To these familiar images are added blood and the destruction of **trees** and **green grass.** Barnes believes these images symbolize war and the bloodshed and destruction of vegetation that accompany it.

Barnes writes:

> At this point in writing, I looked on a chart of history, composed with no reference to this prophecy, and found a singular and unexpected prominence given to *four* such events extending from the first invasion of the Goths and Vandals at the beginning of the fifth century, to the fall of the Western empire, AD 476. The first was the invasion of Alaric, king of the Goths, AD 410; the second was the invasion

⌛ PRETERIST

As the first four seals were set off from the latter three, in that each of the first group revealed a horseman, so the first four trumpets are set off from the last three, in that the latter are referred to as "Woes." The entire series, however, is concerned with the Jewish War of AD 66–70, "the Last Days" of the Jewish commonwealth. Chilton writes that "the first four trumpets apparently refer to the series of disasters that devastated Israel in the Last Days, and primarily the events leading up to the outbreak of war."

Adams writes:

> [The first four of the trumpets] probably predict the several years of ravage and pillage prior to the destruction of Jerusalem itself. In this period, the land suffered terribly. The plagues are reminiscent of those in Egypt, at the birth of the Hebrew nation. Here they mark both the latter's cessation, and the birth of a new nation, the kingdom of God (1 Pet. 2:9, 10).

⏳ FUTURIST

Most dispensational *futurists* take the **hail and fire,** the **trees** and the **green grass** in this scene literally. There are exceptions, however. Walter Scott interprets the third part of the world to be the western confederation of nations, the trees to be great men and leaders, and the grass to be ordinary people. Ironside takes essentially the same view.

Gaebelein, too, departs from a strict literalism:

> Hail (withdrawn heat), fire and blood are all symbols of divine wrath. . . . The green things are symbols of agricultural and commercial prosperity. . . . The third part mentioned repeatedly in these trumpet judgments refers to the [revived] Roman empire. . . . Burning heat may be symbolical of intolerant despotism.

Walvoord objects to the nonliteral methodology of such interpreters:

> The tendency on the part of the expositors has been to read into this judgment a symbol of divine chastening rather than literal hail and fire. The obvious parallel, however, is found in the tenth plague in Exodus 9:18–26. Inasmuch as in the account of Exodus there was literal hail and fire, and the result of the judgment here is the burning up of the third part of trees and all the green grass, there is no

⏳ IDEALIST

Trumpets may serve any number of functions. They might announce a day of remembrance (Lev. 23:24), a triumph (Josh. 6:4), or a coronation (1 Kings 1:34). Most likely, here they represent a warning (e.g., of an invasion from enemy armies). Since these trumpets affect only one-third—or a significant minority—of the created order and of men, the judgments they bring are not final, but serve as warnings of the great judgment to come. Bauckham writes:

> The judgments up to and including that of the sixth trumpet are strictly limited (see 6:8; 8:7–12; 9:5, 15, 18). They are warning judgments, designed to bring humanity to repentance . . . it is clearly stated that they do not in fact have this effect. Those who survive the judgments do not repent. Judgments alone, it is implied, do not lead to repentance and faith.[2]

By contrast, Beale writes:

> These judgments are not intended to evoke repentance but to punish because of the permanently hardened, unrepentant stance of the unbelievers toward God and his people.[3]

Hendriksen epitomizes the view of most in this camp:

> These trumpets of judgment . . . indicate *series* of happenings, that is,

199

⏳ HISTORICIST *(continued)*

of Attila, king of the Huns, "scourge of God," A. D. 447; a third was the sack of Rome by Genseric, king of the Vandals, AD 455; and the fourth, resulting in the final conquest of Rome, was that of Odoacer, king of the Heruli, who assumed the title of King of Italy, AD 476. We shall see, however, on a closer examination, that although two of these—Attila and Genseric—were, during a part of their career, contemporary, yet the most prominent place is due to Genseric in the events that attended the downfall of the empire, and that the second trumpet probably related to him; the third to Attila. These were, beyond doubt, four great periods or events attending the fall of the Roman empire, which synchronize with the period before us.

Most interpreters identify this first trumpet with the military conflicts between the Western Roman Empire and hordes of Goths and Vandals under Alaric. Even the non-Christian historian Edward Gibbon inadvertently used language like that of Scripture in describing these invasions. Gibbon writes of "the tremendous sound of the Gothic trumpet." Rome had not had to confront foreign invaders for eight hundred years. Stunned by the revolt, Rome evacuated Britain to reinforce its northern borders.

The Goths attacked Gaul, Spain, and Italy from the north, burning or

⌛ PRETERIST *(continued)*

It is not necessary to assume that the seven trumpets describe chronological events, as David S. Clark shows:

> It is much better to regard them as all belonging to one time and one event, namely the destruction of the first great persecutor of the Christian church. Christ, in speaking of the fall of Jerusalem, described it in sufficiently alarming terms; and history fills out the event . . . with scenes of crimes, and terror, robbery, and murder, and carnage sufficient to justify such symbols as these.

The destruction of **trees** and the **green grass** may be symbolic of people—even righteous people, if Chilton is correct:

> If the trees and grass represent the elect remnant (as they seem to in 7:3 and 9:4), this indicates that they are not exempt from physical suffering and death as God's wrath is visited upon the wicked. Nevertheless, (1) the Church cannot be completely destroyed in any judgment (Matt. 16:18), and (2) unlike the wicked, the Christian's ultimate destiny is not wrath but life and salvation (Rom. 2:7–9; 1 Thess. 5:9).

On the other hand, there may be reference to the destruction of actual vegetation in the land (a possible translation of **earth** in v. 7). Much of the beautiful foliage and trees around

FUTURIST *(continued)*

solid reason for not taking this judgment in its literal sense.

Ryrie agrees:

It would be very inconsistent to understand these judgments symbolically and interpret the plagues in Egypt plainly and actually. The judgment of the first trumpet presents a grim picture of devastation on the vegetation of the world.

Commenting on the phenomenon of the hail and fire being **mingled with blood,** Ray Stedman points out that the nineteenth-century book, *The Atmosphere,* by Camille Flammarion, documents occurrences of the falling of red rain, in 1744, upon San Pier d'Arena, near Genoa, Italy. The book speculates as to its cause:

A shower of blood is generally a mere fall of vapors tinted with vermilion or red chalk. But when blood actually does fall, which it would be difficult to deny takes place, it is a miracle due to the will of God.[1]

As for the effects of this plague, Kuyper describes the devastation in these terms:

So terrible is this first downpouring of fire and hail that, while not entirely, yet, for a third part nature is utterly destroyed and consumed. At the first trumpet blast all gardens, parks and fields are burned by the fire of the lightning.

IDEALIST *(continued)*

calamities that will occur again and again throughout this dispensation. They do not symbolize single and separate events, but they refer to woes that may be seen any day of the year in any part of the globe. Therefore, the trumpets are synchronous with the seals.

The first four trumpets are directed against "the sources of life which men in their blindness take for granted" (Wilson), or against "nature in its fourfold aspect as regarded by the ancients: land, sea, fresh water, heavenly bodies" (Hobbs).

Most expositors mention the resemblance to the Egyptian plagues. Plummer observes that these judgments, like those of Egypt, depict griefs upon the world, not the trials of the church: "The Church is the true Israel which exists uninjured by these manifestations of God's wrath in the midst of the world of Egyptian wickedness."

As to the timing of these trumpet blasts, Wilcock writes that "the first five Trumpets are likely to resemble the first five Seals in revealing not datable events, but aspects of the world situation which may be true at any time." Earl Morey concurs: "These calamities are symbolic, not literal; they are repetitive throughout history rather than consecutive; again, they will intensify as the Age closes."

The first trumpet affects **the earth,** and brings destruction to vegetation. It

HISTORICIST *(continued)*

destroying everything in their path. The wording of this verse seems particularly suited to the carnage described by Gibbon: "Blood and conflagration and the burning of trees and herbage marked their path." From AD 408 to 410, they besieged the city of Rome three times, sacking the city in 410—the same year that Alaric died.

Matthew Henry expands upon this interpretation by suggesting that the trumpets bring calamities on the church as well as the empire. With reference to the hail, fire, and blood, he says:

> There was a terrible storm; but whether this is to be understood of a storm of heresies, a mixture of monstrous errors falling on the church (for in that age Arianism prevailed), or a storm or tempest of war falling on the civil state, expositors are not agreed.

He suggests that the **trees** and **grass** destroyed in this trumpet judgment could represent the church's clergy and laity, respectively, or great people and common people.

The fraction **a third** has been explained as referring to either the Roman Empire, which was one-third of the then known world (Mede, Bishop Newton), or one-third of the empire itself, namely, the western division (Elliott).

PRETERIST *(continued)*

Jerusalem were destroyed by the Romans in the war and later described by Josephus:

> And now the Romans, although they were greatly distressed in getting together their materials, raised their banks in one-and-twenty days, after they had cut down all the trees that were in the country that adjoined to the city, and that for ninety furlongs round about, as I have already related. And, truly, the very view itself of the country was a melancholy thing; for those places which were before adorned with trees and pleasant gardens were now become a desolate country every way, and its trees were all cut down: nor could any foreigner that had formerly seen Judea and the most beautiful suburbs of the city, and now saw it as a desert, but lament and mourn sadly at so great a change; for the war had laid all signs of beauty quite waste. (*Wars* VI: 1:1)

⏳ **FUTURIST** *(continued)*

Hal Lindsey believes that all of the ecological catastrophes described in this chapter are the direct result of nuclear weapons. He suggests that the **grass** that is burned up would also include grain crops such as wheat, rice, and oats. From the details given in this verse, he extrapolates much related destruction:

> With the massive loss of vegetation will come soil erosion, floods, and mudslides. Air pollution will be immense; the smoke of the fire will fill the atmosphere, and the remaining vegetation will be unable to adequately absorb the hydrocarbons from automobiles and industry. Ecology will be thrown chaotically out of balance. ⏳

⏳ **IDEALIST** *(continued)*

is clear that the command not to harm the trees (7:3) is no longer in force. Such destruction of vegetation, of course, involves the devastation of agricultural products—and, therefore, famine. For this reason, Beale suggests that this trumpet may correspond to the shortages implied in the vision of the third horseman (6:5–6).[4]

Wilcock suggests that the **hail, fire,** and **blood** may "symbolize any kind of destruction which at any time damages the earth on which man lives." Hendriksen writes:

> In all probability this first trumpet indicates that throughout the period extending from the first to the second coming, our Lord, who now reigns in heaven, will afflict the persecutors of the Church with various disasters that will take place on earth, that is, on the land. ⏳

THE SECOND TRUMPET

REVELATION 8:8—9

[8]Then the second angel sounded: And something like a great mountain burning with fire was thrown into the sea, and a third of the sea became blood; [9] And a third of the living creatures in the sea died, and a third of the ships were destroyed.

⌛ HISTORICIST

Barnes writes:

> A *mountain* is a natural symbol of strength, and hence becomes a symbol of a strong and powerful kingdom; for mountains are not only places of strength in themselves, but they anciently answered the purposes of fortified places, and were the seats of power. . . . The effect [of this mountain being cast into the sea] was *as if* one-third of all the fish in the sea were cut off. Of course, this is not to be taken literally. It is designed to describe an effect, pertaining to the maritime portion of the world. . . . The *natural* interpretation would be to apply it to some invasion or calamity pertaining to the sea—to the islands, to the maritime regions, or to commerce.

This **great mountain** (v. 8) is the Vandals (428–468) under their king Genseric, to whom historians refer as "the Tyrant of the Sea." For over six centuries, no hostile ship had disputed Rome's mastery of the **sea.** The Vandals

⏳ PRETERIST

This trumpet can be applied to the destruction of Israel and Jerusalem in the Jewish War of AD 66–70 in both a symbolic and a literal sense. Symbolically, the image of a *mountain* in prophecy often refers to a government or a kingdom. Chilton reminds us that "the nation of Israel was God's 'Holy Mountain,' the 'mountain of God's inheritance' (Exod. 15:17). . . . Mount Zion was an accepted symbol of the nation." Here John sees **a great mountain burning with fire** (v. 8). Jerusalem was burned by the Romans, but even if this were not literally true, fire generally is an emblem of judgment. This mountain in the vision is **thrown into the sea** (v. 8). "The sea" is frequently used in prophecy as a symbol of the Gentile nations, in contrast to "the land," signifying Israel.

The symbolism could depict the Jewish state collapsing and the resultant dispersion of the Jews throughout the Gentile world. Jesus cursed the barren fig tree in the presence of His

FUTURIST

Here too *futurists* are not agreed as to whether to take the language of the passage figuratively or literally or both. Ray Stedman writes:

> If these are literal events, there is also a symbolic dimension to them. . . .The symbol of the mountain-like object falling into the sea probably symbolizes the influence of what is popularly called "the revived Roman Empire."

He then reminds us that the sea is a symbol of the Gentile nations, and concludes that the mountain falling into the sea

> suggests a time when the Antichrist-led coalition will fall upon the Gentiles of the world like a flaming, destroying mountain, conquering the Gentile nations and destroying many Gentile lives.

Gaebelein, too, opts for a symbolic interpretation of the imagery of this trumpet:

> That this is not a literal mountain is obvious. A mountain in Scripture language represents a Kingdom (Isaiah ii:2; Zech. iv:7; Psalm xlvi:2; and especially Jerem. li:25). The sea is typical of nations. Some kingdom, internally on fire, signifying probably revolution, will be precipitated into the restless sea of nations, and the result will be a still greater destruction of life and

IDEALIST

The most common approach to this trumpet is to observe that a mountain, in prophetic and apocalyptic writings, usually represents a kingdom and that fire is a common, generic emblem of judgment. Thus some great kingdom here comes under judgment. It might even represent every kingdom at any time in history that has, or will, come under God's judgment.

A common view is that this is mystery Babylon, Revelation's symbolic representation of the world system, in general, that is here seen collapsing. Certainly Babylon's fall is elsewhere in the book a key theme (14:8; 16:19; ch.18). As the various themes of Revelation are seen represented repeatedly in the parallel sections of of the book, it would not be out of character for this idea to be presented here, as it is, more explicitly, elsewhere.

G. K. Beale (along with numerous others) observes that **a great mountain burning with fire** (v. 8) and cast into the sea is drawn from the images of Babylon's fall in the Old Testament:

> "Behold, I am against you, O destroying mountain, who destroys all the earth," says the LORD. "And I will . . . make you a burnt mountain." . . . The sea has come up over Babylon; she is covered with the multitude of its waves (Jer. 51:25, 42).

Hailey agrees. He writes:

⧖ HISTORICIST *(continued)*

left their ancient home on the Baltic to invade Rome, "destroying the ships and commerce of the Romans, and were distinguished in the downfall of the empire by their ravages on the islands and the sea" (Barnes). In addition to their exploits at sea, the Vandals ravaged Gaul and Spain. As Roman ships were sunk and their mariners slaughtered, portions of the **sea became blood** (v. 8).

Leaning primarily on the account of Gibbon (the leading secular authority on the history of the Roman Empire), Barnes summarizes the Vandals' exploits:

> His general account of the Vandals is this: they are supposed (i. 138) to have been originally the same people with the Goths, the Goths and Vandals constituting one great nation living on the shores of the Baltic. They passed in connexion with them over the Baltic; emigrated to Prussia and the Ukraine; invaded the Roman provinces; received tribute from the Romans; subdued the countries about the Bosphorus; plundered the cities of Bithynia; ravaged Greece and Illyrium, and were at last settled in Thrace under the emperor Theodosius. They were then driven forward by the Huns, and having passed through France and Spain into Africa, conquered the Carthaginian territory, established an independent government, and thence through a long period harassed the neighbouring islands,

⧖ PRETERIST *(continued)*

disciples, which probably symbolized the cursing of the fruitless nation. When His disciples, the next day, pointed out to Him that the tree had withered, Jesus commented: "Assuredly, I say to you, if you have faith and do not doubt . . . if you say to this mountain, 'Be removed and be cast into the sea,' it will be done" (Matt. 21:21). Since this comment is connected to the cursing of the fig tree, it is possible that Jesus was referring symbolically to "this mountain" (i.e., Israel), or, more literally, to the mountain immediately before Him (Zion/Jerusalem) being cast into the sea of Gentile nations as a result of the disciples' prayers. That would agree with verses 3–5 of this chapter, where the prayers of the saints were offered to God, followed by the fire being cast down on the land. Actually, the casting of fire on the land is a feature both of 8:5 and of the first two trumpets.

There also was a more literal fulfillment of the words **a third of the sea became blood** (v. 8) and of the destruction of fish and **the ships** (v. 9). Josephus described a battle in which the Romans pursued many Galileans onto the Sea of Tiberius (Galilee) and slaughtered them there. The words of Josephus, who had never read Revelation, seem almost as if they were calculated to present the fulfillment of this trumpet judgment:

FUTURIST *(continued)*

commerce, which is represented by the ships.

The very literal commitments of Henry Morris come out again in his exposition of this trumpet judgment:

> A mighty mass of rock, hurtling toward the earth, surrounded by combustible gases which ignite as they enter the atmosphere, steered earthward by the angelic host of heaven, seems the most likely physical explanation accessible to us at this time. Maybe a giant meteorite, or asteroid, or even a satellite orbiting one of the other planets, could conceivably be propelled earthward by cosmic forces of which we have little knowledge as yet.

> Although its actual collision with the sea will be in only one impact location, it is evident that the entire world will know about it. People will observe it for some time approaching from space, then entering the earth's gravitational field and spiraling inexorably to the surface itself. Most likely television cameras will be focused on it and the actual splashdown will be seen on TV screens all over the world.

Mounce discourages the attempt to find natural explanations of this phenomenon. He emphasizes that the description is of "an eschatological

IDEALIST *(continued)*

This symbolizes the fall of an eminent unidentified power cast down as Babylon of old; it could be any such city at any period in time. . . . To go beyond this broad application by designating a particular city is unwise, although this pattern fits both Rome and the entire empire when they fell.

Morey suggests that the picture of **a great mountain burning with fire** (v. 8) "suggests a volcano whose ashes pollute the sea." Many commentators have felt that the eruption of Vesuvius in AD 79 may have provided either the source of this imagery or else simply a remarkable example of how this kind of scene can be fulfilled in actual historic events. In this disaster, Pompeii and Herculaneum were covered with lava, many people and fish died as the lava reached the sea, and ships far out at sea were showered with burning embers.

Wilson, however, disagrees:

> To attempt to interpret the blazing mountain in terms of volcanic eruptions, like that of Vesuvius in AD 79, is to misunderstand the nature of such apocalyptic images. The evident meaning of the terrible picture is that the sea can also be used by God to punish and warn mankind. For if the loss of lives and property in all the sea disasters throughout the centuries could be calculated, this vision would not seem at all extravagant.

⧗ HISTORICIST *(continued)*

and the coasts of the Mediterranean by their predatory incursions, destroying the ships and the commerce of the Romans, and were distinguished in the downfall of the empire by their ravages on the islands and the sea. Thus they were moved along from place to place until the scene of their desolations became more distinctly the maritime parts of the empire; and the effect of their devastations might be well compared with a burning mountain moved from its ancient base and then thrown into the sea.

Having captured Carthage, the Vandals pirated the seas for thirty years before returning to pillage Rome for fifteen days, regarding neither age nor sex. The plunder of Rome was taken away on the Vandals' vessels, and the capital was abandoned.

Matthew Henry also offers two possibilities:

By this mountain some understand the leader or leaders of the heretics; others, as Mr. Mede, the city of Rome, which was five times sacked by the Goths and Vandals within the compass of 137 years. . . . In these calamities, a third part of the people (called here the sea or collection of waters) were destroyed. . . . This storm fell heavy upon the maritime and merchandising cities and countries of the Roman empire. 🖉

⧗ PRETERIST *(continued)*

And for such as were drowning in the sea, if they lifted their heads up above the water they were either killed by darts [arrows], or caught by the vessels; but if, in the desperate case they were in, they attempted to swim to their enemies, the Romans cut off either their heads or their hands; and indeed they were destroyed after various manners everywhere, till the rest, being put to flight, were forced to get upon the land, while the vessels encompassed them about (on the sea): but as many of these were repulsed when they were getting ashore, they were killed by the darts upon the lake; and the Romans leaped out of their vessels, and destroyed a great many more upon the land: one might then see the lake all bloody, and full of dead bodies, for not one of them escaped. And a terrible stink, and a very sad sight there was on the following days over that country; for as for the shores, they were full of shipwrecks, and of dead bodies all swelled; and as the dead bodies were inflamed by the sun, and putrefied, they corrupted the air, insomuch that the misery was not only the object of commiseration to the Jews, but to those that hated them, and had been the authors of that misery. (*Wars* III: 10:9)

⧖ FUTURIST *(continued)*

judgment . . . beyond any explanation in terms of natural phenomena." Ryrie (usually a strict literalist) seems to agree:

> It is not necessary to attempt to find something in the realm of experience which can match this description. John really does not say what the instrument of judgment will be, but he clearly reveals the effect of the judgment.

Finding, nonetheless, "something in the realm of experience" with which to compare it, Hal Lindsey points out that the text does not say an actual mountain, but **something *like* a great mountain** (v. 8). He identifies the fulfillment of the effects of the trumpet thus:

> This is probably either an enormous meteor or, more likely, a colossal H-bomb. . . . As much as I would love to be optimistic about a deescalation of the arms buildup, my understanding of Bible prophecy forces me to believe that just the opposite is true. ⊘

⧖ IDEALIST *(continued)*

Beale supports such an approach, arguing that we should not look to literal, contemporary events as the source of the John's imagery, but that the catastrophes are inspired by Old Testament models that use figures of speech.

Wilcock adds that "the particular mention of the loss of shipping . . . may mean that while the first plague was directed against man's environment, the second was directed against his commerce.

Beale agrees in seeing here an interruption in normal commerce, but attributes this interruption to the cutback in resources caused by continuing effects of the agricultural disasters indicated by the imagery of the first trumpet. ⊘

209

THE THIRD TRUMPET

REVELATION 8:10—11

[10]Then the third angel sounded: And a great star fell from heaven, burning like a torch, and it fell on a third of the rivers and on the springs of water. [11] The name of the star is Wormwood. A third of the waters became wormwood, and many men died from the water, because it was made bitter.

⌛ HISTORICIST

The **great star** (v. 10) of this vision is Attila, "the scourge of God." The Romans knew little about the Huns before 440. Their emergence was as sudden as a blazing meteor. Attila assembled his eight hundred thousand men upon the banks of the Danube. As the Vandals were the masters of the sea, Gibbon says, "the Huns were the masters of the great river." They decimated the regions of the Rhine, upper Danube, and Po **Rivers** (v. 10). In the Italian Alps, they shed so much blood as to pollute the waters that have their **springs** there. Some have estimated that three hundred thousand men lay slaughtered in the rivers. One historian wrote: "Many had died, and still continued to die, that drank of the waters, through famine, disease, and pestilence."[5] These details seem to satisfy the demands of the present passage.

Barnes observes:

> In all languages, probably, a *star* has been an emblem of a prince whose virtues have shone brightly,

⌛ PRETERIST

The turning of fresh water sources bitter and toxic may be in part a literal result of the decaying corpses that lay in the Sea of Galilee and in the Jordan River, which flows out of it, as the result of the blood maritime battle described by Josephus (cited in comments on the second trumpet). However, this fouling of the waters has symbolic significance for the nation of Israel. There is probably an intentional allusion to the promise (and implied threat) God made to Israel when they first came out of Egypt. When they came to the bitter waters of Marah, in response to Moses' casting a tree into the waters, God made the waters sweet and wholesome. The meaning of the incident is given in God's words:

> If you diligently heed the voice of the LORD your God and do what is right in His sight, give ear to His commandments and keep all His statutes, I will put none of the diseases on you which I have brought

⧗ FUTURIST

Mounce notes that the **fire** in each of the first three trumpet judgments corresponds to the fire cast down on the earth by the priest-angel just prior to the beginning of the series of trumpet blasts (v. 5).

Throughout the series of trumpet judgments, both Gaebelein and Ironside break ranks with the majority of fellow dispensationalists in adopting the symbolic, rather than the literal, approach to interpretation. Their views, however, are not identical. Gaebelein consistently applies these visions to the religio-political realm, seeing the political Antichrist as occupying center stage, while Ironside understands the fulfillment as applying to the realm of Christendom, with the main personage in view as the Pope, or papal religious system.

With reference to falling of the **great star** (v. 10), Gaebelein writes:

> It is some person who claimed authority and who becomes an apostate, whose fall produces the awful results given here. It may be the final anti-Christ who first may have claimed to be for Israel a great teacher with divine authority and then takes the awful plunge. Worm-wood is his name and the waters became wormwood and bitter. It stands for great corruption.

Ironside explains his position as follows:

⧗ IDEALIST

The third trumpet introduces a great star falling from heaven, as if on fire, and its impact is upon the freshwater sources of earth. Beale reminds us that stars, in apocalyptic literature such as this, represent angels, and goes further to say that such angels corporately represent kingdoms or peoples on earth. Thus the star equals an angel which equals a "legal-like" representative of some sinful people. Its fall in flames, therefore, represents the fall of a people under the judgment of God. In support of this idea, he cites a Hebrew midrash on Exodus 7:16–18 (the plague on the waters of Egypt), which sees the Mosaic plague as a judgment on heavenly beings—namely, the Nile god. These deities are seen as the legal agents of the sinful people who are affected by the plague. He sees the star, in this context, as representing Babylon's representative angel, and thus sees the judgment of Mystery Babylon continuing here from the former trumpet. He thinks that there is here also implication of the famine which he found in the previous trumpet judgments, as well.[7]

The name of the star is Wormwood, a bitter herb, which can be toxic if ingested over a period of time. Wormwood is mentioned in Jeremiah 9:15 and 23:15, and elsewhere in the Old Testament, where it symbolizes "severe affliction resulting from divine wrath."[8]

⌛ HISTORICIST *(continued)*

and who has exerted a beneficial influence on mankind. In all languages also, probably, a meteor flaming through the sky has been an emblem of some splendid genius causing or threatening desolation and ruin. . . . Among expositors there has been a considerable degree of unanimity in supposing the Attila, the king of the Huns, is referred to . . . After Alaric and Genseric, Attila occupies the next place as an important agent in the overthrow of the Roman empire.

Matthew Henry also presents two possibilities:

Some take this to be a political star. . . . Others take it to be an ecclesiastical star, some eminent person in the church, compared to a *burning lamp,* and they fix it upon [the heretic] Pelagius, who proved about this time a falling star, and greatly corrupted the churches of Christ.

Of course, such a suggestion, to be credible, would require that God Himself was as offended as was Henry at the errors of Pelagius, who was, reportedly, in all respects a good Christian, and whose only known sin was that he opposed some of Augustine's theological constructs. Even Augustine himself, Pelagius' chief opponent, praised his upstanding character.

The **springs of water** (v. 10), which become **Wormwood** (v. 11), he

⌛ PRETERIST *(continued)*

on the Egyptians. For I am the LORD who heals you. (Exod. 15:26)

The "healing" of the bitter waters was symbolic of the "healing" of the nation from their bitter bondage.[6] However, God's promise/warning implies that their disobedience to Him will result in His placing upon them the same plagues that he placed on the Egyptians—the waters can be made bitter again. Elsewhere, when describing the curses that Israel could expect if she violated her covenant with God, Moses wrote:

Then the Lord will bring upon you and your descendants extraordinary plagues—great and prolonged plagues—and serious and prolonged sicknesses. Moreover He will bring back on you all the diseases of Egypt, of which you were afraid, and they shall cling to you. (Deut. 28:59–60)

Relevant to this third trumpet judgment are the threats made by God through Jeremiah just prior to the destruction of Jerusalem in his day:

Behold, I will feed them, this people, with wormwood and give them water of gall to drink . . . Behold, I will feed them with wormwood, and make them drink the water of gall. (Jer. 9:15; 23:15)

It is noteworthy that throughout the pages of Revelation, the plagues that come upon the apostates are com-

⧗ FUTURIST *(continued)*

Stars in the prophetic scriptures are religious dignitaries. They that turn many to righteousness are to shine as the stars forever and ever. . . . Here we have a star whose influence over man is so great that when he falls the third part of men are poisoned because of the evil influence of this apostate leader.

Who is this star? While I do not want to try to prophesy, let me give you a suggestion. Who occupies the highest place in the church in the minds of millions of professing Christian people? Many would say, the Pope. Can you imagine what might be the effect on vast numbers of people if tomorrow the newspapers came out with an "Extra" something like this: "The Pope declares that Christianity is all a sham, that religion is just a fraud!"? . . . I do not say certainly it will be so. I am just giving you a hint of what might be.

Ryrie and Morris continue to argue for a more literal application of the words of the text, with which Walvoord agrees:

It seems preferable, however, to view this with a reasonable literalness, as in the case of the second trumpet. The star seems to be a heavenly body or a mass from outer space, understandably burning as it enters the atmosphere of the earth, falling with contami-

⧗ IDEALIST *(continued)*

The judgment brought on by this trumpet blast results in the pollution of the fresh water supplies of the earth. Wilcock says **the waters** (v. 11) are "a symbol of the natural resources which ought to sustain human life." This pollution causes a bitterness so severe that many men are either poisoned by drinking it or die of thirst from unwillingness to drink such fouled waters.

Hendriksen's first suggestion is that this refers to all the ways in which God uses the inland waters (he gives the examples of rivers flooding and damaging property and of epidemics that originate from marshes) as a means of sounding a trumpet warning to man to repent. He also offers a secondary application:

It is, perhaps, possible to expand the meaning of this plague so that . . . it indicates all the calamities which obstruct whatever means man employs in order to satisfy his needs. Water, then, symbolizes that which supplies man's needs, *e.g.*, industry, commerce. Hence, the poisoning of fountains and waters would indicate, among other things, the derangement of industry, commerce, *etc.*

That this condition is caused by the agency of a **great star** (v. 10) underscores "the awe-striking nature of the punishment, and is indicative of the fact

REVELATION 8:10–11

 HISTORICIST *(continued)*

assigns either to "the laws, which are springs of civil liberty" or to "the doctrines of the gospel, the springs of spiritual life."

Adam Clarke is content to catalogue several possibilities:

> This has given rise to various conjectures. Some say the star means Attila and his Huns; . . . others, Eleazer, the son of Annus, spurning the emperor's victims, and exciting the fury of the Zealots [*preterism*]; others, Arius, infecting the pure Christian doctrine with his heresy."

PRETERIST *(continued)*

parable to those with which God afflicted the Egyptians in the days of Moses. The **star,** which was **burning like a torch** (v. 10), is reminiscent of the tree cast into the waters by Moses, but has the opposite effect (Exod. 15:25).

Chilton writes:

> Like the preceding symbol, the vision of the Third Trumpet combines Biblical imagery from the fall of both Egypt and Babylon. . . . The **name** of this fallen star is **Wormwood,** a term used in the Law and the Prophets to warn Israel of its destruction as a punishment for apostasy (Deut. 29:18; Jer. 9:15; 23:15; Lam. 3:15, 19; Amos 5:7). Again, by combining these Old Testament allusions, St. John makes his point: Israel is apostate, and has become an Egypt; Jerusalem has become a Babylon; and the covenant-breakers will be destroyed, as surely as Egypt and Babylon were destroyed.

⏳ FUTURIST *(continued)*

nating influence upon the rivers and waters.

Ladd joins these expositors in identifying the "star" as a meteor falling to earth and contaminating the fresh water sources. Mounce interprets it as "a meteorite symbolizing divine visitation."

Stedman writes that the **great star** (v. 10)

is very likely a comet or comet-like object which breaks up when it enters the atmosphere and scatters itself throughout the earth, falling into the rivers and springs and poisoning them. It is interesting to speculate that the form of poisoning described in these verses might actually be a form of radiation.

Hal Lindsey, characteristic of his prior interpretations, sees in this falling star (as with the burning mountain mentioned previously) a picture of "another thermonuclear weapon which is a part of a series of exchanges between the nuclear powers." ⏳

⏳ IDEALIST *(continued)*

that the judgment is the act of God, and proceeds directly from heaven, and is not to be attributed to merely natural circumstances" (Plummer).

The turning of pure waters **bitter** (v. 11) and undrinkable might reflect the fact that God, in the Old Testament, refers to Himself as "the fountain of living waters" and complains that His people have forsaken Him for idols, which pollutes their worship (Jer. 2:13, 23). Hailey writes: "When men prefer the bitter waters of idolatry to the fountain of the living water, they will receive these bitter waters with the fatal consequences which follow." ⏳

THE FOURTH TRUMPET

REVELATION 8:12

[12]Then the fourth angel sounded: And a third of the sun was struck, a third of the moon, and a third of the stars, so that a third of them were darkened. A third of the day did not shine, and likewise the night.

⧗ HISTORICIST

The **sun,** the **moon,** and the **stars** represent "the political firmament of Rome." The conquest of Rome and the end of its imperial rule were accomplished by the Heruli under the command of Odoacer in the year 476. The last of the western emperors, Romulus-Augustus, was banished, and Odoacer commanded that the name and the office of the Roman emperor of the West should be abolished.

Barnes comments:

> The darkening of the heavenly luminaries is everywhere an emblem of any great calamity. . . . It is not to be *total.* It is not as if the sun, the moon, and the stars were entirely blotted out, for there was still some remaining light. . . . For a third part of the day, and a third part of the night, this darkness reigned; but does not this imply that there would be light again—that the obscurity would pass away, and that the sun, and moon, and stars would shine again? . . . There can be no difficulty in

⧗ PRETERIST

Assigning these events to the times of the Jewish War, Chilton writes: "The imagery here was long used in the prophets to depict the fall of nations and national rulers (cf. Isa. 13:9–11, 19; 24:19–23; 34:4–5; Ezek. 32:7–8, 11–12; Joel 2:10, 28–32; Acts 2:16–21)." He quotes Farrar, who wrote:

> Ruler after ruler, chieftain after chieftain of the Roman Empire and the Jewish nation was assassinated and ruined. Gaius, Claudius, Nero, Galba, Otho, Vitellius, all died by murder or suicide; Herod the Great, Herod Antipas, Herod Agrippa, and most of the Herodian Princes, together with not a few of the leading High Priests of Jerusalem, perished in disgrace, or in exile, or by violent hands. All these were quenched suns and darkened stars.

It is also worthy of mention that the emblems of the darkening of heavenly lights, which so frequently refers to the utter downfall of a nation under judgment, in Old Testament contexts, is a

⌛ FUTURIST

The diminishing of the heavenly lights in this judgment is interpreted by Ironside as a reduction of the light of spiritual perception in the Tribulation, a blinding of those who rejected the all-too-adequate light of the gospel to which they had been exposed.

Gaebelein continues to see the text symbolically:

> The sun is the symbol of the highest authority, the moon, who has not her own light, is symbolical of derived authority and the stars are symbolical of subordinate authority. The symbolical meaning of this trumpet judgment is that all authority within the revived Roman empire will be smitten by the hand from above and as a result there will be the most awful moral darkness.

Walvoord continues to hold out for a more literal application, considering that what we see here is "an eclipse that extends to a third part of the day and a third part of the night." Ryrie similarly suggests:

> The fourth judgment will affect the sun, moon, stars, and the uniformity of the day-night cycle. The sun, moon and stars will be smitten to the extent of one-third with the result that apparently the twenty-four-hour cycle will be shortened to a sixteen-hour cycle.

⌛ IDEALIST

Herschel Hobbs understands this trumpet to apply principally to the fall of the persecuting Roman Empire:

> Such natural calamities were related to the destruction of the Roman Empire, the enemy of God's people. History records that one of the main contributing factors to the downfall of Rome was a series of natural calamities. . . . [Speaking of the eruption of Vesuvius] Pliny said of it that the sky was darkened so that "it was now day elsewhere, but here night blacker and thicker than all nights."

Most idealists, however, apply the calamity more broadly, applying it to God's dealings with any nation at any given time.

This is Hendriksen's understanding of the passage:

> All evils that are due to the abnormal functioning of the heavenly bodies throughout this entire age are here indicated. Thus the entire universe, including even the sun, moon and stars, is used by our Lord as a warning for those who do not serve Him and who persecute His children.

Wilson writes:

> It should be obvious that John is painting a picture and not writing a treatise on astronomy! The darkness prefigures the doom of the ungodly (Isa. 13:10), and is also

⧖ HISTORICIST *(continued)*

applying this to Odoacer, and to his reign—a reign in which, in fact, the Roman dominion in the West came to an end.

The Western Roman Empire came to an end, according to Gibbon, about AD 476 or 479, and Odoacer was "King of Italy" from 476 to 490. Elliott wrote:

> The authority of the Roman name had not yet entirely ceased. . . . There was still a certain, though often faint, recognition of the supreme imperial authority. The moon and the stars might seem still to shine in the West, with a dim reflected light. In the course of the events, however, which rapidly followed in the next half-century, these too were extinguished. ⧖

⧖ PRETERIST *(continued)*

phenomenon here seen to occur only *in part*. One-third means "a significant minority." Whereas these effects would normally accompany the final disaster falling upon Jerusalem, if not reduced to a fraction, this imagery might speak of a partial disaster of the same sort, that falls short of the ultimate end. If the complete darkening of sun and moon referred to the total end of the Jewish State in the fall of Jerusalem, the present trumpet, portraying the same principle, only partially realized, could refer to the fall of multiple Judean cities, or of Galilee, which preceded the final overthrow of the capital city. ⧖

THREE "WOES" ANNOUNCED

REVELATION 8:13

¹³And I looked, and I heard an angel flying through the midst of heaven, saying with a loud voice, "Woe, woe, woe to the inhabitants of the earth, because of the remaining blasts of the trumpet of the three angels who are about to sound!"

⧖ HISTORICIST

This **angel** announces a turning point. The Western Roman Empire has been destroyed in the Gothic period described under the emblems of the first four

⧖ PRETERIST

Most scholars agree that "an eagle flying" is a reading better attested in the manuscripts than **an angel flying** (v. 13). Chilton writes:

FUTURIST *(continued)*

Both Lindsey and Morris seem to believe that the darkness described is a one-third reduction of light throughout the day and the night, such as might result from air pollution. Lindsey proposes the cause for this darkening as "the result from the tremendous pollution in the air left from nuclear explosions." Morris, however, does not see the cause as pollution but as some change in the physical processes that cause the sun to emit light.

IDEALIST *(continued)*

the prelude to the new exodus of God's people from under the hands of their oppressors (cf. 11:8; Luke 21:28). In an age which looks to the stars for guidance, this verse reminds us that God exercises complete control over the solar system.

Wilcock observes, "But the damage is partial ('one third'), not total; which seems to show that the Trumpets are sounding not doom, but warning."

FUTURIST

Most commentators make the point that the word **angel** in this verse is textually doubtful, and ought to be translated as "eagle." While Seiss devotes more than three pages to the significance of eagles and the appropriateness of their use here, most writers feel that the identity of the announcer is not nearly as important as the announcement itself: as terrible as the first four trumpet judgments were, the last three will be much worse. As Tenney observes: "The first four trumpet judgments on the earth are

IDEALIST

As the first four seals, with their horsemen, were set off from the last three, so the first four trumpets are set apart from the last three by this announcement that the latter will be more grievous than the former. This suggests that the calamities which occur throughout history will become more intense as the end approaches.

Specifically, the final three trumpets differ from the previous ones in that they strike the ungodly people directly, rather than merely affecting

REVELATION 8:13

HISTORICIST *(continued)*

trumpets. The final three trumpets, each referred to as a woe, turn our attention to the Eastern Roman Empire and its destruction. After that, the prophecy will turn our view back to the west, where Rome will be seen again in a new form—the papacy (cf. Barnes, 209).

The final trumpets are designated as woes because of the surpassing intensity and duration of the judgments. The first woe is the Saracens' conquest of the southern and eastern third of the empire; the second woe is the Turkish conquest of the remaining third in the east; and the third woe is the judgments of the seven bowls, which will be poured out upon the papacy—identified with the French Revolution and its results.

PRETERIST *(continued)*

The prophetic warnings of Israel's destruction are often couched in terms of eagles descending upon carrion (Deut. 28:49; Jer. 4:13; Lam. 4:19; Hos. 8:1; Hab. 1:8; Matt. 24:28). Indeed, a basic aspect of the covenantal curse is that of being devoured by the birds of the air (Gen. 15:9–12; Deut. 28:26, 49; Prov. 30:17; Jer. 7:33–34; 16:3–4; 19:7; 34:18–20; Ezek. 39:17–20; Rev. 19:17–18).

Though a *historicist*, Adam Clarke accurately puts forth the *preterist* position:

These woes are supposed by many learned men to refer to the destruction of Jerusalem: the first woe—the seditions among the Jews themselves; the second woe—the besieging of the city by the Romans; the third woe—the taking and the sacking of the city, and burning the Temple. This was the greatest of all the woes, as in it the city and Temple were destroyed, and nearly a million men lost their lives.

⧗ FUTURIST *(continued)*

physical in character; the last three are produced by spiritual forces."

Walvoord points out the "warning" character of the first four trumpets. He writes that this verse

> indicates that the first four trumpets are not only judgments in themselves but warnings of the last three trumpets which will be far more severe in character.

Similarly, Mounce observes that the announcement of this verse is "the transition from divine warnings to demonic woes. It previews that ultimate excommunication of unrepentant man to the punishment prepared for the devil and his angels (Matt. 25:41)." ⊘

⧗ IDEALIST *(continued)*

their environment. The first four trumpets might be seen as the shot across the bow, warning the wicked that worse is in store for them if they do not take warning. ⊘

THE FIFTH TRUMPET

REVELATION 9:1—6

¹Then the fifth angel sounded: And I saw a star fallen from heaven to the earth. To him was given the key to the bottomless pit. ²And he opened the bottomless pit, and smoke arose out of the pit like the smoke of a great furnace. So the sun and the air were darkened because of the smoke of the pit. ³Then out of the smoke locusts came upon the earth. And to them was given power, as the scorpions of the earth have power. ⁴They were commanded not to harm the grass of the earth, or any green thing, or any tree, but only those men who do not have the seal of God on their foreheads. ⁵ And they were not given authority to kill them, but to torment them for five months. Their torment was like the torment of a scorpion when it strikes a man. ⁶ In those days men will seek death and will not find it; they will desire to die, and death will flee from them.

⌛ HISTORICIST

To nearly all *historicist* commentators, the **locusts** (v. 3) represent the Saracens (Arabic Muslims) and their campaigns against the Eastern Roman Empire from about 612 to 763. The king (v. 11) that is over them is Mohammed. Adam Clarke says that this locust plague "certainly agrees better with the Saracens than with any other people or nation."

The **star fallen from heaven** (v. 1) is a symbol for a prince who has been degraded and deprived of his rank. Mohammed was of princely pedigree, but the previous generation of his family had lost rule.

In biblical times, actual locust plagues often came from Arabia. Elliott comments: "I say the very word for

⌛ PRETERIST

Besides the physical conflicts and disasters that came upon the Jews in the war against Rome, there was great spiritual and moral deterioration in the Jews' own society.

The **star fallen** (v. 1) clearly is not a literal star, for the personal pronoun **to him** is used regarding the star, as David S. Clark points out:

> This indicates that some personality was represented by that star. It may have been some angel, or some minister of religion like the high priest, or some body of religious teachers that spread unbelief, heresies, false principles that wrecked men's morals and the safety of society . . . This flood of

⏳ FUTURIST

Ironside conjectures that this **fallen star** (v. 1) is the same as the one mentioned under the third trumpet (8:10), whom he identified with the pope. However, while he believes the **key** (v. 1) represents "a system of teaching, and possibly ritual observances connected with it" and thinks that this trumpet describes "the development of apostasy of which [the pope] is evidently the head," yet he does not see the heresy as Catholicism, but "the occult systems of gnostic origin, so largely prevailing and so rapidly spreading at the present time." The **locusts** (v. 3), therefore, "aptly typify or symbolize the spiritual plague of the last days."

Ryrie, Walvoord, and Morris, who preferred a literal interpretation of the burning "mountain" and the falling "star" in the second and third trumpets, agree that the fallen star in this chapter "seems to refer to a person rather than a literal star or meteor" (Walvoord). Lindsey, for the first time up to this point, does *not* see an object that falls from heaven as a nuclear bomb. These writers believe this star to be "none other than Satan himself" (Walvoord, Lindsey). Ryrie explains how this fits with his previous literalism:

> The word [star] is often used to refer to some kind of intelligent creature, usually an angel (cf. 1:20; Job 38:7). Both meanings are perfectly consistent with plain,

⏳ IDEALIST

The star that releases the captives in the abyss in this vision is described as "fallen" (not "falling"). Three verses previously (8:10), a star was seen in the process of falling. There is, obviously, the possibility that this is to be understood chronologically, and that the star that fell when the third trumpet sounded is here seen as having already fallen, whent the fifth trumpet sounds.

This "star" may or may not be identified with "Apollyon," who is described as "the angel of the bottomless pit," later in the vision (v. 11), and who is said to be the "king" over the locusts that erupt from that diabolical pit. The fact that he has **the key to the bottomless pit** (v. 1) might be seen as strongly suggesting the angel of that pit. Alternatively, the angel of the abyss may be an inhabitant of the pit, who is released along with his minions at the sound of the fifth trumpet.

The identification of this fallen star with Satan himself is tempting (no pun intended!), due to the verbal similarity of Jesus' statement to His disciples, wherein He said, "I saw Satan fall like lightning from heaven" (Luke 10:18).

The sovereignty of God, which is a primary emphasis of the whole book, is here demonstrated in the fact that, whether this "star" is a good agent or an evil one, he does not possess the key to the abyss in his own right, but it **was given** (v. 1) to him—i.e., by God. We

223

⌛ HISTORICIST *(continued)*

locust might almost to a Hebrew ear suggest *Arab:* the names of the one and of the other being in pronunciation and in radicals not dissimilar—of the locusts (arbeh), of an Arab (arbi)."

These locusts, quite unlike the natural locust, were **commanded** by their king **not to harm the grass of the earth, or any green thing** (v. 4). A striking parallel appears in Mohammed's instruction in the Koran: "Destroy no palm trees, nor any fields of corn, cut down no fruit trees." This policy was in stark contrast to the slash and burn approach of the Gothic invaders described in the previous trumpet visions (e.g., 8:7). The Saracens were not able to **kill** (v. 5) papal Rome as a political body, but only to torment it for a while. Accordingly, though they desolated the Greek and Latin churches, they could not exterminate them nor gain possession of the empire. Those **who do not have the seal of God in their foreheads** (v. 4), the targets of the tormentors' assaults, according to the *Treasury of Scripture Knowledge,* are "corrupt and idolatrous Christians; against whom the Saracens chiefly prevailed."

As for the **five months** (vv. 5, 10), these are seen as five prophetic months of thirty days each: a total of 150 days, or by the year-for-a-day principle, 150 years. Mohammed adopted the policy of making converts by the sword in 612, from which time the Muslim Arabs

⌛ PRETERIST *(continued)*

locusts that came out of the bottomless pit were moral and spiritual errors. That was doubtless the reason that the servants of God were not hurt by them.

That there was a "flood of . . . moral and spiritual errors" is in fact an understatement, for the sanity and civility of the Jewish society had vanished altogether. Anyone acquainted with the relevant historical facts and with the work of evil spirits in Scripture will be able to see the possibility that a massive demonic delusion accounts for the behavior of the Jews. David Chilton describes the evidence from history that the Jews in the Last Days (AD 66–70) had literally become demonized:

> The entire generation became increasingly demon-possessed; their progressive national insanity is apparent as one reads through the New Testament, and its horrifying final stages in the pages of Josephus' *The Jewish War:* the loss of all ability to reason, the frenzied mobs attacking one another, the deluded multitudes following the most transparently false prophets, the crazed and desperate chase after food, the mass murders, executions and suicides, the fathers slaughtering their own families and the mothers eating their own children. Satan and the host of hell simply swarmed through the land of Israel and consumed the apostates.

FUTURIST *(continued)*

normal interpretation. In English we use this word in the same two ways. Literally, a star means an astronomical entity; and equally literally, though as a figure of speech, we use the word to mean a person, like the star of a football game.

Walvoord, Ryrie, Gaebelein, Tenney, Morris, and others identify the bottomless pit as the abode or prison house of demons. Therefore, they understand the locusts as demonic hordes released against the unrepentant sinners in the Tribulation period. The demons do not **kill** (v. 5), but only **torment** their victims, and are only allowed to afflict **those men who do not have the seal of God on their foreheads** (v. 4), so the 144,000 sealed in chapter 7 will be exempt.

Nondispensationalists, such as Ladd and Mounce, also understand the locusts as demons loosed on the unbelieving world.

Gaebelein graphically describes the implications of this trumpet:

> The light is now completely blotted out and in the darkness coming from the pit of the abyss the demon powers will do their fearful work. Demon possession and the most awful torments for soul and body will be the general thing.

Walvoord emphasizes demon possession as the leading feature of the

IDEALIST *(continued)*

know that only divine authority can provide such a key, since Jesus is the key-holder in 1:18, and it is a good angel (Christ?) who has the power to lock or unlock the abyss in 20:1ff.

This judgment affects men directly, causing **torment** (v. 5), though not death. Hobbs applies this and the former trumpets generally to history, but specifically to the judgment of the Roman Empire:

> It seems likely that the meaning of this event is to portray the *internal decay* within the Roman Empire itself . . . This suggests internal rottenness within the empire which history records was one of the main contributing factors in the fall of the empire. Specifically it was a series of corrupt rulers, all of whom were under the control of the destroyer Apollyon.

A more common interpretation is that the locusts represent demonic forces unleashed upon the earth. The fact that they proceed from the **bottomless pit** (v. 2), or the *abyss*, the prison of the demons, confirms this identification.

Because of the dense smoke that emerged from the opened abyss, **the sun and the air were darkened** (v. 2), even as the influence and power of evil "clouds men's minds and darkens their understandings" (Plummer).

Hendriksen sees the picture to be that of "demons, robbing men of all

HISTORICIST *(continued)*

began to attack the eastern churches and seek to forcibly convert Europe from Christianity to Islam. Their ravages were checked by their defeat at Tours by Charles Martel, in 732. In the year 763, the Muslims ceased their policy of aggression and moved their capital to Baghdad on the Tigris. Thus, "from the time that Mohammed began to propagate his imposture, AD 612, to the building of Baghdad, when they ceased from their ravages, AD 763, are just 150 years" (*Treasury of Scripture Knowledge*).

Even advocates of other approaches who are adamant in their rejection of the *historicist* system of interpretation have admitted the convincing nature of this particular identification, Biederwolf, for example:

> That there is a remarkable parallelism between this prediction and the rise and progress of the Mohammedan power the candid student must admit. Even Kelly, a staunch *futurist*, admits the interpretation to be well founded.

Pieters, also generally critical of *historicism*, concedes:

> Some points in the [*historicist*] interpretation, as developed by these expositors, seem excellently to fit the history, must be frankly conceded. One of the best, in my judgment, is the identification of the fifth trumpet with the rise of Mohammedanism and of the sixth

PRETERIST *(continued)*

David S. Clark writes:

> In the siege of Jerusalem social and civil safeguards were thrown to the winds; and as if they had gone insane, as if possessed with devils, father was set against son and son against father, brother against brother till the inside of the city was a seething hell, and its deliverance impossible.

Jesus, looking toward this event, warned that an onslaught of demons was what His generation could expect if they did not seize the opportunity He was presenting to them to come into His kingdom. Only thus could they walk in the deliverance and victory which they had already begun to experience as a result of His presence with them:

> When an unclean spirit goes out of a man, he goes through dry places, seeking rest, and finds none. Then he says, "I will return to my house from which I came." And when he comes, he finds it empty, swept, and put in order. Then he goes and takes with him seven other spirits more wicked than himself, and they enter and dwell there; and the last state of that man is worse than the first. *So shall it also be with this wicked generation.* (Matt. 12:43–45)

Jay Adams, taking a very different view from that of the majority, suggests

⌛ FUTURIST *(continued)*

passage: "Inasmuch as demons do not have physical shape, what John is seeing must symbolize demonic possession"; and "For the first time in history all those who do not know the Lord Jesus Christ as Saviour will come under demonic possession and affliction."

Referring to the statement that men **will desire to die, and death will flee from them** (v. 6), Walvoord writes: "As is common in demonic affliction as recorded in the Gospels, those in the grip of demons are not free to exercise their own will and therefore are not free to take their own lives." Ryrie, demonstrating loyalty to the literalist hermeneutic, seemingly above and beyond the call of duty, goes further still:

> The effect of this torment is to drive men to suicide, but they will not be able to die. . . . Death will not be possible. Bodies will not sink and drown; poisons and pills will have no effect; and somehow even bullets and knives will not do their intended job.

Kuyper, diverging from the spiritualized approach of most of the above, sees the locust hordes as symbolizing "the terrible military power which, when the antichrist appears, will arrogate dominion to itself over all the earth."

Moorehead also understands the locusts to be an invading army, identifying

⌛ IDEALIST *(continued)*

light, that is, of all true righteousness and holiness, joy and peace, wisdom and understanding." Likewise Hailey writes: "The light of truth which directs men's lives and guides them in the right way, giving peace to the soul, is darkened by the deceptions and delusions set loose by Satan."

Unlike regular locusts, these demonic beasts do not consume **the grass of the earth, or any green thing, or any tree** (v. 4), but rather torment human beings with a torment likened to that inflicted by **scorpions** (vv. 2, 5). Swete writes: "The scorpion takes its place with the snake and other creatures hostile to man, and with them symbolizes the forces of spiritual evil which are active in the world." This assessment seems to be verified by Jesus, when He told the disciples, "Behold, I give you authority to trample on serpents and scorpions, and over all the power of the enemy, and nothing shall by any means hurt you." (Luke 10:19)

Christians are not exempt from the physical maladies that afflict mankind, but the demons have no right to inflict their spiritual harm upon believers. Hobbs points out that "As Israel was safe from the plagues of Egypt, so God's people were protected from these locusts."

In addition to the analogy to Egypt, however, there may be an even closer connection to Ezekiel's vision, in which

HISTORICIST *(continued)*

trumpet with the coming of the Turks.[9]

Matthew Henry takes an entirely different approach to interpreting this vision. Until this point, he has presented the possibility that the trumpets could be describing either political or ecclesiastical events. At this point, he presents only the latter view. He sees the **star fallen from heaven** (v. 1) as Boniface, the third bishop of Rome, who assumed the title of universal bishop. Having forfeited the "keys of the kingdom of heaven," he now has the keys of hell, to unleash damnable doctrines and deception upon the church. This damage is spiritual, not physical; these demonic doctrines do not **kill** (v. 5) people physically, but subject them to spiritual **torment** for a limited period of time (five **months).** Mention might be made at this point of the Roman Catholic interpretation of Bellarmine and other Catholic writers, who identify the locusts with the Lutherans of the Reformation. In this view, Luther himself, who defected from the papal church, is the fallen star of the vision. Seiss, the *futurist*, rebuts this view:

> If Luther was the fallen star, who was the king over the Lutherans? The locusts were to continue "five months," but the Lutherans have wrought now for more than three hundred and fifty years, and still are the particular grief of the Papists. . . . The locusts have stings to

PRETERIST *(continued)*

that the "first woe probably signifies the epidemic spread of disease. This always accompanied war and siege."

Adam Clarke suggests the possibility that the **five months** (v. 5) may be the literal period "from May to September, in the year of the siege," when the Zealots in Jerusalem "produced dreadful contests among the people." David Clark suggests rather that the **five months** simply implies that "this terrible condition was short."

Jay Adams sees the fact that **men will seek death and will not find it** (v. 6) is a possible identification with Luke 23:27–30 and Revelation 6:16, in both of which passages men are said to cry out for the mountains and the hills to fall upon them (which request is not granted). The desire of men to die may also refer to the fact that, during the siege of Jerusalem, the horrendous crimes perpetrated by the inhabitants caused many to wish for the Romans to break through the wall and destroy the city to put them out of their misery.

Alternatively, Chilton dates this five-month period earlier than the siege—that is, before the beginning of the war:

> This may refer in part to the actions of Gessius Florus, the procurator of Judea, who for a five month period (beginning in May of 66 with the slaughter of 3,600 peaceful citizens) terrorized the

⧗ FUTURIST *(continued)*

this horde with that of Gog in Ezekiel 38. He believes Russia will have a key part in this invasion, accompanied by swarms of other nationalities, animated by a satanic spirit and filled with demonic fury.

Though Lindsey's initial comments suggest that he is expecting actual creatures just as described, he mentions (with apparent approval) this idea of modern warfare and military power as a possible alternative: Helicopters!

> That may just be conjecture, but it does give you something to think about! A Cobra helicopter does fit the composite description very well. They also make the sound of "many chariots." [Possibly] . . . the means of torment will be a kind of nerve gas sprayed from its tail. ⧗

⧗ IDEALIST *(continued)*

God's true people were marked on their foreheads just prior to the unleashing of six angelic destroyers, who slaughtered those in Jerusalem who lacked the mark (Ezekiel 9).

The **five months** (v. 5) of the locusts' ravages correspond to the normal lifetime of a natural locust, and is used here symbolically to indicate that the torment of the first woe is to be of limited duration. Wilson observes that "A torment which lasts for five months is a long time, but is still of limited duration."

Men usually avoid death at all costs, yet it overtakes them all. In the picture before us the situation is reversed, for they will desire to die, and death will flee from them (v. 6). Moffatt writes that "The withholding of death, instead of being an alleviation, is really a refinement of torture; so infernal is the pain, that the sufferers crave, but crave in vain, for death. ⧗

HISTORICIST *(continued)*

torment men; the Lutherans have never been tormentors nor persecutors[10] . . . No people have ever suffered from the Lutherans or their doctrines, as to seek death in order to escape their torments, without ability to find it.

PRETERIST *(continued)*

Jews, deliberately seeking to incite them to rebellion. He was successful: Josephus dates the beginning of the Jewish War from this occasion.[11]

DESCRIPTION OF LOCUSTS

REVELATION 9:7—12

[7]The shape of the locusts was like horses prepared for battle. On their heads were crowns of something like gold, and their faces were like the faces of men. [8]They had hair like women's hair, and their teeth were like lions' teeth. [9] And they had breastplates like breastplates of iron, and the sound of their wings was like the sound of chariots with many horses running into battle. [10]They had tails like scorpions, and there were stings in their tails. Their power was to hurt men five months. [11]And they had as king over them the angel of the bottomless pit, whose name in Hebrew is Abaddon, but in Greek he has the name Apollyon. [12] One woe is past. Behold, still two more woes are coming after these things.

HISTORICIST

Elliott and Barnes present reasons why the description of **the locusts** (v. 7) provides a particularly apt symbol of the Islamic hordes. Midianite Arab hordes are likened, as to their numbers, to locusts invading (Judg. 6:5). Islamic tradition speaks of locusts having dropped into the hands of Mohammed, bearing on their wings this inscription: "We are the army of the Great God."

PRETERIST

As was mentioned with regard to the previous section, the **locusts** (v. 7) which are here described in detail, refer to demons set loose in the besieged city of Jerusalem as a judgment against those who had rejected Christ. Seen as such, the distinct features given in these verses can be understood from the *preterist* point of view essentially the same as explained in the *idealist* approach (see column 4).

⌛ FUTURIST

Those who understand these as demonic creatures generally do not attempt to explain the features of **the locusts** (v. 7) as symbolic of anything else, but see them as a straightforward description of their actual appearance. Henry Morris, among them, writes:

> What do these "horses" and "crowns" and "man-faces" represent? Interpreters grope here for possible meanings to these symbols. But these are not written as symbols. . . . John . . . is merely describing what he saw.

Ironside, who sees in this plague a depiction of the rise of New Age heresies under the leadership of a future apostate pope, explains the features of the locusts in accordance with this presupposition:

> Three symbols here intermingle, all of which are very evidently found in the occult systems to which we have referred. Faces as of men would seem to imply intelligence, and these teachers make

⌛ IDEALIST

G.K. Beale points out that the features of this vision, especially the description of the locusts in verses 7–9, are derived from the description of the locust plague referenced in the first two chapters of the book of Joel. He opines that, while scholars are not agreed as to whether Joel's locusts are literal, or whether they represent a human invasion force, the literalness of Joel's usage is immaterial for our consideration of the symbols in Revelation.

The description of the locusts is symbolic of the character of demons: **like horses** (v. 7), they come as an invading army. They wear **crowns of something like gold** (not real gold!), representing their pretended authority. Hailey writes:

> This is the only place in the Book of Revelation where the victory crown (stephanos) is used of any other than Christ and the saints; and even in this instance these are not crowns of permanent victory or of genuine gold . . . The victory of wickedness is only an imitation

⏳ HISTORICIST *(continued)*

Their traditional turbans can be seen as **crowns** (v. 7). The description of having **faces of men** (v. 7) and **hair like women's hair** (v. 8) is seen as a reference to their bearded, long-haired heads. Like the Jews, but unlike Greeks and Romans, the Arabs wore long beards. That they also wore their hair long is well documented. Pliny wrote of the "turbaned Arabs with their uncut hair." The long hair of the Arabs was also spoken of by Ammianus Marcellinus and Jerome in the fourth and fifth centuries respectively. The Arabian poem *Antar* was written in Mohammed's own time. One line of this poem reads: "He adjusted himself, twisted his beard, and folded his hair under his turban, drawing it up from his shoulders." The **breastplates of iron** (v. 9) were literal. The Saracens had iron coats of mail. The Koran says: "God has given you coats of mail to defend you in your wars." The **stings in their tails** (v. 10) may refer to the fact that the Saracens were known to be adept at fighting rearward over the tails of their horses.

Who was the leader, the angel of the pits, then? Barnes writes:

> (a) He was like a star that fell from heaven . . . Would anything better characterize the genius, the power, and the splendid but perverted talent of Mohammed?

⏳ PRETERIST *(continued)*

Though the locusts themselves are no doubt a portrayal of armies of demons that afflicted the whole society of the Jews during their conflicts with the Romans, the description is perhaps mingled with some features of the demonized zealots who made life so miserable for their fellow Jews during the siege. That they have **hair like women's hair** (v. 8) may actually be a reference to their transvestitism, as Josephus describes:

> With their insatiable hunger for loot, they ransacked the houses of the wealthy, murdered men and violated women for sport; they drank their spoils with blood, and from mere satiety and shamelessness gave themselves up to effeminate practices, plaiting their hair and putting on women's clothes, drenched themselves with perfumes and painting their eyelids to make themselves attractive. They copied not merely the dress, but also the passions of women, devising in their excess of licentiousness unlawful pleasures in which they wallowed as in a brothel. Thus they entirely polluted the city with their foul practices. Yet though they wore women's faces, their hands were murderous. They would approach with mincing steps, then suddenly become fighting men, and, whipping out their swords from under their dyed cloaks, they would run through every passerby. (*Wars* IV: 9:10)

⧗ **FUTURIST** (continued)

a great appeal to human reason . . . while actually they themselves follow but sophistical and illogical theories . . . Moreover they are characterized by intense seductiveness and attractive fancies, typified by "the hair of women." . . . But seductive and apparently rational as these systems are when first presented, they prove at last to have teeth like the teeth of lions, tearing to pieces those who put their trust in them . . . These iron breastplates utterly destroy all conscience, or, rather, render them impervious to the shafts of truth.

Ironside is one of those who sees the locusts' **king** (v. 11) as the same angel that opened the pit at the beginning of the chapter. Others consider this king to be a high-ranking subordinate of Satan. Mounce suggests that the name of this leader, **Apollyon** (meaning "Destroyer"), may be a derogatory barb against the Greek god Apollo, of whom the locust was a symbol. He points out that Domitian, whom he believes to have been the emperor reigning when John wrote Revelation, "liked to be regarded as Apollo incarnate." Gaebelein considers the fact that this name is given in both Hebrew and Greek indicates that "both Jew and Gentile . . . come under his power."

⧗ **IDEALIST** (continued)

of the genuine; it is never lasting or true.

Like **men,** whose **faces** they have (v. 7), the demons are intelligent. Like **women** with their long **hair** (v. 8), they can be seductive (1 Tim. 4:1 KJV).

Their teeth, **like lions' teeth** (v. 8), speak of their ferocity (1 Pet. 5:8). **Like scorpions** (v. 10; cf. Luke 10:19), they are malicious.

Their breastplates are **like breastplates of iron** (v. 9), giving the appearance of invulnerability, and it is true that they cannot be resisted by merely human means.

In addition to their refusal to destroy vegetation, these locusts further differ from those of nature in that they had a **king over them** (v. 11), yet "the locusts have no king" (Prov. 30:27). Carpenter writes:

> The sacred writer shows us a plague in which devastation, malice, king-like authority, intelligence, seductiveness, fierceness, strength, meet together under one directing spirit, to torment men.

This king, whose name means "destruction" and "destroyer," may be Satan, though he may also be a high-ranking demon. Wilson writes: "Satan himself does not appear before the vision of the woman and the dragon in ch. 12."

HISTORICIST (continued)

(b) He was a king. That is, there was to be one monarch—one ruling spirit to which all these hosts were subject . . . All those hosts were subject to one mind—to the command of the single leader that originated the scheme.

(c) The name, *Abaddon*, or *Apollyon–Destroyer*, Revelation 9:11. This name would be appropriate to one . . . who wasted so many cities and towns; who overthrew so many kingdoms.

PRETERIST (continued)

The king over the locusts is Satan himself. Jesus had said that the Jewish apostates were children of the devil (John 8:44), and "a synagogue of Satan" (Rev. 2:9; 3:9). David Chilton writes:

Clearly, for Satan's entire host of destroyers to be let loose upon the Jewish nation was a hell on earth indeed. And yet St. John tells us that this outbreak of demons in the land is only **the first Woe.** Even this is not the worst, for **two Woes** (i.e., the sixth and seventh trumpets) **are still coming after these things.**

THE SIXTH TRUMPET

REVELATION 9:13–15

[13]Then the sixth angel sounded: And I heard a voice from the four horns of the golden altar which is before God, [14]saying to the sixth angel who had the trumpet, "Release the four angels who are bound at the great river Euphrates." [15]So the four angels, who had been prepared for the hour and day and month and year, were released to kill a third of mankind.

HISTORICIST

The **third of mankind** (v. 15) upon whom this woe falls is the eastern third, or Grecian portion of what had been the Roman Empire. This was the Byzantine Empire, with its capital at Constantinople.

PRETERIST

It is probable that the figurative language of this vision refers to the Roman armies or their confederates, following upon the demonic "locust" invasions that came upon the apostates of Israel. Many of the troops that came into

FUTURIST

Though some see the **four angels** (v. 14) here as the same four angels in 7:1, who had authority over the four winds, this identification is considered unlikely by Walvoord or Gaebelein. These four are evil angels, presently bound until the moment ordained by God, at which time they will be loosed to kill a third of mankind. This destruction is apparently accomplished through the great army described in the verses immediately following. The mention of the **Euphrates** (v. 14) suggests that the armies come in from the east, as Walvoord writes: "Why should they be bound in or at the Euphrates? The answer seems to be that the vision concerns an invasion from the Orient."

IDEALIST

In Revelation 7:1, we read of four angels who were restraining the destructive powers of God's judgments. Here, we find four angels also associated with judgment events. The difference is that, whereas the earlier four angels held judgment back, these angels seem themselves to be held back, and, when released, become the agents that carry out the judgment events.

The judgment revealed in this trumpet vision involves the river **Euphrates** (v. 14). This was the traditional eastern boundary of the promised land and also of the Roman Empire. It served as a barrier to invaders from the east and therefore symbolizes "restraint upon the forces of evil" (Morey).

235

⧖ HISTORICIST *(continued)*

Shortly before the year 1000, a fierce and numerous people known as the Tartars moved from the area of the Caspian Sea to new settlements on the eastern banks of the Euphrates. Under the leadership of Togrul, the Turkomans or Turkmans, as they came to be called, established a formidable empire in western Asia. The Turkmans conquered Baghdad, the capital of the Saracen empire, in 1055, and converted to the Islamic religion. Persia and India being subjugated, it would have seemed natural for the Turks to expand west across the Euphrates. "Yet for a long time they had now been inactive, and it would seem they had been bound or restrained by some mighty power from moving in their conquests to the West" (Barnes).

Under Togrul's son, Alp Arslan, and his successor, Malek Shah, the Turks crossed the Euphrates and made assaults upon the Byzantine Empire. The Turkish empire in those days was divided into four principalities under Shah's four sons. Almost four hundred years later, in 1453, the Turks—by this time known as the Ottoman Empire—conquered Constantinople, bringing to an end the last vestige of the Roman Empire in the east.

The Turkish hordes are the horsemen (v. 16) depicted in this vision. The increments of time: an **hour,** and a **day,** and a **month,** and a **year** (v. 15) are to be added together. Calculating by the

⧖ PRETERIST *(continued)*

Palestine had been stationed previously at the **Euphrates** (v. 14). David Clark writes:

> The river Euphrates was the boundary between Israel and her ancient captors. It was across the Euphrates that Assyria came and carried Israel into captivity. And it was across the Euphrates that Babylon came and carried Judah into captivity. The great conquerors of Palestine and Egypt had come across the Euphrates in ancient times.

Jay Adams concurs:

> It was across the Euphrates that Israel's conquerors had previously come—Assyria, Babylon, Medo-Persia. Moreover, there were places at this very time where Roman armies were stationed along the Euphrates. Cf. Josephus, *Wars* 7: 1:3. The 10th legion, which participated in the destruction, had been located there.

That this invasion was scheduled so precisely **for the hour and day and month and year** (v. 15) emphasizes that it was a specifically predestined event.

The destruction of Jerusalem was one of the few prophesied events that carried a clear time designation. Daniel's famous prophecy of the "seventy weeks" predicts that "the people of the prince who is to come shall destroy the

⏳ FUTURIST (continued)

Ironside further explains:

These angels are evidently at the present time restraining the great Asiatic hordes from pouring themselves upon the Land of Palestine and Europe. The Euphrates formed the eastern limit of the Roman Empire, and thus was the barrier, as it were, between the East and the West.

Tenney agrees:

The Euphrates was for the empire the boundary between the East and the West, the frontier which the West always had to defend against possible invasion from the warlike hordes that thronged on its border. A second reference to the Euphrates in Revelation 16:12 confirms the idea that the prediction relates to a mass gathering of Oriental peoples by demonic influences against the people of God and the rule of Christ.

In the latter half of the first century, the Roman Empire feared an invasion from the Parthians who were just beyond the Euphrates. The possibility of such an invasion found expression in the popular imagination and the writings of other apocalypses of the same general period as Revelation. Mounce and Ladd point out that there is, however, an important distinction between John's version and those given by the noncanonical apocalyptists: "The latter

⏳ IDEALIST (continued)

The River Euphrates also is mentioned in connection with the sixth "bowl" judgment (16:12), confirming the idealist suggestion of parallelism in the cycles of judgments. According to A. Y. Collins, the sixth trumpet and the sixth bowl refer to "the same event from different points of view."[12]

The timing of this judgment is precisely ordained to occur at an **hour and day and month and year** (v. 15) prescibed by God. This is another affirmation of the sovereignty of God, which continues to pervade the book as a major theme.

The voice that releases these demonic forces comes from the **horns of the golden altar** (v. 13). Earlier, this altar was associated with the prayers of the saints (8:3), so it may be the voice of the saints in prayer that brings this judgment on the earth. It may be that we are to understand the saints to be praying specifically for such disasters to befall the wicked—seemingly exhibiting a thirst for vengeance difficult to harmonize with Christ's command to "love . . . bless . . . do good to" and "pray for" their persecutors (Matt.5:44 / Luke 6:27–28). On the other hand, such occurrences may be entirely at God's prerogative, in answer to the general prayers of all saints, "Your kingdom come; Your will be done on earth . . ." (Matt. 6:10). The prayer that God's kingdom should triumph on earth can

⌛ HISTORICIST (continued)

year-for-a-day method, an **hour** is either one twelfth or one twenty-fourth of a year; a **day** is a year; a **month** is 30 years; and a **year** is either 360 or 365 years, depending upon whose calendar (Jewish or Roman) is followed. Thus the aggregate period totals either 391 years and 15 days, or else 396 years and 106 days.

Elliott and Barnes favor the use of the Julian calendar of 365 days, extending the period of this calamity to 396 years and 106 days. Beginning the reckoning at about 1055, in which the Turks took Baghdad and overturned the empire of the caliphs (Arab rulers), it is thus possible to calculate the end of the period as the year 1453, when Constantinople and the Byzantine Empire fell.

Caringola also sees the period ending with the fall of Constantinople, but he uses the Jewish year of 360 days as the basis for his calculation. Counting backward 391 years from 1453, he arrives at the year 1062, which he says was the year the Turks crossed the Euphrates and began their slaughter. The use of the Jewish year seems consistent with its use of the same elsewhere in Revelation, e.g., 1,260 days equals 42 months equals three and one half years (chaps. 11–13).

The editors of the *Treasury of Scripture Knowledge* begin the period later and use the 360-day year for calculation:

⌛ PRETERIST (continued)

city and the sanctuary. The end of it shall be with a flood [of armies?], and till the end of the war desolations are determined" (Dan. 9:26). These things are said to occur at a specific time connected with the "seventy weeks" (Dan. 9:24).

Jesus also suggested a specific time for the fulfillment of the destruction prophecies. He predicted the destruction of Jerusalem and the temple in Luke 21:6—"the days will come in which not one stone shall be left upon another, that shall not be thrown down." Four of His disciples, Peter, James, John, and Andrew (Mark 13:3), came to Him privately and asked Him "Teacher, but when will these things be? And what sign will there be when these things are about to take place?" (Luke 21:7). His answer is given in what is usually called the Olivet Discourse.

In answer to the question as to what sign would indicate that the destruction of Jerusalem was near, Jesus answered: "When you see Jerusalem surrounded by armies, then know that its desolation is near" (v. 20). As to *when . . . these things [will] be*, His answer was definitive: "Assuredly I say to you, this generation will by no means pass away till all things take place" (v. 32). In fact, Jesus suggested that the invasion of Jerusalem and its destruction was the ultimate theme of all Old Testament prophecy: "For these are the

⌛ FUTURIST *(continued)*

always envision the foreign invasion as an attack against the people of God by pagan hosts while John sees it as a divine judgment upon a corrupt civilization" (Ladd).

The expression **the hour and day and month and year** (v. 15) does not refer to the duration of their carnage but to the fact that this judgment comes exactly at the time God ordained. Ironside elaborates:

> Until that hour strikes, not all the evil machinations of men, not all the ambitions of nations, can bring about the conflict here predicted. But when that hour does strike, no astute statesman's policy, no treaties, no world-federation movements can prevent the dire catastrophe predicted.

In the calamities of the fourth seal, one-fourth of humanity was seen as destroyed. Through the agency of these four demonic angels, a third of those remaining are killed. Through these two judgments alone, the population of the world will have been reduced to one-half its original number. ⌛

⌛ IDEALIST *(continued)*

only mean the displacement and judgment upon those who continue to resist Him.

Because it is the character of these trumpet-judgments to warn rather than finally to destroy, we read that only **a third of mankind** (v. 15) were killed by the agents of destruction about to be described. ⌛

HISTORICIST *(continued)*

[The four angels bound at the Euphrates are the] four sultanies bordering on that river, where they were confined till after the period of the Crusades. . . . The time for which they were prepared . . . amounts to 391 years and 15 days; and from their first conquest over the Christians, AD 1281, to the taking of Cameniec from the Poles, AD 1672 . . . is exactly that period.

At this point, for the first time, Matthew Henry agrees with the majority of *historicists,* in that he identifies these horsemen with the Turks.

PRETERIST *(continued)*

days of vengeance, *that all things which are written* may be fulfilled" (v. 22). Thus *preterists* do not find it to be surprising that God would speak of this invasion as occurring at a time precisely anticipated. Occurring just forty years after the prediction, it fell perfectly into the "this generation" limitation.

DESCRIPTION OF THE ARMY

REVELATION 9:16—19

[16]Now the number of the army of the horsemen was two hundred million; I heard the number of them. [17]And thus I saw the horses in the vision: those who sat on them had breastplates of fiery red, hyacinth blue, and sulfur yellow; and the heads of the horses were like the heads of lions; and out of their mouths came fire, smoke, and brimstone. [18]By these three plagues a third of mankind was killed—by the fire and the smoke and the brimstone which came out of their mouths. [19] For their power is in their mouth and in their tails; for their tails are like serpents, having heads; and with them they do harm.

HISTORICIST

The term **two hundred million** (v. 16) can be translated "two myriad myriads," which can refer to an indefinite number. Elliott says that the Turks and

PRETERIST

The fact is again mentioned (v.18), as in the previous section (v.15), that this plague spells the deaths of **a third of mankind**. Unlike the demon-locusts

FUTURIST

There are two camps with reference to the identification of these bizarre **horsemen** (v. 16): (1) that they are demonic spirits, and (2) that they are literal armies described in figurative terms—probably from the Orient. There are, of course, those also who are undecided. Ryrie writes: "This army might be composed of human beings and it might equally well be an army of demons." Tenney agrees. Among those who lean toward identifying them as spirits are Ryrie, Seiss, and Leon Morris. However, since the locusts of the previous trumpet also were seen as demonic hosts, one is left to wonder why we have two such disparate descriptions of the same phenomenon.

IDEALIST

Some believe (Hobbs and Hailey among them) that the fifth and sixth trumpets are related in that the former describes the internal corruption of a wicked culture, whereas the latter tells of external forces that bring down such a decayed society. Hobbs writes:

> As the locusts symbolized internal decay, so this host symbolized *external opposition* or *foreign invasion.* They were the Parthian cavalry from the land of the Euphrates. Recall that Rome never did conquer these people. A dreadful belief existed within the empire that an invasion by the Parthians would someday destroy the Roman Empire. So this vision is based upon actual historical conditions.

241

⌛ HISTORICIST *(continued)*

Tartars had the custom of using the term *myriads* in the numbering of their troops. Barnes, similarly, writes:

> It has been suggested by Daubuz that in this there may be probably an allusion to the Turkman custom of numbering by *tomans, or myriads.* This custom, it is true, has existed elsewhere, but there is probably none with whom it has been so familiar as with the Tartars and Turks. In the Seljukian age, the population of Samarcand was rated at seven *tomans,* (*myriads,*) because it could send out 70,000 warriors. The dignity and rank of Tamerlane's father and grandfather was thus described, that "they were the hereditary chiefs of a *toman,* or 10,000 horse"—a *myriad,* (Gibbon, iv. 270;) so that it is not without his usual propriety of language that Mr. Gibbon speaks of the *myriads* of the Turkish horse, or of the cavalry of the earlier Turks of Mount Altai, "being, both men and horses, proudly computed by *myriads.*" One thing is clear, that to no other invading hosts could the language here used be so well applied, and, if it were supposed that John was writing *after* the event, this would be the language which he would be likely to employ—for this is nearly the identical language employed by the historian Gibbon.

The color of the breastplates, **fiery red, hyacinth blue, and sulfur yel-**

⌛ PRETERIST *(continued)*

unleashed in the fifth trumpet, which were forbidden to harm men physically, this is a physical army that slaughters people. The fraction "a third" calls to mind the prophecy of Ezekiel, about a previous invasion of Jerusalem, in which a third of the inhabitants were slated for slaughter by the sword (another third would die by famine and pestilence, and the remaining third would go into captivity (Ezek.5:12).

The army is fearsome both in appearance and in numbers, although the number given, **two hundred million** (v. 16), is not to be pressed as a literal calculation. David Clark writes:

> Now it is not certain whether this great army represented confederates of Rome that came from the east and assisted Rome in this Jewish war, or whether it has a general reference to the Roman armies only. . . . But the vision portended war; and war in such gigantic proportions as to overwhelm completely the Jewish state. Two hundred thousand thousand horsemen would be of course impossible; but the number is impressive enough and was doubtless meant chiefly for impression.

Chilton points out that "this army is the fulfillment of all the warnings in the law and the prophets of an avenging horde sent to punish the Covenantbreakers." In Deuteronomy 28, Moses

242

⌛ FUTURIST (continued)

On the other side are those who identify the horsemen with human armies—Walvoord, Gaebelein, Ironside, Tenney, Kuyper, and many others. But the size of the army, being **two hundred million** (v. 16) troops, poses some problems.

Ray Stedman takes the view that it "would be virtually impossible for any one nation—or even a coalition of nations such as NATO—to field such a vast army." Using the Gulf War of 1991 for a comparison, he points out that the combined troops of the thirty-nation United Nations coalition only amounted to about one million persons in uniform. The former Soviet Union had the largest army in the world, numbering about three million men, followed by China with 2.3 million and India with 1.1 million. Stedman concludes that all the armies in the world must be involved in a battle that employs two hundred million troops.

Walvoord, Lindsey, and others, believe that the hordes are forces of Asia, possibly with China dominant. If this theory be adopted, it becomes possible to take the otherwise incredible number, **two hundred million** (v. 16), literally. Walvoord favors so taking it: "Considering the millions of people in the Orient, the literal interpretation is not impossible, especially in view of the population explosion." Lindsey cites an Associated Press article that claimed

⌛ IDEALIST (continued)

It is not necessary to limit the application of this trumpet to invasions against Rome, however. According to the more common view, the vision depicts oft-recurring phenomena. Many expositors, such as Plummer, are of the opinion that the afflictions portrayed here are spiritual in nature:

> The spiritual evils which afflict the ungodly in this life . . . The number of such inflictions is, indeed, great enough to be described as "two myriads of myriads" (v. 16); they destroy a part, but not the greater part (v. 15, "the third part") of men. . . . Such punishment is a foretaste of hell, as seems to be foreshadowed in the "fire and smoke and brimstone" of verses 17, 18.

Carpenter writes that "the aim of the plague is to exhibit the death-working power of false thoughts, false customs, false beliefs, and to rouse men to forsake the false worships, worldliness, and self-indulgence into which they had fallen."

A more commonly held position contrasts the locust invasion of the previous woe with this onslaught of horses. The former unleashed *spiritual* armies of demons against the wicked; the latter brought *physical*, human armies as a punishment and warning upon rebellious mankind.

The horse is an established symbol of warfare in the Bible (cf. Ps. 33:16–17;

⧗ HISTORICIST *(continued)*

low (v. 17), are those "for which the Turks have always been remarkable" (*Treasury*). On the same point, Barnes adds:

> This might, undoubtedly, be applicable to other armies besides the Turkish hordes; but the proper question here is, whether it *would be* applicable to them. The fact of the application of the symbol to the Turks in general must be determined from other points in the symbol which designate them clearly; the only natural inquiry here is, whether this description would apply to the Turkish hosts, for if it would not, that would be fatal to the whole interpretation. On the application of this passage to the Turks, Mr. Daubuz justly remarks, that "from their first appearance the Ottomans have affected to wear warlike apparel of scarlet, blue, and yellow: a descriptive trait the more marked from its contrast to the military appearance of the Greeks, Franks, or Saracens contemporarily.

Matthew Henry joins with Elliott, Barnes, and others in taking the **fire, smoke,** and **brimstone** (v. 18) as a reference to artillery, for great guns were first used by the Turks at the siege of Constantinople. The armies under Sultan Mahomet were armed with sixty-seven cannons. The smallest fired a stone shot weighing 200 pounds. The largest, with a bore of three feet, could

⧗ PRETERIST *(continued)*

warned Israel that violating their covenantal relationship with God would bring great curses upon them (many of the specific details correspond to those in Revelation). The final curse, given in verses 49–68, would be an overwhelming and devastating invasion of foreign armies, who would drive them out of their land and leave them dispersed among all nations. Though the description of the invaders in Deuteronomy 28 is not a verbatim duplicate of the characteristics of this second woe, the effect is the same:

> The Lord will bring a nation against you from afar, from the end of the earth [or "land"—the Euphrates?], as swift as the eagle flies, a nation whose language you will not understand, a nation of fierce countenance, which does not respect the elderly nor show favor to the young. . . . They shall besiege you at all your gates until your high and fortified walls, in which you trust, come down throughout all your land. . . . You shall eat the fruit of your own body, the flesh of your sons and your daughters whom the LORD your God has given you, in the siege and desperate straits in which your enemy shall distress you. . . . And it shall be, that just as the LORD rejoiced over you to do you good and multiply you, so the LORD will rejoice over you to destroy you and bring you to nothing; and you

FUTURIST *(continued)*

that as early as 1961 China was capable of mobilizing a militia of two hundred million troops. Lindsey contemplates: "If the armed militia of China was estimated at 200 million in 1961, what do you suppose it is now?" Such an army would certainly represent the largest multitude of men ever to be under arms in any historic conflict.

Mounce sees no need for such literalism, suggesting that "attempts to reduce this expression to arithmetic miss the point. A 'double myriad of myriads' is an indefinite number of incalculable immensity."

More than one writer has found in the imagery indications of modern weaponry. Stedman writes: "It seems clear that what John envisions for us is the machinery of modern (or future) military destruction translated into the military terminology of his own day." He then suggests the identification of the individual features of the vision with such apparatus as tanks, troop carriers, missile launchers, rocket batteries, helicopter gunships, and so on.

Commenting on the **breastplates of fiery red, hyacinth blue, and sulfur yellow** (v. 17), Walvoord writes: "Some have interpreted the description as John's understanding of a scene in which modern warfare is under way." Regarding the fact that the horses have **heads of lions; and out of their mouths came fire, smoke, and brim-**

IDEALIST *(continued)*

Prov. 21:31; Isa. 31:1; Zech. 9:10). Hendriksen points out that "these are not ordinary horses. They clearly symbolize war engines and war tools of every description." Certainly war is one of those recurring phenomena in history, which Scripture indicates God uses to punish civilizations and warn all men of the universality of death and the need to repent.

The number **two hundred million** (v. 16) is not to be understood literally, any more than are the other features of the vision. Summers has calculated that an actual army of this many men would form a column one mile wide and eighty-five miles long.

The horses' **tails . . . like serpents** (v. 19) are thought to represent the *aftermath* of war. Hailey writes: "Seldom is the serpent poison of war's aftermath completely eradicated; it continues to bear its evil influence."

Rather than representing a single conflict at the end of the age, this battle with its two hundred million horsemen can apply to all wars at all times throughout this dispensation.

Wilcock extends the application further to include every kind of life-extinguishing event that befalls wicked men:

> The death-dealing horsemen of Trumpet 6 are not tanks and planes. Or not only tanks and planes. They are also cancers and

245

⌛ HISTORICIST *(continued)*

hurl a 1,200-pound ball. A few excerpts from Gibbon will suffice to document the role that smoke and fire played in the Turks' assault on Constantinople:

> The incessant volleys of lances and arrows were accompanied with the smoke, the sound, and the fire of their musketry and cannon . . . A circumstance that distinguishes the siege of Constantinople is the re-union of the ancient and modern artillery. The cannon were intermingled with the mechanical engines for casting stones and darts; the bullet and the battering-ram were directed against the same walls; nor had the discovery of gunpowder superseded the use of the liquid and inextinguishable fire. (iv. 344)

> From the lines, the galleys, and the bridge, the Ottoman artillery thundered on all sides; and the camp and city, the Greeks and the Turks, were involved in a cloud of smoke which could only be dispelled by the final deliverance or destruction of the Roman empire. (iv. 350)

The reference to **their power** being in the **tails** (v. 19) of the horses calls to mind the *pashas* by which the authority of high-ranking Turks was exhibited. These are made by attaching two or three horse tails to a pole as a standard. The origin of this custom is related by Ferrario:

⌛ PRETERIST *(continued)*

shall be plucked from off the land which you go to possess. Then the LORD will scatter you among all peoples . . . and among those nations you shall find no rest (vv. 49, 50, 52, 53, 63, 64, 65).

The timing of this invasion may be placed at the very end of the Jewish War, when the Romans actually broke through the wall of Jerusalem and swarmed into the city, or it may refer to the initial invasion of the Romans in AD 66. The former view is amenable to those (e.g., Stuart, Adams, Clark) who see this trumpet as essentially the end of the section dealing with Israel, and who see everything after chapter 11 as dealing with the judgment upon Rome.

David Chilton, who sees the entire book of Revelation as a prophecy of Jerusalem's destruction, takes the latter view. This trumpet does not depict the end of the war, since that will be seen in the seven bowl judgments of chapter 16:

> As it actually worked out in history, the Jewish rebellion in reaction to the "locust plague" of Gessius Florus during the summer of 66 provoked Cestius' invasion of Palestine in the fall, with large numbers of mounted troops from the region near the Euphrates (although the main point of St. John's reference is the symbolic significance of the river in biblical history and prophecy). After ravaging the countryside, his forces arrived at

FUTURIST *(continued)*

stone (v. 17), his comment is: "This again is a description that might be comparable to modern mechanical warfare." After mentioning that **their tails are like serpents, having heads; and with them they do harm** (v. 19), he writes: "Whether these are symbols or the best description John can give of modern warfare, this is an awesome picture of an almost irresistible military force destroying all that opposes it."

Hal Lindsey goes further into detail on these points:

All of these things are a part of a thermonuclear war: smoke represents the immense clouds of radioactive fallout and debris, while brimstone is simply melted earth and building materials. Another thing not clear is exactly who is being attacked. Gaebelein believes that because

> the Land of Israel is nearest it will suffer first, but the revived Roman empire will be the objective of the invading hordes. The "third part" stands for the Roman empire, the coming European confederacy.

If the hordes are under the leadership of the Antichrist, as Moorehead suggests, it is not clear why the revived Roman Empire, alleged also to be the domain of the Antichrist, would come under their attack—but then, whoever said war has to make sense?

IDEALIST *(continued)*

road accidents and malnutrition and terrorist bombs and peaceful demises in nursing homes.

Hendriksen contends:

The general meaning of these trumpets is clear. Throughout the entire period, extending from the first to the second coming, our exalted Lord Jesus Christ . . . will again and again punish the persecutors of the Church by inflicting upon them disasters in every sphere of life.

Concerning the fulfillment of these trumpets, Albertus Pieters writes:

I do not take much interest in locating them here or there in history, for it seems to me I know them. Have we not twice, in 1914–1918 and again in 1939–1945 seen the bottomless pit opened, and the heavens darkened by swarms of evil things that issued from it? Has not the thunder of two hundred million hellish horsemen shaken the earth in our own day?[13]

HISTORICIST *(continued)*

An author acquainted with their customs says, that a general of theirs, not knowing how to rally his troops that had lost their standards, cut off a horse's tail, and fixed it to the end of a spear; and the soldiers rallying at that signal, gained the victory. (Quoted by Barnes)

PRETERIST *(continued)*

the gates of Jerusalem in the month of Tishri—the month that begins with the Day of Trumpets. The army surrounded the city.

This siege did not turn out to be the final one, however, for the Jews repelled the invaders initially, and the war continued until the final siege by Titus in AD 70. The final siege is depicted by the seven bowls later on.

NO REPENTANCE

REVELATION 9:20—21

[20]But the rest of mankind, who were not killed by these plagues, did not repent of the works of their hands, that they should not worship demons, and idols of gold, silver, brass, stone, and wood, which can neither see nor hear nor walk. [21] And they did not repent of their murders or their sorceries or their sexual immorality or their thefts.

HISTORICIST

These verses speak of the impenitence of the apostate churches. "Those of the Latin and Greek churches, who escaped destruction [at the hands of the Saracen and Turkish hordes], still persisted in their idolatrous worship of demons."[14]

Matthew Henry thinks the specific sins of the impenitent—idolatry, murders, sorceries, immorality, and thefts (verse 20)—are particularly applicable to the papal church during this period. The use of images in worship is a form of

PRETERIST

It is hard to imagine any civilization to which God had granted so many inducements to repentance as He had the Jews just prior to the fall of Jerusalem. However, it seems God had given them over to a debased mind (Rom. 1:28), so repentance was no longer among their options.

Instead, as Josephus reports:

Thus were the miserable people beguiled by these charlatans and false messengers of God, while they disregarded and disbelieved the unmis-

FUTURIST

The unbelievers' lack of repentance at this time is truly astonishing. Ironside writes:

> It is a solemn thing to realize that even judgments such as these will have no effect so far as leading men back to God and to repentance is concerned. Punishment does not of itself lead men to repentance.

These verses offer an informative glimpse into the religious and moral conditions during the Tribulation. In our day the same behaviors listed have become dominant problems in Western societies. The New Age Movement encourages the admiration of **idols** and the appeal to demonic agencies for assistance. **Murder** is not only increasing in the cities as a criminal problem, but also in abortion clinics as a social problem. **Sorceries** (from the Greek word

IDEALIST

The list of vices here begins with idolatry, and every other vice has its root in that one. Substituting counterfeit gods for the one holy God has far-reaching moral consequences. Similar lists of sins mentioned here are also mentioned in connection with idolatry in the Bible (e.g., 2 Kings 9:22; Jer.7: 9–10; Hos.4:2; Rom.1:24–29; Gal.5:22; Eph.5:5; Col.3:5).

The seven trumpets are warnings intended to bring men to repentance, and they intensify as the end approaches, but they fail to produce the desired response. C. S. Lewis wrote: "God whispers to us in our pleasures, speaks in our conscience, but shouts in our pains."[15] Plummer notes that a significant portion of mankind is regularly destroyed in the aftereffect of these trumpet woes, "yet," he writes, "how largely they fail to bring men to repentance!"

 HISTORICIST *(continued)*

idolatry; the papal authority was responsible for the **murders** of hundreds of thousands of Albigenses and Waldensians by this time; the **immorality** of the popes leading up to this period was legendary; and the **thefts** could refer to the selling of indulgences.

PRETERIST *(continued)*

takable portents that foreshadowed the coming desolation; but, as though thunderstruck, blind, senseless, paid no heed to the clear warnings of God. (*Wars* VI: v.3)

Josephus also writes:

When the city was encircled and they could no longer gather herbs, some persons were driven to such terrible distress that they searched the common sewers and old dunghills of cattle, and ate the dung they found there; and what they once could not even look at they now used for food. When the Romans barely heard this, their compassion was aroused; yet the rebels, who saw it also, did not repent, but allowed the same distress to come upon themselves; for they were blinded by that fate which was already coming upon the city, and upon themselves also. (*Wars* V: 13:7)

David Clark contrasts the repentance of an old enemy of the Jews with their later refusal to repent:

Old Antiochus Epiphanes, the worst persecutor the Jews ever had, whose memory was a nightmare, when afflicted with a dreadful disease, humbled himself and called on God, and declared if God would heal him he would himself become a Jew and proclaim God's mercy before the world. But these apostates of whom John writes did not repent though doom stared them in the face.

250

⌛ FUTURIST *(continued)*

pharmakia, suggesting the use of consciousness-altering drugs), in illegal forms have defied the control of law enforcement agencies; in a more respectable form, they are taking society by storm through the psychiatric profession's administration of mind-altering drugs to mental patients. Many forms of **sexual immorality** (e.g., promiscuity, homosexuality, divorce and remarriage) have found increasing acceptance in the popular mind. **Theft** remains, as always, a serious problem, aggravated especially by the illegal drug industry. The very sins mentioned as dominant in the Tribulation are those we see on the rise in our world. ⌖

THE LITTLE BOOK AND SEVEN THUNDERS

REVELATION 10:1—4

¹I saw still another mighty angel coming down from heaven, clothed with a cloud. And a rainbow was on his head, his face was like the sun, and his feet like pillars of fire.² He had a little book open in his hand. And he set his right foot on the sea and his left foot on the land, ³ and cried with a loud voice, as when a lion roars. When he cried out, seven thunders uttered their voices. ⁴Now when the seven thunders uttered their voices, I was about to write; but I heard a voice from heaven saying to me, "Seal up the things which the seven thunders uttered, and do not write them."

⌛ HISTORICIST

After Rome fell to the barbarians in 476, as signified in the first four seals, the power of the papacy arose in its place in western Europe. The popes and the system that sustained their authority became incredibly corrupt. In fact, they became the *Antichrist*, the principal opponent of the pure faith of Christ in Europe.

This rise of the papacy has not been mentioned in Revelation until this point. The fall of the Eastern empire in the sixth trumpet now turns our attention back to developments in the West. The prophecies of chapters 10 and 11:1–15 are about the Reformation period in the early sixteenth century. This follows naturally the identification of the second woe with the fall of the Byzantine (Greek) Empire in 1453.

⌛ PRETERIST

This **mighty angel** (v. 1) is, no doubt, Jesus Himself. His face shining **like the sun** is a feature mentioned in the vision of the first chapter (1:16). The **rainbow,** which is now **on his head,** was seen around the throne of God in Revelation 4:3. The angel has **a little book open in his hand** (v. 2), which becomes the primary point of interest in the chapter. He has his left foot **on the land** and his right foot **on the sea** (v. 2). David Chilton explains:

> In the Bible, and especially in the Book of Revelation, "Sea and Land" seem to represent *the Gentile nations* contrasted with *the Land of Israel* (2 Sam. 22:4–5; Ps. 65:7–8; Isa. 5:30; 17:12–13; 57:20; Jer. 6:23; Luke 21:25; Rev. 13:1, 11).

⏳ FUTURIST

Walvoord, with the majority of writers, sees the section that begins here as "a parenthetical section . . . which continues through 11:14. Like chapter 7 it does not advance the narrative but presents other facts which contribute to the total prophetic scene."

The descending **angel** (v. 1) that dominates this scene is thought by some (e.g., Gaebelein, Ironside, Henry Morris, Walter Scott) to be Christ Himself. Others (e.g., Walvoord, Ryrie, J. B. Smith) disagree, believing that "the evidence seems to support the idea that here is a holy angel to whom has been given great power and authority" (Walvoord).

The **little book** (v. 2) in the angel's hand is interpreted in a variety of senses. Walvoord, for example, writes:

> The contents of the little book are nowhere revealed in Revelation, but they seem to represent in this vision the written authority given to the angel to fulfill his mission.

Mounce thinks it "plausible that the little scroll is a message for the believing church and is to be found in the following verses (11:1–13)."

Gaebelein believes that the book "stands for the prophecies in the Old Testament relating especially to Israel during the time of the great Tribu-

⏳ IDEALIST

An interlude falls between the sounding of the sixth and seventh trumpets, as it did between the breaking of the sixth and seventh seals (chap. 7). The subject matter of the interlude does not follow chronologically, but overlaps the period of the sounding of all the previous trumpets.

The **mighty angel** (v. 1) who appears here is either Christ Himself or a special envoy of Christ bearing a striking resemblance to Him (cf. 1:13–16). Those who do not believe it is Christ usually point out that the word **another** (Gr. *allon*) means "another of the same kind" (i.e., as the previous angels mentioned); this could hardly refer to the one who is the Lord over all angels. Hendriksen also points out that John did not worship this angel, as he did Christ (cf. 1:17). This angel has a message for the whole world, indicated by his having a foot on **the land** and a foot on **the sea,** though the open **book** in his hand is said to be **little** (v. 2). Wilson writes: "No great stress should be placed on the diminutive. The 'little' book contains prophecies of worldwide significance (vv. 6, 11), yet it was small enough for John to eat."

The **seven thunders** (vv. 3, 4) represent "the voice of the Lord" (cf. John 12:27–31). The expression probably summarizes the contents of Psalm 29, wherein it is said: "The voice of the LORD is over the waters; the God of glory

⌛ HISTORICIST *(continued)*

Elliott speaks for most Historicist interpreters in identifying the following details: The **mighty angel** (v. 1) can be none other than Christ, since **the little book** (v. 2) in His hand is **open**—and Christ was earlier declared to be the only one in heaven and earth authorized to open the book (5:3). This book is the Bible, which before the Reformation had been confined to a few inaccessible copies written in languages (i. e., Hebrew, Greek, Latin) incomprehensible to common Europeans. During the period immediately following the fall of the Byzantine Empire, the Bible became available (an open book) to the masses after two developments: the invention of the movable type printing press in 1436 or 1437, coupled with the making of several translations into the contemporary European languages. The opening of the Bible to the average man came at the end of a chain of events:

(1) the migration of many Greek scholars to western Europe, coupled with the acceleration of printing in Holland and Germany (1453);

(2) the Greek language first being taught in European universities (1458);

(3) the printing of the Greek New Testament by Erasmus (1516);

(4) Zwingli printing the first Swiss New Testament (1518);

⌛ PRETERIST *(continued)*

But what is this book in his hand? According to David S. Clark:

> Evidently the reasonable explanation is that it was the same book that we saw in the fifth chapter sealed with seven seals; or rather what is left of it. The seven seals have been opened, so this book appears **opened.** We are now in the seventh seal that disclosed seven trumpets and we are in the events of the sixth trumpet. . . . Little remains of the contents of that book and it is now described as "little."

Chilton seems to concur: "The book is thus, essentially, the Book of Revelation itself." Jay Adams, on the other hand, sees the little book as a prophecy separate and additional to the first (contained in chaps. 4–11). The second prophecy, contained in chapters 13–19, concerns the fall of Rome, as the first was concerned with the fall of Jerusalem. At the cry of the angel, we are told that **seven thunders uttered their voices** (v. 3), which Chilton notes

> is itself identified with the Voice in Psalm 29, where some of its phenomenal effects are noted: It shatters cedars in pieces, rocks whole nations with earthquakes, shoots forth mighty bolts of lightning, cracks open the very bowels of the earth, causes animals to calve, and topples the trees, stripping entire forests bare. This adds a dimension to our understanding of

⧗ FUTURIST *(continued)*

lation, what is yet to come upon the earth, culminating in the personal and glorious appearing of the Lord to begin His millennial reign."

Morris, who said that the seven-sealed scroll of the fifth chapter was "the title deed to the earth," suggests that this smaller book may be a "little title deed." It could represent "that portion of Christ's inheritance which is to be awarded to His joint heir, the Apostle John, who appears here in the capacity of a representative Christian believer caught up to heaven at the time of the rapture."

The fact that John was forbidden to write what he heard from the **seven thunders** (v. 4) has caused both curiosity and speculation. Ironside offers an explanation based on the atonement:

> As Mediator of the New Covenant He seals up the utterance of the seven thunders. They speak of judgment due to wayward man, but He Himself has borne the judgment, and those who trust in Him need never know its dreadful secrets.

Walvoord exercises considerably greater caution:

> When John was about to write what he had heard, however, he was instructed not to do so. . . . This illustrates a divine principle that while God has revealed

⧗ IDEALIST *(continued)*

thunders" (v. 3). Altogether, the expression, *the voice of the Lord,* occurs *seven times* in that Psalm (vv. 3, 4, 5, 7, 8, 9).

The sealing of the seven thunders, leaving them unwritten, suggests that "the whole counsel of God has not been revealed (Deut. 29:29; 1 Cor. 13:8–12)" (Morey), or that "never shall we be able to know and to describe *all* the factors and agencies that determine the future" (Hendriksen), or that "God has many unrevealed weapons in His arsenal of judgments to be used at His discretion; man cannot know all of God's ways" (Hailey). Swete writes: "The Seer's enforced reticence witnesses to the fragmentary character of even apocalyptic disclosures. The Seer himself received more than he was at liberty to communicate." The apostle Paul also, when caught up to heaven, "heard inexpressible words, which it is not lawful for a man to utter" (2 Cor. 12:4).

⏳ HISTORICIST *(continued)*

(5) Luther publishing the New Testament in German (1522);

(6) Tyndale's English New Testament and the Swedish Bible (1526);

(7) the Danish Bible (1537);

(8) the "Great Bible" commanded to be placed in every English church (1539); and

(9) the King James Version (1611).

The **loud voice** (v. 3) of this angel is Christ's unmistakable challenge to the doctrines of Roman Catholicism, as enunciated by the Reformers and their precursors, Wycliffe and Huss.

The **seven thunders** (vv. 3, 4) are variously interpreted as: the seven crusades (Vitringa); seven wars between the Reformation and the sounding of the seventh trumpet at the French Revolution (Keith); seven kingdoms that embraced the Reformation, echoing laws confirming the doctrines of Protestantism (Daubuz); the Papal Anathemas denouncing Luther and the Reformation (Elliott, Barnes, and others). According to this last view, John is forbidden to record the papal positions because they are invalid and unworthy of record. Expounding this position, B. W. Johnson writes:

> It is a historic fact that the opening of the book by the Reformation called forth the loudest voices of the seven thunders. The

⏳ PRETERIST *(continued)*

the nature of the Voice from the Cloud: It consists of the heavenly antiphony in which the angelic chorus answers the declarations of the Sovereign Lord.

As to why John was not permitted to record the sayings of the seven thunders, David S. Clark answers:

> No doubt they were too terrible to write. Their ears and hearts are to be spared the description. And we will find in the next chapter that when the end of this scene comes, we are spared the description of the carnage and massacre and madness of that last scene. . . . These very soon became a matter of history, and John did not need to write them in detail.

Chilton gives a less ominous reason for keeping the message of the seven thunders unrecorded:

> The message was intended for St. John's ears only. It was not intended for the Church at large. But what is important here is that God wanted St. John to record the fact that he was not supposed to reveal whatever the seven thunders said. God wanted the church to know that there are some things (many things, actually) that God has no intention of telling us beforehand.

The sealing of the message of the seven thunders also tells us that some things God has in store were not to be

FUTURIST *(continued)*

much, there are secrets which God has not seen fit to reveal to man at this time.

HISTORICIST *(continued)*

anathemas that had been wont to shake the nations were hurled at Luther and his supporters. . . . At first there was a disposition on the part even of Martin Luther, to listen to these thunders as divine, but finally he committed the Papal bull issued against his teachings to the flames to be rejected (*People's New Testament With Notes*).

PRETERIST *(continued)*

fulfilled in John's time. This is in contrast to Revelation 22:10, where John was told, concerning the book of Revelation generally, not to seal it up, because the time was at hand. Thus we are informed that, though the general contents of the book of Revelation dealt with events soon to occur, the seven thunders concerned events not immediately impending.

NO MORE DELAY

REVELATION 10:5–7

⁵The angel whom I saw standing on the sea and on the land raised up his hand to heaven ⁶and swore by Him who lives forever and ever, who created heaven and the things that are in it, the earth and the things that are in it, and the sea and the things that are in it, that there should be delay no longer, ⁷ but in the days of the sounding of the seventh angel, when he is about to sound, the mystery of God would be finished, as He declared to His servants the prophets.

HISTORICIST

As the Jews had been given many centuries to repent of their rebellion against God, so the apostate papal church had been given centuries to mend its ways and return to God. The Jews had killed those who were sent to rebuke them; the papal church had killed thousands who resisted its corrupt doctrines and practices. The ministry of Jesus and His apostles represented the last opportunity for the Jewish nation to repent prior

PRETERIST

The martyrs seen under the altar in chapter 6 were told to wait "a little while longer" until the proper time for vengeance to be taken upon their murderers. Now we read that the little while has passed and **there should be delay no longer** (v. 6). David S. Clark writes:

> Now we see Christ come down with that same book in his hand with every seal opened to declare that the time is up; and the prayers

258

FUTURIST

Kelly identifies the **mystery of God** (v. 7) as "the secret of His allowing Satan to have his own way, and man too (that is to say, the wonder of evil prospering and of good being trodden underfoot)." This view is affirmed by Lindsey and expressed by Gaebelein:

> How great has been that mystery! Evil had apparently triumphed; the heavens for so long have been silent. Satan had been permitted to be the god of this age deceiving the nations. . . . And now the time has come when the mystery of God will be completed.

Walvoord has another opinion:

> The reference to the mystery of God seems to mean truth concerning God Himself which has not been fully revealed. It is often overlooked, however, that the mystery is said to have been "declared to his servants the prophets" (v. 7).

IDEALIST

The most frequent means of identifying **the mystery of God** (v. 7) is to cross-reference with Colossians 2:2, Romans 16:25, and, especially, with Ephesians 3:3–6. There Paul speaks of the union of Jews and Gentiles in one body in Christ as that mystery revealed clearly for the first time to the apostles and prophets of the New Testament era. Robertson believes this mystery refers to "the whole purpose of God in history." Wilson writes that "the consummation of this mystery includes the final judgement of the wicked, and 'the full salvation of the saints in the perfected kingdom' (Beckwith)."

That the mystery of God **would be finished** (v. 7) does not mean that it would terminate, but that it would "be carried out in its entirety" (Hailey).

⧖ HISTORICIST *(continued)*

to its destruction in AD 70. Now the announcement is made that **there should
be delay no longer** (v. 6), that is, that
the papal church was being given its
final opportunity to return to God before coming under divine judgment.
This opportunity was embodied in the
Reformation. It is interesting that Jesus
came to Israel approximately 1,500
years after its founding, and the Reformation came to the church about 1,500
years after its founding.

Elliott translates, "There shall be
time no longer extended," that is, the
time of God's permitting the reign of evil
through the papal Antichrist. As John
was given the revelation of Christ in vv.
1 and 2, and of the Antichrist in v. 3, so
he is, from this point onward, shown in
chronological sequence the events in
the further development of the Reformation. In this, the Reformers are encouraged that the doom of Antichrist
(the papal church) and the consummation of God's purposes are near at hand,
though not yet fully come. ⧖

⧖ PRETERIST *(continued)*

of his saints are to be answered;
and the blood of his martyrs
judged or avenged; and the last
great catastrophe shall fall on the
first great persecutor of the Christian church.

The completion of **the mystery of
God** (v. 7) refers to the fact that the
"predominantly Jewish nature of the
church was to be ended by the destruction of the temple, the distinctive feature in which it centered" (Adams). The
mystery itself, of course, is that of which
Paul frequently speaks, namely, as
Adams writes, "that the Gentiles should
come into the church on an equal foot-
ing with the Jews, not first having to
become Jews themselves—cf. Ephesians
3:3–6."

Chilton similarly identifies this
mystery with Paul's use of the same
term: "This 'Mystery' is a major aspect
of the letters to the Ephesians and Colossians: *the union of believing Jews and
Gentiles in one Church, without distinction.*" ⧖

FUTURIST *(continued)*

The mystery of God which is declared as subject to fulfillment is unfolded therefore in the Old Testament in many passages which speak of the establishment of the kingdom of God on earth. 🕮

JOHN EATS THE BOOK

REVELATION 10:8–11

[8]Then the voice which I heard from heaven spoke to me again and said, "Go, take the little book which is open in the hand of the angel who stands on the sea and on the earth." [9]So I went to the angel and said to him, "Give me the little book." And he said to me, "Take and eat it; and it will make your stomach bitter, but it will be as sweet as honey in your mouth." [10]Then I took the little book out of the angel's hand and ate it, and it was as sweet as honey in my mouth. But when I had eaten it, my stomach became bitter. [11]And he said to me, "You must prophesy again about many peoples, nations, tongues, and kings."

⌛ HISTORICIST

The eating of **the little book** (v. 10) represents the church's reception of the Bible at the time of the Reformation. For the first time, the Scriptures were available to the common man and printed in his own tongue. It was **sweet as honey** in the mouths of those who received it. Having been starved of God's Word for hundreds of years, forced to subsist on legends of saints and traditions of the church, the common Christians in Luther's day were ready to receive the Word of God with relish. The consequence of it becoming **bitter** in the stomach is seen by Barnes and others to refer to the opposition and persecution raised by the Catholic Church against the Protestants.

As John eats this book and receives a further commission, he stands for the ministers of the Reformation, who are

⌛ PRETERIST

The action of eating **the little book** (v. 10), and reference to how it affected the **mouth** and **stomach,** is an imitation of the identical actions of Ezekiel the prophet (see Ezek. 3:1–3, 14). Ezekiel's prophecy was about the destruction of Jerusalem at the hands of the Babylonians in 586 BC. John's similar action also is connected with his prophesying the destruction of Jerusalem, this time by the Romans in AD 70.

John notes that, as he had been told to expect, the book **was as sweet as honey** in the mouth. But after the book was swallowed, his **stomach became bitter** (v. 10). On this detail, David S. Clark writes:

> There were some things glad and some things sad in the events revealed in that book, and about to be revealed. It was a matter of gladness that God heard their prayers and

⌛ FUTURIST

Ryrie suggests that the meaning of John's eating **the little book** (v. 10) "is simply that it is necessary for the prophet of God to let the Word of God affect him first before he ministers it to others." Ironside makes a more universal application:

> It is only as we feed upon and digest the Word of God, that we ourselves are nourished and built up in the truth of our most holy faith, and in a right condition of soul to use that Word for the help and instruction of others.

Since Walvoord considers the book itself "to be a symbol of the Word of God as it is delivered to men, that is, divine revelation already given," he explains John's bittersweet experience in eating it as follows:

> To John the Word of God is sweet, in that it is a word of promise, a word of grace, and a revelation of the love of God. . . . More particularly, however, the Word of God is bitter in that it not only contains promises of grace but, as the book of Revelation itself abundantly illustrates, it reveals the divine judgments which will be poured out on the earth as God deals in wrath with the wicked world.

Mounce writes: "The prospect of no further delay in the fulfillment of God's eternal purposes is sweet indeed. That it will involve a bitter prelude is hard to swallow." 🖉

⌛ IDEALIST

The prophecy of **the little book** (v. 10) that John eats and which he must thereafter speak is thought by some to be found in chapter 11, and by others in chapters 12 through 22.

The alternate sweetness and bitterness of the book in the **mouth** and **stomach** are explained variously. According to Hendriksen:

> The scroll is the Word of God, His gospel in which the mystery of salvation is set forth. That gospel is in itself glorious and sweet. But its proclamation is always followed by bitter persecution. . . . The apostle must not merely understand and digest the message of the gospel; he must experience both its sweetness and the suffering, the cross-bearing, which is always the portion of those who truthfully proclaim it.

Another angle is that of Leon Morris:

> The true preacher of God's word will faithfully proclaim the denunciations of the wicked it contains. But he does not do this with fierce glee. The more his heart is filled with the love of God, the more certain it is that the telling forth of "woes" will be a bitter experience.

The statement that he must **prophesy again** (v. 11) refers to the fact that he has "to some extent set forth God's will in the earlier part of

⧗ HISTORICIST *(continued)*

thereby charged by Christ to preach (prophesy—v. 11) His gospel to many nations and languages. The preaching of the Word was the principal power and distinctive of the Protestant movement. As Barnes notes, preaching was a thing comparatively little known before for many ages. The grand business in the papal communion was not, and is not, *preaching*, but the performance of rites and ceremonies. Genuflections, crossings, burning of incense, processions, music, constitute the characteristic features of all papal churches; the grand thing that distinguishes the Protestant churches all over the world, just in proportion as they *are* Protestant, is *preaching*. ⧉

⧗ PRETERIST *(continued)*

answered their cries, vindicated their cause, and destroyed the persecutors. But it was sad that men did not turn from their sins, sad that such judgments must fall.

The command that John **must prophesy again** (v. 11) is taken by some (e.g., Stuart, Clark, Adams), who see the second half of Revelation as a prophecy of the fall of Rome, to be an indication that the second prophecy will not concern Israel. Hence he is told he must next prophesy about **many peoples, nations, tongues, and kings.** David S. Clark notes that "though this book was ended and all its seals opened there would be other things to follow and we will see that this was true in the next half of Revelation."

Adams elaborates:

> The little book symbolizes an additional and distinct prophecy. . . . The second prophecy is not concerned with a single nation, as was the first, but the downfall of an empire, involving the entire Mediterranean world.

Russell, Chilton, Terry, Carrington, and others, who consider the whole of Revelation to be concerned with the downfall of the Jewish state, believe that the book simply adds an international dimension to the continuing predictions of God's dealings with Israel, particularly stressing the impact of the fall of Jerusalem upon the global gospel mission. ⧉

⌛ **IDEALIST** *(continued)*

the book; and he is now required to proceed with the delivery of his message" (Plummer). The persons to whom John must prophesy are identified by a fourfold enumeration—**peoples, nations, tongues, and kings** (v. 11)—suggesting that all of mankind must hear his message (four being the number of the world).

STRUCTURAL NOTE:

WHERE DOES THE SECTION OF REVELATION BEGINNING WITH CHAPTER 8 END?

All commentators do not outline the Book of Revelation in precisely the same manner. All agree in seeing in chapters 1 through 3 a complete unitary segment. Most also would agree that chapters 4 through 7 or 8:1 comprise a definable division. But the section beginning at chapter 8 with the seven trumpets—where does it close? Most would close it at the end of chapter 11, though there is reason to consider chapters eleven through thirteen or even fourteen as one unit.

We have reached the close of chapter 10, where we expect to read of the sounding of the seventh trumpet. Instead, as we were treated to an interlude between the sixth and seventh seals (chap. 7), so we find an even longer interlude between the sixth and seventh trumpet judgments. This interlude occupies all of chapter 10 and most of 11.

During this interlude, John is given a second book of prophecy, which he is instructed to eat (chap. 10). This is followed by the measuring of the temple (11:1–2) and the discussion of the "two witnesses" (11:3–14). At this point we are introduced to the time period represented variously as three and a half years. The seventh trumpet does not sound until 11:15–18. Chapters 12 and 13 also discuss a period of three and a half years, which may be the same period as that of chapter 11.

Making a clean division between the vision of the seven trumpets (chaps. 8–11) and the segment that focuses on the three and a half years (chaps. 11–13) is difficult, because chapter 11 could be included in either section. On the one hand, chapters 10–11 are an integral part of the vision of the seven trumpets (since the seventh trumpet is sounded at 11:15). On the other hand, chapter 11 seems to belong to the discussion of the period of three and a half years, since the duration of this period is mentioned only in chapters 11 through 13. One possibility is that the three and a half years, first introduced in the interlude between the sixth and seventh trumpets (chap. 11), is expanded upon in what might be viewed as a parenthetical section (chaps. 12–13), to reveal that the period of the ministry of the two witnesses is characterized by persecution. Some, however, would include chapter 14 in the section with chapters 12–13, and see the events of chapter 14 as culminating in the Second Coming of Christ.

At this point, therefore, any attempt at structuring a clear and "clean" outline of the book must remain tentative.

SUMMARY OF CHAPTERS 8–10

Thus concludes the second cycle of sevens (except that the seventh trumpet will not sound until 11:15).

In the view of the *historicists*, the first six trumpet judgments are symbolic of the various foreign invasions against the Roman Empire through the fall of Constantinople in 1453. The open book is the Bible, whose availability to the common people helped further the Reformation's progress.

The *preterist* position sees the trumpets as associated with the Jewish War of AD 66–70, culminating in the fall of Jerusalem in the latter year. The locusts probably refer to demons afflicting the besieged Jews, and the monstrous horses represent the Roman armies. The little book of chapter 10 may anticipate the remainder of the book of Revelation and represent its contents.

Futurists concluded from these chapters that, during the future Tribulation period, judgments of an unprecedented sort will be sent against rebellious humanity. If literal, these judgments will be devastating to nature and catastrophically disruptive of civilization. Some of the trumpet judgments may contain symbolism rather than literal descriptions. The little book is a symbol of God's Word and purposes.

To the *idealist* interpreters, the disasters represented by the trumpets are the various and recurring ways in which God judges sinful mankind through environmental disruptions and natural disasters. These are meant as warnings to induce men to repent. The fulfillment is to found through the entire church age. God's messages of grace and judgment give the book its bittersweet taste.

NOTES

1. Quoted in Ray C. Stedman, *God's Final Word: Understanding Revelation* (Grand Rapids: Discovery House, 1991), 176.
2. Bauckham, *The Theology of the Book of Revelation*, 82.
3. Beale, *The New International Greek Testament Commentary*, 472.
4. Ibid., 474.
5. Quoted by Caringola in *The Present Reign of Jesus Christ*, 119.
6. The bitter herbs at the Paschal meal still remind the Jews of the bitterness of the Egyptian bondage. Their rescue from Egypt by God is referred to as a "healing" in Hosea 11:1–3.
7. Beale, *The New International Greek Testament Commentary*, 479f.
8. Ibid., 480.
9. William E. Biederwolf, *The Second Coming Bible* (Grand Rapids: Baker, 1967), 599; Pieters, *The Lamb, the Woman and the Dragon*, 48.
10. Some Anabaptists might wish to contest this point.
11. Josephus, *Wars* II: 14:919:9.
12. A. Y. Collins, cited by Beale, *The New International Greek Testament Commentary*, 507.
13. Pieters, *The Lamb, The Woman, and the Dragon*, 81.
14. *Treasury of Scripture Knowledge*.
15. C. S. Lewis, *The Problem of Pain* (New York: MacMillan, 1943), 81.

PART IV

THE 1,260 DAYS
REVELATION 11–13

HOW ARE WE TO UNDERSTAND THE PERIOD OF 1,260 DAYS?
WHEN DOES IT OCCUR?

⌛ HISTORICIST APPROACH:

- The measuring of the temple represents the determining of the true remnant church in the midst of the papal church at the time of the Reformation.
- The 1,260 days are actually 1,260 years, being the duration of the power of papal Rome.
- The two witnesses represent the Waldenses, Albigenses, and others who resisted the papacy in the years before the Reformation.
- The woman is the visible church persecuted by Imperial Rome prior to AD 313, and her male child is the true church within her, vindicated by the enthronement of Constantine.
- The beasts each represent different aspects of the papacy.

⌛ PRETERIST APPROACH:

- The 1,260 days is the period of the Jewish War, of Nero's persecution, or both.
- The two witnesses are either historic prophetic witnesses against the Jews prior to the downfall of Jerusalem or a representation of the civil and religious authority in Israel.
- The woman (Israel), gives birth to a child (the church), which flees Jerusalem (during the Jewish War) and is afterward persecuted by the devil.
- The first beast is Rome (or possibly Nero, or both), persecuting the church.
- The second beast is either the cult of the emperor, some zealous Roman procurator, or false prophets in Israel

⌛ FUTURIST APPROACH:

- The 1,260 days refer either to a period of a literal three and one-half years at the end of the Tribulation or to two different periods of that length totaling seven years.

- The two witnesses are two individual prophets yet to appear in Jerusalem—possibly Moses and Elijah or Enoch and Elijah. Alternatively, they may represent a larger witnessing body.
- The woman (faithful Israel) will be forced by persecution from the Antichrist to flee into the wilderness during the Tribulation.
- The first beast is a political world-leader, and the second beast is his religious counterpart, who enforces universal worship of the first beast. (Some futurists take an approach to this section more like that of the idealist approach.)

IDEALIST APPROACH:

- The 1,260 days symbolize the entire church age.
- The two witnesses are the church throughout the church age.
- The woman sustained in the wilderness represents the same.
- The first beast signifies political power that persecutes the church at any time in history and anywhere upon the planet.
- The second beast is false religion and especially that which venerates political power.

THE 1,260 DAYS: INTRODUCTION

CHAPTERS 11–13

In chapters 11–13 of Revelation are repeated references to a period of time alternately designated as "forty-two months," "twelve hundred sixty days," or "a time, and times, and half a time." These are probably three different ways of saying "three and a half years." It is said that the Gentiles will trample the outer court and the holy city for this period (11:2). It is also the duration of the testimony of the two witnesses (11:3), of the preservation of the woman pursued by the dragon (12:6, 14), and of the continuing blasphemies of the beast (13:5).

Some believe that all the references are to the same three-and-a-half-year period. Among *preterists*, some identify the period as that of the Jewish war in rebellion against Rome (AD 66–70).[1] Others think it corresponds to the length of Nero's persecution of the church, which began in November of AD 64 and ended with Nero's death, June 9, AD 68.[2]

Perhaps most *futurists* see here two such periods, totaling seven years. Some would suggest that all the events from Revelation 4:1 through chapter 19 transpire during this period, referring to it as "the Tribulation" and the latter half of the period as "the Great Tribulation"(cf. 7:14).

Historicists understand the 1,260 days as symbolic for the same number of years, citing "the year-for-a-day principle" from Ezekiel 4:6 as their basis. According to this view, the synonymous periods (" forty-two months" and "a time, and times, and half a time") should all be recalculated as 1,260 days, and the days then interpreted as years. While *historicists* are agreed upon this general rule, there is no consensus whatever regarding the beginning and ending of the period thus designated. One suggestion is that the period is the 1,260 years from AD 538, when the Ostrogoths abandoned their siege of Rome, until 1798, when the pope was taken prisoner by the French general under Napoleon.[3] Another is that the 1,260 years began at AD 606, when Phocas decreed himself to be the supreme head of the church.[4] Other opinions place the beginning of the period at AD 1 (Joachin); 455 (Mede); 533 (Cuninghame); 576 (Bengel); 608 (Elliott); 660 (Melancthon); 672 (Guinness); and 727 (Fysh). Matthew Henry endorses the year-for-a-day principle, and suggests that the 1,260 years represent the reign of the Antichrist (the papal church) until the end of the world, but says the beginning of the period is not known.

A common assumption among those who espouse an *idealist* interpretation is to see the forty-two months as symbolic of a period of indefinite length, the whole period of the suffering of the people of God in this dispensation, corresponding to the entire church age. Using three and a half years to describe the church age may be chosen to recall the "three and a half years of terror under Antiochus Epiphanes when the temple was desecrated (June 168 to December 165 BC)."[5]

Alternately, it may be intended to correspond to the actual length of Jesus' earthly ministry, comparing the character of the church's ministry to that of Christ. Some commentators studiously avoid specificity on this point. Homer Hailey simply says that the forty-two months "indicates a broken period of time, a period of trial, persecution, and oppression . . . the period of Roman persecution."[6] Leon Morris, after likening the period to that of Antiochus Epiphanes, concludes, "So John will mean his readers to discern that the trial of the people of God will be of measurable duration and that they will be delivered out of it."[7] Ladd sees value in both the *futurist* and the *idealist* explanations, thus "the three and a half years appear to represent the entire period of the domination of evil but with special reference to the last days of this age."[8]

The decision about which of these opinions is most correct will be inseparably tied to the identification of the two witnesses (chap. 11), of the beast (chap. 13), and of the events described in chapter 12.

THE TEMPLE MEASURED

REVELATION 11:1—2

[1]Then I was given a reed like a measuring rod. And the angel stood, saying, "Rise and measure the temple of God, the altar, and those who worship there. [2]But leave out the court which is outside the temple, and do not measure it, for it has been given to the Gentiles. And they will tread the holy city underfoot for forty-two months."

⧗ HISTORICIST

The **temple of God** (v. 1) throughout the New Testament is always the church (1 Cor. 3:16; 6:19; 2 Thess. 2:4). The distinction between the **temple** and **the court which is outside the temple** (v. 2) is that between the true church and the outward and visible institution of the church. "The symbolism recorded by the apostle evidently describes the measurement of the church, its worship, and of its worshipers by the divine standard of the New Testament."[9]

John was to **measure** three things: (a) the **temple,** (b) the **altar,** and (c) **those who worship there** (v. 1). Barnes writes that this indicates that John is

(a) to take a just estimate of what constitutes the true church, as distinguished from all other associations of men; (b) to institute a careful examination into the opinions in the church on the subject of

⧗ PRETERIST

As at the end of chapter 10, where John's eating of the book repeats Ezekiel's action of centuries earlier, here in chapter 11 John is told to do something else that also has a precedent in Ezekiel. In Ezekiel 40–47 a man measures the temple with a measuring rod. In Revelation 11 John himself is given a reed for the same purpose. In both cases, the action depicts the defining of the true spiritual temple in view of the impending destruction of the physical structure in Jerusalem (by Babylonians in Ezekiel's day, by Romans in John's). David Chilton addresses the significance of this measuring:

Measuring is a symbolic action used in Scripture to "divide between the holy and the profane" and thus to indicate divine protection from destruction (see Ezek. 22:26; 40–43; Zech. 2:1–5; cf. Jer. 10:16; 51:19; Rev. 21:15–16).

⧗ FUTURIST

Alford writes that chapter 11 "is un-doubtedly one of the most difficult in the whole Apocalypse." Many have been perplexed by the task of discover-ing the symbolic meaning of its various features. On the other hand, Walvoord, like most dispensationalists, takes the simple approach of fairly-consistent literalism:

> The great city of 11:8 is identified as the literal Jerusalem. The time periods are taken as literal time periods. The two witnesses are in-terpreted as two individuals. The three and a half days are taken lit-erally. The earthquake is a literal earthquake. The seven thousand men who are slain by the earth-quake are seven thousand individ-uals who die in the catastrophe. The death of the witnesses is literal as are their resurrection and as-cension. These major assumptions provide an intelligent understand-ing of this portion of the prophecy.

Most dispensationalists agree with Walvoord that **the temple** (v. 1) here in view is one that is yet to be rebuilt by the Jews for the reinstitution of the Old Tes-tament sacrificial cultus. Ryrie writes: "This temple is the one which will be rebuilt in Jerusalem (cf. v. 8) during the tribulation and in which ancient Jewish rites will be reinstituted."

John's instructions are to **measure** (v. 1) the *naos*, which is the inner temple consisting in the holy place and the

⧗ IDEALIST

The Greek word for **temple** here is *naos*, which most expositors apply to the holy of holies. It is significant that a refer-ence is made to those **who worship there** (v. 1), since only one person, the Jewish high priest, was entitled to enter the literal holy of holies of the earthly temple. This indicates that we are here presented with a vision of the true habi-tation of God, identified since Pentecost with "the Church of the elect servants of God (1 Cor. 3:16, 17), partakers of the first resurrection, the Church of the first born" (so Alford; cf. 2 Cor. 6:16; Eph. 2:19–22; 1 Tim. 3:15; Heb. 3:6; 1 Pet. 2:5).

As the 144,000 were sealed for preservation (indicating God's aware-ness of the exact number) in the inter-lude of Act 2, so here the true temple of God (the church) is measured (indicat-ing God's awareness of its precise mem-bership) for preservation.

The **court which is outside** (v. 2), however, is not measured, and the **holy city** with it is to be given over for tram-pling by the Gentiles. This unmeasured portion of the temple and the city refers to the visible church members who are not genuine Christians, as Hendriksen explains:

> So the world tramples upon the outside court of merely nominal Christendom. The world invades the false church and takes posses-sion of it. Worldly church mem-

273

⌛ HISTORICIST *(continued)*

sacrifice and atonement—involving the whole question about the method of justification before God; and (c) to take a correct estimate of what constitutes true membership in the church.

This refers to the radical reassessment concerning these matters at the time of the Reformation. Elliott sees the **measuring rod** as a symbol of authority divinely appointed to Luther to **measure** or delineate the new forms of worship that would become a part of the evangelic church. The nonmeasured portion represents the removal from the church of heathen-like, apostate practices like the worship of images, and the exclusion of the papal church itself. This rod was not the creation of Luther or the Reformers, but was **given** (v. 1) to them. The only measure by which such determinations can legitimately be made is the teaching of Christ and His apostles as given in the New Testament. Johnson states:

> The great Reformation planted itself upon the principles maintained by Martin Luther, the Bible as the cornerstone and only rule of faith and practice in the Christian church. Protestantism has not always been true to its principles, but it has always conceded that the final standard of measurement is the Word of God.[10]

⌛ PRETERIST *(continued)*

David S. Clark writes that the act of measuring:

> signified the preservation of all that was good and true about the city and temple; the sifting out for salvation of some elements even in a wicked city ripe for destruction. This is supported by the fact that the worshipers are also included in the measuring.

Jay Adams writes:

> It is possible that verses 1 and 2 may be correctly interpreted as predicting that everything pertaining to the physical temple is to be destroyed except the *naos* (the word used here for "temple") which refers more exactly to the "holy of holies" where the Shekinah glory of God dwelt. This may signify (if correct) that there is no longer need for more than naos worship, where every believer may come boldly to the throne of grace, entering into the most holy place through the name of Christ. At any rate, one thing is definite, verse 2 strikes the same note as that found in Luke 21:24. The temple will be trodden down of the Gentiles.

Clark adds: Here is so plainly the destruction of Jerusalem that it could hardly be put in plainer words.

As there was an interlude between the sixth and seventh seals, depicting the preservation of the 144,000 Jewish

⏳ FUTURIST *(continued)*

holy of holies (Ryrie). Gaebelein writes: "The inner place is symbolical of the faithful remnant of worshippers; the outer court is the symbol of apostate Israel." Therefore a distinction is presumably being drawn between one class of Jews in the Tribulation period and another

Ladd, in company with Gaebelein, Beckwith, Simcox, Zahn, and many others, believes that the measuring is a symbol of preservation and protection, conveying the idea that God will preserve and save the faithful remnant of the Jewish people.

Mounce agrees about the basic significance of the measuring, except that he sees the preservation to refer not to Israel but the church: "For John it means that God will give spiritual sanctuary to the faithful believers (i. e., 'the church, the people of God') against the demonic assault of the Antichrist."

The trampling of the temple and the **holy city** by the Gentiles is said to endure for **forty-two months** (v. 2). Walvoord writes:

> Expositors have differed as to whether the forty-two months are the first half of the seven years or the second half. . . . On the basis of the evidence, it is not possible to be dogmatic. If the point of view is adopted, however, that Revelation is primarily concerned with the latter half of Daniel's seventieth

⏳ IDEALIST *(continued)*

bers welcome the ideas of the world; they feel themselves perfectly at home with the world.

The **forty-two months** (v. 2) "suggests a limited time rather than literal time" (Morey). Wilson writes:

> The time limit which is set for this trial is derived from Daniel 7:25, and refers to the three and a half years of terror under Antiochus Epiphanes when the temple at Jerusalem was desecrated.

Observing that the time periods for the trampling of the holy city by the Gentiles (11:2), the ministry of the two witnesses (11:3), the sojourn of the woman in the wilderness (12:6, 14), and the career of the beast (13:5) are equivalent, Swete writes:

> The time limit serves of course no further purpose than to synchronize the several periods, and to compare them with the greatest crisis through which the Jewish people passed between the Exile and the Fall of Jerusalem.

REVELATION 11:3—6

⌛ HISTORICIST *(continued)*

The words, **they will tread the holy city underfoot for forty-two months** (v. 2), refer to the persecution of the true church by the papal powers, "as *if* the holy city were in the hands of the Gentiles" (Barnes). The **forty-two months** is best understood as 1,260 days (calculating thirty days per month). The year-for-a-day principle would make this 1,260 years. There have been many opinions as to the time of commencement of the period (see "The 1,260 Days: Introduction").

⌛ PRETERIST *(continued)*

believers who escaped and survived the holocaust of AD 70, so here also, between the sixth and seventh trumpets, there is this interlude conveying the same thought in different symbols. The idea, according to Chilton, is that God is "now protecting the True Temple from the outpouring of God's wrath. The outer court (the 'court of the Gentiles') accordingly represents apostate Israel (cf. Isa. 1:12), which is to be cut off from the number of the faithful Covenant people, God's dwellingplace."

THE TWO WITNESSES

REVELATION 11:3—6

[3]"And I will give power to my two witnesses, and they will prophesy one thousand two hundred and sixty days, clothed in sackcloth." [4]These are the two olive trees and the two lampstands standing before the God of the earth. [5]And if anyone wants to harm them, fire proceeds from their mouth and devours their enemies. And if anyone wants to harm them, he must be killed in this manner. [6]These have power to shut heaven, so that no rain falls in the days of their prophecy; and they have power over waters to turn them to blood, and to strike the earth with all plagues, as often as they desire.

⌛ HISTORICIST

There has always been a true church comprised of true worshipers of God and followers of Christ. During the time of papal power, the true Christians who

⌛ PRETERIST

The tale of the two witnesses presents a particularly difficult challenge to the interpreter, as most expositors will concede. Russell says that this passage rep-

276

⧖ FUTURIST *(continued)*

week, this perspective would seem to give weight to the conclusion that this is the latter half of the week or the last three and one-half years prior to the second coming. ⧉

⧖ FUTURIST

Another time indicator appears in this segment. It is a period of **one thousand two hundred and sixty days** (v. 3), which calculates to the same length as the forty-two months in the previous verse. Walvoord, writing of this period, declares that it

> is unquestionably related to either the first three and one-half years or the latter three and one-half years of the seven years of Daniel 9:27. Expositors have differed as to which of the two periods is in view here. From the fact, however, that the two witnesses pour out divine judgments upon the earth and need divine protection lest they be killed, it implies that they are in the latter half of the seven years when awful persecution will afflict the people of

⧖ IDEALIST

The **two witnesses** (v. 3) represent the witnessing church throughout its entire career. As Hendriksen puts it: "These witnesses symbolize the Church militant bearing testimony through its ministers and missionaries throughout the present dispensation."

Though the church is one, the symbol of two witnesses supports the truthfulness of its testimony, since "the testimony of two is true" (John 8:17; cf. Deut. 17:6; 19:15; Matt. 18:16). Also, since Jesus sent His disciples to preach in twos (Luke 10:1), the number two here suggests the missionary thrust of the church on the offensive in the world (Hendriksen).

The duration of their ministry corresponds to the period during which the

⌛ HISTORICIST *(continued)*

stood against its corruptions were a very small minority until the Reformation. The Waldenses, the Albigenses, the Bohemian Brethren, Wycliffe, Huss, and Jerome of Prague all were part of this nonconformist spirit. Elliott and others take the two witnesses to be this long line of witnesses for Christ during the 1,260 years of the papacy prior to the Reformation. Matthew Henry identifies them with "God's eminent faithful ministers, who shall not only continue to profess the Christian religion, but to preach it, in the worst of times."

With reference to the **power** (v. 3) that is given to them, Barnes writes:

This would properly refer to some miraculous power; but still it may be used to denote merely that they would be clothed with the power of causing blessings to be withheld from men, as if rain were withheld; that is . . . God would bring judgments upon men as if they were clothed with this power.

That **fire proceeds from their mouth and devours their enemies** (v. 5) need not be taken any more literally than the words of Jeremiah: "Behold, I will make My words in your mouth fire, and this people wood, and it shall devour them" (Jer. 5:14). So also, the **rain** (v. 6) that they are able to withhold may be taken as spiritual, as when the words of God are likened to rain and dew (Deut. 32:2; Isa. 55:10f).

⌛ PRETERIST *(continued)*

resents "one of the most difficult problems contained in Scripture, and one that has exercised, we may even say baffled, the research and ingenuity of critics and commentators up to the present hour."

Are the two witnesses actually two individuals, or are they symbolic for a group of people, or even for some entity or abstract concept? Moses Stuart understands the meaning of the story to be:

A competent number of divinely commissioned and faithful Christian witnesses, endowed with miraculous powers, should bear testimony against the corrupt Jews, during the last days of their commonwealth, respecting their sins . . . and that the Jews, by destroying them, would bring upon themselves an aggravated and an awful doom.

One clue as to the identity of the witnesses is found in the observation that they are **the two olive trees and the two lampstands** (v. 4). The expression seems to derive from Zechariah 4:11–14, where the figure generally is connected to the high priest Joshua and the governor Zerubbabel. On the other hand, the miracles attributed to them are reminiscent of Moses and Elijah (vv. 5–6). David S. Clark writes:

Now as we study Zechariah we find that he means by these two

278

⏳ FUTURIST *(continued)*

God . . . The punishments and judgments the witnesses inflict on the world also seem to fit better in the great tribulation period.

Gaebelein agrees that this is the last half of the seventieth week of Daniel, but Ironside, Lindsey, and Morris take the other view, here expressed by Ryrie:

There is some disagreement over whether this refers to the first or the last half of the Tribulation. The text does not specify. It seems to this author that it refers to the first since it is the coming of the beast onto the scene in power that terminates their witness (v. 7).

The identity of **the two witnesses** (v. 3) has understandably given rise to a variety of speculations. Most *futurists* take them to be two actual men who will arise to prophesy in Jerusalem in the Tribulation. The similarity of their miracles to those of Moses and Elijah have encouraged some to believe that the witnesses are Moses and Elijah themselves. Moses and Elijah appeared together with Christ on the Mount of Transfiguration, and would aptly represent to the Jewish people the Law and the Prophets, respectively, in whom the Jews put their trust. Elijah's coming was promised in Malachi 4:5–6, which is an added support for his identification with one of the witnesses.

⏳ IDEALIST *(continued)*

outer court and the holy city are trampled (vv. 2–3), which was seen to represent the whole church age (see note on verses 1–2).

The witnesses are **clothed in sackcloth** (v. 3) because they bring a message of repentance.

The **two olive trees** (v. 4) are reminiscent of Zerubbabel and Joshua (Zech. 4:2–14), who were God's agents of restoration after the Exile, as Wilson writes: "In Zechariah the two olive trees represent Zerubbabel the prince and Joshua the priest, who thus symbolize the royal and priestly prerogatives of the church."

The miracles performed by the witnesses (v. 6) recall those of Moses and Elijah, suggesting that the authority and power once vested in the Law and the Prophets is now given to Christ's church (Luke 10:19). Leon Morris writes: "God's servants in the new dispensation have just as great resources as did Moses and Elijah in the old."

The deadly **fire** that **proceeds from their mouth** (v. 5) pictures, on one hand, the fact that whoever sets out to destroy the church will do so to his own undoing—**if anyone wants to harm them, he must be killed in this manner** (v. 5). In addition to the resemblance to Elijah's calling fire from heaven down upon those who had come to capture him (2 Kings 1), this image speaks of the power of their words. God

⧗ HISTORICIST *(continued)*

"There was no knowledge of salvation but by their preaching—no descent of the Spirit but in answer to their prayers; and as the witnesses were shut out of Christendom generally, a universal famine ensued" (The *Seventh Vial,* quoted by Barnes).

The various **plagues** (v. 6) are the calamities that fell upon the papacy from time to time and place to place, when the"heretics" were persecuted. Barnes writes:

> These calamities would seem to have been called down from heaven in answer to their prayers, and in order to avenge their wrongs. And can anyone be ignorant that wars, commotions, troubles, disasters have followed the attempts to destroy those who have borne a faithful testimony for Christ in the dark period of the world here referred to?

Elliott gives a similar explanation, identifying the judgments as "the bloodshed of wars inflicted in God's providence on the enemies of the witnesses."

Caringola points out that, as long as Catholic nations like France and Spain persecuted the true Christians, "there is recorded a continuous account of the shedding of blood along the waterways of Europe. This is why verse 6 states that *'they have power over waters to turn them to blood, and to smite the earth with all plagues . . .'"* (emphasis his).

⧗ PRETERIST *(continued)*

figures the head of the state and the head of the church. Both of these had great power and authority over the hearts and minds and lives of men. Civil and religious authority go far to restrain the evil passions and deeds of men. . . . [The two witnesses] may be thought of as personifications, or as personal representatives of religion and government.

Adams agrees:

> The symbolism under which they appear is taken from Zechariah 4, where the two candlesticks (lampstands) seem to stand for the high priest and the civil head of the people (Joshua and Zerubbabel respectively). Whether the vision of Revelation is a picture of the subjugation of both civil and religious authority during those lawless days, is questionable but possible. The obvious identification of their activities with those of Moses and Elijah, who also may represent civil and religious government, seems to indicate that some interpretation involving this fundamental idea is likely.

David Chilton offers a different suggestion:

> A preliminary conclusion about the two Witnesses, therefore, is that they represent the line of prophets, culminating in John the Baptizer, who bore witness against Jerusalem during the history of

FUTURIST *(continued)*

Some think that it is Elijah and Enoch who appear in this vision. This was the view of the earliest apocryphal writers and the early exegetes of the church. Henry Morris is one modern writer who shares this view. To support this identification, it is stressed that Elijah and Enoch are the only two men who never tasted death, and, since Hebrews 9:27 says "it is appointed for men to die once," these two men must return to fulfill their missed "appointment." However, as Walvoord and Ryrie point out, this argument loses all validity when one considers that "the entire living church at the time of the rapture will go to heaven without dying" (Walvoord).

Not every *futurist* looks for two actual men to fulfill this vision. Mounce writes: "It seems more likely . . . that they are not two individuals but a symbol of the witnessing church in the last tumultuous days before the end of the age."

Others think that two individuals are the *principal* interpretation of the expression, but also leave room for the possibility of including a larger group of witnesses in the picture. Among these is Gaebelein:

> Perhaps the leaders would be two great instruments, manifesting the spirit of Moses and Elijah, endowed with supernatural power, but a larger number of witnesses is unquestionably in view here.

IDEALIST *(continued)*

told Jeremiah: "Behold, I will make My words in your mouth fire, and this people wood, and it shall devour them" (Jer. 5:14). Lenski writes that "the word in the mouth of the Lord's prophet-witnesses may be scorned but it is not an empty sound. Its judgments are fire that devours its enemies." Thus the emperor Julian the Apostate, who vainly tried to reimpose paganism in the Christian Roman Empire, had to confess at last, "You have conquered me, O Galilean!" Wilcock says of these witnesses:

> They are furthermore unquenchable, like the lamps which the prophet Zechariah saw . . . They are untouchable, as is the church of Christ as a whole, though its individual members may be hurt.

⧗ PRETERIST *(continued)*

Israel . . . That these Witnesses are members of the Old Covenant rather than the New is shown, among other indications, by their wearing of sackcloth—the dress characteristic of Old Covenant privation rather than New Covenant fullness.

Chilton goes further to explain that both Moses and Elijah (to whom the witnesses are likened) were in a role preparatory to the coming of Messiah. Moses predicted that "a Prophet like me" (Deut. 18:15) would be raised up after himself—which Prophet was Christ Himself (Acts 3:22ff.; 7:37ff.). Malachi predicted the coming of another Elijah prior to the Messiah's appearing (Mal. 4:5–6), which was fulfilled in John the Baptist (Matt. 11:13–14; 17:12–13). Historically, Moses was succeeded by a *Joshua* (the Hebrew form of the name *Jesus)*, and Elijah was succeeded by one who (like Christ) had a greater anointing of the Spirit than did he himself (2 Kings 2:9). Chilton concludes: "The two Witnesses, therefore, summarize all the witnesses of the Old Covenant, culminating in the witness of John."

Russell actually seeks two literal men in Jerusalem before the fall of that city in AD 70 as the fulfillment of this vision. After surveying the details given, he asserts, "We *have no hesitation in naming St. James and St. Peter* as the

⧗ FUTURIST *(continued)*

Ladd takes this approach as well, allowing that "Possibly there is a blending of the symbolic and the specific" in the passage. He believes the witnesses to be two "actual historical eschatological personages who will be sent to Israel to bring about her conversion." He elaborates that the two witnesses may indeed represent the witness of the church to Israel throughout the age. This witness, however, will be consummated in the end-time by the appearance of two Christian prophets, who will come in the spirit of Moses and Elijah, even as John the Baptist came in the spirit of Elijah. This is apparently Ironside's position as well.

Charles Ryrie summarizes:

> This much is certain: (1) They are persons, for all the other times that the word "witness" is used in the New Testament it is used of persons. They are not movements or powers, but individual persons. (2) It is also certain that they are not named in the text, and this writer feels that the case should be left there. These are two exceptional witnesses raised up by God during the Tribulation and preserved by Him until their ministry is completed.

Walvoord, after surveying the available theories as to the identity of the witnesses, arrives at a position like that of Ryrie:

⌛ PRETERIST *(continued)*

persons indicated." In defense of these identifications, he points out that James, the brother of the Lord, was the most notable leader in the Jerusalem church until his violent death at the hands of the Sanhedrin in the year AD 69. Notwithstanding the strong tradition that Peter died a martyr in Rome (not Jerusalem), Russell marshals eighteen reasons for making Jerusalem "the habitual and fixed residence of St. Peter" and the likely place of his death. Of the legend of Peter's death in Rome, Russell writes:

> It is more than time that it should be relegated to the limbo of fable, with other pious frauds of the same character: That St. Peter's stated abode was Jerusalem is, we think, proved. That he lived up to the verge of the Jewish revolt and war is evident from his epistles. That he died a martyr's death we know from our Lord's prediction; and in his case we may well say that the proverb would hold good, 'It cannot be that a prophet perish out of Jerusalem.' ⌛

⧗ FUTURIST *(continued)*

It seems far preferable to regard these two witnesses as two prophets who will be raised up from among those who turn to Christ in the time following the rapture. ✒

THE DEFEAT OF THE WITNESSES BY THE BEAST

REVELATION 11:7—10

[7]When they finish their testimony, the beast that ascends out of the bottomless pit will make war against them, overcome them, and kill them. [8]And their dead bodies will lie in the street of the great city which spiritually is called Sodom and Egypt, where also our Lord was crucified. [9]Then those from the peoples, tribes, tongues and nations will see their dead bodies three and a half days, and not allow their dead bodies to be put into graves. [10]And those who dwell on the earth will rejoice over them, make merry, and send gifts to one another, because these two prophets tormented those who dwell on the earth.

⌛ HISTORICIST

Barnes understands **when they finish their testimony** (v. 7), to mean "when they should have borne *full* or *ample* testimony." He does not think that this refers strictly to the end of the 1,260 years of papal rule. He argues that such persecutions and "deaths" can apply to "any time *during* the period [of 1,260 years] when it could be said that they had borne a full and ample testimony for the truths of the gospel."

In particular, there was an intensive effort made, beginning with Pope Innocent III in the twelfth century, to exterminate every trace of resistance to the papal authority, such as that of the Waldenses and the Albigenses. At the

⌛ PRETERIST

This is the first passage in Revelation that introduces an evil beast, though chapters 13 and 17 will expand on the concept. Concerning **the beast that ascends out of the bottomless pit** (v. 7), who ultimately manages to silence the voice of the witnesses, Chilton writes:

> The enemy of God and the Church is . . . always **Beast,** in its various historical manifestations. The prophets often spoke of pagan states as terrifying beasts that warred against the Covenant people (Ps. 87:4; 89:10; Isa. 51:9; Dan. 7:3–8, 16–25). All this will be gathered together in St. John's description of Rome and apostate Israel in Revelation 13.

286

FUTURIST

In these verses we encounter the first of thirty-six references to **the beast** (v. 7) in Revelation. Whether this is the same beast as in 13:1 is not certain. Walvoord gives his answer:

> The beast out of the pit is Satan. The beast out of the sea is the world dictator (13:1). The beast out of the land is the false religious leader of that day (13:11). This unholy trinity is the satanic counterfeit of the divine Trinity, the Father, the Son, and the Holy Spirit.

Gaebelein and Ironside identify the beast in this passage with the beast from the sea in 13:1, and they consider both symbolic of the "revived Roman empire" or its ruler, the coming world dictator.

The beast remains powerless to resist the testimony and the judgments of the two witnesses for three and a half years' time. He can do them no harm until **they finish their testimony** (v. 7), showing that, even in an age characterized by apparent satanic authority, God remains entirely sovereign over the affairs and fortunes of His people.

When, however, the beast manages to silence the witnesses with death, the event brings such relief to the guilty consciences of the wicked that it becomes an occasion of global celebration. **Those who dwell on the earth** (v. 10) make merry for three and a half days.

IDEALIST

The beast "appears to represent those antichristian powers in the world which seek to silence the church's witness" (Wilson), or "an incarnation of politico-social evil" (Morey). This beast is treated and described more fully in chapter 13, but here it is seen arising to **make war** (v. 7) against the two witnesses. Since *making war* is generally a term referring to a conflict between two armies, this would seem to confirm that the witnesses are not two individuals (for then it would not be a war but a personal assault upon two men), but a greater company (i.e., the church).

When their **testimony** is complete (v. 7), God permits the church to experience apparent defeat. This period of defeat is measurable in days as opposed to the years of their ministry, both of which bear a symbolic similarity to the duration of Christ's ministry and death. Swete observes that the **three and a half days** (v. 9) during which the witnesses lie dead, though only a brief period, is "long enough to bear the semblance of being complete and final." Wilcock also sees this time as one of attack on the church:

> Scripture does seem to envisage a time (this is the first clear indication of it in Revelation) when at the very end of history an unexampled onslaught will be mounted against the church, and she will to all appearances "go under" . . . We shall

⧗ HISTORICIST *(continued)*

third Lateran Council of 1179, war was declared against the heretics, followed, in 1231, by the Inquisitions.

As the Scripture predicts that their enemies would **not allow their dead bodies to be put into graves** (v. 9), so history bears out. Christian burial was denied by papal decree to those who were regarded as heretics. This denial of burial was decided at both the third and fourth Lateran Councils, in 1179 and 1215, respectively. Also in the papal decree of Gregory IX, in 1227, and the decree of Pope Martin, following the Council of Constance, in 1422

> The Council ordered that Wycliff's body should be exhumed . . . and the ashes of Huss, instead of burial, should be collected and cast into the Lake of Constance—I may add that Savanarola's ashes were similarly cast into the Arno, AD 1492, and that in the first Bull entrusted to the Cardinal Cajetan, against Luther, as well as that afterward, this was one of the declared penalties, that both Luther and his partizans [sic] should be deprived 'ecclesiasticae sepulturae' [Christian burial].[11]

By the year 1514, these attempts to silence the witnesses appeared to have succeeded. Elliott quotes the Catholic historian, Cardinal Pallavicini, as to the state of affairs at the beginning of the sixteenth century:

⧗ PRETERIST *(continued)*

The witnesses' testimony, though tormenting to the apostate Jews, cannot be cut short. The witnesses are overcome and killed, but not until **they finish their testimony** (v. 7). This fact would seem to fit with Chilton's thesis that the witnesses represent the line of Old Testament prophets until John, or that of Russell that the witnesses were two individuals. It works less well with the position of Clark and Adams, who identified the witnesses as the religious and civil government of Israel.

The ongoing opposition to the prophetic witness, which had continued through the centuries prior to Christ's coming, was focused in the opposition of the Jews and Romans to the Lord's anointed. His death was the occasion of rejoicing for many segments of society. Pilate and Herod—who formerly had hated each other—were reconciled to each other when Jesus died (Luke 23:12). Chilton continues:

> At Christ's death all manner of people rejoiced and mocked: the rulers, the priests, the competing religious factions, the Roman soldiers, the servants, the criminals; all joined in celebrating His death (cf. Matt. 27:27–31, 39–44; Mark 15:29–32; Luke 22:63–65; 23:8–12, 35–39); all sided with the Beast against the Lamb (John 19:15).

⌛ FUTURIST *(continued)*

The **dead bodies** (v. 8) are even left unburied, that their foes may gloat over them. Walvoord explains:

> In the effort to capitalize as much as possible on their death, their bodies are exhibited in the streets for three and one-half days contrary to all reasonable laws of humanity. Apparently great throngs of people come to witness the bodies of the two witnesses whom they so greatly feared in life ... Apparently the celebration is worldwide. By means of television and the transmission of pictures throughout the world by communication satellites and other means, the entire earth will see graphically the dead bodies of the two witnesses.

Seiss observes:

> The exposure of their dead bodies tells of a most extraordinary malignity and spite, and attests the extraordinary potency and effectiveness of the objects of it. It shows at once a devilishness of unwonted intensity in the people, and a terribleness of efficiency in the Witnesses in provoking a fiendishness and resentment so monstrous and unrelenting that it could not be placated by their death, but continued to reek and vent itself upon their lifeless remains after they were dead.

⌛ IDEALIST *(continued)*

hear more of it, and of the Beast who initiates it (verse 7), in chapter 20.

This is not a case of the "gates of hell" prevailing fully over the true church, which Jesus promised would never happen (Matt. 16:18), for, as Hendriksen writes:

> The beast will not kill every believer. But the Church itself, as a mighty organization for the dissemination of the gospel and regular ministry of the Word, will be destroyed.

The words **their dead bodies** (vv. 8, 9) occur three times. In the first two cases, the expression in Greek is singular—"their dead body"—confirming that these two represent one corporate body, the church, the body of Christ. **The great city** (v. 8) is not literal Jerusalem, but "the world in rebellion against God" (Morey)—or "that secular city which has the character of Sodom and Egypt" (Wilson)—in contrast to the city of God, New Jerusalem, which is the church.

Wilcock observes:

> It may not be altogether fanciful to see in the church's experience a reflection of Christ's experience, in his three days of death following three years of ministry, since his place of suffering is explicitly identified with hers (verse 8).

⧗ HISTORICIST *(continued)*

In the *West* the true faith flourished, with scarce any contamination attaching to it: there remaining only, almost invisible, certain minute stains of ignoble and despised heresies, followed by a little flock of rustic and rude men: the remnant either of the Waldenses, or of the followers of John Huss, who had been condemned and burned a century before.

A papal bull was issued in 1513 calling the remaining Bohemian brethren to present their cause before the 9th Session of the Fifth Lateran Council. None appeared, which fact was hailed as a sign that the triumph of Rome was complete. At the session, which occurred on May 5, 1514, in the words of Elliott:

> The orator of the session ascended the pulpit; and, amidst the applause of the assembled council, uttered that memorable exclamation of triumph—an exclamation which . . . was never, I believe, pronounced before, and certainly never since—*"Iam nemo reclamat, nullus obsistit"*—"There is an end of resistance to the Papal rule and religion; opposers there exist no more;" and again, "The whole body of Christendom is now seen to be subjected to its Head [the Pope]."

Pope Leo X responded to this announcement with the following state-

⧗ PRETERIST *(continued)*

The location of the witnesses' death is said to be in Jerusalem, as most would understand the reference to **where also our Lord was crucified** (v. 8). The city is also identified **spiritually** with **Sodom** and **Egypt.** The first of these names is applied to Israel in Isaiah 1:10, but where, prior to this, is the name *Egypt* applied to the Jews? David Chilton answers:

> Commentators are generally unable to find Bible references comparing Israel (or Jerusalem) to Egypt, but this is the old problem of not being able to see the forest for the trees . . . The language of Revelation itself . . . speaks of the Egyptian plagues being poured out upon Israel (8:6–12; 16:2–12). The war of the Witnesses with apostate Israel and the pagan states is described in the same terms as the original Exodus from Egypt (cf. also the Cloud and the pillar of fire in 10:1). Jerusalem, the once-holy, now apostate city, has become pagan and perverse, an oppressor of the true Covenant people.

On the matter of the witnesses' corpses lying unburied and then rising from the dead and ascending into heaven, Russell admits that this cannot be shown to have happened to James and Peter, with whom he has identified the witnesses. But neither can the possibility be eliminated by existing evidence, as Russell explains:

⧗ IDEALIST *(continued)*

John describes the rejoicing of **those who dwell on the earth** (v. 10) at the apparent triumph of evil over the church, which has so long confronted them with the claims of Christ. The sending of **gifts** (v. 10) as a token of celebration was a common custom in ancient times (cf. Esth. 9:19, 22). Swete notes:

> Such a sense of relief is not seldom felt by bad men when a preacher of righteousness or a signal example of goodness is removed, though good breeding may prevent outward manifestation of joy.

Great emphasis is placed upon the exulting of the wicked over the witnesses' death—perhaps in order to amplify their chagrin when they witness the witnesses' resurrection. Plummer writes: "the triumph will be brief; it will but usher in the end and the final subjugation of the devil." ⧉

291

HISTORICIST *(continued)*

ment: "All which considered, our soul exults in the Lord: and we judge that thanks should be given to God for it, and that, among all the faithful in Christ, there should be those signs of joy which on similar occasions are wont to be observed." After this, the pope and the others made great festivity, and the pope granted plenary papal indulgence. This was a striking fulfillment to the passage under consideration. The **great city,** where the dead bodies of the two witnesses lie unburied, is "papal city."

PRETERIST *(continued)*

If we are asked, Did this miracle take place with respect to the martyred witnesses of Christ, St. James and St. Peter? we can only answer, We do not know . . . We therefore quit the subject with this one observation: Four-fifths at least of the description of the Apocalypse suit the known history of St. James and St. Peter, and no one can allege that the remainder may not be equally appropriate.

THE VINDICATION OF THE TWO WITNESSES

REVELATION 11:11—14

[11]Now after the three and a half days the breath of life from God entered them, and they stood on their feet, and great fear fell on those who saw them. [12]And they heard a loud voice from heaven saying to them, "Come up here." And they ascended to heaven in a cloud, and their enemies saw them. [13]In the same hour there was a great earthquake, and a tenth of the city fell. In the earthquake seven thousand people were killed, and the rest were afraid and gave glory to the God of heaven. [14]The second woe is past. Behold, the third woe is coming quickly.

⧗ HISTORICIST

The bodies of the two witnesses lay dead for **three and a half days** (v. 11). According to the year-for-a-day principle, this means *three and a half years.* From May 5, 1514, the date that the Fifth Lateran Council declared, "There is an end of resistance to the Papal rule and religion; opposers there exist no more!" until October 31, 1517, when Luther nailed the 95 Theses to the door of the Wittenberg church, was precisely three years and 180 days (one-half of a 360-day year).

They stood on their feet (v. 11): To describe the mighty revolution of the Reformation as a rising from the dead of the faithful church seems an appropriate symbol. Barnes gives three reasons to see in the Reformers' testimony a "standing up again" of those martyrs

⧗ PRETERIST

Chilton associates the death of the witnesses with the death of Christ Himself, as the enemy's apparent victory over the discomforting, ages-long, prophetic witness against Jerusalem by the whole line of the prophets. The rejoicing of the world over the witnesses' destruction he compares with that of all of Christ's enemies at His death. With reference to their resurrection, he writes:

> The attempt to destroy the Witnesses seemed to be successful, not only in silencing individual prophets, but in abolishing the Testimony of the Covenant itself. . . . Yet the evil time is brief, being limited to a mere three and a half days . . . Through the resurrection of Christ, the Church and her Testimony became unstoppable. In union with Christ in His Ascension to glory

FUTURIST

The resurrection of the witnesses is a spectacle that will be viewed with awe and horror by the world. Ryrie paints the picture:

> It is not difficult to imagine the scene. A crowd will be standing around or filing past their bodies lying in the street. Undoubtedly there will be radio and television coverage. Suddenly they will stand up . . . The two witnesses will disappear out of sight in the cloud of glory.

Before the newspapers can report the story or the commentators write

> their interpretations there will be another great event to cover, an earthquake centering in Jerusalem which destroys a tenth part of the city and kills seven thousand men.

On the point that **the rest were afraid and gave glory to the God of heaven** (v. 13), Henry Morris writes:

> The two witnesses had stood by "the God of the earth" (11:4). Now "the God of heaven" had stood by them. The unbelieving multitudes had been forced to give glory to the God of heaven, though they had put to death His servants.

Walvoord comments:

> Even though they recognize the power of the God of heaven, it does not seem to indicate that they have

IDEALIST

Many times in history the witnessing church has appeared to be beaten by the world system, only to arise again and be vindicated as God's indestructible witness. Leon Morris writes: "Each such resurrection strikes consternation into the hearts of her oppressors."

In a figurative sense, Christian martyrs could be said to be "resurrected and exalted" by the honor often shown them after their deaths—even as the Jews, having slain their prophets, later adorned their tombs as shrines (cf. Matt. 23:29–31). Swete writes that the final triumph of the church "has been partly anticipated in the sight of the world by the tribute paid to the victims of a persecution, sometimes within a few years after their dishonour and death . . . Paganism saw the men it had hated and killed called up to heaven before its eyes."

Ultimately, the church will literally rise to meet the Lord in the air (1 Thess. 4:16–18). Hendriksen writes: "In connection with Christ's second coming the Church is restored to life, to honour, to power, to influence." This may be preceded by a brief period of serious global persecution of the church, as in this chapter.

The vindication of the witnesses is followed by **a great earthquake** (v. 13), which kills seven thousand men, and the fall of **a tenth of the city.** Hendriksen writes: "This is probably simply

⧗ HISTORICIST *(continued)*

who had opposed the papacy in the preceding centuries: (a) it was the same kind of testimony, to the same truths and against the same evils; (b) it was borne by men of the same spirit and character; and (c) it was borne with the same fearlessness, facing the same kind of opposition and persecution.

Speaking of those who would bear witness to the truth after his death at the stake, John Huss said, "And I, awakening as it were from the dead, and rising from the grave, shall rejoice with exceeding great joy." Appropriately, Pope Hadrian, at the Diet of Nuremberg in 1523, declared, "The heretics Huss and Jerome seem now to be alive again in the person of Luther." As Cuninghame put it,

> At the commencement of the 16th century, Europe reposed in the deep sleep of spiritual death, under the iron yoke of the Papacy. There was none that moved the wing, or opened the mouth, or peeped; when suddenly in one of the universities of Germany the voice of an obscure monk was heard, the sound of which rapidly filled Saxony, Germany, and Europe itself, shaking the very foundations of the Papal power, and arousing men from the lethargy of ages. (quoted by Barnes)

Barnes applies the call to the witnesses, **Come up here** (v. 12), and their

⧗ PRETERIST *(continued)*

(Eph. 2:6), **they went up to heaven in the Cloud, and their enemies beheld them.** . . . The story of the two witnesses is therefore the story of the witnessing Church.

Following the ascension of the witnesses, John records **a great earthquake,** and that **a tenth of the city fell** (v. 13). *Preterist* interpreters associate this with the fall of Jerusalem. It is not clear, however, whether this passage deals with the final and complete destruction of the city. Regarding the fraction "a tenth," Chilton writes:

> Actually, the whole city fell in AD 70; but, as we have seen, the Trumpet-judgments do not yet reach the final end of Jerusalem, but (apparently) go only as far as the first siege of Jerusalem, under Cestius. In conformity to the nature of the Trumpet as an alarm, God's taking a "tithe" of Jerusalem in the first siege was a warning to the City.

David S. Clark states that "This continues the terrors in the city's destruction." One result of the earthquake is the deaths of **seven thousand people** (v. 13). This number may be symbolic, since seven is the number of completeness and one thousand a figure for "many." Chilton suggests that the number "represents the exact reverse of the situation in Elijah's day. In 1 Kings 19:18, God told Elijah that seven thou-

FUTURIST *(continued)*

come to a point of true faith in Christ.

Ryrie adds:

Some may be converted because of this experience, but some will simply recognize divine power without personal repentance.

Hal Lindsey, on the other hand, believes the phenomenon will bring about the true conversion of many of the Jews.

IDEALIST *(continued)*

a symbolic representation of the alarming happenings on the very eve of the final judgment."

⏳ HISTORICIST *(continued)*

subsequent ascension heavenward to "the various influences that served to establish and confirm the Reformation, and to introduce the great principles of religious freedom, giving to that work ultimate triumph, and showing that it had the favor of God." Elliott sees the ascension of the two witnesses as a symbolic way of describing the church's "calling up to political ascendancy and power." He refers to a decree by the Roman emperor, called the Pacification of Nuremberg, through which full toleration was granted to the formerly persecuted Protestants.

The **great earthquake** (v. 13) is a reference to the political convulsions that rocked Europe after the Reformation. Specifically, two consequences of this earthquake are mentioned: (a) **a tenth of the city fell** (v. 13), meaning a partial reduction in the power of the papal "city," which Barnes applies to the fact that "a considerable portion of the colossal Papal power suddenly fell away." Caringola sees the "tenth" as a reference to the Church of England declaring itself independent of Rome in 1529—making England the first nation to break away from the rule of the popes; and (b) **seven thousand men were killed** (v. 13), which are understood by Elliott as seven chiliads, meaning provinces or countries. The seven chiliads that fell away from Rome were Holland, Zealand, Utrecht, Frieseland,

⏳ PRETERIST *(continued)*

sand in Israel remained faithful to the Covenant."

J. Stuart Russell relates what he feels may be a related incident:

> It is a remarkable fact that we find in Josephus an account of an incident which occurred during the Jewish war which in many respects bears a striking resemblance to the events described in this passage . . . The statement of Josephus is as follows:

> During the night a terrific storm arose; the wind blew with tempestuous violence, and the rain fell in torrents; the lightnings flashed without intermission, accompanied by fearful peals of thunder, and the quaking earth resounded with mighty bellowings. The universe, convulsed to its very base, appeared fraught with the destruction of mankind, and it was easy to conjecture that these were portents of no trivial calamity.

Taking advantage of the panic caused by the earthquake, the Idumeans, who were in league with the Zealots, who occupied the temple, succeeded in effecting an entrance into the city, when a fearful massacre ensued. "The outer court of the temple," says Josephus, "was inundated with blood, and the day dawned upon eight thousand five hundred dead."

> We do not quote this as the fulfillment of the scene in the vision,

298

⌛ HISTORICIST *(continued)*

Groningen, Overyssel, and Guiderland, the provinces of the Union of Utrecht.

⌛ PRETERIST *(continued)*

although it may be so; but to show how much the symbols resemble actual historical facts.

THE SEVENTH TRUMPET
REVELATION 11:15—19

[15]Then the seventh angel sounded: And there were loud voices in heaven, saying, "The kingdoms of this world have become the kingdoms of our Lord and of His Christ, and He shall reign forever and ever!" [16]And the twenty-four elders who sat before God on their thrones fell on their faces and worshiped God, [17]saying, "We give you thanks, O Lord God Almighty, the One who is and who was and who is to come, because You have taken Your great power and reigned. [18]The nations were angry, and Your wrath has come, and the time of the dead, that they should be judged, and that You should reward Your servants the prophets and the saints, and those who fear Your name, small and great, and should destroy those who destroy the earth." [19]Then the temple of God was opened in heaven, and the ark of His covenant was seen in His temple. And there were lightnings, noises, thunderings, an earthquake, and great hail.

⌛ HISTORICIST

The sixth trumpet, which sounded in chapter 9, verse 13, has included all the events from that point through chapter 11, v. 14. The intervening material has depicted a period of 1,260 years, during which time the papal church persecuted the true church, and in the midst of which the Reformation occurred. Also, during a considerable portion of the same period, the Turks have made war

⌛ PRETERIST

Though it is announced that **the kingdoms of this world have become the kingdoms of our Lord and of His Christ** (v. 15), this is not a declaration that the entire earth has at this point come under the forcible and conscious rule of Christ, as at the end of time. The time frame is that of the fall of Jerusalem in AD 70. The meaning of the declaration is given by David S. Clark:

FUTURIST

Virtually all *futurists*, being premille-narians (Abraham Kuyper, an amillen-nialist, being a rare exception), see the trumpet of the **seventh angel** (v. 15) as heralding the Second Coming of Christ to put down all opposition, take the au-thority of the nations to Himself and es-tablish His millennial kingdom on earth. The mention of the Second Com-ing at this point has raised questions about the chronological structure of Revelation. Walvoord writes:

> The question that remains . . . is how can the kingdoms of the world become at this point the kingdoms of Christ when, as a matter of fact, the seven vials [bowls] are seem-ingly to be poured out? The an-swer as indicated previously seems to be that just as the seven trum-pets are comprehended in the sev-enth seal so the seven vials [bowls] are comprehended in the seventh trumpet.

Heading off an apparent discrep-ancy between the statement that **He shall reign forever and ever** (v. 15), and the belief that the reign of Christ is generally associated with the 1,000 years of chapter 20, Walvoord writes:

IDEALIST

This trumpet brings in the final con-summation of the reign of God: **and He shall reign forever and ever** (v. 15). It is the close of act 3 of the drama. This is the second picture Revelation has given of the end (cf. 6:12–17). Here, however, there is no actual description of the judgment scene. Rather than give us the details of the devastation, this trum-pet, as Lenski says, "does something greater, it pictures a scene in heaven *after* the judgment and lets us hear what the judgment signifies for God and his Christ, for the obdurate world, and for Christ's prophets and saints."

In the anthem sung by **the twen-ty-four elders** (vv. 16–18), many man-uscripts omit the phrase **and who is to come** (v. 17). If these manuscripts are to be followed, then the Lord is now sim-ply referred to as **the One who is and who was,** because, having returned already at this point, there is no further reason to predict His coming.

The **ark of His covenant** (v. 19) seen in the heavenly temple, is men-tioned here as a reminder of God's faith-fulness to His covenant people (the church). The chapter ends with a great

⧗ HISTORICIST *(continued)*

against papal Europe, conquering "a third of mankind"—a conflict beginning about 1062 and continuing until the Treaty of Carlowitz, in 1699.

It is finally time for us to hear the sounding of **the seventh trumpet** (v. 15), which brings to an end the first series of visions. The story of the church can only be regarded as completed when there is a final judgment upon the ages-long enemy of the gospel and a vindication of those who have remained faithful through much tribulation. This passage depicts this development as being an occasion of great rejoicing and worship in heaven. Christ, who has endured the opposition of the apostate church, finally fulfills the longing of every godly soul; He has **taken** [His] **great power and reigned** (v. 17).

Most significantly, this trumpet brings us to the end of the age. The sounding of the seventh trumpet does not refer to a momentary, staccato blast, but to an extended period, which includes the pouring out of the seven bowls of wrath, the last of which brings the end of the world. The bowls, which are described in detail in chapter 16, begin to be fulfilled in the French Revolution at the end of the eighteenth century, but the last few still await fulfillment at the coming of the Lord.

The last verse of this chapter should be the beginning of chapter 12, because it introduces a new series of visions, as

⧗ PRETERIST *(continued)*

The first great opposer is swept away, and "the kingdoms of this world,"—no, rather the rule or sway of this world belongs to Christ. Now the kingdom was really given to Christ at his ascension; but two things had to happen before it was rightly on its way as a world conquering power. The first was spiritual, the outpouring of the Spirit at Pentecost; and the second was physical, the breaking down of the barrier of Judaism in the fall of the first great opposer. Then Christianity became a world religion.

This is also the line of reasoning taken by Chilton:

> Thus the Kingdom of God, the "Fifth Kingdom" prophesied in Daniel 2, becomes universalized . . . The final dissociation of Christianity from Judaism means that it is now a worldwide religion. The Kingdom of Christ now begins the process of encompassing and enveloping all kingdoms of the world.

There may be a tendency to read in the expression, **the time of the dead, that they should be judged** (v. 18), a reference to the final resurrection and judgment of all the dead at the final coming of Christ. This is not necessarily its meaning, however. As David S. Clark explains:

> ["The dead" are] not all the dead as if this were the final judgment at the

⌛ FUTURIST *(continued)*

The millennial reign, while it extends for only one thousand years, is in some sense continued in the new heaven and the new earth. Never again will the earth be under the control and overLordship of man.

Another problem associated with a premillennial understanding of this passage is that there appears to be, in verse 18, a resurrection of the dead and a judgment. Dispensationalism teaches that the Christians are raised at the Rapture, prior to the Tribulation (cf. Rev. 4:1), and that the wicked are raised at the end of the Millennium (20:12–13). However, this passage seems to place the resurrection and judgment at the end of the Tribulation. On dispensational assumptions, this is seven years too late to involve the church, and 1,000 years too early to be the wicked. How does one harmonize these things?

Walvoord considers that the "context seems to indicate that the resurrection of the righteous dead is especially in view rather than that of the wicked dead, who are not raised until after the millennium." And who are these "righteous dead," if not the church? Hal Lindsey answers:"The believers of the Old Testament and those who become believers during the Tribulation will be resurrected and rewarded at the end of the Tribulation, when Jesus returns to the earth as King of Kings."

⌛ IDEALIST *(continued)*

display of the power of God in the form of **lightnings, noises, thunderings, an earthquake, and great hail** (v. 19), which Alford calls "the solemn salvos, so to speak, of the artillery of heaven."

303

⧗ HISTORICIST *(continued)*

did 4:1. The fourth chapter opens with the announcement, "I looked, and behold, a door standing open in heaven." This series of visions opens with a similar statement: **the temple of God was opened in heaven** (v. 19). B. W. Johnson comments:

> There is to be a revelation of facts connected with the temple of God. We have already shown that the reference is not to the Jewish temple, which no longer existed, but to the spiritual temple, the church of Jesus Christ . . . The *thunders, earthquake,* etc., foreshadow the commotions, revolutions, and judgments which will take place in the fulfillment of the symbols."[12]

⧗ PRETERIST *(continued)*

end of the world, (we will find that at the end of chap. 20) but this refers to those martyred dead who had fallen in the persecutions. In chapter 6 we saw them under the altar in heaven praying: "How long, O Lord, holy and true, dost thou not judge and **avenge** our blood on them that dwell on the earth?" Now here it is said, "And the time of the dead is come that they should be judged or **avenged** and that thou shouldst reward thy servants that fear thy name."

Chilton also affirms that this is "not the final judgment of the Last Day, but rather the historical vindication and avenging of the martyred saints, those who had suffered at the hands of ungodly Israel, as Jesus had foretold."

A consequence of this judgment upon the earthly temple was that **the temple of God was opened in heaven** (v. 19). Commenting on this phrase, Russell writes:

> That is as much as to say, the local and temporary passes, but is succeeded by the heaven/ and eternal; the earth/ and figurative is superseded by the spiritual and true . . . No sooner is the "first tabernacle" swept away than the temple in heaven is opened, and even the sacred ark of the covenant, the shrine of the divine Presence and Glory, is revealed to the eyes of men. Access into the holiest is no longer forbidden, and we have

FUTURIST *(continued)*

This thesis posits that there are at least three resurrections: one of the church, prior to the Tribulation; a second of the Old Testament and Tribulation saints, at Christ's coming at the end of the Tribulation; and a third resurrection at the end of the Millennium, involving the wicked dead. (The raising of the two witnesses, if placed in the middle of the Tribulation, would raise the tally to a total of four resurrections.)

To escape the need for three resurrections, Gaebelein, Ironside, Morris, and others see in this seventh trumpet both the commencement and the end of the Millennium. The Second Coming of Christ is at the beginning, and the resurrection and judgment come at the end.

Ironside writes: "The eighteenth verse covers the entire millennium and carries us on to the judgment of the wicked dead, to the end of time . . . The day of judgment will be a thousand years long."[13]

PRETERIST *(continued)*

boldness to enter into the holiest by the blood of Jesus.

As we move into chapter 12, it is clear that the scene is significantly changed. A new section of the book is broached. Though he does not speak for *preterists* like Russell, Terry, and Chilton, Jay Adams gives a glimpse of how many *preterists* understand the structure of Revelation at this juncture:

By way of anticipation, it may be said that the first prophecy ends with chapter 11; chapter 12 is transitional, and chapter 13 marks the beginning of the second prophecy. Everything about the first prophecy has to do with Judaism; everything about the second pertains to the Roman empire. Only a brief perusal of the two sections is necessary to confirm this.

THE BIRTH OF THE MALE CHILD

REVELATION 12:1—6

[1]Now a great sign appeared in heaven: a woman clothed with the sun, with the moon under her feet, and on her head a garland of twelve stars. [2]Then being with child, she cried out in labor and in pain to give birth. [3]And another sign appeared in heaven: behold, a great, fiery red dragon having seven heads and ten horns, and seven diadems on his heads. [4]His tail drew a third of the stars of heaven and threw them to the earth. And the dragon stood before the woman who was ready to give birth, to devour her Child as soon as it was born. [5]She bore a male Child who was to rule all nations with a rod of iron. And her Child was caught up to God and His throne. [6]Then the woman fled into the wilderness, where she has a place prepared by God, that they should feed her there one thousand two hundred and sixty days.

⌛ HISTORICIST

Elliott, Barnes, and others see this vision and the two that follow as retrogressive, that is, they provide supplemental and explanatory information on a time already covered in previous portions of the book. Barnes identifies this as the beginning of a second series of visions, the first series having been contained in chapters 4–11, which concerned themselves primarily with the outward state of the church—that is, secular and political developments that affected the fortunes of the church. This second set of visions, contained in chapters 12–19, looks at the same time period with a concern for observing the *internal* affairs of the church—both the visible,

⌛ PRETERIST

At this point, two groups of *preterists* part company in their interpretation of the material. The two camps are as follows:

First, there are those, like David Chilton, Milton Terry, J. Stuart Russell, and Philip Carrington, who believe that the remaining chapters (through chap. 19) continue the prophecy of the destruction of Jerusalem (identifying *Babylon* also with Jerusalem). Chilton affirms that "the second half of the Book of Revelation covers much the same ground as the first, but from a different perspective." In defining the nature of the distinct perspectives of each portion, Milton Terry writes:

⏳ FUTURIST

The woman seen in this vision is the second of four women mentioned in the book of Revelation (the others being Jezebel, 2:20; the harlot, 17:4; and the bride, 19:7).

Many have thought the woman represents the church, or, as some holiness people would understand it, the professing church, in contrast to the true overcoming company of the last days, whom they identify collectively with the **male Child** (v. 5). In defense of this latter identification, it is pointed out that there is a promise to the overcomers in the church at Thyatira that they, with Christ, "shall rule . . . with a rod of iron" (Rev. 2:27), as is also declared of the male Child here.

The majority of *futurists* take the **woman** (v. 1) to be Israel, and her **Child** (v. 5) to be Christ. This is the view of Gaebelein, Walvoord, Ryrie, Ironside, Moorehead, Lindsey, and most dispensationalists. The support for this identification of the woman is found in the description of her as being **clothed with the sun, with the moon under her feet, and on her head a garland of twelve stars** (v. 1). This has obvious reference back to Joseph's dream in Genesis 37:9, in which the sun and moon and twelve stars (eleven plus Joseph) represented the family of Jacob, the people of Israel. That the Child is Christ is supported by the fact that He is **to rule all nations with a rod of iron**

⏳ IDEALIST

Chapters 12 through 14 (or, possibly, 15:4) make up act 4 of the drama. Some place the beginning of the Act at 11:19. Alford remarks that "the principal details of this section are descriptive rather than prophetical, relating to things past and passing."

The birth of Christ is depicted in this passage, though His entire earthly career is passed over, jumping directly from His birth to His ascension and enthronement in heaven (v. 5). The point is to show that Satan, who made an effort to destroy Jesus from His birth onward (e.g., when Herod slaughtered the infants of Bethlehem), entirely failed to prevent Christ's triumph and the establishment of His kingdom.

The travailing **woman** (v. 1) is either the believing remnant of Old Testament Israel, through whom Christ was brought into the world, or "an ideal symbol of God's people in both dispensations" (Wilson). The **sun** clothing her, the **moon under her feet,** and the **garland of twelve stars** (v. 1) clearly recall Joseph's dream (Gen. 37:9), in which the sun, moon, and stars represented Joseph's immediate family, namely Israel.

The woman's **labor** and **pain** (v. 2) represent the afflictions endured by Israel throughout pre-Christian history, while they awaited the birth of the Messiah.

Waiting to kill and eat the woman's Child as soon as it is born is **a dragon**

⌛ HISTORICIST *(continued)*

external church and the true, faithful church.

The **woman** (v. 1) in this vision is the true church at a time when there was great promise of growth and success (represented by the fact that she was **with child** and about to **give birth**—v. 2). **Heaven** (v. 1) refers to the political firmament: the **sun** and the **moon** being representative of the highest authorities (the Roman rulers who are seen adorning and supporting the church at the time indicated), and the **stars** representing lesser authorities (the ecclesiastical rulers and bishops who are at that time recognized as dignified authorities). The **male Child** (v. 5) is representative of the children of the church, seen as a body politic raised to dominant power.

The **dragon** (v. 3) is a fit image for any heathen persecutor, but here represents Imperial Rome, which, through persecution of the church, sought to prevent the realization of its "male Child" destiny."The real enemy here referred to is, undoubtedly, Satan . . . but here it is Satan in the form of some fearful opponent of the church that would arise at a period when the church was prosperous, and when it was about to be enlarged" (Barnes). The fact that the dragon **drew a third of the stars of heaven** (v. 4) with its tail suggests symbolically that the persecuting power at the time designated dominated only a

⌛ PRETERIST *(continued)*

Part First has revealed the Lamb of God under various symbols, glorious in power, opening the book of divine mysteries, avenging the martyred saints, and exhibiting the fearful judgments destined to come upon the enemies of God. Everything is viewed as from the throne of the King of heaven, who sends forth his armies and destroys the defiant murderers of his prophets and burns up their city (comp. Matt. 22:7).

Part Second reveals the Church in conflict with infernal and worldly principalities and powers, surviving all persecution, and triumphing by the word of her testimony, and, after Babylon the harlot falls and passes from view, appearing as the wife of the Lamb, the tabernacle of God with men, glorious in her beauty and imperishable as the throne of God.[14]

The second camp would consist of Moses Stuart, Jay Adams, David S. Clark, and others who believe that *Babylon* is the city of Rome and that the remaining chapters assume that the judgment on Jerusalem, the first great persecutor of the saints, is complete. The second great persecutor of the church, imperial Rome, is thus to be conquered in the visions that lie ahead. On this assumption, chapter 12 makes a smooth transition between the two sections. Beginning with the flight of

⧗ FUTURIST *(continued)*

(v. 5), a promise first made to Christ in Psalm 2:9 and repeated in Revelation 19:15.

Both Ladd and Mounce, who are not dispensationalists, also understand the child to be Christ, but they see the woman, not as national Israel, but as the "messianic community, the ideal faithful Israel" (Mounce). This apparently means that the faithful remnant in Israel throughout the ages is pictured as God's instrument for bringing the Messiah into the world.

There is little difficulty in identifying the **dragon** (v. 3) with Satan, since he is named in verse 9. However, the particular circumstance of his **having seven heads and ten horns** is thought by many to extend the identification in some way to the first beast of the next chapter—which is usually associated with the revived Roman Empire of the end-times.

The action of the dragon in casting down **a third of the stars** (v. 4) is capable of more than one interpretation, as Ryrie shows:

> The problem is, what are the stars? They could be the luminous bodies seen in the heavens, in which case this event would be some sort of judgment involving a meteor shower on earth. But sometimes stars refer to angelic beings (as 9:1; Job 38:7; and possibly Rev. 1:20). If that is the reference here,

⧗ IDEALIST *(continued)*

(v. 3) who is unambiguously identified as Satan in verse 9. Lenski agrees with this identification:

> The pregnant woman is the church which is pregnant with the promise of the Messiah beginning with Genesis 3:15. Satan's one aim was "to devour" or destroy this Messiah.

The dragon's **seven heads** (v. 3) speak of universal (seven) authority (heads); **ten horns** speak of political or military strength; the **seven diadems** refer to political authority.

The **third of the stars** (v. 4) cast down represent (probably) the portion of angels who fell with Satan originally (2 Pet. 2:4; Jude 6). The birth of the **male Child** (v. 5) is that of Jesus in Bethlehem. Hendriksen writes: "Nearly all commentators of all schools agree that the child is Christ." The dragon is frustrated by the ascension of Jesus to heaven, so he is forced to vent his rage upon the church which remains on earth. The woman's flight **into the wilderness** (v. 6), where she is sustained for three and a half years, speaks of God's care of the church throughout the church age. ◎

311

⌛ HISTORICIST *(continued)*

third of the political "heaven." If it drew all of the stars, this would suggest universal dominion. This identifies the proper time frame, thinks Elliott, with the time of Maximim, the ruler of the Asiatic third of the Roman Empire in 313, while the church in the remaining two-thirds of the empire enjoyed toleration and protection under Constantine.

This persecution could not, however, prevent the destiny of the church from being realized, for **her Child was caught up to God and His throne** (v. 5). This symbolizes the enthronement of Constantine over the entire empire in 324. His avowedly Christian throne, like that of Solomon, might well be called the throne of God, and Christianity was "caught up" to the place of supremacy in the empire. Non-Christian historian Gibbon remarks: "The gratitude of the church has exalted the virtues of the generous patron who seated Christianity on the throne of the Roman world." Constantine and his successors, like Theodosius, ruled the heathen **with a rod of iron** (v. 5), eventually ending all toleration of paganism.

For the flight of the woman **into the wilderness**, see comments on verses 14ff. ⌀

⌛ PRETERIST *(continued)*

Jewish Christians from doomed Jerusalem, the chapter depicts the dragon's continuing war against them, leading to his employment of the Roman emperors in the effort to destroy the church in chapter 13. Adams writes:

> Chapter 12 carries the reader from Jerusalem to Rome. This is a long trip culturally as well as geographically. Hence, a transitional chapter, weaving the two together by revelation of spiritual forces and movements behind the scenes, is quite necessary, as well as appropriate.

There is little disagreement among *preterist* expositors as to who the **woman** (v. 1), the **dragon** (v. 3), and the **male Child** (v. 5) are in the vision. The woman is usually identified with the faithful remnant of Old Testament Israel, since the male Child (understood as Christ) is born as the result of her **labor** and her **pain** (v. 2). This travailing of the woman is understood to refer to the centuries of affliction suffered by the faithful Jews as they awaited the coming of their Messiah.[15] The observation that she **cried out in labor** (v. 2) "has reference to the [Old Testament] Church's official declaration of the Word of God, the prophecy that she uttered as she travailed in birth" (Chilton).

The dragon has **seven heads and ten horns** (v. 3). This seems to make

FUTURIST *(continued)*

then the event described is the revolt of Satan in which he took with him in rebellion a third of the angels (cf. Jude 6; 2 Pet. 2:4).

The principal problem attaching to this second view is the time element of the passage, which *futurists* understand to be the end of the age. The fall of disobedient angels obviously occurred long ago, for Jude and Peter describe it as being past in their day. Walvoord is more chronologically consistent in his interpretation:

> The tail of the dragon is declared to draw a third part of the stars of heaven and cast them to the earth. This seems to refer to the gathering under his power of those who oppose him politically and spiritually involving his temporary subjugation of a large portion of the earth.

The attempt of the dragon **to devour** (v. 4) the Child at his birth is best understood as a reference to Satan's plot to kill Christ in His infancy, revealed in Herod's slaughter of the innocents in Bethlehem. From this early event, the narrative skips over the entire life of Christ to his ascension: **her Child was caught up to God and His throne** (v. 5).

The meaning of the woman's fleeing **into the wilderness** (v. 6) and being preserved there is taken by liter-

⌛ PRETERIST *(continued)*

him the combination of all four of Daniel's beasts (Daniel 7), which sported, altogether, seven heads (there were four on the third beast) and ten horns (these were all on the fourth beast). The beasts of Daniel had actually represented four successive world empires: Babylon, MedoPersia, Greece, and Rome, which, says Chilton, "were all stages in the dragon's attempt to establish his illicit empire over the world. . . . He was the great Beast, of which they had been only partial images."

After the birth of Christ, the narrative skips to the ascension, since the purpose of the vision is not to retell the life of Christ, but to reveal its sequel with reference to the warfare of His church.

The flight of the woman into the wilderness after Christ's ascension represents the escape of the Jewish believers from the doomed city prior to its destruction. Thus the wrath of the dragon is expended upon the city only after his real target, the Christians, has relocated to safety. Jay Adams writes that the sixth verse

> foretells how God plans to preserve his own, rescuing them from the fierce attack upon Jerusalem. The destruction of the city was a Satan-inspired attack, which, in the providence of God, was used for purposes of judgment upon a rebellious people. It may be viewed,

314

⌛ FUTURIST *(continued)*

alists to mean that the Jewish people will be persecuted by the Antichrist and will flee for refuge into the wilderness of southern Palestine. Many (including Walvoord, Ryrie, Lindsey), with no stated scriptural reason, identify the place that they will take refuge as the city of Petra in the Jordanian wilderness south of the Dead Sea.[17] That this flight is accomplished on "two wings of a great eagle" (see v. 14) suggests an ultramodern scenario to Hal Lindsey:

> Some kind of massive airlift will rapidly transport these fleeing Jews across the rugged terrain to their place of protection. Since the eagle is the national symbol of the United States, it's possible that the airlift will be made available by aircraft from the U. S. Sixth Fleet in the Mediterranean.

The prevailing opinion is that the **one thousand two hundred and sixty days** (v. 6), during which the woman is fed in the wilderness, is the second half of the seventieth week of Daniel 9:24–27, and corresponds, therefore, to the final three and a half years prior to the Second Coming of Christ. Mounce, less specifically, observes that the preservation of the woman is of a "duration corresponding to the period of persecution."

This means, of course, that the vision has skipped without warning from

315

⏳ PRETERIST *(continued)*

therefore, either from the side of Satan's persecution or God's wrath.

The woman remains safe in the wilderness during the period of tribulation in Israel, a time that has already been identified (see notes at 11:2, 3) as three and a half years. In 11:2, this period was called "forty-two months," whereas here, as in 11:3, it is spoken of as **one thousand two hundred and sixty days** (v. 6). David S. Clark writes: "This 1260 days is a term borrowed from Daniel where it was a period of persecution, and has become the symbol of any period of persecution"—though, as we have seen, it was also the literal length of the Jewish War (AD 66–70) and of Nero's persecution of the church.[16] 🔄

⧗ FUTURIST *(continued)*

the ascension of Christ (v. 5) to consideration of events just prior to His return (v. 6).

Weidner explains: "The thought here that this man-child is to rule all the nations with a rod of iron brings by anticipation this very period of the final end before us." Moorehead affirms this conclusion: "The chapter touches the first advent and then sketches the events that pertain to the time of the second advent." Ironside, too, writes: "as in other prophecies, the entire present dispensation is passed over in silence."

G. E. Ladd considers that the vision before us "completely transcends the usual categories of time and space. It is not meant to be a foretelling of history but a representation of the struggle in the spiritual world which lies behind history." In this, as in many other remarks, he agrees with advocates of the *idealist* approach. ⧉

WAR IN HEAVEN

REVELATION 12:7–12

[7]And war broke out in heaven: Michael and his angels fought with the dragon; and the dragon and his angels fought, [8]but they did not prevail, nor was a place found for them in heaven any longer. [9]So the great dragon was cast out, that serpent of old, called the Devil and Satan, who deceives the whole world; he was cast to the earth, and his angels were cast out with him. [10]Then I heard a loud voice saying in heaven, "Now salvation, and strength, and the kingdom of our God, and the power of His Christ have come, for the accuser of our brethren, who accused them before our God day and night, has been cast down. [11]And they overcame him by the blood of the Lamb and by the word of their testimony, and they did not love their lives to the death. [12]Therefore rejoice, O heavens, and you who dwell in them! Woe to the inhabitants of the earth and the sea! For the devil has come down to you, having great wrath, because he knows that he has a short time."

HISTORICIST

Barnes provides the following explanation for this segment:

> The meaning is, that a state of things would exist in regard to the church, which would be well represented by supposing that such a scene should occur in heaven; that is *as if* a war should exist there between the great enemy of God and the angels of light, and *as if* being there vanquished, Satan should be cast down to the earth, and should there exert his malignant power in a warfare against the church. The general idea is, that this warfare would be *primarily* against heaven, as if he fought with the angels in the very presence of God.

PRETERIST

The **war in heaven** (v. 7) is not chronologically subsequent to the flight of the woman into the wilderness. Chilton writes:

> On the contrary, St. John unveils this scene in order to explain the preceding verse—to show why the woman had to flee into the wilderness. Once that is explained, in verses 7–12, he returns to the theme of the flight of the woman.

Citing the work of Hengstenberg and Carrington, Chilton makes an extensive case for the identification of Michael with Jesus Himself. Russell also affirms this as a probability. Christ has

FUTURIST

The scene shifts unexpectedly from earth to heaven. At some point in connection with the events of the previous verses, **war broke out in heaven** (v. 7) between God's angels and the forces of Satan. The angels are seen as under the command of **Michael,** the only angel in Scripture that is called "the archangel" (Jude 9), and who is first introduced in Daniel. In fact, if Walvoord is correct, this scene is identical to one depicted in the book of Daniel:

> The event here prophesied was predicted by Daniel the prophet in Daniel 12:1, where it is recorded that Michael shall "stand up, the great prince which standeth for the children of thy people." This event marks the beginning of the Great Tribulation defined in Daniel 12:1. It is undoubtedly the same event as in Revelation 12.

The warfare in heaven brings the happy result of Satan and his angels being **cast out** (v. 9) of heaven and confined to earth. As Walvoord mentioned above, he sees this event occurring in the middle of the Tribulation, or the beginning of what he calls the "great tribulation." In this, the majority of dispensationalists seem to agree with him. Gaebelein dates this downfall of Satan at the time of the fifth trumpet:

IDEALIST

This retells the spiritual conflict depicted in verses 1–6, but from the heavenly perspective. Wilcock writes: "The opposition of verse 7 is the opposition of verse 4b seen at a different depth of focus."

Michael and his angels (v. 7) prevailed over the kingdom of darkness, as Christ ministered, died, and arose on earth, the last event being the "casting out" of the accuser (John 12:31). But if the victory is Christ's, why is it depicted as if accomplished by Michael in the heavenlies? G. B. Caird likens Michael to the staff officer who removes Satan's flag from the heavenly map of battle in response to the Field General's real victory at the cross.

The announcement that **salvation . . . strength . . . the kingdom . . . have come** (v. 10) celebrates Christ's resurrection victory over Satan and the beginning of the New Covenant age (Col. 2:15; Heb. 2:14).

Satan, here alone called **the accuser of our brethren** (v. 10), until the death of Christ was able to accuse God's people before the throne of God (Job 1–2; Zech. 3:1); now, because of the atonement, he has lost all grounds for accusation (Rom. 8:31–34), as Hendriksen explains:

> Satan is "hurled down from heaven" in this sense, namely that he has lost his place as an accuser of the brethren. Whereas Christ was

⌛ HISTORICIST *(continued)*

Elliott identifies this **war in heaven** (v. 7) with the time of Christianity's conflict with heathenism in the days of Julian the Apostate, the emperor who sought to reestablish paganism in the empire from 361 until 363. The casting out of the dragon was the end of that conflict, marked by the downfall of paganism at Julian's death in 363. Julian's dying words were, "O Galilean, thou hast conquered!"

The song of rejoicing is that of the Christians at the time of that victory, celebrating the establishment of **the kingdom of our God** (v. 10), which is to be understood as Rome under Christian rulers. The dragon is not finished bringing troubles upon the church, however. It is announced that further **woe** is to be expected for **the inhabitants of the earth and the sea** (v. 12).

In Elliott's opinion, this woe refers to heretical persecutors arising from within the church and to the Gothic scourge soon to come.

Barnes, however, gives the future peril a different face:

> I regard this, therefore, as referring to the time of the rise of the Papacy, when, *but* for the formidable, corrupting, and destructive power, it might have been hoped that the church would have spread all over the world. 🔲

⌛ PRETERIST *(continued)*

been symbolized previously as a "mighty angel" (cf. 10:1), so also here, the symbol of Christ is that of "the archangel" (as Michael is called in Jude 9). Explaining that archangel does not mean "a member of a superior class of angels," but rather "Chief of the angels," Chilton suggests that the title is equivalent to "Commander of the LORD's army" in Joshua 5:13–15. The fact that He is here seen leading the angels of heaven as a victorious army against the satanic kingdom further suggests the identification with the Lord, since Christ is seen in this same role elsewhere (see 19:11–16).

Because **the great dragon was cast out** (v. 9) as a consequence of the battle, we can pinpoint the heavenly battle as being at the same time as the accomplishment of the atonement at the death and resurrection of Christ. One of several evidences of this is found in Jesus' statement (recorded by the same author): "Now is the judgment of this world; *now the ruler of this world will be cast out*" (John 12:31). Another evidence appears in the announcement that **Now salvation, and strength, and the kingdom of our God, and the power of His Christ have come** (v. 10). This also coincides with the atonement. In addition, other New Testament authors confirm that a victory of this sort over Satan was accomplished by Christ in His death (cf. Col. 2:15; Heb. 2:14–15).

⧗ FUTURIST *(continued)*

Satan is then cast out into the earth and his angels are cast out with him. It is identical with what we have seen already under the fifth trumpet, the star fallen out of heaven, opening the pit of the abyss with the darkening smoke and the locust swarms coming forth.

Ironside, by contrast, places this event as early as the Rapture of the church, at the very beginning of Daniel's seventieth week:

These evil hosts are continually endeavoring, by deception, to keep Christians from enjoying their present portion in Christ, but when the church is caught up, they will be ignominiously driven from what we might call the "outer court of heaven" and cast down upon the earth.

A voice in heaven declares the significance of Satan's defeat: **Now salvation, and strength, and the kingdom of our God, and the power of His Christ have come** (v. 10). In what sense is this true in the middle of the Tribulation? Walvoord explains:

The salvation mentioned as now impending refers not to salvation from the guilt of sin but to salvation in the sense of deliverance and completion of the divine program.

⧗ IDEALIST *(continued)*

born and rendered satisfaction for sin, Satan has lost every semblance of justice for his accusations against believers.

Satan's activity is now limited to the earthly level, accusing believers' consciences against themselves and seeking to bring them under self-condemnation. In response to such attacks, the believer pleads the merits and accomplishments of **the blood of the Lamb** (v. 11). This constitutes the *defensive* aspect of the present warfare of the believer. The **word of their testimony** (evangelism) is the *offensive* warfare of the church. They **did not love their lives to the death** demonstrates that the Christian's victory is measured, not necessarily in personal survival, but in faithful martyrdom.

Bauckham writes:

Throughout the period martyrdom played a major role in the success of the Christian Gospel . . . the fact of the martyrs' willingness to die and the way in which they died were seen to cohere with the nature of the religious message they believed.[18]

Satan's defeat and casting out from heaven is occasion for rejoicing by those who are in heaven, but **woe to the inhabitants of the earth and the sea** (v. 12), because the devil continues his malicious work upon earth

⏳ PRETERIST *(continued)*

The death of Christ did not put Satan entirely out of business, but it ended his career as **the accuser of our brethren** (v. 10), his principal role in pre-Christian times (cf. Job 1—2; Zechariah 3). The blood of Christ has undermined the grounds of every charge that Satan might bring against the brethren. "Who shall bring a charge against God's elect? It is God who justifies. Who is he who condemns? It is Christ who died, and furthermore is also risen, who is even at the right hand of God, who also makes intercession for us" (Rom. 8:33–34).

Satan is cast to the earth. He cannot accuse the saints before God any longer, for **they overcame** his accusations by appeal to the atoning **blood of the Lamb** (v. 11). They also take territory from the satanic kingdom **by the word of their testimony** (that is, by preaching the Gospel), and by their willingness to die rather than be intimidated by persecution (v. 11).

A woe is proclaimed upon **the inhabitants of the earth [or land]** (v. 12), since the thwarted dragon is now limited in his range of activity and will vent his wrath both upon the saints and upon the apostate Jews. His intention is to stamp out the church before it can extend itself as a global entity. Since Jesus indicated that this would be accomplished within a single generation (Matt. 16:28; 24:34), the dragon has only **a short time** (v. 12) to stamp out

FUTURIST *(continued)*

Though salvation and power have come, and though Satan has been defeated in the heavenlies, the fighting is not over. In his office as **the accuser of our brethren** (v. 10), Satan can no longer stand in heaven, but he continues his attack against the Tribulation saints on earth. They are ready for him, however; they stand their spiritual ground and even overcome their attacker **by the blood of the Lamb and by the word of their testimony** (v. 11).

This victory of the saints over their accuser, however, is entirely spiritual. Physically, it is he who seems to prevail (cf. 13:7). The winners are those who keep their faith intact until they die—who do **not love their lives to the death** (v. 11).

Satan will vent his wrath against **the inhabitants of the earth and the sea** because **he knows that he has a short time** (v. 12). As to how short the time is, and what the devil expects his fate to be when the time runs out, Walvoord expresses the opinion of the majority:

> The short time or season (Gr., *kairos*) refers to the time of the great tribulation after which Satan will be bound for the duration of the millennial kingdom.

IDEALIST *(continued)*

with greater vigor than before, knowing only too well **that he has a short time** (v. 12). The following verses stress the malice that this desperate foe directs toward the church throughout this dispensation, and Leon Morris explains that the troubles of the persecuted righteous arise not because Satan is too strong, but because he is beaten. He is doing all the harm he can while he can. But he will not be able to do this for much longer.

⌛ PRETERIST *(continued)*

the infant movement. Thus he goes to war with the remaining seed of the woman, as Russell explains:

> Translating the symbols into common language, they appear to signify that the progress of Christianity in the land aroused the hostility of Satan and his emissaries, and led to more active persecution of the disciples of Christ. ✍

THE WOMAN PERSECUTED, BUT PRESERVED

REVELATION 12:13–17

[13]Now when the dragon saw that he had been cast to the earth, he persecuted the woman who gave birth to the male Child. [14]But the woman was given two wings of a great eagle, that she might fly into the wilderness to her place, where she is nourished for a time and times and half a time, from the presence of the serpent. [15]So the serpent spewed water out of his mouth like a flood after the woman, that he might cause her to be carried away by the flood. [16]But the earth helped the woman, and the earth opened its mouth and swallowed up the flood which the dragon had spewed out of his mouth. [17]And the dragon was enraged with the woman, and he went to make war with the rest of her offspring, who keep the commandments of God and have the testimony of Jesus Christ.

⌛ HISTORICIST

The flight of the woman **into the wilderness** (v. 14) is variously understood. Elliott interprets this as suggesting a serious decline in the true piety and the

⌛ PRETERIST

Verse 13 picks up the narrative where verse 6 left off, that is, with the flight of the woman into the wilderness. As Chilton points out,

FUTURIST

Having read of the heavenly defeat of Satan, and his being cast to earth, in verses 7–12, we now return to the woman in the wilderness, where the narrative left her in verse 6. Verse 14 simply repeats the information of verse 6, adding only a few details, like the fact that her flight was made possible by **two wings of a great eagle.** (See Hal Lindsey's comments cited on verse 6.) Ironside, Walvoord, and others remind us that such imagery was used in Exodus 19:4 and in Deuteronomy 32:11–12 to describe God's care for Israel in bringing her out of Egypt and protecting her in the wilderness of Sinai.

Mounce suggests that the woman's flight in this section "may in part reflect the escape of the Palestinian church to Pella in AD 66," but he spiritualizes the meaning of the preservation: "The intent of the verse, however, is not so

IDEALIST

The devil, having lost any authority over the planet he may ever have possessed, vents his rage in a futile effort to destroy the witnessing church (now represented by **the woman** and **the rest of her offspring**—v. 17). Swete writes: "If he cannot directly attack the Woman's Son, he can hurt the Son through the Mother (cf. Matt. 25:45; Acts 9:4)."

The woman's flight on the **two wings of a great eagle** (v. 14) recalls the same imagery used in connection with Israel's flight from Egypt into the wilderness (Exod. 19:4). That she is **nourished** (v. 14) there in the wilderness (where crops generally cannot be grown and providing for oneself becomes less possible that in settled life) continues this imagery, in that Israel was also fed—with manna—during her wilderness sojourn. Earlier in

⧖ HISTORICIST *(continued)*

spiritual state of the church shortly after the triumph of Christianity in the Roman Empire. Thus the church at that time vanished "in its distinctive features from public view." The **two wings** (v. 14) given to protect the church refer to the eastern and western divisions of the empire, in both of which the church at this time enjoyed protection under Theodosius the Great.

With reference to the **flood** (v. 15) sent out against the woman by the dragon, Henry H. Halley writes: [it] "may refer to Persecutions of the Church by Roman Empire"—and the help received by the woman from **the earth** (v. 16) "may allude to Conversion of Emperor Constantine and Christianization of Roman Empire, which put an end to the Persecutions."

Elliott regards the persecution of **the woman who gave birth to the male Child** (v. 13) as the persecution that occurred under heretical Arian emperors, whose downfall and disappearance from the Roman world is symbolically signified in that **the earth opened its mouth and swallowed up the flood which the dragon had spewed out of his mouth** (v. 16).

Elliott interprets the continuing warfare against **the rest of her offspring** (v. 17) as Satan's efforts to subvert the doctrines of men like Augustine and Vigilantius.

⧖ PRETERIST *(continued)*

Preterist commentators have traditionally seen this passage in terms of the escape of the Judean Church from the Edomite and Roman invasions during the Jewish War, when, in obedience to Christ's commands (Matt. 24:15–28), the Christians escaped to shelter in the caves of the desert.

Dean Alford sides with this *preteristic* understanding of this passage:

I own that considering the analogies and the language used, I am much more disposed to interpret the persecution of the woman by the Dragon of the various persecutions by the Jews which followed the Ascension, and *her flight into the wilderness* of the gradual withdrawal of the Church and her agency from Jerusalem, finally consummated by the flight to the mountains on the approaching siege, commanded by our Lord Himself.

In the earlier narrative of the chapter, Satan has always been "the dragon," but now, having been cast down to earth, he is referred to as **the serpent** (in verses 14 and 15; though he is **the dragon** again in verses 16 and 17). David S. Clark sees a deliberate and emphatic contrast here: "The Devil is represented as a crawling serpent; but the church as flying on wings."

The **wings of a great eagle** (v. 14), which carry the woman to safety, are

⏳ FUTURIST *(continued)*

much the flight of the church as the provision of God for her sustenance." The passage demonstrates that God will provide "to those facing martyrdom a place of spiritual refuge and enablement to stand against Satan."

As for the **flood** (v. 15) of water spewed from the dragon's mouth, and the opening of the earth to help the woman, J. B. Smith and Ryrie see this as a literal flood of water, intended "to drown people out of their wilderness refuge."

Ironside interprets the flood of water to mean "evil teachings . . . in contrast to the water of life given by our Lord Jesus Christ":

> We may get the idea of this if we recall the fact that today myriads of Jews are being carried away by that Satanic flood from the mouth of the dragon known as Christian Science. So in the days of the great tribulation, Satan will try to swamp and destroy Israel as a nation by the evil teachings he will spread through the world.

Gaebelein, Henry Morris, and Hal Lindsey understand the "flood" to represent "the overflowing horde of men and weapons sent after the Jews in the wilderness by the beast" (Morris). These attackers, however, will be thwarted by an actual chasm opening in the earth

⏳ IDEALIST *(continued)*

Revelation, mention has been made of God feeding believers with "hidden manna" (see at 2:17).

This period of God's provision is again (as in verse 6) said to be three and a half years, here described as **a time and times and half a time** (v. 14). Of all the times this length of time is mentioned in Revelation, Alford believes this to be the instance which least lends itself to a literal calculation of three and a half calendar years:

> The conflict is that between Satan and the Church, whose seed . . . is God's Christian people, and is it likely that a few days or years will limit the duration of a prophecy confessedly of such wide import?

Lenski, with most others, applies this period to the time from Christ's enthronement (v. 5) to the time of the final judgment.

Hendriksen thinks this time element is a reminder of the days of Elijah, Ahab, and Jezebel, when the prophet's decree stopped the rain and he was supernaturally sustained by God in exile for this same length of time (1 Kings 17, 18; cf. Luke 4:25; James 5:17).

The **water . . . like a flood** (v. 15) sent out by the dragon to sweep away the church is either "the peoples of the world" (Morey), or a "stream of lies, delusions, religious 'isms,' philosophical falsehoods, political utopias, quasi-sci-

⌛ HISTORICIST *(continued)*

Barnes presents a different explanation. By this point in the narrative, the dragon has become the papacy:

> It is unnecessary to say that, after the Pagan persecutions ceased, and Christianity was firmly established in the empire; after Satan saw that all hope of destroying the church in that manner was at an end, his enmity was vented in another form—in the rise of the Papacy, and in the persecutions under that—an opposition to spiritual religion no less determined and deadly than that which had been waged by Paganism.

To Barnes, the woman's flight is not the disappearance of true piety in the church, but rather the disappearance into obscurity of the uncompromised Christians persecuted by the papacy. The expression **a time and times and half a time** (v. 14) is equivalent to the 1,260 days of verse 6, and is understood to be the same number of years. During that time the true spiritual church would survive in the form of small, obscure, and persecuted sects such as "the Waldenses and Albigenses, the Bohemian brethren, and kindred people; in deserts and places of obscurity." Barnes does not venture to suggest the beginning of this period. "If that could be ascertained with certainty, there would be no difficulty in determining when it would come to an end."

⌛ PRETERIST *(continued)*

an echo of the exodus in which God told Israel that He had carried them out of Egypt *on eagles' wings* (Exod. 19:4). Like the woman in this vision, Israel had been delivered from the dragon (cf. Ps. 74:13–14; Ezek. 32:2) and sustained by God in the wilderness.

In an attempt to destroy the woman, the serpent sent **a flood** out of his mouth, hoping she might thus **be carried away by the flood** (v. 15). This is a general reference to the devil's campaigns against the church.

Satan's attempt to destroy the church, however, was as abortive as was Pharaoh's schemes against Israel, for **the earth [or "land"] opened its mouth and swallowed up the flood** (v. 16).

Milton Terry comments:

> The great thought in all these images is that divine power is put forth to deliver and sustain the New Testament Church of God in the day of her persecution—the same power that of old wrought the miracles of Egypt, and of the Red Sea, and of the wilderness.

David S. Clark explains similarly:

> God is never short of means. All the resources of earth and heaven are at his command. Here we see how the providences of the world are on the side of God's church. The stars in their courses fought against Sisera [Judges 5:20],

328

⧗ FUTURIST *(continued)*

and swallowing them, or, as Gaebelein suggests:

> There will be other agencies in the earth by which this Satanic attempt . . . will be frustrated. These agencies will probably be those nations who have believed the final message, the Gospel of the Kingdom.

Walvoord departs here from his usual literalism:

> It is more plausible that this passage should be understood in a symbolic way. The flood cast after Israel is the total effort of Satan to exterminate the nation, and the resistance of the earth is the natural difficulty in executing such a massive program. The nature of the terrain in the Middle East, including many areas not heavily populated, provides countless places of refuge for a fleeing people.

Frustrated in his effort to destroy the entire Jewish race, Satan turns his special wrath against **the rest of her offspring,** those Jews **who keep the commandments of God and have the testimony of Jesus Christ** (v. 17). This gives us some idea of the reason that dispensationalists refer to the Great Tribulation as "the time of Jacob's trouble."[19]

⧗ IDEALIST *(continued)*

entific dogmas" (Hendriksen), which has been, along with overt persecution, one of the principal challenges faced by the church throughout history, as Wilson explains:

> The proverbial deceit of the serpent is manifested in a stream of deadly delusions which would engulf the church if they were not providentially diverted. This river of lies is the satanic parody of the river of life which flows from the heavenly throne.

By opening the earth to swallow the opposition (v. 16), God is symbolically seen as saving the church from such dangers, as he preserved Israel from apostasy (Num. 16:1–3, 31–33). There is here, again, a direct connection to the language associated with the exodus. When the Israelites celebrated their deliverance in song, and recollected the drowning of the pursuing Egyptians in the Red Sea, they sang poetically that "The earth swallowed them" (Exod. 15:12).

Unable to destroy the church as an entity, the dragon makes war on individual believers, **the rest of her offspring** (v. 17). Swete writes: "If he can neither unseat the Throned Christ nor destroy the Church, yet individual Christians may enjoy no such immunity." Though individual Christians succumb to martyrdom, the message of

329

HISTORICIST *(continued)*

Caringola suggests that the period began in 254 and ended in 1514. Many other suggestions have been offered.

The **flood which the dragon had spewed out of his mouth** (v. 16) and the earth's intervention to protect the woman is generally understood to reflect God's protection and preservation of the true remnant even against overwhelming odds.

As for the **war with the rest of her offspring** (v. 17), De Wette observes: "The church, as such, he could not destroy; therefore he turned his wrath against individual Christians, to bring as many of them as possible to death."

PRETERIST *(continued)*

which may refer to the storms that helped Israel win her battle; and here the earth puts forth her helping hand to save God's people and God's cause. The God of the church is the God of nature, and the God of providence; and he can command them in any exigency that may arise.

The escape of the Jewish Christians from the holocaust did not make the devil give up his warfare and admit defeat. He continued his attack against not only the woman (the Jewish church) but also **the rest of her offspring** (v. 17). This must refer to the Gentiles brought into God's family through the Jewish remnant church, as Jay Adams explains:

> Failing in his purpose to destroy the "sealed ones" by the Jerusalem holocaust, he turns against "the remnant of her seed" (v. 17). This is the Gentile church, true spiritual Israel, the present seed of Abraham.

IDEALIST *(continued)*

Revelation is that the Church triumphs in history and in eternity. ⟳

THE BEAST FROM THE SEA

REVELATION 13:1—4

[1]Then I stood on the sand of the sea. And I saw a beast rising up out of the sea, having seven heads and ten horns, and on his horns ten crowns, and on his heads a blasphemous name. [2] Now the beast which I saw was like a leopard, his feet were like the feet of a bear, and his mouth like the mouth of a lion. The dragon gave him his power, his throne, and great authority. [3]And I saw one of his heads as if it had been mortally wounded, and his deadly wound was healed. And all the world marveled and followed the beast. [4]So they worshiped the dragon who gave authority to the beast; and they worshiped the beast, saying, "Who is like the beast? Who is able to make war with him?"

⌛ HISTORICIST

That the **beast** from **the sea** (v. 1) is closely identified with Rome will scarcely be disputed by members of most interpretive schools. The description of the monster deliberately connects with the fourth beast of Daniel 7, in that both have **ten horns** and both are noted for their blasphemies and their persecution of the saints (cf. Dan. 7:7, 25). Virtually all conservative scholars identify that fourth beast of Daniel with the Roman Empire. In addition, the beast in the present passage has **seven heads,** which are later explained to represent "the seven mountains" upon which the harlot sits (Rev. 17:9). Probably no commentator in history has failed to point out Rome's well-known reputation as

⌛ PRETERIST

Rather than **I stood** (v. 1), most scholars prefer the textual reading **he stood** (i.e., the dragon). Russell writes: "This is not unimportant. The dragon, foiled in his attempt to destroy the woman and her seed, stations himself on the sands of the sea, looking out for a potent auxiliary enlisted in his service." The symbol of **the sea** (v. 1) is generally regarded as an emblem of the Gentile world, from which Daniel's four beasts arose (Daniel 7:1ff.). So it is a Gentile power that is here represented by **a beast** (v. 1). Together with the information about this beast given in the seventeenth chapter, most expositors have found it relatively easy to decode the symbolism. Seeking an individual to

FUTURIST

The **beast rising up out of the sea** (v. 1) calls to mind the four beasts of Daniel 7, also described as "from the sea," with "sea" usually understood as a symbol of the Gentile nations, as Biederwolf notes (and in contrast to "the land," which often refers to Israel):

> By the vast majority of commentators the sea is taken, and rightly, as symbolic of the disordered and confused life of the Gentile nations of the world.

Walvoord confirms this opinion, but adds that:

> Others take it as a reference to the Mediterranean, namely, that the beast will arise from the Mediterranean area. Probably both are true in that the beast is a Gentile and does come from the Mediterranean scene.

Expositors have had no difficulty connecting the beast to the Roman Empire. This is partly because of his similarity to the fourth beast of Daniel, who represents Rome, and partly due to the detailed explanation given in Revelation 17, as Mounce explains:

> For John the beast was the Roman Empire as persecutor of the church . . . Yet the beast is more than the Roman Empire . . . The beast has always been and will be in a final intensified manifesta-

IDEALIST

The preferred reading of the opening words of this chapter is, "And *he* stood," meaning the dragon, who calls forth assistance from land and sea in the form of two monstrous beasts. This first beast, arising **out of the sea** (v. 1), is intended to represent "an incarnation of politicosocial evil" (Morey), or any governmental system at any time that opposes the kingdom of God.

The sea is a standard symbol for the nations of the Gentile world (cf. Isa. 17:12; 60:5). The political systems of the world habitually set themselves "against the LORD and against His Anointed" (Ps. 2:2). Wherever and whenever the church is persecuted by governmental power, there you have the activity of Satan through a manifestation of this beast.

Beale mentions the common practice of expositors to assume that John's description of this beast is inspired by the ancient Canaanite myths about a seven-headed sea monster called Leviathan (mentioned in various Old Testament texts (e.g., Ps.74:13–14; Isa.27:1). However, he suggests that the imagery is more likely taken from the four beasts of Daniel[25]—which would seem to be more in line with Revelation's general tendency to rebirth imagery from the apocalyptic canon of the Old Testament. In support of this point, Beale cites Caird's words: "no Jewish or Christian writer could use the lens of this

⧗ HISTORICIST *(continued)*

"the city upon seven hills." It is true that the description of this beast differs somewhat from that of the fourth beast in Daniel, although the differences are not sufficient to preclude identifying this beast with that Roman beast in Daniel.

In addition to the beasts in these opening verses, this chapter reveals a second beast in verse 11. *Historicists* have put forward three principal possibilities for the interpretation of these two beasts.

One view, advocated by Victorinus, Grotius, Wette, Bede, and others, holds that both beasts represent Rome in its pagan days, the second beast being a picture of the pagan priesthood.

The second possibility, taken by Barnes, Cuninghame, and others, is that this first beast out of the sea is representative of pagan Rome, and the second beast out of the land is the revival of Roman paganism in the form of the papacy.

A third view sees both beasts as different aspects of papal Rome. The first beast is the papacy in its exercise of *political* power; the second is the same entity in its exercise of *ecclesiastical* power through its priesthood. This is the view of Vitringa, Bengel, Elliott, and others.

That the first beast is the papacy was the consistent doctrine of most Protestants for many centuries. Those who supported this identification in-

⧗ PRETERIST *(continued)*

fulfill the demands of the passage, Russell enumerates fourteen clues from the text and concludes:

> It would be strange if such a number of marked and peculiar characteristics could be applicable to more than one individual, or if such an individual could be so obscure as not to be immediately recognized. He must be sought among the greatest of the earth; he must be the foremost of his day, the observed of all observers; he must fill the highest throne and rule the mightiest empire. His period, too, is fixed: it is the last days of the Jewish polity, close upon the final catastrophe.

However, the narrative seems at times to favor an individual, and at others a larger entity as the historical referent of the beast. No *preterist* expositor has failed to see the allusion of the passage to the empire of Rome, among them Jay Adams:

> That the wild beast from the sea is the Roman empire is clear. Farrar notes no less than sixteen marks in the text of Revelation itself which prove this.

The merging of the two ideas—of an individual and an empire—is not inappropriate in the single symbol, however, as Chilton writes:

> This Beast . . . is not just an institution, but a person; specifically, as

FUTURIST *(continued)*

tion, the deification of secular authority.

Ladd adds a slightly idealist twist, but believes essentially the same thing:

> The beast is both Rome and the eschatological antichrist—and, we might add, any demonic power which the church must face in her entire history.

While Mounce and Ladd are not dispensationalists, if they were, they likely would have prefaced the words "Roman Empire" with the word "revived." Dispensationalism asserts that the world empire of the Tribulation period will be a revival of old, pagan Imperial Rome, under a Roman head. Gaebelein presents this view, as does Walvoord, who writes:

> This passage is first of all a revelation of the revived Roman Empire in its period of worldwide dominion, but more especially this paragraph directs attention to the evil character who exercises satanic power as the world dictator.

It seems apparent that, if a man is to win the admiration of the world, as the passage describes, he must be a charming and charismatic leader. Ironside expresses the view of most:

> After the church has been caught up to meet the Lord, one man [will arise] who will combine in himself

⧗ IDEALIST *(continued)*

myth except as it had been reground by Daniel."[26]

The beast's color (scarlet, like the dragon; cf. 12:3; 17:3) and the number of his **heads** and **horns** (also the same as those of the dragon) indicate that he is the governmental incarnation of Satan himself (12:3), thinly disguised in political systems or personalities. Hendriksen writes:

> The first beast . . . represents the persecuting power of Satan operating in and through the nations of this world and their governments. The second symbolizes the false religions and philosophies of this world. Both these beasts oppose the Church throughout this dispensation; yet the apostle describes them in terms that indicate the form which they assumed during the closing decade of the first century AD.

Wilson agrees, but adds detail that seems to place him, momentarily, with Mounce and Ladd in the futurist camp:

> [This beast] represents the persecuting power of human government, first as manifested in the Roman Empire, and later to be realized in full in the reign of Antichrist.

The description of the beast clearly is derived from that of the four beasts in Daniel 7:1–7, which also came out of the sea, and which, among them, bore the

⏳ HISTORICIST *(continued)*

cluded Martin Luther, John Wycliffe, John Knox, William Tyndale, John Calvin, John Wesley, Roger Williams, Fox's Book of Martyrs, the translators of the King James Bible, John Bunyan, the Westminster Confession, Sir Isaac Newton, Charles Spurgeon, David Benedict's *History of the Baptist Denomination*, Bishop J. C. Rylie, Dr. Martin Lloyd-Jones. Of this longstanding consensus, Steve Wohlberg is the Director of White Horse Media, writes:

> According to 400 years of Protestant scholarship (which shouldn't be taken lightly), the beast is here now and has been operating for over a thousand years. Again, this prophecy is not against sincere people who don't fully understand the Bible—but against a system that leads away from direct faith in Jesus Christ alone for salvation and has introduced many subtle traditions into the Christian Church.[20]

The main propagator of the historicist approach to Revelation in modern times is the Seventh-Day Adventist Church. Though better known for their promotion of seventh-day Sabbath observance, the identification of the papacy with the beast of Revelation is a cornerstone of their eschatological claim to being the restoration of pure Christianity in the end-times. On the present passage, the founder of that movement, Ellen G. White, wrote:

⏳ PRETERIST *(continued)*

we shall see, it is the Emperor Nero. This is because, particularly the way the Bible looks at things, the two could be considered as one . . . [T]he Empire was embodied and represented in the reigning Caesar (Nero). Thus St. John's prophecy can shift back and forth between them, or consider them both together, under the same designation.

Even if Rome is introduced at this point, not all *preterists* believe, as do Adams and Clark, that the concern of the Apocalypse has now shifted from the doom of Jerusalem to the judgment of Rome. Others, such as Milton Terry, think Rome is only brought into the picture as a chief agent of the judgment that came upon Jerusalem in AD 70:

> We should keep in mind that in all this prophetic symbolism we have before us *the Roman empire as a persecuting power*. This Apocalypse is not concerned about the history of Rome.

It has been observed that the beast draws together features of each of Daniel's four beasts. The first, Babylon, was represented as a lion; this beast has a **mouth like the mouth of a lion** (v. 2). It is interesting that, when Paul was discussing his release from imprisonment under Nero, he remarked, "I was delivered out of *the mouth of the lion*" (2 Tim. 4:17).

⧗ FUTURIST *(continued)*

the statesmanship of a Caesar, the military genius of a Napoleon, and the personal attractiveness of a Chesterfield. This man will head a combination of ten powers, formed, as before mentioned, from the nations that have sprung out of the old Roman Empire.

The animal-like traits of the beast (v. 2) combine the components of all four of Daniel's beasts. This is observed by Gaebelein, who writes:

> This revived Roman empire is an amalgamation of parts of the previous world empires. The preceding ones are absorbed by the last, the Roman empire . . . The ten horns are the ten kingdoms which will exist in that empire . . . The heads represent the seven forms of government which have characterized the empire in the past, the seventh becomes the eighth.

Unlike the ancient Roman Empire, and all others that have sought to bring all nations under their authority, the revived Roman Empire will succeed in winning the allegiance and admiration of **the whole world** (v. 3). As Walter Scott writes:

> The authority of the dragon, and his far-reaching influence, go far beyond the geographical limits of the ten kingdoms. The beast to whom he delegates his authority, exercises a commanding influ-

⧗ IDEALIST *(continued)*

resemblance to a lion, a bear, a leopard, and a ten-horned monster. In Daniel, each of these represented a successive Gentile world empire. It seems that, by combining the characteristics of the four beasts, this vision "must indicate all antichristian governments" (Hendriksen). Wilcock describes this creature as:

> a beast whose power is not that of wealth or influence, but that of government ("diadems" and a "throne") . . . and whose authority is worldwide (verse 7). We see in him the principle of power politics: in a word: the state. For John this meant, of course, the Roman Empire; but every succeeding generation of Christian people knows some equivalent of it.

John explains that **the dragon gave him his power** (v. 2). Swete comments: "The Dragon works through the Beast as his agent; the war is of Satan's making, but the Empire is his tool for waging it."

Historically, not all persecution of Christians has come through official state policies of hostility toward them. Some persecution (including that already noted in the letters to Smyrna and Philadelphia) is spontaneous, and comes as a result of the resentment or hatred felt toward believers by their unbelieving neighbors. In fact, in Paul's day, it was possible to seek refuge from

⧗ HISTORICIST *(continued)*

In the sixth century the papacy had become firmly established. Its seat of power was fixed in the imperial city, and the bishop of Rome was declared to be the head over the entire church. Paganism had given place to the papacy. The dragon had given to the beast "his power, and his seat, and great authority." Revelation 13:2.[21]

A Seventh-Day Adventist publication, presenting a *historicist* approach to Revelation, asserts that the beast's deadly wound was inflicted by Napoleon's General Berthier in 1798.[22] The recovery of the papacy began "in 1929, when Mussolini executed the 'Concordat of 1929' with the papacy, restoring to them their properties and power."[23]

However, as we have principally been following the views of Elliott and Barnes to this point, we will amplify upon these two positions.

Notwithstanding minor differences, Elliott and Barnes would substantially agree on most of the following points: Elliott explains **the sea** (v. 1) from which the beast rises as the flood of Gothic invasions. The **ten horns** (v. 1) picture Rome as comprised of ten subordinate kingdoms. These are conceived, by Barnes, as existing just after the Gothic invasions, but prior to the rise of the papacy, and by Elliott, as arising out of the papal "head" around AD 532. These ten kingdoms are: the

⧗ PRETERIST *(continued)*

It has puzzled many that one of the beast's heads **had been mortally wounded,** but the wound had **healed** (v. 3) so that the beast lived on (v. 14). Some have felt that John was taken in by the popular contemporary myth that Nero would return to conquer Rome again after his apparent death—but this denies the book any validity as a revelation of God and reduces it to the creative expression of John's personal opinions. Such an interpretation is certainly not necessary. Even if Nero is the head mortally wounded, it is not he who personally survives the wound, but the beast that survives the wounding of one of its heads. At the death of Nero, the Roman Empire was thrown into violent convulsions of civil war and anarchy, in which three emperors succeeded one another within the space of less than 18 months. The recovery of the empire under Vespasian was a marvel to all—the beast of the empire had survived the mortal wounding of one of its heads (Nero).

Alternatively, there is the possibility of identifying the wounded head with Julius Caesar, as David S. Clark does:

> If [the beast] is the Caesar dynasty, as it evidently is, then the head, or king, with the deadly wound was clearly Julius Caesar the founder of the empire. And the wound of that head, the killing of Julius Caesar, did not kill the beast at all; the

338

⧗ FUTURIST *(continued)*

ence all over the earth—reaching even to the limits of heathendom.

The world's admiration of the beast stems from his amazing recovery from a **deadly wound** (v. 3). This could refer to a rising from the dead, possibly after an assassination. This is a common view, expressed, for example, by Ryrie:

> In 11:7 he was seen coming out of the abyss, and that coincides with his restoration to life here. He apparently actually dies, descends to the abyss and returns to life. The world understandably wonders after him.

Weidner expands on this thought:

> Just as Paul maintained that Jesus Christ was declared to be the Son of God by His resurrection from the dead (Rom. 1:4), so in the times of the Antichrist stress will be laid on the fact that though this first beast had received his death-stroke, nevertheless he had lived again and that therefore he had established his right to claim divine majesty and worship.

A common alternative explanation of the meaning of the beast's recovery from his deadly wound is expressed by Walvoord:

> The wounding of one of the heads seems instead to be a reference to the fact that the Roman Empire as

⧗ IDEALIST *(continued)*

such spontaneous persecution in the Roman justice system (Acts 22:25–29; 25:11), and government officials were occasionally the defenders of the rights of Christians against those who wished to harm them (Acts 18:12–16).

However, when persecution of the saints becomes a governmental policy, then the persecuted have no recourse to legal protections and have nowhere to hide. State persecution of the Church has thus always been one of Satan's most devastating means of discouraging the Church, often driving her underground, as under some of the emperors, or the modern Communist States.

The beast's **seven heads** (v. 1) speak of the various manifestations of the beastly spirit in successive empires: Old Babylonia, Egypt, Assyria, Babylon, Persia, Greece, and Rome. Since the beast was seen to have recovered from the mortal wounding of **one of his heads** (v. 3) in John's day, it is probable that Rome is the head that recovered from this blow. The wound itself would be the death of Nero in AD 68, at which time Rome's career as persecutor seemed to have ended, but it was revived under Domitian. Even Rome's survival as an empire was threatened by the revolutions and political upheavals that immediately followed Nero's death. However, stability was regained when Vespasian came to power (AD 69–79), as Moffatt explains:

⌛ HISTORICIST *(continued)*

AngloSaxons, the *Franks,* the *Alleman Franks,* the *BurgundicFranks,* the *Visigoths,* the *Suevi,* the *Vandals,* the *Ostrogoths,* the *Bavarians,* and the *Lombards.*

The seven hills, according to 17:9–10, represent not only seven mountains but also seven kings. The seven kings are really the seven forms of government under which Rome had historically existed, namely, *kings, consuls, dictators, decemvirs, military tribunes,* and the *imperial* form current in John's day. These are the first six heads. The seventh would be Diocletian and his three colleagues. This seventh head received a **deadly wound** (v. 3) when Julian the Apostate (the last heathen emperor) fell and the decree of Theodosius brought an end of tolerance of pagan ritual religion in the empire. This should have been the death of the beast. However, the **deadly wound was healed** (v. 3) by the revival of pagan practices through the influence of the papacy in the days of Charlemagne. The fact that the beast was **worshiped** along with its sponsor, **the dragon,** is not taken to mean worship in a religious sense, but the general homage and admiration accorded to one esteemed as a superior. ▨

⌛ PRETERIST *(continued)*

deadly wound was healed. Though Julius Caesar was killed as a protest against autocracy, it did not destroy it in the least; the empire lived on, and Julius was followed by other Caesars more autocratic than he would have dared to be.

A third explanation is found in David Chilton, who believes that the mortal wound of the Roman Empire was delivered by the phenomenal success of the gospel in the early days, when even members of Caesar's own household came into the faith (Phil. 4:22):

> In fact, Tiberius Caesar even formally requested that the Roman Senate officially acknowledge Christ's divinity.[24] . . . The Beast had received the head-wound, the wound unto death—yet it still lived.

The worship of the dragon and of the beast (v. 4) refers to the statism that characterized much of the empire, especially in Asia Minor, where temples to the Caesars abounded. ▨

340

FUTURIST *(continued)*

such seemingly died and is now going to be revived.

IDEALIST *(continued)*

The vitality of the pagan empire, shown in its power of righting itself after the revolution, only added to its prestige. The infatuation of loyalty, expressing itself in the worship of the emperor as the personal embodiment of the empire, grew worse and worse.

The resilience of the beast causes the whole world to marvel. It seems as if nothing can resist the awesome power of the State. The military prowess, policing capability, and persecuting power of the state intimidates many into compliance. "You can't fight city hall" is a milder version of what is intended by the words **who is able to make war with him?** (v. 4).

THE BEAST'S WAR WITH THE SAINTS

REVELATION 13:5—10

[5]And he was given a mouth speaking great things and blasphemies, and he was given authority to continue for forty-two months. [6]Then he opened his mouth in blasphemy against God, to blaspheme His name, His tabernacle, and those who dwell in heaven. [7]It was granted to him to make war with the saints and to overcome them. And authority was given him over every tribe, tongue, and nation. [8]All who dwell on the earth will worship him, whose names have not been written in the Book of Life of the Lamb slain from the foundation of the world. [9]If anyone has an ear, let him hear. [10]He who leads into captivity shall go into captivity; he who kills with the sword must be killed with the sword. Here is the patience and the faith of the saints.

⌛ HISTORICIST

Both Daniel (7:25) and Revelation refer to the **blasphemies** (v. 5) associated with this beast. In New Testament times, blasphemy was defined as making oneself equal to God (John 10:33) and claiming the authority to forgive sins (Luke 5:21).

Statements made by various popes[27] that illustrate the nature of this blasphemy would include that made by Pope Nicholas V (1397–1455):

> The Roman Pontiff judges all men, but is judged by no one. . . . I have the authority of the King of Kings. I am all in all and above all . . . Wherefore, if those things that I do be said not to be done of man

⌛ PRETERIST

Many Roman emperors permitted, encouraged, or enforced the worship of themselves, at least in their assumption of divine titles like Sebastos (meaning "one to be worshiped") and *divus*, *Deus*, and *Theos* (all meaning "god"). Thus we read of the beast's **blasphemies** (v. 5). It is further indicated that **all who dwell on the earth [or land]** participate in his worship (v. 8).

Chilton points out that "worship" can be understood in terms of "everyday, practical allegiance and obedience." This is certainly what our "spiritual worship" (NKJV "reasonable service") to God is said to be in Romans 12:1–2. The Jews, by refusing allegiance

⌛ FUTURIST

The **forty-two months** (v. 5) is the second half of the Tribulation period, which portion is usually called "the Great Tribulation." But it is not necessary to limit the career of the beast to this period. Walvoord presents the dispensational position:

> It is probable that the person who heads the revived Roman Empire comes into power before the beginning of the entire seven-year period of Daniel 9:27, and as such enters into covenant with the Jewish people. His role as world ruler over all nations, however, does not begin until the time of the Great Tribulation. From that point, he continues forty-two months until the second coming of Christ terminates his reign.

Gaebelein writes:

> This empire will be revived in the first part of the final seven years. We saw this under the first seal. Here is the beginning of the forty-two months the dragon gives to him his power, and his throne, and great authority. It becomes now fully possessed by Satan.

That the latter part of the beast's career is characterized by **blasphemies** (v. 5) connects him with the *little horn* of Daniel 7, who had a "mouth speaking pompous words" (Dan. 7:8), and with the *man of sin*, who "opposes and exalts himself above all that is

⌛ IDEALIST

Governments love to "play God," to command the admiration and loyalty of their subjects, and to assume to themselves ever more numerous prerogatives—including those which belong to God alone. Not a few empires have required that their subjects actually worship them as deities (as did Pharaoh of Egypt, Nebuchadnezzar of Babylon, Darius of Media-Persia, and numerous Roman emperors), or that they discontinue the worship of the true God in deference to the state's wishes (as modern Communist states have attempted to do).

Though Paul tells us that governments are ordained by God to enforce good conduct and restrain and punish criminal behavior (Rom. 13:1–7; cf. 1 Pet. 2:13–14), under Satan's influence, they misuse their power. Wilcock writes:

> [Satan] puts blasphemies in the mouth of the state, so that it proclaims "I am God" by demanding from its subjects a total, unconditional allegiance, such as those whose names are written in the Lamb's book of life will never give to any but Christ.

The repeated use of the words **was given** (vv. 5, 7) and **was granted** (v. 7) emphasize that the power of evil is not absolute, but contingent upon God's sovereign allowance. The beast is granted the ability to **make war with the saints and to overcome them** (v. 7), as Wilson explains:

⧗ HISTORICIST *(continued)*

but of God, what can you make me but God? . . . I conclude, commanding, declaring, and pronouncing, to stand upon necessity of salvation, for every creature to be subject to me.

Nor are such statements confined to history long past. Pope Leo XIII, in his apostolic letter of June 20, 1894, claimed: "We hold the place of Almighty God on earth." His successor, Pius X, likewise boasted, "The Pope . . . is Jesus Christ himself, hidden under the veil of flesh." On April 30, 1922, Pope Pius XI said, "You know that I am the Holy Father, the representative of God on earth, the Vicar of Christ, which means that I am God on earth."

The beast's blasphemous career is said to be **forty-two months** (v. 5) in duration. That is 1,260 days, which, following the day-for-a-year hermeneutic, translates into 1,260 years. We have encountered this same period twice in chapter 11 and twice in chapter 12. In those places, as here, it refers to the period of conflict between the true witnessing church and the apostate papal establishment.

Many divergent conjectures have been offered up in the attempt to mark the beginning and end of this period. Cuninghame and Caringola identify the beginning of the period as the year 533, the year in which the Eastern emperor Justinian elevated the bishop of

⧗ PRETERIST *(continued)*

to Christ and choosing allegiance to Caesar, became guilty of worshiping the beast. Given the opportunity to own Christ as their king before Pilate, the Jews proclaimed, "We have no king but Caesar!" (John 19:15). Alfred Edersheim in a book published before 1923 writes: "With this cry Judaism was, in the person of its representatives, guilty of denial of God, of blasphemy, of apostasy. It committed suicide."[28]

For a while, the beast was permitted by God **to make war with the saints and to overcome them** (v. 7). This war took the form of the persecution of the church by the Roman Empire, and especially by Nero, shortly before the destruction of Jerusalem.

Concerning the latter, historian Philip Schaff writes:

Some Christians were arrested, confessed their faith, and were "convicted . . ." says Tacitus, "of the crime . . . of hating the human race."[29] Their Jewish origin, their indifference to politics and public affairs, their abhorrence of heathen customs, were construed into an *"odium generis humani"* [hatred of the human race] . . . there began a carnival of blood such as even heathen Rome never saw before or since . . . A "vast multitude" of Christians was put to death in the most shocking manner. Some were crucified, probably in mockery of the punishment of Christ, some sewed up in the skins of wild beasts and

⌛ FUTURIST *(continued)*

called God" (2 Thess. 2:4). "But the God whom he denies has limited his sway," Ironside notes, "for power will be given him only 'to continue forty and two months'; that is, for three and a half years, the last half of Daniel's 70th week."

The Great Tribulation will be the hardest times of persecution the Jews have ever known. The beast's **war with the saints** (v. 7) is to be identified with the dragon's war against the woman and the rest of her offspring in 12:17. This "Big Brotherlike" dictator, no doubt through his command of the latest technologies, will be able to monitor every human being on earth, seeking to identify every noncompliant citizen.

In our irreligious and secularized time, it is hard to imagine a time in which **all who dwell on the earth will worship** (v. 8) anything or anyone! However, as Tenney explains:

> The worship of the beast is compulsory, being imposed upon the world by conquest (13:7), by propaganda (13:12), by lying miracles (13:13–15), and by social and economic pressure (13:16–17). This coercion constitutes the last great attempt to unify all religions under one general system with a powerful, visible, personal object of worship who is also the head of the state and in whose hands rests the power of life and death over his subjects.

⌛ IDEALIST *(continued)*

He was given the power to persecute and kill the saints, but not to overcome their faith. Thus the beast enjoys only an apparent success; the real victory belongs to the saints who remain faithful unto death (12:11).

Hendriksen sees this not only as an ongoing, ages-long principle, but more specifically, the overcoming of the church is understood to apply to the condition at the end of the dispensation:

> Throughout the entire gospel age . . . the governments of this world place themselves on the throne; arrogate to themselves the authority that belongs to God . . . and blaspheme God and heaven. This condition will finally result in the complete destruction of the Church as a mighty and influential organization for the spread of the gospel. For finally every tribe and people and tongue and nation will worship antichristian government (Rev. 13:7 and 11:7 should be compared).

The duration of the beast's career, **forty-two months** (v. 5), is identical to the length of time that the holy city is trampled (11:2), that the two witnesses preach (11:3), and that the woman is sustained by God in the wilderness (12:6, 14). It has been mentioned previously that this symbolic figure means the whole period from the First Coming to the Second Coming of Christ, the spe-

⧗ HISTORICIST *(continued)*

Rome to be "head of all the holy Churches, and of all the holy priests of God." This was the first time that the Roman bishop was given an official authority above the bishops elsewhere in Christendom. It prepared the way for the rise of the full-blown papal supremacy, which emerged under Pope Boniface III, according to Guinness. By adding 1,260 years to this date, one reaches the year 1793. This was the time of the French Revolution, which *historicists* take to be the judgments upon the papacy depicted as the seven bowls of wrath in Revelation 16.

The ability to **make war with the saints and to overcome them** (v. 7) is also attributed to the little horn of Daniel 7:25. Historicists emphasize the unknown number of persons slain by the Church of Rome during the Middle Ages and the Reformation. Dissenters were persecuted, beaten, tortured, and mutilated, and killed by various means for the greater part of 1,000 years. They were burned, crushed, and impaled; their women were raped and dismembered, and their children killed before their eyes.

Caringola, using Foxe's *Book of Martyrs* and Guinness' *The Approaching End of the Age,* has catalogued a few of the atrocities of the Roman Church in slaughtering her opponents (The actual statistics may be disputed): By order of the popes, tens of thousands of Vaudois

⧗ PRETERIST *(continued)*

exposed to the voracity of mad dogs in the arena. The satanic tragedy reached its climax . . . Christian men and women, covered with pitch or oil or resin, and nailed to posts of pine, were lighted and burned as torches for the amusement of the mob while Nero, in fantastical dress, figured in a horse race, and displayed his art as charioteer. Burning alive was the ordinary punishment of incendiaries; but only the cruel ingenuity of this imperial monster, under the inspiration of the devil, could invent such a horrible system of illumination.[30]

David S. Clark explains:

The Devil had gone to make war, or to persecute the seed of the woman which keep the commandments of God. Accordingly he does it through this great world power, the empire of Rome. Rome becomes the Devil's agent. History tells us of the persecutions of Rome; how Paul was beheaded, and Peter crucified head downwards; how the Christians were thrown to the lions, exposed to the cold, drowned in rivers, thrown into cauldrons of boiling oil, daubed with pitch and burned for torchlights; how every conceivable torture was inflicted on them; how all the might and power of the Roman empire were exerted to extirpate them, till the church at length conquered its persecutor.

FUTURIST *(continued)*

The call, **If anyone has an ear, let him hear** (v. 9), resembles the warning at the end of each of the seven letters in chapters 2 and 3, except that the earlier statements ended with the additional phrase "what the Spirit says to the churches." Walvoord states:

> The omission of the phrase "unto the churches" in 13:9 is most significant and tends to support the teaching that the church, the body of Christ, has previously been raptured and is not in this period. The exhortation in Revelation 13 is much wider. It is to anyone who will listen, and the message is not addressed to the church as such but to the entire world.

Ryrie describes v. 10 as "a word of great comfort":

> The captor will be taken captive; the killer will be killed. When God's purposes are finished through the beast, God will take him captive and confine him to the lake of fire. The knowledge of this is the patience and faith that sustains the saints who endure these persecutions.

IDEALIST *(continued)*

cific number chosen possibly recalls the length of the persecution under Antiochus Epiphanes, or the length of the drought in the days of Elijah, or the length of Nero's persecution, or even the length of Jesus' public ministry. Of this latter suggestion, Wilcock reasons:

> If it be reckoned that something over three years elapsed between his baptism and his ascension, then "three and a bit years", or three and a half years, would be an excellent symbol for the period between the church's "baptism" at Pentecost and her "ascension" to meet the Lord when he returns.

He who leads into captivity shall go into captivity (alternatively rendered "If anyone is to be taken captive, to captivity he goes"); **he who kills with the sword must be killed with the sword** (v. 10). This has been understood variously. It may be that it foretells the fate of the beast, i.e., that he who captures and kills will someday be captured and killed by one greater than himself, thus relieving the church of its oppressor. Alternatively, it may be an exhortation to the Christians to patiently endure imprisonment and martyrdom without resorting to self-defensive violence. The second member of the axiom, echoing as it does the words of Jesus in Matthew 26:52, would support this conclusion. Wilson understands it in this latter sense:

347

HISTORICIST *(continued)*

were massacred in Northern Italy (1237–1342); Lollards were terribly persecuted in England (1300–1413); thousands of Hussites were killed in Bohemia (1421); and the Spanish Inquisition burned alive 31,912 and tortured 300,000 Protestants (1481–1808). In Piedmont, 3,000 Vaudois were burned and suffocated in a cave (1488). Fifty thousand German Protestants were hanged, burned, or buried alive by Emperor Charles V (1546). In England, Catholic queen "Bloody Mary" burned alive over 300 Protestants (1555). In the St. Bartholomew's Day Massacre, in France, 60,000 were butchered (1572). In Magdeburg, Germany, 20,000 Protestants were massacred (1631). Irish Roman Catholics mercilessly martyred 40,000 Protestants (1641). This sampling of the beast's war shows why **the patience and the faith of the saints** (v. 10) are called for.

As the popes led many **into captivity,** and slew many **with the sword** (v. 10), so there were popes who were taken into captivity and suffered violent and ignoble deaths. In 1798, when Napoleon conquered Italy, the pope was among those taken prisoner.

PRETERIST *(continued)*

In this passage again (v. 5) we encounter the time period equivalent to three and a half years, which Adams interprets:

> Since many were about to face a period of great persecution, they are encouraged to endure by the comforting revelation that though it will be severe, it will be short. The time of the dragon's authority to overcome the saints is only 42 months.

David Chilton writes:

> The period of 42 months . . . is a symbolic figure in prophetic language, signifying a time of trouble, when the enemies of God are in power, or when judgment is being poured out, while God's people wait for the coming of the Kingdom. . . . Its prophetic usage is not primarily literal, although it is interesting that Nero's persecution of the Church did in fact last a full 42 months, from the middle of November 64 to the beginning of June 68. This period of 42 months thus corresponds (but is not necessarily identical) to the 42 months/ 1,260 days of 11:2–3 and the "time, times, and half a time" of 12:14.

⧗ IDEALIST *(continued)*

If any man is destined for captivity, then he must be willing to accept it in a spirit of humble submission (cf. Jer. 15:2). . . . To meet the persecution inflicted by the beast in this spirit demonstrates the steadfast endurance and unwavering faith of the saints.

THE SECOND BEAST

REVELATION 13:11–15

[11]Then I saw another beast coming up out of the earth, and he had two horns like a lamb and spoke like a dragon. [12]And he exercises all the authority of the first beast in his presence, and causes the earth and those who dwell in it to worship the first beast, whose deadly wound was healed. [13]He performs great signs, so that he even makes fire come down from heaven on the earth in the sight of men. [14]And he deceives those who dwell on the earth by those signs which he was granted to do in the sight of the beast, telling those who dwell on the earth to make an image to the beast who was wounded by the sword and lived. [15]He was granted power to give breath to the image of the beast, that the image of the beast should both speak and cause as many as would not worship the image of the beast to be killed.

HISTORICIST

As stated previously, *historicist* scholars have differed among themselves with reference to the identity of the two beasts. Regardless of their opinion about the identity of the first beast, however, the majority would seem to identify the second with papal Rome or the priesthood of the Roman Church.

After the establishment of Roman Catholic domination in the sixth century, the Bishop of Rome would do anything in his power to maintain and expand his influence. The Beast had to be worshiped and made Holy, in order to be revered and feared. That way, the Bishop of Rome would maintain his leading position in the order of things forever. The Holy Roman Empire was created to last forever, and it was

PRETERIST

While the beast from the sea is not difficult to identify, the same cannot be said for the second beast, who rises up **out of the earth [or land]** (v. 11). *Preterist* expositors have advanced at least three positions. The most frequently encountered view suggests that this beast is a symbol for "the cult of the emperor," that is, that organized force within the empire that sought to enforce the worship of the Caesars. The second beast's **two horns like a lamb** (v. 11) suggest a religious nature more that a political one. Among those who make this identification is David S. Clark:

> This suggests religious activities. And so this second beast is rightly recognized as the Pagan religion or pagan priesthood . . . The Pagan

350

⧗ FUTURIST

As if the appearance of the first beast did not portend enough disaster, we now see another beast—less terrifying at first sight, having only **two horns like a lamb** (v. 11), but still very ominous, speaking **like a dragon.** Ryrie interprets its features in this way: "The horns suggest strength, though less strength than the first beast, and the lamb may allude to an appearance of meekness or innocence and may also indicate his character as an imitation of the Lamb of God."

It is generally held that this beast is a religious leader—or even a counterfeit messiah—in contrast to the largely political character of the first beast. It seems apparent that the second beast is to be identified with the "false prophet" in 16:13, 19:20, and 20:10.

Most common among *futurist* scholars is the opinion that this beast, like the first, is an individual. Walvoord is typical of this persuasion: "The identification of the second beast as the head of the apostate church is indicated in many ways in the book of Revelation." Walvoord uses a lengthy quotation from Alford to imply approval of the suggestion that this beast may be the head of the Roman Catholic Church.

Some believe that the second beast, rather than the first, should be identified as the Antichrist. In this view, he would be a Jew posing as the long-awaited Jewish messiah. Gaebelein is of this opinion:

⧗ IDEALIST

The second beast supports the first, but is different in form and strategy. While the first beast is ferocious looking and terrifying, the second seems harmless **like a lamb** (v. 11). Its innocuous appearance is misleading, however, and like the false prophets of whom Jesus warned, its words **like a dragon** (v. 11) tell more about its nature than does its lamblike appearance (compare Matt. 7:15–20 with Matt. 12:33–37).

The fact that its two horns are said to contribute to its "lamb-like" appearance raises the question of why, if it is a mimickry of Christ, the lamb, is it not depicted as having seven horns, as did the Lamb in 5:6? Beale suggests, as a partial answer, that the horns are limited to two in order to parody the two witnesses, two lampstands and two olive trees of 11:3–4. The fact that this beast performs signs—particularly that **he even makes fire come down from heaven**—is seen also as a possible counterfeiting of the same activity of the two witnesses (11:5). Beale also thinks the two horns may recall the "ram that had two horns" of Daniel 8:3.

Hendriksen identifies this beast:

The second beast is the false prophet (19:20). It symbolizes false religion and false philosophy in whichever form these appear throughout the entire dispensation.

⌛ HISTORICIST *(continued)*

created to bring the whole world under the influence of Rome.

In the empire that sprang up under Charlemagne, through the influence of the papacy, there was a return of the Roman world to paganism, but in its Christianized form. This was also the revived head that had formerly received a deadly wound. Or, to shift the imagery, in the new manifestation of the Roman persecuting spirit, as embodied in the papal system, we see the **image** (v. 14) of the first beast given life and **breath** (v. 15).

This **beast** has **two horns like a lamb** (v. 11). Thus far, it mimics the Lamb, Jesus Christ. As a point of interest, bishops since the time of Pope Gregory (590) wore a pallium of lamb's wool and abbots wore a miter with two points and were known as the *Goruti* ("the horned ones"). Jesus had warned his disciples to be vigilant against the appearance of "false prophets, who come to you in sheep's clothing" (Matt. 7:15). This beast is elsewhere called the "false prophet" (Rev. 16:13; 19:20; 20:10). Jesus said that, notwithstanding the sheeplike appearance, "inwardly they are ravenous wolves." Like the donkey in Aesop's fable, who donned a lion's skin and succeeded in terrifying his fellow animals until he had the poor judgment to undertake an impressive roar, the false prophet's true colors are made apparent by what proceeds out of the

⌛ PRETERIST *(continued)*

religion gave animus to the persecution of those who did not worship at the heathen shrines, and was hand in glove with the civil power in persecuting the Christian church.

Jay Adams concurs:

The symbolism probably depicts the cult of the emperor which was very strong in Asia Minor. This cult demanded emperor worship.

A second opinion is that of J. Stewart Russell, who considers the rising of the beast out of "the land" to necessitate a geographical origin in Israel. Russell affirms: "He can be no other than the Roman procurator or governor of Judea under Nero, and the particular governor must be sought at or near the outbreak of the Jewish war."

Two candidates would seem qualified by these criteria to be the second beast: Albinus and Gessius Florus, the latter being the better possibility. Writes Russell:

Each was a monster of tyranny and cruelty, but the latter outdid the former. Before Gessius Florus came into office, the Jews counted Albinus the worst governor who had ever ground them by his oppression. After Gessius Florus came they thought Albinus almost a virtuous man in comparison.

FUTURIST *(continued)*

The second beast is a Jew. . . . The sphere of the second beast is Palestine. . . . This second beast is the final, personal Antichrist. . . . He is a counterfeit lamb and his two horns are an imitation of the priestly and kingly authority of Christ. He is the one of whom our Lord spoke (John v:43). He is the man of sin, the son of perdition described by Paul in 2 Thess. ii. He must be a Jew or his claim to being Israel's true Messiah would not be accepted by the Jews.

Walvoord disputes this idea:

There is no evidence that either of the beasts is a Jew. . . . It would seem quite unlikely that either of the two beasts of Revelation 13 will be a Jew inasmuch as they both persecute the Jewish people and are the final Roman rulers of the times of the Gentiles.

Walvoord seems to represent the majority of dispensational interpreters when he writes:

Among premillennial expositors, the trend seems to be to identify all of these terms [the *man of sin* (2 Thess. 2:3), *the little horn* (Dan. 7:8), *the prince that shall come* (Dan. 9:26), *the willful king* (Dan. 11:36ff.), *Antichrist* (1 John 2:18)] with the first beast and relegate the second beast to a subordinate role as a religious, rather than a political ruler.

IDEALIST *(continued)*

Wilson calls this beast "false religion as the servant of the secular power." He writes:

In John's day the beast operated through the priests who acted as the propagandists of the Caesar-cult by aping a spiritual power which they did not possess in the interests of a persecuting state.

On this point, Mounce and Ladd (usually in the *futurist* camp) agree with the *idealist* identification. Ladd suggests that this beast represents organized religion, prostituted for evil ends, employed to support civic power. Mounce writes, "The false prophet stands for the role of false religion in effecting the capitulation of mankind to the worship of secular power. It is the universal victory of humanism."

Ramsay writes:

The Province of Asia in its double aspect of civil and religious administration, the Proconsul and the Commune [the two horns], is symbolized by the monster described in 13:11.

Hobbs adds to the picture:

It is easy to identify this beast . . . This beast symbolized the Roman "Commune" or "Concilia." This was an official body set up in the provinces to enforce emperor-worship.

⧗ HISTORICIST *(continued)*

mouth (Matt. 7:16; 12:33–34). Thus the lamblike appearance is offset by the fact that this beast **spoke like a dragon** (v. 11).

This beast is said to **perform great signs** (v. 13), in order to enforce the worship of the Beast. A partial list of alleged miracles said to have occurred in relation to Catholicism could include the following: images have come down and lit their own candles (could this be called "making **fire come down from heaven**"—v. 13?); crucifixes have spoken; idols have sweat, turned their eyes, moved their hands, opened their mouths, healed sicknesses, raised the dead, mended broken bones (does this sound like giving **breath** to an **image,** so as to allow it to **speak**—v. 15?); the *stigmata* has appeared on hands and feet of persons; Mary has appeared to many, healed their sicknesses, etc. Many of these things are still being claimed in modern times.

The reference to **fire** coming **down from heaven** is thought, by some, to refer to the Pope's pretending to have to the prerogative of bringing the fires of damnation upon men and nations—a prerogative allegedly exercised in numerous damning anathemas, interdicts and excommunications pronounced upon sinners and dissenters from the papal authority. The fact that the Roman Church claims to possess the apostolic authority either to

⧗ PRETERIST *(continued)*

Russell is quite prepared to defend his opinion against those who might object that the particular actions of the second beast are not known to correspond to those of Gessius Florus:

> Josephus, indeed, has not preserved all the facts, which, if we had them, would no doubt vividly illustrate all the particulars of the apocalyptic portraiture of the second beast. But we scarcely need them. Force, fraud, cruelty, imposture, tyranny are attributes which too certainly might be predicted of such a procurator as Florus. Perhaps the traits most difficult to verify are those that relate to the compulsory enforcement of homage to the emperor's statue and the assumption of miraculous pretensions. Yet even here all we know is in favor of the description being true to the letter.

A third possible identification of the second beast is that of David Chilton, who, like Russell, states that the coming of the beast "out of the land" must refer to Israel, but sees its appearance **like a Lamb** (v. 11) to be a reference to false prophets. Jesus said: "Beware of false prophets, who come to you in sheep's clothing, but inwardly they are ravenous wolves" (Matt. 7:15). This beast is later called "the false prophet" (Rev. 16:13; 19:20; 20:10). Chilton seems to take the beast here to represent the Jewish religious system and leadership collectively as a false agent of God.

⌛ FUTURIST *(continued)*

Ryrie considers the power of the beast to make **fire come down from heaven on the earth** (v. 13) to be a deliberate "duplication of the power of the two witnesses to show the world that he has as much power as they had." One way in which the false prophet will corrupt religion will be by commanding that **an image to the beast** (v. 14) be made and worshiped on the threat of death for noncompliance. Walvoord points out that: "This image, referred to three times in the chapter, is mentioned seven more times in the book of Revelation (14:9, 11; 15:2; 16:2; 19:20; 20:4)."

In addition to requiring the construction and veneration of the image, the false prophet proceeds to **give breath to the image of the beast** (v. 15) so that it is even given the ability to **speak,** which to Ryrie may indicate:

a supernatural miracle (performed by the power of Satan) which actually gives life to the image. Or, the word [for "breath"] may be translated "wind" and indicate some magical sleight of hand which the second beast performs that gives the appearance of real life to this image. The speech and movements of this image could easily be manufactured.

Walvoord takes a similar view:

The intent of the passage seems to be that the image has the appearance of life manifested in breath-

⌛ IDEALIST *(continued)*

Of this body, Summers informs us:

John and his readers knew what this imperial cult meant since it was better organized and enforced in Asia Minor than in any other part of the Roman Empire. It was composed of deputies whose duty was to build images of Domitian, altars at the images, and legislate in any way they considered best to enforce the state religion.

Homer Hailey writes:

However, a representation of this form of paganism probably does not exhaust its significance, for its spirit is reflected in all forms of false worship which followed, including the papacy and many other systems of false religion.

This beast performs **great signs** (v. 13) in the sight of men, by which he **deceives those who dwell on the earth** (v. 14). The specific examples of calling fire from heaven and causing an image to speak may either be taken literally of actual tricks and ventriloquism performed by staged chicanery or as occult power. Since the dragon is behind it, it is possible that actual supernatural signs are intended, though, as Wilson tells us: "The trickery of magic was practiced by all the religious charlatans of the day."

Alternatively, they may be intended only as a symbolic way of saying that false religions will give various convincing evidences of their divine origins.

⌛ HISTORICIST *(continued)*

"retain" or to "forgive" the sins of men (John 20:23) means that all men stand in jeopardy of the fire (that is, the judgment) from heaven (originating from God) that must consume those who sin, unless they find favor in the eyes of the Roman Institution.

Protestant commentators (e.g., Elliott, Barnes, Vitringa, Cuninghame) have generally understood these to be fake miracles done by the second beast, though demonic power could account for the presence of actual supernatural occurrences.

The second beast also requires the death of all those who will not bow to the authority of the Roman Church. Though the papacy no longer has the political power to carry out such widespread persecutions against dissenters, there have, nonetheless, been centuries in the past during which such dissent was dangerous. The movements led by men like Peter Waldo, Jan Hus, Wycliff, and others, in opposition to papal authority, were often hunted and persecuted unto death by the church's agencies, such as the Jesuits, who conducted various Inquisitions. ▨

⌛ PRETERIST *(continued)*

Upon the points that this beast exercises all the authority of the first beast (v. 12), and exercises supernatural powers (v. 13), Chilton writes:

> The Jewish leaders, symbolized by this beast from the Land, joined forces with the Beast of Rome in an attempt to destroy the Church (Acts 4:24–28; 12:1–3; 13:8; 14:5; 17:5–8; 18:12–13; 21:11; 24:1–9; 25:2–3, 9, 24). . . . The Book of Acts records several instances of miracle-working Jewish false prophets who came into conflict with the Church (cf. Acts 8:9–24) and worked under Roman officials (cf. Acts 13:6–11); as Jesus foretold (Matt. 7:22–23), some of them even used His name in their incantations (Acts 19:13–16).

The making of **an image to the beast** (v. 14), or an image of the beast (v. 15), the giving breath to the image, and the requirement that all men worship it are difficult features to correlate with any action known to have occurred in Israel in the first century. This need not be taken literally, however, and can simply refer to the Jews' general homage to Rome's authority, as Chilton observes:

> The idolatrous character of apostate Israel is assumed throughout the message of the New Testament. The Apostle Paul specifically accuses the Jews of lawlessness and apostasy in Romans 2. In verses 21–22, he says: "You, therefore,

⌛ FUTURIST *(continued)*

ing, but actually it may be no more than a robot. The image is further described as being able to speak, a faculty easily accomplished by mechanical means.

These comments fail to note, however, that the very ease with which technology today can generate speech and robotic movement would seem to remove any occasion of marvel at the ability of the second beast to manufacture such phenomena.

In Gaebelein's opinion, the image will probably be set up outside of Palestine, possibly in Rome. Most dispensationalists (e.g., Weidner), however, think that this image will be set up in the rebuilt temple in Jerusalem, constituting it the "abomination of desolation" spoken of by both Daniel (9:27; 11:31; 12:11) and Jesus (Matt. 24:15). 📖

⌛ IDEALIST *(continued)*

This False Prophet enforces worship of **an image of the beast** (v. 15) on pain of death. This imagery is taken from Daniel 3, where Nebuchadnezzar, king of Babylon, required **the universal worship** of an image (probably of himself) or face execution. This identification is encouraged by the frequency with which Daniel's imagery reappears in Revelation, and the prominence of "Babylon" as the major antagonist in both books.

The most persistent antichristian religious and philosophical sentiments will be those that align themselves with nationalism and statism—all of which confer upon the state a godlike virtue. Dissenters are usually persecuted out of existence. Sometimes state religions actually represent their governments or rulers with literal statues, though the image need not be a literal statue. 📖

⌛ **PRETERIST** *(continued)*

who teach another, do you not
teach yourself? . . . You who abhor
idols, do you rob temples?"

THE MARK OF THE BEAST

REVELATION 13:16—18

[16]He causes all, both small and great, rich and poor, free and slave, to receive a mark on their right hand or on their foreheads, [17]and that no one may buy or sell except one who has the mark or the name of the beast, or the number of his name. [18]Here is wisdom. Let him who has understanding calculate the number of the beast, for it is the number of a man: His number is 666.

⌛ HISTORICIST

It takes only a slight acquaintance with the literature on Revelation and eschatology to know two things: (1) that the characters of the Greek, Hebrew, and Latin languages also served instead of numerals to designate numeric values, and (2) that a great number of names throughout history have, by being reduced to their numerical values, been shown to equal the mysterious number **666** (v. 18). Many attempts have been made to solve the mystery of the meaning of the number of the beast. The earliest solution known to historians was that proposed by Irenaeus in the second century, who believed it to be the name *Lateinos* [Greek for "Latin"]. He wrote:

⌛ PRETERIST

The exhortation, **Let him who has understanding calculate the number of the beast,** is one of the clearest indicators that the fulfillment of these prophecies belongs to the first century AD. John obviously did not expect his readers who had **understanding** (v. 18) to have any difficulty in identifying the Beast, since they could simply calculate the meaning of this cryptogram. If the beast was not contemporary with the readers, it would not only be impossible, but also a cruel tease, for John to tell them that they could calculate this number and discover the true identity of the beast. As Chilton points out, John "did not expect them to figure

⧗ FUTURIST

Many see in this passage a prediction of a cashless, worldwide economy in which credit/debit numbers assigned to individuals around the world replace the use of actual currency. Modern innovations in the banking industry may be leading in this direction. Eventually this number will be placed on the body of its possessor, possibly as an implanted computer chip or a laser-tattoo, in order to eliminate the possibility of theft or credit card fraud. Ryrie offers the basis for this literal view: "The word 'mark' means an impress made by a stamp, like a brand used on slaves and animals." But not all, including Weidner, take it as a literal mark upon the skin:

> Most commentators think that we dare not interpret here literally of an actual mark impressed,—that as in the case of the servants of God no actual visible mark is intended, so here the mark signifies, as Alford says, "rather conformity and addiction to the behests of the beast.'"

Without this number, it will be impossible for anyone to do business, placing men under intense economic pressure to conform, which Biederwolf

⧗ IDEALIST

The proof of compliance with the antichristian system is the acceptance of a **mark on their right hand or on their foreheads** (v. 16). Interpreters such as Wilcock do not find it necessary to understand this mark as any more visible or literal than is the "seal" (7:3) or the "name" (14:1) on the foreheads of the Christians:

> As the invisible seal of the Spirit confirms the divine ownership of God's servants (7:3), so the mystical mark of the beast confirms those who thus sell themselves to the "system."

Receiving the beast's mark is synonymous with proclaiming one's servitude to the beast (cf. 14:9, 11; 20:4). In the Roman world, a slave was often branded in a conspicuous part of the body (the hand and the forehead were the parts least likely to be covered with clothing) with the brand or mark of his owner. The devil's people thus bear his "mark"—that is, they exhibit the unmistakable evidence of who their master is, and God's servants (14:1) similarly exhibit the proof of who their Master is. What is it that "marks" men out as

⧗ HISTORICIST *(continued)*

"It seems to me very probable; for this is a name of the last of Daniel's four kingdoms; they being *Latins* that now reign." This solution to the mystery has satisfied most of the *historicist* writers as well. Barnes writes:

> This appellation, originally applied to the language only, was adopted by the Western kingdoms, and came to be that by which they were best designated. It was the Latin world, the Latin kingdom, the Latin church, the Latin patriarch, the Latin clergy, the Latin councils. To use Dr. More's words, "They *Latinize* everything: mass, prayers, hymns, litanies, canons, decretals, bulls, are conceived in Latin. The Papal councils speak in Latin, women themselves pray in Latin. The Scriptures are read in no other language under the Papacy than Latin. In short, all things are Latin." With what propriety, then, might John, under the influence of inspiration, speak, in this enigmatical manner, of the new power that was symbolized by the beast as *Latin.*

For centuries, the **mark** (v. 16) of being Roman Catholic was that one worshiped in the Latin language, regardless what language one commonly spoke, or whether one even could understand the Latin liturgy! The receiving of this mark on the **hand** or **foreheads** (v. 16) may merely be an allusion to the practice, common in

⧗ PRETERIST *(continued)*

out the name of some 20th-century official in a foreign government."[33]

One of the major evidences for identifying the beast with Nero is this information about **the number of his name** (v. 17). Here using English characters, the Hebrew form of "Caesar Nero" is *Nrwn Osr* (pronounced "Neron Kaiser"). The value of the seven Hebrew letters is 50, 200, 6, 50, 100, 60, and 200, respectively. The total is thus 666. This is the solution advocated by David S. Clark, Jay Adams, Kenneth Gentry, David Chilton, and most others.

Most likely, the code utilized the *Hebrew* form rather than the Greek or Latin form of the name to avoid detection from Roman authorities, who would know both Latin and Greek, but not Hebrew. The readers of the book, however, knew considerable Hebrew, judging from the many symbols taken from the Old Testament and also John's use of Hebrew words like *Armageddon, amen, hallelujah, Satan* (a Hebrew name, used in addition to the Greek word for *devil*), and Abaddon (in addition to its Greek counterpart Apollyon). The Hebrew language has exerted so great an influence over the writing of Revelation, in fact, that some scholars have even speculated that John originally wrote it in Aramaic (his native tongue and a cognate of Hebrew).

Chilton summarizes the earliest historical opinions:

FUTURIST *(continued)*

envisions as including something of a mandatory labor union: "The Antichrist will control the labor market. In order to buy or sell one will have to join the organization of which the Antichrist is the head."

Walvoord adds that "the mark is simply a token that they are beast worshipers, and it serves as an identification necessary to conduct business and to purchase the necessities of life. It is another device to force all people to worship the beast."

Mounce seems to think that the implied "economic boycott seems to be a harassment of believers rather than a means of putting to death." But most understand the text to teach that those who do not conform will have to face death. Those who do conform, receiving the mark, will face worse consequences than death in being cast into the lake of fire (14:10–11). As Gaebelein puts it:

> The most terrible persecution is connected with this idol-worship. The most awful tyranny exists then, for all commerce is controlled by the Beast. Whoever does not have the mark . . . on hand and forehead cannot buy nor sell, and whoever does not worship the Beast will be killed. And those who worship the Beast and receive the mark are lost souls.

The meaning of the beast's number **666** (v. 18) has been debated and

IDEALIST *(continued)*

servants of one or the other? Hendriksen well explains:

> The forehead symbolizes the mind, the thoughtlife, the philosophy of a person. The right hand indicates his deed, action, trade, industry, etc. Therefore receiving the mark of the beast on the forehead or right hand indicates that . . . either preeminently in what he thinks, says, writes or more emphatically in what he does—this antichristian spirit becomes evident.

Those who do not participate in the world's activities and philosophies in any age can expect persecution and ostracism. The indication of this ostracism is found in the mention of one of its forms, that they may not **buy or sell** (i.e., economic boycott—v. 17). The poverty of church of Smyrna (2:9) may have been due to just such economic pressures. Summers continues to make specific application to the time of Domitian:

> Worshiping the emperor was a test at every phase of life. Christians were boycotted in the market for the refusal to bear the mark of the emperor. Marriage settlements, wills, transfers of property—none of these were legal without the stamp of the emperor.

The mark is either **the name of the beast** or **the number of his name** (v. 17). It is not necessary to assume by

⏳ **HISTORICIST** *(continued)*

ancient times, of slaves or soldiers bearing a mark or the name of their owner or emperor upon their hands (Actius and Ambrose bear testimony to this), or, in some cases, upon the forehead (as confirmed by Valerius Maximus and Ambrose).[31]

Writes Barnes:

> Applied to the Papacy, the meaning is, that there would be some mark of distinction; some indelible sign; something that would designate, with entire certainty, those persons who belonged to it, and who were subject to it. It is hardly necessary to say that, in point of fact, this has eminently characterized the Papacy. All possible care has been taken to designate with accuracy those who belong to that communion, and all over the world, it is easy to distinguish those who render allegiance to the Papal power.

The forbidding to **buy or sell** (v. 17) is explained by the fact that the popes have often forbidden commercial intercourse with heretics or Protestants. Barnes writes: "It has been common in Rome to prohibit, by express law, all traffic with heretics." Pope Alexander III, at the Third Lateran Council in 1178, ordered that "no man presume to entertain or cherish them in his house, or land, to exercise traffic with them." The same pope, presiding over the synod of Tours, passed a law concerning the

⏳ **PRETERIST** *(continued)*

All the earliest Christian writers on the Apocalypse, from Irenaeus down to Victorinus of Pettau and Commodian in the fourth, and Andreas in the fifth, and St. Beatus in the eighth century, connect Nero, or some Roman emperor, with the Apocalypse Beast.[34]

When we survey the possible candidates among the Roman rulers, there do not appear to be any who so admirably fit the detailed description of the beast—nor whose names could plausibly be reduced to the gematria 666, other than Nero. Since Nero was contemporary with John and his readers, there can be little doubt that they would readily make this association. "'Even late-date advocate Donald Guthrie, who rejects the Nero theory, grants that this variant gives the designation Nero 'a distinct advantage.'"[35]

As for the impossibility of buying or selling by those lacking the mark (v. 17), David Clark writes:

> This was to boycott or ostracize the Christians, and deprive them of the common rights of citizens, or the common rights of humanity. The pressure of economic distress was to be laid on them to compel them to conform.

Chilton notes:

> Similarly [the Jewish leaders] organized economic boycotts against those who refused to submit to

⌛ FUTURIST *(continued)*

applied myriads of ways. John Nelson Darby, the father of the modern dispensational system, acknowledged that he did not know what it represents:

> I confess my ignorance as to the number six hundred and sixty-six. I cannot present you with anything satisfactory to myself. We find, answering to the number six hundred and sixty-six, the words *apostasy* and *tradition;* but I cannot say anything positive on the point.

J. B. Smith, after mentioning that the six Roman numerals (I, V, X, L, C, D) add up to 666, points "to the possibility of a Roman being the antichrist. . . . All the numerals from 1 to 36 total 666. *Beast* in the evil sense occurs exactly 36 times (6X6) in Revelation."

Attempts have been made to identify the number 666 with the names of many persons of ancient or modern history. One popular opinion is that the Antichrist will be a reincarnation of Nero or Judas Iscariot. Many modern historical figures have been shown to have names that can, by ingenious calculations, be made to conform to this diabolical cipher. Ryrie, with good cause, observes: "So many identifications have been made of 666 with characters of history as to make them all unreliable coincidences."

More popular among modern expositors is the suggestion that the num-

⌛ IDEALIST *(continued)*

the language used that the literal name or a literal cipher must be intended. The number 666 is often interpreted as follows: "Six" is the number of incompleteness (unlike "seven," which represents perfection or completeness). The number is repeated three times to intensify the idea of human imperfection. Each digit in the number **666** (v. 18) falls short of the symbolic number of perfection: 7. Since it is **the number of a man** (v. 18), 666 symbolizes man's imperfection.

This explanation, however, is weakened by the consideration that the text, in the Greek, does not present three sixes, but, rather the number six-hundred sixty-six (600 + 60 + 6). Thus, there is no presentation of three "sixes" in the original text.

The number may have been chosen here because of its association with Nero (see *preterist* comments), though pointing to him only as a representative type of satanic states in any age that oppose Christianity. Wilcock writes: "The number 666 does not mean Nero or Caligula or Rome. It simply means the beast, false religion."

363

HISTORICIST *(continued)*

Waldenses, that "no man should presume to receive or assist them in selling or buying." At the Council of Constance, Pope Martin V issued a decree requiring that "they permit not the heretics to have houses in their districts, or enter into contracts, or carry on commerce."[32]

Various *historicists* have suggested many other names as possible explanations of the number 666, but nearly all point toward the papacy as the beast. Some others have included: (1) Latin Basileia [Latin kingdom]; (2) Apostaths [Apostate]; (3) the Hebrew word for"Roman"—all of which can be shown to total 666.

Andreas Helwig (1572–1643) explained the mystic number 666 by reference to the pope's official Latin title: *Vicarius filii Dei* (translated: "Vicar of the Son of God"). The Roman numeral value of this title (i.e., V= 5, I= 1, C= 100, L= 50, D= 500, all other letters = 0) totals exactly 666. This title reportedly was written upon the crown known as the "Triple Tiara" worn by the popes at their coronations. In the seventeenth century, it was expunged from the miter.

PRETERIST *(continued)*

Caesar as Lord, the leaders of the synagogues"forbidding all dealings with the excommunicated,"[36] and going so far as to put them to death.

⏳ FUTURIST *(continued)*

ber six represents man, who falls short of the perfection that the number seven would represent. Among these is Gaebelein:

> But what does the number 666 mean? If we were to state all the different views on this number and the different applications we would have to fill many pages and then we would not know what is right and wrong. . . . The number 666 signifies man's day and man's defiance of God under Satan's power in its culmination.

SUMMARY OF CHAPTERS 11–13

The section falling in the center of the book of Revelation concerns itself with a period of time that is represented as 1,260 days (or equivalents). There are widely differing opinions as to what is signified by this time period.

On the one hand, *preterists* and *futurists* take this period quite literally—that is, they see it as an actual period of three-and-a-half years. Of course, the *preterist* applies it to a period in the past, while the *futurist* anticipates the fulfillment in the future. The former will usually see this period either as the time of Nero's persecution of the church (AD 65–68), or as the length of the Jewish War (AD 66–70), both of which answer pretty well to the exact length of time indicated. The *futurists* apply these numbers to a future tribulation period, just prior to Christ's Second Coming. In some cases, three-and-a-half years is viewed as the whole length of the tribulation, but, more often, two periods of that length are joined together to make the total length of the tribulation seven years—identified with the "seventieth week" of Daniel 9. The "beast" of *preterism* is Nero; whereas the "beast" of *futurism* is a coming, antichristian and anti-Jewish dictator.

By contrast, *historicists* follow the year-for-a-day interpretive method, and transform 1,260 days into a period of 1,260 years. These are then identified with the centuries during which the papacy held sway over the Western church and persecuted its dissenters (from around 532 to about 1792).

Idealists take the number as entirely symbolic and see it as representing the entire Gospel Age, from the first coming of Christ to the second. The trampling of Jerusalem, the two witnesses, the woman surviving in the wilderness, and the blasphemous career of the beast are all seen as conditions prevailing throughout the Christian Era.

NOTES

1. E.g., David S. Clark, *The Message from Patmos: A Postmillennial Commentary on the Book of Revelation* (Grand Rapids: Baker, 1989), 75.

2. E.g., Kenneth Gentry, *The Beast of Revelation*, 53ff.

3. Jim Pinkoski, *The Prophecies of Daniel and Revelation* (Frederick, MD: Amazing Facts, 1986).

4. *Treasury of Scripture Knowledge*.

5. Wilson, *Revelation*, 95.

6. Homer Hailey, *Revelation: An Introduction and Commentary* (Grand Rapids: Baker, 1979), 252, 288.

7. Morris, *The Revelation Record*, 147.

8. Ladd, *A Commentary on the Revelation of John*, 154.

9. B. W. Johnson, *The People's New Testament With Notes*, quoted in Caringola, *The Present Reign of Jesus Christ*, 457.

10. *Ibid.*

11. Elliott, *Horae Apocalyptica*, Vol. III, 435.

12. *The People's New Testament with Notes*, quoted in Caringola, *The Present Reign of Jesus Christ*.

13. These teachers still have a total of three resurrections because there is the resurrection and Rapture of the two witnesses, which they place in the midst of the tribulation.

14. *Biblical Apocalyptics: A Study of the Most Notable Revelations of God and of Christ in the Canonical Scriptures* (New York: Eaton & Mains, 1896), 381.

15. Russell is one of the few dissenters to this party line. He takes the woman and the child both to be alternate symbols of the same entity, namely, the Judean church, which escaped to Pella prior to the siege in AD 70.

16. This began in November of AD 64 and ended with Nero's death June 9, 68.

17. If this is true, they should be easy enough to find, if their persecutors would trouble themselves to read the commentaries.

18. Bauckham, *The Theology of the Book of Revelation*, 151.

19. The time of Jacob's trouble" is a phrase found only in Jer. 30:7, in Scripture, and may be a reference to the Babylonian captivity of the Jews in the sixth century BC.

20. Posted, at the time of this writing, at http://www.whitehorsemedia.com/articles/?d=31# .ULLLk6WIXeM

21. E. G. White, *The Great Controversy* (DeLand, FL: Laymen For Religious Liberty), 54.

22. The period refers to the 1,260 years from AD 538, when the Ostrogoths abandoned their siege of Rome, until 1798, when the Pope was taken prisoner by the French general under Napoleon.

23. Pinkosky, *The Prophecies of Daniel and Revelation*, 26.

24. Chilton documents this point in a footnote, citing Tertullian's *Apology*, book 5: "Unless gods give satisfaction to men, there will be no deification for them: the god will have to propitiate the man. Tiberius, accordingly, in whose days the Christian name made its entry into the world, having himself received intelligence from Palestine of events which had clearly shown the truth of Christ's divinity, brought the matter before the Senate, with his own decision in favor of Christ. The Senate, because it had not given the approval itself, rejected his proposal. Caesar held to his opinion, threatening wrath against all accusers of the Christians. Consult your histories."

25. Beale, *The New International Greek Testament Commentary*, 683.

26. G. B. Caird, *The Language and Imagery of the Bible* (Philadelphia: Westminster, 1980), 229.

27. The following quotes of the popes are cited by various *historicist* authors.

28. Edersheim, *The Life and Times of Jesus the Messiah*, n.p.

29. Compare the modern attempts to paint Christian positions about certain sins as "hate speech."

30. Philip Schaff, *History of the Christian Church*, vol.1 (Peabody, MA: Henrickson, 1858), 381–82.

31. These ancient authorities are quoted in Latin by Barnes in "Revelation" in Notes, 333.

32. Documented in Elliott, *Horae Apocalyptica*, Vol. III, 220f.

33. David Chilton, *Paradise Restored: A Biblical Theology of Dominion* (Tyler, TX: Dominion Press, 1985), 180.

34. David Chilton, *The Days of Vengeance: An Exposition of the Book of Revelation* (Fort Worth, TX: Dominion Press, 1987), 351.

35. Gentry, *The Beast of Revelation*, 35. See also Donald Guthrie, *New Testament Introduction*, 3rd ed. (Downers Grove, IL: InterVarsity, 1970), 959.

36. Austin Farrer, *The Revelation of St. John the Divine* (London: Oxford University Press, 1964), 157.

PART V

THE SEVEN LAST PLAGUES
REVELATION 14—16

WHAT DO THESE BOWLS OF WRATH REPRESENT?
WHEN DO THESE EVENTS OCCUR?

HISTORICIST APPROACH:

- In general, the seven bowls of wrath find fulfillment in the judgment upon the papacy (Babylon), beginning with the French Revolution and the Napoleonic Wars and concluding yet in the future.

PRETERIST APPROACH:

- The judgments of these bowls are largely against Jerusalem, culminating in its fall in AD 70, though the fifth bowl touches the Roman Empire as well—probably referring to the chaotic state of affairs that prevailed after Nero's suicide.
- Alternatively, this section says nothing about the fall of Jerusalem and refers strictly to the judgment of God upon pagan Rome.

FUTURIST APPROACH:

- The bowls represent future, global judgments that in their devastating effect are unparalleled in history.
- These occur at the very end of the Tribulation period, culminating in World War III, or the Battle of Armageddon.
- This war is the last battle to be fought by mankind, and it will be ended by the personal appearing of Christ as He comes to establish His millennial kingdom.

IDEALIST APPROACH:

- There is a relationship between the bowl judgments and the trumpet judgments. The former may be a recapitulation of the latter.
- The principal distinction between the trumpets and the bowls is that the former are partial in their effects and serve to warn the wicked of their spiritual danger, whereas the latter are complete and represent final judgment upon the unrepentant.

- The same event in history may serve as a trumpet judgment for one person (a mere warning) and as a bowl judgment for another (a final judgment, resulting in death).
- The disasters described recur in history repeatedly.

THE LAMB AND THE REDEEMED

REVELATION 14:1–5

[1]Then I looked, and behold, a Lamb standing on Mount Zion, and with Him one hundred and forty-four thousand, having His Father's name written on their foreheads. [2]And I heard a voice from heaven, like the voice of many waters, and like the voice of loud thunder. And I heard the sound of harpists playing their harps. [3]They sung as it were a new song before the throne, before the four living creatures, and the elders; and no one could learn that song except the hundred and forty-four thousand who were redeemed from the earth. [4]These are the ones who were not defiled with women, for they are virgins. These are the ones who follow the Lamb wherever He goes. These were redeemed from among men, being firstfruits to God and to the Lamb. [5]And in their mouth was found no deceit, for they are without fault before the throne of God.

HISTORICIST

The close of chapter 13 was not encouraging. Those who resisted the papacy were seen as being "killed" and "overcome" and excluded from commerce by the beast. It is a bleak picture, but one which is now to be offset by the uplifting visions of this chapter. The first of these sees **the one hundred and forty-four thousand** (v. 1)—triumphant on **Mount Zion** with Christ, the **Lamb.**

PRETERIST

The first vision of this chapter, depicting the 144,000 with the **Lamb standing on Mount Zion** (v. 1), is reminiscent of the second psalm. The psalm speaks of the kings and rulers vainly rebelling against and resisting God and the Messiah, but declares that God laughs at their futile efforts to unseat Him from his sovereign position. God tells them, "Yet I have set My King on My holy hill

⧗ FUTURIST

The place this chapter occupies in the structure of the book is unique, in that it has no organic connection with the chapters immediately preceding (chaps. 12–13) or with those following (chaps. 15–16).

Tenney sees the chapter as an illustrative parenthesis in the book:

> The "parenthetical" material of chapter 14 consists of a series of short visions which are really commentaries on the various aspects of the main action of the book. They are not intended to describe a series of actions in chronological order, but are glimpses of various phases of the conflict.

Ryrie writes, "This chapter is something like a table of contents of the things in the remainder of the book."

Many expositors (e.g., Seiss, Ironside, Gaebelein, Walvoord, Ryrie, Morris) agree that the **one hundred and forty-four thousand** (v. 1) in this vision are the same saints as were seen sealed in chapter 7.

Tenney offers two possible identifications:

> If they are identical with the 144,000 mentioned in chapter 7 they represent Jewish believers who have kept their purity of worship and who have come to know the Messiah through great suffering . . . If they can be identified with the "man child" who is "caught up

⧗ IDEALIST

Chapter 14 can be seen as culminating the section before it or as introducing that which follows. Or it can stand alone. It contains elements that were introduced earlier in the book (i.e., the 144,000, cf. chap. 7) and also elements that have not previously been discussed but which will be the focus of later chapters (i.e., the fall of Babylon, v. 8, cf. chaps. 16–18). Milton S. Terry, though technically a *preterist*, sees the chapter in the *idealist* sense, as a victorious culmination:

> The revelation of the three great foes, the dragon, the beast from the sea, and the beast from the land, is followed immediately by a sevenfold disclosure of victory and judgment in the heavens. The purpose of these visions and voices from heaven is obviously to show that the powers of the heavens are mightier than those of the infernal serpent and his associates. The trinity of hostile forces, armed with many lying wonders, might seem from a human point of view invincible. But John, like the young servant of Elisha when confronted with the horses and chariots and immense host of the king of Syria, is here admonished that they which are with the persecuted Church are more and mightier than they which make war against her (cf. 2 Kings 6:15–17).

Whether the **Mount Zion** (v. 1), where the **Lamb** is seen standing with the

371

⏳ HISTORICIST (continued)

Elliott (along with most) identifies this group with that of the same number seen in chapter 7, who were there sealed on their foreheads. They are the true elect of God, bearing His name on their foreheads in distinction from those who follow the beast, and display his mark. Their number is symbolic, and no doubt represent the true followers of Christ living over the entire period of the beast's horrible reign, who "from the earliest Papal times, have yet had the peculiar fitness of special reference to that [era] when Christ's saints began to see themselves more openly separated from the Romanists than before. . . . the time, I mean, of the Waldenses, Wicliffites, Hussites."[1]

Some (e.g., Vitringa, Grotius) understand the mountain to represent the heavenly venue of departed saints, as does Barnes:

> The manifestation of *the blessed with the Lamb in eternal glory* is intended to give believers who are on earth and exposed to persecution on the part of the Dragon, a pledge inspiring courage and patience, that if they remain faithful they too shall attain to that glory.

Caringola and others take Mount Zion simply as "a symbol of the true Christian church," citing the use of the same expression to this effect in Hebrews 12:22. If the 144,000 are identified with the **harpists playing their**

⏳ PRETERIST (continued)

of Zion" (v. 6). Despite all the efforts of the dragon and the beast to eliminate the church, the Judean believers stand secure with the Lord in victory.

David S. Clark explains the purpose of the chapter and its relation to chapter 7:

> It is plain that here in the fourteenth chapter we have a duplicate of the scene of the seventh chapter; and evidently for the same reason. This is for the encouragement of the persecuted church on earth.

Jay Adams expands on this chapter's purpose:

> But why are the Jewish saints referred to in the second, or Roman section of the Apocalypse? For a similar reason to that which necessitated the mention of the innumerable Gentile multitude in the Jewish portion. They are introduced here to show that as God cared for his own during the former trial so too he would be concerned with his servants during the Roman ordeal.

Those who are singing in verses 2 and 3 are said to sing a song that **no one could learn** (v. 3) except the 144,000. David S. Clark sees the mystery of redemption in this song:

> That no one could learn their song was doubtless because it was the song of redemption; the angels might look with admiration and

FUTURIST *(continued)*

unto God and unto his throne" (12:5), they are a select group of believers, born in tribulation, and separated from the general body of the people of God by their peculiar faith and piety.

But Gaebelein disagrees:

A good many have made of this company a portion of the Church, a first fruits, who, according to this theory, have lived separated lives and are caught up into heaven, while the other believers, who did not live as near to God as they did, will have to suffer in the great tribulation.

The **Mount Zion** (v. 1) pictured here is taken either as the literal mountain in Israel by that name, or as heaven. Walvoord (in agreement with Gaebelein, Weidner, Ironside, Morris, and others) holds the first of these views:

Preferable is the view that this is a prophetic vision of the ultimate triumph of the Lamb following His second coming, when He joins the 144,000 on Mount Zion at the beginning of His millennial reign.

Ryrie (in company with Tenney, Kuyper) understands it as heaven:

But since Zion is used of the heavenly Jerusalem (Heb. 12:22) and since these 144,000 are before the throne (v. 3) it seems more natural

IDEALIST *(continued)*

144,000, is terrestrial or celestial is disputed. Alford thinks that the company previously introduced to us in chapter 7 is here seen again on earth:

I would call attention of the reader to the fact, essential to the right understanding of the vision, that the harpers and the song are in heaven and the 144,000 on earth.

This conclusion does not seem to reflect the majority opinion, however, as Hengstenberg shows:

As certainly as the voice from heaven in verse 2 is the voice of the 144,000, so certainly must the Mount Zion where the Lamb stands with them be the heavenly one. According to verse 3 the throne of God is on Mount Zion, but this belongs to the heavenly Zion and not to the earthly.

The heavenly venue of the throng seems to be confirmed by the statement that these people **were redeemed from the earth** (v. 3). The fact that the number of those redeemed is the same as the number of those sealed in chapter 7 serves to assure that all those upon whom God has placed his seal will ultimately be saved. Not one is missing.

In contrast to those who bore the name of the beast on their foreheads (13:16), these have the **Father's name** (v. 1) upon theirs, signifying their allegiance to God rather than to the beast.

⧗ HISTORICIST *(continued)*

harps (v. 2), then they must be in heaven, since the latter are said to be singing **before the throne, before the four living creatures, and the elders** (v. 3). But the identification is not certain. The harpists are singing the **new song** (v. 3), whereas the 144,000 seem to be in the position to **learn that song** (v. 3)—i.e., from the harpists. Therefore Elliott and De Wette may be correct in assuming that the harpists are singing *in heaven* while the 144,000 are on earth.

Commenting on the text that says **no one could learn that song except the hundred and forty-four thousand (v. 3),** Adam Clark writes:

> As none but genuine Christians can worship God acceptably, because they approach Him through the only Mediator, so none can understand the deep things of God but such; nor can others know the cause why true believers exult so much in God through Christ, because they know not the communion which such hold with the Father and the Son through the Holy Ghost.

Elliott takes the position that the **new song** is the blessed doctrine of the Reformation: *Christ our righteousness.*

Their being **virgins** (v. 4) is understood not as meaning that they are necessarily unmarried and celibate, but that they **were not defiled with**

⧗ PRETERIST *(continued)*

wonder on the work of redemption, but they have no experience of it.

J. Stewart Russell thinks that the wording of this passage influenced the writer of the epistle to the Hebrews, a suggestion which, if true, tends to establish the pre-AD 70 date of writing for Revelation:

> Is it possible to believe that the writer of the Epistle to the Hebrews had not this vision in his thoughts when he wrote that noble passage, "Ye are come unto mount Zion, the city of the living God, the heavenly Jerusalem," etc.? The points of resemblance are so marked and so numerous that it cannot possibly be accidental. The scene is the same,—Mount Zion; the *dramatis personae* are the same,—"the general assembly and church of the firstborn, which are written in heaven," corresponding with the hundred and forty and four thousand who bear the seal of God. In the epistle they are called "the church of the firstborn;" the vision explains the title,—they are "the *firstfruits* unto God and to the Lamb;" the first converts to the faith of Christ in the land of Judea.

The virginity of this company is not with reference to their physical singleness, but rather to their refusal to associate with the harlot (Jerusalem or Rome; see notes in chap. 17).

to understand Zion as the heavenly city.

Whereas chapter 7 revealed little about them beyond their number and nationality, this description emphasizes their character. In deliberate contrast to those at the end of the previous chapter, who had the number or name of the beast on their foreheads, this company is seen with God's name **on their foreheads** (v. 1). The 144,000 are **not defiled with women, for they are virgins** (v. 4). This is not likely to refer to sexual virginity, since their virginity is contrasted with defilement. Married people would not be virgins, but neither are they defiled by being married (Heb. 13:4). Gaebelein expresses the opinion of most when he writes: "They did not defile themselves with the corruptions and idolatries prevalent on the earth. They kept themselves from spiritual fornication." Walvoord elaborates:

> In like manner Israel is referred to frequently in the Bible as "the virgin daughter of Zion" (Lam. 2:13), and as the "virgin of Israel" (Jer. 18:13; 31:4, 21; Amos 5:2).

Ryrie explains that the word **firstfruits** (v. 4) means:

> They are a token offering to God, which indicates that a larger harvest would follow. The first converts of a country are called firstfruits of the larger number to be won (Rom.

The **new song** (v. 3) is the song of New Testament redemption (contrast with Moses' song in Exodus 15 celebrating redemption from Egyptian bondage). That **no one could learn that song** (v. 3) other than the redeemed ones attests that the song of redemption "can only be sung by those who have experienced its joys" (Wilson).

The state of virginity (v. 4) as applied to the church is spiritual, not physical, meaning they have not participated in the fornication of idolatry, in contrast to "all nations" in verse 8.

They are said to be **firstfruits to God and to the Lamb** (v. 4). Wilson thinks that this cannot mean there are more to follow, since the 144,000 comprise all the saints of the entire dispensation. Instead, *firstfruits* carries the more general sense of "an offering to God." Hendriksen sees the term similarly, indicating that the firstfruits suggests a setting apart prior to the remainder of the harvest, i.e., the final judgment (cf. vv. 14–20). The 144,000 were set apart from men in general as God's portion from the earth.

Remembering the pastoral purpose of the book as a message to suffering Christians contemporary with John, Hobbs writes concerning this passage: "Thus the suffering saints of Asia saw a foretaste of their own glory. And it gave them courage and patient endurance." A guileless man is not a

⌛ HISTORICIST *(continued)*

women. Sexual relations in marriage do not defile (Heb. 13:4), and these, therefore, have simply avoided illicit sexual activity and are morally pure, as De Wette explains:

> The sense cannot be that all these 144,000 had lived an unmarried life; for how could the apostle Peter, and others who were married, have been excluded? But the reference must be to those who held themselves from all impurity . . . which, in the view of the apostles, was closely connected with idolatry.

The expression, **being firstfruits to God and to the Lamb** (v. 4), is understood by Barnes to mean that the 144,000 were "not to be regarded as the *whole* of the number that was saved, but that they were *representatives* of the redeemed." 🔲

⌛ PRETERIST *(continued)*

In particular, the use of the label **firstfruits to God and to the Lamb** (v. 4) points to the identification of the 144,000 with the first Jewish believers, as Adams explains:

> The 144,000 cannot be interpreted as Jews who will some day escape persecution in a yet future age. In no intelligible sense could such a group of Jews be considered "firstfruits." Historically, the firstfruits of the Christian church were among the Jews—in fact among the very Jews who are here mentioned: those in Jerusalem, who escaped the destruction in 70 AD. How artificial to twist "firstfruits" into the very *last* fruits of the Christian era!

Milton Terry identifies the group a little more narrowly:

> The confessors and martyrs of the apostolic Church, who overcame by reason of their testimony and the blood of the Lamb, are thus declared to be a first fruits, a choice selection out of the innumerable company of saints. The purpose of the Apocalypse was to give special encouragement to these virgin spirits. 🔲

⏳ FUTURIST *(continued)*

16:5; 1 Cor. 16:15) . . . Apparently they indicate the harvest of many other Israelites (remember that they are Jews, not Gentiles) who will turn to the Lord at the end of the tribulation and during the millennium (Isa. 2:3; Zech. 8:22).

⏳ IDEALIST *(continued)*

sinless man; he is one who has nothing to hide. When sin is all confessed and judged in the presence of God, guile is absent. And so this guileless company is described as without fault before the throne of God.

THE EVERLASTING GOSPEL

REVELATION 14:6—7

⁶Then I saw another angel flying in the midst of heaven, having the everlasting gospel to preach to those who dwell on the earth—to every nation, tribe, tongue, and people—⁷saying with a loud voice, "Fear God and give glory to Him, for the hour of His judgment has come; and worship Him who made heaven and earth, the sea and springs of water."

⌛ HISTORICIST

Barnes looks for a future fulfillment of this vision:

> For the fulfillment of this, therefore, we are to look to a period subsequent to the rise and fall of that great Antichristian power symbolized by the beast and his image . . . The main idea is, that when God shall be about to cause his gospel to spread through the world, there will be, as it were, a solemn judgment on that Antichristian power which had so long resisted the truth and persecuted his saints.

In the mind of Elliott and others, however, this **angel** (v. 6) represents the missionary era and the Great Awakening in the time of the Wesleys, Whitefield, Edwards, and Finney.

Adam Clarke, writing in 1831, speculated:

⌛ PRETERIST

The preaching of **the everlasting gospel** (v. 6) is not literally done by angels in heaven, but by the church, of which the angel in this verse is representative. This gospel, some believe, may not be the message that we usually think of by that name, as David S. Clark writes:

> Is this the gospel of salvation to the world . . . what we usually mean by the term "everlasting gospel?" It might seem so because of the very terms used, "everlasting gospel." Or is his gospel the announcement of the doom and judgment of the persecutor? This view is favored by the words which he actually speaks for he says: "The hour of his (God's) judgment is come," that is, on the persecutor.

On the other hand, most expositors would see this as a reference to the regular message of salvation that Christ

⧗ FUTURIST

Gaebelein writes:

> The Angel must not be taken as a literal angel. The preaching of any Gospel to those who dwell on earth is never committed to angels, but to men.

Some dispensationalists, who affirm two legitimate "gospels" (i.e., the "gospel of grace" and the "gospel of the kingdom") have sought to explain the term **the everlasting gospel** (v. 6) variously.

Gaebelein distinguishes it from the "church-age" gospel:

> This has nothing to do with the preaching of the Gospel during this church-age . . . It is everlasting because it concerns the Creator as the only object of worship.

In contrast, Ironside sees it as identical with the church's gospel:

> This everlasting gospel is not to be distinguished from the gospel that has been proclaimed throughout the centuries. In truth, the very fact that it is called "everlasting" shows that it is identical with the gospel as proclaimed from the beginning . . . that God is sovereign, and man's happiness consists in recognizing His authority. To this blessed fact is added, in the present dispensation, the full truth of the gospel of the grace of God. The gospel of the kingdom is but another aspect of this same news from

⧗ IDEALIST

The **angel flying in the midst of heaven** preaching **the everlasting gospel** (v. 6), is not a literal angel, but a symbol for a general concept. Wilson thinks that the gospel here referred to is not the gospel so often spoken of in the New Testament, but "a call to the earth's inhabitants to awake to the reality of God's rule before it is too late" (cf. Acts 14:15). Hobbs writes: "This gospel was not the gospel of salvation. It was a pronouncement that the hour of God's judgment had come." Wilcock writes: "It is the absolutely basic gospel. . . . It is the hypothetical gospel with which Christ challenged the lawyer in Luke 10:28—'Do this, and you will live.'" Hailey takes issue with the above opinions:

> This is the only occurrence of the word "gospel" in any of John's writings. It raises the question whether this is the gospel revealed throughout the New Testament which was to be preached to all the world, or a special message to be announced just before the end time. However, it is evident that it could not be the latter for the faith has been once for all delivered to the saints (Jude 3) . . . and if an angel from heaven preaches any other gospel, he stands anathema, devoted to destruction (Gal. 1:8).

The word "gospel," prior to its use as a Christian term, referred to a public pronouncement of good tidings (such as

⧗ HISTORICIST *(continued)*

The vision seems truly descriptive of a late institution entitled "The British and Foreign Bible Society," whose object it is to print and circulate the Scriptures of the Old and New Testaments through all the habitable world, and in all the languages spoken on the face of the earth.

Ellen G. White, sees this preaching of the gospel as the preaching of the precursors of the Seventh-Day Adventist Movement, beginning in 1844, proclaiming the necessity of observing the seventh-day (Saturday) Sabbath.[2]

The announcement that **the hour of His judgment has come** (v. 7) refers to the impending destruction of Babylon (see v. 8). This great preaching movement was taking place, especially in England and America, just prior to the time that we see the pouring out of the bowls of wrath upon the papal system on the Continent through the French Revolution.

Henry H. Halley, in *Halley's Bible Handbook*, with his peculiar penchant for superfluous capitalization, writes of this vision:

This seems to symbolize General Evangelization of the Whole World in the Whole Gospel Era. Yet, coming just before the announcement of the Fall of "Babylon" (14:8), may it not be a picture of our Modern Era of World-Wide Missions?

⧗ PRETERIST *(continued)*

told His disciples to preach, and which he indicated would be preached in all the world before "the end comes" (Matt. 24:14). Russell is among these expositors:

There is a manifest allusion here to the fact predicted by our Lord that, before the coming of "the end," the Gospel of the kingdom would first be preached in all the world . . . "for a witness to all nations" (Matt. xxiv. 14). This symbol, therefore, indicates the near approach of the catastrophe of Jerusalem,—the arrival of the hour of Israel's judgment.

David Chilton concurs:

Contrary to the speculations of several expositors, there is no reason to suppose that this is something other than the Gospel of which the New Testament constantly speaks . . . Every element in it [is] an aspect of the New Testament message: **Fear God** (Luke 1:50; 12:5; Acts 10:35), **and give Him glory** (Matt. 5:16; 9:8; 15:31), **because the hour of His judgment has come** (John 12:23, 31–32; 16:8–11); **and worship Him who made the heaven and the earth and the sea** . . . All this bears striking resemblance to what is recorded of the apostolic Gospel (cf. Acts 14:15; 17:24–31). ⧗

⧗ FUTURIST *(continued)*

heaven, emphasizing particularly the Lordship of Christ.

This statement raises the important question of the relationship between "the Lordship of Christ" and the gospel in the present dispensation.

Walvoord appears to reject both of the above alternatives, offering a third:

> The everlasting gospel seems to be neither the gospel of grace nor the gospel of the kingdom, but rather the good news that God at last is about to deal with the world in righteousness and establish His sovereignty over the world.[3]

Though himself a dispensationalist, Henry Morris takes his fellows to task on their handling of the definition of the gospel:

> Paul, in fact, had warned that if an angel from heaven came preaching some other gospel than the same gospel which he (Paul) had preached, that angel should be rejected as one accursed by God (Gal. 1:8). This, plus the fact that John himself . . . called the angel's message the everlasting gospel, is conclusive proof that this gospel is the true and only gospel. ⧉

⧗ IDEALIST *(continued)*

might be announced by a town crier). Beale suggests that this angel's heralding of the everlasting gospel is deliberately in contrast to the non-eternal "gospel" of the Roman beast. He points out that the birthday of Caesar Augustus was officially hailed as signaling "the beginning of good news for the world"—the advent of a new era. As Caesar's "gospel" required that men maintain allegiance to him, so this Gospel requires that men **worship Him who made heaven and earth, the sea and springs of water.** ⧉

⌛ HISTORICIST *(continued)*

Note, while the Pretender-Lamb's [the beast's] method of conquest was to kill those who would not worship him (13:15), the weapon of the Lamb is the Simple Preaching of the Gospel (14:6). 📖

BABYLON IS FALLEN

REVELATION 14:8

[8]And another angel followed, saying, "Babylon is fallen, is fallen, that great city, because she has made all nations drink of the wine of the wrath of her fornication."

⌛ HISTORICIST

This is the first mention of **Babylon** in Revelation, so we have not thus far been given the keys to unlock the mystery of its meaning. As the beast was mentioned in 11:7, before he had been properly introduced (13:1ff.); so also his mistress, the harlot Babylon, is here mentioned prior to her formal introduction (chap.17).

The identification of this power, and its fall, are the great subjects of chapters 17 and 18, respectively. For reasons to be given later, *historicist* interpreters for several centuries tended to equate the Babylon of the Apocalypse with papal Rome. Halley suggests that the reason the first mention of Babylon is referring to the end of its career is that Babylon

⌛ PRETERIST

With this first reference in Revelation to that great city **Babylon,** a symbol is introduced over which *preterists* are not in full agreement. For reasons that shall be listed later (see note at 17:1ff.), J. Stuart Russell and others (Terry, Chilton, etc.) believe Babylon to be a symbolic designation for Jerusalem. Chilton says that "the evidence that the prophetic **Babylon** was Jerusalem is nothing short of overwhelming." Milton Terry concurs:

> As Jesus in Matthew 24:14 said that the end of this city [Jerusalem] and the pre-Messianic age would follow the preaching of the Gospel among the nations, so in this Apocalypse the proclamation

⧖ FUTURIST

Ryrie writes:

> The repetition of "is fallen" empha-
> sizes the certainty of the utter de-
> struction of Babylon. This is
> anticipatory since Babylon's actu-
> al fall is connected with the out-
> pouring of the seventh [bowl].

Walvoord suggests that Babylon, in the first half of the Tribulation period, may be the apostate church, which will be destroyed in the middle of the Tribulation. In the second half of the Tribulation, Walvoord is more inclined to see Babylon as an actual city—perhaps Rome, or even a rebuilt Babylon on its historic site on the Euphrates—which is to be destroyed at the end of the Great Tribulation.

Ironside holds to the view that Babylon is a religious system:

> Just as Babylon of old was the
> fountainhead of idolatry, so is
> mystic Babylon today the mother
> of all false religious teaching in
> Christianity. In the time of the
> end it will be headed up in one
> great false church—that worldly

⧖ IDEALIST

Wilson sees **Babylon** as a symbol for human society organized against God. Hendriksen considers it to represent "the world as centre of seduction."

Wilcock writes: "Suffice it to say for the present that Babylon is another picture of the beast from the sea, the world system which is in rebellion against God."

Beale explains:

> In the Apocalypse, Rome and all
> wicked world systems take on the
> symbolic name "Babylon the
> Great." Indeed, this symbolic in-
> terpretation of Babylon is assured
> beyond reasonable doubt by the
> prophecies of God's judgment on
> historical Babylon, which fore-
> told that Babylon "will be deso-
> late forever" and "not rise again"
> (Jer. 28:39 LXX; Jer. 50:39–40;
> 51:24–26, 62–64; so also Isa.
> 13:19–22).[4]

Ancient Babylon was the center of idolatry, the occult, immorality, and rebellion against God. It thus became a fitting symbol for the rebellious world

⌛ HISTORICIST *(continued)*

was such a horrible thing that the writer thought best to assure his readers that it would have only Temporary Existence before he undertook to tell them about it.

On the charge that **she has made all nations drink of the wine of the wrath of her fornication,** Clarke writes:

> There is an allusion here to a custom of impure women, who give love potions to those whom they wish to seduce and bind to their will; and these potions are generally of an intoxicating nature, greatly inflaming the blood, and disturbing the intellect . . . And papal Rome has been not less active in disseminating her superstitions. She has given her rituals, but not the everlasting gospel, to most nations of the earth.

The judgment alluded to briefly in this verse is anticipatory of the judgment series upon Babylon that is detailed in chapter 16. ⌛

⌛ PRETERIST *(continued)*

of the fall of **Babylon the Great** follows immediately after that of the eternal Gospel.

Russell also identifies Babylon as Jerusalem:

> This is plainly another declaration of the same impending catastrophe, only more distinctly indicating the doom of the guilty city—the great criminal about to be brought to judgment.

David S. Clark, on the other hand, takes the view of many others (Moses Stuart, Jay Adams, etc.) that the increased attention to Babylon in the second half of Revelation should be taken as a mystic reference to Rome, the persecuting city after the fall of Jerusalem:

> Rome was called Babylon because [she was] sort of a duplicate of old Babylon, in that she was a persecutor of God's people, she was intensely idolatrous, and she was doomed to overthrow for her sins.

Further arguments over the identification of this Babylon must await the commentary on chapter 17. At this point it is clear that the fall of a great persecuting city is jubilantly announced by a heavenly messenger. ⌛

⧗ FUTURIST *(continued)*

church, which has proved so unworthy and false to her Lord, is to be broken absolutely to pieces, to be utterly destroyed.

Mounce sees in Babylon a reference to "Rome, a contemporary Babylon, a symbol for the spirit of godlessness, the final manifestation of secular humanism." Ladd says that Babylon stands for "the capital city of the final apostate civilization, the symbol of human society organized politically, economically, and religiously in opposition to and in defiance of God."

⧗ IDEALIST *(continued)*

system, which in every age opposes God's kingdom, but which is already judged and fallen, so far as God's eternal perspective is concerned.

The compound expression **the wine of the wrath of her fornication** combines two metaphors. On the one hand, as a harlot (cf. chap. 17), the intoxication of her paramours is a part of her seduction. On the other, she and her clients will be made drunken with the contents of God's cup of wrath (v. 10; cf. Jer. 25:15).

FIRE AND BRIMSTONE FOR THE BEAST'S WORSHIPERS

REVELATION 14:9–12

[9]Then a third angel followed them, saying with a loud voice, "If anyone worships the beast and his image, and receives his mark on his forehead or on his hand, [10]he himself shall also drink of the wine of the wrath of God, which is poured out full strength into the cup of His indignation. He shall be tormented with fire and brimstone in the presence of the holy angels and in the presence of the Lamb. [11]And the smoke of their torment ascends forever and ever; and they have no rest day or night, who worship the beast and his image, and whoever receives the mark of his name. [12]Here is the patience of the saints; here are those who keep the commandments of God and the faith of Jesus.

⌛ HISTORICIST

Those who have demonstrated their allegiance to the papacy by taking the distinctive **mark** (v. 9—see notes at 13:16–18) will suffer eternal damnation. Babylon, in chapter 17, will be seen as holding a "cup full of abominations and the filthiness of her fornication" (17:4), by which "the inhabitants of the earth were made drunk" (17:2), and she herself is "drunk with the blood of the saints" (17:6). In this vision, her followers, who have drunk from "the cup of her fornication," ultimately drink of the **wine of the wrath of God** from **the cup of His indignation** (v. 10). One cannot drink from the cup of the

⌛ PRETERIST

Though this may be a reference to persons suffering eternally in hell (a traditional association with these verses), the imagery might refer to the permanent destruction of the city Babylon—whether Jerusalem or Rome—and those in it who participated in its worship of the beast. That they must **drink of the wine of the wrath of God** (v. 10) may allude to the practice of giving wine to condemned criminals just before they were crucified (cf. Mark 15:23). In this case it would be a sign of impending death and judgment. That **the smoke of their torment ascends forever and**

386

⌛ FUTURIST

The judgment described is for anyone who **worships the beast and his image** (v. 9, 11). As Tenney says,

> A clear line of division is drawn on the basis of worship: those who worship the beast (14:11), and those who worship God (14:7). The primary emphasis of Revelation is on this point.

The eternal judgment upon those who take the mark of the beast is declared here in graphic detail. There are not many passages in the Bible that bring out the horrors of ultimate damnation as intensely as does this one. The offenders will be made to **drink of the wine of the wrath of God** (v. 10). It was common practice in all ancient Mediterranean societies to dilute wine with several parts water before drinking it, but not in this case. The wrath of God for these people will be served up **full strength,** meaning "this wine is not to be tempered with water. There is no element of grace or hope or compassion blended with the judgment" (Biederwolf).

Verse 11 strongly affirms that those who reject God's mercy will experience an eternity of torment to regret it. Because there is a call for **patience** on the part of the **saints** (v. 12), Mounce maintains that this is "a warning to both the pagan population (vv. 15, 17) and those within the church (vv. 12, 13)" of God's eternal wrath on those who deny faith in Christ and worship the beast.

⌛ IDEALIST

The phrase **poured out full strength** (v. 10), as a modifier for **the wine** of God's wrath, presents a paradoxical expression. Two literal translations are "mixed undiluted" or "mingled unmixed." The first word refers to the ancient practice of mixing wine with spices to increase its potency. The second word refers to the practice of diluting wine with water, a customary practice at meals. The wrath of God is thus poured out unmitigated and undiminished—i.e., not tempered with mercy—for those who remain in the camp of the beast to the end. Hendriksen writes:

> Here on earth this wrath is still mixed with grace. The Lord makes His sun to rise on the evil and the good, and sends rain on the just and the unjust (Matt. 5:45). By and by, in hell, the wrath will be unmixed.

No passage in Scripture more vividly portrays the traditional doctrine of eternal torment in hell than do verses 10 and 11 here. While we find similar language in a description of the temporal downfall of Edom (cf. Isa. 34:10), where it is no doubt symbolic, that does not prevent this passage from using the terms literally. Hobbs observes: "reality is always greater than the symbol, whether it be of heaven or hell. If hell is not real fire, then it is something worse than fire."

⌛ HISTORICIST *(continued)*

harlot without also drinking from the cup of God's indignation.

Clarke sees in these words "an allusion to the poisoned cup that certain criminals were obliged to drink, on which ensued speedy death."

The reference to **fire and brimstone** (v. 10) may be literal, though Barnes, Vitringa, Grotius, and others think it to be the eternal pangs of remorse and conscience.

Clarke points out, without committing one way or another on the literalness of the fire and brimstone, "an allusion to the punishment of Sodom and Gomorrah for their unnatural crimes." Also of the eternally ascending smoke: "Still an allusion to the destruction of Sodom and Gomorrah." 🔲

⌛ PRETERIST *(continued)*

ever (v. 11) may not be intended literally, as Chilton explains:

> The imagery of their permanent doom is taken from the utter destruction of Sodom and Gomorrah by fire and brimstone, when "the smoke of the land ascended like the smoke of a furnace" (Gen. 19:28; cf. its symbolic use in Isa. 34:9–10, describing the fall of Edom).

If one argues that Sodom's smoke did not ascend "forever and ever," it should be noted that Jude spoke of Sodom and Gomorrah as "suffering the vengeance of eternal fire" (Jude 7). The context in Jude does not indicate that the verse refers to the personal damnation of the inhabitants, but rather the visible destruction of the cities as a historical witness to God's wrath toward sin.

Chilton compares the expression **they have no rest day or night** (v. 11) to the ceaseless activity of the four living creatures, who "do not rest day or night" in praising God (Rev. 4:8). 🔲

⧗ IDEALIST *(continued)*

This punishment of the wicked should provide an incentive for **the patience of the saints** (v. 12). Swete writes: "The Caesar-cult supplied the Saints with a test of loyalty which strengthened and matured those who were worthy of the name."

BLESSED ARE THE DEAD

REVELATION 14:13

¹³Then I heard a voice from heaven saying to me, "Write: 'Blessed are the dead who die in the Lord from now on.'" "Yes," says the Spirit, "that they may rest from their labors, and their works follow them."

⧗ HISTORICIST

The declaration of a blessing on those **who die in the Lord from now on** is not intended to suggest that those who had died in Christ in previous times were not blessed. Particularly during times of great persecution that are to come, however, those who escape them by Christian death are to be regarded as blessed, as Barnes writes:

> It is much to be able to say of the dead that they are 'blessed.' There is much in death that is sad; we so much dread it by nature; it cuts us off from so much that is dear to us; it blasts so many hopes; and the grave is so cold and cheerless a resting-place, that we owe much to a system of religion which will enable us to say and to feel, that it is a blessed thing to die. Assuredly we should be grateful for any system of religion which will enable us thus to speak of those who are dead; which will enable us, with corresponding feeling, to look forward to our own departure from this world.

⧗ PRETERIST

The emphasis of this announcement appears to be upon the phrase **from now on,** in contrast to some previous time. It is possible that this simply means that there is blessing for the righteous "from the point of death onwards" (i.e., "to die is gain . . . to be with Christ, which is far better"—Phil. 1:21, 23), as David S. Clark writes:

> Yes, though you are thrown to the lions in the amphitheatre, though you are daubed with pitch and burned for a torchlight at a garden party, though your head rolls from the block at the stroke of the executioner's axe,—yes even thus you are blessed a thousand times above your persecutors.

If the fall of Jerusalem has been the subject of this chapter to this point, then it would follow naturally that this passage considers the impact of the Old Covenant's passing upon the postmortem experience of believers. Remembering that "the way into the Holiest of All was not yet made manifest while the

⧗ FUTURIST

This verse contains the second beatitude of seven to be found in Revelation. The others are at 1:3; 16:15; 19:9; 20:6; 22:7, 14.

There is a general teaching of Scripture that those who **die in the Lord** are blessed, for to live is Christ and to die is gain (Phil. 1:21). The modifying phrase, **from now on,** seems to speak of those who die after a certain point in history: namely, those who die as martyrs in the most trying days of the Great Tribulation.

To those facing this ultimate test of loyalty to Christ, the words of Jesus to His disciples are relevant:

> If anyone desires to come after Me, let him deny himself, and take up his cross, and follow Me. For whoever desires to save his life will lose it, but whoever loses his life for My sake will find it. For what profit is it to a man if he gains the whole world, and loses his own soul? (Matt.16:24–26)

Mounce comments that "faithfulness to Christ issues in martyrdom, but the faithful dead are blessed." "Those who die in the Lord," says Walvoord, "are described as resting from their labors with the rewards of their work following them." ⧗

⧗ IDEALIST

Martyrdom is not specifically mentioned in this verse (only dying **in the Lord**, which is more general. However, that martyrdom is a leading motif of Revelation cannot be denied, the earliest references to the subject occurring in 2:10, 13, and the last reference in 20:4–6. Those who die faithful to Christ, especially in martyrdom, are the "overcomers" or "conquerors" commended at the end of each of the seven letters (chs.2–3). "They overcame [Satan] . . . and they did not love their lives to the death" (12:11). Of these conquerors, Bauckham writes:

> Christians are expected to conquer as Christ did. Each of the messages to the seven churches in chapters 2–3 had included a promise of eschatological reward to 'the one who conquers' . . . and the last of these . . . reads: 'To the one who conquers, I will give a place with me on my throne, just as I myself conquered and sat down with my Father on his throne' (3:21).[5]

The unidentified **voice from heaven** proclaiming this second of seven beatitudes may be that of the Lamb. The declaration presents the blessed rest that dying Christians enter **from now on,** meaning either from the time of Christ's sacrificial death on the cross, or possibly, from the point of their own death onwards. The Spirit's voice answers in affirmation. ⧗

391

⧗ HISTORICIST *(continued)*

It is notable that **their works follow them,** since there is little else that will:

> [The man who dies] can take with him none of his gold, his lands, his raiment; none of the honors of this life; none of the means of sensual gratification. All that will go with him will be his character, and the results of his conduct here, and, in this respect, eternity will be but a prolongation of the present life. (Barnes) ✒

⧗ PRETERIST *(continued)*

first tabernacle was still standing" (Heb. 9:8), Chilton writes:

> By the work of Christ, heaven has been opened to God's people. The *limbus patrum,* the afterlife abode of the Old Testament faithful (the "bosom of Abraham" of Luke 16:22), has been unlocked and its inhabitants freed (cf. 1 Pet. 3:19; 4:6). Death is now the entrance to communion in glory with Christ and the departed saints. ✒

THE HARVEST AND THE VINTAGE

REVELATION 14:14—20

[14]Then I looked, and behold, a white cloud, and on the cloud sat One like the Son of Man, having on His head a golden crown, and in His hand a sharp sickle. [15]And another angel came out of the temple, crying with a loud voice to Him who sat on the cloud, "Thrust in your sickle and reap, for the time has come for You to reap, for the harvest of the earth is ripe." [16]So He who sat on the cloud thrust in His sickle on the earth, and the earth was reaped. [17]Then another angel came out of the temple which is in heaven, he also having a sharp sickle. [18]And another angel came out from the altar, who had power over fire, and he cried with a loud cry to him who had the sharp sickle, saying, "Thrust in your sharp sickle and gather the clusters of the vine of the earth, for her grapes are fully ripe." [19]So the angel thrust his sickle into the earth and gathered the vine of the earth, and threw it into the great winepress of the wrath of God. [20]And the winepress was trampled outside the city, and blood came out of the winepress, up to the horses' bridles, for one thousand six hundred furlongs.

⌛ HISTORICIST

Adam Clarke writes:

> It is supposed that, from this verse to the end of the chapter, the destruction of Rome is represented under the symbols of harvest and vintage; images very frequent among the ancient prophets, by which they represented the destruction and excision of nations. See Joel 3: 12–14; Isa. 17: 5; and Matt. 13:37.

This picture of harvest is the consummation of all things, when the enemies of the church will be cut off. The

⌛ PRETERIST

The vision of Christ **on the cloud** (v. 14) is not referring to His Second Coming, since He is not said to be "coming" on the cloud, but seated, as enthroned in glory. The vision depicts judgment action pertaining to the fall of Jerusalem in the first century. Chilton writes:

> These verses [14–16] form the centerpiece of the whole section, verses 6–20. We have seen three angels making proclamation to the Land of Israel (vv. 6–13); three more will appear, to perform symbolic actions over the Land (vv. 15, 17–20).

⏳ FUTURIST

All are agreed that the vintage here is a horrendous judgment upon the wicked, but opinions are divided as to the meaning of the grain harvest. Is it a picture of judgment or is it a depiction of the ingathering of saints before judgment falls?

Ryrie, Mounce, Gaebelein, Seiss, Petingill, and others, take the first view. Ryrie writes: "The picture here is that all the false religion of man is fully ripe and ready for harvest."

With reference to **One like the Son of Man** (v. 14), most commentators (e.g., Walvoord, Gaebelein, Ironside, Weidner, Moorehead, Ryrie, and others) agree that this is none other than Christ Himself.

That an **angel** (v. 15) would give commands to Christ does not seem appropriate, until we observe that this angel **came out of the temple,** suggesting that it is simply bearing a message from God to the Son.

In verse 16, the harvest, presumably of grain, is accomplished. A number of expositors believe that this reaping is to be distinguished from the gathering of the vintage in verses 17–20. This ingathering, they believe, refers to the gathering of the elect. Wordsworth writes: "It is the manifestation of God's love in the gathering of the good wheat into the heavenly barn." This view is also taken by Ironside, Tenney, Weidner, Moorehead, Biederwolf, and Ladd.

⏳ IDEALIST

This is the third picture of the final judgment at Christ's coming (cf. 6:12–17; 11:15–18). The church is first raptured (v. 16), then the wicked are gathered to judgment (vv. 17–20).

There are not many who will object to the identification of the one seen sitting on the cloud (v. 14) with Christ. Wilson speaks for nearly all when he says: "This description could apply to no one but Christ."

Some have objected to the seeming inappropriateness of Christ being told what to do by a mere **angel** (v. 15). However, the objection does not give proper weight to the fact that the angel proceeds directly from **the temple,** i.e., the presence of God. Plummer writes:

> The angel acts as the messenger of the will of God to Christ in his capacity as the Son of man, because the command is one concerning the times and seasons which the Father hath kept in his own power.

That the first harvest is that of grain, in contrast to that of the grapes which follows (vv. 17–20), is likely, and agrees with the order of events in the Jewish agricultural year. Some (e.g., Dana, Summers, Moffatt) think the entire picture of harvest is concerned with judgment upon the wicked, though Wilson and Beckwith think the grain harvest includes the harvest of both the righteous and the wicked at the end of the age (cf.

⌛ HISTORICIST *(continued)*

idea already has been presented earlier in the book, through various forms and images. Here the image is that of two harvests.

Halley points out that this chapter opened with a vision of the "firstfruits" of the harvest, and ends with the complete grain harvest and grape gathering. In Israel, the wheat was harvested in the spring and the fruit in the late summer. The command, **Thrust in Your sickle and reap** (v. 15), echoes the words of Joel 3:13: "Put in the sickle, for the harvest is ripe."

This undoubtedly refers to the ingathering of the wheat harvest, and is a picture of the reception of the righteous into the kingdom. "The design is to state that the Redeemer will gather in a great and glorious harvest, and by this assurance to sustain the hearts of his people in times of trial and persecution" (Barnes).

Next we see the harvest of fruit— **the vine of the earth** (v. 18)—which is crushed for wine, as an evident image of the crushing of the wicked. Halley writes: "The 'Harvest' seems to be of the Saved. The 'Vintage,' of the Lost The 'Winepress' is of the Wrath of God on the Wicked."

We have previously read that the wicked shall "drink of the wine of the wrath of God" (v. 10). The metaphor shifts here so that the wine from the press is actually the **blood** (v. 20) of

⌛ PRETERIST *(continued)*

There is some question whether the harvest (vv. 14–16) and the gathering of the vine for treading (vv. 17–20) symbolize different events or are two ways of describing the same event. David S. Clark favors the latter option:

> Does the first scene represent the gathering of the righteous and the second represent the gathering of the wicked? Or do both stand for the judgment of the wicked? Since we are dealing with the judgment of an evil power, the latter view may be best.

If, however, the best reason for identifying both parts of the vision with punitive judgment is that "we are dealing with the judgment of an evil power," then we might well question the conclusion, since the whole book being about the judgment of an evil power has not prevented the intrusion of visions which show the brighter side of things, viz., the salvation of the righteous (cf. chaps. 7, 12, 19–22). Many expositors believe that the reaping of verses 14–16 has to do with the salvation of the believers, or their gathering to safety (the escape of the Judean Christians to Pella in AD 66–70), while the vintage vision of verses 17–20 depicts the judgment upon the city of Jerusalem in AD 70. Russell expresses this view:

> As the "harvest of the land" denotes the salvation of the faithful

⏳ FUTURIST *(continued)*

Moorehead, taking a midtribulational view of the Rapture, writes:

> 1 Thess. 4:13–18 is another account of this majestic scene, the gathering of God's people into His everlasting kingdom by resurrection and translation. This does not occur before the Great Tribulation, but it does occur before the wrath of God is poured out.

The vintage of the earth, in verses 17–20, is collected by an angel with a sickle, rather than, as in the first case, by the Son of Man with His sickle. When the angel lowers his sickle, it comes up bearing upon its blade **the vine of the earth** which is then cast into the **winepress of the wrath of God** (v. 19), where it is **trampled outside the city** (v. 20). What is the vine of the earth? Ironside writes: "this vine is apostate Israel." Others, like Walvoord, take the vine of the earth to be a more general reference to the wicked, regardless of race. Walvoord writes: "This is obviously a picture of the ultimate judgment of the wickedness of men at the time of the second coming of Christ."

Ryrie writes: "In verse 20 this judgment is specified not as hell but as something that occurs on earth (" trodden without the city"—Jerusalem). It apparently is a reference to the war of Armageddon (cf. 19:17–19)."

⏳ IDEALIST *(continued)*

Matt. 13:30, 39), and the vintage of the grapes is a close-up view of the judgment of the wicked in particular. Beckwith writes: "The figure is comprehensive, including in a word the whole process of the winding up of the ages, and the recompense of both the good and the bad." Edward McDowell thinks this may, in addition to being a picture of the end of the age, apply to God's activity in history as well. He writes:

> God is continuously executing judgment among men separating the righteous from the unrighteous, *calling* his own to himself and sending the wicked to the place of perdition.[6]

Most (e.g., Alford, Milligan, Swete, Hobbs, Wilcock, Hailey, etc.) understand the first harvest to be the eschatological ingathering of the righteous. This occurs at the appropriate time in history, namely, **when the harvest of the earth is ripe** (v. 15). This recalls a number of passages in the New Testament that employ a similar metaphor. Jesus' parable of the growing seed emphasized that the harvest at the end of the age would happen "when the grain ripens" (Mark 4:29). James wrote:

> Therefore be patient, brethren, until the coming of the Lord. See how the farmer waits for the precious fruit of the earth, waiting patiently for it until it receives the

⧗ HISTORICIST *(continued)*

those being judged. Here at the end of the world, the picture shows the destruction of the wicked on the last day. That the blood is said to flow **up to the horses' bridles (v. 20)** is, no doubt, intended to be a hyperbole—for the likes of which there are literary precedents. Clarke writes:

> A hyperbolical expression, to denote a great effusion of blood. The Jews said, "When Hadrian besieged the city called Bitter, he slew so many that the horses waded in blood up to their mouths."

The distance, one thousand six hundred furlongs (v. 20) has been variously interpreted. The distance (about two hundred miles) is taken by some to be the breadth of Italy, but others do not look at this as a literal dimension. Some take the number 1,600 to be symbolic of the universality of the judgment, as it is 40 x 40 (40 being the number of judgment). Barnes takes neither of these views, but believes that the details are given merely for effect, to convey the enormity of the disaster:

> The idea is, that there would be a slaughter so great, as it were, as to produce a lake or sea of blood; that the enemies of the church would be completely and finally overthrown, and that the church, therefore, delivered from all its enemies, would be triumphant. ⧗

⧗ PRETERIST *(continued)*

people of God, so the "vintage of the land" denotes the destruction of His enemies . . . The harvest corresponds with the reaping of the wheat and its safe gathering into the barn [Matt. 13:30]; in other words, it is the fulfillment of the prediction, "The Son of man shall send his angels, and they shall gather together his elect from the four winds" (Matt. 24:31–34), an event which was to take place before the passing of that generation.

Chilton points out that "the emphasis falls not on judgment but on blessing, the gathering in of the elect . . . The word for gather is, literally, *to synagogue.*" Some have thought it strange that Christ, the Lord over all angels, would take instructions from an angel who urges Him to **Thrust in Your sickle and reap** (v. 15). However, the angel simply represents the church praying in obedience to Christ, who commanded that believers "pray the Lord of the harvest to send out laborers into His harvest" (Matt. 9:38). In response to the request, laborers are in fact sent and **the earth (or *land*) was reaped** (v. 16). Next, the sickle is applied to **the vine of the earth (or *land*)** (v. 19), which is an image of Israel (cf. Isa. 5:1–7), and its treading represents the slaughter of the inhabitants of the land, especially Jerusalem, by the Romans. As Russell points out:

⌛ FUTURIST *(continued)*

Gaebelein concurs: "The battle of Armageddon comes into view for the first time in verse 20."

It is difficult to decide how literally the description of the carnage should be taken. That the blood of the slain should "come" **up to the horses' bridles** (v. 20) may mean that there are rivers of blood whose depth reach this measure (which Ryrie estimates at about four and a half feet). Ryrie believes this to be the correct understanding.

Walvoord does not feel that this understanding is likely to be correct. He writes:

> It seems quite impossible that the blood will flow in depth as high as the horses' bridles, and it is better to understand this simply as a liberal spattering of blood.

Biederwolf summarizes:

> The expression is meant perhaps as a mere measure, as Simcox says,—that any horseman riding there would find his horse bridle-deep in blood. Some have conceived of the blood as having been merely splashed as high up as the bridles of the horses. The idea in any case is that an exceedingly great slaughter is predicted.

The **city** (v. 20), outside of which this slaughter takes place, is thought by most (e.g., Walvoord, Ryrie, Gaebelein,

⌛ IDEALIST *(continued)*

early and latter rain [i.e., until it ripens]. (James 5:7)

Hendriksen writes:

> Matthew 3:12 is a sufficient commentary: "And he will gather his wheat into his garner." Thus the sickle was thrown to the earth, and the earth was reaped and the elect were gathered to Him.

Since the grapes gathered in the second phase of this harvest (vv. 17ff.) are thereafter **trampled** (v. 20), it is clear that they represent the wicked, who are judged at the coming of Christ. Hendriksen writes: "The vine of the earth symbolizes the entire multitude of evil men; its grapes are the individual unbelievers."

To participate in the second phase of reaping, **another angel** comes from **the temple** (v. 17), and yet **another angel . . . from the altar** (v. 18). Beckwith writes: "He comes from the altar, upon which was offered the incense accompanying the prayers of the saints for judgment."

Wilcock writes:

> The grape harvest, which is destined for the wine press of God's wrath and produces a monstrous tide of blood, is the reaping of the wicked; the land will be a blood bath from end to end (perhaps 1,600 *stadia*, or furlongs, means

⏳ PRETERIST *(continued)*

The angel commissioned to destroy does not gather the clusters, but cuts down the vine itself, and casts it altogether into the "great wine-press of the wrath of God." The wine-press is trodden; and this is represented as taking place outside the city, as the sin-offering was burned outside the camp, and as the criminal was executed outside the gate, being accursed (Heb. xiii. 11–13).

The identification of this imagery with the destruction of Jerusalem can hardly be missed, since the same language is used concerning the fall of the same city to the Babylonians in 586 BC: "The Lord trampled as in a winepress the virgin daughter of Judah" (Lam. 1:15). The **blood** (v. 20) of these grapes flows throughout the land of Israel (probably the allusion intended by the **one thousand six hundred furlongs**) in a great sea of carnage. Russell writes:

> This is terrible in symbol and almost literal in its historic truth. It was a people that was thus 'trampled' in the fury of divine wrath. Where was there ever such a sea of blood as was shed in that exterminating war of Vespasian and of Titus? The carnage, as related by Josephus, exceeds all that is recorded in the sanguinary annals of warfare . . . If we had not the testimony of an eyewitness, who certainly could have no interest in

⏳ FUTURIST *(continued)*

Ironside, Weidner, Moorehead, Simcox) to be Jerusalem.

The breadth of the bloodbath, **one thousand six hundred furlongs** (v. 20), is said to be 175 miles (Ryrie) or 200 miles (Walvoord). To what this measurement applies is not stated. Ironside writes: "This is said to be the actual length of the land of Palestine." Though this view is widely held, Biederwolf points out that the actual length of Israel, north to south, is "160 Roman miles—140 English miles." He believes that, since four is "the world number," 1,600 should be understood as "a square number merely denoting completeness and universality; four times four hundred, or four times four times one hundred, or forty times forty."

Walvoord has another approach. He writes:

> The area covered, 1,600 furlongs, is apparently 200 miles, and specifies that the area within a 200 mile radius from Jerusalem will be the center of the final carnage where the armies of the world will be gathered at the time of the second coming of Christ . . . There is no reason . . . for limiting the battle to the precise boundary of the holy land, and there is really no serious problem here in taking the distance literally.

⏳ IDEALIST *(continued)*

the length of Canaan, the 200 miles "from Dan to Beersheba").

The detail that this trampling takes place **outside the city** (v. 20) is explained by Hobbs by the unimaginative suggestion that "This was the usual place for the winepress." Wilson suggests, however, that the figure "probably refers to the exclusion of the wicked from the society of the redeemed."

Many suggestions have been made as to the meaning of the **one thousand six hundred furlongs** (v. 20). The number is taken by many (e.g., Hendriksen, Wilson, and many others) to be symbolic, derived from the square of four (the number of the earth) multiplied by the square of ten (referring to completeness). Plummer tells us that this number conveys the idea of "completeness as regards the created world, and the inability of anyone to escape God's judgment." ⏳

PRETERIST *(continued)*

exaggerating the ruin of his people or defaming their character, it would scarcely be possible to believe that these symbols were not overcharged. But no one can read that tragic story without recognizing there the very transactions that are here written in symbol, and which amply attest the reality and truth of the prophecy.

Carrington writes:

In AD 70 the Vine of Israel is cut down and trampled in the Winepress; but this destruction is the culmination of a process which has lasted over forty years; it began Outside the City, when one whom they despised and rejected trod the Winepress alone, and of the people there was none with Him. It was in that moment that Jerusalem fell.

THE SONG OF MOSES AND THE LAMB

REVELATION 15:1—4

[1]Then I saw another sign in heaven, great and marvelous: seven angels having the seven last plagues, for in them the wrath of God is complete. [2]And I saw something like a sea of glass mingled with fire, and those who have the victory over the beast, over his image and over his mark and over the number of his name, standing on the sea of glass, having harps of God. [3]They sing the song of Moses, the servant of God, and the song of the Lamb, saying, "Great and marvelous are Your works, Lord God Almighty! Just and true are Your ways, O King of the saints! [4]Who shall not fear You, O Lord, and glorify Your name? For You alone are holy. For all nations shall come and worship before You, For Your judgments have been manifested."

⌛ HISTORICIST

This chapter is closely connected to the previous chapter and introduces the chapter that follows. Clarke makes the following structural observation:

> Under the emblems of harvest and vintage God's judgments on the enemies of His Church have already been pointed out; but these are further signified by the seven [bowls], which are called *the seven last plagues* of God. The *seven last plagues* appear to fall under the seventh and last trumpet. As the seventh seal contained the seven trumpets, so the seventh trumpet contains the seven [bowls]. And as seven angels sounded the seven trumpets, so seven angels are appointed to pour out the seven

⌛ PRETERIST

This chapter gives a prelude to the judgment of the seven bowls. There was a heavenly scene of victory in chapters 4–5, just prior to the breaking of the seven seals, and a similar prelude in 8:1–6 anticipated the seven trumpets.

The bowl judgments are said to be the **seven last plagues** (v. 1), and they will bring about the final end of the once faithful city Jerusalem. The time frame is the end of the Jewish War (AD 70). As Chilton writes:

> There is no reason to assume that these must be the "last" plagues in an ultimate, absolute, and universal sense; rather, in terms of the specifically limited purpose and scope of the Book of Revelation,

⌛ FUTURIST

The vision depicting the final series of judgments is preceded by this heavenly vision. The fact that the **sea of glass** is now seen to be **mingled with fire** (v. 2) is explained by Walvoord: "Here the sea mingled with fire speaks of divine judgment proceeding from God's holiness." Ryrie presents another view: "Here [the sea of glass] is mingled with fire, perhaps referring to the fiery persecution which these people had suffered under the beast."

The vision next presents **those who have the victory over the beast** (v. 2). To the dispensationalist, this cannot refer to the church, which is raptured prior to the rise of the Antichrist, so these must be those who are converted during the Tribulation period. Most (e.g., Walvoord, Gaebelein, Ironside, Ladd) understand these people to have been put to death by the beast, but living in heaven, either as disembodied spirits, or as Ironside suggests, having "been raised from the dead, and raptured during the tribulation period." Tenney comments:

> Whether they are martyred dead whose spirits live before God, or whether they are a translated group is not stated. One thing is noticeable: the concluding retribution does not fall until they have been removed from the scene. They may experience the wrath of the devil (12:12) and the persecu-

⌛ IDEALIST

The judgment represented by the upcoming vision is referred to as the **last plagues** (v. 1). Many take this to indicate the last judgment acts in history, i.e., at the end of time. Alford writes:

> There can be no doubt here, not only that the series reaches on to the time of the end, but that the whole of it is to be placed very close to the same time. It belongs by its very conditions to the time of the end.

Wilson writes:

> The entire vision (chaps. 15, 16) is a great and marvelous portent because the wrath of God reaches its goal in the endtime judgements [sic] which are symbolized by these last seven plagues.

Hendriksen, on the other hand, thinks that the *finality* of these plagues is not with reference to history in general, but to individual sinners who have not repented following the trumpet warnings that God has sent. Every unrepentant sinner eventually exhausts God's patience, bringing final judgment upon his life. Hendriksen writes:

> Throughout the history of the world God's final wrath again and again reveals itself: now it strikes this one, then another . . . Thus conceived, we notice that the vision of the bowls of wrath runs parallel with all the others and

⧗ HISTORICIST *(continued)*

[bowls], angels being always the ministers of Providence. This chapter contains the opening vision which is preparatory to the pouring out of the vials.

As in chapter 14, we see visions calculated to reassure the church of its ultimate triumph in God's purposes, and of the final destruction of the antichristian power (the papacy) that has harassed the saints through much of the church's history. This latter concept is introduced by the appearance of the **seven angels having the seven last plagues** (v. 1), whose role is depicted in chapter 16. That these are announced to be the "last plagues" does not necessarily mean the closing of the affairs of the world, but those final judgments that will wind up the affairs respecting the beast and his image.

We recognize the scene of the vision to be the throne room of God because of the reappearance of the **sea of glass** (v. 2—seen before the throne in Rev. 4:6). There is the added detail that the sea of glass is **mingled with fire,** suggesting the judgment ready to proceed from God's throne. Standing before the throne are **those who have the victory over the beast** (v. 2), who represent "those who in the long dominion of the Papal power, and amidst all its arts and corruptions—its threats and persecutions—had remained steadfast in the truth, and who might thus be said to have gained *a victory"* (Barnes).

⧗ PRETERIST *(continued)*

they comprise the final outpouring of God's wrath, His great cosmic Judgment against Jerusalem, abolishing the Old Covenant world-order once and for all.

A singing company is seen in heaven, having gotten **the victory over the beast** (v. 2)—probably through martyrdom. Their song (or songs) is/are characterized as **the song of Moses . . . and the song of the Lamb** (v. 3). It is, of course, the Lamb, and not Moses, who was instrumental in the deliverance of which they sing. To most commentators, the reference to Moses calls to mind again the exodus and reminds us that Jerusalem had become the new Egypt (Rev. 11:8). The original "song of Moses" was the song of deliverance sung by the Israelites when they found themselves permanently free from their former oppressor (cf. Exodus 15). As Egypt had lost "horse and rider" in the Red Sea, so Jerusalem's horses had been bridle-deep in a virtual sea of blood (a truly *red* sea!—Rev. 14:20).

While most commentators refer the "song of Moses" to that celebration of the Israelites upon their escape from Egypt, in Exodus 15, yet few recall that there was a second "song of Moses" recorded in Deuteronomy 32—a song very often quoted, or alluded to, in the New Testament.[7] As the earlier song rejoiced in *deliverance* for

FUTURIST *(continued)*

tion of the beast (13:15), but they do not experience the wrath of God.

Have we seen these people before? Gaebelein thinks they are the martyr-harpers seen in Revelation 14:2–3. Ironside thinks they "are, perhaps, identical with the two witnesses of chapter 11." Petingill identifies them with the innumerable company in Revelation 7:9. Weidner and Moorehead combine the opinions of Gaebelein and Petingill.

Their song is called **the song of Moses,** which recalls the Exodus, and also **the song of the Lamb** (v. 3). Walvoord writes:

> The fact that "song" . . . is repeated with a definite article in both cases would lead to the conclusion that two songs are in view, rather than one, both being sung by the martyred throng. The former recounts the faithfulness of God to Israel as a nation in recognition that a large number of Israelites are among these martyred dead. The song of the Lamb speaks of redemption from sin made possible by the sacrifice of the Lamb of God, and would include all saints.

Gaebelein summarizes: "The song of Moses (Exod. xv) is the song of an earthly deliverance and the song of the Lamb concerns a spiritual deliverance."

IDEALIST *(continued)*

like them covers the entire dispensation.

That the saints are in heaven is clear from the fact that they are seen standing on the **sea of glass** (v. 2), which was earlier seen before the throne of God (4:6). Here, however, the crystal sea is said to be **mingled with fire.** Hendriksen writes that this image "symbolizes God's transparent righteousness revealed in judgments upon the wicked."

The song the redeemed sing is one song, not two. Yet it is called **the song of Moses . . . and the song of the Lamb** (v. 3) because the deliverance God wrought through Moses in the Exodus foreshadowed the salvation accomplished by Christ at the cross. Wilson writes:

> The continuity of God's saving purpose in both dispensations means that the Old Testament phrases which make up the hymn can be applied to the greater exodus which he accomplished through Christ.

The song of the redeemed predicts that **all nations shall come and worship** before God when His **judgments have been manifested** (v. 4). Lenski writes: "The teaching of Scripture is that in the end the whole universe shall acknowledge the righteousness of all God's acts and verdicts.

REVELATION 15:1–4

HISTORICIST *(continued)*

The song of the saints celebrates the justice of God in His dispensation of judgments, for they sing, **Just and true are Your ways, O King of the saints! (v. 3).** Of this theme, Clarke writes: "Every step God takes in grace or providence is according to justice, and He carefully accomplishes all His threatenings and all His promises; to this He is bound by His truth."

PRETERIST *(continued)*

Israel, the second predicted the *disasters* that would come upon them when they would later apostasize from the covenant (vv. 23–25), which apostasy reached its culmination in their rejection of the Messiah and abandoning Him to death. The predicted disasters fell in the form of the Roman invasion and destruction of the Jewish nation and religion (compare Deut. 32:32 with Rev.14:18ff.).

If this is the song referred to here, then it is set in stark contrast from "the song of the Lamb." In a sense, the fulfillment of the threats of Moses' song overlap the introduction of Christ's. The overthrow of the Old Covenant coincided with the establishing of the New Covenant.

THE ANGELS HAVING THE SEVEN LAST PLAGUES

REVELATION 15:5—8

[5]After these things I looked, and behold, the temple of the tabernacle of the testimony in heaven was opened. [6]And out of the temple came the seven angels having the seven plagues, clothed in pure bright linen, and having their chests girded with golden bands. [7]Then one of the four living creatures gave to the seven angels seven golden bowls full of the wrath of God who lives forever and ever. [8]The temple was filled with smoke from the glory of God and from His power, and no one was able to enter the temple till the seven plagues of the seven angels were completed.

⌛ HISTORICIST

The seven last plagues are contained within the seventh trumpet of 8:1, which extends to the end of secular history and the ultimate triumph of Christ. The **bowls** (v. 7) given to the angels are to be poured out in chapter 16. Though they are emptied in rapid succession in the vision, they represent earthly events that unfold over a period of two or more centuries, beginning with the French Revolution in the eighteenth century and extending to events not yet accomplished in history. As the seven trumpet judgments were sent for the destruction of pagan Rome, the events represented by the bowls of wrath are designed for the punishment and destruction of the beast, that is, papal Rome.

⌛ PRETERIST

Though the King James Version referred to the containers from which these plagues are poured as "vials," it is now generally agreed that the Greek word refers to a vessel that is more broad than tall, like a bowl. David Chilton thinks the intended picture is that of a *chalice*, defending his opinion as follows:

> I have called these seven containers **Chalices** (rather than *vials* [KJV] or *bowls* [NASV]) to emphasize their character as a "negative sacrament" . . . [The] wicked are condemned in 14:10 to "drink the *wine* of the wrath of God, which is mixed in full strength in the cup of His anger"; and, when the plagues are poured out, the "Angel of the waters" exults in the appropriate-

⧗ FUTURIST

The reason that **the temple** is opened (v. 5), as Ryrie points out, is "to reveal seven angels coming out. This emphasizes the fact that the judgments of God are not vindictive but vindicative." Ironside writes:

> The mention of the tabernacle of the testimony brings Israel again before us, and reminds us that these judgments are in order to the carrying out of God's covenant with His ancient people Israel, when the nations that have oppressed them must be punished.

At this point one of the living creatures presents the seven angels with **seven golden bowls full of the wrath of God** (v. 7). Mounce reminds us that in Revelation 5:8 "the golden bowls were full of incense representing the prayers of the saints . . . John may be calling our attention to the relationship between prayer and divine retribution." Ladd points out that these bowls of wrath are to be regarded the third woe, which is associated with the seventh trumpet. ⧗

⧗ IDEALIST

John sees that **the temple . . . in heaven was opened** (v. 5), not to grant access to worshipers, but to allow the priestlike angels of doom to emerge to receive the **seven golden bowls** of wrath from the hand of **one of the four living creatures** (v. 7). The **smoke** that filled the temple, like that which accompanied the dedication of both the tabernacle and Solomon's temple, precluded anyone being permitted to **enter the temple** (v. 8) for the time being.

Of this debarring of entry to God's presence in the temple, Milligan writes: "God cannot be approached at the moment when he is revealing Himself in all the terrors of His indignation." Moffatt writes:

> Smouldering fires of indignation are now on the point of bursting into punishment from the arsenal of anger. Hence, till the plagues are over, God's presence is unendurable. ⧗

⧗ HISTORICIST *(continued)*

John sees that the temple in heaven **was filled with smoke from the glory of God** (v. 8), recalling the times in the Old Testament when the tabernacle and the temple were visited by the Shekinah cloud. As on those occasions none could enter or minister in the sanctuary (Ex. 40:34f.; 1 Kings 8:10f.), here also we are told **no one was able to enter the temple till the seven plagues of the seven angels were completed.** "The meaning here seems to be, that no one would be permitted to enter to make intercession—to turn away his wrath—to divert him from his purpose" (Barnes). ⧉

⧗ PRETERIST *(continued)*

ness of God's justice: "For they poured out the blood of saints and prophets, and Thou hast given them blood to drink" (16:6). A few verses later, St. John returns to the image of "the cup of the wine of His fierce wrath" (16:19).

Just prior to the outpouring of the bowls, the temple fills with **smoke from the glory of God** (v. 8). This harks back to the dedication of the tabernacle (Exod. 40:34–35) and Solomon's temple (1 Kings 8:10–11), in both of which cases, as here, no one could enter the sanctuary. David S. Clark writes: "This was no doubt to show that no intercession would now avail for the doomed sinners. Their day of grace was past." ⧉

THE FIRST BOWL

REVELATION 16:1—2

[1]Then I heard a loud voice from the temple saying to the seven angels, "Go and pour out the bowls of the wrath of God on the earth." [2]So the first went and poured out his bowl upon the earth, and a foul and loathsome sore came upon the men who had the mark of the beast and those who worshiped his image.

⧗ HISTORICIST

This is the beginning of the series of calamities that have befallen and have yet to befall the papacy in the course of its gradual overthrow. The **men who had**

⧗ PRETERIST

Throughout this section, *preterists* are divided concerning the recipient of these judgments. On the one hand, as we have mentioned earlier, several

FUTURIST

Tenney observes:

> The seven bowls (chaps. 15, 16) are a closely knit series following each other in rapid succession. They parallel the trumpets in their spheres of action, but they are more intense.

From the description of the events resulting from the pouring out of the first bowl, the general question arises whether we are given a symbolic or a literal picture of the events that will transpire. Though dispensationalists prefer to follow a literal hermeneutic

IDEALIST

Since no one was able to enter the temple until the seven bowls were poured out (cf. 15:8), it must be that the **voice from the temple** giving orders to **the seven angels** (v. 1) is that of God Himself. Like the seven trumpets that sounded in chapters 8 through 11, these bowls resemble the plagues of Egypt, reminding the reader that the evil world under Satan's dominion resembles the Pharaoh's oppressive reign, from which God's people have been delivered. It has often been pointed out that the domains affected by the

HISTORICIST *(continued)*

the mark of the beast, and those who worshiped his image (v. 2) has been understood to mean "those who sustained the civil or secular power to which the Papacy gave life and strength, and from which it, in turn, received countenance and protection" (Barnes).

Robert Flemming, in the first decade of the eighteenth century, published two books from the *historicist* viewpoint, entitled, *Apocalyptic Key* and *The Rise and Fall of the Papacy*. Prior to this, about 1690, Flemming informed King William III of England that the bowls of judgment in this chapter of Revelation would begin to be poured out on the Latin kingdom in the year 1793–94, and that it would begin, if not in Italy, in France. This he calculated by using the year-for-a-day method, beginning with the decree of Justinian that made the bishop of Rome supreme over all bishops (AD 533). Counting 1,260 years forward, he predicted a particular year about a century after his own time—a year that saw the beginning of the French Revolution.

The majority of *historicist* commentators, including Elliott, Barnes, and Cuninghame, relate this vision to the French Revolution, seen as one of the major blows in modern history weakening the papal power, but not yet eradicating it entirely.

France was always more significant than most other nations to the

PRETERIST *(continued)*

expositors believe that Jerusalem remains the object of wrath here as in the earlier chapters. Others hold that, while the first half of the book dealt with Jerusalem, the second has shifted its interest to the fall of Rome, that second great persecutor (after Jerusalem) of the church. Jay Adams is among those who espouse the latter view:

> Chapter 16 describes the judgments upon the fall of Rome. The pouring out of the bowls of wrath, in section two, parallels (though in no way recapitulates) the sounding of the trumpets in section one. These two sequences alone represent judgment *action* and therefore alone predict the actual judgment *periods* upon Jerusalem and Rome respectively.

Russell, who is of the "Jerusalem" camp, writes: "It is to be observed that the area affected by these plagues is 'the land,' that is Judea, the scene of the tragedy."

Depending upon which view one takes, those who have **the mark of the beast** (v. 2) would be either the loyal citizens of the Roman Empire generally, or else just the Jews in Palestine who had rejected Christ in favor of giving their allegiance to Rome ("We have no king but Caesar!"). Assuming that one of the themes of the Apocalypse is that Jerusalem has become the new Egypt and the church the new Israel, the

FUTURIST *(continued)*

whenever possible, some become uncertain at this point in the narrative—sometimes allowing for both a literal and a symbolic interpretation. For example, Ironside writes:

> I do not profess to be able to tell you just how much we are to take as symbolic, and how much as literal, in this septenary series of judgments.

Gaebelein takes a similar approach to the question:

> While it is undoubtedly true that we have symbols also in these [bowl] judgments, it is nevertheless possible that some of these plagues may have, besides the symbolical, also a literal meaning.

On the other hand, Walvoord, Ryrie, Seiss, and others remain fairly consistent to their literalistic commitments throughout these bowl visions. Seiss writes:

> The greatest plagues of judgment of which we read in the past were those poured out upon ancient Egypt. They were literal plagues, which happened according to the terms in which they are recorded . . . The last plagues must therefore be literal too.

Some, considering the sores in the first bowl to be literal boils upon literal bodies, look to an entirely supernatural

IDEALIST *(continued)*

numbered trumpets and their corresponding bowls are the same. The obvious difference is that each of the trumpets adversely affected only a third of whatever domain they touched, whereas the bowls produce utter and total ruin. Wilcock contrasts the trumpets with the bowls, pointing out that the former "were God's warnings. The plagues poured out of the Bowls are total, because the opportunity for repentance has gone . . . These are no longer warnings but punishments."

This correlation between the trumpets and bowls suggests to Hendriksen that the two series are parallel, occuring simultaneously throughout the Christian dispensation. He writes:

> Whoever refuses to be warned by the trumpets of judgment . . . is "destroyed" by the bowls of wrath. For one individual a certain calamity may be a trumpet of judgment [that is, a warning merely], while for someone else the same event may be a bowl of wrath [that is, the ultimate means of final destruction].

In Hendriksen's view, **a foul and loathsome sore** (v. 2) represents "vicious and incurable ulcers or any other incurable disease" by which men die and are cast into hell. Hailey takes the boils symbolically. He writes:

⧗ HISTORICIST *(continued)*

sustenance of the papal system. The popes themselves have often referred to the king of France as "the eldest son of the church." The condition of France has often been a bellwether for the continent. Napoleon said, "A revolution in France is sooner or later followed by a revolution in Europe."

In the French Revolution, **a foul and loathsome sore** (v. 2), that is, the moral corruption, atheism, and general dissolution of society, spread over those countries where the beast and his image were principally worshiped. Barnes discusses the meaning of the word "sore" as being an ulcer or boil of painful character, such as those associated with the plague. He then cites from Burke's *Letters on a Regicide Peace,* in which the author had no intention of drawing any parallel with this scene in the Apocalypse, and yet used the following expressions in describing the French Revolution: "the epidemic of atheistical fanaticism," "the malignant French distemper," "a plague, with its fanatical spirit of proselytism, that needed the strictest quarantine to guard against it." The Revolution was aimed at the power of the papacy, and in five years two million people were slain, including twenty-four thousand priests. Forty thousand churches were made into stables. The power of the popes in France was shattered. ⧉

⧗ PRETERIST *(continued)*

plague pictured here parallels that which came upon Egypt in Exodus 9:8–12. It seems more than coincidental that this very plague was threatened against Israel when Moses was enumerating the judgments that he would send upon them if they proved unfaithful to his covenant:

> The LORD will strike you with the boils of Egypt, with tumors, with the scab, and with the itch, from which you cannot be healed. . . . The LORD will strike you in the knees and on the legs with severe boils which cannot be healed, from the sole of your foot to the top of your head (Deut. 28:27, 35).

That these sores resisted healing can be seen in the fact that the people still were suffering from them when the fifth bowl is poured out upon them in verse 11.

The principal significance of this plague would probably be symbolic, though such literal boils and rashes almost certainly became an epidemic in the besieged Jerusalem, where sanitation was the first luxury to be lost. With dead bodies piled in rotting heaps throughout the city, and the streets running with rivers of blood and sewage, it is no wonder that infectious diseases of every sort were rampant and unchecked. ⧉

⏳ FUTURIST *(continued)*

source for the affliction. Others find some naturalistic explanation. Lindsey takes the latter approach:

> The rash of malignant sores could easily be caused by the tremendous radioactive pollution in the atmosphere. After the bombings of Nagasaki and Hiroshima thousands of people developed hideous sores because of the radioactivity.

Gaebelein spiritualizes the sores:

> All the internal corruption will be outwardly manifested . . . and as a sore is a vile thing to behold, we may think of the great vileness connected with the moral, apostate conditions in the earth, which God will permit to break out.

But Ironside suggests a spiritual and a literal fulfillment: "What a scene of death and desolation, whether we think of it as physical or spiritual, or both."

The sores inflicted by this plague are apparently incurable by human means, since the victims of the plague are still languishing in torment when the fifth bowl is poured out (see v. 11). ⏳

⏳ IDEALIST *(continued)*

> As in the human body where sores break out from an accumulation of impurities that permeate the whole body, so also in this case it is the corruption of the world breaking out.

Hobbs, who is partially a late date *preterist*, nonetheless applies the vision beyond his short-range application to the fall of the Roman Empire. The seven angels are God's "messengers of wrath" sent forth "to execute judgment upon the Roman Empire, and beyond that upon all the forces of evil at the end of the age." He does not take the sores of this plague literally, but writes:

> This symbolic way of picturing judgment would comfort John's contemporaries. But it also gives assurance to all believers throughout the ages who are persecuted by the devotees of political and material forces. ⏳

THE SECOND BOWL

REVELATION 16:3

[3]Then the second angel poured out his bowl on the sea, and it became blood as of a dead man; and every living creature in the sea died.

⧖ HISTORICIST

That the sea would become **blood as of a dead man** is not to be understood literally, but as imagery "implying that the ocean would become discoloured, and indicating that this was the effect of blood shed in great quantities on its waters" (Barnes). Since these bowls represent plagues of judgment upon the papacy, Barnes feels the "proper application . . . would be the complete destruction or annihilation of the naval force that contributed to sustain the Papacy. This we should look for in respect to the naval power of France, Spain, and Portugal, for these are the only Papal nations that have had a navy."

Fulfillment of this prophecy is found in the series of great naval disasters that swept away the fleets of France, the most formidable naval power that had ever existed under papal rule. For details of this, we cite Elliott:

> Meanwhile the great *naval* war between France and England was in progress; which, from its commencement in February, 1793, lasted for above twenty years, with

⧖ PRETERIST

The precise relationship between the seven trumpets and the seven bowls is difficult to determine. Clearly there is a general correspondence between the successive elements affected, although the trumpets' effect is only partial (one-third), while the bowls affect the whole. It is remotely possible that the bowls are to be seen as another look at the same events represented by the trumpets, though this seems unlikely in view of the difference just mentioned and the fact that the bowls are specifically associated with "the seven last plagues" (15:1). Possibly the trumpets depict preliminary calamities that fall upon Israel during the Jewish War, while the bowls present plagues associated with the final and utter devastation of Jerusalem.

For those who see the second half of Revelation as depicting the fall of Rome, the difference in the extent of the two sets of judgments would be explained in terms of the trumpets being upon Jerusalem, and the bowls, more universally, upon the empire at large.

FUTURIST

This bowl, like the second trumpet, affects the sea. Whereas, in the second trumpet, one-third of the sea became blood, we here read of the whole sea undergoing the same transubstantiation. At this point, there is the possibility of a symbolic or literal interpretation. Gaebelein is in company with many others when he writes:

> The sea represents the Gentiles. These will now experience the wrath of God. See the plague in Egypt (Exod. vii:17–25.) That was a literal thing; but not so here. Some apply it to the continued carnage which will be one of the leading features of the final history of the times of the Gentiles.

Biederwolf writes:

> Perhaps most commentators interpret all these [bowl] judgments symbolically, making the sea in this instance represent the nations in a restless state and this [bowl] as designating the moral and spiritual death among the nations. The future alone can decide the question, but the close resemblance to the Egyptian plagues suggests that the fulfillment may be a literal one.

Though favoring a more natural interpretation, even Walvoord must admit to the possibility that the expression, **it became blood,** is not entirely literal. He points out:

IDEALIST

As the second trumpet affected the sea in Revelation 8:8, so also this bowl is poured out **on the sea,** resulting in the total putrefaction of that body of water. Pointing out that the first beast also arose from "the sea," some (e.g., Hailey) suggest that the sea may symbolize all of humanity. In this view, the vision "brings into focus the utter putrefaction of a dead society."

Hendriksen suggests that this bowl simply shows that when God brings final punishment and death upon unrepentant sinners, He sometimes uses the sea as an instrument. Shipwrecks, sea battles, tsunamis, and other sea disasters serve as a bowl judgment, a messenger of death, upon wicked men whose time to repent has expired— while the same disasters will have a different impact upon survivors or those who hear of them, serving as trumpet warnings to bring them to repentance. He writes: "This happens again and again throughout history."

Alternatively, Hobbs suggests: "This judgment may suggest the destruction of sources of physical sustenance—the sea was a major source both of food and of the means of commerce."

G.K. Beale points out that these judgments have to do with the downfall of Babylon (see 16:19), which he views as a symbol of "the World System." He identifies this bloodying of the sea with judgment on the World System in the

⧗ HISTORICIST *(continued)*

no intermission but that of the short and delusive peace of Amiens; in which war the maritime power of Great Britain was strengthened by the Almighty Providence that protected her to destroy everywhere the French ships, commerce and smaller colonies; including those of the fast and long-continued allies of the French, Holland and Spain . . . Altogether in this naval war, from its beginning in 1793, to its end in 1815, it appears that there were destroyed near 200 ships of the line, between 300 and 400 frigates, and an almost incalculable number of smaller vessels of war and ships of commerce. The whole history of the world does not present such a period of naval war, destruction, and bloodshed.

Among the British victories over the French during that time, the following stand out:

1793—the greater part of the French fleet at Toulon destroyed by Lord Hood;

1794—victory of Lord Howe over the French off Ushant;

1794—the taking of Corsica and nearly all the smaller Spanish and French West Indies;

1795—the capture of the Cape of Good Hope by Lord Bridgeport, and the defeat of the French and Dutch fleet sent to recover them;

⧗ PRETERIST *(continued)*

The turning of the sea to blood is a more extensive result than that of the second trumpet. There is a resemblance, of course, to the first plague upon Egypt, wherein the Nile turned to blood (Exod. 7:17–21). However, in the present case, as Chilton points out, "the blood is not running in streams, but instead is **like that of a dead man:** clotted, coagulated, and putrefying." The blood of the dead, to the Jews, would be the ultimate in uncleanness, so the image may simply mean that the whole of Judea has become covered with uncleanness—and even has become like the sea, which is usually a symbol for the Gentile nations.

An interesting literal parallel to this description is found in Josephus (which we previously cited in the commentary on Rev. 8:8–9). Josephus describes a battle that occurred upon the Sea of Galilee in which the Romans overtook the fleeing Jews in boats and massacred them in the water. Josephus writes:

And for such as were drowning in the sea, if they lifted their heads up above the water they were either killed by darts, or caught by the vessels; but if, in the desperate case they were in, they attempted to swim to their enemies, the Romans cut off either their heads or their hands; and indeed they were destroyed after various manners

⏳ FUTURIST *(continued)*

It is possible that the sea does not become literally human blood but that it corresponds to it in appearance and loathsomeness . . . The reference to the sea may be limited to the Mediterranean, but the same word would be used if the judgment extended to all large bodies of water.

Stedman writes:

We have already seen foreshadows of this phenomenon in the so-called "red tide" which scientists have occasionally observed in the Caribbean and other seas sheltered by land masses. There is a microorganism which, given the right set of conditions, multiplies precipitously, turning the water a deep scarlet. All sea life in the affected area dies.

Hal Lindsey, continuing to follow the nuclear war motif that characterizes much of his exposition, writes: "We can only speculate as to whether a direct judgment of God or a tremendous nuclear exchange will affect marine life to this extent." Gaebelein, however, advocates caution in the employment of speculations:

How little we can say of all these awful scenes of wrath coming upon the earth. It is far better to acknowledge our ignorance in some of these matters than to indulge in fanciful speculations. ⏳

⏳ IDEALIST *(continued)*

economic sphere. In support of this emphasis on economic issues, he reminds us that the first beast, of Revelation 13, emerged from "the sea" (13:1), and his "mark" primarily had an economic impact upon his servants (13:17). This mark has been brought to our attention again in the discussion of the first bowl (16:2). Likewise, the fall of Babylon, in chapter 18, is said to particularly shatter the dreams of merchants (18:11, 15), and maritime commerce—"as many as trade on the sea"(18:17)

Pointing out the "striking" parallelism between the second trumpet and the second bowl, he writes: "the second trumpet and the second bowl have to do with the same kind of judgment. The primary difference is the trumpet's partial effect and the bowl's total affect."[8]

Leon Morris, making the same comparison, writes:

When the second trumpet was blown, something like a mountain was hurled into the sea, a third of the waters became blood and a third of the creatures in and on the sea died (8:8–9). On this occasion there is no mention of one-third or of any other proportion. We are now face to face with finality. Everything in the sea died.[9]

Applying these judgments to the entire "inter-advent age" (that is, the time between the first and second comings of Christ), he says that the trumpet and

⧗ HISTORICIST *(continued)*

1797—the victory over the Spanish fleet off Cape St. Vincent, and of the Dutch at Camperdown;

1798—Lord Nelson's victory of the Nile;

1801—Lord Nelson's victory at Copenhagen;

1805—Lord Nelson's annihilation of the French fleet at Trafalgar.

With such a wealth of historical facts, it seems altogether appropriate that symbols such as appear in this passage should be used in their description.

⧗ PRETERIST *(continued)*

everywhere, till the rest, being put to flight, were forced to get upon the land, while the vessels encompassed them about (on the sea): but as many of these were repulsed when they were getting ashore, they were killed by the darts upon the lake; and the Romans leaped out of their vessels, and destroyed a great many more upon the land: one might then see the lake all bloody, and full of dead bodies, for not one of them escaped. And a terrible stink, and a very sad sight there was on the following days over that country; for as for the shores, they were full of shipwrecks, and of dead bodies all swelled; and as the dead bodies were inflamed by the sun, and putrefied, they corrupted the air, insomuch that the misery was not only the object of commiseration to the Jews, but to those that hated them, and had been the authors of that misery. (*Wars* III: 10:9)

⧗ IDEALIST *(continued)*

bowl, taken together, stress that the economic disaster that can occur partially, can occur universally also, throughout the present age. ⧗

THE THIRD BOWL

REVELATION 16:4—7

⁴Then the third angel poured out his bowl on the rivers and springs of water, and they became blood. ⁵And I heard the angel of the waters saying, "You are righteous, O Lord, the One who is and who was and who is to be, because You have judged these things. ⁶For they have shed the blood of saints and prophets, and You have given them blood to drink. For it is their just due." ⁷And I heard another from the altar saying, "Even so, Lord God Almighty, true and righteous are Your judgments."

⌛ HISTORICIST

This judgment and the third trumpet both are said to affect **the rivers and springs** (v. 4—cf. 8:10). In considering the third trumpet, we looked for a fulfillment occurring in that region of Europe where the rivers and streams have their origins. The fulfillment was identified there with the invasion of Attila and the Huns (see notes at 8:10–11). So also, the fulfillment of this vision should be sought within those same portions of Europe.

The time frame of the first four bowls roughly coincide, all beginning with the French Revolution, but each bowl depicts a separate aspect of the crisis that came upon the papacy at that time. France, not content to keep her revolutionary philosophy to herself, sought to impose it upon neighboring nations. Beginning in 1793, France launched invasions against Germany, Austria, Switzerland, and Northern Italy. It was in the invasion of Italy that

⌛ PRETERIST

Though some *preterists* understand this judgment, along with the others of this series, to be directed against the Roman Empire and its capital city, those who see Jerusalem's fall throughout the passage seem to have the advantage here, whether viewing it literally or figuratively.

The pollution of the water sources did occur during the siege of Jerusalem, and streams of actual blood flowed through the city. This can be seen as a literal fulfilling of this vision, though it is possible that a symbolic meaning is intended as well. Chilton writes:

> Water is a symbol of life and blessing throughout Scripture, beginning from the story of creation and the Garden of Eden. In this plague, the blessings of Paradise are reversed and turned into a nightmare; what was once pure and clean becomes polluted and unclean through apostasy.

⏳ FUTURIST

As the third trumpet made one-third of the freshwater sources bitter, so the third bowl turns them entirely into **blood** (v. 4). We are again faced with the possibility of taking a symbolic approach, as does Gaebelein when he writes: "All the joys of life, typified by rivers and fountains of water, are poisoned and corrupted." But Walvoord exhorts us to hold out, as before, for a literal fulfillment:

> Though some have taken rivers and fountains to be symbolic, there is no reason for not taking this in the literal sense as the sea in the second [bowl] and the men in the first [bowl].

Angels proclaim God's justice in giving the rebels blood to drink, since they have demonstrated their bloodthirsty character by killing the righteous saints who prophesied against them (vv. 5–6). Walvoord writes:

> Even as the saints are worthy of rest and reward, so the wicked are worthy of divine chastening and judgment. The bloodletting during the great tribulation, as saints are slaughtered by the thousands, is without parallel in the history of the human race.

This gloomy assessment of the body count during the tribulation period seems justified, if the futurists are correct in taking a literal interpretation of

⏳ IDEALIST

Idealists do not generally commit to any specific belief as to the fulfillment of a plague like this one. Most see the imagery of a judgment **on the rivers and springs of water,** with the result that **they became blood**(v. 4), as merely a device to show God's ability to suit the punishment to the crime of the sinners. Hendriksen's view would identify the fulfillment of this judgment with any occurrence through which men are destroyed by rivers and inland waters (drowning, poisoning).

However, apart from mentioning the likeness of this plague to the first Egyptian plague, most skip over the question of how this gruesome picture is to correlate with historical realities and focus upon the statement of **the angel of the waters** (v. 5). Swete writes: "The spirit of the waters is so far from resenting the plague that he bears witness to the justice which inflicts it." Summers and Hobbs interpret these judgments as primarily falling upon the Roman Empire, and secondarily applying to other cases. Summers writes, concerning the precise justice of this bowl, as declared by the angel of the waters:

> [God] visits punishment in accordance with sin: Once the Empire had made the blood of the martyrs run like water; now all the Empire can find to drink is blood—and they deserve it. God's judgments are righteous.

⧗ HISTORICIST *(continued)*

Napoleon began his career of victories, from which Rome has never recovered.

These wars occurred on the Rhine, the Po, and the Alpine streams of Piedmont and Lombardy, the region. Barnes writes: "One has only to look upon a map of Northern Italy to see that there is no other portion of the world which would more naturally be *suggested* when speaking of a country abounding in 'rivers and fountains of water.'" B. W. Johnson writes: "In the year 1796, a general, age 27, led a French army across the Alps. On the river system of Italy, on the Rhone, the Po and its tributaries, he battled with the Austrians and their allies. It is remarkable that every one of his great conflicts were fought upon the rivers."[10] The affected regions were all papal states and territories.

Another feature of the location should be that it is a place where many Christian martyrs have died, since **they have shed the blood of saints** (v. 6). The judgment upon the region is declared to be a just retribution for the shedding of their blood. It is a matter of history that in the region of the fountains of the Rhine, the Danube, and the Po Rivers, multitudes of saints were slaughtered at the command of the popes. These martyrs included Lutherans, Moravians, Hussites, Albigenses, Waldenses, Vaudois, and Huguenots. For more detail, see note at 13:6–7.

Barnes writes:

⧗ PRETERIST *(continued)*

The factor that most powerfully points to Jerusalem in AD 70 is the announcement in verse 6 concerning those upon whom the calamity falls. Russell writes:

The local and national character of the transactions represented in the vision is distinctly brought out in ver. 6. When the third angel turns the rivers into blood, the angel of the waters is heard acknowledging the retributive justice of this plague,—[**For they have shed the blood of saints and prophets**]. This "killing of the prophets" was the very sin of Israel, and of Jerusalem, nor is there any other city or nation against which this particular crime can be alleged as its peculiar characteristic. This impeachment decisively fixes the allusion in the vision to the Jewish people, and to that fearful period in their history when it might be truly said that their rivers ran with blood.

Chilton agrees, adding:

The characteristic crime of Israel was always the murder of the prophets (cf. 2 Chron. 36:15–16; Luke 13:33–34; Acts 7:52): Jesus named this fact as the specific reason why the blood of the righteous would be poured out in judgment upon that generation (Matt. 23:31–36) . . . Joining the angel in praise comes the voice of **the Altar** itself, where the blood of the

FUTURIST *(continued)*

many earlier passages. The bloodletting would not only include the martyred saints, who become the beast's victims (13:7, 10), but, additionally, an almost infinitely larger number of the world's general population! One-quarter of the earth's population are killed, in Revelation 6:8, followed by the violent deaths of another third of the remainder of mankind, in Revelation 9:15. These two passages alone reduce the total world population by 50 percent. The deaths of over 3.5 billion people over so short a space would indeed be "without parallel in the history of the human race."

This bowl, with its turning of all sources of potable water into (undrinkable) blood would seemingly kill off all survivors of these previous calamities within a matter of days.

IDEALIST *(continued)*

The **altar** (v. 7) is here heard speaking its agreement because it was earlier associated with the prayers of the saints for justice to be done (cf. 6:9). Part of God's answer to those cries was the sending of the trumpet judgments, which were intended to warn the wicked to repent. Now in the bowls we see the final answer to those prayers, as God pours out unrelenting vengeance upon the unrepentant.

427

HISTORICIST *(continued)*

In the times of Papal persecutions these valleys had been made to flow with the blood of the saints; and it seemed, at least, to be a righteous retribution . . . that the very fountains and streams which had before been turned into blood, by the slaughter of the friends of the Saviour, should now be reddened with the blood of men slain in battle.

PRETERIST *(continued)*

saints and prophets had been poured out [cf. 6:9–11].

THE FOURTH BOWL

REVELATION 16:8—9

⁸Then the fourth angel poured out his bowl on the sun, and power was given to him to scorch men with fire. ⁹And men were scorched with great heat, and they blasphemed the name of God who has power over these plagues; and they did not repent and give Him glory.

HISTORICIST

The time of this vision's fulfillment overlaps the time of the second and third bowls (i.e., the years following the French Revolution), and all three focus upon some aspect of the judgment coming upon papal Rome. The main actor in the present verses is **the sun** (v. 8), which is generally a symbol for a prominent ruler. Elliott writes:

> [T]here was predicted in the [bowl] before us the darkening, partially or entirely, either of that power among the ten Papal kingdoms

PRETERIST

There is no record of the sun's heat literally increasing to a dangerous and scorching degree at any time associated with the fall of Jerusalem or of Rome. If the sun is taken as a symbol of mighty political or religious leaders, however, this passage could certainly refer to the oppression and tyranny exercised by the leaders of the zealot sects that terrorized ("**scorched**"—v. 9) the citizens inside the besieged city of Jerusalem, if that is the geographical and chronological setting of these judgments.

FUTURIST

Gaebelein writes:

> Some apply this literally, but the symbolic meaning is to be preferred . . . The sun here is not the physical sun, but means, as under the fourth trumpet, the supreme authority governing them (the Roman empire). . . . The government, Satan-ruled as it is, becomes now the source of the most awful torment to those who are under its dominion.

Ironside supports the symbolic approach of Gaebelein as well:

> The sun is the supreme source of light, and this implies that that which should have been for man's comfort becomes a curse instead, and the means of his bitter suffering.

Some expositors take the increase of the sun's heat in a literal sense. Stedman and Lindsey find probable natural

IDEALIST

Commentators of this approach studiously avoid specifically identifying the effects of this bowl **on the sun** (v. 8) with any actual reality in history or human experience. Most point out that this fourth bowl resembles the fourth trumpet in the fact that the sun is affected in both cases—although the intensification of the sun in this case is the exact opposite of the diminishing of the sun's light that occurred with the sounding of the fourth trumpet (8:12).

The sun is now made to **scorch men** (v. 8). As the heavenly bodies were said to have fought against Sisera (Judg. 5:20), so the sun is used here to hurt and ultimately kill unrepentant men. Though Hendriksen does not specify how he understands the fulfillment of this bowl judgment, his general interpretation of the previous bowls would suggest that this one applies to all the cases in history in which people died of

HISTORICIST *(continued)*

that might be considered as most properly the sun in the symbolic firmament of Papal Christendom, that is, of the *German Emperor*; or perhaps of the sovereigns of these Papal kingdoms, more in the general . . . In 1806, the year after the battle of Austerlitz, we read of the renunciation by the German Emperor, on Napoleon's requirement . . . of his title of *Emperor of the Holy Roman Empire* and of *Germany.* So the Holy Roman Empire, as it was called, having lasted 1,000 years from the time of Charlemagne, was declared to be no more, and the *imperial sun* of Papal Christiendom darkened . . ." (Italics in original)[11]

PRETERIST *(continued)*

Isaiah is not likely to be speaking literally when he promises obedient Israel that they "shall neither hunger nor thirst, *Neither heat nor sun shall strike them*; For He who has mercy on them will lead them, Even by the springs of water He will guide them." (Isa. 49:10).

Seeing Israel as the afflicted venue, Chilton writes:

> This too is a reversal of a basic covenantal blessing that was present in the Exodus, when Israel was shielded from the heat of the sun by the Glory-Cloud, the Shadow of the Almighty (Exod. 13:21–22; cf. Ps. 91:1–6).

God, in fact, threatened that the breaking of the covenant by Israel would bring upon them God's judgment in this very form: "The Lord will strike you . . . with scorching" (Deut. 28:22).

Alternatively, if the judgment of the fall of Rome is in view, the image may represent the tyranny of Roman leaders or the ruthlessness of those Gothic and Vandal kings that attacked Rome and brought about her downfall.

FUTURIST *(continued)*

causes for the sun's increased power to harm mankind. Stedman writes:

> Every now and then great flares of nuclear fire burst outward from the surface of the sun, interacting with the earth's magnetic field and causing disruption in radio communication. Apparently a solar flare of immense magnitude creates intense heat upon the earth. Given the reported depletion of protective ozone that is now taking place in the earth's upper atmosphere, this heat may be accompanied by an increase in ultraviolet radiation from the sun which would produce severe sunburns.

Hal Lindsey, too, in keeping with his general method, gives a fully naturalistic interpretation:

> I believe that in a full-scale nuclear exchange the balance of the atmosphere will be radically upset, and this could be one of the things that is implied here.

IDEALIST *(continued)*

exposure to the elements—perishing in deserts without water, succumbing to cancer through damaging solar rays, etc.

Hobbs writes: "As the center of our solar system, the sun is the source of all physical and natural life. But instead of being a blessing it becomes a curse. This judgment encompasses the whole scope of natural life." Hailey reminds us that the martyrs had long since reached a place of safety where "the sun shall not strike them, nor any heat" (7:16).

It is no surprise to find that those affected by this judgment **did not repent** but rather **they blasphemed** (v. 9). It is this very stubbornness that has required God to employ these measures against them.

THE FIFTH BOWL

REVELATION 16:10—11

¹⁰Then the fifth angel poured out his bowl on the throne of the beast, and his kingdom became full of darkness; and they gnawed their tongues because of the pain. ¹¹They blasphemed the God of heaven because of their pains and their sores, and did not repent of their deeds.

⌛ HISTORICIST

The near-unanimous opinion of the Protestant interpreters of the past was that **the throne of the beast** (v. 10) is a reference to Rome. The scene of the calamities described here must be Rome or Italy. The **darkness** that fills the beast's kingdom is, in the words of Barnes, "Confusion—disorder—distress, for darkness is often the emblem of calamity."

Following an outbreak of revolutionary sentiment in Rome, on December 27, 1797, Berthier, the commander-in-chief of the French troops, received orders from the Directory to advance rapidly into the ecclesiastical states. The multitudes tumultuously demanded the overthrow of the papal authority, and the French troops were invited to enter. The French, upon entering Rome, commenced the systematic pillaging of the city. The churches, convents, and the palaces of the cardinals and nobility were laid waste. The spoiling of Rome by

⌛ PRETERIST

If the announcement of the third bowl seemed to support the opinion of those who see the fall of Jerusalem throughout this series of judgments (see note at verse 6), this fifth bowl appears to support the contention of those who find in this section the judgments against pagan Rome. Virtually all *preterists* understand **the throne of the beast** (v. 10), upon which this bowl is poured, to be a reference to the city of Rome. David Chilton, who believes that the fall of Jerusalem is still the principal concern of Revelation at this point, admits:

Although most of the judgments throughout Revelation are aimed specifically at apostate Israel, the heathen who join Israel against the Church come under condemnation as well. Indeed the Great Tribulation itself would prove to be "the hour of testing, that hour which is to come upon *the whole world*, to test those who dwell upon *the Land*" (3:10).

FUTURIST

While the first four bowls affected the forces of nature (men, sea, rivers, sun), the fifth bowl affects the political power of the beast. Moorehead says that "judicial blindness smites his kingdom; madness and defiance rule." Gaebelein adds that his throne and his kingdom is deluged with wrath. All becomes darkness. The boast had been "Who is like unto the Beast? Who is able to make war with him?" (13:4). Here God unexpectedly answers this rhetorical question with a literal answer. There is none that can stand against Him in battle. However, this is not the complete judgment of the two beasts. That comes later (19:20).

But the darkness may be literal, and this judgment may come to accomplish a specific strategic purpose, as Lindsey states:

> I believe there's a reason for God's blackout of this Revived Roman Empire: the darkness will allow the movement of 200 million Oriental soldiers into the area of the Middle East, the subject of the next judgment.

However, why the two hundred million Chinese would be able to navigate the many thousands of miles trek overland in the darkness, while the technology of Western Europe would be incapable of detecting them presents a

IDEALIST

The parallels between the seven trumpets and the seven bowls have been noted throughout the series. Likewise here, we find people torments by pain and engulfed in darkness. Though not identical in their source, the effects of the fifth trumpet are similar. The demonic locust invasion also "darkened" the sky (9:2) and brought unbearable "torment" (9:5) upon the rebels under judgment.

Swete points out that the first four bowls differ from the last three, in that the former are related to, and adversely affect, various realms of nature (the land, the sea, the rivers, the sun), while the latter are "more directly political."

Leon Morris writes:

> It is possible that we should take the darkening in this plague to denote the waning of the power of the beast, and this will be further stressed in the remaining plagues.[14]

The **throne of the beast** (v. 10), upon which this judgment falls, means, according to Hendriksen, "the centre of antichristian government. When Assyria falls, or Babylon, or Rome, the whole universe of the impenitent seems to collapse." Hobbs, Hailey, and others who mix the *idealist* approach with the late-date *preterist*, apply this event to the punishment of pagan Rome, but do not limit the application to Rome alone.

433

⧗ HISTORICIST *(continued)*

the French exceeded that carried out earlier by the Goths or the Vandals.

Robbed of all defense, in 1798 Pope Pius VI, who was above eighty years old, was ordered to dispossess himself of all his temporal authority. Refusing this, he was forcibly removed, "dragged from the altar in his palace, his repositories all ransacked and plundered, the rings even torn from his fingers, the whole effects of the Vatican and Quirinal inventoried and seized, and the aged pontiff conducted, with only a few domestics, amid the brutal jests and sacrilegious songs of the French dragoons, into Tuscany."[12] The pope died in exile at age 82.

Throughout Europe, from 1798 to 1866, the authority of the papal system progressively deteriorated. In 1870 the Italian troops conquered Rome and incorporated it into the Kingdom of Italy.

It is a tribute to this approach to Revelation that Robert Fleming calculated the very dates of these events, using the year-day method, a century before their occurrence. In the book *Apocalyptical Key,* or *The Pouring Out of the Vials,* first published in 1701, Fleming wrote:

> [The Pope] cannot be supposed to have any [bowl] poured upon his seat immediately (so as to ruin his authority so signally as this judgment must be supposed to do) until the year 1848. . . . But yet we are

⧗ PRETERIST *(continued)*

The **darkness** (v. 10) that comes upon the kingdom of the beast is a familiar symbol in the prophetic scriptures representing political turmoil and the overthrow of rulers. Such a crisis actually occurred in Rome when Nero committed suicide, in AD 68. The power vacuum created by this incident nearly tore the empire apart. The historian Tacitus refers to the "worldwide convulsions" that rocked the empire in the year following Nero's death. The year AD 69 came to be known as "the year of the four emperors" because of the rapid rise and fall of a series of self-appointed successors to Nero—Galba, Otho, and Vitellius, none of whom reigned more than six months. F. W. Farrar speaks of "the horrors inflicted upon Rome and Romans in the civil wars by provincial governors":

> Such were Galba, Otho, Vitellius, and Vespasian. Vespasian and Mucianus deliberately planned to starve the Roman populace; and in the fierce struggle of the Vitellians against Sabinus and Domitian, and the massacre which followed, there occurred the event which sounded so portentously in the ears of every Roman—the burning to the ground of the Temple of the Capitoline Jupiter, on December 19th, AD 69. It was not least of the signs of the times that the space of one year saw wrapped in flames the two most hallowed

⏳ FUTURIST *(continued)*

mystery almost as great as any in the Book of Revelation.

The mention here of **pains and their sores** (v. 11) relates to the ongoing effects of the first plague. Biederwolf writes: "This verse shows that the first three plagues are still continuing: the sores are still in force. It shows that the bowls are cumulative and not successive." Despite the loss of sea life, light, and fresh water, and the presence of painful boils all over the people, they still **did not repent** (v. 11). We are reminded of obstinate cases, like Pharaoh in Exodus, whose hearts can remain hardened through seemingly any disaster. The recalcitrance, in this case, as in Pharaoh's, may be due to God's hardening of their hearts, although this need not be assumed. Man's own wickedness can be so great as to be unreformable by any earthly means. "Darkness and anguish do not tend to soften men's hearts, or lead them to confess their sins," Ironside comments. "Their very suffering but stirs them up to blaspheme God the more."

Walvoord adds:

> Though they are declared once more in verse 21 to have blasphemed God, this is the last reference to their failure to repent (cf. 2:21; 9:20–21; 16:9). The Scriptures plainly refute the notion that wicked men will quickly repent

⏳ IDEALIST *(continued)*

Hobbs writes, "What is pictured here as happening to Rome eventually will happen to all anti-God forces in the earth." Hailey adds:

> This throne was the seat of world power, which would have been thought of by the saints of John's day as the world rule from Rome. But this throne should not be restricted to Rome only; for wherever world power is worshiped, there the beast has his throne.

The effect of this bowl upon the beast's empire is that **his kingdom became full of darkness** (v. 10). The darkness apparently was accompanied by physical sensation of pain as well, causing the sufferers to gnaw their tongues **because of the pain** (v. 10). This recalls the Egyptian plague that resulted in three days of darkness "which even may be felt" (Exod. 10:21–22).

Since the worshipers of the beast preferred to live in spiritual darkness rather than in the light of the knowledge of God, it is a fitting retribution that the darkness they loved becomes a means of torment for them.

Once again those who were suffering under the mighty hand of God declined to choose the one option that could have relieved them: they **did not repent of their deeds** (v. 11) ☙

⌛ HISTORICIST *(continued)*

not to imagine that this will totally destroy the Papacy (though it
will exceedingly weaken it), for we
find that still in being and alive
when the next [bowl] is poured
out.

However, this judgment upon the
power of the Roman Church did not dis-
courage her from perpetuating her
blasphemies, for she continued innovat-
ing new heresies even during and after
this time. Two examples that some see
of the blasphemous declarations that
emerged about this time are the doctrines of the Immaculate Conception of
Mary (1854) and of the infallibility of
the pope when speaking *ex cathedra*
(1870). Since these doctrines attribute
to mere humans (Mary and the popes)
qualities that rightly belong only to God
(sinlessness and infallibility, respectively), one is justified in declaring that
such decrees fulfill the terms of the text:
they blasphemed the God of heaven
(v. 11).

⌛ PRETERIST *(continued)*

shrines of the ancient world—the
Temple of Jerusalem and the Temple of the great Latin god.[13]

Alternatively, the disasters upon
the Roman capital pictured here might
refer to the invasions that led to the ultimate fall of Rome in the fifth century.
This time frame would fit that of the expositors who feel that the destruction of
Rome is the subject of this second half of
Revelation. 🔯

 **FUTURIST** *(continued)*

when faced with catastrophic warnings of judgment.

THE SIXTH BOWL

REVELATION 16:12—16

[12]Then the sixth angel poured out his bowl on the great river Euphrates, and its water was dried up, so that the way of the kings from the east might be prepared. [13]And I saw three unclean spirits like frogs coming out of the mouth of the dragon, out of the mouth of the beast, and out of the mouth of the false prophet. [14]For they are spirits of demons, performing signs, which go out to the kings of the earth and of the whole world, to gather them to the battle of that great day of God Almighty. [15]"Behold, I am coming as a thief. Blessed is he who watches, and keeps his garments, lest he walk naked and they see his shame." [16]And they gathered them together to the place called in Hebrew, Armageddon.

⌛ HISTORICIST

Halley observes that the garden of Eden and, later Babylon, were both situated at the **great river Euphrates** (v. 12), which also figures prominently in this bowl judgment, at the end of history (to the *historicist* that is the point in history to which this series of judgments has brought us). He writes:

> The Garden of Eden, where the human race originated, and Babel, where earthly Government began its rebellion against God, were in the Euphrates Valley. Thus human history will come to an end where it began.

The strange beatitude, **Blessed is he who watches, and keeps his garments, lest he walk naked and they see his shame (v. 15)** is rendered more intelligible by Adam Clarke:

⌛ PRETERIST

The **great river Euphrates** (v. 12) figured significantly in the sixth trumpet judgment (cf. 9:14) as it does in the sixth bowl. The drying up of the Euphrates was the stratagem of Cyrus the Persian, the conqueror of historical Babylon in 536 BC. Cyrus diverted the flow of the waters of the Euphrates out of the river's bed, which ran under the wall surrounding Babylon. The river being dried up allowed Cyrus to march his troops under the wall, taking Belshazzar completely by surprise, and taking the city without serious resistance. There is no compelling reason to believe that the literal drying of the Euphrates is required to meet the demands of this passage, as David S. Clark shows:

⌛ FUTURIST

The sixth trumpet called attention to the Euphrates River also and mentioned two hundred million horsemen prepared for battle. As Gaebelein writes, the drying up of the river precipitates the movement of these troops from the East to participate in the final World War—usually called the "Battle of Armageddon," after the place named in verse 16. He writes: "The drying up of the Euphrates seems therefore to mean the removal of the barrier, so that the predicted gathering of the nations may take place (Joel 3:2)."

Opinions as to the identification of **the kings from the east** (v. 12) are surveyed by Ironside:

> Who are the kings of the East? Various theories have been suggested. Some consider they may be the so-called lost ten tribes of Israel, returning to their land. Others, the dominions of Persia, Afghanistan, and so on. It is significant that the word rendered "the east" is really"the sunrising." Is it only a coincidence that, for a millennium at least, Japan has been known as "the kingdom of the rising sun"? May not the Mongolian races, possibly allied with India, be the kings of the East, here depicted as coming in conflict with the powers of the West?

Walvoord has no difficulty with this suggestion:

⌛ IDEALIST

The end of the series of bowl judgments is one of the few portions of Revelation where most approaches reach a measure of agreement. The *preterists* would be the exception. However, *historicists*, *futurists*, and *idealists* often see the events of this sixth bowl as occurring at or near the end of history.

On the other hand, it is sometimes argued that the events in this passage, like those in many other parts of Revelation, are seen as recurring phenomena throughout the course of history. Sometimes both ideas are affirmed: demonically-inspired warfare occurs repeatedly throughout the age, but the time of the end will see the greatest of these conflicts, just prior to the coming of Christ.

The imagery behind the drying up of the **river Euphrates** (v. 12) has been explained variously. Swete writes:

> It is possible that his mind runs also on the story told by Herodotus (i.191) of the capture of Babylon by Cyrus, who marched into the city across the drained bed of the Euphrates; a new Babylon is to be surprised, and the drying up of the river marks the removal of the last obstacle to its fall.[19]

Another common expedient is to suggest that it was to expedite the movement of invading forces that **the river Euphrates** was seen to be dried up. Leon Morris reminds us that "In the

HISTORICIST *(continued)*

Here is a plain allusion to the office of him who was called the prefect or overseer of the mountain of the Temple. His custom was to go his rounds during the watches of the night; and if he found any of the Levites sleeping on his watch, he had authority to beat him with a stick and burn his vestments. Such a person being found on his return home *naked*, it was at once known that he had been found asleep at his post, had been beaten, and his clothes burned; thus his *shame* was seen—he was reproached for his infidelity and irreligion.

Since Barnes's interpretation of the fifth bowl took in events right up to his own day (1851), he believes that the remainder of the prophecies were to be fulfilled in or after his time. As in the sixth trumpet, he believed that the **Euphrates** points to the Turkish power. In this identification, he represents the views of almost all *historicists.* For example, Cachemaille wrote:

It seems manifest that the same Turkish Power is here intended as was described under the Sixth Trumpet. . . . Now, as the next great event after the outpouring of the Fifth Vial on the Seat of the Beast, that is, on Papal Rome, it was foreshown that the symbolic waterflood of that great river was to begin to be dried up; that is, that the population and area of the Turkish Empire were, from one

PRETERIST *(continued)*

We may remember in this connection that the doom of old Babylon was achieved by turning aside the waters of the Euphrates. As we use the word Waterloo as a symbol of defeat, they may have used the drying of the Euphrates as a symbol of defeat.

Jay Adams joins David Clark in understanding the Babylon of Revelation to be pagan Rome and this bowl judgment to be the preparation for the downfall of the Roman Empire in the fifth century AD:

It is quite appropriate that the fall of the last world power be described in terms of the first, since, in a very real sense, it is not merely the fall of Rome, but the end of the Satanic world empire which is predicted. This began with Babylon, the head of Daniel's image, and ends with the kingdom of God, which smashes the image, and breaks it in pieces. The whole image falls as the stone strikes it.

On the other hand, Chilton, Russell, Carrington, Terry, and others identify the Babylon of Revelation with Jerusalem, and therefore see this bowl as related to its destruction in AD 70. Chilton sees a double reference in the drying up of the Euphrates:

The image of the drying of the Euphrates for a conquering army is taken, in part, from a stratagem of

⧗ FUTURIST *(continued)*

The rising power of parts of the Orient in our day in countries such as Japan, China, India, as well as lesser nations, makes such an invasion a reasonable prediction.

Hal Lindsey also confirms this scenario:

> There will likely be a coalition of powers from the Eastern countries and it will probably be led by Red China. Their way is cleared for a rapid forced march and "banzai charge" by the drying up of the Euphrates River. This sort of thing has been made technically possible by the Russians' recent construction of a dam near the headwaters of the Euphrates.

The vision of the **three unclean spirits like frogs** (vv. 13–16) is possibly a parenthesis. Gaebelein declares this to be so; Walvoord does also:

> In verses 13–16 John has an additional vision introduced by the phrase "and I saw" which is parenthetical in nature but a commentary upon the sixth [bowl] and somehow related to it.

Ryrie explains that the "mention of the kings of the east introduces an excursus on Armageddon (vv. 13–16)."

These froglike demons are assigned to seduce the leaders of **the earth** and of **the whole world** into participating in **the battle of that great day of God**

⧗ IDEALIST *(continued)*

Old Testament a mighty action of God is frequently associated with the drying up of waters, as the Red Sea (Exod. 14:21), the Jordan (Josh. 3:16–17), and several times in prophecy (Isa. 11:15; Jer. 51:36; Zech. 10:11)." This is not to say that the literal Euphrates River must thus be affected in fulfillment of this vision. The Euphrates merely symbolizes an obstruction to invaders, as Hengstenberg explains:

> [The Euphrates] is mentioned here merely in respect to the hindrance it presented to the march of the ungodly power of the world into the Holy Land, against the Holy City; against the Church.

The Romans feared a Parthian invasion from beyond the Euphrates River. Furthermore, it was rumored, after Nero's suicide, that he had not really died or else would be resurrected and that he would lead an invasion against Rome from this very region. This was called the *Nero redivivus* myth. Many expositors see allusions to this myth throughout the Revelation. If they are correct, one must conclude either that John mistakenly took this story as valid, or that he used it, without believing it, as a picture of the eventual fall of the Roman Empire. Referring to this Nero myth, Wilson writes of verse 12:

⧗ HISTORICIST *(continued)*

cause or another, to begin to be diminished.[15]

Barnes and Elliott speculate that **the kings from the east** (v. 12), who obtained access of passage by the drying up of the river, might speak of those kings who, as Isaiah and the Psalms declare, will bring gifts and homage to the messiah (Ps. 72:10–11; Isa. 60:4–6, 9, 11). Barnes identified the drying up of the Euphrates with "some such decay of the Turkish power as would be followed by the conversion of the rulers of the East to the gospel." He and Elliott see the beginning of this process in the internal revolt and insurrection in the Turkish Empire that began in 1820.

The **three unclean spirits like frogs** (v. 13) Elliott sees as signifying: (1) the spirit of infidelity coming from the mouth of the dragon; (2) the spirit of popery proceeding from the mouth of the beast; and (3) the spirit of the priestcraft coming from the mouth of the false prophet. All three of these manifested themselves with great intensity in France, England, and other lands, beginning about 1830 and continuing to the present.

Barnes identifies the three spirits as paganism, the papacy, and Islam. He said that Islam was a particularly apt identification, since one of these spirits comes **out of the mouth of the false prophet** (p. 13), which is an

⧖ PRETERIST *(continued)*

Cyrus the Persian. . . . The more basic idea, of course, is the drying up of the Red Sea (Exod. 14:21–22) and the Jordan River (Josh. 3:9–17; 4:22–24) for the victorious people of God. Again there is the underlying note of tragic irony: Israel has become the new Babylon, an enemy of God that must now be conquered by a new Cyrus, as the true Covenant people are miraculously delivered and brought into their inheritance.

Carrington feels that this detail of the vision "surely represents nothing but the return of Titus to besiege Jerusalem with further reinforcements."[17] Josephus informs us that thousands of the troops that Titus brought in were actually from the region of the Euphrates.[18]

The armies are gathered to battle through the influence of **three unclean spirits like frogs** (v. 13), originating from the devil and his two chief cohorts. The mention of "frogs" may allude to the second Egyptian plague (Exod. 8:1–15), which would agree with the assumption that Jerusalem, "which is spiritually called . . . Egypt" (11:8), is the city under attack in the vision. Natural Egypt was judged with natural frogs; spiritual Egypt is afflicted by "spiritual frogs."

These demonic spirits gather **the kings of the earth [or land] and of the whole world** (v. 14) to the place called **Armageddon** (v. 16) to partici-

⏳ FUTURIST *(continued)*

Almighty (v. 14). The involvement of every nation on earth is taken literally by many.

This battle does not have to mean a single conflict, but rather, as Walvoord points out:

> The evidence . . . seems to point to the conclusion that this is a climax of a series of military events described in Daniel 11:40–45, where the reference to the "tidings out of the east" (Dan. 11:44) may have this invasion in view.

Since the nations of the whole world will be effectively under a single government during the Tribulation, how will it be possible for there to be a world war at the end of the Tribulation? Two answers have been put forward:

One answer suggests that the armies, all loyal to the beast, are gathered in anticipation of the Second Coming of Christ to make war against Him and His heavenly armies (17:14; 19:19). That the battle is against Christ seems to fit with Ladd's opinion that the drying up of the river is symbolic of the removal of the barrier which holds back the pagan hordes, the kings of the east, who join forces with the kings of the whole world to battle with the Messiah.

The other possibility is that the final war will be one of rebellion and insurrection on the part of many nations against the beast's authority (Dan.

⏳ IDEALIST *(continued)*

What follows shows that Nero will indeed return—not literally, but in the shape of that persecuting ruler who will be the last opponent of the people of God . . . Here the kings from the east represent the Parthian provincial governors, who are probably to be identified with the ten kings of 17:12, 13.

Of course, the question must be asked whether the warfare associated with this bowl is spiritual or physical. On this question, there is not a consensus among *idealists.*

Summers explains that the reference to **the kings from the east** (v. 12) "is symbolical of the army-host in the hand of God to do battle with [that is, on the side of] God."

Hobbs agrees with Summers that the kings "must be seen as forces fighting for God, because they figure in the larger idea of Rome's overthrow," but adds, "This is expanded in the apocalyptic thought to declare the final triumph of Christ over all evil forces in the universe."

Alford, taking issue with such ideas, writes:

> To suppose the conversion of the Eastern nations or the gathering together of Christian princes to be meant, or to regard the words as referring to any auspicious event, is to introduce a totally incongruous feature into the series of bowls

⧗ HISTORICIST *(continued)*

appropriate designation for *the Prophet* Mohammed. Barnes understands **the battle of that great day of God Almighty** (v. 14) in the place called **Armageddon** (v. 16), as not a real military war, but a metaphor for the spiritual conflict in the last days:

> It is by no means necessary to suppose that what is here represented will *literally* occur. There will be a mustering of spiritual forces; there will be a combination and a unity of opposition against the truth; there will be a rallying of the declining powers of Heathenism, Mahometanism [sic], and Romanism, *as if* the forces of the earth . . . were assembled in some great battlefield.

It is hard to know whether Adam Clarke was open to this being a literal war or something else. Writing prior to 1810 (the year of the first publication of his commentaries), he had already heard so many disparate and mistaken identifications of the battle of Armegeddon that he was obviously cynical as to the possibility of positive identification. He wrote:

> But what is the battle of Armageddon? How ridiculous have been the conjectures of men relative to this point! Within the last twenty years this battle has been fought at various places, according to our purblind seers and self-inspired

⧗ PRETERIST *(continued)*

pate **in the battle of that great day of God Almighty** (v. 14).

There are several significant allusions here. Neither those who see the import of this series of bowls to be the fall of Jerusalem in AD 70 nor those who apply these passages to the fall of Rome in the fifth century understand Armageddon to mean the literal place in northern Israel. The name is understood as a pregnant symbol. Meaning "the mountain of Megiddo," it seems to refer to Mount Carmel, where Jezebel's prophets were defeated by Elijah, since this is the nearest hill to the plain of Megiddo. This plain was the site of many significant battles, including the defeat of the Canaanites by Deborah and Barak (Judg. 5:19), and the battles in which the wicked king Ahaziah (2 Kings 9:27) and the good king Josiah (2 Chron. 35:20–25) were killed. Although we now use "the Battle of Armageddon" as a virtual synonym for "World War III," Jay Adams writes that "the battle mentioned at the conclusion of the chapter has nothing to do with the second coming of Christ."

Russell considers this battle to be that in which Jerusalem was destroyed by the Romans:

> The scene of the conflict also, "Armageddon,"—a name that is associated with one of the darkest and most disastrous days in the history of Israel, the field of

⧗ FUTURIST *(continued)*

11:40–45). This is Walvoord's preferred explanation: "More probably, it reflects a conflict among the nations themselves in the latter portion of the great tribulation as the world empire so hastily put together begins to deteriorate."

"Behold, I am coming as a thief" (v. 15). It is surprising to find this saying of Christ inserted into the narrative at this point. Perhaps this was to indicate the close chronological connection between the battle of Armageddon and the Second Coming of Christ, as Ladd thinks:

> Jesus himself interjects a word to the church, both to warn His people and to assure them of the realities behind the immediate historical events . . . This verse is an interruption in the context of the passage to give the church its proper perspective.

Mounce elaborates:

> When all the forces of the beast are gathered for the last battle, the believers will enter a period of supreme crisis . . . The faithful are admonished to be on the alert with spiritual preparedness required to disarm the deceptive propaganda of Satan and his henchmen.

Armageddon (v. 16), which is Hebrew for "Mountain of Megiddo" or "Mountain of Magedon," has been taken symbolically by some to mean,

⧗ IDEALIST *(continued)*

which confessedly represents *judgment,* the seven last plagues.

From the mouths of the infernal "trinity" proceed **three unclean spirits like frogs** (v. 13). As Ahab was drawn to the battle in which he died by the sending of a lying spirit into the mouths of his prophets (1 Kings 22:21–33), so God releases these **spirits of demons** (v. 14) into all the world to gather the kings of the whole world **to the battle** in which they are to die (cf. 19:20–21).

The announcement from Christ, **Behold, I am coming** (v. 15), comes somewhat unexpectedly in this description of the looming battle, though it is not inappropriate, since, in this view of things, the conflict here described will be in progress when Christ returns. Alford writes:

> This great gathering of the beast and of the kings of the earth against God and the Lamb is the signal for the immediate and glorious appearing of the Lord. And therefore follows in the next verse an exhortation to be ready and clad in garments of righteousness when He comes.

That the name **Armageddon** (v. 16) is symbolic is suggested by the fact that no translation of this Hebrew word is given here (cf. 9:11). The word means the Mountain of Megiddo, but there is

HISTORICIST *(continued)*

prophets! At one time it was Austerlitz, at another Moscow, at another Leipsic, and now Waterloo! And thus they have gone on, and will go on, confounding and being confounded.

Some twentieth-century *historicists*, however, have interpreted Armageddon as a literal armed conflict of international proportions. In 1926, for example, Alexander Hardie wrote: "The last Great War of 1914–1918, which convulsed and disgraced humanity, was doubtless the predicted Armageddon."[16]

Robert Caringola, one of the relatively few commentators in the past fifty years to write from the *historicist* position, also finds fulfillment of these later bowl judgments within this century. He agrees with other *historicists* in finding the Turkish Empire implied in the reference to the Euphrates. Living a century and a half later than Barnes, however, gives him the advantage of hindsight in identifying how the Turkish Power fell. On the drying of the Euphrates, Caringola writes:

In 1917–18 the once great Turkish Empire, which had its roots in the Euphrates river, was defeated by British Empire troops under General Edmund Allenby. In October 1917 he launched an attack on the Turkish forces controlling Palestine. This battle was fought in the

PRETERIST *(continued)*

Megiddo, the emblem of defeat and slaughter, lies in Jewish territory. That name of evil omen was meet to be the type of that final field of blood on which Israel as a nation was doomed to perish.

David S. Clark also assumes that the passage deals with Rome's destruction:

It is a place famous for battle and slaughter. . . . It would mean in those days what Waterloo means to us, and would be used in the same way. . . . Any great disaster to a warring nation is an Armageddon. The Confederacy met its Armageddon at Gettysburg, and the Germans met their Armageddon at the Marne. . . . Its use here would indicate a place or scene of great slaughter. I take it that it is used here in the symbolical sense, but meant that Rome was coming to her Armageddon where she would go down in battle and slaughter.

In the midst of the description of the preparations for war, Jesus interjects a warning that He will come **as a thief** (v. 15). This need not be a reference to His Second Coming any more than the identical words in Revelation 3:3 were a reference to that event. Jesus pronounces a beatitude upon those who keep their **garments** so as not to be walking **naked** and have people see their **shame** (v. 15). This may refer back to His comments to some of the churches

⏳ FUTURIST *(continued)*

"Mount of Slaughter." Mounce writes: "HarMagedon is symbolic of the final overthrow of all the forces of evil by the might and power of God."

Most *futurists*, however, identify it with an actual location, as does Ironside:

> It refers to the mountain that overlooks the valley of Esdraelon—the great plain of Jezreel in the northern part of the land of Palestine, which Napoleon Bonaparte said would make an ideal battleground for all the armies of the world.

Walvoord would not fully agree with Napoleon upon this point, but does not find any problem with this location being the main hub of a broader warfare:

> The area, though it is a large one, is not sufficient for all the armies of the world, though the valley of Esdraelon is fourteen miles wide and twenty miles long. What this Scripture seems to indicate is that this area is the central point for the military conflict which ensues. Actually the armies are deployed over a 200-mile area up and down from this central location (cf. 14:20). At the time of the second coming, some of the armies are in Jerusalem itself (Zech. 14:1–3). ⏳

⏳ IDEALIST *(continued)*

no mountain upon the plain that bears that name, as Leon Morris explains:

> No place of this is name is known, and the term is surely symbolic. But its meaning is uncertain. John tells us that it is a Hebrew word, and the two most favoured suggestions are that it means 'mountain of Megiddo' . . . or 'the city of Megiddo' . . . The former seems closer to the Hebrew, but unfortunately no mountain appears to be called 'the mountain of Megiddo.'[20]

This seems to further support the notion that the name is used for effect (suggesting a place of slaughter) rather than to geographically locate the battleground. Beckwith calls it "an imaginary name for designating the scene of the great battle between Antichrist and the Messiah."

Hendriksen has seen in all of the bowls the recurring phenomena of mortal disasters by which God brings men to their final ends (deaths). He believes that Armageddon symbolizes the repeated judgments of God against the enemies of His people. Giving as examples the destruction of Sennacherib's 185,000 by an angel of the Lord and the Maccabean victory over the Syrians, he writes:

> For this cause, HarMagedon is the symbol of every battle in which, when the need is greatest and believers are oppressed, the Lord

HISTORICIST *(continued)*

Gaza-Beersheba sector with the result that Jerusalem surrendered to Allenby. . . . The once mighty Turkish Empire was forever "dried up" and ceased to exist as a result of World War I.

Caringola points out that the October Revolution of the Bolsheviks also occurred in 1917, marking the beginning of the world Communist movement, which he believes to be one of the unclean spirits that gathers the nations to a future battle of Armageddon. The other two unclean spirits are said to be Judaism and Islam. These, together with Communism, are "all hostile to Christianity and are irreconcilable; ultimately they will war each other into oblivion." The final war of Armageddon will be the "consummation of the arms age."

PRETERIST *(continued)*

in chapter 3. The Laodiceans were counseled to buy "white garments, that you may be clothed, that the shame of your nakedness may not be revealed" (3:18). The overcomers in Sardis were told that they "shall be clothed in white garments" (3:5). This same church had been told that if they failed to watch, Jesus would come upon them "as a thief" (3:3).

Jesus told His disciples that some of them standing with him "shall not taste death" before they "see the Son of Man coming in His kingdom" (Matt. 16:28). This could not have been fulfilled much later than AD 70, since most of the generation of the disciples would have died by that time. This "coming" of the Son of Man could refer to the judgment upon Jerusalem.

IDEALIST *(continued)*

suddenly reveals His power in the interest of His distressed people and defeats the enemy. As we have indicated, this sixth bowl, as well as the preceding ones, is evident again and again in history. Yet, like the other bowls, it reaches its final and most complete realization just before and in connection with the last day.

Hendriksen also considers this final Armageddon to be the same battle described in Revelation 11:7ff.; 19:11ff.; and 20:7ff

THE SEVENTH BOWL

REVELATION 16:17—21

[17]Then the seventh angel poured out his bowl into the air, and a loud voice came out of the temple of heaven, from the throne, saying, "It is done!" [18]And there were noises and thunderings and lightnings; and there was a great earthquake, such a mighty and great earthquake as had not occurred since men were on the earth. [19]Now the great city was divided into three parts, and the cities of the nations fell. And great Babylon was remembered before God, to give her the cup of the wine of the fierceness of His wrath. [20]Then every island fled away, and the mountains were not found. [21]And great hail from heaven fell upon men, every hailstone about the weight of a talent. Men blasphemed God because of the plague of the hail, since that plague was exceedingly great.

⌛ HISTORICIST

Historicists, like futurists, believe that the fulfillment of this bowl judgment is yet to come. Since a highly symbolical form of expression has characterized the book throughout the earlier portions, it is to be assumed that the same method of expression prevails here. As the earlier visions, for the most part, could only be clearly understood with the aid of historical knowledge of the events after their fulfillment, it is unlikely that we should accurately surmise, before their occurence, the exact events foreseen in this vision.

Elliott explains that, as the bowl is poured out **into the air** (v. 17), this signifies "a convulsion, vitiation, and darkening of the moral and political atmosphere of Western Europe." He says

⌛ PRETERIST

The announcement, **It is done!** (v. 17) brings us to the long-anticipated culmination of what had seemed an endless stream of judgments. We finally see the fall of **the great city** which is **great Babylon** (v. 19). But who is actually intended by this designation? Throughout this second half of the Apocalypse, we have been tracing two alternative opinions held among preterists. Jay Adams is among those who see the great city as Rome:

> Verse 19 unmistakably pinpoints the topic under discussion. The fall of the "great city" (cf. also 17:18), the "city of the nations" (the correct textual reading is undoubtedly singular), and "great Babylon"

⧗ FUTURIST

The seventh and final bowl is poured into the air (v. 14). Walvoord agrees with Gaebelein, when the latter writes:

> This is Satan's sphere. His power and dominion is now dealt with in wrath. While Satan was cast out of heaven, he may still maintain part of the atmosphere immediately above the earth, thus upholding his claim as the prince of the power of the air (Eph. ii:2).

In addition to the **noises and thunderings and lightnings** (v. 17) reported in various strategic places in Revelation (8:5; 11:19), there is now described **a great earthquake** (v. 18), unparalleled in history as to its destructive effects. Hal Lindsey gives an explanation consistent with his interpretations up to this point:

> The earth could be shaken either by a literal earthquake or by a full-scale nuclear exchange of all remaining missiles. I lean toward the nuclear conflict.

Stedman adds to this scenario:

> This judgment—particularly coming as it does on the heels of the Battle of Armageddon—probably describes the effect of nuclear warfare, which would release vast clouds of poisonous radiation upon the earth.

One effect of this earthquake is the division into three parts of **the great city** (v. 19) and **great Babylon** comes

⧗ IDEALIST

Though most of the results of this bowl are described as affecting the earth, the bowl itself is poured out **into the air** (v. 17). Hailey suggests that the air is symbolic of the realm of Satan's power, who is called "the prince of the power of the air" in Ephesians 2:2.

It is done! (v. 17) means that the series of plagues is completed and the judgment of God upon His enemies has reached its final manifestation. The repeated phenomena of **noises and thunderings and lightnings** (v. 18) were first found proceeding from the throne of God at Revelation 4:5. They were repeated in 8:5, where they were joined by an earthquake. At 11:19, the same phenomena, including the earthquake, were repeated, with "great hail" added to the list. In the present passage we find the final occurrence of these phenomena—noises, thunderings, lightnings, **earthquake** (v. 18) and **great hail** (v. 21)—but special emphasis is placed on the magnitude of the earthquake and on the size of the hailstones.

The **great earthquake . . . such as had not occurred since men were on the earth** (v. 18) actually is described as destroying the **cities of the nations** (v. 19) and removing **every island** and mountain (v. 20). Lenski writes: "No city, even on the most remote island, no fortress of the antichristian empire on a single mountain height escaped the destructive final

451

⧗ HISTORICIST *(continued)*

that the **thunderings, lightnings,** and **noises** (v. 18) represent the wars and tumults that will follow. The storm of **hail** (v. 21), he thinks, indicates a judgment from the north. This suggests to his mind that France, the most northerly of the papal kingdoms, will be one of the chief players in the outworking of the implied disaster. Other expositors think that Russia may be in view (comparing this passage with Ezek. 38:9, 15, which is thought to refer to the Russians as "Gog"). Elliott remains open to this possibility as well.

Barnes, by contrast, takes the reference to "the air" to suggest that "as storms and tempests seem to be engendered in the air, so this destruction would come from some supernatural cause, as if the whole atmosphere should be filled with wind and storm." Caringola removes the *supernatural* element in the disaster, and asserts, "Many scholars believe that this speaks metaphorically of the curse and devastation wrought by aerial bombardment."

Caringola believes that the effects of this warfare will be to "bring down all illegitimate governments." Barnes and others see this bowl, like the previous ones, as applying to the downfall of Babylon—that is, papal Rome. The **earthquake** (v. 18), the disappearance of **every island** (v. 20), and the great storm of **hail** (v. 21) all are symbolic of

⧗ PRETERIST *(continued)*

can mean nothing but the fall of Rome.

The fall of pagan Rome occurred in the year 476, which would be the year of the fulfillment of this vision if Adams' view is correct.

The other option held among *preterist* scholars is that the great city Babylon is symbolic for Jerusalem, and the catastrophe described here is thus dated AD 70, when the Romans destroyed the city and massacred or deported all of the inhabitants. A number of considerations collectively support this suggestion.

First, there is the **great earthquake** (v. 18). The writer of Hebrews points out that, as the giving of the Old Covenant at Sinai was accompanied by the shaking of the earth, so also the dissolution of that covenant would be accompanied by an even greater shaking of both earth and heaven (Heb. 12:26–28). The Old Covenant vanished away (see Heb. 8:13) amid great tumult when Titus' troops destroyed the temple in Jerusalem along with the city. It would be appropriate for the Apocalypse to use the symbol of a great earthquake to depict this development. The famous Puritan writer, John Owen, understood this earthquake in this way:

> It is therefore *the heavens of the Mosaical worship*, and the Judaical churchstate, with the *earth of their political state* belonging thereunto,

452

⧗ FUTURIST *(continued)*

under the wrath of God. The wording allows "great Babylon" and "the great city" to be seen as the same city or as two different cities, as Walvoord explains:

> Some have taken both references to indicate Babylon, others have identified the first great city of the verse as Jerusalem . . . Whether this refers to Rome, which is spiritual Babylon or, as some have understood it, to a rebuilt city of Babylon on the Euphrates, it is clear in any case that Babylon is the special object of the judgment of God. . . . The fact that the judgment is an earthquake seems to indicate that a literal city is in view, either Rome or rebuilt Babylon, and that the judgment results in its physical destruction.

As a consequence of the earthquake, we read that **every island fled away, and the mountains were not found** (v. 20), which indicates, according to Ironside:

> The utter destruction of every spiritual and religious institution that man has built up apart from God. It is the absolute overthrow of civilization, and the complete wreck of all man's hopes to bring in even livable conditions in this world, while rejecting the Lord Jesus Christ.

Ryrie agrees:

> Everything that man has built will crumble before his eyes. Quite

⧗ IDEALIST *(continued)*

wrath." As Wilcock puts it: "Bowl 6 brought wholesale destruction; Bowl 7 brings total erasure." Swete observes:

> Writing in a century remarkable for the number and severity of its earthquakes, and to men whose country was especially subject to them, St John is careful to distinguish this final shock from even the greatest hitherto known.

Wilcock considers this to be the shaking predicted in Haggai 2:6, and expounded in Hebrews 12:26–27, which says:

> He has promised, saying, "Yet *once more I shake not only the earth, but also heaven.*" Now this, "Yet *once more,*" indicates the removal of those things that are being shaken, as of things that are made, that the things which cannot be shaken may remain.

With the **great city . . . divided into three parts** and **the cities of the nations** (v. 19) in ruin, this event brings antichristian civilization to an end. The statement that **great Babylon was remembered** (v. 19) suggests that the lingering question in the hearts of God's people, "Has God forgotten about the sins of the wicked?" is answered in the final judgment at the Second Coming. Hobbs and Summers consistently identify Babylon with Rome, though Hobbs writes:

⧗ HISTORICIST *(continued)*

the awesome and fearful character of the judgment, as Elliott writes:

> It seems to me very possible that there may be here, too, that which shall literally answer to the prediction. Compare the as yet unfulfilled prophecy of Isa. 30:30. But the analogy of all the Apocalyptic prefigurations requires primarily a *symbolic* explanation.

The division of the **great city** into **three parts** (v. 19) is explained as "the final breaking up of that decemregal form of the Papal empire, which has now characterized it for nearly thirteen centuries, into a new and tripart form" (Elliott).

Alternately, Barnes understands this three-part division as meaning that, when the time comes for the total destruction of the papacy, "there will be a threefold judgment—either a different judgment in regard to some threefold manifestation of that power, or a succession of judgments, *as if* one part were smitten at a time" (Barnes). Likewise, the cities of the nations are those cities the world over that have been under the power of the papacy. Barnes summarizes:

> The *fulfillment* of what is here stated will be found, according to the method of interpretation proposed, in the ultimate overthrow of the Papacy. The process described in this chapter is that of

⧗ PRETERIST *(continued)*

that are here intended. . . . This was the greatest commotion and alteration that God ever made in the heavens and earth of the church, and which was to be made only once.[21]

It is further significant to the identification of the city in question that it was **divided into three parts** (v. 19), a detail that has little discernible application to Rome or any other city than Jerusalem. Applied to the latter, it is an echo of Ezekiel 5:1–12, where the prophet was required to shave his hair from his head, divide it into three parts, and conduct a symbolic action upon each part. One third of the hair was burned, another third was to be chopped up with a sword, and the remaining third was to be scattered into the wind. Ezekiel was told by God: "This is Jerusalem" (Ezek. 5:5). In 586 BC some of the inhabitants of Jerusalem were burned inside the city, some were slain by the swords of the Babylonians, and the rest were scattered among the nations. That which occurred to Jerusalem in 586 BC happened again in AD 70.

In another sense, the besieged city was literally divided into three parts of warring factions among the entrapped Jews. As Carrington notes:

> This refers to the division into three factions, which became acute after the return of Titus. While Titus was besieging it from

literally the whole world will collapse around him, yet he will persist in thinking he is still the master of his own fate without any need for God.

The **great hail** (v. 21), if literal, is like none ever seen in history. Yet, as Biederwolf points out, "There is . . . no incontrovertible reason for not taking the hailstones in a literal sense," as do Gaebelein, Walvoord, Weidner, Simcox, and many others.

Hailstones of a hundred pounds each could kill sinners but not bring them to repentance, for we read the familiar refrain: **men blasphemed God** (v. 21). And this will be their dying posture.

After this judgment, "the next event is that prophesied in 19:11 where Christ Himself descends from heaven to take over His kingdom on earth," writes Walvoord. Ryrie concurs:

> The conclusion of this series of judgments brings us to the second coming of Christ. This is described in chapter 19, but John is first given a vision of the details concerning Babylon which has been mentioned several times before. 📖

No such physical judgment as John pictures falling upon the city of Rome is recorded in history up to this time. Should the "eternal city" be destroyed completely at some future time, the destruction would still be beside the point. John was using the figure of the seat of the persecuting empire to depict the final, complete destruction of all powers, both earthly and cosmic, which oppose Christ and his people.

With the foundations of the earth shaken and broken up, it remains for the superstructure of sinful civilization to be broken into pieces by hailstones **about the weight of a talent** (v. 21) each—about one hundred pounds. Such hailstones, if literal, would grind all plants, animals, men, and most structures to powder. There is probably an echo here of Isaiah 28:17—"The hail will sweep away the refuge of lies."

Of this total picture of devastation, Hendriksen writes: "The meaning is that in the final judgment the entire empire of evil is destroyed. It goes down into utter ruin."

Rather than repent and seek God's mercy in their final hour, the reprobate inhabitants of earth employ their dying breaths in blaspheming God (v. 21). Swete observes:

> Even Pharaoh had shown signs of repentance under the hail (Exod.

HISTORICIST *(continued)*

successive calamities that would weaken it and prepare it for its fall; then a rallying of its dying strength; and then some tremendous judgment . . . that would completely overthrow all that was connected with it.

PRETERIST *(continued)*

without, the three leaders of rival factions were fighting fiercely within: but for this the city might have staved off defeat for a long time, even perhaps indefinitely, for no great army could support itself for long in those days in the neighborhood of Jerusalem; there was no water and no supplies. The fighting within the city delivered it quickly into the hands of Titus.[22]

This is the second time in Revelation that we encounter **great Babylon** (v. 19; cf. 14:8). Whether this city is Jerusalem or Rome is further explored in our treatment of chapter 17.

A fascinating passage from Josephus may shed light on the prediction of hailstones weighing **about the weight of a talent** (v. 21). This is about a hundred pounds, and may not refer to literal hail. Many believe there is reference here to the hundred-pound, white stones hurled over Jerusalem's walls by Roman Catapults, according to the account of Josephus.[23]

⧖ **IDEALIST** *(continued)*

9:27), though he relapsed into impenitence as soon as it had ceased; but the age of the last plague blasphemed while it suffered.

SUMMARY OF CHAPTERS 14–16

Thus concludes the final cycle of sevens.

The *historicist* view has seen the final overthrow of the papacy depicted in these final judgments. The language is symbolic, referring to the French Revolution and subsequent events in European history—as well as some yet future—which bring the papal power to a complete end.

The *preterist* position divides between those who see this as a continuation of the prophecy of the downfall of Jerusalem, and those who believe that subject was left behind in chapter 11. The latter opinion sees this section as representing God's judgment upon the Roman Empire.

Futurists find in these chapters the very end of the Tribulation period. Just prior to the return of Christ, unprecedented judgments will be sent against the rebellious, Satan-worshiping subjects of the Antichrist. The climax will be the final great Battle of Armageddon, involving millions of troops from the majority of militarized nations. Christ will bring this war to a sudden end at His coming.

Idealist interpreters find a recapitulation of the trumpets series here, with an increase in intensity. These "last plagues" may be "last" in the sense of occurring at the end of time, or merely in the sense that, for certain individuals, whenever in history they occur, they are the last stroke of personal judgment from God.

NOTES

1. Elliott, *Horae Apocalypticae*, Vol. III, 260.
2. E. G. White, *The Great Controversy* (DeLand, FL:Laymen For Religious Liberty, 1888/1990), 389.
3. Walvoord does not make it clear why the good news that God is about to "establish His sovereignty over the world" should be distinguished from "the gospel of the kingdom," why such time-sensitive information should be called "the everlasting gospel," nor why either should be distinguished from "the gospel of grace."

4. Beale, *The New International Greek Testament Commentary*, 755.

5. Bauckham, *The Theology of the Book of Revelation*, 76.

6. Edward McDowell, *The Meaning and Message of the Book of Revelation* (Nashville: Broadman, 1951), 150.

7. E.g., Deut. 32:17 (1 Cor. 10:20); Deut. 32:21 (Rom. 10:19); Deut. 32:35f. (Rom. 12:19; Heb. 10:30); Deut. 32:43 (Rom. 15:10).

8. Beale, *The New International Greek Testament Commentary*, 815.

9. Morris, *The Revelation of St. John*, 187.

10. *The People's New Testament With Notes.*.

11. Elliott, *Horae Apocalyptica*, Vol. III, 341f.

12. Alison's *History of Europe*, vol. 1, 542–46.

13. Quoted by Chilton in *The Days of Vengeance*, 406.

14. Morris, *The Revelation of St. John*, 190.

15. *The Visions of Daniel and the Revelation Explained.*

16. In *A Study of the Book of Revelation* (Los Angeles: Times-Mirror Press, 1926), v.

17. Quoted in Chilton, *The Days of Vengeance*, 408.

18. Josephus, *Wars* III: 1:3; 111:4:2; V: 1:6; VII: 1:3.

19. Quoted in Morris, *The Revelation of St. John*, 191.

20. Ibid., 193.

21. Quoted in Chilton, *The Days of Vengeance*, 413–14.

22. Ibid., 415–16.

23. See Josephus, *Wars* V: 6:3—"The engines [catapults], that all the [Roman] legions had ready prepared for them, were admirably contrived; but still more extraordinary ones belonged to the tenth legion: those that threw darts and those that threw stones, were more forcible and larger than the rest, by which they not only repelled the excursions of the Jews, but drove those away that were upon the walls also. Now, *the stones that were cast were the weight of a talent,* and were carried two furlongs and farther. The blow they gave was no way to be sustained, not only by those that stood first in the way, but by those that were beyond them for a great space. As for the Jews, they at first watched *the coming of the stone, for it was of a white color,* and could therefore not only be perceived by the great noise it made, but could be seen also before it came by its brightness; accordingly the watchmen that sat upon the towers gave them notice when the engines was let go, and the stone came from it, and cried out aloud in their own country language, *"THE SON COMETH:"* so those that were in its way stood off, and threw themselves, the down upon the ground; by which means, and by their thus guarding themselves, the stone fell down and did them no harm. But the Romans contrived how to prevent that by blacking the stone, who then could aim at them with success, when the stone was not discerned beforehand, as it had been till then; and so they destroyed many of them at one blow."

PART VI

THE GREAT BABYLON
REVELATION 17—19

WHO OR WHAT DOES BABYLON REPRESENT? WHEN DO THESE EVENTS OCCUR?

⧖ HISTORICIST APPROACH:

- The fall of Babylon the harlot is the overthrow of the papal system of religion and government—yet to be seen in the future. These chapters feature the divergent reactions of the godly and the ungodly to this final vindication of true religion.
- The rider on the white horse represents the ongoing conquests of Christ through His Word, or else His continuing campaign of judgment upon other enemies.

⧖ PRETERIST APPROACH:

- Babylon is identified either with Rome or with Jerusalem.
- If the former, these chapters describe the downfall of the Roman Empire and especially of the city of Rome, the harlot.
- If Babylon is Jerusalem, these visions depict the burning of that city by the Romans and the mixed reactions of the wicked and the righteous.

⧖ FUTURIST APPROACH:

- Babylon may represent the Catholic Church or some great apostate religious entity forming under the Antichrist in the end times.
- Alternatively, Babylon may be a city—either a restoration of the ancient Babylon or a revived Rome.
- In any case, this great enemy of truth and righteousness will be destroyed in the end of the Tribulation, to the chagrin of the wicked but the rejoicing of the righteous.
- Jesus visibly returns to earth in chapter 19, riding a white horse.

⧖ IDEALIST APPROACH:

- Babylon represents the world system as the seducer of the godly.
- Its destruction at the end of the age is depicted in terms of its current manifestation in John's time: Rome.
- The ultimate judgment upon this harlot comes through Christ at His Second Coming, who is the rider on the white horse.
- Alternately, the rider may represent Christ's more gradual conquests over the world system through the preaching of the gospel.

THE VISION OF THE HARLOT

REVELATION 17:1–6

[1]Then one of the seven angels who had the seven bowls came and talked with me, saying to me, "Come, I will show you the judgment of the great harlot who sits on many waters, [2]with whom the kings of the earth committed fornication, and the inhabitants of the earth were made drunk with the wine of her fornication." [3]So he carried me away in the Spirit into the wilderness. And I saw a woman sitting on a scarlet beast, which was full of names of blasphemy, having seven heads and ten horns. [4]The woman was arrayed in purple and scarlet, and adorned with gold and precious stones and pearls, having in her hand a golden cup full of abominations and the filthiness of her fornication. [5]And on her forehead a name was written: MYSTERY, BABYLON THE GREAT, THE MOTHER OF HARLOTS AND OF THE ABOMINATIONS OF THE EARTH. [6]I saw the woman, drunk with the blood of the saints and with the blood of the martyrs of Jesus. And when I saw her, I marveled with great amazement.

⌛ HISTORICIST

Barnes points out that this chapter "properly commences a more detailed description of the judgment inflicted on the formidable antichristian power referred to in the last chapter, though under a new image."

Matthew Henry summarizes the significant points of the description of this woman, with brief comments:

> was written on her forehead. It was the custom of impudent harlots to hang out signs, with their names, that all might know what they were. Now in this observe, (1.) She is named from her place of resi-

⌛ PRETERIST

Though the fall of Babylon has been announced in 14:8 and described in 16:19, another whole section is required to tell the story more thoroughly. Chapters 17–19 reveal the destruction of Babylon in greater detail, the precursor to the marriage of the Lamb to a new bride. Appropriately, the chaste bride is contrasted with the wicked city depicted as a **great harlot** (v. 1). In order to gain this insight, John is transported in vision **into the wilderness** (v. 3). David S. Clark points out:

FUTURIST

This passage obviously involves a parenthetical look at events prior to the pouring out of the bowls in chapter 16. With the seventh bowl comes the Second Coming of Christ, which will be described in greater detail in 19:11ff. The power of the harlot apparently belongs to the first half of the Tribulation period, and her destruction falls within the middle, or at the beginning of "the Great Tribulation."

The harlot is called **Mystery, Babylon the Great** (v. 5), but the meaning of this name is much debated.

Babylon is widely regarded to be, in some sense, a symbol of Rome (supported by data that comes later in verses 9 and 18), but not all agree as to the specific sense in which Rome fits into the vision.

Many, including Ryrie, Gaebelein, and Ironside, agree with Walvoord, who understands the harlot to be a religious entity, a coalition of apostate churches, headquartered in Rome and, most probably, dominated by the Vatican:

> The description of the woman as arrayed in purple and scarlet and decked with gold, precious stones, and pearls is all too familiar to one acquainted with the trappings of ecclesiastical pomp today and especially of high officials in the Roman Catholic and Greek Orthodox churches. . . . It has been noted by many writers that the iniquitous and pagan rites of Babylon

IDEALIST

Bauckham notes:

> The two major symbols for Rome, which represent different aspects of the empire, are the sea-monster ('the beast': especially chapters 13 and 17) and the harlot of Babylon (especially chapters 17–18). The beast represents the military and political power of the Roman Emperors. Babylon is the city of Rome, in all her prosperity gained by economic exploitation of the Empire. Thus the critique in chapter 13 is primarily political, the critique in chapters 17–18 primarily economic, but in both cases also deeply religious. The beast and the harlot are intimately related. The harlot rides on the beast (17:3), because the prosperity of the city of Rome at the Empire's expense and her corrupting influence over the Empire rest on the power achieved and maintained by the imperial armies.[6]

The announcement of **the judgment of the great harlot** (v. 1) must have taken John by surprise, since no mention has previously been made even of her existence. Some have found a contradiction in the fact that John is informed that he is about to witness the judgment of the great Harlot—yet, most of the vision of chapter 17 has nothing to do with that judgment. For the most part, the vision portrays the lavish prosperity of the Harlot. Only one verse (16) mentions her judgment. Wilson believes

⧗ HISTORICIST *(continued)*

dence—*Babylon the great.* But, that we might not take it for the old Babylon literally so called, we are told there is a mystery in the name; it is some other great city resembling the old Babylon. (2.) She is named from her infamous way and practice; not only a harlot, but a mother of harlots, breeding up harlots, and nursing and training them up to idolatry, and all sorts of lewdness and wickedness—the parent and nurse of all false religion and filthy conversation. 5. Her diet: she satiated herself with *the blood of the saints and martyrs of Jesus.* She drank their blood with such greediness that she intoxicated herself with it; it was so pleasant to her that she could not tell when she had had enough of it: she was satiated, but never satisfied.

This woman, as suggested above, by Henry, is a religious entity, or a church. However, she is not the true Church of Jesus Christ, but an apostate institution that has strayed from her husband's bed and betrayed His trust. If the true remnant church is like a chaste bride (chap. 21), the unfaithful church is likened to a harlot. Bishop Wordsworth did not overstate the case when he wrote:

> It cannot be doubted that our most eminent divines have commonly held and taught that the apocalyptic prophecies concerning Babylon were designed by the Holy Spirit to

⧗ PRETERIST *(continued)*

Sometimes he was carried away into **heaven** to see visions; but the thing he was about to see now had no affinity with heaven, and he could not see such a scene as this in heaven, so he was taken to a wilderness as a more appropriate place, and one more in congruity with what he was about to see.

The **scarlet beast** (v. 3) is undoubtedly the same beast from the sea that was described in chapter 13. The details of its description are identical to that in chapter 13, except that nothing was stated earlier about the color of the beast. Identifying the beast as imperial Rome, J. Stuart Russell writes: "The *scarlet* colour . . . may easily be recognized as the symbol of Imperial dignity." David S. Clark writes: "This is the same beast, he is scarlet now, perhaps in allusion to the blood he had shed; and this beast, as we have seen, was the empire of Rome."

Though *preterists* like Russell and Clark agree upon the identity of the beast as Rome, they do not agree as to the identity of **the woman** (vv. 3, 4, 6) who rides the beast. Clark, Moses Stuart, Jay Adams, and others believe the woman to be the imperial city of Rome, whereas the beast represents the empire. These writers connect the Roman persecution of the church with the statement that the woman was **drunk with the blood of the saints and with the blood of the martyrs** (v. 6).

⧗ FUTURIST *(continued)*

crept into the early church and were largely responsible for the corruptions incorporated in Roman Catholicism from which Protestantism separated itself in the Middle Ages.

Ryrie agrees:

It is hard to escape the conclusion that the Roman church is the harlot. But this is not the whole picture, for the apostate church is not merely the Roman church. It will include other groups in a family relationship with their mother.

Elsewhere in Scripture, the word **harlot** (v. 1), when not speaking of an actual woman, generally refers to apostate Judaism,[5] and alludes to the practice of spiritual adultery, usually including the worship of idols, as Walvoord writes:

The symbolism of spiritual adultery is not ordinarily used of heathen nations who know not God, but always of people who outwardly carry the name of God while actually worshiping and serving other gods.

Other commentators interpret Babylon principally in political, cultural, or commercial terms, a representative of the anti-God systems of man in any age. Ladd considers Babylon to be the symbol of human civilization with all its pomp and circumstance, organized in opposition to God, and Tenney agrees:

⧗ IDEALIST *(continued)*

that John's **amazement** (v. 6) at the sight of the woman was occasioned by his expectation to see the announced "judgment of the great harlot," whereas the spectacle actually presented to him was that of the harlot's glories and triumphs in her sin.

Beale answers this objection by pointing out that this announcement does not pertain to chapter 17 alone, but to the larger literary unit of 17:1—19:4, which is definitely dominated by that judgment. This larger section is "a large interpretive review of the sixth and seventh bowls,"[7] which have previously described the downfall of Babylon.

The Harlot's position **on many waters** (v. 1) echoes a literal truth about ancient Babylon (cf. Jer. 51:13; Ps. 137:1), which straddled the Euphrates and its series of canals, though here the waters represent "peoples, multitudes, nations, and tongues" (v. 15).

The **fornication** committed by the **kings of the earth** (v. 2) refers to their "purchasing the favor of Rome by accepting her suzerainty and with it her vices and idolatries" (Swete).

In order to view the spectacle of the harlot's judgment, John is transported to **the wilderness** (v. 3) or a desert place. Martin Kiddle comments that the wilderness

represents the perpetual condition of Christian detachment from the

HISTORICIST *(continued)*

describe the Church of Rome. . . .
And it was maintained by those in
that learned age who were most
eminent for sober moderation and
Christian charity, as well as profound erudition.[1]

The **wilderness** (v. 3), or desert
place, Elliott sees as a reference to the
Campagna—the low plain surrounding
the city of Rome—which is in a desolate
state even to this day. This condition
began with the rise of the ten-horned
beast of Western anti-Christianity, upon
whose back the harlot church of Rome
rose to supremacy, and has continued
since that time.

This woman is ornately bedecked
with **purple and scarlet, and
adorned with gold and precious
stones and pearls** (v. 4), like the great
basilicas of the Roman Catholic Church.
Adam Clarke writes: "This strikingly
represents the most pompous and costly
manner in which the Latin church has
held forth to the nations the rites and
ceremonies of its idolatrous and corrupt
worship." Elliott, Vitringa, and Bengel,
with many others, see the purple and
scarlet as depicting the actual color of
the robes worn by the popes and the
cardinals.

Commenting on the inscription,
**THE MOTHER OF HARLOTS AND
OF THE ABOMINATIONS OF THE
EARTH,** John Wesley writes

PRETERIST *(continued)*

Clark writes:

> Here is her persecution. She was
> intoxicated with a fanatical zeal to
> exterminate the Christians . . .
> thousands on thousands executed
> in every form of torture. No won-
> der the word scarlet comes into the
> scene.

Russell, on the other hand, like Chilton, Carrington, Terry, and others,
holds that Jerusalem is the harlot Babylon. Russell is adamant that Rome does
not fit the symbol of the harlot Babylon
nearly as admirably as does Jerusalem,
marshaling a great deal of evidence to
support this assertion. His chief arguments are these:

1. The fall of Rome does not fall within
   the things "which must shortly
   take place," which is the stated subject matter of the Apocalypse (cf.
   1:1);

2. The Olivet Discourse, which Russell
   conceives as a shorter treatment of
   the same subject matter as Revelation, does not include a discussion
   of the fate of Rome (see Matthew
   24; Mark 13; Luke 21);

3. As Revelation presents a series of
   contrasts—a Lamb vs. a dragon;
   the Father's name vs. the beast's
   name on people's foreheads; the
   bride vs. the harlot—so also the
   Apocalypse contrasts two cities,

⧗ FUTURIST *(continued)*

To say that Rome is the final interpretation of this symbolism would not do justice to the text. The great harlot represents more than one city and more than one era of history. . . . To the reader it would convey the sum total of pagan culture, social, intellectual, and commercial, that had opposed and oppressed the people of God from time immemorial. . . . the actual city of Babylon, and perhaps Rome also, were the best examples of it in their day.

Ryrie writes:

The name is used for more than a city in these chapters; it also stands for a system. This is much the same as the way Americans speak of Wall Street or Madison Avenue. They are actual streets, but they also stand for the financial and advertising enterprises.

Mounce identifies Babylon as "a dominant world system based on seduction for personal gain over against the righteous demands of a persecuted minority . . . the final intensified expression of worldly power":

Every great center of power which has prostituted its wealth and influence restores to life the spirit of Babylon, which will provide the social, religious, and political base for the last attempt of Antichrist to establish his kingdom.

⧗ IDEALIST *(continued)*

affairs of civilization. . . . It is from the "desert" that the Christian is able to view civilization clearly, as it really is.[8]

The woman is seen as **sitting on a scarlet beast** (v. 3), which is apparently the same as the beast from the sea that was described in chapter 13. The only new feature of the description of the beast in this passage is its color "scarlet," which, if synonymous with "red," is the same color as the dragon in Revelation 12:3, yet another indicator linking this beast with Satan.

Along with the description of the harlot's gaudy attire, perhaps her most interesting feature is that **on her forehead a name was written** (v. 5) identifying her with Babylon, which has been mentioned briefly twice before (cf. 14:8; 16:19).

Wilson notes that the prostitutes of Rome customarily wore a headband with their names written upon it. Hobbs confirms this, mentioning Seneca and Juvenal as his sources.

Almost all expositors of this approach see in the description of the harlot (vv. 7ff.) a picture of Rome, though the image is extended by many to include a broader entity as well. Hailey writes: "There can be little or no doubt that the Babylon of this section is Rome; and Rome itself is a symbol of the great world city of lust and seduction." Hobbs,

⧗ HISTORICIST *(continued)*

Benedict 13th, in his proclamation of the jubilee, AD 1725, explains this sufficiently. His words are, "This catholic and apostolical Roman church is the head of the world, the *Mother* of all believers, the *Faithful Interpreter* of God, and *Mistress* of all churches." . . . But God somewhat varies the style (i.e., from Pope Benedict 13th), "The *Mother of Harlots*"—the parent, ringleader, patroness, and nourisher of many daughters, that closely copy after her.

As the Mother of Harlots, she is the church from which other impure (even Protestant) churches have been spawned, as Clarke writes:

> This inscription being written upon her forehead is intended to show that she is not ashamed of her doctrines, but publicly professes and glories in them before the nations; she has indeed a whore's forehead, she has refused to be ashamed. The inscription upon her forehead is exactly the portraiture of the Latin church.

Her cup is full of abominations, which Elliott identifies with indulgences, the worship of relics, and other sacrilegious practices introduced by the Roman church. "Abominations" in the Old Testament is a term for idolatrous images.

Even if we take "harlot" in its natural sense of sexual immorality, its use

⧗ PRETERIST *(continued)*

Babylon and the New Jerusalem. The latter is the church. The earthly Jerusalem is clearly in view in earlier chapters. To bring Rome into the picture at this point would introduce a third city and destroy the symmetry of the book;

4. As a symbolic name for Jerusalem, Babylon would be as fitting as Sodom and Egypt, which were applied to Jerusalem earlier (11:8);

5. The phrase "that great city" was used of Jerusalem earlier (11:8), as it is used repeatedly in these chapters regarding Babylon;

6. In chapter 14, the winepress was trodden "outside the city" (14:20), which almost all understand to refer to Jerusalem, yet the only "city" named earlier in that chapter is Babylon (14:8), hence, Babylon equals Jerusalem;

7. The division of Babylon into "three parts" in 16:19 best fits Jerusalem (see notes at that passage; cf. Ezek. 5:1–12);

8. The appellation "the harlot" is an established label for Jerusalem from the Old Testament (cf. Isa. 1:21; 57:8; Jer. 2:2, 20); it could never be applied to Rome or any Gentile city, since they have never been in a covenant relationship with God. As Chilton writes: "The metaphor of

466

⧗ FUTURIST *(continued)*

The systems of man have many aspects. With Ryrie and others, Walvoord said that the Babylon in chapter 17 and the Babylon in chapter 18 are not identical, representing different manifestations of the Babylonian spirit. Walvoord writes:

> It is helpful to consider chapter 17 as dealing with Babylon as an ecclesiastical or spiritual entity and chapter 18 as dealing with Babylon as a political entity.

The **scarlet beast** (v. 3), it is generally agreed, is the same beast that arose from the sea in chapter 13. Clearly the harlot and the beast are not identical, since the woman here is seen **sitting on** (v. 3) the back of the beast. Walvoord says:

> Her position, that of riding on the beast, indicates on the one hand that she is supported by the political power of the beast, and on the other that she is in a dominant role and at least outwardly controls and directs the beast.

Ryrie confirms this interpretation:

> The startling feature of this scene is that the [harlot] is sitting on the beast, indicating that she will have power over the man of sin. This event must occur during the first part of the tribulation before the man of sin overthrows religion and requires everyone to worship him. ⓠ

⧗ IDEALIST *(continued)*

too, writes: "Unless one sees Rome as symbolic of all powers arrayed against God, he will miss John's full message." Hendriksen takes Babylon to represent:

> the world viewed as the embodiment of "the lust of the flesh, the lust of the eyes, and the vainglory of life." . . . Babylon, then, is the world as the centre of seduction at any moment in history, particularly during this entire dispensation.

Alford breaks rank in this instance, and sides with the *historicists* in that he writes: "I do not hesitate therefore . . . to maintain that interpretation which regards papal and not pagan Rome as pointed out by the harlot of this vision."

It can be said that Rome, under several of its emperors, became **drunk with the blood of the saints and . . . of the martyrs of Jesus** (v. 6). This is also true of world governments throughout history, though Wilson suggests that this line probably refers to those slain by Nero.

Leon Morris writes:

> Now John fixes his eyes firmly on the end time. He concerns himself not with the apparent triumph of evil, but with its final and complete overthrow. He sees God as casting down every stronghold and hurling his judgments against the wicked. No might of theirs avails. God is completely triumphant.[9] ⓠ

⌛ HISTORICIST *(continued)*

here is appropriate, since sexual criminality has been common in the Vatican during certain periods. Pope John XII (955–963) was "guilty of almost every crime; violated virgins and widows, high and low; lived with his father's mistress; made the Papal Palace a brothel; was killed while in the act of adultery by the woman's enraged husband."[2]

Elliott and most others understand the fact that the harlot is **drunk with the blood of the saints and with the blood of the martyrs of Jesus** (v. 6) as a clear reference to the bloody persecutions perpetrated by the Roman church through the centuries. H. Grattan Guinness states: "It has been calculated that the popes of Rome have, directly or indirectly, slain on account of their faith fifty millions of martyrs."[3]

⌛ PRETERIST *(continued)*

harlotry is exclusively used in the Old Testament for a city or nation that has abandoned the Covenant and turned toward false gods; and with only two exceptions[4] . . . the term is always used for faithless Israel";

9. Jerusalem sat upon seven hills as truly as did Rome;

10. If "the kings of the earth" be understood to mean "the rulers of the land (Israel)," then Jerusalem, as appropriately as Rome, could be said to be "that great city" in 17:18 (see note there);

11. The expression "that great city which reigns over the rulers of the land" (v. 18) is fully equivalent to that which is said of Jerusalem in Lamentations 1:1—"Who was great among the nations! The princess among the provinces";

12. The Jews of Jerusalem were idolatrous, as was Rome;

13. No city other than Jerusalem could be charged with the blood of the prophets and saints and apostles (see 17:6; 18:20, 24).

THE MYSTERY OF THE HARLOT EXPOUNDED

REVELATION 17:7—11

[7]But the angel said to me, "Why did you marvel? I will tell you the mystery of the woman and of the beast that carries her, which has the seven heads and ten horns. [8]The beast that you saw was, and is not, and will ascend out of the bottomless pit and go to perdition. And those who dwell on the earth will marvel, whose names are not written in the Book of Life from the foundation of the world, when they see the beast that was, and is not, and yet is. [9]Here is the mind which has wisdom: The seven heads are seven mountains on which the woman sits. [10]There are also seven kings. Five have fallen, one is, and the other has not yet come. And when he comes, he must continue a short time. [11]The beast that was, and is not, is himself also the eighth, and is of the seven, and is going to perdition."

⌛ HISTORICIST

This woman sits on the seven-headed beast, which has been readily identified with Rome, often called the seven-hilled city. The beast **was, and is not, and will ascend out of the bottomless pit** (v. 8), meaning, "The Roman Empire was the beast, or idolatrous persecuting power, when under the pagan emperors; it ceased to be so when it became Christian; and became so again under the Roman pontiffs, and shall 'go to perdition.'"[10]

Elliott, Newton, Cuninghame, Mede, Guinness and others take the seven kings to represent the seven forms of government under which the Roman Empire existed during the course of its history.

⌛ PRETERIST

The focus of these verses shifts from interest in the identity of the harlot to that of the beast upon which she is seen riding. There is little controversy about identifying this beast with Rome, though various expositors differ in the way they draw this identification from the data of the passage. The principal concern in verses 7 through 11 has to do with the meaning of the seven heads of the beast as **mountains** (v. 9) and **kings** (v. 10). David S. Clark writes:

> We had the beast located geographically on the seven hills, which meant Rome. Now we have him located in history to tell us what period of Rome we are deal-

⧗ FUTURIST

The reference to the seven mountains (v. 9) is generally regarded as an unmistakable clue that Rome is intended, since Rome from ancient times was called "the city on the seven hills." This view will be found in Ryrie, Gaebelein, Petingill, Simcox, Moorehead, and many others.

Seiss disagrees:

> A flimsier basis for such a controlling and all-conditioning conclusion is perhaps nowhere to be found. The seven *hills* of the city of Rome, to begin with, are not *mountains*, as everyone who has been there can testify; and if they were, they are no more characteristic of the situation of Rome than the seven hills are characteristic of Jerusalem. But the taking of them as literal hills or mountains at all is founded upon a total misreading of the angel's words.

Seiss (and, seemingly, Walvoord) said that the seven **mountains** (v. 9), being described also as seven **kings** (v. 10), implies not literal mountains, but empires that have risen in succession in history. The five that had fallen in John's day would thus be Egypt, Assyria, Babylon, Medo-Persia, and Greece. This would still identify the current empire to be the Roman, since that is the sixth. The seventh is not yet come. Of these seven powers, Seiss writes:

⧗ IDEALIST

Wilson suggests that the beast is described in terms reminiscent of Nero, who is thus a symbol of the Antichrist. The **seven heads are seven mountains** (v. 9)—usually identified with Rome, but believed by many to extend by interpretation to the various world empires which have each been "peaks" in their respective periods. Milligan, Hengstenberg, and others who see the beast as the embodiment of the antiGod spirit of secular power, have suggested this interpretation, among them Hendriksen:

> The seven heads have a twofold symbolical significance. They indicate both the present embodiment of the beast [Rome in John's day] and all of its embodiments throughout history.

In the ages-long history of the beast, five of its heads (kingdoms) have already **fallen, one is, and the other has not yet come** (v. 10). The fallen empires in John's day were Ancient Babylonia, Assyria, New Babylonia, Medo-Persia, and Greco-Macedonia (Hendriksen). The one not yet fallen, of course, was Rome. As for the seventh, Hendriksen speculates that it may be the collective title for all antichristian governments from the fall of Rome until the final empire of Antichrist, which is the eighth. He asks, perhaps rhetorically, "Does the clause 'and is of the seven' indicate that, in some sense, one of the

HISTORICIST *(continued)*

The five already fallen are kings, consuls, dictators, decemvirs, and military tribunes. The sixth, present in John's day, was that of the military emperors, or Caesars. Of this succession of governmental forms, Guinness writes:

> Seven kings formed the first head, and lasted 220 years; consuls, tribunes, decemvirs, and dictators, were the next four heads, and governed Rome in turn for nearly 500 years; sixty-five emperors followed, and ruled the Roman world for 500 years more.[11]

Scholars differ in their identification of the seventh form. Bishop Newton saw the seventh as "the Dukedom of Rome." Cuninghame equates it with the Christian emperors from Constantine to Augustulus. Mede understands it as the Western government after the division of the empire into East and West. Elliott conceives the seventh to be that ushered in under Diocletian, which received its death wound in Julian through the Christian emperor Theodosius. The eighth form is thus identified as the papacy, beginning with Gregory; in it Elliott sees the persecuting power of the former emperors, restored to life.

PRETERIST *(continued)*

ing with. And there is no period of Rome's history that will fit this description but the dynasty of the Caesars. . . . John says five of these kings are fallen, viz. Julius Caesar, Augustus, Tiberius, Caligula, Claudius, all these five had passed away when John wrote this book; and one is, viz. Nero, who was then on the throne; and one is yet to come, Galba, and when he cometh, he shall continue a short space. Accordingly Galba succeeded Nero, and his short space was a reign of seven months.

J. Stuart Russell, attempts to identify seven mountains upon which Jerusalem sits, and manages to name only four, but Chilton writes:

> It is not at all necessary, with Russell (The *Parousia*, 492), to seek seven mountains in Jerusalem as the fulfillment of this statement. The Harlot is seated on the Beast, and thus on the seven hills of Rome; in other words, apostate Judaism, centered in the City of Jerusalem, is supported by the Roman Empire.

Russell is also in his own camp with reference to the meaning of the *seven kings*, about whom he said:

> From the appointment of Cuspius Fadus to the outbreak of the Jewish war, there were seven governors who bore supreme rule in Jerusalem and Judea . . . They are related to the beast as Romans and as

⏳ FUTURIST *(continued)*

By these seven great powers then, filling up the whole interval of this world's history, this Harlot is said to be carried. On these she rides, according to the vision. It is not upon one alone, nor upon any particular number of them, but upon all of them, the whole seven-headed Beast, that she sits . . . They were each and all the lovers, supporters, and defenders of organized falsehood in religion, the patrons of idolatry, the foster friends of all manner of spiritual harlotry.

Among *futurists* there are also some (e.g., Gaebelein) who understand the seven kings in the same sense as do the *historicists,* namely, as seven forms of government under which Rome had existed throughout its history.

The unexpected reference to **the eighth** (v. 11) apparently refers to the man himself, who is the leader of the seventh or final world empire. ▣

⏳ IDEALIST *(continued)*

former antichristian empires will be reestablished?"

Beckwith takes the kings to be individual rulers of Rome, though he believes that the number seven is symbolic:

> The Roman empire must fill out its destined place in history, it must have its complete tale of kings denoted by the typical number seven; then Antichrist comes, who succeeds the Roman empire which he destroys; he forms an eighth ruler added to the seventh . . . but at the same time he is "of the seven," inasmuch as he is one of the seven (Nero) reincarnate.

Concerning the eighth being **of the seven** (v. 11), Milligan's approach differs from those of either Hendriksen or Beckwith:

> The preposition *"of"* is to be understood in its common acceptance in John's writings, as denoting origin, identity of nature: as Primasius puts it, "the beast is the essence, the concentrated expression of the seven, the embodiment of their spirit. ▣

473

PRETERIST *(continued)*

deputies; and they are related to the woman as governing powers. It is now easy to see how Nero himself, the beast from the sea, or foreign tyrant, may be said to be the eighth, and yet of the seven. 🌀

THE MYSTERY EXPOUNDED (CONTINUED)

REVELATION 17:12—18

[12]"The ten horns which you saw are ten kings who have received no kingdom as yet, but they receive authority for one hour as kings with the beast. [13]These are of one mind, and they will give their power and authority to the beast. [14]These will make war with the Lamb, and the Lamb will overcome them, for He is Lord of Lords and King of kings; and those who are with Him are called, chosen, and faithful." [15]And he said to me, "The waters which you saw, where the harlot sits, are peoples, multitudes, nations, and tongues. [16]And the ten horns which you saw on the beast, these will hate the harlot, make her desolate and naked, eat her flesh and burn her with fire. [17]For God has put it into their hearts to fulfill His purpose, to be of one mind, and to give their kingdom to the beast, until the words of God are fulfilled. [18]And the woman whom you saw is that great city which reigns over the kings of the earth."

 HISTORICIST

As Halley observes:

> 'Babylon" is stated to be the great city reigning over the kings of the earth (17:18), which, at the time, was Rome . . . The City of Rome, first Pagan, then Papal, has been the Dominating Power of the

PRETERIST

In these verses the explanation shifts from a consideration of the beast's seven heads to his **ten horns** (v. 12). These are also said to represent as many **kings,** but apparently of a different sort from those in verse 10. According to Russell:

⧗ FUTURIST

We are now told that the beast's **ten horns** represent an equal number of **kings** (v. 12). But how do these differ from the seven kings symbolized by the heads of the beast? Walvoord explains:

> These kings in contrast to the seven heads of the beast are kings who rule not in succession but simultaneously at the end time. By comparison with chapter 13, it will be seen that this is the form of the Roman Empire just preceding the world empire.

Most dispensationalists equate these ten horns with the ten toes of the image in Nebuchadnezzar's dream (Daniel 2) and the ten horns on the fourth beast that Daniel saw rising from the sea (Daniel 7). They are confederate with the beast (v. 13) and will ultimately be made to **make war with the Lamb** (v. 14) at the Battle of Armageddon (cf. 19:17–21). This war, of course, will be won by the Lamb since He alone is the victorious **Lord of Lords and King of kings** (v. 14). Ryrie writes: "Christ's titles, 'King of kings' and 'Lord of Lords,' are

⧗ IDEALIST

Wilson believes that the **ten kings** (v. 12) probably are to be identified with the "kings from the east" mentioned in 16:12. Summers identifies them as representing the "power of the Empire" (i.e., the Roman Empire of John's day). Hobbs agrees, but specifies that the ten kings are the former rulers of territories that became subject to Rome, permitted to retain authority only as puppets of Rome. Swete makes the same identification.

Alford, in this instance agreeing with the *futurists*, identifies the ten as a future coalition of ten European kingdoms that will grow out of the fourth beast of Daniel 7:23:

> In the precise number and form here indicated, they have not yet arisen, and what changes in Europe may bring them into the required number and form is not for us to say.

On the other hand, many (e.g., Hengstenberg, Milligan) join Hendriksen, who considers ten a number to be taken symbolically, representing all the

⏳ HISTORICIST *(continued)*

World for Two Thousand Years, 200 BC. to AD 1800.[12]

The **ten kings** (v. 12) are actually ten kingdoms summed up in their kings. These are ten Romano-Gothic kingdoms existing in AD 532: the *Anglo-Saxons*, the *Franks*, the *Alleman-Franks*, the *Burgundic-Franks*, the *Visigoths*, the *Suevi*, the *Vandals*, the *Ostrogoths*, the *Bavarians*, and the *Lombards*. Elliott points out that the number has varied slightly in subsequent history, but the number ten was nonetheless maintained as the number comprising the Western Roman or papal kingdoms. In the sixth century, these ten RomanoGothic kingdoms appropriated to themselves the Roman diademic badge of sovereignty.

These ten "kings" will ultimately be seen as playing a key role in the destruction of the Harlot, who is identified as the papal (false) church (v. 16), but, prior to that, they make war against the *true* Church. This is characterized as a war waged against **the Lamb** (v. 14), though the form it took was, no doubt, the persecution of the saints by pagan Rome. The faithful saints, whose warfare is spiritual, not carnal (cf., Rev.12:11), are the instruments through which the Lamb ultimately defeats pagan Rome. Matthew Henry emphasizes the grandeur of this victory:

⏳ PRETERIST *(continued)*

This symbol signifies the auxiliary princes and chiefs who were allies of Rome and received commands in the Roman army during the Jewish war . . . It is not incumbent to produce the exact number of *ten*, which, like seven, appears to be a mystic or symbolic number.

Turning our attention back to the harlot, we learn that the **waters which you saw, where the harlot sits, are peoples, multitudes, nations, and tongues** (v. 15). This would fit the identification of the woman with Rome neatly enough, as would the statement in verse 18. However, those who think the harlot to be Jerusalem are quick to show how these verses fit their position as well, as Chilton explains:

Jerusalem could truly be portrayed as seated on "many waters" (i.e., the nations) because of the great and pervasive influence the Jews had in all parts of the Roman Empire before the destruction of Jerusalem. Their synagogues were in every city.

The woman is seen to be destroyed by the ten horn-kings of the beast that previously had carried her in verse 16. They **hate the harlot** (v. 16), destroy, strip, eat, and burn her with fire.

Ezekiel made an identical prediction concerning the harlot Jerusalem:

⧖ FUTURIST *(continued)*

especially significant in light of the Lordship the beast will assume over these kings."

The **waters** (v. 15) upon which the harlot sat are next defined as **peoples, multitudes, nations, and tongues.** According to Ladd,

> Rome could be said to be seated on many waters in the sense that she drew her strength and sovereignty from her conquest of many nations; but it will be even more true of eschatological Babylon, who will seduce all the world to worship that which is not God.

Gaebelein writes that the Roman church

> even now can boast of her children among all nations. She gets her support from the whole world. And when she gets her revival she will have a still greater dominion. The kings of the earth then yield once more to her spiritual fornication.

Walvoord here departs from his customary practice of interpreting references to rivers, streams, and fountains of waters literally:

> Generally speaking, when water is mentioned in Revelation, it should be taken literally. The fact that a symbolic meaning is specifically assigned to it here indicates that this is the exception to the usual rule.

⧖ IDEALIST *(continued)*

antichristian *cultural* powers on earth which would arise after the breakup of the Roman Empire:

> The ten kings are really all the mighty ones of this earth in every realm: art, education, commerce, industry, government, in so far as they serve the central authority.

On the question of the identity of the ten kings, the jury is still "out." Whoever they may be, however, it is clear that they **make war with the Lamb** (v. 14), which suggests initially persecution of the Lamb's followers, though the Lord Himself appears later to dispense with His enemies personally (19:11ff.).

The woman sits upon, or rules over, many **peoples, multitudes, nations, and tongues** (v. 15). Swete points out that Rome's "greatest danger lay in the multitudes which were under her sway, and out of which would arise the 'ten kings' who were to bring about her downfall."

Leon Morris writes:

> Wicked men are not just one happy band of brothers. Being wicked, they give way to jealousy and hatred. At the climax their mutual hatreds will result in mutual destruction.

We get a fascinating glimpse at the sovereignty of God in His direction of political history in the comment: **God**

⌛ HISTORICIST *(continued)*

The victory is justly aggrandized. 1. By the vast multitude who paid obedience and subjection to the beast and to the [harlot]. She sat upon (that is, presided over) many waters; and these waters were so many multitudes of people, and nations, of all languages; yea, she reigned not only over kingdoms, but over the kings, and they were her tributaries and vassals, v. 15, v. 18. 2. By the powerful influence which God hereby showed he had over the minds of great men. Their hearts were in his hand, and he turned them as he pleased; for, (1.) It was of God, and to fulfil his will, that these kings *agreed to give their kingdom unto the beast;* they were judicially blinded and hardened to do so. And, (2.) It was of God that afterwards their hearts were turned against the [harlot], to hate her, and to *make her desolate and naked, and to eat her flesh, and burn her with fire;* they shall at length see their folly, and how they have been bewitched and en-slaved by the papacy, and, out of a just resentment, shall not only fall off from Rome, but shall be made the instruments of God's provi-dence in her destruction.

The burning of the woman **with fire** (v. 16) by the ten kings is conceived by Elliott to refer to the spoiling and burning of Rome by the Gothic powers in the fifth and sixth centuries. It is mentioned in the future tense, because

⌛ PRETERIST *(continued)*

I will gather all your lovers with whom you took pleasure . . . I will gather them from all around against you and will uncover your nakedness to them . . . They shall also strip you of your clothes, take your beautiful jewelry, and leave you naked and bare. . . . They shall burn your houses with fire . . . and I will make you cease playing the harlot. (Ezek. 16:37–41)

To many, none but Rome could, in John's day, be described as **that great city which reigns over the kings of the earth (v. 18).** By contrast, Chilton defends the identification of the city with Jerusalem:

Revelation is not a book about poli-tics; it is a book about the Covenant. Jerusalem *did* reign over the na-tions. She *did* possess a Kingdom which was above all the kingdoms of the world. She had a covenantal priority over the kingdoms of the earth. . . . When Israel was faithful to God, offering up sacrifices for the nations, the world was at peace; when Israel broke the Cov-enant, the world was in turmoil. The Gentile nations recognized this (1 Kings 10:24; Ezra 1:4–7; cf. Rom. 2:17–24).

Russell takes another approach to defending the identification of Jerusalem with the harlot city. He points out that the expression "kings of the earth" in the Greek is found not only throughout

FUTURIST *(continued)*

When the beast has no further use for his mistress Babylon, he will turn his loyal dogs, the ten horns, upon her, and she will be killed and her body ravaged and burned, as Ryrie writes:

> Religious Babylon, who sought political alliances and power will in the end be destroyed by a political alliance. It will be these ten nations who "make her desolate."

The statement that the ten kings will **eat her flesh** (v. 16) is possibly an allusion to the fact that Jezebel's flesh was eaten by dogs, rather than given a decent burial. Gaebelein suggests this, and holds that this harlot and "Jezebel" in 2:20 both are symbols for Roman Catholicism. The destruction of the harlot apparently takes place in the middle of the Tribulation, spelling the end of all religious worship other than that directed to the beast. Ryrie writes:

> For the first half of the tribulation she will reign unchallenged; but at the middle of the tribulation, the beast (the man of sin) will see her as a challenge to his own power and program. So with his league of ten nations he will destroy the harlot and set himself up to be worshiped.

Walvoord elaborates:

With the beginning of the second half of the week, the ruler of the revived Roman Empire, who is the

IDEALIST *(continued)*

has put it into their hearts to fulfill His purpose (v. 17), as Moffatt writes:

> A divine overruling controls all political movements (cf. 11:2; 13:5, 7) . . . The irony of the situation is that the tools of providence are destroyed, after they have unconsciously served their purpose (as in Isa. 10:12f.).

Beale, takes issue with *preterists*, who see Babylon as Jerusalem, and with the historicists and many *futurists*, who see the Harlot as the corrupt church, on the basis that this woman is said to reign **over the kings of the earth** (v. 18). He asserts that neither Jerusalem nor the church can admirably fit this description, and that it is better understood to refer to "the entire evil economic-religious system of the world throughout history."[13]

The common identification of **great city** (v. 18) with Rome of John's day is contested by many. Alford believes this to be impossible because the devastation described here never happened to pagan Rome.

On the other hand, Bauckham does not think that the details of the fall of Babylon should be understood literally:

> The last of the seven bowls results in the fall of Babylon in an earthquake of unprecedented proportions (16:17–21). If we took this as literal prediction, we should soon find it contradicted by later images

479

⧗ HISTORICIST *(continued)*

this destruction was still in the future from John's perspective, but it is past with reference to the time of the papal church, which is the time pictured in the vision.

Others understand this burning as future to the time of the vision, a description of the final overthrow of the Romish system. This would thus refer to the calamities that began with the French Revolution (as seen in the bowl judgments) and might find its fulfillment in the future through a socialistic or communistic European commonwealth (Caringola).

Calling the harlot **that great city which reigns over the kings of the earth** (v. 18), would seem to identify the woman, beyond all question, as Rome. The particular identification of her with *papal* Rome seems supported by the fact that, of the twenty-one mentions of harlotry in the Bible, eighteen refer to the apostate people of God, either Israel or the church (Alford). Even the three exceptions may be more apparent than real, as Simcox has pointed out. Examples of these references include: Isaiah 1:21; Jeremiah 2:20; Ezekiel 16 and 23; and Micah 1:7. ▨

⧗ PRETERIST *(continued)*

Revelation but also in Acts 4:26–27, in which Herod and Pontius Pilate are identified by the very same expression. Plainly, then, in Acts the expression means "the leaders or rulers of the *Land* (i.e., of Israel). If that is the phrase's meaning here in verse 18, then Jerusalem surely can be said to be the city that reigns over the rulers of Israel. ▨

⧖ FUTURIST *(continued)*

political head of the world empire and is himself designated also as "the beast," is able to proclaim himself dictator of the whole world. In this capacity he no longer needs the help and power of the church. . . . Many find a parallel revelation in Daniel 11:36–39 where the willful king likewise puts aside all other deities in favor of the worship of himself.

⧖ IDEALIST *(continued)*

of the downfall of Babylon. In 17:16, Babylon, now portrayed as a harlot, is stripped, devoured and burned by the beast and the ten kings. The traditional punishment of a harlot is here superimposed on the image of a city sacked and razed to the ground by an army. Chapter 18 extends the image of a city besieged and burned to the ground.[14]

BABYLON IS FALLEN

REVELATION 18:1—3

¹After these things I saw another angel coming down from heaven, having great authority, and the earth was illuminated with his glory. ²And he cried mightily with a loud voice, saying, "Babylon the great is fallen, is fallen, and has become a dwelling place of demons, a prison for every foul spirit, and a cage for every unclean and hated bird! ³For all the nations have drunk of the wine of the wrath of her fornication, the kings of the earth have committed fornication with her, and the merchants of the earth have become rich through the abundance of her luxury."

⌛ HISTORICIST

The declaration that Babylon is already **fallen** (v. 2) does not mean that the actual destruction of that city is past (since it is still said to be future in v. 21). It means, rather, that its judgment is sufficiently imminent to justify the use of the prophetic past tense, as Cachemaille explains:

> At the time corresponding with the opening of this chapter, the actual sudden destruction of Babylon has not yet taken place. There is first (vv. 2, 3) some awful change in her for the worse, some great moral downfall, now proclaimed far and wide over the earth. Then (vv. 4–7) a warning voice to any of God's people who may still be in her, at their peril; together with a declaration of the retributive character of the judgment now imminent.[15]

Barnes, by contrast, contends: "The idea is that of utter desolation; and the

⌛ PRETERIST

The fall of **Babylon** (v. 2), according to how one has dealt with the previous relevant passages, is either the fall of Rome in the year 476 (Luiz de Alcazar, David S. Clark, Jay Adams, Moses Stuart), or the destruction of the Jewish polity and religion at the fall of Jerusalem in AD 70 (Chilton, Russell, Terry, et al.). For the defense of the respective positions, see commentary at chapter 17.

The fact that Babylon has become a habitation of **every foul spirit** and **every unclean and hateful bird** (v. 2) is known to be true of Jerusalem, and Israel in general, which was first overrun by demons around the time Christ was due to be born. It is notable that, despite the infrequency of the mention of "evil spirits" in the Old Testament, such spirits seemed to come out in force to oppose Jesus during His ministry. It is as though the demons, in anticipation of Christ's

⧗ FUTURIST

Opinions differ as to whether the **angel coming down from heaven** (v. 1) is the Lord himself or simply an important created being. More important, probably, is the content of his announcement: **Babylon the great is fallen, is fallen** (v. 2). The repetition of the phrase "is fallen" is thought by Seiss to suggest

> two separate parts or stages of the fall, answering to the two aspects in which Babylon is contemplated, referring first to Babylon in mystery, as a *system* or spirit of false worship, and second to Babylon as *a city*, in which this system or spirit is finally embodied.

The idea that "Mystery Babylon" in chapter 17 is not identical to the commercial entity called "Babylon" in this chapter is not uncommon among *futurist* expositors. Those who draw a distinction, however, are not unanimous as to the precise nature of the difference. Ryrie writes:

> The emphasis in chapter 17 is on the religious and political aspects of Babylon and in 18 on the commercial aspect. Babylon is both a city and a system. . . . In addition, there is another difference between these two chapters. In chapter 17 it was the beast and his allies who destroyed the harlot Babylon. Here it is God who destroys this aspect of Babylon.

⧗ IDEALIST

The angel who here announces the fall of Babylon seems to have not only **great authority** (v. 1), but also an infectious radiance, for **the earth was illuminated with his glory.** Swete observes: "So recently has he come from the Presence that in passing he flings a broad belt of light across the dark earth." The announcement that **Babylon the great is fallen, is fallen** (v. 2), in a terse form, was encountered earlier (cf. 14:8), but without elaboration. Here it becomes the topic sentence of an extended oracle and lamentation.

The extended lamentation is a collage of fragments taken from multiple Old Testament messages of doom. Richard Bauckham observes:

> It is a remarkable fact, for example, that John's great oracle against Babylon (18:1–19:8) echoes every one of the oracles against Babylon in the Old Testament prophets, as well as the two major oracles against Tyre.[16]

In a footnote, he provides the Old Testament references to which he has alluded. On Babylon: Isa.13:1–14:23; 21:1–10; 47; Jer. 25:12–38; 50–1; On Tyre: Isaiah 23; Ezek. 26–28.

Commenting on verse 2, which says that Babylon **has become a dwelling place of demons, a prison for every foul spirit, and a cage for every unclean and hated bird,** Swete writes:

⧗ HISTORICIST *(continued)*

meaning here is, that spiritual Babylon—Papal Rome (ch. xiv. 8)—will be reduced to a state of utter desolation resembling that of the real Babylon."

Since we are told that **the earth was illuminated** (v. 1) with the glory of the angel who announces the downfall of Babylon, some commentators, including Elliott, Vitringa, and Daubuz, expect that "there will be a diffusion of great religious light" (Elliott), which will result in widespread conversions to true Christianity, just prior to the destruction of the papal system, and/or following it.

That Babylon is said to have become the dwelling place of **demons, and every foul spirit, and every unclean and hated bird** (v. 2) is a spiritualized allusion to Isaiah 13:21–22, which speaks of the fall of the literal Babylon in Mesopotamia.

The mention that all the nations have drunk of the wine of the wrath of her fornication (v. 3) harks back to Jeremiah 51:7: "Babylon was a golden cup in the LORD's hand, that made all the earth drunk. The nations drank her wine; therefore the nations are deranged.

Barnes writes:

> It is not necessary to suppose this of the city of Rome itself—for that is not the object of the representation. It is the *Papacy*, represented under the image of the city and having its seat there. *That* is to be

⧗ PRETERIST *(continued)*

coming, had invaded the Land of Israel, hoping to impede His mission. Of course, they were no match for Him, and His ministry to Israel could be characterized as the liberation of a "man" from demonic bondage (an image Jesus used with reference to His own generation—Matt.12:43ff.). That "man's" (Israel's) rejection of Christ caused an even greater number of demons to return to afflict him, as Jesus predicted (Matt.12:45). As a consequence, of this surrender to demonic forces, Jerusalem also was reduced to ground level, again as Christ predicted (Matt. 24:2), allowing the region to become the haunt of the desert creatures considered unclean in the Jews' religion. No such literal fulfillment of these words has been demonstrated with regard to Rome.

The statement, however, that **the merchants of the earth have become rich through the abundance of her luxury** (v. 3), seems to fit Rome better than Jerusalem. Certainly Rome could most naturally be said to have had a major impact upon the world's economy. On the other hand, Jerusalem was charged with committing **fornication** with **the kings of the earth** (v. 3) in Old Testament times (Ezek. 16:14–15, 26, 28–30; 23:12–21). The prophet used this imagery to explain God's reason for bringing judgment upon Jerusalem by the hands of the Babylonians in 586 BC. It would seem appropriate that the New

⧗ FUTURIST *(continued)*

Walvoord follows a similar reasoning:

After the disposal of Babylon in its religious form by its destruction at the hands of the beast, the prophetic revelation in chapter 18 then deals with Babylon as a political force also destined for destruction at a later date.

Walvoord gives two reasons for distinguishing between the Babylon in chapter 17 and that in this chapter. First, there is mourning mentioned in connection with the Babylon in this chapter, whereas none seems to be associated with the fall of Babylon in chapter 17. His second reason is:

The destruction of Babylon in chapter 18 should be compared with the preceding announcement in 16:19 where the great city is divided and the cities of the Gentiles fall. This event comes late in the great tribulation, just prior to the second coming of Christ, in contrast to the destruction of the harlot of chapter 17 which seems to precede the great tribulation. 🖉

⧗ IDEALIST *(continued)*

The evil spirits, watching over fallen Rome like night birds or harpies that wait for their prey, build their eyries in the broken towers, which rise from the ashes of the city.

Hailey writes: "Such a prison of unclean spirits stands in contrast to the holy city into which nothing unclean or abominable shall enter (21:27)."

Verse 3 reminds us that the **kings of the earth** and **the merchants of the earth** have consorted with the harlot (also mentioned in v. 2 of the previous chapter), though the specific point that the merchants **have become rich** through this association is a new detail, which sets the stage for their lamenting over her fall in verses 11–16. 🖉

HISTORICIST *(continued)*

destroyed as utterly as was Babylon of old; that will become as odious, and loathsome, and detestable as the literal Babylon, the abode of monsters is.

 PRETERIST *(continued)*

Testament apostle/prophet would employ the same language in describing a near-identical event, the destruction of Jerusalem by the Romans.

COME OUT OF HER

REVELATION 18:4—8

⁴And I heard another voice from heaven, saying, "Come out of her, my people, lest you share in her sins, and lest you receive of her plagues. ⁵For her sins have reached to heaven, and God has remembered her iniquities. ⁶Render to her just as she rendered to you, and repay her double according to her works; in the cup which she has mixed, mix double for her. ⁷In the measure that she glorified herself and lived luxuryously, in the same measure give her torment and sorrow; for she says in her heart, 'I sit as queen, and am no widow, and will not see sorrow.' ⁸Therefore her plagues will come in one day—death and mourning and famine. And she will be utterly burned with fire, for strong is the Lord God who judges her."

HISTORICIST

The call, **Come out of her, my people,** recalls Isaiah's and Jeremiah's exhortations for the Jewish exiles to leave Babylon to return to their own land (Isa. 48:20; Jer. 51:6, 45).

Barnes makes the application to the Roman church:

As applicable to Papal Rome, in view of her impending ruin, this means (a) that there might be found in her some who were the true people of God; (b) that it was

PRETERIST

There is nothing in these verses to specifically encourage the identification of Babylon with Rome, although there is nothing to forbid it either. The entire chapter is filled with allusions to Old Testament oracles against Babylon, Tyre, Sodom, and Jerusalem. The specific details do not need to be pressed as applicable to the present case if we accept the meaning that, in principle, the judgment of this city is like God's historical judgments upon great cities of the past.

⌛ FUTURIST

The appeal, "Come **out of her, my people**" (v. 4), is to whatever godly people may still have survived and not been translated late in the Tribulation, just prior to the final destruction of the world system at the coming of Christ, as Ryrie writes:

> In its primary interpretation this appeal will be addressed to those believers who will be living in the tribulation days and who like believers in every age will be tempted to compromise.

In v. 4, two reasons are given for separation from Babylon: (1) to avoid being seduced and becoming a participant in **her sins;** (2) to avoid receiving a portion in **her plagues.** With reference to the comment that **her sins have reached to heaven** (v. 5), Walvoord observes that the verb "reached" is "Gr., *kollaō*, literally 'glued' or 'welded together,'" i.e., piled one on another as bricks in a building," which makes this an allusion to the Tower of Babel, where Babylon had its beginning (Gen. 11:5–9).

⌛ IDEALIST

The warning goes out to God's people regarding the doomed city to **Come out of her, my people, lest you share in her sins, and lest you receive of her plagues** (v. 4). Seeing the prophecy addressed to the fall of Rome, Hobbs believes this passage calls for "the complete separation of the saints of Asia from their pagan neighbors. They were to have nothing to do with idolatry and other evils."

Many others see the exhortation's intention as extending far beyond the time of John's original readers. Hailey writes: "The call of the voice John heard was not instruction to leave the city of physical Rome, for wherever one goes he is amidst people of the world." Wilson clarifies that

> to come out of Babylon does not require local removal from the place itself (1 Cor. 5:10), but is rather a demand to the churches for complete moral separation from her iniquities so that they do not participate in her plagues (Isa. 51:11; Jer. 51:45; 2 Cor. 6:17).

487

⧖ HISTORICIST *(continued)*

their duty to separate wholly from her—a command that will not only justify the Reformation, but which would have made a longer continuance in communion with the Papacy, when her wickedness was fully seen, an act of guilt before God; (c) that they who remain in such a communion cannot but be regarded as partaking of her sin; and (d) that if they remain, they must expect to be involved in the calamities that will come upon her. There never was any duty plainer than that of withdrawing from Papal Rome; there never has been any act attended with more happy consequences than that by which the Protestant world separated itself forever from the sins and the plagues of the Papacy.

Verses 6 and 7 are simply stating that the punishment of Babylon will be proportionate, though double, to her wicked activities. The prediction that she will be **utterly burned with fire** (v. 8) is likely to be figurative, according to Barnes, though he says it not impossible that Rome will ultimately be burned with fire. Vitringa cites an opinion held among the rabbis that Rome would thus come to its end. Gibbon documents the belief of early Christians that "the country of the Scipios and Caesars should be consumed by a flame from heaven, and the city of the seven hills, with her palaces, her temples, and

⧖ PRETERIST *(continued)*

On the other hand, some features in these verses fit well with the assumption that Babylon is Jerusalem just prior to AD 70. The call to **Come out of her, my people** (v. 4) not only echoes similar exhortations concerning ancient Babylon (cf. Isa. 48:20; Jer. 50:8; 51:6), but also Christ's instructions to the disciples to flee from the condemned city at the first sign of its imminent doom (cf. Luke 21:20–23). The epistle to the Hebrews as a whole (and especially passages like Heb. 12:25–29; 13:13–14) constitutes just such a call as that found here.

The statement that **her sins have reached to heaven** (v. 5) is an apparent allusion to God's assessment of Sodom in Genesis 18:21, and Sodom has already been used as a symbolic name for Jerusalem (Rev. 11:8). One of the provisions of the New Covenant was God's promise that "I will remember no more" the sins and iniquities of His people (Jer. 31:34). This is one of the "better promises" (Heb. 8:6) by which the New Covenant outshines the first. Contrarily, it can be said of her who related to God on the basis of the Old Covenant, and violated it, that **God has remembered her iniquities** (v. 5). This was Jerusalem.

That God has determined to **repay her double** (v. 6) for her sins is another link to Jerusalem and Judah, of whom the prophet said, "I will repay double for

⏳ FUTURIST *(continued)*

The punishment of Babylon will be proportionate, **just as she rendered to you** (v. 6), but the measurement will be mixed in the cup of wrath double strength. The particular means of destruction, that **she will be utterly burned with fire** (v. 8), as well as other features of this chapter, echo the lament over Babylon in Jeremiah 50 and 51. It is said that these prophecies have never historically been fulfilled upon ancient Babylon, which gives reason for some to expect an actual rebuilding of that city in the end-times, and this new Babylon will be destroyed suddenly by fire. One of those expecting such a rebuilding is Henry Morris:

> The scriptures do not describe the source of such a devastating fire, but it surely can be no ordinary fire. The buildings of Babylon will certainly be of fireproof construction, yet they will be completely incinerated. Possibly the earthquake belches fire and brimstone from the earth's mantle. Possibly nuclear missiles stored in Babylon are somehow detonated. Perhaps it is all strictly supernatural fire from heaven.

⏳ IDEALIST *(continued)*

Lenski writes:

> The constant danger confronting God's people is to be taken in by the antichristian seduction which seeks to entice and entangle them.

Hendriksen writes:

> The admonition to leave Babylon is addressed to God's people in all ages (cf. Isa. 48:20; 52:11; Jer. 50:8, 41–44; Zech. 2:7). From this fact it appears that Babylon is not only the city of the end time. It is the world, as centre of seduction, in any age.

As Babylon of old had its origins in the Tower of Babel, the goal of which was to reach to heaven, so the spiritual Babylon has finally achieved the ancient goal—its **sins have reached to heaven** (v. 5)!

The boast of this Babylon, **I sit as queen and am no widow, and will not see sorrow** (v. 7), echoes that of ancient Babylon, according to Isaiah 47:7–9:

> And you [Babylon] said, "I shall be a lady forever. . . . I am and there is no one else besides me; I shall not sit as a widow, nor shall I know the loss of children." 🕮

HISTORICIST *(continued)*

her triumphal arches, should be buried in a vast lake of fire and brimstone."

 PRETERIST *(continued)*

their iniquity and their sin" (Jer. 16:18) and, "Bring on them the day of doom, and destroy them with double destruction!" (Jer. 17:18).

That the calamity comes **in one day** (v. 8) is not to be taken too literally, as Chilton writes:

> The term Day here does not signify some specific duration of time; but it is used here to indicate relative suddenness, as well as emphasizing that the destruction of Jerusalem would be no random occurrence: it was coming as a Day of Judgment.

FORNICATORS LAMENT; APOSTLES AND PROPHETS AVENGED

REVELATION 18:9—24

[9]"The kings of the earth who committed fornication and lived luxuriously with her will weep and lament for her, when they see the smoke of her burning, [10]standing at a distance for fear of her torment, saying, 'Alas, alas, that great city Babylon, that mighty city! For in one hour your judgment has come.' [11]And the merchants of the earth will weep and mourn over her, for no one buys their merchandise anymore: [12]merchandise of gold and silver, precious stones and pearls, fine linen and purple, silk and scarlet, every kind of citron wood, every kind of object of ivory, every kind of object of most precious wood, bronze, iron, and marble; [13]and cinnamon and incense, fragrant oil and frankincense, wine and oil, fine flour and wheat, cattle and sheep, horses and chariots, and bodies and souls of men. [14]The fruit that your soul longed for has gone from you, and all the things which are rich and splendid have gone from you, and you shall find them no more at all. [15]The merchants of these things, who became rich by her, will stand at a distance for fear of her torment, weeping and wailing, [16]and saying, 'Alas, alas, that great city that was clothed in fine linen, purple, and scarlet, and adorned with gold and precious stones and pearls! [17]For in one hour such great riches came to nothing.' Every shipmaster, all who travel by ship, sailors, and as many as trade on the sea, stood at a distance [18]and cried out when they saw the smoke of her burning, saying, 'What is like this great city?' [19]They threw dust on their heads, and cried out, weeping and wailing, and saying, 'Alas, alas, that great city, in which all who had ships on the sea became rich by her wealth! For in one hour she is made desolate.' [20]Rejoice over her, O heaven, and you holy apostles and prophets, for God has avenged you on her." [21]Then a mighty angel took up a stone like a great millstone and threw it into the sea, saying, "Thus with violence the great city Babylon shall be thrown down, and shall not be found anymore. [22]The sound of harpists, musicians, flutists, and trumpeters shall not be heard in you anymore. No craftsman of any craft shall be found in you anymore, and the sound of a millstone shall not be heard in you anymore. [23]And the light of a lamp shall not shine in you anymore, and the voice of bridegroom and

bride shall not be heard in you anymore. For your merchants were the great men of the earth, for by your sorcery all the nations were deceived. [24]And in her was found the blood of prophets and saints, and of all who were slain on the earth."

HISTORICIST

Much of the imagery in this section comes from passages in Ezekiel 27 and 28 referring to the fall of the city of Tyre. Papal Rome is here likened to Tyre with respect to its pride, luxury, and economic strength.

The **burning** (vv. 9, 18) of the city is to be taken as the downfall of the papal power, whether figurative, as Barnes thinks, or with actual fire. Vitringa and Daubuz equate this burning with the catastrophic burning mentioned in 17:16, in which the harlot was set aflame by the ten kings. Elliott, however, rejects this interpretation. He thinks papal ecclesiastical Rome will be destroyed by a combination of an earthquake and of volcanic fire and smoke of divine origin. He raises two objections to the view of Vitringa and Daubuz: (1) "How could the kings well have been her burners now, when in fact they were her mourners?" and (2) if the fire is of human agency, "whence all the terror and standing afar off of the kings, merchants, and shipmasters?"

Among the goods no longer to be available from Babylon are **gold and silver, precious stones and pearls** (v. 12). The historian Gibbon mentions such stones and pearls as being among

PRETERIST

This lengthy section brings out these principal features:

(a) Babylon falls suddenly—**in one hour!** (vv. 10, 17, 19);

(b) The fall of Babylon will be permanent and irrevocable (vv. 11, 14, 21, 22, 23);

(c) Babylon had once been associated with an abundance of luxury commodities (vv. 11–17);

(d) The fall will be the occasion of great lamentation for **the kings of the earth [or *land*]** (v. 9), for **the merchants of the earth [or *land*]** (vv. 11, 15), and for **every shipmaster . . . sailors, and as many as trade on the sea** (v. 17);

(e) The same event will be an occasion for rejoicing and vindication for the **holy apostles and prophets** (v. 20) and the **prophets and saints** (v. 24).

Most of the above features fit reasonably well either with the assumption that Babylon is Rome or that Babylon is Jerusalem. Points (c) and (d) might seem to fit Rome better than Jerusalem, whereas points (a) and (b) fit Rome less perfectly than Jerusalem. Point (e) can as readily be applied to either Jerusalem or Rome.

The principal objections to the identification with Rome would be that

⧗ FUTURIST

Several expositors believe it likely that ancient Babylon in modern Iraq may be rebuilt in the last days, attaining its former glory and becoming the commercial center of the world. Gaebelein is certain that Babylon will be rebuilt, while Ryrie considers it "a matter of debate." Tenney and others state it as a possibility. In view of alternative theories, Walvoord considers it "simpler to postulate a rebuilt Babylon as fulfilling literally the Old Testament prophecies as well as that embodied in this chapter." Haldeman writes: "Rome will be the political [and] Babylon the commercial, capital of Antichrist's kingdom."[19] Tenney agrees:

> Babylon is the symbol and epitome of a pagan culture, but it may also be a very real place. Perhaps the latter days will see the construction of a great world metropolis, the seat of final world empire and the summation of all that the ingenuity of man can devise. If so, Babylon is yet to come in its final manifestation.

Abraham Kuyper writes that the location of "that great city" will "certainly . . . neither be Babylon nor Rome." Biederwolf considers the suggestion of a rebuilt Babylon as "not to be seriously considered."

Of the weeping and mourning of the **merchants** (v. 11) and **shipmasters** (v. 17) over the destruction of Babylon, Ryrie writes:

⧗ IDEALIST

This dirge is modeled after the lamentation over Tyre in Ezekiel 27. The section closes with a call for the saints to **rejoice** (v. 20) in their vindication at the fall of their enemy, but the chapter mainly focuses upon the grief and chagrin of those sympathetic to Babylon, the **kings** (vv. 9–10), **merchants** (vv. 11–16), and **shipmasters** (vv. 17–19), who formerly had plied a profitable trade with the mistress city. Wilson, who links Babylon closely with Rome, writes:

> Here the client kings of Rome wail over the fall of their seducer and protector ('the strong city'), because it has brought their own power and influence to a swift end.

Placing **the souls of men** (v. 13) at the end of the list of commodities may suggest that, of all the articles bought and sold, the lowest value was placed upon human life. The value attributed to human life in Rome can be seen in the great numbers of slaves, prostitutes, and victims of the amphitheater that fed Rome's insatiable thirst for affluence, pleasure, and entertainment.

Milligan calls into question the strict identifying of Babylon with Rome, arguing that pagan Rome was never the great commercial city suggested in chapter 18, and that it did not cease to purchase goods even after its pagan condition ended.

⧗ HISTORICIST *(continued)*

the articles that contributed to the luxury of Rome. He speaks of "precious stones, among which the pearl claimed the first rank after the diamond." But spiritual Babylon traffics not only in material goods but in **the souls of men** (v. 13), through "the sale of indulgences, dispensations, absolutions, masses, [papal] bulls, etc."[17]

The imagery of casting a **millstone** (v. 21) into the water harks back to Jeremiah 51:63–64, where a similar act is used to predict ancient Babylon's fall:

> Now it shall be, when you have finished reading this book, that you shall tie a stone to it and throw it out into the Euphrates. Then you shall say, "Thus Babylon shall sink and not rise from the catastrophe that I will bring upon her. And they shall be weary."

The list of familiar sights and sounds that shall not **be found . . . anymore** (vv. 22f.) in Babylon deliberately echoes in detail the very similar predictions in Jeremiah 7:34 and 25:10. The statement, **by your sorcery all the nations were deceived** (v. 23), is explained by Barnes:

> It is a common representation of Papal Rome that she has *deceived* or *deluded* the nations of the earth . . . and no representation ever made accords more with the facts as they have occurred. The word *sorceries* here refers to the

⧗ PRETERIST *(continued)*

Rome did not fall suddenly (point a), nor permanently (point b). These points are anticipated by David S. Clark, along with other "Babylon=Rome" advocates:

> Rome was frequently sacked and burned, captured again and again, and in her fall there was the suddenness of calamity, and the gradualness of decline. That a city called Rome exists in the present day, does not nullify this interpretation. The old persecuting Rome fell. The enemy of God and the church received her punishment.

Jay Adams writes:

> The passages in which these ideas occur are poetical—in fact are in the form of a funeral dirge. Allowance must be made for poetic language which was never intended to be taken precisely.

The objections to Jerusalem being Babylon would rest upon the fact that Jerusalem was not so much of a commercial center (point c) as was Rome, nor did the fall of Jerusalem cause an economic crisis for the kings, merchants, and shipmasters of the earth (point d).

In answer to the first objection, it may be said that the demands of the passage do not require that the city in question be the greatest commercial center *in the world*—only that it was a wealthy, cosmopolitan trading city, by

⌛ FUTURIST *(continued)*

The merchants of the earth weep and sorrow, for they see the source of their "careless ease" vanishing before their eyes. This motive for their lamentation is plainly stated in 11b. It is not that they care about Babylon, but they do care about their businesses. . . . This will be a stock market crash on a worldwide scale, and in the face of it the thoughts of unsaved men will only turn to how their interests are affected.

In verses 12 and 13, twenty-eight commodities are listed that will no longer be available from Babylon. Most of them are luxury items, suggesting the great affluence and opulence of the Antichrist's economic empire, as Gaebelein writes:

And in studying the articles of the commerce of apostate Christendom we notice that these are nearly all articles of luxury. The greatest panic has then come and there will be no recovery of the market.

While the loss of these things causes the lost men and women of the earth to mourn and lament, the same event gives the occasion for rejoicing by God's people, because **God has avenged** (v. 20) them upon her, as Tenney writes:

The kings and merchants mourn because their luxury and power have been destroyed, and thus

⌛ IDEALIST *(continued)*

Hendriksen emphasizes the connection with Rome less than the more general application to the world as seducer *in general:*

When Babylon perishes, the economic chaos is complete; the world of the unbeliever, on which he has pinned his hopes and built his trust, collapses! This is true with respect to the fall of every Babylon—whether it is literal Babylon, or Nineveh, or Rome.

The phrase **for God has avenged you on her** (v. 20) should be translated "God has judged your judgment on her." Caird sees this as an application of the law of malicious witness (Deut. 19:16–19), which demanded that if a man had been found to have borne false testimony against his brother, he would be punished with the very penalty that he intended for his brother to suffer. Rome had laid false charges against the Christians, even condemning innocent saints to death. The penalty for that perjury is now exacted upon Rome in the form of Rome's own death. Summers and Hobbs—who have seen in the previous verses the fall, first of the Roman Empire, then of Rome's allies—take the **great millstone** (v. 21) to represent the capital city itself, and its disappearance of the "eternal city" into the sea as the last vestige of the empire.

⌛ HISTORICIST *(continued)*

various arts, the tricks, impostures, and false pretenses by which this has been done.

The guilt of the recipient of these judgments and her worthiness to suffer them is summed up in the statement, **in her was found the blood of prophets and saints, and of all who were slain** (v. 24). Cachemaille writes,

> That the Church of Rome has shed more innocent blood than any other institution that has ever existed among mankind, will be questioned by no Protestant that has a complete knowledge of history . . . These atrocities were not perpetrated in the brief paroxysms of a reign of terror, or by the hand of obscure sectaries, but were inflicted by a triumphant Church, with every circumstance of solemnity and deliberation.[18] ⌛

⌛ PRETERIST *(continued)*

whose business international merchants were made rich. These things were certainly true of Jerusalem.

David Chilton writes:

> The wealth of Jerusalem was a direct result of the blessings promised in Leviticus 26 and Deuteronomy 28. God had made her a great commercial center, but she had abused the gift. While there are similarities between the list of goods here and that in Ezekiel 27:12–24 (a prophecy against Tyre), it is likely that the items primarily reflect the Temple and the commerce surrounding it.

When we remember that "kings of the earth" and "merchants of the earth" can be translated as "rulers of the Land (i.e., of Israel)" and "merchants of the Land (i.e., of Israel)," respectively, the arguments against identifying Babylon with Jerusalem seem less conclusive. ⌛

⌛ **FUTURIST** *(continued)*

their hope of a civilization of complete comfort has vanished. Babylon, their earthly and sensual paradise, has been destroyed, and they are left inconsolable. On the other hand, the angel bids the people of God to rejoice, because God has finally avenged the blood of His people on their chief enemy.... The removal of Babylon thus makes way for the city of God, the civilization that God produces through regeneration. ⌕

⌛ **IDEALIST** *(continued)*

Hendriksen, Wilcock, and others, however, understand Babylon more universally as the seductive world system and its demise as the end of the world at the coming of Christ. Hendriksen explains the casting of the stone **into the sea** (v. 21) as a means of indicating how "thoroughgoing and complete will be Babylon's fall. Never will the great millstone be retrieved. Thus, this wicked world, as the centre of seduction, will perish forever." Wilcock agrees:

> The tumult of the waters, as the great boulder is hurled into the sea, dies down flat calm. . . . The stone sinks beneath the surface, and civilization is as though it had never been. ⌕

THE MARRIAGE OF THE LAMB HAS COME

REVELATION 19:1—10

[1]After these things I heard a loud voice of a great multitude in heaven, saying, "Alleluia! Salvation and glory and honor and power belong to the Lord our God! [2]For true and righteous are His judgments, because he has judged the great harlot who corrupted the earth with her fornication; and He has avenged on her the blood of His servants shed by her." [3]Again they said, "Alleluia! Her smoke rises up forever and ever!" [4]And the twenty-four elders and the four living creatures fell down and worshiped God who sat on the throne, saying, "Amen! Alleluia!" [5]Then a voice came from the throne, saying, "Praise our God, all you His servants and those who

fear Him, both small and great!" ⁶And I heard, as it were, the voice of a great multitude, as the sound of many waters and as the sound of mighty thunderings, saying, "Alleluia! For the Lord God Omnipotent reigns! ⁷Let us be glad and rejoice and give Him glory, for the marriage of the Lamb has come, and His wife has made herself ready." ⁸And to her it was granted to be arrayed in fine linen, clean and bright, for the fine linen is the righteous acts of the saints. ⁹Then he said to me, "Write: 'Blessed are those who are called to the marriage supper of the Lamb!'" And he said to me, "These are the true sayings of God." ¹⁰And I fell at his feet to worship him. But he said to me, "See that you do not do that! I am your fellow servant, and of your brethren who have the testimony of Jesus. Worship God! For the testimony of Jesus is the spirit of prophecy."

⏳ HISTORICIST

The call for God's friends to rejoice in the downfall of Babylon was issued in Revelation 18:20. In these opening verses we read of the response to that exhortation. The four occurrences of **Alleluia!** in the first six verses are the only times that word appears in the New Testament. Verses 7 through 10 announce that the time has come for **the marriage of the Lamb** (v. 7), a term found nowhere else in Scripture, though the idea of Christ taking a bride is not unique to this passage (cf. Matt. 9:15; 22:2ff.; John 3:29; 2 Cor. 11:2; Eph. 5:25–27).

With the fall of the papal system, the church is prepared to join Christ in further conquests of the nations through the gospel and to celebrate His triumphal reign. Since **Alleluia** (v. 1) is a Hebrew word, it suggests to Elliott, Vitringa, Daubuz, and others, that the Jews are to have a prominent part in

⏳ PRETERIST

David Chilton presents a side-by-side comparison of the first six verses of this passage with the last five verses (15–19) of chapter 11, seeking to establish the identity of subject matter in the two passages which represent the closing visions of the two major sections of the book. There are six elements in each passage:

1. **loud voices . . . in heaven** (11:15; 19:1);

2. the declaration of the commencement of the reign of God (11:15, 17; 19:1, 6);

3. the **twenty-four elders** fall on their faces and worship (11:16; 19:4);

4. the avenging of **the blood of His servants** is announced (11:18; 18:24; 19:2);

⌛ FUTURIST

Here were have the first reference to **the marriage of the Lamb** (v. 7), and we must identify the participants. Gaebelein writes:

> But who is the bride about to become the Lamb's wife? Some teach that it is Israel to be united with the Lord in the closest bonds. But these expositors forget that the scene is a heavenly one. This marriage does not take place on earth where the faithful remnant looks up expecting Him to appear for their deliverance, but this marriage is in glory.

Gaebelein, despite this statement, fully expects the broken marital relationship between God and Israel to be restored, and that God will take back his adulterous wife of the Old Testament "in the day of her national repentance when the Lord comes." This national repentance, however, will not bring Israel into fellowship with the church, which—as dispensationalism teaches—is eternally separate from the redeemed Israel. However, the bride of the Lamb in this passage is acknowledged to be "the Church of the New Testament." Most dispensationalists (e.g., Walvoord, Ryrie, Ironside) would agree with Tenney on this identification:

> The "marriage of the Lamb" is certainly figurative of the ultimate union of Christ with His people. The word "church" is not used

⌛ IDEALIST

For the fifth time in the Book of Revelation, this chapter brings us to the end, when Christ returns (cf. 6:12ff.; 11:15ff.; 14:14ff.; 16:17ff.), closing Act 6.

Two aspects of this event are presented in the two parts of the chapter. The opening verses (1–10), proclaim the wedding day for Christ and His church; in verses 11–21, it is the day of doom for the followers of the beast.

Hendriksen explains in some detail the Jewish marriage customs of apostolic times, from which the biblical imagery is derived. It begins with the betrothal of the bride to the groom. This is as binding as marriage itself (Ex. 22:16), so those thus betrothed are called husband (2 Cor. 11:2) and wife (Luke 2:5).[21] The period of betrothal allows the groom to pay the dowry to the father of the bride and gives the bride opportunity to prepare for the wedding. After an interval of betrothal, the groom comes with his friends to the bride's home, from which he conveys her back to his own home or that of his parents. There the wedding supper is held and the marriage consummated. Hendriksen applies these particulars to the marriage of Christ and the church:

> Throughout the entire Old Testament dispensation the wedding was announced. Next, the Son of God assumed our flesh and blood: the betrothal took place. The price—the dowry—was paid on

499

⌛ HISTORICIST *(continued)*

this song. Elliott writes: "the Jews will probably just at, or after this catastrophe, be converted and join, and perhaps take the lead in, the earthly Church's song of praise on the occasion."

Matthew Henry inclines to the same opinion:

> Some think this refers to the conversion of the Jews, which they suppose will succeed the fall of Babylon; others, to the general resurrection: the former seems more probable.

The **marriage of the Lamb** (v. 7) is variously understood, depending upon the millennial leanings of the scholars. It either represents the future state of the true church after the fall of the papacy "as if in permanent union with her glorious head" (Barnes), or it may refer to the true church at present, in a relationship to be intensified in the future. Caringola writes: "In Christ, we have already attained to this event. Yet the prophecy signifies that the church, at this point of triumph, attains to permanent union with her head and Lord." Barnes observes:

> Papal Rome has just been represented as a gay and meretricious woman; and there is a propriety, therefore, in representing the true church as a pure bride, the Lamb's wife, and the final triumph of that church as a joyous marriage. . . .
> All the preparations had been

⌛ PRETERIST *(continued)*

5. reference to God's **servants . . . who fear Him, small and great** (11:18; 19:5);

6. loud noises, including **thunderings** (11:19; 19:6).

The final point in chapter 11 is the opening of the heavenly temple (v. 19). At the end of this section, **the marriage of the Lamb** (v. 7) is announced. Chilton concludes: "The appearance of the Bride, prepared for marriage, is thus equivalent to the opening of the Temple and the full establishment of the New Covenant." An intriguing and unique element of this segment is the introduction of the marriage of the Lamb, a concept not previously hinted at in Revelation, though the unfaithful harlot has received much attention. Chilton writes:

> *The destruction of the Harlot and the marriage of the Lamb and the Bride—* the divorce and the wedding—*are correlative events.* The existence of the Church as the congregation of the New Covenant marks an entirely new epoch in the history of redemption. God was not now merely taking Gentile believers into the Old Covenant (as He had done under the Old Testament economy). Rather, He was bringing in "the age to come" (Heb. 2:5; 6:5), the age of fulfillment . . . With the final divorce and destruction of the unfaithful wife in AD 70, the

FUTURIST *(continued)*

here, but the bride can scarcely mean anything else.

Dispensationalists take the timing of the marriage to be "immediately after the rapture of the church" (Ironside), although they also believe that the Rapture occurred fifteen chapters earlier (Rev. 4:1), whereas the marriage is not announced until the end of the Tribulation. Since the church is the bride at this marriage, it remains to identify **those who are called to the marriage supper of the Lamb** (v. 9). Walvoord identifies the guests with "the saints of past and future ages" and writes:

> The unfounded notion that God treats all saints of all ages exactly alike is hard to displace in the theology of the church. The fact that the divine purpose is not the same for Israel, the Gentile believers, or the church of the present age is plainly written in the Word of God.

Ladd, with whom Mounce agrees, disagrees with this position:

> A recent commentator [Walvoord] sees here a distinction between the church (the bride) and the invited guests (the saints of the Old Testament and millennial periods). This ignores the fluidity of metaphorical language. . . . Christ is both the Lamb and the shepherd of the sheep (Rev. 7:17) and a conquering warrior as well (Rev. 19:11ff.). So the church is both the bride and those invited.

IDEALIST *(continued)*

Calvary. And now, after an interval which in the eyes of God is but a little while, the Bridegroom returns and "It has come, the wedding of the Lamb."

Moffatt writes: "The marriage day of Christ and his church is the day of his second advent."

The fourth beatitude in the book (19:9) is reserved for the guests who are invited to participate in the wedding feast, as Milligan writes:

> It may be a question whether we are to distinguish between the bride herself and those who appear to be spoken of as guests at the marriage supper. But the analogy of Scripture, and especially of such passages as Matt. 22:2; 26:29, lead to the conclusion that no such distinction can be drawn. Those who are faithful to the Lord are at once the Lamb's bride and the Lamb's guests.

Wilson agrees: "This beatitude makes apparent the fluidity of biblical metaphors, for the saints are not only the bride, but are also the guests at the wedding." Lange explains this anomaly: "The Church in its unitous form is the Bride; in its individual members it consists of guests."

The **fine linen** (v. 8) worn by the bride is explained by Swete to consist of "the sum of the saintly acts of the members of Christ, wrought in them by His Spirit."

HISTORICIST *(continued)*

made for a permanent and uninterrupted union with its Redeemer,
and the church was henceforward
to be recognized as his beautiful
bride, and was no more to appear
as a decorated harlot—as it had
during the Papal supremacy.

Observing the fluidity of the metaphor, Halley points out that "At the
Marriage Supper, Individuals are spoken of as Guests (9); but Collectively
they are called the Bride (7)."[20]

John foolishly falls down before the
angel to worship him, for which he is
roundly rebuked. As part of the reason
for not worshiping this divine messenger, John is told **"For the testimony of
Jesus is the spirit of prophecy."** This
enigmatic statement is helpfully paraphrased by Matthew Henry thus:

> *"I am thy fellow-servant, and of thy
> brethren which have the testimony of
> Jesus*—I am a creature, thine
> equal in office, though not in na-
> ture; *I*, as an angel and messenger
> of God, *have the testimony of Jesus*,
> a charge to be a witness for him
> and to testify concerning him,
> and thou, as an apostle, having
> *the Spirit of prophecy*, hast the
> same testimony to give in; and
> therefore we are in this brethren
> and fellow-servants."

Caringola says the rebuke John received for nearly worshiping the angelic
messenger should stand as a reminder

PRETERIST *(continued)*

marriage of the Church was firmly
established.

A prerequisite of the coming of the
marriage day is that **His wife has
made herself ready** (v. 7). Chilton
comments:

> The duty of the apostles during
> the Last Days was to prepare the
> Church for her nuptials. Paul
> wrote of Christ's sacrifice as the
> redemption of the Bride: He
> "loved the Church and gave Him-
> self up for her; that He might
> sanctify her, having cleansed her
> by the washing of water with the
> Word; that He might present to
> Himself the glorious Church,
> having no spot or wrinkle or any
> such thing; but that she should
> be holy and blameless" (Eph.
> 5:25–27). Paul extended this im-
> agery in speaking to the Corin-
> thians about the goal of his
> ministry:"I am jealous for you
> with godly jealousy; for I be-
> trothed you to one Husband, that
> to Christ I might present you as a
> pure virgin" (2 Cor. 11:2–3).

The preparedness of the bride involves two distinct aspects. On the one
hand, the **righteous acts** that comprise her wedding attire are a gift of
grace **granted** (v. 8) to her by God. On
the other, she **has made herself
ready** (v. 7). These bring out both
man's (1 Tim. 4:16; 1 John 3:3) and
God's (Col. 1:22; Eph. 5:26) agency in

⧗ FUTURIST *(continued)*

All of these things overwhelm John, prompting him to almost worship the angel giving him the information. For this error he is sharply rebuked and told that **the testimony of Jesus is the spirit of prophecy** (v. 10). The meaning of this enigmatic statement is given by Ryrie as: "the study of prophecy should witness to Jesus." Gaebelein paraphrases it: "All prophecy concerns the Lord Jesus Christ." ◎

⧗ IDEALIST *(continued)*

The angel's words of rebuke to John, **I am your fellow servant, and of your brethren who have the testimony of Jesus** (v. 10) parallels the similar statement in 22:9, where the angel states: "I am your fellow servant, and of your brethren the prophets." This suggests that those who are credited with bearing the testimony of Jesus are not simply all the believers, but more specifically the Christian *prophets*, which helps make sense of the following comment: **the testimony of Jesus is the spirit of prophecy** (v. 10).

The difficulty presented by this comment is the ambiguity of the use of the genitive, which may be subjective or objective. If the former, then the testimony is that given *by* Jesus; if the latter, it is the testimony of others *about* Jesus. Taking the genitive as subjective, Wilson believes that this can be paraphrased: "the testimony given by Jesus is the word that the Spirit puts into the mouths of the prophets." Taken as an objective genitive, it would be paraphrased something like: "All true prophecy testifies about Jesus (i.e., He is the focus and primary interest of all true prophecy)." ◎

⧗ HISTORICIST *(continued)*

of the sinfulness of worshiping any created being or thing—" something the great apostate church failed to learn. Man, who is created in God's image, is to worship Christ only—not popes, saints, angels, relics, Mary." ⧉

⧗ PRETERIST *(continued)*

the sanctification of the church (cf. 1 Thess. 5:15–24). ⧉

THE RIDER ON THE WHITE HORSE

REVELATION 19:11—21

[11]Now I saw heaven opened, and behold, a white horse. And He who sat on him was called Faithful and True, and in righteousness He judges and makes war. [12]His eyes were like a flame of fire, and on His head were many crowns. He had a name written that no one knew except Himself. [13]He was clothed with a robe dipped in blood, and His name is called The Word of God. [14]And the armies in heaven, clothed in fine linen, white and clean, followed Him on white horses. [15]Now out of His mouth goes a sharp sword, that with it He should strike the nations. And He Himself will rule

(continued on page 505)

⧗ HISTORICIST

The riding forth of Christ on the **white horse** (v. 11) is understood either as the ongoing victories accomplished by the church through the Word of God, the **sharp sword** (v. 15) that proceeds **out of His mouth,** or else it is Christ's continuing judgment upon His enemies as He conquers the nations at Armageddon, as described in Revelation 16:16. In either case, the horse is symbolic.

⧗ PRETERIST

While some preterists see all references to the coming of Christ as being fulfilled in AD 70, most *preterist* commentators expect an actual coming of Christ in the future—much as do those who take other approaches to Revelation.

These expositors, however, do not generally see the Second Coming of Christ in the passage before us. The coming of Christ on a white horse may them with a rod of iron. He Himself treads the winepress of the fierceness and wrath of Almighty God. [16]And He has on His robe and on His thigh a name written: KING OF KINGS, AND LORD OF LORDS. [17]Then I saw an angel standing in the sun; and he cried with a loud voice, saying to all the birds that fly in the midst of heaven, "Come and gather together for the supper of the great God, [18]that you may eat the flesh of kings, the flesh of captains, the flesh of mighty men, the flesh of horses and those who sit on them, and the flesh of all people, both free and slave, both small and great." [19]And I saw the beast, the kings of the earth, and their armies, gathered together to make war against Him who sat on the horse and against His army. [20]Then the beast was captured, and with him the false prophet who worked signs in his presence, by which he deceived those who received the mark of the beast and those who worshiped his image. These two were cast alive into the lake of fire burning with brimstone. [21]And the rest were killed with the sword which proceeded from the mouth of Him who sat on the horse. And all the birds were filled with their flesh.

⌛ FUTURIST

When the heavens open, John sees Christ, accompanied by **the armies in heaven** (v. 14), coming in victory and judgment to establish his millennial kingdom on earth. Certainty about the identity of the rider on the white horse (v. 11) is established beyond question by the threefold manner in which He is named. First, He is called **Faithful and True** (v. 11). Second, He has a name

⌛ IDEALIST

Few persons appearing in Revelation are more universally identified by expositors than the rider upon this **white horse** (v. 11). Though a number of names are assigned to Christ, as **Faithful and True** (v. 11) and **the Word of God** (v. 13), He possesses, additionally, **a name written that no one knew except Himself** (v. 12). To explain this statement, Swete writes: "Only the Son

505

⧗ HISTORICIST *(continued)*

In the first case, the horse may symbolize the church as Christ's vehicle in the earth (cf. Zech. 10:3). Caringola advocates this interpretation:

> The militant Church is determined to wage spiritual warfare until we attain a final victory and all Christ's enemies are conquered, but our warfare is not with carnal weapons, 2 Corinthians 10:4, 5.

Barnes acknowledges that, in Revelation 1:16, "The sword seems to be an emblem of his *words* or *doctrines*, as penetrating the hearts of men," but that "here it is an emblem of a work of destruction wrought on his foes." In the references to his **robe dipped in blood** (v. 13) and **He Himself [treading] the winepress** (v. 15), Barnes points out the apparent allusion to Isaiah 63:1–3:

> Who is this who comes from Edom,
> with dyed garments from Bozrah.
> This one who is glorious in His apparel, traveling in the greatness of His strength?
> "I who speak in righteousness, mighty to save."
> Why is your apparel red, and Your garments like one who treads in the winepress?
> "I have trodden the winepress alone, and from the peoples no one was with Me.
> For I have trodden them in My anger, and trampled them in My fury;

⧗ PRETERIST *(continued)*

be thought of by many as the quintessential vision of the Second Coming at the end of the present age, but most *preterists* agree with Jay Adams, who believes it applies to the continuing warfare of the church through the proclamation of the gospel following the fall of Babylon in the previous chapters:

> That this does not describe a physical coming such as the second advent is apparent from at least two facts: first, Christ is nowhere else said to return upon a *horse*. He did not ascend this way, and he is to return *as he ascended.* . . . Secondly, the conflict described here is spiritual, not physical (unlike that which will transpire at the second advent). This is a battle waged and won by the *Word of God.* This is clear from the reference to the Word as the weapon which issues from the mouth of the Savior—cf. verses 15 and 21.

David S. Clark agrees:

> Now I submit the question: Is this not the conquering power of the gospel and the triumph of Christianity? The sword of the Spirit which is the word of God, by preaching, and teaching, and testimony conquers the world for Christ.

Reminding us of the earlier battle scenes in Revelation, Clark continues:

⧗ FUTURIST *(continued)*

that **no one knew except Himself** (v. 12), indicating that "no human name can express what He is in Himself" (Gaebelein). Third, **His name is called The Word of God** (v. 13), which is the most unmistakable title of all, harking back to the opening verses of John's Gospel.

The armies that **followed Him on white horses** (v. 14) may be saints, defined strictly as "the church" (J. B. Smith); or saints defined more broadly as the church, the saints of former dispensations, and the Tribulation saints (Ironside, and possibly Gaebelein and Ryrie). They may be angels (Kuyper, Ladd), or they might be the church together with angels (Walvoord, Mounce).

The decision concerning the meaning of the **sharp sword** (v. 15) that John sees coming **out of His mouth,** with which Christ will **strike the nations,** is split between two possibilities. Nondispensational writers like Mounce agree with Ladd's symbolic identification of the sword:

> The only weapon involved in this warfare is the word of Christ. The language looks back to Isa. 11:4: "And he shall smite the earth with the rod of his mouth, and with the breath of his lips he shall slay the wicked." Here is a symbolic representation of victory by the power of the word which is impossible to be literally envisaged.

⧗ IDEALIST *(continued)*

of God can understand the mystery of His own Being."

Those who accompany Christ (v. 14) are believed by some (e.g., Hendriksen) to be the holy angels. Others (Alford, Milligan) understand the glorified saints to be in the company as well. Wilson excludes the angels altogether from the company and identifies the armies with the overcomers of 17:14, "the redeemed who follow the Lamb wherever he goes (14:4)."

Concerning the significance of the sharp sword (v. 15) that proceeds from His mouth, that with **it He should strike the nations,** Carpenter writes: "The sword is now wielded for but one work—the *word* that Christ spoke will judge men at the last day (John 12:48)." Hendriksen concurs: "This sword is not the comforting story of the gospel. It is symbolical of destruction, as is clearly indicated by the entire context."

Three Old Testament metaphors are blended in v. 15: First, that He strikes **the nations** with the weapon that proceeds from His mouth recalls Isaiah 11:3, 4; second, **He Himself will rule them with a rod of iron,** alluding to Psalm 2:9, which has previously been alluded to in 2:27 and 12:5; third, **He Himself treads the winepress of the fierceness and wrath of Almighty God** refers back to Isaiah 63:1–6, which depicts Christ treading the grapes "alone." This last phrase sug-

⌛ HISTORICIST *(continued)*

Their blood is sprinkled upon My garments, and I have stained all my robes."

Though this passage says that Christ has "trodden the winepress alone" and "no one was with Me," whereas the vision under consideration depicts **the armies in heaven** (v. 14) following with Him, it should be noted that the clothing of those who are with Him was white and clean (v. 14), while His was **dipped in blood** (v. 13). On this point, Barnes writes:

> These hosts of the redeemed on white horses accompany him to be witnesses of his victory, and to participate in the joy of the triumph, not to engage in the work of blood.

The gathering of the carrion fowl to eat flesh suggests that a great destruction of God's enemies is anticipated here. Most significantly, we see the final end of **the beast** and **the false prophet** (v. 20). The beast, according to Barnes, "here, as all along, refers to the Papal power; and the idea is that of its complete and utter overthrow *as if* the leader of an army were taken captive and tormented in burning flames, and all his followers were cut down on the field of battle." ⍾

⌛ PRETERIST *(continued)*

We saw the dragon going forth to make war upon the woman (the church) and her seed (12:17). We saw the beast and the false prophet bring all the powers at their disposal to crush the church of God. But that was only one side of the lines. The battle was not so one-sided as that. Here is a better leader with his army. The foe will be met with a better army and a better weapon than his own, and we will see presently what the outcome of the conflict will be.

The calling of **the birds . . . for the supper of the great God** (v. 17) is no doubt intended as a contrast to the marriage feast referred to in verse 9. Jay Adams writes: "Chapter 19 is the story of two suppers. They contrast sharply. One is a joyous marriage feast; the other the carnage of vultures."

Chilton, who sees the losers of this battle—those who become food for birds—as Israel in AD 70, reminds us:

> A basic curse of the covenant is that of being eaten by birds of prey (cf. Deut. 28:26, 49). Israel is now a sacrificial corpse (Matt. 24:28), and there is no longer anyone who can drive away the scavengers (cf. Gen. 15:11; Deut. 28:26). John's language is borrowed from God's invitation through Ezekiel "to every bird and beast of the field" to devour the corpses of His enemies (Ezek. 39:17–20).

FUTURIST *(continued)*

Ladd realizes, however, that a battle in which "the only weapon involved" is "the word of Christ" focuses attention on spiritual warfare—the conquest of the gospel over the darkness of the world. Going too far toward a spiritualized approach may undermine the notion of a sudden violent struggle at the Parousia. Ladd therefore tempers his position, adding:

> The radical spiritualization of this concept which sees a conflict of human ideologies in human history and the triumph of Christianity does not accord with the nature of apocalyptic thought.

To Mounce, the word in this case is not the gospel in its triumphal forward movement, but the "sharp sword symbolizes the lethal power of His word of judgment." This is Biederwolf's position as well, who calls the sharp sword "the Word of God in its judging power, its avenging power." Dispensationalist Ironside also acknowledges the sword to represent "His word."

On the other hand, dispensational writers Ryrie, Walvoord, Gaebelein, and Lindsey all decline to identify this sword with the word of Christ, though they do link it with Isaiah 11:4 and Psalm 2:9. Ryrie considers the sword to indicate Christ's authority.

Walvoord devotes more words to discussing the kind of sword suggested

IDEALIST *(continued)*

gests that the armies of heaven (v. 14) who are with Christ do not participate in the trampling (i.e., destructive judgment) of the wicked, but are merely spectators.

Christ returns at a time when **the beast** (v. 19) and his confederates are **gathered together to make war** with Christ. Hendriksen understands this to represent "the persecuting power embodied in the government and directed against Christ and His Church. . . . Hence, the apostle sees the whole world of unbelief gathered for the final assault upon the Church." This is the same battle referred to in parallel sections as occurring at the end of the Christian dispensation (11:7ff.; 14:14ff.; 16:14ff.; 20:7ff.). Swete writes:

> Those who take note of the tendencies of modern civilization will not find it impossible to conceive that a time may come when throughout Christendom the spirit of Antichrist will, with the support of the State, make a final stand against a Christianity which is loyal to the Person and teaching of Christ.

This battle ends when Christ casts the beast and the false prophet **alive into the lake of fire** (v. 20). Hengstenberg understands these beings to be other than human:

> The term "alive," without bodily death, confirms the idea that the

PRETERIST *(continued)*

A fitting conclusion to the presentation of the *preterist* approach and of its ramifications is provided by David S. Clark:

> Let the church remember that this rider on the white horse is the living Jesus, that he is in the forefront of every battle, that just as he conquered the beast and the false prophet, so he will conquer every enemy. . . . The rider on the white horse is still riding on. Let the church follow, clothed in linen, white and clean.

⌛ FUTURIST *(continued)*

by the Greek word than to any consideration of its meaning: "Here the word is used symbolically to represent a sharp instrument of war with which Christ will smite the nations and establish His absolute rule." He does not attach any significance to the sword protruding from the mouth, unless it is found in his statement: "It represents unyielding absolute government under which men are required to conform to the righteous standards of God."

Though **the beast, the kings of the earth, and their armies** (v. 19) foolishly join in the battle against Christ and His armies, the outcome is not in question. In the end, **the beast** and **the false prophet** are captured and consigned to the **lake of fire** (v. 20), while the rest of those resisting Christ are **killed with the sword** (v. 21) out of the mouth of Christ. As the gruesome scene closes, **the birds,** which were summoned for the purpose in verses 17–18, **were filled with their flesh** (v. 21). ⌛

⌛ IDEALIST *(continued)*

beast and the false prophet are not human individuals at all, but purely ideal forms. A human individual cannot enter hell alive.

Hendriksen understands this imagery to mean that "at Christ's second coming Satan's persecution of the Church [symbolized in the beast] and his power to deceive on earth [represented by the false prophet] shall cease forever . . . never again to appear anywhere outside hell."

The followers of the opposition are first slain (2 Thess. 1:7–8) and then cast into the lake of fire (20:15; 2 Thess. 1:9). Before being resurrected to damnation, however, their bodies are subjected to the indignity of being eaten by birds (vv. 17–18, 21; cf. Deut. 28:26; 1 Sam. 17:44, 46; 1 Kings 14:11; etc.) ⌛

SUMMARY OF CHAPTERS 17–19

These chapters describe the conclusion of the careers of Christ's earthly enemies, the beasts and Babylon.

Historicists see this segment as a protracted celebration of the future downfall of papal Rome, the centuries-long opponent of God and persecutor of the saints. Christ is seen riding forth in victory, making further conquests through His Word throughout the world.

On *preterist* suppositions, Babylon may be Rome, the imperial city, which was to be sacked and destroyed by its subject nations. Otherwise, Babylon represents apostate Jerusalem, sacked and burned by the Romans. The choice between these options rests upon the decision whether the second half of Revelation has turned attention from the fall of Jerusalem to the fall of Rome. There is no consensus on this point.

Futurists differ as to the identity of Babylon. It may be the ancient Babylon in Iraq or ancient Rome revived in the last days. It may represent the Roman Catholic Church or some world council of churches that has defected from Christ and persecutes His followers. Regardless of the exact identification, these chapters exult in the wicked system's demise and foresee the victorious return of Christ from heaven in chapter 19.

The *idealist* interpretation sees Babylon as the seductive world system, described in terms reminiscent of Rome, its chief expression in John's day. This system seeks both to seduce and to persecute the church, but will succumb to the power of Christ either at His Second Coming or gradually through the progress of the gospel.

NOTES

1. Quoted in Caringola, *The Present Reign of Jesus Christ*, 234–35.
2. Halley, *Halley's Bible Handbook*, 774.
3. H. Grattan Guiness in *The Approaching End of the Age*, 5th ed., (n.p. 1881), 212.
4. The two exceptions are Tyre (Isa. 23:15–17) and Nineveh (Nahum 3:4). It is notable that both of these pagan cities, Tyre (See 1 Kings 5:1–12; 9:13; Amos 1:9) and Nineveh (Jon. 3:5–10), had at one time been in covenant with God.
5. Cf. Isa. 1:21; 2:20; Jeremiah 3; Ezekiel 23; etc.
6. Bauckham, *The Theology of the Book of Revelation*, 35f.
7. Beale, *The New International Greek Testament Commentary*, 847.
8. *The Revelation of St. John* (Mofatt New Testament Commentary).

9. Morris, *The Revelation of St. John*, 196.

10. *Treasury of Scripture Knowledge.*

11. Guinness, *The Approaching End of the Age*, 170.

12. Halley, *Halley's Handbook of the Bible*, 731, 732.

13. Beale, *The New International Greek Testament Commentary*, 888.

14. Bauckham, *The Theology of the Book of Revelation*, 20f.

15. Cachemaille, *The Visions of Daniel and Revelation Explained*, 616.

16. Bauckham, *The Theology of the Book of Revelation*, 5.

17. *Treasury of Scripture Knowledge.*

18. Cachemaille, *The Visions of Daniel and Revelation Explained*, 620, 622.

19. I. M. Haldeman, *A Synopsis of the Book of Revelation.*

20. Halley, *Halley's Bible Handbook*, 734.

21. Thus reads Luke 2:5 in the Textus Receptus. The Alexandrian text omits the word "wife."

PART VII

THE MILLENNIUM

REVELATION 20

WHAT IS THE MEANING OF THE "1,000 YEARS"?
WHEN DO THESE EVENTS OCCUR?

PREMILLENNIAL APPROACH:

- The binding of Satan is yet future. It will take place when Christ returns.
- The 1,000 years is a literal period during which Christ will reign on earth from Jerusalem, with His people.
- The loosing of Satan will bring the Millennium to its climax, followed by the resurrection and judgment of the wicked at the Great White Throne.
- The new heavens and new earth will be created after the Millennium, i.e., 1,000 years after Christ's Second Coming.

AMILLENNIAL APPROACH:

- The binding of Satan represents the victory of Christ over the powers of darkness accomplished at the cross.
- The 1,000 years is symbolic of a long, indeterminate period, corresponding to the age of the church (now).
- Satan will be loosed briefly to wreak havoc and to persecute the church in the end of the present age.
- The fire coming from heaven and consuming the wicked is symbolic of Christ's Second Coming.
- A general resurrection and judgment of the evil and the good will occur at Christ's coming, followed by the creation of new heavens and a new earth.

POSTMILLENNIAL APPROACH:

- Some interpret the chapter essentially as do the amillennialists, but with an added note of optimism about the success of the gospel in the present age.
- Others see the binding of Satan to represent a future point in time when the successful preaching of the gospel will have effectively reduced Satan's influence to nothing.

- The 1,000 years may or may not be a literal duration, but speaks of the future glorious age, prior to the Second Coming, in which the influence of the gospel will have universal sway.
- A final attempt on the part of a loosed Satan at the end of the age will get nowhere.
- A general resurrection and judgment will occur at the coming of Christ.

Our study of Revelation to this point has taken the form of a comparison of four interpretive approaches to the judgment events prophesied in chapters 4 through 19. The respective approaches proceed upon entirely different assumptions about the time frame, the geographical extent, and the duration of the judgments depicted as seals, trumpets, and bowls of wrath.

For many readers, however, the most interesting question to be resolved in the book of Revelation concerns the meaning of the final chapters, and particularly chapter 20. Unfortunately for our adopted arrangement, the four categories considered throughout our treatment thus far cannot be applied to these final chapters (just as it could not in the opening three chapters). This is not because there is unanimity among interpreters upon these chapters—on the contrary, the interpretation of these final chapters comprises what is arguably the chief controversy in eschatological studies, if not in all evangelical theology.

Our problem arises from the fact that none of the four approaches treated in the earlier chapters monolithically adheres to a single interpretation of Revelation 20, which is unique among the chapters of the Bible in that it speaks of the 1,000-year reign of the saints, commonly called the *Millennium*. Controversy attaches to almost every feature of this Millennium—e.g., its purpose, its venue, its character, its duration—but the major schools of thought have taken their names from their distinctive opinions as to the *timing* of the Millennium *vis-à-vis* the Second Coming of Christ. There are essentially three options. Each of these can present impressive exegetical arguments in its defense, each has been advocated by impressive conservative scholars, and each has enjoyed its own period of prominence in the thinking of the Western church.

1. *Premillennialists* (or *premillenarians*) understand the 1,000 years to follow the return of Christ. Thus, they believe in a *premillennial* return of Christ (before the Millennium). Among those who hold to this view, there are two major varieties: the dispensational and the historic *premillennialists.* The principal points of departure between these two groups is that the former believe in a special status of the nation Israel in the redemptive work of God in the end-

times, resulting in a restored millennial temple in Jerusalem complete with Levitical priests and animal sacrifices, whereas the historic premillenarians see the church, rather than ethnic Israel, as prominent in the millennial period. Dispensationalists also are distinctive in holding that the church will be raptured out of the earth seven years prior to the commencement of the Millennium, whereas other *premillennialists* see the Rapture of the church as occurring simultaneously with the descent of Christ to earth at the establishment of the millennial order.

2. *Postmillennialists* also find in Revelation 20 a consummation of history in the 1,000-year reign of the saints, but they believe that Christ will accomplish this through the church's fulfilling of its gospel mission, prior to His return. The 1,000 years of peace will be accomplished through no other agency than that which is already in the possession of the church, i.e., the Word of God and the Holy Spirit. The world will become *Christianized*, either as the result of worldwide revival and mass conversions, or through the imposition of Christian ideals by converted rulers and Christian governments—or both. The former prospect was suggested by Jonathan Edwards and most early *post-millennialists*, while the latter is emphasized by many modern *postmillennialists*, especially of the Christian Reconstructionist variety. It is averred

that Christ will return at the end of the Millennium (His coming is thus *postmillennial*).

3. *Amillennialism*, which means "no millennium," takes its name from its denial that there will be a special golden age of literally 1,000 years, either before or after the return of Christ. Revelation 20 is understood symbolically or spiritually, so that the reign of the saints depicts either the vindicated martyrs reigning from heaven in the present age, or earthly believers achieving spiritual victory over personal sin during the same period. The time frame is seen to be the whole time between Christ's first and second advents. Thus the binding of Satan at the beginning of the Millennium is associated with the First Coming of Christ, and the "fire from heaven" at the end of the Millennium is associated with His Second Coming.

In addition to the treatment of Revelation 20, each millennial position has its own way of understanding the Old Testament prophets' prediction of a messianic kingdom age. Virtually all of the Old Testament prophets as well as the Psalms anticipate a golden age of great peace and justice ruled over by the expected Messiah. Premillenarian interpreters may apply these passages to the future Millennium (as the dispensationalists do), or see them fulfilled at least partially in the church age as well as the Millennium (as do some historic *premillennialists). Amillennialists* generally assume all such prophecies are fulfilled during the entire age of the church, assigning spiritual meanings to the terminology of the prophecies. *Postmillennialists* may apply them either to the entire church age or specifically to the golden age at the end of the present dispensation.

The impossibility of treating the millennial question under the four headings that have commanded our attention in the earlier chapters will be seen in the fact that *amillennialist* theologians, for example, can interpret the book of Revelation according to any one of the four approaches. *Amillennialists* like Luther and Calvin interpreted Revelation according to the *historicist* method. Other *amillennialists,* like Jay Adams, take the *preterist* approach to Revelation. Abraham Kuyper was unusual among *amillennialists,* in that he took the *futurist* approach. Very many *amillennialists,* like Hendriksen, Wilcock, Hailey, Hobbs, Morey, and others, follow a more *idealist* approach to Revelation. Likewise *postmillennialism* has been espoused by adherents of more than one approach to Revelation, as has *premillennialism* (e.g., Ladd, who mixes *preterism, futurism,* and the *idealist* approach).

Thus the categories pertaining to the four approaches to the Apocalypse simply do not transfer to the millennial debate. This is because Revelation 20,

like many other prophecies in Scripture, deals with the ultimate question of God's kingdom being established upon the earth. The interpretation of Revelation 4–19, on the other hand, is concerned only with the timing of the Great Tribulation, whether it be placed early or late in the church age, or whether it is coextensive with the whole of the church age. Thus the timing of the Tribulation and the timing of the kingdom of God are separate and independent concerns.

Regardless of which conclusion the reader may reach concerning the interpretation of Revelation as whole, resolving the matter of the Millennium in chapter 20 requires an assessment of entirely different considerations. Conclusions reached upon the strongest grounds about the meaning of the earlier portion of Revelation will not dictate any particular interpretation of the meaning of chapter 20.

It is not my intention to undertake a second book focusing upon the merits and demerits of each millennial system. This has already been done admirably by several authors.[1] Since the comparison of the three millennial views is distinct from the consideration of the four distinctive approaches to Revelation, the treatment of chapters 20 through 22 requires a modified format. Instead of a four-way comparison, we will switch to a three-way comparison of chapter 20, and an even more integrated commentary on chapters 21 and 22 for reasons that will be apparent when we come to that section. I will treat each of the millennial views somewhat broadly, attempting to avoid being bogged down in discussions of the intricacies of each argument, which would require a separate volume. This more cursory treatment will not lean as heavily upon the citation of a multitude of expositors as did the earlier material in this book.

THE BINDING OF THE DRAGON

REVELATION 20:1–3

¹Then I saw an angel coming down from heaven, having the key to the bottomless pit and a great chain in his hand. ²He laid hold of the dragon, that serpent of old, who is the Devil and Satan, and bound him for a thousand years; ³and he cast him into the bottomless pit, and shut him up, and set a seal on him, so that he should deceive the nations no more till the thousand years were finished. But after these things he must be released for a little while.

PREMILLENNIAL

Then (v. 1) suggests a chronological sequence following the events in chapter 19:10ff., where Christ was seen in His Second Coming upon a white horse, subduing His enemies and defeating the Antichrist and the False Prophet. Hence, the events of which we now read are to occur after the Second Coming of Christ.

John sees an unnamed **angel coming down from heaven in possession of the key to the bottomless pit** (v. 1), or the *abyss*, and sporting **a great chain** for the purpose of putting Satan out of commission for a time. It is not necessary to know the identity of this angel, but Michael was **seen to** gain the mastery over Satan in chapter 12, and it is possible that he is the mightiest of God's angels—he alone in Scripture being called "the archangel" (Jude 9).

AMILLENNIAL

Then I saw (v. 1) speaks only of the order in which the visions were presented to John, not the chronology of its fulfillment. As chapter 12 describes the birth of Christ after many chronologically later events are described in previous chapters, so this chapter goes back to the beginning of the Christian dispensation and looks at Christ's victory over Satan, accomplished at the cross.

The **angel** who comes down to bind Satan may be Michael, who is depicted as defeating the dragon in the parallel vision of chapter 12, or may represent Christ Himself,[2] the true conqueror of the devil, or may simply symbolize the general fact of Satan's having been overpowered.

Several elements in the passage seem to demand a nonliteral interpretation. First, the devil, a spiritual being, is

POSTMILLENNIAL

Then (v. 1) conveys the idea that the events about to be described are to occur after the events described in the immediate preceding context. Thus the successful preaching of the gospel worldwide, resulting in the subordination of all nations to the authority of Christ, precedes His Second Coming. The Second Coming of Christ will be seen in verses 9ff. of this chapter, but the events before us in the present verses are to find fulfillment before that. The Englishman often credited with the founding of this school of thought, Daniel Whitby (1638–1725), identified the events of this chapter as following the seventh trumpet in chapter 11. Followed by Jonathan Edwards (1703–1758) in America, Whitby taught that the preaching of the gospel will, at some future point, successfully convert the majority of sinners. Satan's influence will thus be effectively bound upon earth, that he should deceive the nations no more (v. 3) for a lengthy period. A. H. Strong expressed this view:

> Through the preaching of the gospel in all the world, the kingdom of Christ is steadily to enlarge its boundaries, until Jews and Gentiles alike become possessed of its blessings, and a millennial period is introduced in which Christianity generally prevails throughout the earth.[6]

521

PREMILLENNIAL *(continued)*

The location of the bottomless pit is unrevealed, although many feel that it must have its opening somewhere upon earth, since this opening is referred to twice in Revelation (v. l; cf. 9:1). In chapter 9, the abyss was opened by a "star" that fell "from heaven to the earth," suggesting the earth as the location of the pit. The star that fell in chapter 9 was "given" the key to the bottomless pit, because, being an evil angel, he did not possess it by right but by grant from God. The angel in chapter 20, however, is not seen receiving, but "having" the key. While this does not preclude his having received it earlier (and may even imply it), it may suggest a more innate right to possess and use the key on the part of this angel.

Having **laid hold of the dragon** (v. 2), the angel deftly discharges his commission to bind him **for a thousand years.** There will be more to say later about this thousand years, but suffice it to say that the language clearly indicates that the disabling of Satan is very thorough. In addition to the restriction imposed by the chain, the devil is further eliminated by being **cast . . . into the bottomless pit, and shut . . .** up in it with **a seal** [set] **on him** (v. 3). This does not mean that there will be no sin in the Millennium, for as Biederwolf writes: "This refers to Satan's complete banishment from earth, so that while sin is still to exist in individuals, it is no longer to be

AMILLENNIAL *(continued)*

depicted as being bound by **a great chain** (v. 1), whereas one would think of spiritual beings as not being susceptible to confinement by physical restraints.[3] A second indicator of the symbolism in the passage is the reference to Satan (as elsewhere in the book) as both a **dragon** and a **serpent** (v. 2), neither of which is any more a literal description of this spiritual being than is "a Lamb . . . having seven horns and seven eyes" (cf. 5:6), a literal description of the man Jesus Christ. We are further dissuaded from a literal interpretation of the passage by the fact that many of its features, e.g., **a thousand years** (v. 2), **a pit**, and a **seal** (v. 3) are used elsewhere in Scripture in a symbolic manner.[4]

The nature of the binding itself is not absolute, so as to preclude every activity of Satan. It is specifically limited in the passage to the devil's power to **deceive the nations** (v. 3) for the duration of the period. That Jesus in some sense bound Satan during His ministry is affirmed by Christ Himself. Jesus describes His ministry of deliverance to the demon—possessed as analogous to the plundering of a strong man's house by an invader (Matt. 12:29). Here the strong man is clearly Satan and the intruder is Christ. Jesus explains parabolically that a necessary first step was to bind the strong man, who otherwise would not allow his house to be pil-

POSTMILLENNIAL *(continued)*

This **thousand years** (vv. 2, 3) speaks of that future period.

David S. Dark sees this chapter as beginning a new section, not, as the *amillennialist* suggests, to recapitulate a time period discussed earlier, but looking to the end of the Christian era, long after Christ has subdued Jerusalem and Rome (in chaps. 11 and 19). Dark suggests that the capture of the beast and the false prophet occurred at the fall of pagan Rome, but that the binding of Satan remains to be fulfilled in the future. Most other *postmillennialists* (like the *premillennialists)* see no break between the chapters, but a progression leading naturally from the end of chapter 19 into chapter 20. All agree with Dark, however, in saying: "We therefore conclude that there will be a millennium and that it will result from the preaching and teaching of the gospel, when 'the earth shall be full of the knowledge of the Lord.'"

R. J. Rushdoony also believes in this golden era at the end of the church age, but takes a different approach to the interpretation of Revelation 20. He sees this chapter almost exactly as does the *amillennialist.* He writes: "Thus Revelation 20 is in a sense a recapitulation of the entire book." He sees the binding of Satan as having already occurred in the past, when Christ was on earth. The thousand years apparently is seen, with the *amillennialist,* as the entire church

PREMILLENNIAL *(continued)*

a power forming a fellowship, and thus making a kingdom of sin and Satan."

The sealing of the prison, like the sealing of the tomb of Christ (cf. Matt. 27:66), suggests a forbidding of any to tamper with it on command of the highest authority. The effect of this incarceration of Satan is that he should deceive the nations no more till the thousand years were finished (v. 3). This clearly indicates the presence of nations after the destruction of the Antichrist in 19:21—perhaps those that did not participate in the conflict. These will be, according to Alford, "the quiet and willing subjects of the kingdom," who will again be seduced when the thousand years are over (vv. 7ff.).

There can be no doubt that the nations still experience satanically inspired deception today, which challenges any interpretation of this vision that would make Satan to be currently bound. Weidner declares: "If any one thing is clear, it is this, that the power of Satan has as yet not been bound." "If he is bound today," it is often said, "the chain is too long."

By way of anticipation, we are forewarned at this point that we have not yet seen the end of Satan's career, for, after the Millennium **he must be released for a little while** (v. 3). There will be one final rebellion following the thousand years of Christ's peaceful reign on earth before the eternal new creation will come. @

AMILLENNIAL *(continued)*

laged. The implication is that Jesus' casting out of demons provides proof that He had already "bound" Satan. This binding of Satan, however, does not involve a literal incarceration preventing all movement. In the analogy, "binding" refers only to rendering his opponent incapable of resistance. The parallel account in Luke replaces the metaphor of binding the strong man with that of stripping the strong man of his armor and weapons (Luke 11:22). Thus, according to Christ's own teaching, the imagery of "binding Satan" conveys the fact that Satan has been rendered incapable of successfully resisting the forward advance of God's kingdom. Additional passages in the New Testament use similar images to describe the decisive victory of Christ over His foes. Colossians 2:15 exults in the fact that Christ "disarmed principalities and powers" through the cross, and Hebrews 2:14 states that Jesus endured death so that He might thereby "destroy[5] him who had the power of death, that is, the devil."

The meaning of this binding of Satan, then, is that Christ, at His first advent, brought about a conclusive victory, leaving Satan impotent to prevent the success of God's kingdom. The imagery of this passage is simply a more vivid dramatization of this concept, in keeping with the apocalyptic style of the book itself. @

POSTMILLENNIAL *(continued)*

age. The principal difference between his view and that of the *amillennialist* is that the latter makes no prediction about the ultimate success of the gospel in converting the world, whereas Rushdoony, with all *postmillennialists*, believes that the church will bring all things under the dominion of Christ. It would seem that this view of Revelation 20 differs from that of classical *postmillennialism* only in restricting the golden age to the end portion of the "thousand years" (which represents the whole church age), whereas the older postmillennialism identifies the thousand years with the golden age at the end of the church age and the end of the world. In one sense, Rushdoony's view could be called *optimistic amillennialism*.[7] with reference to the interpretation of this chapter. Benjamin B. Warfield also took an approach similar to this. ⧉

THE THOUSAND-YEAR REIGN

REVELATION 20:4—6

[4]And I saw thrones, and they sat on them, and judgment was committed to them. Then I saw the souls of those who had been beheaded for their witness to Jesus and for the word of God, who had not worshiped the beast or his image, and had not received his mark on their foreheads or on their hands. And they lived and reigned with Christ for a thousand years. [5]But the rest of the dead did not live again until the thousand years were finished. This is the first resurrection. [6]Blessed and holy is he who has part in the first resurrection. Over such the second death has no power, but they shall be priests of God and of Christ, and shall reign with Him a thousand years.

PREMILLENNIAL

There is much dispute over the identity of the persons who were seen seated upon the thrones (v. 4), whether they were (a) God, Christ, and the angels; (b) the twenty-four elders (cf. Rev. 4:4); (c) the martyrs and those who refused to worship the beast (mentioned later in the verse); or (d) all the saints of both the Old and the New Testaments (cf. Matt. 19:28). The last view mentioned seems to be preferred by most expositors (e.g., Alford, Milligan, Gaebelein, Weidner, etc.).

The right of judging **was committed to them** (v. 4), which suggests that they participated with Christ in the judicial rule of the nations during the Millennium. In that John also saw **those who had been beheaded and who**

AMILLENNIAL

Two views prevail among *amillennialists* concerning the venue of the saints in this vision. The older view, proposed by Augustine, is that the picture is that of the spiritual reign of believers on earth in the present age, symbolizing the victory through which it is written that "we are more than conquerors through Him who loved us" (Rom. 8:37).

An alternative view, attributed originally to the nineteenth-century German scholar Kliefoth, is that the vision describes the blessedness of the departed saints in heaven after death, but prior to the resurrection. This is the more widespread view today among *amillennialists.*

The thrones (v. 4) are apparently in heaven, as were those in Revelation

POSTMILLENNIAL

The thousand years spoken of here refer to the progressive victory of the gospel in the world, especially in the latter part of the present age. Gentry writes:

> Postmillennialism expects the proclaiming of the Spirit-blessed gospel of Jesus Christ to win the vast majority of human beings to salvation in the present age. Increasing gospel success will gradually produce a time in history prior to Christ's return in which faith, righteousness, peace, and prosperity will prevail in the affairs of people and of nations. After an extensive era of such conditions the Lord will return.[9]

The meaning of **the first resurrection** (vv. 5, 6) is not a unanimously settled matter among *postmillennial* writers. It is said of the martyrs that they **lived and reigned** (v. 4) for the thousand years, which is taken by some to mean that the future victory and revival of Christianity after its earlier history of persecution amounts to nothing less than a rebirth of the cause for which the martyrs died. John Jefferson Davis writes: "The 'first resurrection,' then, refers to the future restoration and vindication of the cause for which the martyrs died."[10] Barnes similarly writes:

> They were exalted in their principles and in their personal happiness in heaven, *as if* they occupied

PREMILLENNIAL *(continued)*

had not worshiped the beast, it has been speculated that they might be here standing before the court being assessed "as to how far they were worthy of being called to the first resurrection" (Lange). However, it is more likely that they belong to the larger company of those sitting on the thrones and are singled out as worthy of particular mention. The reference to their being beheaded may represent any form of martyrdom, not restricting the number to those actually decapitated.

The meaning of the expression **they lived** (v. 4) is hotly debated. *Premillennialists* prefer to translate the expression **they came to life**, meaning "they lived [again]," and identify it with the **first resurrection** of verses 5 and 6. This is the resurrection of the saints to reign on earth (cf. 2:26–27; 5:10) during the Millennium. It is to be followed at the end of the thousand years by the resurrection of the wicked for the judgment of the Great White Throne (vv. 11ff.), hence **the rest of the dead did not live again until the thousand years were finished** (v. 5). Whereas the *amillennialist* and the *postmillennialist* do not consider this "first resurrection" to be physical, it seems inconsistent to make this resurrection out to be a spiritual one while acknowledging the resurrection at the end of the thousand years to be physical, as Alford writes:

AMILLENNIAL *(continued)*

4:4, upon which the twenty-four elders sat. Likewise, the souls of those who had been beheaded for Christ are no doubt seen in heaven here, as they were in Revelation 6:9. The only place for the disembodied souls of saints since the accomplishment of our redemption has been in heaven, and the only time frame during which such souls can be found there (*sans* bodies) is from the point of their deaths till the time of their resurrection at the Second Coming of Christ. Thus the time frame would seem to be the present age of the church, from John's own century to the time of the resurrection.

This is the period is referred to as **a thousand years** (v. 4). The number "a thousand" is frequently used in Scripture without the intention of conveying statistical information. It is given as the number of generations to which God keeps His covenants (Deut. 7:9), the number of hills upon which God owns the cattle (Ps. 50:10), the number of enemies that one Israelite shall chase (Josh. 23:10), etc. Furthermore, the expression "a thousand years" is never used elsewhere in Scripture for an actual number of years, but only to suggest the idea of a very long time (cf. Ps. 90:4; Eccl. 6:6; 2 Pet. 3:8). So also here, the reign of the victorious martyrs during the time of Satan's incarceration is simply a very long time, as the figure "a thousand years" generally means.

POSTMILLENNIAL *(continued)*

the throne with Him and shared its honors and triumphs.

An older view of Daniel Whitby, followed by A. A. Hodge in the nineteenth century and James Snowden in the early twentieth century, was that the first resurrection refers to a revival of the martyr spirit. As explained by Strong, verses 4 and 5 of this chapter refer to

> a period in the latter days of the church militant when, under special influence of the Holy Ghost, the spirit of the martyrs shall appear again, true religion be greatly quickened and revived, and the members of Christ's churches become so conscious of their strength in Christ that they shall, to an extent unknown before, triumph over the powers of evil both within and without.[11]

When v. 5 says the rest of the dead did not live again until the thousand years were finished, it may mean, as Dark understands it:

> Christ's cause and people were dominant during the thousand years, and Satan's allies were subdued till the thousand years were ended, and after that they rose to power again. . . . They . . . rose to their old time power and persecution.

Rushdoony takes the view of many *amillennialists* that the first resurrection

529

PREMILLENNIAL *(continued)*

As regards the text itself, no legitimate treatment of it will extort what is known as the spiritual interpretation now in fashion. If in a passage where two resurrections are mentioned, where certain souls lived at the first, and the rest of the dead lived only in the end of a specified period after the first—if in such a passage the first resurrection may be understood to mean *spiritual* rising with Christ, while the second means literal rising from the grave; then there is an end to all significance in language, and Scripture is wiped out as a definite testimony to anything.

It is acknowledged by some (e.g., Milligan and Fausset) that the vision of the souls (v. 4) of those who had been beheaded must refer to disembodied souls, but this only means that John saw them first in their disembodied states in heaven, whereas they now are seen experiencing the physical resurrection.

Though Lange takes the number symbolically, the thousand years (v. 4) may be as readily taken literally as any of the other time indicators in the Book of Revelation. Stuart writes:

> The great question whether this is to be taken literally or symbolically, is one that must be settled by the analogy of the book in regard to specific periods. We have seen that the famous period of three and one-half years is to be understood, in all probability, in its

AMILLENNIAL *(continued)*

These were those who refused to worship the beast or to wear **his mark** (v. 4), which means those who refused to compromise despite the world's intimidation (see *historicist* and *idealist* commentaries at chapter 13).

The phrase **they lived and reigned with Christ** (v. 4) is thought by some (i.e., *premillennialists*) to be better translated "they *came to life* and reigned with Christ." This version is followed by many leading Bible translations. If this latter translation is chosen, the reference will be said to teach a rising of these saints from the dead prior to the resurrection detailed at the end of this chapter. This reading would support only the *premillennial* position, in that it would show that these persons, were resurrected before the Millennium.

This problem for the amillennialist may be resolved in more than one way. First, it may be that their "coming to life" refers to their entrance into heaven at the point of their death and does not speak of their physical resurrection at the coming of the Lord. Alternatively, it is entirely possible to retain the translation "they lived" as simply stating that they *lived on* in heaven beyond the point of their earthly deaths. Either translation, "they lived" or "they came to life," can be justified grammatically.[8]

The first resurrection (v. 5) may refer to the life of the departed saints in heaven or merely to the principal

POSTMILLENNIAL *(continued)*

is a figurative way of referring to the re-generation of the believer, whereas Benjamin B. Warfield held the view, also found among some *amillennialists,* that the first resurrection is the entrance into heavenly joys and that these verses present a picture of the souls of the redeemed safe in heaven. This appears to be the view of David S. Dark also.

Chilton points out that the "first resurrection" may be a reference back to Christ's own resurrection from the dead. Paul refers to Christ as "the firstfruits of those who have fallen asleep" (1 Cor. 15:20) and as "the firstborn from the dead" (Col. 1:18). As Chilton says, when Christ arose, "He rose from the dead, and resurrected all believers with Him." Thus the beatitude is not pronounced upon those who have risen from the dead, but rather **he who has part in the first resurrection** (v. 6). Every believer "has part in" the resurrection of Christ—those souls seen in heaven illustrate that the life they have received while on earth continues, uninterrupted by death, in heaven. Chilton raises a pertinent question, only to answer it:

> Does this reign of the saints take place in heaven or on earth? The answer should be obvious: *both!* The saints' thrones are in heaven, with Christ (Eph. 2:6); yet, with their Lord, they exercise rule and dominion on earth (cf. 2:26–27; 5:10; 11:15).

531

PREMILLENNIAL *(continued)*

literal sense. . . . Here, then, assuming a similar usage with respect to numbers, we may suppose
that the thousand years may be
taken in their ordinary sense, or at
least for a very long period.

Though this will be long enough
for the producing of many millennial
generations of people, individual life
spans apparently will be greatly increased over those currently known.
Isaiah 65:20 tells us: "No more shall an
infant from there live but a few days,
nor an old man who has not fulfilled
his days; for the child shall die one hundred years old."

Peter wrote that with the Lord one
day is "as a thousand years, and a thousand years as a day" (2 Pet. 3:8). This
may mean that the Millennium, coming after six thousand years of world
history, should be regarded as the anti-
type of the seventh day, which followed
the six days of creation.

A particular blessedness and holiness accrues to the one **who has part
in the first resurrection** (v. 6), because only they live in the Millennium
and will escape **the second death** to
live on in the New Jerusalem in the new
creation. The reference to their being
holy may reflect that **they shall be
priests** (v. 6), since priests were holy
unto the Lord. It is important to note
that those thus designated are **priests
of God and of Christ**, a phraseology

AMILLENNIAL *(continued)*

feature of the time period as a whole in
terms of the privileges of living saints as
well. The Scriptures elsewhere teach
that there will be only one physical resurrection at the end of time, which will
include the righteous and the unrigh-
teous (cf. John 5:28–29; Acts 24:14–15;
compare "the last day" in John 6:39, 40,
44, 54, and 12:48). We find this resurrection of bodies from their graves at
the end of the Millennium (v. 13). It follows that there can be no other physical
resurrection than that mentioned at
the end of the chapter and that the "first
resurrection" mentioned in verses 5
and 6 must therefore be a spiritual one.
Such a conclusion is justified by the fact
that the Christian's experience of regeneration is frequently spoken of in terms
of a spiritual rising from death to life (cf.
John 5:24; 11:34–35; Eph. 2:5–6; Col.
2:13; 3:1; Rom. 6:4–5, 13).

**But the rest of the dead did not
live again** (v. 5). This either means (a)
that the blessedness of the saints was
never experienced by the unsaved (until
the thousand years were finished being
taken only as a contrast to the state of
the saints during the same period, but
not implying a change at the end of the
period), or it means (b) that, while the
saints enjoy two resurrections (the first
being spiritual rebirth and the second
being the physical resurrection at the
end of time), the lost know no such "first
resurrection" and have only the physi-

POSTMILLENNIAL *(continued)*

Having been resurrected with Christ, Christians are to rule and to promote His rule in the world at this present time. Chilton, Rushdoony, and other Christian Reconstructionists believe that this rule of the saints on earth will ultimately take the form of "a Christian Republic, where God's law rules."[12] The application of the Mosaic civil ordinances to modern case law is one of the principal concerns of this wing of *postmillennialists*—in anticipation of a time when "all kings shall fall down before Him; / All nations shall serve Him" (Ps. 72:11). If the rulers of the world are going to seek to honor God in their lawmaking, the church must be prepared to inform them of how civil law can best conform to the divine standard revealed in the Mosaic statutes

533

PREMILLENNIAL *(continued)*

providing a strong indicator of Christ's co-equal deity with God. 🔊

AMILLENNIAL *(continued)*

cal resurrection ahead of them at the end of the present dispensation (a "resurrection of condemnation," according to Christ—John 5:29).

That the saints shall reign with Him a thousand years (v. 6) suggests that the church, seen collectively, in some sense participates with Him in His reign over history during the entire church age. 🔊

SATAN AGAIN "AT LARGE"

REVELATION 20:7–10

[7]Now when the thousand years have expired, Satan will be released from his prison [8]and will go out to deceive the nations which are in the four comers of the earth, Gog and Magog, to gather them together to battle, whose number is as the sand of the sea. [9]They went up on the breadth of the earth and surrounded the camp of the saints and the beloved city. And fire came down from God out of heaven and devoured them. [10]The devil, who deceived them, was cast into the lake of fire and brimstone where the beast and the false prophet are. And they will be tormented day and night forever and ever.

PREMILLENNIAL

Now when the thousand years have expired, Satan will be released from his prison (v. 7). Some understand this final revolt to be exceedingly brief and fierce, but not successful in interrupting the reign of the saints. Others see the

AMILLENNIAL

We had been forewarned, in verse 3, that **when the thousand years have expired, Satan will be released from his prison** (v. 7). This speaks of a brief period of indeterminate duration at the end of the Christian era, during

POSTMILLENNIAL

The short period described as following the millennial period appears to be a complete reversal of the gains implied by previous verses. There are some, of the postmillennial persuasion, who see these time references, not as actual chronological periods, but as the indicating the relative strength of the Gospel (1,000 years) and of Satan's futile resistance (a little while) during the entire age of the church. However, the classic postmillennialism (as represented, for example, by the Puritans) actually sees a brief and abortive rebellion occurring just prior to the Second Coming of Christ.

Now when the thousand years have expired (v. 7)—that is, toward the very end of the long period of Christian ascendancy—the release of Satan from his prison will result in a return to his old activities, for he **will go out to deceive the nations** (v. 7), the very

PREMILLENNIAL *(continued)*

temporary interruption of the reign of the believers, only to be resumed with Christ after the final battle of Gog and Magog in the coming new heavens and earth. The reason for God's permitting Satan this last brief respite seems to be to prove the character of those generations of men born during the Millennium and never previously having been tempted to rebellion. Since those deceived by the devil at this time are the nations which are in the four corners of the earth (v. 8), some expositors[13] suggest that they comprise only those which are located so far from the center of Christ's reign as to never have come under His rule. Others think these to be the same nations which had until this time been subject to Christ, but which later apostatize when seduced by the devil.[14] Gaebelein says that many people during the Millennium will serve the divine government with feigned loyalty out of fear, all the while maintaining sin in their hearts and longing for the time when they can rise up to overthrow Christ's authority.

Gog and Magog (v. 8) are previously known to us only from Ezekiel 38 and 39, where they come down from the uttermost northern parts to invade Israel in the last days. Most understand the battle of Gog and Magog in Ezekiel to occur early in the Tribulation, prior to Armageddon, thus making Ezekiel's battle a different one from the one

AMILLENNIAL *(continued)*

which Satan will be permitted to resist the church on a global scale. If Adams is correct, this corresponds to the rise of "the man of sin, the son of perdition" whom Paul described as being "restrained" at the present, but who is to be later "unrestrained" to deceive the world and to oppose all that is called God (2 Thess. 2:6–12).

Satan's release to deceive the nations (v. 8) would seem to constitute the ultimate setback for the church, as the majority of the world devolves to a pagan state comparable to that which prevailed before the first coming of Christ.

All nations will endeavor to defeat the camp of the saints (v. 9). This may be warfare of a spiritual sort, but since such battle against the church meant persecution in Revelation 11:7 and 13:7, it is likely that persecution of the church on a grand scale is what is in view here as well. The beloved city (v. 9) is the New Jerusalem described more fully in chapter 21, which is an image of the church (cf. 21:9–10; Heb. 12:22ff.).

The career of this rebel force and their diabolical leader comes to a final end with the Second Coming of Christ, here depicted with the words fire came down from God out of heaven and devoured them (v. 9). The Second Coming of Christ will be "in flaming fire taking vengeance on those who do not know God, and on those who do not obey the

POSTMILLENNIAL *(continued)*

thing he had been restricted from doing in verse 3. He finds no shortage of sympathy from the nations, for they follow him *en masse* **as the sand of the sea** (v. 8).

Satan's confederacy is called **Gog and Magog** (v. 8), names taken from the prophecy of Ezekiel 38 and 39. In Ezekiel Gog is the name of a ruler, and Magog the name of his people. For this reason, Gog and Magog may simply be a way of saying "prince and people."

This final revolt of the previously suppressed forces of evil targets the church of Jesus Christ, which is here symbolically designated as the **camp of the saints and the beloved city** (v. 9). This battle may speak of a spiritual conflict between truth and error waged entirely in the realm of ideas and culture, or it may refer to political persecution of Christians. Rushdoony writes:

> Some see a defeat of the saints and a victory for Satan in the end times, but only by importing other Bible passages into this text, all with doubtful reference, since they can be referred more intelligently to the Jewish war or "the great Tribulation," is such an interpretation possible. We are here told only of an attempt, and the attempt is now described as Satan's attempt.

Chilton writes:

PREMILLENNIAL *(continued)*

described here. If so, then these nations will have recovered their former strength during the Millennium, after suffering a crushing defeat in the earlier campaign.

The attack is **against the camp of the saints** (v. 9), who are apparently viewed as camped around the city, mobilized for her defense, **and the beloved city**. The city is Jerusalem. *Premillennial* expositors are nearly unanimous in identifying it with the earthly Jerusalem and not with the heavenly Jerusalem seen descending in chapter 21.

This battle is not fought by the saints protecting their city, but by God, for **fire came down from God out of heaven and devoured** (v. 9) the armies of Satan. This resembles the results and the method of destruction of the enemy in Ezekiel's battle of Gog and Magog as well: "I will rain down on him, on his troops, and on the many peoples who are with him, flooding rain, great hailstones, fire and brimstone" (Ezek. 38:22). This battle being ended, the time has come for the final judgment of all the lost and their consignment, along with Satan, to the lake of fire (v. 10). 🔲

AMILLENNIAL *(continued)*

gospel" (2 Thess. 1:8). It is the "day of the Lord . . . in which the heavens will pass away with a great noise, and the elements will melt with fervent heat; both the earth and the works that are in it will be burned up" (2 Pet. 3:10). This coming of the Lord with its attendant burning up of the earth clearly could not have occurred at the beginning of the Millennium since, in such a case, there would be no venue for the playing out of the earthly drama in this chapter.

At the coming of Christ in fiery judgment, **the devil** (v. 10) is not going to be temporarily chained but, rather, he is to be **cast into the lake of fire**. This appears to be the meaning of Isaiah 27:1:

> In that day the LORD with His severe sword, great and strong, will punish Leviathan the fleeing serpent, Leviathan that twisted serpent; and He will slay the reptile that is in the sea. 🔲

POSTMILLENNIAL *(continued)*

The apostates rebel, and Satan's forces briefly surround the Church; but there is not a moment of doubt about the outcome of the conflict. In fact, there is no real conflict at all, for the rebellion is immediately crushed: **Fire came down from heaven and devoured them**, as it had the wicked citizens of Sodom and Gomorrah.

Will the fire from heaven be literal? Augustine taught that the fire was symbolic for the unwavering resolve of the faithful not to apostasize or yield obedience to those who rage against them.[15] There is no reason to exclude the possibility of actual fire, since such is said to accompany Christ in His coming in judgment at the end of the world (2 Thess. 1:8; 2 Pet. 3:10, 12).

THE END OF THE WORLD

REVELATION 20:11—15

[11]Then I saw a great white throne and Him who sat on it, from whose face the earth and the heaven fled away. And there was found no place for them. [12]And I saw the dead, small and great, standing before God, and the books were opened. And another book was opened, which is the Book of Life. And the dead were judged according to their works, by the things which were written in the books. [13]The sea gave up the dead who were in it, and Death and Hades delivered up the dead who were in them. And they were judged, each one according to his works. [14]Then Death and Hades were cast into the lake of fire. This is the second death. [15]And anyone not found written in the Book of Life was cast into the lake of fire.

PREMILLENNIAL

The **great white throne** (v. 11) is probably the same throne seen in Revelation 4:2, though it may not have the same Occupant. In that earlier vision, the One that was seated upon the throne was distinguished from Christ, the Lamb (cf. 5:13). Clearly it was God the Father who handed the sealed scroll to Christ in Revelation 5:7. It may be that the One here seen seated upon the throne is also the Father (as think Alford, Hengstenberg, Simcox, Weidner), but it may also be Christ—a view preferred by Fausset, Lange, Stuart, Gaebelein, Barnes, and Milligan. In favor of this latter opinion, Christ was said to be seated with His Father upon His throne in Revelation 3:21, and again, in 21:5–8, the speaker from the throne would appear to be Christ, since He identifies

AMILLENNIAL

The judgment of the **great white throne** (v. 11) is not a special judgment to be distinguished from other judgments of the close of the age (e.g., a separate *bema* judgment of the believers only, some thousand years earlier), but simply a description of the only ultimate judgment at the coming of Christ, involving believers and unbelievers (cf. Matt. 25:31; Rom. 2:5–10; Rev. 11:18). The "great white throne" is thus not a technical label to distinguish this event from others like it, but merely a statement of the color of the throne (white), suggesting purity, upon which God, or Christ, is seen seated at the last day (John 12:48). The glory of the Lord at this point is such that **the earth and the heaven fled away** (v. 11) from before His face. This in itself indicates that

540

POSTMILLENNIAL

The final judgment is to take place at the actual *postmillennial* coming of Christ at the end of the world. Here Jesus is seen upon a **great white throne** (v. 11). That the One upon the throne is Christ seems to be suggested by the fact that the throne is said to be white, whereas Jesus was earlier seen seated upon a "white cloud" (14:14) and upon a "white horse" (6:2; 19:11). Jesus said that the Father has committed "all judgment" to the Son (John 5:27) and that "When the Son of Man comes in His glory . . . then He will sit on the throne of His glory" (Matt. 25:31). What follows in the remainder of the parable of Matthew 25 is the judgment of the sheep and the goats, which corresponds to this scene in Revelation. Paul said that Christ "will judge the living and the dead at His appearing and His kingdom" (2 Tim. 4:1).

At his coming in glory **the earth and the heaven fled away** (v. 11), corresponding to the burning up of the present heavens and earth that Peter associates with the Second Coming (2 Pet. 3:10, 12) and the destruction of the man of sin by the "brightness of His coming" (2 Thess. 2:8).

Whereas the *premillennialist* believes this final judgment to include only the wicked (the righteous having already been resurrected at the beginning of the Millennium), the language of the passage: **the dead, small and**

PREMILLENNIAL *(continued)*

Himself as "the Alpha and the Omega, the Beginning and the End" (21:6) as did Christ in chapter 1.

The glory of Christ (or God) is so intense as to dissolve the universe (cf. 2 Pet. 3:10, 12), so that John declares that **the earth and the heaven fled away** (v. 11). These will be permanently removed, so that there was found no place for them. In the opening verse of the next chapter, the old heavens and earth are said to be "passed away." This makes place for the creation of a new heavens and earth.

John next sees the **dead** (v. 12), who were earlier referred to as "the rest of the dead" (v. 5), who had not experienced the first resurrection. Now that the world is at an end, the time for their resurrection and judgment has come. Alford writes:

> That this judgment refers to the wicked dead alone there can be no doubt from a plain exegesis of the word *"dead"* and from the context. All the righteous who had been resurrected and caught up before the Millennium as well as those who had died during the Millennium and those who were alive at the close of the Millennium will be there also, not, however, to be judged (John 5:24), but to have their judgment confirmed.

There is a noted differentiation between **the books** (v. 12) from which

AMILLENNIAL *(continued)*

the Second Coming did not occur a thousand years earlier. Why would not the glory of the returning Christ have brought about this flight of the natural world into nonexistence at that earlier time? It can hardly be thought that his glory at his coming will be less intense than it would be a thousand years later. Since the coming of the Lord is in fact the end of the natural universe (2 Pet. 3:10–13), we read that **there was found no place for them** (v. 11), making way for a new heaven and a new earth to occupy the place left vacant by their dismissal (21:1).

The fact that John **saw the dead** (v. 12) arise and come **before God** to be judged proves that it is at this point, and not a thousand years earlier, that the Second Coming is seen. The judgment is everywhere associated with Christ's Second Coming in Scripture (cf. Matt. 25:19, 31; 2 Thess. 1:8ff.; 2 Tim. 4:1).

The presence of **books as well as the Book of Life** (v. 12) suggests that there will be more than one category of persons standing judgment. The presence of the Book of Life seems to imply the presence of the righteous, whose names are to be found there, while we are also told explicitly that John also saw there those who were **not found written in the Book of Life** (v. 15).

This judgment, then, wherein **the dead were judged according to their works** (v. 12), includes believers

542

POSTMILLENNIAL *(continued)*

great (v. 12), and that the **sea gave up the dead who were in it, and Death and Hades gave up the dead** (v. 13) seems calculated to stress the universality of the event. The Bible everywhere affirms that the righteous and the wicked will be resurrected at the same time (e.g., John 5:28–29; Acts 24:15) and face judgment on the same occasion (e.g., Matt. 16:27; 25:31ff.; Rom. 2:5–10), and the same is taught here. The presence of **the Book of Life** (v. 12) at this judgment confirms that the righteous are here in the judgment along with the wicked.

Not only Satan, but also his confederates, **Death and Hades** (v. 14), will be forever consigned to the **lake of fire**, along with **anyone not found written in the Book of Life** (v. 15). Thus all of Christ's enemies are destroyed, never to rise again, fulfilling that great *postmillennial* promise concerning Christ that "He must reign till He has put all enemies under His feet. The last enemy that will be destroyed is death" (1 Cor. 15:25–26).

Because of the vast number of the saved, especially during the millennial period, the actual number of the lost, who end up in the lake of fire, will be a negligible percentage of all humanity who have ever lived: "In the immense range of God's dominion, good is the rule, and evil is the exception. Sin is a speck upon the azure of eternity; a spot

543

PREMILLENNIAL *(continued)*

the dead were judged, and the Book of Life, which contained none of their names. The latter was mentioned in the promise made to the overcomers in the church of Sardis (3:5). It apparently is the register of all those whom the Lamb has redeemed. Jesus told the disciples, "Rejoice because your names are written in heaven" (Luke 10:20). The church is composed of those "who are registered in heaven" (Heb. 12:23). The names of those who are judged at this final "great white throne judgment" apparently all are absent from the Book of Life. The reason for there being only one Book of Life but a plurality of "the books" may be that the names of the saved are fewer than those of the lost, or else that the Book of Life contains only a list of names, while the books contain the names as well as the deeds of the wicked, for, when the books were opened, **the dead were judged according to their works** (v. 12).

Neither those who had been put out of sight by burial nor those fed to the fishes at sea will be able to remain hidden from the final judgment, for the **sea gave up the dead who were in it, and Death and Hades delivered up the dead who were in them** (v. 13). This may correspond to the words of the prophet:

> For behold, the Lord comes out of His place to punish the inhabitants of the earth for their iniquity;

AMILLENNIAL *(continued)*

as well as unbelievers, despite the clear teaching of Scripture that salvation is not attained through works (cf. Eph. 2:8–9; Titus 3:5). It is an equally clear teaching of Scripture that a Christian is known by his works as surely as is an unsaved man (Jas. 2:15–18; Titus 1:16; 2:14). Therefore Christians who are saved by grace through faith will be proven to be so as the result of an examination of their works (Matt. 16:27; 25:31ff.; 1 Pet. 1:17).

With the inauguration of the new heavens and new earth at the coming of Christ, there is such a complete victory over death, the final foe (1 Cor. 15:26), that even the places rendered unclean by having harbored the bodies of the dead, the **sea** and **Hades** (v. 13), are eliminated (v. 14; 21:1). In addition, all who in their lifetimes persisted in the paths of death will attain the thing they were all their lifetime inadvertently pursuing: **the second death** (v. 14). ◉

POSTMILLENNIAL *(continued)*

upon the sun. Hell is only a corner of the universe."[16]

David S. Dark writes:

> If it is objected that here we have no mention of the destiny of the righteous and therefore they could not have been in this scene, we reply that the book of Revelation does not end here, and that the story is to be continued and we shall see the destiny of the righteous in the portion that is yet to come. 🕮

PREMILLENNIAL *(continued)*

the earth will also disclose her blood, and will no more cover her slain (Isa. 26:21).

Death and Hades (v. 14) were revealed in the fourth seal as riding upon the pale horse and slaying a fourth part of mankind (Rev. 6:8). Here, in verse 13, they are personified again as demonic powers that had previously held the dead captive, but now had to surrender their prey. This diabolical duo, like the beast and the false prophet before them (cf. 19:20) and like Satan himself (v. 10), are cast into the lake of fire (v. 14). Thus fulfilling that prediction of the apostle Paul: "The last enemy that will be destroyed is death" (1 Cor. 15:26). The lake of fire is now identified with **the second death** (v. 14), which had been mentioned in verse 6.

The only use to which the Book of Life is put in Revelation is that it is searched to see which names are **not found written** in it (v. 15). The other two references in Revelation to the Book of Life (3:5; 22:19) also focus negatively upon the absence (or removal) of names from this book; being found in it is one's only hope of not being **cast into the lake of fire** (v. 15).

SUMMARY OF CHAPTER 20

Thus concludes what has been called the most controversial chapter in the Bible.

In the view of the *premillennialists,* the golden age of peace and righteousness will not and cannot be realized until Jesus personally returns. He will then bind Satan for 1,000 years and reign over this earth with a rod of iron. The saints who rule with Him will be the righteous who have experienced resurrection earlier at His coming. Satan will be given one last chance at the end of this time and will succeed in deceiving many people, but his rebellion will be supernaturally crushed and he will be eternally judged.

The *amillennial* position takes the Millennium to represent the present age, extending from the First to the Second Advents of Christ. Christ bound Satan (to speak symbolically) when He lived and died on earth long ago. In the future, Satan will again be loosed to bring mischief upon the church, but the Second Coming of Christ will result in Satan's demise and will issue in an eternal new creation devoid of evil, death, or any curse.

Postmillennialists believe (when not agreeing completely with the amillennial interpretation) that there will be a future golden age during which Satan will be bound and peace and righteousness will prevail throughout the earth. This will not be accomplished by the personal return of Christ, but by the power of the gospel preached through the church to all nations. After 1,000 years (more or less) of this glorious arrangement, Satan will launch an abortive attempt to destroy the work of God again. His judgment will be at the return of Christ, followed by a resurrection and judgment of all people

NOTES

1. See, especially, *The Meaning of the Millennium: Four Views,* Robert G. Clouse, ed.; and *The Millennial Maze,* Stanley J. Grenz , both InterVarsity Press, Downers Grove, IL. See also *Mysterious Apocalypse,* Arthur Wainwright, Abingdon, Nashville.
2. The view of Augustine, Andreas, Vitringa, and Hengstenberg
3. Notwithstanding passages like Jude 6 and 2 Peter 2:4, where "chains" are probably to be understood symbolically as well.
4. For "1,000 years," cf. Ps. 90:4; 2 Pet. 3:8. For the use of a "pit," cf. Ps. 7:15; 9:15; 35:7; 40:2; 55:23; 69:15; 88:6; Prov. 22:14; Isa. 24:22; 38:17; Zech. 9:11. For "seal," cf. John 3:33; Rom. 4:11; 1 Cor. 9:2; 2 Tim. 2:19; Rev. 6:3, 5, 7, 9, etc.

5. The Greek verb *katargeo,* used here, means "to reduce to inactivity"—a parallel concept to that of binding, and no more a reference to an absolute inactivity of the devil than that intended in our present passage.

6. In his *Systematic Theology* (Philadephia: Griffith & Rowland, 1909), 3:1008.

7. Chilton, who takes a view of the millennium similar to that of Rushdoony, struggles to properly label the position—finding both "optimistic amillennialist" and "non-chiliastic postmillennialist" too vocally unwieldy—settling for "generic" postmillennialism.

8. The Greek verb in question is the aorist active indicative of *zaō* (to live). This can be either ingressive or constantive in its present form. If the former, it means "came to life." If the latter, then "lived" is the correct translation. The word in the same form appears two other times in Revelation. In Rev. 2:8, it is used of Christ, who was dead and "lives" or else "came to life," depending on the meaning of the word. Both translations work in this context, though "lives" works better in juxtaposition with "was dead." If the meaning were "came to life," the first verb should have been "died" (thus both verbs would share equal strength of the active voice). The other occurrence is at Rev. 13:14, where the beast who had been "wounded by the sword" nonetheless "lived" or "came to life." The former suggests that he survived the injury, whereas the latter presupposes that the beast was actually killed and resurrected. One of the beast's heads looked "as if it had been mortally wounded" (13:3), but this is not the same thing as affirming that the wound had in fact proved fatal. Even if the wound did prove fatal, it was only one of seven heads that sustained the injury—the beast himself survived. Thus the word "lived" or "lived on" seems best to fit the circumstances of the context of 13:14. Even if these conclusions could be established, they would not prove anything about the use of the word in our present context. However, since the word for "live" and the word for "reign" which are joined in the phrase, are both in the same verbal form (aorist active indicative) and since the action of the second verb ("reigned") in the passage refers to the constant activity of the whole period, rather than simply its beginning, "they lived and reigned" seems more appropriate a translation than does the alternative: "they came to life and began to reign . . . for a thousand years." It was their reigning—not their *beginning* to reign—that lasted a thousand years. Thus, from the amillennial perspective, the verb most likely speaks of their continuing to live in heaven with Christ even though they had died on earth.

9. Kenneth Gentry, "Postmillennialism," in *Three Views on the Millennium and Beyond.* (Grand Rapids: Zondervan, 1999), 13f.

10. John Jefferson Davis, *Christ's Victorious Kingdom* (Grand Rapids: Baker, 1986), 98.

11. Strong, *Systematic Theology,* 3:1013.

12. James B. Jordan, *The Law of the Covenant* (Tyler, TX: Institute for Christian Economics, 1984), 26–27.

13. E.g., Alford, Lange, Vitringa, Stuart.

14. The view of Fausset, Barnes, Hengstenberg.

15. St. Augustine in *The City of God,* xx.12.

16. W. G. T. Shedd, *Dogmatic Theology,* vol. 2.

PART VIII

THE NEW CREATION

REVELATION 21—22

WILL THERE BE A LITERAL NEW HEAVENS AND NEW EARTH?
WHAT IS THE NEW JERUSALEM?

LITERALIST:

- Some take the descriptions in these chapters fairly literally, as applied to a brand new planet and universe, which will be created after the close of the Millennium (*premillennialists*) or else at the Second Coming (some *amillennialists* and some *postmillennialists.*)
- The New Jerusalem described here will be the eternal home of the redeemed.

NON-LITERALIST:

- Some spiritualize the whole vision, applying it to a nonmaterial state of existence in heaven.
- Others take the "New Heaven and the New Earth" to represent what Paul called " a New Creation" (2 Cor. 5:17)—that is, the condition of those who are in covenant with God and Christ through the New Covenant, the "Old Heaven and the Old Earth" (meaning the Old Covenant) having passed away.
- The New Jerusalem represents the church itself, represented under the imagery of a new Holy of Holies—the tabernacle of God with men—in its present earthly existence.

As with the rest of Revelation, there is no consensus among expositors regarding the closing chapters of the book. However, as with the case of chapter 20, the disagreement among scholars does not divide along the lines of the four camps that have been compared and contrasted in the greater part of this book. The new heavens and the new earth have been interpreted in essentially three ways: (a) literally of a future material universe after the coming of Christ (so most *futurists* believe); (b) symbolically of heaven, the abode of the glorified saints; or (c) spiritually of the New Covenant community (the church) that has replaced the Old Covenant community of Israel. Many tend to take the first position as the primary meaning and to acknowledge secondarily a spiritual application to the present believing community, which has already "tasted of the powers of the age to come" (Heb. 6:5), but which still awaits the establishment of the literal "new heavens and a new earth in which righteousness dwells" (2 Pet. 3:13) at the return of Christ or after the Millennium. Chilton holds to the validity of both applications, though he makes the spiritual one the principal interpretation, writing:

> Thus, when St. John tells us that he saw "a new heaven and earth," we should recognize that the primary significance of that phrase is symbolic, and has to do with the blessings of salvation.

Let us look at the evidence for each of these views individually:

(a) *The literal.* Among futurists, and especially the dispensationalists, there is broad agreement that these chapters describe fairly precisely the creation of a new universe after the coming of Christ (actually, in their view, after the Millennium, which itself followed the coming of Christ). The focus is terrestrial, as the majority of the details point in the direction of an earthly city to which the kings and the nations bring their treasures as gifts for the worship of God.

Thus Gaebelein writes: "We now come to the revelation concerning the final and eternal state of the earth." Ray Stedman writes: "The good news is that God is preparing a new world for us to inhabit after our old world passes away." Weidner writes: "The purified and renewed earth has become the abode of glorified humanity and the tabernacle of God is with man."

The earth, in this vision, is restored to a condition like that which prevailed in the garden of Eden before the fall. It is watered by a great river, as we also read of the region of Eden (22:1; cf. Gen. 2:10); the "tree of life" is found there, as in Eden (22:2); and "there is no more curse" (22:3), as was the case before the Fall in Eden.

Biederwolf is apparently quoting G. Campbell Morgan[1] when he writes: "It would seem as though we must take these things literally because there is no other way to take them."[2] Yet, not only would a minority of scholars agree with the statement that "there is no other way to take them," but Biederwolf's commentary itself later takes much of the language nonliterally. For example, about the expression "the twelve tribes of the children of Israel" (v. 12): "Spiritual Israel of course is here symbolized by the names of the actual tribes of Israel."[3] Similarly, when discussing the fact that the city is said to be as tall as it is wide (v. 16), and responding to the attempts of some to tinker with the figures, Biederwolf writes: "Inasmuch as the description must be taken symbolically there is no need to attempt to reduce the enormous dimensions given here."[4] Thus, it is difficult to maintain a consistent standard of literal interpretation, even if one is basically committed to doing so.

(b) *The symbolic.* Russell takes an approach opposite that of the literalist: "Plainly we have here a representation in which symbolism is carried to its utmost limits; and he who would deal with such gorgeous imagery as with prosaic literalness is incapable of comprehending them." Russell is among those who would apply the vision under consideration to heaven. While many who espouse the literal view find no difficulty in applying the word "heaven" to what they really understand to be a renewed physical earth,[5] Russell seems specifically to reject the idea of a physical earth as the eternal abode of the saints and applies all the imagery to heaven itself:

> There are, indeed, certain phrases which at first seem to imply that earth is the scene where these glories are manifested . . . but, on the other hand, the whole conception and description of the vision forbid the supposition of its being a terrestrial scene.

The evidence he gives seems ambiguous at best. First, he insists that these chapters must necessarily belong to the category of "things which must shortly come to pass" (that is, close to the time of writing), even though he allows that portions of chapter 20 look to events more distant from John's day.

Second, he makes much of the fact that the heavenly Jerusalem, so prominent in this vision, is always elsewhere said to be in heaven (e.g., Gal. 4:26; Heb. 12:22–23). He seems to miss the point that the Jerusalem which has ever previously been located in heaven is here seen to be "coming down out of heaven" (21:2), presumably to earth. Notwithstanding the slenderness of this evidence, Russell writes: "Clearly, therefore, the holy city is the abode of the glorified; the inheritance of the saints in light, the mansions of the Father's house, prepared for the home of the blessed."

Those who anticipate a physical new earth would have no problem accepting the above language, though they would say that all of these will be experienced in a neo-terrestrial setting. This, however, is not how Russell sees it: "We therefore conclude that the vision sets forth the blessedness and glory of the heavenly state, into which the way was fully opened at the 'end of the age.'"[6]

(c) *The spiritual.* The "spiritual" view of the new creation is simply applying the images which appear to be talking about heaven, the earth, a city, a river, trees, and so on, to the spiritual new creation—the church. The passage is represented as a figurative portrait of a spiritual reality manifested here and now in the state and experience of the individual believer, who is already "a new creation" (2 Cor 5:17), and the New Covenant church collectively.

Some expositors who understand the vision in this way consider the "first heavens and the first earth," which have passed away, to be the preconversion state of the believer. Others see the defunct Old Covenant system of Judaism as the older "creation," now replaced with the new order under Christ. Chilton cross-references the passage with many other portions of Scripture to establish his thesis.

There is no reason that the first and third options (or the second and third, for that matter) cannot be understood as both being suggested by the passage. Just as the physical tabernacle was a shadow of the spiritual realities of the New Covenant, the new heavens and earth, when they come into physical existence, could prove to be physically structured so as to mimic those spiritual realities instituted by Christ at the cross and currently enjoyed by believers. As Chilton puts it, "The final reality of the eschatological New Creation is also the present reality of the definitive-progressive New Creation." Believers have, after all, already "tasted of the powers of the age to come" (Heb. 6:5).

With these options in view, we now turn to the passage itself.

OVERVIEW OF NEW CREATION

REVELATION 21:1—8

[1]Now I saw a new heaven and a new earth, for the first heaven and the first earth had passed away. Also there was no more sea. [2]Then I, John, saw the holy city, New Jerusalem, coming down out of heaven from God, prepared as a bride adorned for her husband. [3]And I heard a loud voice from heaven saying, "Behold, the tabernacle of God is with men, and He will dwell with them, and they shall be His people. God Himself will be with them and be their God. [4]And God will wipe away every tear from their eyes; there shall be no more death, nor sorrow, nor crying. There shall be no more pain, for the former things have passed away." [5]Then He who sat on the throne said, "Behold, I make all things new." And He said to me, "Write, for these words are true and faithful." [6]And He said to me, "It is done! I am the Alpha and the Omega, the Beginning and the End. I will give of the fountain of the water of life freely to him who thirsts. [7]He who overcomes shall inherit all things, and I

will be his God and he shall be My son. [8]But the cowardly, unbelieving, abominable, murderers, sexually immoral, sorcerers, idolaters, and all liars shall have their part in the lake which burns with fire and brimstone, which is the second death."

The concept of a new heaven and a new earth (v. 1) is first given clear expression in Isaiah and is later mentioned by Peter, probably alluding to Isaiah (2 Pet. 3:13). God first speaks of His intention to "plant the heavens, lay the foundations of the earth, and say to Zion, 'You are My people'" (Isa. 51:16). Since this is uttered after the first heaven and earth were created, this must speak of planting a new heaven and earth. Chilton understands it to be a reference to the establishment of the Jewish religion and polity, since the creation of this heaven and earth is stated to be a result of the Exodus (v. 15). This is possible, though the wording ("that I may . . .") seems to suggest an action that God still anticipated performing after Isaiah's day. This could refer to the establishment of the New Covenant, since certain elements of the New Covenant order are said to be something that God "creates" (Isa. 4:5; 57:19). Also, the specific promise of "new heavens and a new earth," found exclusively in Isaiah 65:17 and 66:22, fall within a portion of Isaiah which New Testament writers applied to the present age.[7]

In saying **the first heaven and the first earth had passed away** (v. 1) John may simply be repeating what was implied in the previous chapter, where John saw the throne of God, "from whose face the earth and the heaven fled away. And there was found no place for them" (20:11). While this may be understood literally, it is also possible to apply it spiritually, since, in connection with declaring the believer to be "a new creation," Paul also says, "old things have passed away" (2 Cor. 5:17). It also may refer, depending upon an interpreter's presuppositions, to the Old Covenant system, which the author of Hebrews said was "ready to vanish away" (Heb. 8:13).

Many readers are disappointed to find that on the new earth there was no more sea (v. 1). Most seem to take this in the absolute sense that the new creation has no sea at all (Augustine, Alford, Bede, Barnes, Fausset, Gaebelein, Sadler, Weidner, etc.). Bede says (and Alford and Weidner imply) that the sea was dried up in the global conflagration of which Peter writes in 2 Peter 3. Sadler points out that this means the three-quarters of the earth's surface now covered with water will no longer be uninhabitable. Though convinced that there will be literally no oceans, Ray Stedman speculates that "there may be large bodies of fresh water, perhaps even larger than Great Lakes, that we may enjoy in the new heaven and the new earth."

Alternatively, Biederwolf thinks it likely that "there was no more sea" only in the sense that the first heaven and the first earth were "no more." Not only had the former heavens and earth (or *land*) passed away, but the *former* sea as well. With this interpretation, we may infer that, as a new heaven and earth had replaced the old, so also a new sea had replaced the old one.

Many take the sea symbolically as representing the nations and peoples of the Gentiles. According to this theory, only the spiritual Israel remains of all the nations that once covered the planet. The glory of the Lord thus fills the earth as the waters once covered the sea (Hab. 2:14).

The mixing of metaphors in **the holy city, New Jerusalem . . . prepared as a bride adorned for her husband** (v. 2) is arresting. That a city could be dressed in bridal attire is difficult to picture with the mind. Yet it is not the first time the images of a city and a woman have been joined in describing one entity. In Revelation 17, the great harlot was also Babylon, and a divine interpreter explained that "the woman whom you saw is that great city" (17:18). The figure of a woman to represent a city goes back to the Old Testament, where Jerusalem is referred to as "the virgin, the daughter of Zion" (Isa. 37:22).

The present passage, however, takes us even further into the realm of symbolism, for in this case not only does the woman represent a city, but the city also represents something else. Since the New Jerusalem is later described as "the Lamb's wife" (v. 9), we can readily identify the symbol with the church, which is the bride of Christ (Eph. 5:31–32). Yet, while the church is located on earth, its foundation and the root from which it springs is in heaven. Thus it ever emanates or descends from heaven. The descent mentioned here, however, does not seem to be timeless and perpetual.

The bride is here **prepared as a bride adorned for her husband** (v. 2), suggesting the wedding day. In chapter 19, the announcement was made that the marriage of the Lamb had come and his wife had made herself ready (19:7), yet no description of the wedding or the bride was offered. This vision seems to pick up where that one left off, for here we see the procession of the bride in her readiness to be joined to her husband.

The timing of this event would most naturally be taken to be the same as that of chapter 19, where most interpreters have seen the Second Coming of Christ. However, millennialists (both post–and pre–) have taken chapter 20 (the Millennium) to refer to events following chapter 19 and preceding this chapter. If so, then it would seem that the marriage was announced as present before the Millennium (in 19:7), but does not really occur until after the Millennium (here). The *amillennialist* escapes this problem. To him the Second Coming occurred in chapter 19, but his interpretation of chapter 20 as a synopsis of the church age makes this passage also a reference to events occurring at the Second Coming. This verse is expanded upon in verses 9 through 21.

The declaration **Behold the tabernacle of God is with men** (v. 3) informs us that God's ancient promises made in Leviticus and Ezekiel are fulfilled in this event. In Leviticus 26:11, Israel was told conditionally that, if they remained obedient, God would set His tabernacle among them and would not abhor them. The destruction of Solomon's temple and the removal to Babylon in 586 BC was God's way of revoking this privilege because of the Jews' disobedience. While in Babylon, however, Ezekiel prophesied that there would come a time of ultimate restoration of God's people under the terms of the New Covenant, resulting in the renewal of the original privilege: "My tabernacle also shall be with them; indeed I will be their God, and they shall be my people" (Ezek. 37:27). Many interpreters apply Ezekiel 37 to the Millennium, though the repetition of Ezekiel's words in this place would favor a fulfillment in the new creation.

Some have so construed the promise **God will wipe away every tear from their eyes** (v. 4) as to teach that there will be tears in heaven. Biederwolf, however, suggests that the words simply mean "that He will so constitute things that no more tears will be shed." This seems to be confirmed by the explanation that **there shall be no more death, nor sorrow, nor crying. There shall be no more pain** (v. 4). The causes of present mourning and crying are eradicated forever.

There is also a present realization of these truths, since, for the Christian, Christ has "abolished death" (2 Tim. 1:10), so that "whoever lives and believes" in Christ "shall never die" (John 11:25). As for sorrow, grief, and pain, our relationship with God through Christ has even transformed these experiences so that, while we do still mourn the loss of loved ones, we do not "sorrow as others who have no hope" (1 Thess. 4:13).

The former things (v. 4) belonging to the old creation **have passed away** along with it (cf. v. 1). All the worse for those who had set their hearts upon "the things in the world" (1 John 2:15). John earlier warned his readers (possibly as a result of having had this vision) that "the world is passing away, and the lust of it; but he who does the will of God abides forever" (1 John 2:17). God has renewed **all things** (v. 5) to correspond appropriately to the new creation. Biederwolf comments: "The former state of things . . . will be changed

555

and the change will extend of course to everything."

This also applies to the Christian now, of whom Paul writes, "old things have passed away; behold, all things have become new" (2 Cor. 5:17). With the emphasis upon "all things," he points out that the Christian is not simply given a ticket to heaven and a new set of religious rituals, but every area of his life is targeted for renewal as the result of his participation in the new life. Making this same point, Philip Schaff eloquently wrote:

> Religion is not a single, separate sphere of human life, but the divine principle by which the entire man is to be pervaded, refined and made complete. It takes hold of him in his undivided totality, in the center of his personal being; to carry light into his understanding, holiness into his will, and heaven into his heart; and to shed thus the sacred consecration of the new birth, and the glorious liberty of the children of God, over his whole inward and outward life. No form of existence can withstand the renovating power of God's Spirit. There is no rational element that may not be sanctified; no sphere of natural life that may not be glorified.[8]

The language of these verses also can apply to the passing away of the old covenantal order, which has been so completely replaced by the new order that God commands His people: "Do not remember the former things, nor consider the things of old. Behold I will do a new thing" (Isa. 43:18–19). No place remains for the old covenant, as the writer of Hebrews explains: "In that He says, 'A new covenant,' He has made the first obsolete. Now what is becoming obsolete and growing old is ready to vanish away" (Heb. 8:13).

As Jesus declared upon the cross, "It is finished" (John 19:30), and upon the fall of Babylon the Great a loud voice from the temple cried, "It is done!" (Rev. 16:17), so now, with reference to the perfecting of the bride and the completion of God's purposes in history, it is again affirmed, It is **done!** (v. 6). The speaker is thought by some (e.g., Lange, Milligan, and others) to be God, but the remainder of the verse would seem to identify him as Christ (so think Barnes, Stuart, and others). The speaker identifies himself as **the Alpha and the Omega, the Beginning and the End** (v. 6), which title belonged to Christ in the opening chapter (cf. 1:8, 17–18; 22:13, 16). Further, the promise, **I will give of the fountain of the water of life freely to him who thirsts** (v. 6), is clearly the same as that made twice by Jesus in John's Gospel (cf. John 4:10, 14; 7:37f.). Also, the phrase **He who overcomes** (v. 7) is characteristic of the phraseology in the promises made by Christ in the letters to the seven churches (cf. 2:7, 11, 17, 26; 3:5, 12, 21).

That the overcomer **shall inherit all things** (v. 7) is the natural consequence of the other part of the statement: **he shall be My son.** The inheritance is given to the sons. Paul develops this thought in Rom. 8:15–17:

> For you did not receive the spirit of bondage again to fear, but you received the Spirit of adoption by whom we cry out, "Abba, Father." The Spirit Himself bears witness with our spirit that we are children of God, and if children, then heirs—heirs of God and joint heirs with Christ, if indeed we suffer with Him, that we may also be glorified together.

The blessing of the overcomer is followed by the cursing of the non-overcomers. **The cowardly** (v. 8) are in contrast to those who have been faithful unto death. Thus the cowardly are equated by many (e.g., Alford, Bengel, De Wette, Stuart, Hengstenberg, Milligan) with apostates, who defect from the gospel rather than enduring hardship as good soldiers of Jesus Christ. The **unbelieving, abominable, murderers, sexually immoral, sorcerers, idolaters, and all liars** have an inheritance as well: as the tribes of Israel each obtained a portion in the land of Canaan, these **shall have their part in the lake which bums with fire and brimstone.** The identification of the lake of fire with **the second death** (v. 8) is repeated, having been made first in Rev. 20:14.

One way of understanding the structure of these final chapters is to see this whole segment (vv. 1–8) as an outline or summary of the remaining portion of the book. A remarkable correspondence exists between the progression of thought in these first verses and in the remaining chapters. Compare, after the introductory statement in verse 1:

Content	In verses 1–8	In the remainder
New Jerusalem	v. 2	21:9–21
God dwells among men	v. 3	21:22–27
Renewal of the world	v. 5a	22:1–5
"These words are true and faithful"	v. 5b	22:6–10
Work completed: "I am Alpha and Omega"	v. 6a	22:11–15
Final blessing: water of life to all who thirst	v. 6b–7	22:16–17
Final curse upon the rebellious	v. 8	22:18–19

THE NEW JERUSALEM

REVELATION 21:9—21

[9]Then one of the seven angels who had the seven bowls filled with the seven last plagues came to me and talked with me, saying, "Come, I will show you the bride, the Lamb's wife." [10]And he carried me away in the Spirit to a great and high mountain, and showed me the great city, the holy Jerusalem, descending out of heaven from God, [11]having the glory of God. Her light was like a most precious stone, like a jasper stone, clear as crystal. [12]Also she had a great and high wall with twelve gates, and twelve angels at the gates, and names written on them, which are the names of the twelve tribes of the children of Israel: [13]three gates on the east, three gates on the north, three gates on the south, and three gates on the west. [14]Now the wall of the city had twelve foundations, and on them were the names of the twelve apostles of the Lamb. [15]And he who talked with me had a gold reed to measure the city, its gates, and its wall. [16]The city is laid out as a square; its length is as great as its breadth. And he measured the city with the reed: twelve thousand furlongs. Its length, breadth, and height are equal. [17]Then he measured its wall: one hundred and forty-four cubits, according to the measure of a man, that is, of an angel. [18]The construction of its wall was of jasper; and the city was pure gold, like clear glass. [19]The foundations of the wall of the city were adorned with all kinds of precious stones: the first foundation was jasper, the second sapphire, the third chalcedony, the fourth emerald, [20]the fifth sardonyx, the sixth sardius, the seventh chrysolite, the eighth beryl, the ninth topaz, the tenth chrysoprase, the eleventh jacinth, and the twelfth amethyst. [21]The twelve gates were twelve pearls: each individual gate was of one pearl. And the street of the city was pure gold, like transparent glass.

It is significant that the invitation **Come, I will show you the bride, the Lamb's wife** (v. 9) came from **one of the seven angels who had the seven bowls,** for it was one of those angels (possibly the same one) who earlier had said to John, "Come, I will show you the judgment of the great harlot" (17:1).

This provides a structural link, deliberately placing the harlot in juxtaposition with the bride.

Another link to the earlier passage is seen in John's being carried away in the Spirit to a great and high mountain (v. 10), in contrast to 17:3—"So he carried me away in the Spirit into the wilderness." The bride-city is elevated upon a mountain, "beautiful in elevation, the joy of the whole earth" (Ps. 48:2), while the harlot city is situated in a barren wasteland.

John's seeing the holy Jerusalem, descending out of heaven from God (v. 10) was mentioned earlier (cf. v. 2), though the only description given there was that the city was adorned as a bride. Here, the attire of the bride is seen to be her having the glory of God (v. 11). The Shekinah that once rested upon the temple in earthly Jerusalem has departed from that institution and come to alight upon the church, the new temple of the Holy Spirit and the new City of God. The inheritance and hope of the New Testament believer is the hope of obtaining the glory of God (Rom. 2:7; 5:2; 8:18; Col. 1:27; 1 Thess. 2:12; 2 Thess. 2:14; Heb. 2:10; 1 Pet. 5:1, 10). This speaks of the likeness of Christ Himself seen upon His people (Rom. 8:29; 2 Cor 3:18; Phil. 3:21; 2 Pet. 1:19; 1 John 3:2).

The light radiating from the glorious bride-city is compared to the radiance of **a most precious stone, like a jasper stone, clear as crystal** (v. 11), which probably refers to a diamond. The believing remnant is likened to jewels in the Old Testament. In Malachi 3:16–17, it is said of those who fear the Lord and meditate on His name, "'They shall be Mine,' says the LORD of hosts, 'on the day that I make them my jewels.'"

The context in Malachi suggests that the reference is to the Jewish believers in Christ, who escaped the desolation of the capital city in AD 70. In this place also some find grounds for seeing the bride as the surviving church at the time of the destruction of the old Jewish polity.

The city is described as surrounded by **a great and high wall** (v. 12). This is applicable to the church as a spiritual city even today. In speaking of the spiritual Jerusalem, God predicted "and you shall call your walls Salvation" (Isa. 60:18), and "I . . . will be a wall of fire around her, and I will be the glory in her midst" (Zech. 2:5). If Salvation is the wall—indeed, God Himself is the wall—of the city, then the city and its wall appear to be spiritual in nature. This would be a figurative means of expressing the reality of the believer's security in the City of God.

The wall of the city has **twelve gates** (v. 12) that have written upon them **the names of the twelve tribes of the children of Israel.** In Isaiah, the same passage that calls the city's wall "Salvation" goes on to say, "And your gates [shall be called] Praise" (Isa. 60:18). The most important of the twelve tribes was Judah, whose name means "Praise." In Isaiah, the city's gates are named after this tribe; in Revelation, the gates bear the names of all twelve tribes. There may be no conflict here, since in Judah, that is, in Christ, who is of that tribe, all the "twelve tribes" of the spiritual Israel are included. The attachment of the tribal names to the gates may suggest that through Israel God made a way for the world to enter the City of God, for "salvation is of the Jews" (John 4:22). Of course, this is only another way of saying that salvation is through Jesus Christ, who sprang from the Jewish race.

It is expedient that there should be **three gates on the east, three gates on the north, three gates on the south, and three gates on the west** (v. 13), to speak of universal access into the church, for Jesus predicted that "They will come from the east and the west, from the north and the south, and sit down in the kingdom of God" (Luke 13:29).

The positioning of the **twelve foundations** (v. 14) of the city has been disputed. On the one hand, they may be stacked one upon another in twelve layers. Alternatively, each of them individually may support a portion of the wall running between two gates. There would be twelve such portions of the wall, each resting upon its own foundation. This is how Alford, Biederwolf, De Wette, Swete, Simcox, Weidner, and some others understand the imagery.

Further evidence for identifying the city with the church is seen in the city foundations that have upon them the names of **the twelve apostles of the Lamb** (v. 14). This detail communi-

cates pictorially what Paul said more directly, that the church is "built upon the foundation of the apostles and prophets" (Eph. 2:20). This is the city for which Abraham looked: "the city which has foundations, whose builder and maker is God" (Heb. 11:10).

The measuring of **the city, its gates, and its wall** (v. 15) recalls Ezekiel 40:3, where an angelic messenger carried a measuring line and a reed to measure the gates and walls of "something like the structure of a city" (Ezekiel 40:2) and the temple in it. It seems likely that this vision corresponds to that of Ezekiel, although *premillennialists* generally apply Ezekiel's to the Millennium and this one to the state of things after the Millennium.

Like the angel in Ezekiel, this angel measured the city himself (v. 17), whereas John had been given a reed and asked to do the measuring in 11:1. In that earlier place, John was made to measure the temple, but here the whole city is measured because the whole city is the temple. Biederwolf writes: "The measuring shows that the discourse is of something real, and that the city is not to be resolved into mere thought and imagination."

The shape of the city was a square, or actually a cube, because **its length, breadth, and height are equal** (v. 16). The dimensions are said to be **twelve thousand furlongs** each direction. Those who take the passage more literally look for a future metropolis that measures fifteen hundred miles in each direction, including its height. Its wall would be only **one hundred and forty-four cubits** (v. 17), or about 216 feet, tall—which makes the city thousands of times taller that its surrounding wall. This would prevent the wall from obscuring the glory of the city.

Many think it unreasonable to translate these numbers into modern units and then apply them literally to the city. Swete writes: "Such dimensions defy imagination and are permissible only in the language of symbolism." Stuart writes: "Everything shows that a literal exegesis in such a case as the present, excepting merely so far as to get a proper idea of the grandeur and the congruity of the image, is entirely out of the question." Chilton writes: "The numbers are obviously symbolic, the multiples of twelve being a reference to the majesty, vastness, and perfection of the Church."

It is important to note that the city's cube shape was also the shape of the Holy of Holies. Since John sees no temple in the city (v. 22), we may imply that the whole city is the temple, or more specifically, the holy of holies. It is the place of the glory of God (cf. v. 11). This is the nature of the church today—it is the place of God's residence (Eph. 2:20–21; 1 Tim. 3:15; Heb. 3:6; 1 Pet. 2:5), where God communes with men. Earlier, John had measured the holy of holies (the *naos*) for its protection and preservation. In this vision, the *naos* is again measured, indicating its permanence, but it is now identified with the City of God, the church of Jesus Christ.

Part of the adorning of the bride is her jewelry. Though the jewels could have been mentioned in connection with the bride imagery, they are here incorporated instead into the city motif. The walls, foundations, and gates are all made of great gemstones. This harks back to a prophecy of the Old Testament concerning the church:

O you afflicted one,
Tossed with the tempest, and not
    comforted,
Behold, I will lay your stones with
    colorful gems,
And lay your foundations with
    sapphires.
I will make your pinnacles of
    rubies,
Your gates of crystal,
And all your walls of precious
    stones. (Isa. 54:11–12)[9]

The specific gems mentioned in the two passages differ, but the idea is obviously the same in both places. Of the New Jerusalem we read that its wall was of jasper; and the city was pure gold, like clear glass (v. 18), which amplifies the information previously given in verse 11. The light of the city was said to be like that of a jasper stone, which we now understand to be the material from which the wall is constructed. But the city itself was of gold, so thoroughly purified as to become transparent. This is an image used to describe the refined character of the sanctified believer (Job 23:10; Zech. 13:9; Mal. 3:3; 1 Pet. 1:7; Rev. 3:18).

The twelve gems comprising the foundations call to mind the twelve gems worn upon the breast of the high priest, though again the individual stones are not identical (cf. Exod. 28:15–21). Since these same stones bear the names of the twelve apostles, it could be understood as a statement about the leadership of the people of God having transferred from the high priesthood of the temple to the apostles of the church.

There may be symbolic significance to the fact that **the twelve gates were twelve pearls** (v. 21). Unlike the previously named gems, pearls are created organically. A rough grain of sand irritating the tissues of the oyster causes the secretion of a substance that transforms the source of irritation into a pearl. The pearl thus may stand for affliction turned to benefit, even as silver and gold refined by fire are used in Scripture for the same concept. The gates are the means of entry into the city. If the pearl is understood in this light, we have a picture of one of Paul's preaching themes: "We must through many tribulations enter the kingdom of God" (Acts 14:22).

In Scripture a way of life is frequently called a path, a way, a highway, or a road (e.g., Prov. 4:18; Isa. 35:8). Therefore it is reasonable to understand **the street of the city** (v. 21) as representing the way of life of those who comprise the New Jerusalem. This street **was pure gold, like transparent glass,** which speaks of the godly character and behavior that comes from enduring the refining fires of tribulation.

THE HABITATION OF GOD

REVELATION 21:22—27

[22]But I saw no temple in it, for the Lord God Almighty and the Lamb are its temple. [23]The city had no need of the sun or of the moon to shine in it, for the glory of God illuminated it. The Lamb is its light. [24]And the nations of those who are saved shall walk in its light, and the kings of the earth bring their glory and honor into it. [25]Its gates shall not be shut at all by day (there shall be no night there). [26]And they shall bring the glory and the honor of the nations into it. [27]But there shall by no means enter it anything that defiles, or causes an abomination or a lie, but only those who are written in the Lamb's Book of Life.

On the statement, I saw **no temple in it** (v. 1), Russell writes:

> Some of the features [of this vision] are evidently derived from the visionary city beheld by Ezekiel; but there is this remarkable difference, that whereas the temple and its elaborate details occupy the principal part of the Old Testament vision, no temple at all is seen in the apocalyptic vision—perhaps for the reason that where all is most holy no one place has greater sanctity than another, or because where God's presence is fully manifested, the whole place becomes one big temple.

Rather than going to a particular place to worship and appearing before God "in the sanctuary," today one needs only be found "in God" or "in Christ" to worship acceptably, for **the Lord God Almighty and the Lamb are its temple** (v. 22).

As the creation was originally illuminated by the glory of God himself prior to the creation of the heavenly lights (Gen. 1:3 [cf. 2 Cor. 4:6], 14ff.), so this New Jerusalem **had no need of the sun or of the moon to shine in it, for the glory of God illuminated it** (v. 23). It is illuminated by the One who declared himself to be the "Light of the world" (John 8:12); **the Lamb is its light.** The absence of natural light and having only the glory of God (the Shekinah) to provide light is another feature that links the imagery of the city with that of the Holy of Holies (see on v. 16). Without the light of God's presence, that room was cast into absolute darkness.

563

A helpful way of treating this segment is to look at it alongside an Old Testament passage with which it coincides. Compare the details point-by-point with Isaiah, chapter 60:

Isaiah 60	Revelation 21
the sun shall no longer be your light by day, nor for brightness shall the moon give light to you; but the Lord will be to you . . . light (v. 19)	the city had no need of the sun or of the moon to shine in it for the glory of God illuminated it (v. 23)
the Gentiles shall come to your light (v. 3)	the nations of those who are saved shall walk in its light (v. 24)
kings shall minister to you (v. 10) the glory of Lebanon shall come to you (v. 13)	the kings of the earth bring their glory and honor into it (v. 24)
your gates shall be open continually . . . not shut day nor night (v. 11)	Its gates shall not be shut at all by day (there shall be no night there) (v. 25)
the wealth of the Gentiles shall come to you (v. 5)	they shall bring the glory and the honor of the nations into it (v. 26)
also your people shall be all righteous (v. 21)	there shall by no means enter it anything that defiles . . . (v. 27)

In Isaiah 60, all of this is precipitated by the dawning of the glory of the Lord in a glorious new day (Isa. 60:1–3). This day was seen to dawn with the birth of John the Baptist and Jesus (cf. Luke 1:76–78; Matt. 4:13–16). Both passages then would appear to speak, albeit in symbolic terms, of the realities of the New Covenant age. The coming of the Gentiles into the church and the submission of kings to Christ has been in progress for nearly two thousand years now.

RENEWAL OF THE WORLD

REVELATION 22:1—5

[1]And he showed me a pure river of water of life, clear as crystal, proceeding from the throne of God and of the Lamb. [2]In the middle of its street, and on either side of the river, was the tree of life, which bore twelve fruits, each tree yielding its fruit every month. The leaves of the tree were for the healing of the nations. [3]And there shall be no more curse, but the throne of God and of the Lamb shall be in it, and His servants shall serve Him. [4]They shall see His face, and His name shall be on their foreheads. [5]There shall be no night there: They need no lamp nor light of the sun, for the Lord God gives them light. And they shall reign forever and ever.

This chapter, through verse 5, continues and concludes the description of the new creation, a prominent feature of which was **a pure river of water of life, clear as crystal, proceeding from the throne** (v. 1). This image of a river flowing out of Jerusalem is found in three separate Old Testament prophets, which must therefore all be describing the same time period and phenomenon.

Several physical issues strongly suggest that this river is symbolic rather than literal. For one thing, according to Ezekiel 47, the volume of water increases the farther the river flows from its source. Taken literally, it would require that the water multiply itself almost as Jesus multiplied the loaves, since the quantity must increase without any additional influx from other sources. Since the water is "living water" (Zech. 14:8) rather than ordinary water, we could allow the possibility of its reproducing itself in the manner of all other living things, though this seems a doubtful conclusion.

Another evidence that we are not reading of a literal river of water is that in Joel 3:18 this river is described as watering the Valley of the Acacias, which Numbers 25:1 locates in Moab, across the Jordan River from Jerusalem. In order for this river to reach from Jerusalem to Moab, one would have to posit the removal of the Jordan, a contingency never hinted at in Scripture, or else this river would have to flow across the Jordan to water the region on the other side. Since it is a physical impossibility

565

for one river to cross another, as two roads do, we are compelled to consider a symbolic interpretation of the river.

To understand the symbolism of this river, one need only consult John's Gospel, where Jesus, standing up at the Feast of Tabernacles, said: "If anyone thirsts, let him come to Me and drink. He who believes in Me, as the Scripture has said, out of his heart will flow rivers of living water." John adds the following explanatory note: "But this He spoke concerning the Spirit" (John 7:37–39). Thus the river of living water flowing out of Jerusalem apparently would represent the activity and blessings of the Holy Spirit flowing from God's throne in the heart of the believer.

The **tree of life** (v. 2) lacks the definite article, and thus seems to be used collectively of many trees of the one kind. This presumption seems confirmed by comparison to the parallel vision in Ezekiel 47:7—"There, along the bank of the river, were very many trees on one side and the other." John says the trees are in the middle of its street, and on either side of the river (v. 2). Barnes and Stuart picture the river running through the city, with a street running parallel on either side, with the line of trees planted in a row between the riverbanks and the street on either side. Alford, Biederwolf, Seiss, and Weidner, on the other hand, picture the river flowing through the broad street with a row of trees on

either bank. The decision on this point would appear to be of vanishingly small consequence.

The certainty of the identification of the tree in this vision with those in Ezekiel's is seen in Ezekiel 47:12:

> Along the bank of the river, on this side and that, will grow all kinds of trees used for food. . . . They will bear fruit every month, because their water flows from the sanctuary. Their fruit will be for food, and their leaves for medicine.

The trees bear monthly their **twelve fruits** (v. 2), which many (e.g., Stuart, Swete, Milligan, Weidner, and others) understand to be the food that the saints will eat to sustain themselves in their glorified bodies. The purpose of **the leaves of the tree** is considerably more nebulous. They are said to be **for the healing of the nations** (v. 2), but the question intrudes itself, *what nations?* If we take this to mean that humanity in the new creation will be organized into discreet political nations, then these are matters of which we have little or no additional information.

On the other hand, if "nations" is understood simply in the sense of "the Gentiles," then it may simply be a reference to the church saints of Gentile extraction in the holy city. Weidner considers the reference to be to "the converted Gentiles who are among the glorified saints." This view seems to enjoy the favor of most expositors, including Milligan:

> It is impossible to think that the nations here spoken of have yet to be converted. They have already entered the New Jerusalem, and that they are healed can signify no more than this, that they are kept in constant soundness of health by what is here administered to them.

Taken, however, as a symbolic picture of the New Covenant blessings in the present age, the leaves of the tree could refer simply to the fact that as the gospel advances, the kingdom, like a mustard tree (Matt. 13:31–32) or a great cedar (Ezek. 17:22–23), spreads its branches, providing all nations a place of refuge and healing under the shadow of its leaves (cf. Ezek. 31:4–6; Dan. 4:11–12).

The removal of the **curse** (v. 3) seems to refer to the curse upon the earth pronounced in the garden of Eden (Gen. 3:15ff.). If, however, the New Covenant community is being contrasted here with the old Judaism, this may refer to the curse that came upon Israel for her covenant unfaithfulness, leaving only the uncursed, obedient remnant to enter the joys of the new creation.

Jesus promised that the pure in heart would see God (Matt. 5:8), and it is here declared that He makes good on that promise: **They shall see His face, and His name shall be on their foreheads** (v. 4). The seal of God's name upon the foreheads of the 144,000 was brought to our attention in chapter 14, but we here see that this is the privilege and standing of all of the inhabitants of the city, meaning either that the 144,000 represent all the saved, or else that they at least enjoy no greater privilege than do the remainder of those saved. As was mentioned earlier (21:23), so we are again told that **there shall be no night there** (v. 5) as well as that **they need no lamp nor light of the sun, for the Lord God gives them light.**

Here again the saints are said to **reign forever and ever** (v. 5). They were previously seen reigning in chapter 20, during the Millennium. To the *amillennialist*, the reign of the saints in chapter 20 could be understood as their reigning in heaven in the intermediate state before Christ returned, whereas they now reign in resurrected bodies upon the renewed planet earth. The *premillennialist* already had them reigning on earth in chapter 20, so it can only be implied that they reign in this passage "in a higher sense than during the Millennium" (Biederwolf; also Alford, Stuart, Weidner).

AFFIRMATION OF GOD'S WORD

REVELATION 22:6—10

⁶Then he said to me, "These words are faithful and true." And the Lord God of the holy prophets sent His angel to show His servants the things which must shortly take place. ⁷"Behold, I am coming quickly! Blessed is he who keeps the words of the prophecy of this book." ⁸Now I, John, saw and heard these things. And when I heard and saw, I fell down to worship before the feet of the angel who showed me these things. ⁹Then he said to me, "See that you do not do that. For I am your fellow servant, and of your brethren the prophets, and of those who keep the words of this book. Worship God." ¹⁰And he said to me, "Do not seal the words of the prophecy of this book, for the time is at hand."

Verses 6 through 21 form an epilogue to the book of Revelation. The prophecy and message of the book has been given in completeness, and few things remain to be said that are not mere repetitions of points made earlier. Yet the epilogue has some significant features, including some things relevant to the interpretation of the book as a whole.

In these closing paragraphs, the identity of the speakers of various statements becomes somewhat confusing. At times (e.g., vv. 6, 9–11), the words seem to be those of the angel-guide— still one of the seven who poured out the bowls (cf. 21:9)—and at others, (e.g., vv. 7, 12, 16) the speaker is clearly Jesus. Even John may have become confused at points, since he again fell down to worship the speaker and had to be reminded again that the speaker was not God, but a mere servant (vv. 8–9).

The reaffirmation that **these words are faithful and true** (v. 6) appears to be spoken by the angel here, although they are the echo of the identical declaration made by God Himself in 21:5. The authenticity of the messenger is affirmed by the statement that he was sent by the Lord God of the holy prophets, which also emphasizes the continuity of the prophetic Spirit's activity from the Old Testament times to the New. As was mentioned in the opening verse of the book, the events predicted are **things which must shortly take place** (v. 6), a fact which requires a variety of explanations from those who

568

find the fulfillment at various times in history or the future (see commentary at 1:1, 3). The theme of the book from 1:7, that He will come in the clouds, is here emphasized as having a speedy fulfillment: **Behold, I am coming quickly!** (v. 7). On the meaning of this "coming," see commentary at 1:7.

The sixth beatitude of the book, **Blessed is he who keeps the words of the prophecy of this book** (v. 7) is essentially the same as the first one in 1:3.

It is remarkable that, in verses 8 and 9, John made precisely the same mistake (seeking to worship the angel) for which he had been sternly rebuked earlier (cf. 19:10), and now receives the same rebuke again. This may give us some notion of the extent to which the magnificence of the visions distracted him and interfered with his normal rational activity.

The command not to **seal the words of the prophecy of this book** (v. 10) stands apparently in deliberate contrast to the instructions Daniel received at the end of his book. The prophecies of Daniel were not to have an immediate fulfillment in his own time. Therefore the angel instructed him, "But you, Daniel, shut up the words, and seal the book until the time of the end" (Dan. 12:4). John is to treat his book differently than did Daniel because, in the case of Revelation, the time is at hand (v. 10). Austin Farrer writes: "Indeed, these are the very days for which Daniel wrote, and St. John has been inspired to 'unseal' him." Biederwolf implies that what was "at hand" in John's day was not the time of the fulfillment, but the time for the book to be "diffused, read and explained."

GOD'S WORK COMPLETED

REVELATION 22:11—15

[11]"He who is unjust, let him be unjust still; he who is filthy, let him be filthy still; he who is righteous, let him be righteous still; he who is holy, let him be holy still." [12]"And behold, I am coming quickly, and My reward is with Me, to give to every one according to his work. [13]I am the Alpha and the Omega, the Beginning and the End, the First and the Last." [14]Blessed are those who do His commandments, that they may have the right to the tree of life, and may enter through the gates into the city. [15]But outside are dogs and sorcerers and sexually immoral and murderers and idolaters, and whoever loves and practices a lie.

Verse 11 underscores the nearness of the events just mentioned, as if so little time remains that one could hardly hope to repent before the judgment falls. Russell writes: "So imminent is the end that it is intimated that now it is too late for any alteration in the state or character of men; such as they are so must they continue." Alford writes:

> The saying has solemn irony in it (compare Matt. 26.45), the idea being that the time is so short that there is hardly any room for any change, but down in its depths the lesson conveyed is, "Change while yet there is time."

Alternatively, Fausset believes that the statement **He who is unjust, let him be unjust still; he who is filthy, let him be filthy still; he who is righteous, let him be righteous still; he who is holy, let him be holy still** (v. 11) is noting that the "punishment of sin is sin and the reward of holiness is holiness." Farrer, on the other hand, suggests that it constitutes a prayer "that the world may come out black and white, so as to be ripe for judgment."

Upon declaring once again that His coming will be soon, Jesus adds that He will give to every man a reward **according to his work** (v. 12). That the judgment of men is upon the basis of their works is an oft-repeated theme in the New Testament (cf. Matt. 16:27; 25:31ff.; Rom. 2:6; 1 Pet. 1:17; Rev. 20:13).

The seventh and final beatitude of the book blesses **those who do His**

commandments (v. 14) and promises **that they may have the right to the tree of life, and may enter through the gates into the city.** Entrance to the church and participation in eternal life are thus said to be the portion of those who are obedient to the commandments of God (cf. Matt. 19:17; 28:20; Luke 6:46; John 8:31; 1 John 2:3–4). Many would favor the Alexandrian reading of this verse, which replaces "do His commandments" with "wash their robes." However, since the spotless garments of the true bride are "the righteous acts of the saints" (19:8),

the call for obedient righteousness remains the thrust of the verse regardless which reading is chosen.

Those excluded from the City of God are characterized as **dogs** (a term the Jews used to characterize Gentiles, but which Paul applied to the Judaizers— Phil. 3:2), **and sorcerers and sexually immoral and murderers and idolaters, and whoever loves and practices a lie** (v. 15). That such behavior effectively bars one's entrance into the kingdom of God is also clearly declared by Paul (cf. 1 Cor. 6:9–10; Gal. 5:19–21).

FINAL BLESSING

REVELATION 22:16—17

[16]"I, Jesus, Have Sent My Angel to testify to you these things in the churches. I am the Root and the Offspring of David, the Bright and Morning Star." [17]And the Spirit and the bride say, "Come!" And let him who hears say, "Come!" And let him who thirsts come. Whoever desires, let him take the water of life freely.

Christ calls Himself **the Root and the Offspring of David** (v. 16), the meaning of which has occasioned disagreement. That the Messiah was to be the offspring of David was central to Jewish orthodoxy (cf. Matt. 22:42), but what does the expression "Root . . . of David" suggest? Many hold that this speaks of the root from which David himself, or

the Davidic dynasty, arose, so that "Root and Offspring of David" means "both the Source and Culmination of the Davidic line" (Chilton). Biederwolf disagrees:

Not the root in the sense that David sprang from Him, as a tree does from a root, but in the sense that He was the "root-shoot" of

571

David, or that He Himself sprang from David, as a sprout starts up from a decayed and fallen tree.

In addition, Christ assumes the title, the **Bright and Morning Star** (v. 16), which takes its imagery either from Venus, which is sometimes visible in the morning and was called the "morning star" by the ancients, or from the sun, which is the star that heralds the dawn. Balaam had prophesied of a Star that would arise in Jacob (Num. 24:17), which is generally regarded as a prophecy about Christ. Jesus promised Himself in this terminology to the overcomers of the Thyatiran church (Rev. 2:28), and Peter wrote of the hope that eventually the day will dawn and the "morning star" will rise in the believers' hearts (2 Pet. 1:19). This may refer to the ultimate glorification of the believer in the image of Christ at His coming (1 John 3:2), the result of a progressive transformation "into the same image from glory to glory" currently occurring in the lives of those who love Him (2 Cor. 3:18).

The **Spirit and the bride say, "Come!"** (v. 17)—but to whom are they speaking? The final occurrence of the word "come" in this verse is clearly addressed to those who thirst, so that many interpreters understand the whole verse to be addressed to such. This would mean that the invitation to come to Christ is made by the Spirit, by the bride (the church), and by those who hear and respond to the invitation. Stuart and Swete believe that **him who hears** refers not to the one who hears the voice of the Spirit and the bride, but to the one who hears the book of Revelation when it is read in the churches.

Alternatively, the Spirit and the bride may be beckoning Christ to "come." He has just promised that He would come quickly (vv. 7, 12), and the final petition in the book is that of John praying for Jesus to come quickly (v. 20). In this view, the him who hears would be Christ, who hears the plea of the Spirit and the bride, and who in turn invites the thirsty to Come! in order to **take the water of life freely**. Such an invitation was previously given by Jesus in John 7:37f. and in Revelation 21:6 (see note at that verse).

FINAL CURSE

REVELATION 22:18—19

[18]For I testify to everyone who hears the words of the prophecy of this book: If anyone adds to these things, God will add to him the plagues that are written in this book; [19]and if anyone takes away from the words of the book of this prophecy, God shall take away his part from (he Book of Life, from the holy city, and from the things which are written in this book.

The severe curse called upon anyone who **adds to these things** (v. 18) or who **takes away from the words of the book of this prophecy** (v. 19), has been invoked by some expositors against those who differ from them in the interpretation of the apocalyptic vision, though it is hard to believe that any sincere attempt to interpret the symbols of the book would incur such wrath from God as these words suggest. It is probable that the strict safeguards are intended less for the interpreter of the book than the integrity of its transmission by copyists, as Stuart writes:

> The practice of tampering with books of such a nature must have been somewhat frequent in the region where the Apocalypse was published; otherwise there would be something not perfectly natural in the severity of the interdict before us.

Swete elaborates:

It is not uncommon for writers to protect their works by adding a solemn abjuration to the scribes to correct the copies carefully, and in no case to mutilate or interpolate the original. If the solemn warning of the present verse was intended in this sense, it has signally failed, for in no other book of the New Testament is the text so uncertain as in Revelation. It is, however, no error in judgment that is condemned, nor merely intellectual fault, but the deliberate falsification or misinterpretation.

Many have seen in these verses a declaration that with these words the canon of Scripture is to be closed, as if **this book** (v. 18) were intended to mean the Bible itself. There are several reasons to doubt this meaning:

1. Revelation may not have been chronologically the last book of the Bible to be written. While no one knows for sure, some have argued from internal evidences that the books of John, James, Hebrews, and 2 Peter may allude

to Revelation, which would require their being written later. In any event, there is no way of ascertaining that Revelation was the last canonical book to be written, and assurance of this fact would be required in order to credit this interpretation;

2. There is no way that John's readers would have understood "this book" to mean the collected writings of the New Testament, since no such book of collected writings existed until centuries later. Even when early canons were formed in the first centuries of the church, they did not include the book of Revelation until the Council of Carthage in the AD 390s;

3. The punishment for adding to "this book" is to have the **plagues that are written in this book** (v. 18) added to oneself. Presumably, "this book" in both cases refers to one and the same book. The mention of "plagues" written in the book strongly suggests the book of Revelation, since plagues are a dominant feature of Revelation, whereas few other books in the Bible discuss or describe any kind of plague;

4. There are similar warnings not to add to God's words all the way back in Deuteronomy and in Proverbs.[10] Yet many books of the Bible—including the entire New Testament—were written after these warnings. This suggests that the words do not announce the closing of the scriptural canon.

Since the major criterion for New Testament canonicity is apostolic authority, and since the apostles have all long since died, we must agree that the canon will allow no future entries. However, this verse in Revelation cannot without violence be pressed to teach this fact.

The penalty for removing words from the book is that **God shall take away his part from the Book of Life, from the holy city, and from the things which are written in this book** (v. 19). A promise was made to the overcomers in Sardis that their names would not be blotted out of the Book of Life (3:5). Here we are told specifically that it is possible for some to have their part in the Book of Life taken away. As the implications of these statements upon the Calvinist-Arminian debate concerning the perseverance of the saints are not within the range of our study of this book, we will leave it to the writers of other—longer—books to sort out the meaning of this threat.

CONCLUSION

REVELATION 22:20—21

[20]He who testifies to these things says, "Surely I am coming quickly." Amen. Even so, come, Lord Jesus! [21]The grace of our Lord Jesus Christ be with you all. Amen.

To these words we can add only our own "Amen."

SUMMARY OF CHAPTERS 21–22

Opinions concerning the meaning of the New Creation in these chapters do not divide along the lines of the four approaches nor of the three millennial interpretations covered in the earlier sections of this commentary.

Futurists will mostly take the language literally, applying all to a physical reality that will be brought into existence when God's purposes for the present created order have been completed.

Those of the other three approaches *(historicist, preterist,* and *idealist)* may agree with the literalist interpretation, but may also tend toward one or another nonliteral approach. Some make the new creation out to be the church in the present era of the New Covenant. Others take it to be the heavenly abode of all who are saved, described in terrestrial symbolism.

NOTES

1. If so, he accidentally omitted quotation marks.
2. Biederwolf, *The Second Coming Bible,* 708.
3. Ibid.
4. Ibid.
5. E.g., streets of gold and gates of pearl are frequently said to describe "heaven," though literalism would make them features of a physical city on a renewed earth.
6. In Russell's view, "the end of the age" refers to the end of the Old Testament age, finally culminating in AD 70 with the destruction of Jerusalem.

7. E.g., compare

Isa. 65:23	with	1 Cor. 15:58
Isa. 65:25	with	Luke 10:19
Isa. 66:1f.	with	I Tim. 3:15
Isa. 66:8	with	Gal. 4:26
Isa. 66:11	with	Matt. 5:6
Isa. 66:12	with	John 14:27
Isa. 66:15f.	with	Matt. 22:7
Isa. 66:18	with	Matt. 8:11
Isa. 66:19	with	Col. 1:27
Isa. 66:20	with	Rom. 15:16

8. Philip Schaff, *The Principle of Protestantism* [1845], trans. John Nevin (Philadelphia: United Church Press, 1964)..

9. That the church is here pictured seems a necessary conclusion to be drawn from Paul's quotation of the first verse of the chapter in Gal. 4:27 and his application of it to the Gentiles of the New Covenant church

10. Deut. 4:2, "You shall not add to the word which I command you, nor take from it, that you may keep the commandments of the Lord your God which I command you." Deut. 12:32, "Whatever I command you, be careful to observe it; you shall not add to it nor take away from it." Prov. 30:6, "Do not add to His words, lest He rebuke you, and you be found a liar."

BIBLIOGRAPHY

Some of the resources used in the preparation of this book are listed below. In order to maintain objectivity in presentation as much as possible, I have directly cited authors holding the respective positions. When quoting directly from these sources, the last name of the author will be found either in the text or in the notes. Where no page number is given, the quoted material is taken from the source *in situ*.

Adams, Jay. *The Time is at Hand*. Phillipsburg, NJ: Presbyterian and Reformed Publishing, 1966. [*preterist*]

Alford, Henry. *The Revelation* in *The Greek Testament*. Revised by Everett R Harrison. Chicago: Moody,, 1958. [*idealist*]

Ashcraft, Morris. *Hebrews:Revelation* in *The Broadman Bible Commentary* (hereafter *BBC*). Vol. 12. Clifton J. Alien, gen. ed. Nashville: Broadman, 1972. [*preterist*]

Barnes, Albert. *"Revelation"* in *Notes on the New Testament* (hereafter *Notes*). Grand Rapids: Baker, 1884–85). [*historicist*]

Barnhouse, Donald Grey. *Revelation: An Expository Commentary*. Grand Rapids: Zondervan,1971. [*futurist*]

Bauckham, Richard. *The Theology of the Book of Revelation*. Cambridge: Cambridge University Press, 1993. [*idealist/late-date preterist*]

Beale, G. K. *The New International Greek Testament Commentary: The Book of Revelation*. Grand Rapids: Eerdmans, 1999. [idealist]

Beasley-Murray, George R. *The Book of Revelation (New Century Bible)*. London: Oliphants: Marshall, Morgan and Scott, 1974.

Beckwith, Isbon T. *The Apocalypse of John*. Grand Rapids: Baker, 1967.

Biederwolf, William E. *The Second Coming Bible*. Grand Rapids: Baker, repr. 1972.

Boring, M. Eugene. *Revelation* in *Interpretation: A Bible Commentary For Preaching and Teaching*, James Luther Mays, ed. Louisville: John Knox, 1989.

Bowman, J. W. *Revelation* in *The Interpreter's Dictionary of the Bible*. Vol. 4. Nashville: Abingdon, 1962.

Bruce, Frederick F. *Revelation* in *The International Bible Commentary*. Grand Rapids: Zondervan, rev. 1986.

Caird, G. B. *The Revelation of St. John the Divine*. New York: Harper & Row, 1966.

Caringola, Robert. *The Present Reign of Jesus Christ: A Historical Interpretation of the Book of Revelation*. Springfield, MO: Abundant Life Ministries Reformed Press, 1995. [*historicist*]

Carrington, Philip. *The Meaning of the Revelation*. London: SPCK, 1931. [*preterist*]

Carpenter, W. Boyd. *The Revelation of St. John* in *Ellicott's Commentary on the Whole Bible*. Vol. 8. C. J. Ellicott, ed. Grand Rapids: Zondervan, 1959.

Chilton, David. *The Days of Vengeance: An Exposition of the Book of Revelation* (Fort Worth, Tex.: Dominion Press, 1987). [*preterist*]

Clark, David S. *The Message From Patmos: A Postmillennial Commentary on the Book of Revelation*. Grand Rapids: Baker, 1989. [*preterist*]

Clarke, Adam. *Adam Clarke's Commentary on the Holy Bible.* Abridged by Ralph Earle. Grand Rapids: Baker, 1967. [*historicist*]

Clouse, Robert G. *The Meaning of the Millennium: Four Views.* Downers Grove, IL: InterVarsity, 1977.

Elliott, E. B. *Horae Apocalyptica.* 4 vols. London: Seeley, Burnside, and Seeley, 1847. [*historicist*]

Elwell, Walter A., ed. *Evangelical Commentary on the Bible.* Grand Rapids: Baker, 1989.

Farrer, Austin. *The Revelation of St. John the Divine.* Oxford: Clarendon, 1964.

Gaebelein, Arno C., *The Revelation: An Analysis and Exposition of the Last Book of the Bible.* Neptune, NJ: Loizeaux Brothers, 1915. [*futurist*]

Gentry, Kenneth. *The Beast of Revelation.* Tyler, TX.: Institute for Christian Economics, 1989. [*preterist*]

———. *Before Jerusalem Fell: The Dating of the Book of Revelation.* Tyler, TX: Institute for Christian Economics, 1989. [*preterist*]

Grenz, Stanley J. *The Millennial Maze: Sorting Out Evangelical Options* (Downers Grove, IL: InterVarsity, 1992).

Hailey, Homer. *Revelation: An Introduction and Commentary.* Grand Rapids: Baker, 1979. [late-date *preterist/ idealist*]

Hendriksen, William. *More Than Conquerors: An Interpretation of the Book of Revelation.* Grand Rapids: Baker, 1939. [*idealist*]

Henry, Matthew. *Acts to Revelation* in *Matthew Henry's Commentary on the Whole Bible.* Vol. 6. Old Tappan, NJ: Revell). [*historicist*]

Hobbs, Herschel H. *The Cosmic Drama.* Waco, TX: Word Books, 1971. [late-date *preterist/ idealist*]

Ironside, H. A. *Lectures on the Revelation.* Neptune, NJ: Loizeaux Brothers, 1920. [*futurist*]

Ladd, George Eldon. *A Commentary on the Revelation of John.* Grand Rapids: Eerdmans, 1972. [generally *futurist*]

Lenski, R. C. H. *The Interpretation of St. John's Revelation.* Minneapolis: Augsburg, 1943. [*idealist*]

Lindsey, Hal. *There's a New World Coming: A Prophetic Odyssey.* Eugene, OR: Harvest House, 1973. [*futurist*]

Miller, Fred P. *Revelation: A Panorama of the Gospel Age.* Clermont, FL: Moellerhaus, 1991. [*historicist*]

Milligan, William. *The Book of Revelation.* London: Hodder & Stoughton, 1889. [*idealist*]

Moffatt, James. *Revelation* in *The Expositor's Greek Text.* Grand Rapids: Eerdmans, 1974).

Morey, Earl. Notes on *Revelation* in *The Spirit-Filled Life® Bible.* Jack W. Hayford, gen. ed. Nashville: Thomas Nelson, 1991. [*idealist*]

Morris, Henry M. *The Revelation Record: A Scientific and Devotional Commentary on the Book of Revelation.* Wheaton, IL: Tyndale House, 1983. [*futurist*]

Morris, Leon. *The Revelation of St. John.* Grand Rapids: Eerdmans, 1969. [*idealist*]

Morris, S. L. *The Drama of Christianity.* Richmond, Va.: Presbyterian Committee of Publication, 1928. [*idealist*]

Mounce, Robert H. *The Book of Revelation in The New International Commentary on the New Testament.* Grand Rapids: Eerdmans, 1977. [*futurist*]

Pieters, Albertus. *The Lamb, the Woman, and the Dragon.* Grand Rapids: Zondervan, 1937. [late-date *preterist/ idealist*]

Pinkoski, Jim. *The Prophecies of Daniel and Revelation.* Frederick, MD: Amazing Facts, Inc., 1986. [*historicist*, Seventh-Day Adventist]

Plummer, A. and C. Clemance. *Revelation* in *The Pulpit Commentary.* London: Kegan Paul, 1890.

Ramsay, W. M. *The Letters to the Seven Churches of Asia.* Grand Rapids: Baker, 1963.

Rushdoony, Rousas John. *Thy Kingdom Come: Studies in Daniel and Revelation.* (Fairfax, VA.: Thoburn, 1978. [*Idealist]*

Russell, J. Stewart. *The Parousia: A Critical Inquiry into the New Testament Doctrine of our Lord's Second Coming.* Grand Rapids:, 1887, repr. 1983. [*preterist*]

Ryrie, Charles Caldwell. *Revelation.* (Chicago: Moody, 1968. [*futurist*]

Seiss, J. A. *The Apocalypse: Lectures on the Book of Revelation.* Grand Rapids: Zondervan, 1957. [*futurist*]

Stanley, John E. *Revelation* in *Asbury Bible Commentary.* Eugene Carpenter and Wayne McCown, general eds. Kansas City, MO: Beacon Hill.

Stedman, Ray C. *God's Final Word: Understanding Revelation.* Grand Rapids: Discovery House, 1991. [*futurist*]

Strauss, Lehman. *The Book of the Revelation.* Neptune, NJ.: Loizeaux Brothers, 1964. [*futurist*]

Stuart, Moses. *A Commentary on the Apocalypse.* 2 vols. Andover, MA: Alien, 1845. [*preterist*]

Summers, Ray. *Worthy Is the Lamb: An Interpretation of Revelation.* Nashville: Broadman, 1951. [late-date *preterist/ idealist*]

Swete, H. B. *The Apocalypse of St. John.* New York: Macmillan, 1906. [late-date *preterist/ idealist*]

Tenney, Merrill C. *Interpreting Revelation.* Grand Rapids: Eerdmans, 1957. [*futurist*]

Terry, Milton S. *Biblical Apocalyptics: A Study of the Most Notable Revelations of God and of Christ in the Canonical Scriptures.* New York: Eaton & Mains, 1898. [preterist]

The Treasury of Scripture Knowledge. Old Tappan, NJ: Revell. [*historicist*]

Wainwright, Arthur W. *Mysterious Apocalypse.* Nashville: Abingdon, 1993.

Walvoord, John. *The Revelation of Jesus Christ.* Chicago: Moody, 1966. [*futurist*]

Wilcock, Michael. *I Saw Heaven Opened: The Message of Revelation.* Downers Grove, IL: InterVarsity, 1975. [*idealist*]

Wilson, Geoffrey B. *Revelation.* Durham, England: Evangelical Press, 1985. [*idealist*]

SCRIPTURE INDEX

Subject and Author Index